The Ultimate Ninja Foodi

Cookbook for Beginners

1500 Easy & Tasty Ninja Foodi Recipes for Beginners and Advanced Users to Pressure Cook,

Steam & Crisp, Air Fry, Bake/Roast, Sear/Sauté, and More

Janet Thorp

TABLE OF CONTENTS

Introduction 1

Fundamentals of Ninja Foodi XL Pressure Cooker Steam Fryer 2

4-Week Diet Plan 7

Chapter 1 Breakfast Recipes 9

Chapter 2 Vegetable and Sides Recipes 31

Chapter 3 Poultry Recipes 53

Chapter 4 Beef, Pork, and Lamb Recipes 80

Chapter 5 Fish and Seafood Recipes 106

Chapter 6 Snacks and Appetizer Recipes 128

Chapter 7 Dessert Recipes.. 146

Chapter 8 Soup, Stew, and Chili Recipes 168

Conclusion... 178

Appendix 1 Measurement Conversion Chart 179

Appendix 2 Air Fryer Cooking Chart 180

Appendix 3 Recipes Index 181

Introduction

So far, Ninja Foodi XL Pressure Cooker Steam Fryers haven't been used as much as they could be in integrated cooking systems that work well. They are usually made of thick aluminum or stainless steel, which makes them heavier and more expensive than regular pots. They could also be hard to make in a lot of developing countries. Prices are rarely less than 20 US dollars, and high-end items can easily cost more than 200 US dollars. In places where Ninja Foodi XL Pressure Cooker Steam Fryers aren't used very often, their relatively high prices make it hard for them to spread. People use Ninja Foodi XL Pressure Cooker Steam Fryer more in cities, where fuel has to be paid for in cash, and in rural areas, where they can quickly cook local food. This is especially true in Asia (China, Nepal, and India).

Markets all over the world sell different models of pressure cookers. To find the best model, you must consider price, size, the primary type of stove used (electric, gas, or fire), durability, and maintenance.

This cookbook is the best way to learn how to use a pressure cooker and cook with it. This cookbook will help you get the variety of tasty recipes and instructions on how to clean it after use. In short, you will find precise information along with you need to know about your pressure cooker in this book.

Ninja Foodi XL Pressure Cooker Steam Fryers are unique pots that can be sealed so that air can't get in. It lets pressure inside build up. The pot lid is firmly attached to the pot body by a mechanical device with screws or parts that fit together. A silicone ring or seal between the cover and the pot keeps steam from escaping. When you increase the temperature, the pressure of the moisture inside the pot builds up until it is higher than atmospheric pressure. This lets the temperature go well above the boiling point. With this design, you can save time, energy, and materials. In a pressure cooker, food cooks faster because the temperature can quickly go above 110°C. Also, less steam gets out between the pot and the lid, so less water is needed to cook the food.

What Is Ninja Foodi XL Pressure Cooker Steam Fryer

A fireless cooker, like a heat-retaining bag or box, can also be used with a pressure cooker (discussed later). A test done in Tajikistan found that this combination saved 80% of fuel. If the pot is put into a bag or box that keeps heat in before the pressure valve lets the steam out, no steam energy is lost. For example, instructions for boiling water, how long it takes to cook after the water boils, and how long the pot needs to stay in the heat bag. This information depends on the altitude, the food to be cooked, and the type of pressure cooker and heat retention bag.

Ninja Foodi XL Pressure Cooker Steam Fryer can also be used to make traditional dishes. But users need user training and awareness training to learn how to cook traditional dishes with the new equipment. One best way to do this would be to give out a pressure cooker cookbook with traditional recipes. As the air pressure is lower at higher altitudes, the temperature at which water boils is more down there. So, cooking takes longer and more fuel, or the food doesn't get done. Depending on the altitude, the food must boil for between one-fourth and one-fifth of the average time to soften it.

Benefits of Ninja Foodi XL Pressure Cooker Steam Fryer

The steam and air fry can't perform both at the same time, which is a really hectic task (the moisture would counteract the super crisp technology of the air fryer, obviously). The air fry setting on this appliance is said to have "the perfect balance of temperature control and hot air flow for crispy, golden results with little or no added oil."

It also has a unique steam function, so you can roast a chicken and potatoes in it and then quickly steam some vegetables while the chicken and potatoes rest. But it's not just for quickly steamed greens. The water tank holds 1.1 liters, enough to steam for up to 85 minutes (hello, dumplings, fish, and more!). Oh, and it can also be "BBQ." The deluxe reversible rack makes meat and vegetables as juicy and tender as you want with different position with no smoke and smell.

It has an extra-large, family-sized capacity and can pressure cook, air fry, and steam, all under one SmartLid. It makes meals faster with up to 70% faster than slow cooking, 40% faster than traditional cooking methods, and 25% faster for artisan bread and cakes. Attached Deluxe Reversible Rack cook twice as much or make 3-part full meals at the touch of a button—you can get mains, sides, and desserts. Its advanced Steamcrisp technology make it even easier to steam and crisp simultaneously for faster and juicier results that don't dry out. Slide to open the 14 functions and 3 cooking modes in one lid with the SmartLid slider.

Ninja Foodi XL Pressure Cooker Steam Fryer with SmartLid, an 8-quart Cooking Pot, a 5-quart Cook & Crisp Basket, and a Deluxe Reversible Rack.

Healthier Cooking

Most people buy a Ninja Foodi XL Pressure Cooker Steam Fryer because they want to cook healthier food. Since the cooking process uses very little oil, this is a great way to replace unhealthy deep-fried foods with something more beneficial.

Fried foods, like breaded chicken tenders and fried fish, still need to be sprayed with a bit of oil so that the breading gets evenly crispy as it cooks, but you use a lot less fat. Also, you don't have to fry French fries or tater tots deep to make them nice and crispy.

Rapid, Secure, and User-Friendly

At first, the Ninja Foodi XL Pressure Cooker Steam Fryer was meant to replace a deep fryer. Even though that was great, it wasn't enough to convince most people who needed one since they often don't use a deep fryer at home.

We all wish we had more time to cook, while we don't. This is why ready-made meals and takeout are so popular, even though we all know they are bad for us. If you frequently prepare frozen and breaded dishes like onion rings and chicken tenders, you will appreciate this the most. In order to avoid a soggy mess, the food you prepare in the Ninja Foodi XL Pressure Cooker Steam Fryer gets crisped up.

A light misting of cooking oil on the surface of the dish before cooking is all that's required to create a crunchy, crispy crust. This method is ideal for cooking frozen breaded or fried foods. You can reheat pizza, so give it a shot! As it warms the slice through, it crisps the bottom crust and properly revitalizes the toppings. It's as good as the first day it was released.

Very Versatile

A healthy alternative to deep frying is the Ninja Foodi XL Pressure Cooker Steam Fryer, which is capable of much more. With this device, you can prepare practically anything, including curries, desserts, whole spaghetti squash, and fried chicken. Yes, it's a terrific way to prepare store-bought frozen items like French fries, tater tots, and pizza rolls. It's so easy that even kids can complete it. Dinner is taken care of.

Faster Than Oven Cooking

One of the best things about a Ninja Foodi XL Pressure Cooker Steam Fryer is that it heats up quickly and gets hot.

The moving air also helps the food cook evenly, brown, and crispy without having to do much. This means that you'll be able to cook faster. A Ninja Foodi XL Pressure Cooker Steam Fryer is faster than an oven because it can get hot quickly and is smaller than an oven. Most ovens take up to 10 minutes to heat up, but the Ninja Foodi XL Pressure Cooker Steam Fryer doesn't need to be heated up before most recipes.

Put your food in the basket, slip it into the air fryer, choose your cooking time, and in 10 to 15 minutes you'll have a delicious meal. It's an excellent tool for making snacks quickly and easily. For a party or a snack after school, it's easy to turn it on, put in your favorite snack, and wait a few minutes for it to be done.

Easy and Efficient Reheat
You can cook anything in a Ninja Foodi and use it to reheat food, making it even more helpful. You might want to use a Ninja Foodi XL Pressure Cooker Steam Fryer to reheat food for several reasons.

It's an easy and quick way to reheat food. It keeps food from overcooking or burning. It's simple. It keeps food crispy and fresh tasting. No one in the world likes cleaning up after cooking, right? This unpleasant job can take away a lot of the pleasure of a great meal. So, you'll be happy to know that a good Ninja Foodi XL Pressure Cooker Steam Fryer is also very easy to clean after use.

Easy to Clean
Cleaning up after cooking is the worst thing in the world. This unpleasant job can take away a lot of the pleasure from a great meal. So, you'll be glad to hear that a good Ninja Foodi XL Pressure Cooker Steam Fryer is also very easy to clean after use.

You can clean it every time using it for cooking, you won't have to clean it as often as other pots and pans. Just put soapy water in the basket and use a sponge that won't scratch to clean the inside and outside. Some of the baskets that come with the Ninja Foodi XL Pressure Cooker Steam Fryer can even be cleaned in the dishwasher.

You should also clean it more thoroughly once or twice a month, including the cooking coil, depending on how often you use it. Cleaning the oven is not complicated or time-consuming if you do it often.

Cooking Functions
Pressure: Quickly cook food while preserving softness.

Steam & Crisp: It allows you to make whole meals with just one touch, vegetables, and proteins that are juicy and crisp, and fresh artisan bread.

Steam & Bake: Bake cakes and quick breads with less fat and more fluffiness with steam.

Air Fry: This method allows food to maintain its crispiness and crunchiness while using very little to no oil.

Broil: Apply intense heat from above in order to brown and caramelize the surface of the meal.

Bake/Roast: Treat the appliance like an oven and use it to make tender meats, baked treats, and a variety of other foods.

Dehydrate: For wholesome snacks, dehydrate meats, fruits, and veggies.

Proof: Establish a setting in which the dough can rest and rise before being used.

Sear/Sauté: Use the appliance as a burner to simmer sauces, sauté vegetables, and brown meats.

Steam: Cook delicate items at a high temperature while being gentle.

Sous Vide: What literally translates to "under vacuum," is a function that allows food to be cooked more slowly while being contained in a plastic bag and placed in an expertly controlled water bath.

Slow Cook: Cook your food for a more extended time at a lower temperature. Yoghurt is manufactured by pasteurizing and fermenting milk to make it creamy.

Yogurt: Get creamy homemade yogurt by pasteurizing and fermenting milk in the unit.

Keep Warm: When the steam, slow cook, or pressure cooking cycle is complete, the appliance will automatically transition to the keep warm setting. After the function has begun, you can stop this transition from happening automatically by pressing the button labelled "stay nice."

If the timer runs for one hour or less, it will count for minutes and seconds. Only minutes will be counted if the clock runs for longer than an hour. After 12 hours, this function will stop functioning.

Operating Buttons

SMARTLID SLIDER: The available features for each set will light up as you move the slider.

DIAL: After deciding on a mode with the slider, you can use the dial to go between the various functions until the one you want is highlighted. Once this is done, the mode you choose will be highlighted.

LEFT ARROWS: To change the temperature of the cooking process, use the up and down arrows.

RIGHT ARROWS: To change the amount of time spent cooking, use the up and down arrows located to the right of the display.

START/STOP button: Press to start cooking, and pressing the button while the unit cooks will stop the current cooking function.

POWER: The Power button pauses all cooking modes and turns off the appliance.

Step-By-Step Instructions

Accessory Assembly Instructions

Deluxe Reversible Rack

Arrange the Deluxe Reversible Rack such that the lower layer is at the bottom. Ingredients should be placed in the lower section of the rack. Pass the deluxe layer through the standard layer's grips. If you need extra counter space for cooking, move the remaining components to the top secret tier.

Cook & Crisp Basket

To clean the diffuser, first remove two of the diffuser's fins from the groove on the basket, then firmly pull the diffuser down on itself. To put together the Cook & Crisp Basket, position the basket so that it is sitting atop the diffuser, and then press down firmly.

Lid Opening and Closing Instructions

To open and shut the lid, pull down on the handle that is located above the slider. When the slider is in the position for the Ninja Foodi XL Pressure Cooker Steam Fryer and AIR FRY/ STOVETOP function, the top can be opened and closed at your convenience. The lid can't be opened when the slider is under PRESSURE.

The lid won't open until the whole unit is no longer under pressure. The smart slider won't move to the right until the

pressure is gone from the unit. When the unit is no longer under pressure, it will show "OPN LID" on the screen.

Before First Use

1. Take off and throw away the unit's packaging, stickers, and tape.

2. Pay close attention to the instructions, warnings, and essential safety measures to avoid getting hurt or damaging your property.

3. Use warm soapy water to clean the silicone ring, removable cooking pot, Cook & Crisp Basket, deluxe reversible rack, and condensation collector, and then thoroughly rinse and dry each of these components. Under NO circumstances should the dishwasher be used to clean the bottom of the range.

4. The silicone ring can be put in either way because it has two sides. Place the silicone ring around the outside edge of the lid on the bottom of the rack. Make sure it's in and lays flat under the silicone ring rack.

Take Out the Condensation Collector and Put It Back In Place.

The condensation collector should be inserted into the cooker base's slot. Slide it out each time you use it so you may wash your hands with it.

Take the Anti-Clog Cap Off and Putting It Back On.

The anti-clog cap keeps the valve inside the lid from getting clogged and keeps food from splattering on the user. It should be cleaned with a cleaning brush after every use. To take it off, hold the anti-clog cap with your thumb and bent index finger, then turn your wrist in a clockwise direction. To put it back in, put it where it belongs and press down on it. Before using the unit, ensure the anti-clog cap is correct.

Water Test Beginning the Process of Cooking Under Pressure

New users should perform a water test to get comfortable with pressure cooking.

1. Put the pot in the cooker base and fill it with 3 cups of water at room temperature.

2. Put the lid back, lock it, and move the slider to the PRESSURE setting.

3. Ensure the pressure release valve is in the SEAL (or Pressure functions) position.

4. When the valve is put in place, it will be loose. This is fine.

5. High (Hi) pressure will be the default for the unit. Use the down arrow on the right to change the time to 2 minutes. To start, press START/STOP.

6. The word "PrE" and progress bars will appear on this display to indicate that the device is increasing its pressure.

7. When all of the members of the unit are under pressure, the timer will begin counting down. When the cooking time runs out, the unit will beep and show "End" before letting the pressured steam out quickly. When the pressure release valve is about to open, an alarm will go off. When the pressure release valve is opened, steam will come out. Move the slider to the right when the screen says "OPN Lid" to open the lid. Then take off the top.

Quick Pressure Release & Natural Pressure Release

The Natural Pressure Release

When the cooking is done under pressure, the steam will naturally come out of the unit as it cools. The release time will depend on the food and liquid. The Ninja Foodi will switch to Keep Warm mode during this time. If you want to turn off Keep Warm mode, press the KEEP WARM button. When the pressure has been released naturally, the unit will show "OPN Lid."

Quick Pressure Release

ONLY use if your recipe says to. When the cooking is done under pressure, and the KEEP WARM light is on, rotate or turn the pressure release valve or rotator to the VENT position to immediately let the stress out of the pot. Even after letting the pressure out naturally or using the pressure release valve, there will still be some steam in the unit. When the lid is going to be opened, this steam will escape.

Using Pressure Function

Pressure

1. Press the Power button after inserting the power cord into a wall outlet to turn on the device.

2. Put the ingredients and at least 1 cup of liquid, as well as any other needed items, in the pot. DO NOT fill the jar up past the line "PRESSURE MAX."

3. Close the lid. Next, turn the pressure release valve to the SEAL setting. Move the slider to the PRESSURE setting. To choose Hi or LO, use arrows buttons. Then use the up and down arrows to adjust the cook time.

4. To begin the cooking process, press the START/STOP button. When you turn the Ninja Foodi on, the pressure within will start to build. On the screen, you will see the letters "PrE" as well as progress bars. When the unit has pressurized, the timer will begin counting down.

5. When the allotted amount of time for cooking has passed, switch the pressure release valve to the VENT position. The unit will beep and switch automatically to Keep Warm

mode. The timer will also start counting up.

6. When the unit shows "OPN Lid," the pressure has been released, and you can open the lid by moving the slider to the right.

Using Steamcrisp Functions

After you have connected the power cord to an available outlet in the wall and pressed the Power button, the device will begin to operate.

Steam & Crisp

1. Put in the ingredients based on the recipe. Move the slider to STEAMCRISP. The STEAM & CRISP function will be chosen by default. The time and temperature will be set to their defaults. Use arrows on the left side of the screen to select a temperature between 300°F and 450°F in 5-degree increments.

2. To make changes to the cooking time in increments of one minute, up to an hour long, use the arrows buttons. To begin the cooking process, press the START/STOP button. The "PrE" and progress bars on the screen show that the unit is making steam. How long something needs to moisture depends on how many things are in the pot. When the unit has reached the right level of smoke, the display will show the temperature you set, and the timer will start to count down. When the cooking time runs out, the unit will beep and say "End" for 5 minutes. Use the up arrow to add more time if your food needs more time. The unit will not heat up first. Now, we know how to make recipes from Ninja Foodi XL Pressure Cooker Steam Fryer. Let us make try to make anything with steps.

Bake/Roast

1. Equip the pot with all of the necessary implements and components. Put the lid back on. Then, using the dial, choose BAKE/ROAST after moving the slider to the AIR FRY/STOVETOP position. The temperature will automatically be set to the present value. Choose a temperature in increments of 5 degrees by using the arrow buttons to select a value between 250 and 400 degrees Fahrenheit.

2. To modify the cook time, use the arrow buttons to go from up to 1 hour in increments of 1 minute, and then from 1 hour to 4 hours in intervals of 5 minutes.

3. Press START/STOP to begin cooking

4. The unit will beep when cook time reaches zero, and "End" will flash 3 times on the display.

Dehydrate

1. Position the deluxe reversible rack in the lower position, and after that, add a layer of ingredients to the shelf.

2. While still holding it by its handles, position the deluxe layer so that it rests on the reversible rack. After that, add another

layer of ingredients on top of the first layer, and cover the container with the lid.

3. To dehydrate the food, turn the dial to DEHYDRATE after moving the slider to the AIR FRY/STOVETOP position. The temperature will automatically be set to the present value. Choose a temperature between 80 and 195 degrees Fahrenheit using the arrow buttons to make adjustments in 5-degree increments.

4. To alter the cook time in 15-minute increments from 1 hour to 12 hours, use the arrow buttons.

5. To start the cooking process, press the START/STOP button.

6. The unit will beep when cook time reaches zero, and "End" will flash 3 times on the display.

Proof

1. Put the dough in the pot or the Cook & Crisp Basket, and then cover it with the lid.

2. Using the dial, select PROOF after first moving the slider to the AIR FRY/STOVETOP position.

3. The temperature will automatically be set to the preset value. Choose a temperature in increments of 5 degrees by using the arrows buttons to select a value between 75 and 95 degrees Fahrenheit.

4. To modify the proof time in minute increments between 20 minutes and 2 hours, use the arrow buttons. The minimum proof time is 20 minutes, and the maximum proof time is 2 hours. Press START/STOP to begin cooking.

5. The unit will beep when cook time reaches zero, and "End" will flash three times on the display.

Sear/Sauté

1. Put the ingredients in the cooking pot. Either open the lid of the appliance or use the slider to select AIR FRY/STOVETOP, or use the dial to select SEAR/SAUTÉ.

2. The default temperature setting will display. To choose "Lo1," "2," "3," "4," or "Hi5," use the arrows for that.

3. Press START/STOP button to begin cooking and end the function after cooking. To switch to another cooking function, use the slider and select your cooking method.

Frequently Asked Questions

Why does it take so much time for the unit to build up its pressure? How much time passes before the pressure starts to rise?

Cooking times vary based on the temperature, the cooking pot's current temperature, and the temperature or quantity of the ingredients. Check that the silicone ring is completely seated and that it is flush against the lid. You should be able to spin the call by giving it a light tug, provided that it was put appropriately.

Inadequate liquid prevents the unit from pressurizing. Why does the time go so slowly?

You can also set hours rather than minutes. When selecting the time, the display window will show HH: MM and the time will also change by increase/decrease in minute increments.

How will I know when the machine starts to pressurize?

The display will show a progress bar of building pressure. The letters "PrE" and flashing lights appear on the screen whenever you use the Pressure function or Steam function. This indicates the machine is generating pressure when using PRESSURE or STEAM. When the main unit has build pressure, your cook time will start. A lot of steam comes from the unit when using the Steam function. Smoke is customary which release through the valve during cooking so don't panic for that.

Why can't I open the lid while releasing pressurizing?

The lid will not unlock before the appliance is depressurized as a safety measure. Set the pressure release valve to VENT to swiftly discharge the pressurized steam. Steam will suddenly erupt from the pressure release valve. The unit will be ready to

open when the smoke is finally let out.

Is it normal for the pressure release valve to be slack?

Yes. The loose fit of the pressure release valve is deliberate; it makes switching from SEAL to VENT quick and straightforward and helps regulate pressure by releasing a tiny quantity of steam during cooking to produce outstanding results. When cooking under pressure, please make sure it is in the SEAL position, and when fast releasing, confirm that is turned as far as possible toward the VENT position. The device hisses and cannot build pressure. A pressure release valve should be turned to the SEAL setting, so double-check this. After doing this, if you still hear a loud hissing sound, the silicone ring may not be entirely in place. To halt cooking, press START/STOP, VENT if necessary, and lift the lid. Please ensure the silicone ring is placed correctly and flatly underneath the rack by applying pressure on it. Once everything is put in place, you should be able to spin the call by giving it a slight tug. Instead of counting down, the device is counting up. The Ninja Foodi is in "Keep Warm" function after the cooking is finished.

How much time does it take the unit to depressurize?

The pressure release depends on the food quantity in the cooking pot and can vary from recipes. If the unit takes longer time than usual to depressurize, Switch off and release all the pressure before opening the lid.

Helpful Tips for Users

Make sure that the ingredients are spread out in the bottom of the cooking pot in an even layer without overlapping one another so that the browning will be consistent. It is important to remember to shake the pan halfway through the allotted cooking time if the elements overlap.

To prevent smaller items from being lost through the deluxe reversible rack, we advise first placing them in a pouch made of parchment paper or aluminum foil and then wrapping them. After the food has been cooked, select the Keep Warm option to keep it at a warm temperature that is still safe for consumption. To avoid the food inside from drying out, we suggest keeping the lid closed and use this function just before serving it. To reheat meals, use the function labelled "Reheat." After each usage, the appliance needs to be thoroughly cleaned.

1. Unplug the appliance from the wall outlet before beginning the cleaning process.

2. To clean the cooker base and the control panel, clean them with a damp cloth.

3. With some water and dish soap, you may clean the pressure release valve and anti-clog cap.

4. If food residue is stuck on the cooking pot, fill the pot with water and allow it to soak before cleaning. DO NOT use scouring pads. If scrubbing is required, use liquid dish soap or a non-abrasive cleaner with a nylon pad or brush.

5. Air-dry all parts after each use.

4-Week Diet Plan

Week 1

Day 1:
Breakfast: Healthy Egg Muffins
Lunch: Seasoned Artichoke
Snack: Spinach with Parsley Dip
Dinner: Saucy Turkey Leg
Dessert: Carambola Chips

Day 2:
Breakfast: Spinach Muffins
Lunch: Sweet Potatoes with nuts
Snack: Broccoli Pecorino Toscano bites
Dinner: Turkey with Gravy
Dessert: Dark Brownies

Day 3:
Breakfast: Cheese Rolls
Lunch: Broccoli Feta Balls
Snack: Crispy Cocktail Meatballs
Dinner: Almond-Coated Fish
Dessert: Grilled Pineapple

Day 4:
Breakfast: Eggs Dish
Lunch: Herbed Olives
Snack: Crispy BBQ Smokies
Dinner: Beef Greens Bowl
Dessert: Chocolate Mug Cake

Day 5:
Breakfast: Pepper Bread
Lunch: Cauliflower Cheese Tots
Snack: Crispy Calamari Appetizer
Dinner: Sesame Salmon
Dessert: Walnut Bread

Day 6:
Breakfast: Broccoli Quiche
Lunch: Pita Chips
Snack: Grandma's Crispy Wings
Dinner: Regular Pad Thai
Dessert: Chocolate-Covered Bacon

Day 7:
Breakfast: Fried PB&J Sandwich
Lunch: Salmon Jerky
Snack: Spinach Chips
Dinner: Baked Beef
Dessert: Sweet Tapioca

Week 2

Day 1:
Breakfast: Blueberry Muffins
Lunch: Ricotta Cheese Potatoes
Snack: Scallops Bacon Kabobs
Dinner: Spicy Buffalo Wings
Dessert: Spice Monkey Bread

Day 2:
Breakfast: Bell Pepper Cups
Lunch: Traditional Broccoli Salad
Snack: Cocktail Wieners
Dinner: Chicken Sausages
Dessert: Strawberry Shortcake

Day 3:
Breakfast: Mushroom Boat Eggs
Lunch: Taco Broccoli
Snack: Bacon Fat Bombs
Dinner: Easy Burgers
Dessert: Coconut Pie

Day 4:
Breakfast: Spinach- Rollups
Lunch: Grilled Cheese
Snack: Crispy Ranch Kale Chips
Dinner: Marinated Shrimp
Dessert: Almond Pears

Day 5:
Breakfast: Pancake Hash
Lunch: Roasted Broccoli
Snack: Picnic Chicken Chunks
Dinner: Air-Fried Turkey
Dessert: Sweet Potato Donut

Day 6:
Breakfast: Meatloaf Slices
Lunch: Cheese Stuffed Peppers
Snack: Asian Short Ribs
Dinner: Lamb Skewers
Dessert: Fried Pancake Oreos

Day 7:
Breakfast: English Bacon Breakfast
Lunch: Sesame Carrots
Snack: Mustard Wings
Dinner: Mayo Fish Sticks
Dessert: Banana Cake

Week 3

Day 1:
Breakfast: Spinach Cheddar Quiche
Lunch: Lemony Broccoli Salad
Snack: Trail Chex Snack
Dinner: Mexican Brisket Salad
Dessert: Zesty Raspberry Muffins

Day 2:
Breakfast: Parmesan Omelet
Lunch: Cauliflower Mash
Snack: Pickle Chips
Dinner: Lamb Avocado Bowl
Dessert: Blackberry Granola Crisp

Day 3:
Breakfast: Cheesy Bacon Muffins
Lunch: Roasted Bell Peppers
Snack: Barbecue Chips
Dinner: Fish Fillets With Dill Sauce
Dessert: Tangy Fruit Salad Jam

Day 4:
Breakfast: Broccoli- Frittata
Lunch: Potato Patties
Snack: Chicken Bites
Dinner: Cola Pulled Pork
Dessert: Toasted Flakes

Day 5:
Breakfast: Mexican Casserole
Lunch: Herbed Green Beans
Snack: Crispy Zucchini Crackers
Dinner: Mussels in White Wine
Dessert: Honey Chocolate Cookies

Day 6:
Breakfast: French Toasts
Lunch: Greek Olives
Snack: Bacon Chaffle
Dinner: Easy Crab Cakes
Dessert: Quick Peanut Butter Cookies

Day 7:
Breakfast: Chili Egg Bake
Lunch: Air Fried Bell Peppers
Snack: Cheese Sticks
Dinner: Buffalo Chicken
Dessert: Rhubarb Cream Pie

Week 4

Day 1:
Breakfast: Cheddar Coconut Biscuits
Lunch: Broccoli Cheese Gnocchi
Snack: Shrimp Sesame Toasts
Dinner: Indian Chicken Marsala
Dessert: Ricotta Vanilla Cookies

Day 2:
Breakfast: Cranberry Nutty Grits
Lunch: Stuffed Mushrooms
Snack: Cheese Quesadillas
Dinner: Easy Chicken Paillard
Dessert: Chocolate Pudding Cake

Day 3:
Breakfast: Kale Cream Eggs
Lunch: Scrambled Spinach Eggs
Snack: Crispy Cauliflower
Dinner: Fish Nuggets
Dessert: Mini Cheesecakes

Day 4:
Breakfast: Bacon Knots
Lunch: Cheesy Asparagus
Snack: Grilled Meatball
Dinner: Mozarella Chicken
Dessert: Orange Custard

Day 5:
Breakfast: Sweet Potato Toast
Lunch: Cheese Broccoli Pizza
Snack: Crispy Zucchini Fries
Dinner: Beef Marinara Wraps
Dessert: Cinnamon Plum

Day 6:
Breakfast: Bacon Egg Cups
Lunch: Crispy Sweet Potatoes
Snack: Brie and Artichoke Dip
Dinner: Shrimp Kebabs
Dessert: Easy Pecan Cobbler

Day 7:
Breakfast: Italian Frittata
Lunch: Mushroom Puff Pastry
Snack: Eggplant Crisps
Dinner: Mushroom Stuffed Turkey
Dessert: Homemade Pecan Nutella

Chapter 1 Breakfast Recipes

10 Spinach Egg Frittata
10 Creamy Egg Cups
10 Egg Breakfast
10 Cheesy Broccoli Casserole
10 Pork Wrapped Scotch Eggs
10 Broccoli- Frittata
10 Creamy Cauliflower Frittata
10 Turkey Scramble
11 Cheddar Coconut Biscuits
11 French Toasts
11 Cheese Egg Scramble
11 Chili Egg Bake
11 Morning Herbed Eggs
11 Chicken Muffins
11 Eggs with Kalamata Olives
11 Portobello Eggs
12 Cheddar Breakfast
12 Eggplant Pepper Spread
12 Coconut Crusted Fish Sticks
12 Cauliflower Frittata With Almond Mike
12 Kielbasa Egg Scramble
12 Mozarella Egg Bake
12 Brussel Sprouts Egg Bake
12 Walnut Granola
13 Dill Bacon Bites
13 Pork Casserole
13 Tomato Egg Omelet
13 Soft-Boiled Eggs
13 Argula Cream Spread
13 Pepper Eggs
13 Swiss Chard Egg Frittata
13 Zucchini Spread
13 Omelet with Herbs
14 Cheese Rolls
14 Dill Egg Omelet
14 Coconut Crusted Mozarella Sticks
14 Spinach Muffins
14 Spinach Cheese Quesadilla
14 Breakfast Egg Pizza
14 Kale Cream Eggs
14 Bell Peppers Salad
15 Wrapped Bacon with Eggs
15 Sweet Cinnamon Muffins
15 Cajun Sausage
15 Tomato Breakfast Wrap

15 Cheese & Avocado Melt
15 Eggs Ham
15 Blueberry Muffins
16 Parmesan Bread
16 Pita Bread
16 Artichoke Pizza
16 Pepperoni Cheese Pizza
16 Strawberry Morning Toast
17 Pepper Bread
17 Peach Vanilla Fritters
17 Turkey Sausage Roll-Ups
17 Hush Puffs
17 Sweet Potato Toast
18 Chocolate Rolls
18 Baked Eggs
18 Walnut Apple Muffins
18 Bacon Knots
18 Air Fried Grapefruit
18 Broccoli Quiche
19 Blueberry Morning Muffins
19 Ham Cornmeal Muffins
19 Toast Sticks
19 Oat Muffins
19 Orange Creamy Rolls
19 Breakfast Scotch Eggs
20 Cheesy Bacon Muffins
20 Jelly stuffed Muffins
20 Egg Quesadillas
20 Pork Quiche Cups
20 Mushroom Boat Eggs
21 Fried PB&J Sandwich
21 Spinach- Rollups
21 Ham Eggs
21 Flaxseed Muffins
21 Walnut Vanilla Pancake
21 Western Cheese Omelet
22 Chicken Hash
22 Breakfast Eggs with Cream
22 Sesame Flax Meal Porridge
22 Pancake Hash
22 Creamy Seed Porridge
22 Breakfast Chicken Sandwich
22 Rice Paper Breakfast
23 Parmesan Omelet
23 Almond Egg Bread
23 Kale Fritters

23 Morning Sausages
23 Bacon Egg Cups
23 Spinach Cheddar Quiche
24 Zucchini Hash
24 Coconut Porridge
24 Egg Scramble
24 Liver Pate
24 Meatloaf Slices
24 Spinach Parsley Omelet
24 Minced Beef Sandwich
25 Beef Chili
25 Bacon Burger
25 English Bacon Breakfast
25 Italian Frittata
25 Broccoli Tofu Scramble
25 Healthy Blueberry Oat Mini Muffins
26 Veggies on Toast
26 Tropical Oats
26 Farro with Berries and Walnuts
26 Eggs and Sausage Muffins
26 Mexican Casserole
26 Cheesy Bacon Quiche
27 Porridge
27 Bell Pepper Cups
27 Tomato and Spinach Healthy Breakfast
27 Eggs Dish
27 Omelet Cups
27 Spinach-Feta Cups
28 Ham Casserole
28 Soft Eggs
28 Garlic Toast
28 Classical Hard-Boiled Eggs
28 Traditional French Eggs
28 Delightful Eggs
28 Healthy Egg Muffins
29 Cranberry Nutty Grits
29 Tasty Tomato Spinach Quiche
29 Mayo Egg Salad
29 Cheesy Meaty Sausage Frittata
29 Baked Egg
29 Baked Cheesy Hash Brown Bake
30 Bacon and Sausage Omelet
30 Delicious Mushroom Frittata

Spinach Egg Frittata

Prep Time: 8 minutes. | Cook Time: 20 minutes. | Serves: 4

1 tablespoon avocado oil	6 eggs, beaten
½ teaspoon chili flakes	2 cups spinach, chopped

1. Place the Cook & Crisp Basket in your Pressure Cooker Steam Fryer. 2. In a suitable mixing bowl, mix chili flakes with eggs and spinach. 3. Then brush your Ninja Foodi Pressure Cooker Steam Fryer Cook & Crisp Basket with avocado oil. 4. Pour the prepared egg mixture in the Cook & Crisp Basket and transfer to your Ninja Foodi Pressure Cooker Steam Fryer. 5. Put on the Smart Lid on top of the Ninja Foodi Steam Fryer. 6. Move the Lid Slider to the "Air Fry/ Stovetop". 7. Cook the eggs at 365°F/185°C on "Air Fry" Mode for about 20 minutes. 8. Serve warm.
Per Serving: Calories: 400; Fat: 20 g; Total Carbs: 36 g; Fiber: 5 g; Sodium: 675 mg; Protein: 22 g

Creamy Egg Cups

Prep Time: 10 minutes. | Cook Time: 3 minutes| Serves: 2

2 eggs	teaspoon smoked paprika
1 tablespoon cream cheese 1	

1. Place the Cook & Crisp Basket in your Pressure Cooker Steam Fryer and place a reversible rack in it. 2. Crack the eggs into the ramekins and top them with smoked paprika and cream cheese then place in the Ninja Foodi Steam Fryer. 3. Put on the Smart Lid on top of the Ninja Foodi Steam Fryer. 4. Move the Lid Slider to the "Air Fry/Stovetop". 5. Cook the eggs in your Ninja Foodi Pressure Cooker Steam Fryer at 400°F/200°C on "Air Fry" Mode for about 3 minutes.
Per Serving: Calories: 111; Fat: 2 g; Total Carbs: 12 g; Fiber: 1 g; Sodium: 024 mg; Protein: 7 g

Egg Breakfast

Prep Time: 5 minutes. | Cook Time: 20 minutes. | Serves: 4

2 bell peppers, sliced	1 teaspoon avocado oil
4 eggs, beaten	½ teaspoon white pepper

1. Place the Cook & Crisp Basket in your Pressure Cooker Steam Fryer. 2. Brush the Ninja Foodi Cook & Crisp Basket with avocado oil. 3. Then mix the bell peppers with white pepper and put inside your Ninja Foodi Cook & Crisp Basket. 4. Put on the Smart Lid on top of the Ninja Foodi Steam Fryer. 5. Move the Lid Slider to the "Air Fry/Stovetop". 6. Pour the beaten eggs over the bell peppers. Cook on "Air Fry" Mode at 360°F/180°C for about 20 minutes.
Per Serving: Calories: 280; Fat: 11g; Total Carbs: 23g; Fiber: 1g; Sodium 214 mg; Protein: 18 g

Cheesy Broccoli Casserole

Prep Time: 10 minutes. | Cook Time: 20 minutes. | Serves: 4

2 cups broccoli, chopped	½ cup Cheddar cheese, shredded
4 eggs, beaten	1 teaspoon avocado oil
1 teaspoon chili flakes	

1. Place the Cook & Crisp Basket in your Pressure Cooker Steam Fryer and set a reversible rack inside. 2. Brush the Ninja Foodi Cook & Crisp Basket with avocado oil from inside. 3. Then mix broccoli, eggs, chili flakes, and cheese in a suitable mixing bowl. 4. Put this mixture into Cook & Crisp Basket and place it in the Pressure Cooker Steam Fryer. 5. Move the Lid Slider to the "Air Fry/Stovetop". 6. Cook the casserole at 370°F/185°C on "Air Fry" Mode for about 20 minutes.
Per Serving: Calories: 180; Fat: 11 g; Total Carbs: 14 g; Fiber: 3 g; Sodium: 287 mg; Protein: 6 g

Pork Wrapped Scotch Eggs

Prep Time: 15 minutes. | Cook Time: 20 minutes. | Serves: 4

4 medium eggs, hard-boiled,	peeled

2 cups pork	½ teaspoon salt
1 teaspoon dried basil	2 tablespoons almond flour

1. Place the Cook & Crisp Basket in your Pressure Cooker Steam Fryer. 2. In a suitable mixing bowl, mix pork with basil, salt, and almond flour. 3. Then make 4 balls from the meat mixture. 4. Fill every meatball with cooked egg and put it in your Ninja Foodi Pressure Cooker Steam Fryer. 5. Put on the Smart Lid on top of the Ninja Foodi Pressure Cooker Steam Fryer. 6. Move the Lid Slider to the "Air Fry/ Stovetop". 7. Cook the meal at 375°F/190°C on "Air Fry" Mode for about 20 minutes.
Per Serving: Calories: 153; Fat: 1 g; Total Carbs: 5 g; Fiber: 2 g; Sodium: 0245mg; Protein: 11 g

Broccoli- Frittata

Prep Time: 10 minutes. | Cook Time: 20 minutes. | Serves: 2

1 tablespoon olive oil	½ teaspoon salt
1½ cups broccoli florets, chopped	¼ teaspoon black pepper
½ cup sliced brown mushrooms	6 eggs
¼ cup chopped onion	¼ cup Parmesan cheese

1. Place the Cook & Crisp Basket in your Pressure Cooker Steam Fryer and set a reversible rack inside. 2. In an 8-inch nonstick cake pan, mix the olive oil, broccoli, mushrooms, onion, salt, and pepper. 3. Stir until the vegetables are coated with oil. 4. Place the mixture in the Ninja Foodi Cook & Crisp Basket. 5. Put on the Smart Lid on top of the Ninja Foodi Steam Fryer. 6. Move the Lid Slider to the "Air Fry/ Stovetop". 7. Cook on "Air Fry" Mode at 400°F/200°C for about 5 minutes until the vegetables soften. 8. Meanwhile, in a suitable bowl, whisk the eggs and Parmesan until mixed. 9. Pour the prepared egg veggie mixture into the pan and shake gently to distribute the vegetables. Cook on "Air Fry" Mode at 350°F/175°C for 15 minutes until the eggs are set. 10. Remove from your Ninja Foodi Pressure Cooker Steam Fryer and let sit for about 5 minutes to cool slightly. Use a silicone spatula to gently lift the frittata onto a plate before serving.
Per Serving: Calories 343; Fat 13.1 g; Sodium 1333 mg; Carbs 5.7g; Fiber 0.1g; Sugar 0.2g; Protein 43.6g

Creamy Cauliflower Frittata

Prep Time: 10 minutes. | Cook Time: 14 minutes. | Serves: 4

4 eggs, beaten	½ cup cauliflower, chopped
1 tablespoon cream cheese	½ teaspoon chili flakes
½ cup heavy cream	½ teaspoon avocado oil

1. Place the Cook & Crisp Basket in your Ninja Foodi Pressure Cooker Steam Fryer and place a reversible rack in it. 2. In a suitable mixing bowl, mix eggs with cream cheese, heavy cream, and chili flakes. 3. Brush the Cook & Crisp Basket with avocado oil and put the cauliflower inside. Flatten it in one layer. 4. Place it in the Ninja Foodi Fryer. 5. Then pour the egg mixture over the cauliflower. 6. Put on the Smart Lid on top of the Ninja Foodi Steam Fryer. 7. Move the Lid Slider to the "Air Fry/Stovetop". 8. Cook the meal at 370°F/185°C on "Air Fry" Mode for about 14 minutes.
Per Serving: Calories: 187; Fat: 8 g; Total Carbs: 21 g; Fiber: 1 g; Sodium: 338 mg; Protein: 9 g

Turkey Scramble

Prep Time: 10 minutes. | Cook Time: 25 minutes. | Serves: 2

1-pound turkey	shredded
2 teaspoons avocado oil	2 eggs, beaten
2 cups of coconut milk	1 teaspoon black pepper
1 cup Monterey jack cheese,	

1. Place the Cook & Crisp Basket in your Ninja Foodi Pressure Cooker Steam Fryer and place a reversible rack in it. 2. Brush Cook & Crisp Basket with avocado oil. 3. After this, mix turkey with coconut milk, cheese, eggs, and black pepper. 4. Put the prepared mixture in the Cook & Crisp Basket and flatten gently then place in the Ninja Foodi Steam Fryer. 5. Put on the Smart Lid on top of the Ninja Foodi Steam Fryer. 6. Move the Lid Slider to the "Air Fry/Stovetop". 7. Cook the turkey On "Air Fry" Mode at 370°F/185°C for about 25 minutes.
Per Serving: Calories: 531; Fat: 15 g; Total Carbs: 81 g; Fiber: 2 g; Sodium: 1125 mg; Protein:18 g

Cheddar Coconut Biscuits

Prep Time: 15 minutes. | Cook Time: 8 minutes. | Serves: 4

½ cup coconut flour
¼ cup Cheddar cheese, shredded
1 egg, beaten
1 tablespoon cream cheese

1 tablespoon coconut oil, melted
¾ teaspoon baking powder
½ teaspoon cardamom

1. Place the Cook & Crisp Basket in your Ninja Foodi Pressure Cooker Steam Fryer. 2. Mix all the recipe ingredients in a suitable mixing bowl and knead the dough. 3. Then make 4 biscuits and put them in your Ninja Foodi Pressure Cooker Steam Fryer. 4. Put on the Smart Lid on top of the Ninja Foodi Steam Fryer. 5. Move the Lid Slider to the "Air Fry/Stovetop". 6. Cook the meal at 390°F/200°C on "Air Fry" Mode for about 8 minutes. Shake the biscuits from time to time to avoid burning.
Per Serving: Calories: 435; Fat: 16 g; Total Carbs: 61 g; Fiber: 2 g; Sodium: 85 mg; Protein: 9 g

French Toasts

Prep Time: 12 minutes. | Cook Time: 9 minutes. | Serves: 2

⅓ cup coconut flour
1 egg, beaten
¼ teaspoon baking powder
2 teaspoons sugar

¼ teaspoon cinnamon
1 teaspoon mascarpone
1 tablespoon butter, softened

1. Place the Cook & Crisp Basket in your Pressure Cooker Steam Fryer. 2. In a suitable mixing bowl, mix coconut flour with egg, baking powder, sugar, cinnamon, and mascarpone. 3. Then grease the baking cups with butter and pour the coconut flour mixture inside. 4. Put on the Smart Lid on top of the Ninja Foodi Steam Fryer. 5. Move the Lid Slider to the "Air Fry/Stovetop". 6. Cook on "Air Fry" Mode at 365°F/185°C for about 9 minutes until the mixture is set.
Per Serving: Calories: 389; Fat: 17 g; Total Carbs: 60 g; Fiber: 3 g; Sodium: 241 mg; Protein: 11 g

Cheese Egg Scramble

Prep Time: 10 minutes. | Cook Time: 20 minutes. | Serves: 6

1 cup of coconut milk
1 teaspoon avocado oil
2 tablespoons mascarpone

1 cup cheddar cheese, shredded
3 eggs, beaten

1. Place the Cook & Crisp Basket in your Pressure Cooker Steam Fryer. 2. Brush the Ninja Foodi Cook & Crisp Basket with avocado oil. 3. Then mix coconut milk with mascarpone, cheese, and eggs. 4. Put on the Smart Lid on top of the Ninja Foodi Steam Fryer. 5. Move the Lid Slider to the "Air Fry/Stovetop". 6. Pour the liquid in the Ninja Foodi Cook & Crisp Basket. Cook it at 350°F/175°C on "Air Fry" Mode for about 20 minutes.
Per Serving: Calories: 183; Fat: 6 g; Total Carbs: 24 g; Fiber: 3 g; Sodium: 269 mg; Protein: 9 g

Chili Egg Bake

Prep Time: 5 minutes. | Cook Time: 6 minutes. | Serves: 5

5 eggs
1 teaspoon chili flakes

1 teaspoon avocado oil

1. Place the Cook & Crisp Basket in your Ninja Foodi Pressure Cooker Steam Fryer and place a reversible rack in it. 2. Brush the Ninja Foodi Cook & Crisp Basket with avocado oil and crack the eggs into 5 small ramekins. Transfer them to the basket. 3. Put on the Smart Lid on top of the Ninja Foodi Steam Fryer. 4. Move the Lid Slider to the "Air Fry/Stovetop". 5. Sprinkle the eggs with chili flakes. Cook on "Air Fry" Mode at 360°F/180°C for about 6 minutes.
Per Serving: Calories: 180; Fat: 11 g; Total Carbs: 14 g; Fiber: 3 g; Sodium: 287 mg; Protein: 9 g

Morning Herbed Eggs

Prep Time: 10 minutes. | Cook Time: 20 minutes. | Serves: 4

8 eggs
1 teaspoon dried basil
1 teaspoon black pepper

1 teaspoon dried oregano
1 teaspoon avocado oil

1. Place the Cook & Crisp Basket in your Ninja Foodi Pressure Cooker Steam Fryer. 2. Brush the Ninja Foodi Cook & Crisp Basket with avocado oil from inside. 3. Then crack the eggs inside and top them with black pepper and dried oregano. 4. Put on the Smart Lid on top of the Ninja Foodi Steam Fryer. 5. Move the Lid Slider to the "Air Fry/Stovetop". 6. Cook on "Air Fry" Mode at 355°F/180°C for about 20 minutes.
Per Serving: Calories: 460; Fat: 20 g; Total Carbs: 26 g; Fiber: 3 g; Sodium: 126 mg; Protein: 28 g

Chicken Muffins

Prep Time: 10 minutes. | Cook Time: 10 minutes. | Serves: 6

1 cup chicken
½ cup Cheddar cheese, shredded
1 teaspoon dried oregano
½ teaspoon salt

1 tablespoon butter, softened
1 teaspoon dried parsley
2 tablespoons coconut flour

1. Place the Cook & Crisp Basket in your Ninja Foodi Pressure Cooker Steam Fryer. 2. Mix all the recipe ingredients in a suitable mixing bowl and stir until homogenous. 3. Then pour the muffin mixture in the muffin molds and transfer the molds in your Ninja Foodi Pressure Cooker Steam Fryer. 4. Put on the Smart Lid on top of the Ninja Foodi Steam Fryer. 5. Move the Lid Slider to the "Air Fry/Stovetop". 6. Cook on "Air Fry" Mode at 375°F/190°C for about 10 minutes.
Per Serving: Calories: 531; Fat: 15 g; Total Carbs: 81 g; Fiber: 2 g; Sodium: 1125 mg; Protein: 18 g

Eggs with Kalamata Olives

Prep Time: 5 minutes. | Cook Time: 20 minutes. | Serves: 4

4 eggs, beaten
2 Kalamata olives, sliced

1 teaspoon avocado oil
½ teaspoon paprika

1. Place the Cook & Crisp Basket in your Ninja Foodi Pressure Cooker Steam Fryer. 2. Brush the Ninja Foodi Cook & Crisp Basket with avocado oil and pour the eggs inside. 3. Sprinkle the eggs with paprika and top with olives. 4. Put on the Smart Lid on top of the Ninja Foodi Steam Fryer. 5. Move the Lid Slider to the "Air Fry/Stovetop". 6. Cook on "Air Fry" Mode at 360°F/180°C for about 20 minutes.
Per Serving: Calories: 240; Fat: 4 g; Total Carbs: 43 g; Fiber: 8 g; Sodium: 85 mg; Protein: 2 g

Portobello Eggs

Prep Time: 10 minutes. | Cook Time: 14 minutes. | Serves: 2

2 garlic cloves, minced
1 tablespoon olive oil
¼ teaspoon dried thyme
2 Portobello mushrooms, sliced
2 Roma tomatoes, halved lengthwise
Salt and black pepper

2 large eggs
2 tablespoons grated Pecorino Romano cheese
1 tablespoon fresh parsley, for garnish
1 teaspoon truffle oil (optional)

1. Place the Cook & Crisp Basket in your Ninja Foodi Pressure Cooker Steam Fryer. 2. Move the Lid Slider to the "Air Fry/Stovetop". 3. Mix the olive oil, garlic, and thyme in a suitable bowl. Till the mushrooms and tomatoes are coated, brush the mixture over them. Add salt and black pepper to taste. 4. Place the vegetables in the basket of your Ninja Foodi Pressure Cooker Steam Fryer, cut side up. 5. Each mushroom has an egg in the center, which is then covered in cheese. 6. Put on the Smart Lid on top of the Ninja Foodi Steam Fryer. 7. Move the Lid Slider to the "Air Fry/Stovetop". 8. Until the vegetables are soft and the whites are crisp, cook on "Air Fry" Mode at 400°F/200°C for 10 to 14 minutes. Chop the tomatoes when they are cold enough to handle, then arrange them on top of the eggs. Just before serving, scatter parsley over top and, if like, sprinkle with truffle oil.
Per Serving: Calories 178; Fat 14.6 g; Sodium 67 mg; Carbs 12.4g; Fiber 4.8 g; Sugar 6.1g; Protein 2.9 g

Cheddar Breakfast

Prep Time: 5 minutes. | Cook Time: 25 minutes. | Serves: 4

4 eggs, beaten
1 teaspoon avocado oil

2 ounces Cheddar cheese, shredded

1. Place the Cook & Crisp Basket in your Pressure Cooker Steam Fryer and place a reversible rack in it. 2. Brush the ramekins with avocado oil. 3. Then mix eggs with cheese and pour the mixture inside ramekins. 4. Put on the Smart Lid on top of the Ninja Foodi Steam Fryer. 5. Move the Lid Slider to the "Air Fry/Stovetop". 6. Cook on "Air Fry" Mode at 355°F/180°C for about 25 minutes.
Per Serving: Calories: 326; Fat: 23 g; Total Carbs: 10 g; Fiber: 2 g; Sodium: 781 mg; Protein: 22 g

Eggplant Pepper Spread

Prep Time: 15 minutes. | Cook Time: 20 minutes. | Serves: 4

3 eggplants
1 teaspoon chili flakes
1 teaspoon salt

½ teaspoon black pepper
2 tablespoons avocado oil

1. Place the Cook & Crisp Basket in your Ninja Foodi Pressure Cooker Steam Fryer. 2. Peel the eggplants and rub them with salt. 3. Put on the Smart Lid on top of the Ninja Foodi Steam Fryer. 4. Move the Lid Slider to the "Air Fry/Stovetop". 5. Cook the eggplants in your Ninja Foodi Pressure Cooker Steam Fryer at 365°F/185°C on "Air Fry" Mode for about 20 minutes. 6. Then chop the eggplant and put it in the blender. 7. Add all the remaining recipe ingredients and blend the mixture until smooth.
Per Serving: Calories: 190; Fat 9.3 g; Total Carbs: 3.1 g; Sugar 1 g; Protein: 25.2 g; Cholesterol 132 mg

Coconut Crusted Fish Sticks

Prep Time: 15 minutes. | Cook Time: 10 minutes. | Serves: 4

8-ounce cod fillet
1 egg, beaten
2 tablespoons coconut shred

1 teaspoon dried oregano
½ teaspoon salt
1 teaspoon avocado oil

1. Place the Cook & Crisp Basket in your Ninja Foodi Pressure Cooker Steam Fryer. 2. Cut the cod fillet into sticks. 3. Then mix salt with dried oregano and coconut shred. 4. Dip the cod sticks in the beaten egg and coat in the coconut shred mixture. 5. Put on the Smart Lid on top of the Ninja Foodi Steam Fryer. 6. Move the Lid Slider to the "Air Fry/Stovetop". 7. Sprinkle the cod sticks with avocado oil. Cook in your Ninja Foodi Pressure Cooker Steam Fryer at 400°F/200°C on "Air Fry" Mode for about 10 minutes.
Per Serving: Calories: 190; Fat 9.3 g; Total Carbs: 3.1 g; Sugar 1 g; Protein: 25.2 g; Cholesterol 132 mg

Cauliflower Frittata With Almond Mike

Prep Time: 5 minutes. | Cook Time: 25 minutes. | Serves: 4

2 cups cauliflower, chopped
2 ounces Monterey Jack cheese, shredded

4 eggs, beaten
1 cup organic almond milk
1 teaspoon dried oregano

1. Place the Cook & Crisp Basket in your Ninja Foodi Pressure Cooker Steam Fryer. 2. In a suitable mixing bowl, mix dried oregano with almond milk and eggs. 3. Pour the liquid in the Ninja Foodi Cook & Crisp Basket and add cauliflower and cheese. 4. Put on the Smart Lid on top of the Ninja Foodi Steam Fryer. 5. Move the Lid Slider to the "Air Fry/Stovetop". 6. Close the lid. Cook the meal at 350°F/175°C on "Air Fry" Mode for about 25 minutes.
Per Serving: Calories: 280; Fat: 22 g; Total Carbs: 1 g; Fiber: 0 g; Sodium: 366 mg; Protein: 19 g

Kielbasa Egg Scramble

Prep Time: 10 minutes. | Cook Time: 8 minutes. | Serves: 4

8 eggs, beaten
1 teaspoon dried parsley
3 ounces kielbasa, chopped

1 teaspoon coconut oil
1 teaspoon dried oregano

1. Place the Cook & Crisp Basket in your Ninja Foodi Pressure Cooker Steam Fryer. 2. Put on the Smart Lid on top of the Ninja Foodi Steam Fryer. 3. Move the Lid Slider to the "Air Fry/Stovetop". 4. Then toss coconut oil in the Ninja Foodi Cook & Crisp Basket and melt it. 5. Add kielbasa. Cook it at 385°F/195°C on "Air Fry" Mode for about 2 minutes per side. 6. After this, add eggs, parsley, and oregano. 7. Stir the mixture well. Cook it for about 4 minutes. Stir the meal again.
Per Serving: Calories: 320; Fat: 14 g; Total Carbs: 19 g; Fiber: 1 g; Sodium: 258 mg; Protein: 25 g

Mozarella Egg Bake

Prep Time: 5 minutes. | Cook Time: 20 minutes. | Serves: 4

1 cup Mozarella, shredded
4 eggs

1 teaspoon coconut oil, softened
½ teaspoon black pepper

1. Place the Cook & Crisp Basket in your Ninja Foodi Pressure Cooker Steam Fryer. 2. Put on the Smart Lid on top of the Ninja Foodi Steam Fryer. 3. Move the Lid Slider to the "Air Fry/Stovetop". 4. Grease the Ninja Foodi Cook & Crisp Basket with coconut oil and crack eggs inside. 5. Sprinkle the eggs with black pepper and Mozarella. 6. Cook the meal at 360°F/180°C on "Air Fry" Mode for about 20 minutes.
Per Serving: Calories 199; Fat 17.9g; Sodium 525mg; Carbs 1.1g; Fiber 0.3g; Sugar 0.6g; Protein 9.9g

Brussel Sprouts Egg Bake

Prep Time: 5 minutes. | Cook Time: 20 minutes. | Serves: 4

1-pound Brussel sprouts, shredded
8 eggs, beaten
1 teaspoon avocado oil

1 teaspoon turmeric
½ teaspoon salt

1. Place the Cook & Crisp Basket in your Ninja Foodi Pressure Cooker Steam Fryer. 2. Mix all the recipe ingredients and stir until homogenous. 3. Put on the Smart Lid on top of the Ninja Foodi Steam Fryer. 4. Move the Lid Slider to the "Air Fry/Stovetop". 5. Pour the mixture in the Ninja Foodi Cook & Crisp Basket. Cook on "Air Fry" Mode at 365°F/185°C for about 20 minutes.
Per Serving: Calories: 323; Fat: 14.2g; Total Carbs: 2.1g; Fiber: 0.3g; Sugar: 0.6g; Protein: 44.3g

Walnut Granola

Prep Time: 15 minutes. | Cook Time: 60 minutes. | Serves: 4

½ cup pecans, chopped
½ cup walnuts or almonds, chopped
¼ cup unsweetened flaked coconut
¼ cup almond flour
¼ cup flaxseed or chia seeds
2 tablespoons sunflower seeds

2 tablespoons melted butter
¼ cup Swerve sugar replacement
½ teaspoon cinnamon
½ teaspoon vanilla extract
¼ teaspoon nutmeg
¼ teaspoon salt
2 tablespoons water

1. Place the Cook & Crisp Basket in your Ninja Foodi Pressure Cooker Steam Fryer. 2. Move the Lid Slider to the "Air Fry/Stovetop". 3. Cut a piece of parchment paper to fit inside your Ninja Foodi Cook & Crisp Basket. 4. In a suitable bowl, mix the coconut, nuts, almond flour, flaxseed or chia seeds, sunflower seeds, butter, Swerve, cinnamon, vanilla, nutmeg, salt, and water until mixed. 5. Spread the prepared granola on the parchment paper and flatten to an even thickness. 6. Put on the Smart Lid on top of the Ninja Foodi Steam Fryer. 7. Move the Lid Slider to the "Air Fry/Stovetop". 8. Cook on "Air Fry" Mode at 250°F/120°C for about an hour until golden throughout. 9. Remove from your Ninja Foodi Pressure Cooker Steam Fryer and allow to cool. 10. Serve.
Per Serving: Calories 134; Fat 11 g; Sodium 14 mg; Carbs 8.7g; Fiber 4.2g; Sugar 4.5g; Protein 2.2 g

Dill Bacon Bites

Prep Time: 10 minutes. | Cook Time: 12 minutes. | Serves: 4

10-ounce bacon, chopped
1 teaspoon dried dill

4 teaspoons cream cheese
1 teaspoon dried oregano

1. Place the Cook & Crisp Basket in your Ninja Foodi Pressure Cooker Steam Fryer. 2. Put on the Smart Lid on top of the Ninja Foodi Steam Fryer. 3. Move the Lid Slider to the "Air Fry/Stovetop". 4. Put the bacon in your Ninja Foodi Pressure Cooker Steam Fryer in one layer. Cook on "Air Fry" Mode for about 12 minutes at 375°F/190°C. Shake the bacon from time to time to avoid burning. 5. Then mix bacon with remaining ingredients and make the balls (bites)
Per Serving: Calories: 280; Fat: 22 g; Total Carbs: 1 g; Fiber: 0 g; Sodium: 366 mg; Protein: 19 g

Pork Casserole

Prep Time: 15 minutes. | Cook Time: 25 minutes. | Serves: 6

2 jalapeno peppers, sliced
2 cups pork
1 cup Cheddar cheese, shredded

1 teaspoon coconut oil
1 teaspoon chili flakes
½ teaspoon turmeric

1. Place the Cook & Crisp Basket in your Ninja Foodi Pressure Cooker Steam Fryer. 2. Grease the Ninja Foodi Cook & Crisp Basket with coconut oil. 3. Then mix pork with jalapeno peppers, chili flakes, and turmeric. 4. Put the mixture in the Ninja Foodi Cook & Crisp Basket and flatten it. Top the mixture with Cheddar cheese. 5. Put on the Smart Lid on top of the Ninja Foodi Steam Fryer. 6. Move the Lid Slider to the "Air Fry/Stovetop". 7. Cook the casserole at 380°F/195°C on "Air Fry" Mode for about 25 minutes.
Per Serving: Calories 241; Fat 16.8 g; Sodium 225 mg; Carbs 8g; Fiber 0.4g; Sugar 1.1g; Protein 15.4g

Tomato Egg Omelet

Prep Time: 5 minutes. | Cook Time: 20 minutes. | Serves: 4

6 eggs, beaten
1 tomato, chopped
1 teaspoon coconut oil, melted

½ teaspoon dried dill
½ teaspoon salt

1. Place the Cook & Crisp Basket in your Ninja Foodi Pressure Cooker Steam Fryer. 2. Mix eggs with dried dill and salt. 3. Grease the Ninja Foodi Cook & Crisp Basket with coconut oil and pour the egg mixture inside. 4. Put on the Smart Lid on top of the Ninja Foodi Steam Fryer. 5. Move the Lid Slider to the "Air Fry/Stovetop". 6. Add chopped tomatoes. Cook the omelet for about 20 minutes at 365°F/185°C.
Per Serving: Calories 199; Fat 17.9g; Sodium 525mg; Carbs 1.1g; Fiber 0.3g; Sugar 0.6g; Protein 9.9g

Soft-Boiled Eggs

Prep Time: 5 minutes. | Cook Time: 16 minutes. | Serves: 2

6 eggs

1. Place the Cook & Crisp Basket in your Ninja Foodi Pressure Cooker Steam Fryer. 2. Put the eggs in the Ninja Foodi Cook & Crisp Basket. 3. Put on the Smart Lid on top of the Ninja Foodi Steam Fryer. 4. Move the Lid Slider to the "Air Fry/Stovetop". 5. Cook on "Air Fry" Mode at 250°F/120°C for about 16 minutes.
Per Serving: Calories 161; Fat 7.9 g; Sodium 595 mg; Carbs 10.8g; Fiber 1.7g; Sugar 0.5g; Protein 13.2g

Argula Cream Spread

Prep Time: 5 minutes. | Cook Time: 10 minutes. | Serves: 4

2 tablespoons heavy cream
3 cups arugula, chopped
2 tablespoons dried oregano

1-ounce pork rinds
1-ounce Parmesan, grated

1. Place the Cook & Crisp Basket in your Ninja Foodi Pressure

Cooker Steam Fryer. 2. Mix all the recipe ingredients in the Ninja Foodi Cook & Crisp Basket. 3. Put on the Smart Lid on top of the Ninja Foodi Steam Fryer. 4. Move the Lid Slider to the "Air Fry/Stovetop". 5. Cook on "Air Fry" Mode at 365°F/185°C for about 10 minutes. 6. Then carefully mix the cooked mixture again and blend with the help of the immersion blender to get the spread texture.
Per Serving: Calories 220; Fat 13.5 g; Sodium 1395 mg; Carbs 6.9g; Fiber 1.7g; Sugar 3.8g; Protein 19.7g

Pepper Eggs

Prep Time: 10 minutes. | Cook Time: 12 minutes. | Serves: 4

1 teaspoon cayenne pepper
1 tablespoon butter, melted

8 eggs

1. Place the Cook & Crisp Basket in your Ninja Foodi Pressure Cooker Steam Fryer. 2. Then brush the Ninja Foodi Cook & Crisp Basket with butter and crack the eggs inside. 3. Sprinkle the eggs with cayenne pepper. 4. Put on the Smart Lid on top of the Ninja Foodi Steam Fryer. 5. Move the Lid Slider to the "Air Fry/Stovetop". 6. Cook on "Air Fry" Mode at 395°F/200°C for about 12 minutes.
Per Serving: Calories 122; Fat 7.5 g; Sodium 465 mg; Carbs 9g; Fiber 3.8g; Sugar 2.8g; Protein 7.4g

Swiss Chard Egg Frittata

Prep Time: 5 minutes. | Cook Time: 20 minutes. | Serves: 4

6 eggs, beaten
4-ounce Swiss chard, chopped
¼ cup coconut cream

1 teaspoon coconut oil, melted
½ teaspoon turmeric
½ teaspoon salt

1. Place the Cook & Crisp Basket in your Ninja Foodi Pressure Cooker Steam Fryer. 2. In a suitable mixing bowl mix all the recipe ingredients except coconut oil and make the small fritters. 3. Brush it with coconut oil and put the fritters inside. 4. Put on the Smart Lid on top of the Ninja Foodi Steam Fryer. 5. Move the Lid Slider to the "Air Fry/Stovetop". 6. Cook on "Air Fry" Mode at 385°F/195°C for about 10 minutes per side.
Per Serving: Calories 179; Fat 7.5 g; Sodium 242 mg; Carbs 16g; Fiber 0.6g; Sugar 6.8g; Protein 10.6g

Zucchini Spread

Prep Time: 10 minutes. | Cook Time: 15 minutes. | Serves: 4

4 zucchinis, chopped
1 teaspoon garlic powder

1 tablespoon avocado oil
½ teaspoon salt

1. Place the Cook & Crisp Basket in your Ninja Foodi Pressure Cooker Steam Fryer. 2. Mix zucchini with garlic powder, avocado oil, and salt. 3. Put on the Smart Lid on top of the Ninja Foodi Steam Fryer. 4. Move the Lid Slider to the "Air Fry/Stovetop". 5. Put the mixture in your Ninja Foodi Pressure Cooker Steam Fryer. Cook on "Air Fry" Mode at 375°F/190°C for about 15 minutes. 6. Then blend the cooked zucchini until you get smooth spread.
Per Serving: Calories 38; Fat 2.6 g; Sodium 120 mg; Carbs 3.1g; Fiber 0.6g; Sugar 1.7g; Protein 11.7g

Omelet with Herbs

Prep Time: 10 minutes. | Cook Time: 18 minutes. | Serves: 3

6 eggs, beaten
1 tablespoon coconut milk
1 teaspoon Herbs de Provence

1 teaspoon coconut oil
1-ounce Parmesan, grated

1. Place the Cook & Crisp Basket in your Ninja Foodi Pressure Cooker Steam Fryer. 2. Grease the Ninja Foodi Cook & Crisp Basket with coconut oil. 3. Mix eggs with coconut oil and Herbs de Provence. Pour the liquid in your Ninja Foodi Pressure Cooker Steam Fryer. 4. Put on the Smart Lid on top of the Ninja Foodi Steam Fryer. 5. Move the Lid Slider to the "Air Fry/Stovetop". 6. Then top it with Parmesan. Cook the meal at 365°F/185°C on "Air Fry" Mode for about 18 minutes.
Per Serving: Calories 202; Fat 15.9g; Sodium 720 mg; Carbs 3.9g; Fiber 1.3g; Sugar 1.6g; Protein 12.4g

Cheese Rolls

Prep Time: 15 minutes. | Cook Time: 10 minutes. | Serves: 4

4 eggs, beaten
½ teaspoon coconut oil, melted

½ teaspoon chili flakes
2 tablespoons cream cheese

1. Place the Cook & Crisp Basket in your Ninja Foodi Pressure Cooker Steam Fryer. 2. Mix eggs with chili flakes. 3. Put on the Smart Lid on top of the Ninja Foodi Steam Fryer. 4. Move the Lid Slider to the "Air Fry/Stovetop". 5. Then brush the Ninja Foodi Cook & Crisp Basket with coconut oil. 6. Make 4 crepes from egg mixture. Cook at 395°F/200°C on "Air Fry" Mode in your Ninja Foodi Cook & Crisp Basket. 7. Then spread the cream cheese over every egg crepe and roll.
Per Serving: Calories 96; Fat 5.8 g; Sodium 65 mg; Carbs 5.6g; Fiber 0.3g; Sugar 1.7g; Protein 36.4g

Dill Egg Omelet

Prep Time: 10 minute | Cook Time: 15 minutes. | Serves: 4

8 eggs, beaten
1 tablespoon dill, dried

¼ cup of coconut milk
½ teaspoon coconut oil, melted

1. Place the Cook & Crisp Basket in your Ninja Foodi Pressure Cooker Steam Fryer. 2. Mix eggs with dill and coconut milk. 3. Brush the Ninja Foodi Cook & Crisp Basket with coconut oil and pour the egg mixture inside. 4. Put on the Smart Lid on top of the Ninja Foodi Steam Fryer. 5. Move the Lid Slider to the "Air Fry/Stovetop". 6. Cook the omelet for about 15 minutes at 385°F/195°C.
Per Serving: Calories 341; Fat 26.8 g; Sodium 525 mg; Carbs 9.8g; Fiber 0.4g; Sugar 1.1g; Protein 15.4g

Coconut Crusted Mozarella Sticks

Prep Time: 15 minutes. | Cook Time: 6 minutes. | Serves: 6

2 eggs, beaten
10 ounce Mozarella, cut into sticks

2 tablespoons coconut shred

1. Place the Cook & Crisp Basket in your Ninja Foodi Pressure Cooker Steam Fryer. 2. Dip Mozarella sticks in the eggs and then coat in the coconut shred. Repeat the same step one more time. 3. Put the sticks inside. 4. Put on the Smart Lid on top of the Ninja Foodi Steam Fryer. 5. Move the Lid Slider to the "Air Fry/Stovetop". 6. Roast at 400°F/200°C on "Air Fry" Mode for about 3 minutes per side.
Per Serving: Calories 208; Fat 10.5 g; Sodium 1755 mg; Carbs 26.9g; Fiber 4.1g; Sugar 2.5g; Protein 2.9g

Spinach Muffins

Prep Time: 10 minutes. | Cook Time: 15 minutes. | Serves: 4

1 cup Cheddar cheese, shredded
1 cup spinach, chopped
6 eggs, beaten

1 teaspoon coconut oil, melted
1 teaspoon dried oregano

1. Place the Cook & Crisp Basket in your Ninja Foodi Pressure Cooker Steam Fryer. 2. In a suitable mixing bowl, mix Cheddar cheese with spinach, eggs, and dried oregano. 3. Brush the molds of the muffin with coconut oil and put the muffins mixture inside. 4. Put on the Smart Lid on top of the Ninja Foodi Steam Fryer. 5. Move the Lid Slider to the "Air Fry/Stovetop". 6. Cook on "Air Fry" Mode at 385°F/195°C at 350°F/175°C for about 15 minutes.
Per Serving: Calories 235; Fat 18.5 g; Sodium 64 mg; Carbs 9.6g; Fiber 4.1g; Sugar 2.4g; Protein 11.9g

Spinach Cheese Quesadilla

Prep Time: 10 minutes. | Cook Time: 3 minutes. | Serves: 2

2 tortillas
¼ cup Cheddar cheese, shredded

½ cup spinach, chopped
1 teaspoon avocado oil

1. Place the Cook & Crisp Basket in your Ninja Foodi Pressure Cooker Steam Fryer. 2. Brush the Ninja Foodi Cook & Crisp Basket with avocado oil. 3. Then mix Cheddar cheese with spinach and put over the tortillas. Fold the tortillas and put in your Ninja Foodi Cook & Crisp Basket. 4. Put on the Smart Lid on top of the Ninja Foodi Steam Fryer. 5. Move the Lid Slider to the "Air Fry/Stovetop". 6. Cook the tortillas at 400°F/200°C on "Air Fry" Mode at 350°F/175°C for about 3 minutes.
Per Serving: Calories 281; Fat 15.5 g; Sodium 262 mg; Carbs 27.5g; Fiber 2.2g; Sugar 5g; Protein 8.5g

Breakfast Egg Pizza

Prep Time: 10 minutes. | Cook Time: 24 minutes. | Serves: 4

4 large eggs
1 tablespoon water
½ teaspoon garlic powder
½ teaspoon onion powder
½ teaspoon dried oregano
2 tablespoons coconut flour
3 tablespoons grated Parmesan

cheese
½ cup shredded provolone cheese
1 link cooked turkey sausage, chopped (about 2 ounces)
2 sun-dried tomatoes, chopped
2 scallions, thinly sliced
Olive oil

1. Place the cooker's pot in your Pressure Cooker Steam Fryer and set a reversible rack inside. 2. Layer Cook & Crisp Basket with parchment paper and lightly coat the paper with olive oil. 3. In a suitable bowl, whisk 2 of the eggs with the water, garlic powder, onion powder, and dried oregano. Add the coconut flour, breaking up any lumps with your hands as you add it to the bowl. 4. Blend the egg mixture before adding the coconut flour. Add the Parmesan cheese and stir. Give the mixture some time to rest so that it becomes thick and dough-like. 5. Transfer the mixture to the Cook & Crisp Basket. Use a spatula to spread it evenly and slightly up the sides of the Cook & Crisp Basket. 6. Put on the Smart Lid on top of the Ninja Foodi Steam Fryer. 7. Move the Lid Slider to the "Air Fry/Stovetop". 8. Cook on "Air Fry" Mode until the crust is set but still light in color, about 10 minutes. Top with the cheeses, sausage, and sun-dried tomatoes. 9. Break the remaining 2 eggs into a suitable bowl, then slide them onto the pizza. Return the pizza to your Ninja Foodi Pressure Cooker Steam Fryer. 10. Put on the Smart Lid on top of the Ninja Foodi Steam Fryer. 11. Move the Lid Slider to the "Air Fry/Stovetop". 12. Cook on "Air Fry" Mode at 400°F/200°C for about 14 minutes until the egg whites are set and the yolks are the desired doneness. Top with the scallions and allow to rest for about 5 minutes before serving.
Per Serving: Calories 187; Fat 10.9 g; Sodium 2512 mg; Carbs 12g; Fiber 1.7 g; Sugar 4.9g; Protein 13.7g

Kale Cream Eggs

Prep Time: 10 minutes. | Cook Time: 20 minutes. | Serves: 4

1 cup kale, chopped
6 eggs, beaten
¼ cup heavy cream

½ teaspoon black pepper
½ teaspoon coconut oil

1. Place the Cook & Crisp Basket in your Ninja Foodi Pressure Cooker Steam Fryer and place a reversible rack in it. 2. Grease ramekins with coconut oil. 3. Then mix kale with eggs and heavy cream. Add black pepper. 4. Pour the mixture in the ramekins. 5. Put on the Smart Lid on top of the Ninja Foodi Steam Fryer. 6. Move the Lid Slider to the "Air Fry/Stovetop". 7. Cook on "Air Fry" Mode at 375°F/190°C for about 20 minutes.
Per Serving: Calories 149; Fat 12 g; Sodium 132 mg; Carbs 10.5g; Fiber 2.6g; Sugar 4.6g; Protein 1.5g

Bell Peppers Salad

Prep Time: 5 minutes. | Cook Time: 10 minutes. | Serves: 4

1 cup bell pepper, chopped
1 teaspoon avocado oil
1 teaspoon olive oil

1 teaspoon dried cilantro
½ cup Mozarella, shredded

1. Place the Cook & Crisp Basket in your Ninja Foodi Pressure Cooker Steam Fryer. 2. Mix bell pepper with avocado oil and put it in your Ninja Foodi Pressure Cooker Steam Fryer. 3. Put on the Smart Lid on top of the Ninja Foodi Steam Fryer. 4. Move the Lid Slider to the "Air Fry/Stovetop". 5. Cook the vegetables for about 10 minutes at 385°F/195°C. Shake the bell peppers from time to time. 6. Then mix cooked bell peppers with olive oil, cilantro, and Mozarella. Shake the cooked salad.
Per Serving: Calories 117; Fat 5.8 g; Sodium 10 mg; Carbs 9.9g; Fiber 3.3g; Sugar 3.3g; Protein 6.7g

Wrapped Bacon with Eggs

Prep Time: 15 minutes. | Cook Time: 4 minutes. | Serves: 2

2 eggs, hard-boiled, peeled	1 teaspoon black pepper
4 bacon slices	2 lettuce leaves
1 teaspoon cream cheese	

1. Place the Cook & Crisp Basket in your Ninja Foodi Pressure Cooker Steam Fryer. 2. Put the bacon slices in your Ninja Foodi Pressure Cooker Steam Fryer. 3. Put on the Smart Lid on top of the Ninja Foodi Steam Fryer. 4. Move the Lid Slider to the "Air Fry/Stovetop". 5. Cook on "Air Fry" Mode at 400°F/200°C at 350°F/175°C for about 2 minutes per side. 6. Then wrap the eggs in the bacon and put on the lettuce leaves. 7. Add cream cheese and black pepper and fold the lettuce leaves.
Per Serving: Calories 281; Fat 15.5 g; Sodium 262 mg; Carbs 27.5g; Fiber 2.2g; Sugar 5g; Protein 8.5g

Sweet Cinnamon Muffins

Prep Time: 10 minutes. | Cook Time: 10 minutes. | Serves: 4

⅓ cup coconut flour	1 teaspoon cinnamon
2 tablespoons sugar	4 eggs, beaten
¼ teaspoon baking powder	1 tablespoon coconut oil, softened

1. Place the Cook & Crisp Basket in your Ninja Foodi Pressure Cooker Steam Fryer. 2. Mix all the recipe ingredients in a suitable mixing bowl. 3. Then transfer the mixture in the muffin molds. 4. Put on the Smart Lid on top of the Ninja Foodi Steam Fryer. 5. Move the Lid Slider to the "Air Fry/Stovetop". 6. Cook on "Air Fry" Mode in your Ninja Foodi Pressure Cooker Steam Fryer at 375°F/190°C for about 10 minutes.
Per Serving: Calories 216; Fat 6.9 g; Sodium 31 mg; Carbs 38.5g; Fiber 5.6g; Sugar 6.7g; Protein 6.7g

Cajun Sausage

Prep Time: 10 minutes. | Cook Time: 20 minutes. | Serves: 8

1½ pounds 85% lean turkey	1 teaspoon Creole seasoning
3 cloves garlic, chopped	1 teaspoon dried thyme
¼ onion, grated	½ teaspoon paprika
1 teaspoon Tabasco sauce	½ teaspoon cayenne

1. Place the Cook & Crisp Basket in your Ninja Foodi Pressure Cooker Steam Fryer. 2. In a suitable bowl, mix the turkey, garlic, onion, Tabasco, Creole seasoning, thyme, paprika, and cayenne. Mix with clean hands until mixed. Shape into 16 patties, about ½ inch thick. 3. Put on the Smart Lid on top of the Ninja Foodi Steam Fryer. 4. Move the Lid Slider to the "Air Fry/Stovetop". 5. Working in batches, arrange the prepared patties in a single layer in your Ninja Foodi Cook & Crisp Basket. Pausing halfway through the cooking time to flip the half-cooked patties, cook on "Air Fry" Mode at 370°F/185°C for about 15 to 20 minutes until a thermometer inserted into the thickest portion registers 165°F/75°C.
Per Serving: Calories 283; Fat 6.6g; Sodium 693mg; Carbs 8.5g; Fiber 1.4g; Sugar 3.4g; Protein 45.2g

Tomato Breakfast Wrap

Prep Time: 15 minutes. | Cook Time: 13 minutes. | Serves: 4

8 ounces (about 12 slices) reduced-sodium bacon	8 large romaine lettuce leaves
8 tablespoons mayo	4 Roma tomatoes, sliced
	Salt and black pepper

1. Place the Cook & Crisp Basket in your Ninja Foodi Pressure Cooker Steam Fryer. 2. Spread the bacon strips in a single layer in your Ninja Foodi Cook & Crisp Basket. 3. Put on the Smart Lid on top of the Ninja Foodi Steam Fryer. 4. Move the Lid Slider to the "Air Fry/Stovetop". 5. Cook on at 350°F/175°C "Air Fry" Mode for about 10 minutes. 6. Spread a tablespoon of mayo on each of the lettuce leaves and top with the tomatoes and cooked bacon. Season with salt and black pepper. 7. Roll the lettuce leaves as you would a burrito,

securing with a toothpick if desired.
Per Serving: Calories 164; Fat 16.9 g; Sodium 99 mg; Carbs 3.2g; Fiber 0.8g; Sugar 0.2g; Protein 2.3g

Cheese & Avocado Melt

Prep Time: 10 minutes. | Cook Time: 5 minutes. | Serves: 2

1 avocado	1 tablespoon heavy cream
4 slices cooked bacon, chopped	¼ cup shredded Cheddar cheese
2 tablespoons salsa	

1. Place the Cook & Crisp Basket in your Ninja Foodi Pressure Cooker Steam Fryer. 2. Slice the avocado in half then discard the pit. To ensure the avocado halves do not roll in the basket, slice a thin piece of skin off the base. 3. In a suitable bowl, mix the bacon, salsa, and cream. Divide the mixture between the avocado halves and top with the cheese. 4. Place the avocado halves in the Ninja Foodi Cook & Crisp Basket. 5. Put on the Smart Lid on top of the Ninja Foodi Steam Fryer. 6. Move the Lid Slider to the "Air Fry/Stovetop". 7. Cook on "Air Fry" Mode at 400°F/200°C for about 3 to 5 minutes until the cheese has melted and begins to brown. Serve warm.
Per Serving: Calories 469; Fat 34.1 g; Sodium 1242 mg; Carbs 23.5g; Fiber 0.6g; Sugar 0; Protein 19.2g

Eggs Ham

Prep Time: 15 minutes. | Cook Time: 15 minutes. | Serves: 2

4 slices deli ham	(optional)
¼ cup shredded Cheddar cheese	Salt and black pepper
4 large eggs	A little vegetable oil
1 tablespoon chopped fresh parsley	

1. Place the Cook & Crisp Basket in your Ninja Foodi Pressure Cooker Steam Fryer. 2. Lightly coat 4 silicone muffin cups with vegetable oil. 3. Layer each cup with a ham slice, tearing it into a few smaller pieces, if necessary, to ensure an even fit. (It's OK if the ham extends slightly above the top of the cup.) Sprinkle 1 tablespoon of cheese into the bottom of each cup, then crack an egg into each. 4. Put on the Smart Lid on top of the Ninja Foodi Steam Fryer. 5. Move the Lid Slider to the "Air Fry/Stovetop". 6. Cook on "Air Fry" Mode at 400°F/200°C for about 15 minutes until the whites are set and the yolk is cooked to the desired doneness. Scatter parsley on top, if desired, and season to taste with salt and pepper.
Per Serving: Calories 170; Fat 13.1 g; Sodium 6 mg; Carbs 14.8 g; Fiber 2.5g; Sugar 9g; Protein 1.9g

Blueberry Muffins

Prep Time: 10 minutes. | Cook Time: 20 minutes. | Serves: 6

1¼ cups almond flour	3 tablespoons melted butter
3 tablespoons Swerve sugar replacement	1 tablespoon milk
1 teaspoon baking powder	1 tablespoon fresh lemon juice
2 large eggs	½ cup fresh blueberries
	Vegetable oil

1. Place the Cook & Crisp Basket in your Ninja Foodi Pressure Cooker Steam Fryer. 2. Lightly coat 6 silicone muffin cups with vegetable oil. Set aside. 3. In a suitable mixing bowl, mix the almond flour, Swerve, and baking powder. Set aside. 4. In a separate small bowl, mix well the eggs, butter, milk, and lemon juice. Add the egg mixture to the flour mixture and stir until just mixed. Fold in the blueberries and let the batter sit for about 5 minutes. 5. Spoon the prepared muffin batter into the muffin cups, about two-thirds full. 6. Put on the Smart Lid on top of the Ninja Foodi Steam Fryer. 7. Move the Lid Slider to the "Air Fry/Stovetop". 8. Cook on "Air Fry" Mode at 350°F/175°C for about 20 to 25 minutes, until a toothpick inserted into the center of a muffin comes out clean. 9. Remove the basket from your Ninja Foodi Pressure Cooker Steam Fryer and let the muffins cool for about 5 minutes before transferring them to a wire rack to cool completely.
Per Serving (1 muffin): Calories 274; Fat 9.5 g; Sodium 3542 mg; Carbs 6.3g; Fiber 0.9g; Sugar 4.6g; Protein 40.5g

Parmesan Bread

Prep Time: 10 minutes. | Cook Time: 30 minutes. | Serves: 6 to 8

½ cup unsalted butter, melted
¼ teaspoon salt
¾ cup grated Parmesan cheese
3 to 4 cloves garlic, minced
1 tablespoon chopped fresh parsley
1 pound frozen bread dough, defrosted
Olive oil
1 egg, beaten

1. Mix the melted butter, salt, Parmesan cheese, garlic and chopped parsley in a suitable bowl. 2. Roll the prepared dough out into a rectangle that measures 8 inches by 17 inches. 3. Spread the butter mixture over the prepared dough, leaving a half-inch border un-buttered along one of the long edges. Roll the prepared dough from one long edge to the other, ending with the un-buttered border. Pinch the seam shut tightly. Shape the log into a circle sealing the ends by pushing one end into the other and stretching the prepared dough around it. 4. Cut out a circle of aluminum foil that is the same size as the Ninja Foodi Pressure Steam Fryer basket. Brush the foil circle with oil and place an oven safe ramekin or glass in the center. 5. Transfer the prepared dough ring to the aluminum foil circle, around the ramekin. This will help you make sure the prepared dough will fit in the basket and maintain its ring shape. Use kitchen shears to cut 8 slits around the outer edge of the prepared dough ring halfway to the center. Brush the prepared dough ring with egg wash. 6. Brush the sides of the Cook & Crisp Basket with oil and transfer the prepared dough ring, foil circle and ramekin into the basket. 7. Slide the Cook & Crisp Basket back into the Pressure Steam Fryer, but do not turn it on. Let the prepared dough rise inside the Pressure Steam Fryer for around 30 minutes. 8. After the bread has proofed in the Ninja Foodi Pressure Steam Fryer for around 30 minutes. 9. Put on the Smart Lid on top of the Ninja Foodi Steam Fryer. 10. Move the Lid Slider to the "Air Fry/Stovetop". Select the "Air Fry" mode for cooking. 11. Cook the bread ring on the "Air Fry" mode at 340°F/170°C for 15 minutes. Flip the bread over by inverting it onto a plate or cutting board and sliding it back into the cook & crisp Basket. 12. Air-fry for another 15 minutes. Serve Warm.
Per serving: Calories: 334; Fat: 10.9g; Sodium: 354mg; Carbs: 20.5g; Fiber: 4.1g; Sugar 8.2g; Protein 06g

Pita Bread

Prep Time: 10 minutes. | Cook Time: 48 minutes. | Serves: 8

2 teaspoons active dry yeast
1 tablespoon sugar
1½ cups warm water
3¼ cups all-purpose flour
2 teaspoons salt
1 tablespoon olive oil
Salt, to taste

1. Dissolve the yeast, sugar and water in the bowl of a stand mixer. Let the mixture sit for around 5 minutes to make sure the yeast is active. Mix the flour and salt in a suitable bowl, and add it to the water, along with the olive oil. Mix with the prepared dough hook until mixed. 2. Knead the prepared dough until it is smooth. Transfer the prepared dough to an oiled bowl, cover and let it rise in a warm place until doubled in bulk. 3. Place the Cook & Crisp Basket in your Pressure Cooker Steam Fryer. 4. Divide the prepared dough into 8 portions and roll each portion into a circle about 4-inches in diameter. Don't roll the balls too thin, or you won't get the pocket inside the pita. 5. Brush both sides of the prepared dough with olive oil, and sprinkle with salt if desired. 6. Put on the Smart Lid on top of the Ninja Foodi Steam Fryer. 7. Move the Lid Slider to the "Air Fry/Stovetop". Cook one at a time on "Air Fry" Mode at 400°F/200°C for 6 minutes, 8. flipping it over when there are two minutes left in the cooking time.
Per serving: Calories: 284; Fat: 9g; Sodium: 441mg; Carbs: 7g; Fiber: 4.6g; Sugar 5g; Protein 19g

Artichoke Pizza

Prep Time: 10 minutes. | Cook Time: 18 minutes. | Serves: 2

2 tablespoons olive oil
3 cups fresh spinach
2 cloves garlic, minced
1 (8-ounces) pizza dough ball
½ cup grated mozzarella cheese
¼ cup grated Fontina cheese
¼ cup artichoke hearts, chopped
2 tablespoons grated Parmesan
cheese
¼ teaspoon dried oregano
Salt and black pepper, to taste

1. Heat the oil in a suitable sauté pan on the stovetop. Add the spinach and half the garlic to the pan and sauté for a few minutes, until the spinach has wilted then transfer to a bowl. 2. Place the Cook & Crisp Basket in your Pressure Cooker Steam Fryer. 3. Line the Ninja Foodi Pressure Steam Fryer basket with aluminum. Brush the foil with oil. Shape the prepared dough into a circle and place it on top of the foil. 4. Brush the prepared dough with olive oil and transfer it into the Ninja Foodi Pressure Steam Fryer basket with the foil on the bottom. 5. Put on the Smart Lid on top of the Ninja Foodi Steam Fryer. 6. Move the Lid Slider to the "Air Fry/Stovetop". Cook the prepared pizza dough on "Air Fry" mode at 390°F/200°C for around 6 minutes . 7. Turn the prepared dough over, remove the aluminum foil and brush again with olive oil. Air-fry for 4 minutes. 8. Add the mozzarella and Fontina cheeses over the prepared dough. Top with the spinach and artichoke hearts. Sprinkle the Parmesan cheese and dried oregano on top and drizzle with olive oil. Put on the Smart Lid on top of the Ninja Foodi Steam Fryer. Move the Lid Slider to the "Air Fry/Stovetop". Cook on "Air Fry" mode at 350°F/175°C for around 8 minutes, until the cheese has melted and is browned. 9. Serve.
Per serving: Calories: 372; Fat: 20g; Sodium: 891mg; Carbs: 29g; Fiber: 3g; Sugar 8g; Protein 17g

Pepperoni Cheese Pizza

Prep Time: 10 minutes. | Cook Time: 18 minutes. | Serves: 2

1 (8-ounces) pizza dough ball
Olive oil
½ cup pizza sauce
¾ cup grated mozzarella cheese
½ cup thick sliced pepperoni
⅓ cup sliced pickled hot banana peppers
¼ teaspoon dried oregano
2 teaspoons honey

1. Place the Cook & Crisp Basket in your Pressure Cooker Steam Fryer. 2. Cut out a piece of foil the same size as the bottom of the Ninja Foodi Pressure Steam Fryer basket. Brush the foil circle with olive oil. Shape the prepared dough into a circle and place it on top of the foil. Dock the prepared dough by piercing it several times with a fork. Brush the prepared dough with olive oil and transfer it into the "cook & crisp basket" with the foil on the bottom. 3. Put on the Smart Lid on top of the Ninja Foodi Steam Fryer. Move the Lid Slider to the "Air Fry/Stovetop". Select the "Air Fry" mode for cooking. 4. Air-fry the plain pizza dough at 390°F/200°C for around 6 minutes. Turn the prepared dough over, remove the aluminum foil and brush again with olive oil. Air-fry for an additional 4 minutes. 5. Spread the pizza sauce on top of the prepared dough and sprinkle the mozzarella cheese over the sauce. Top with the pepperoni, pepper slices and dried oregano. 6. Put on the Smart Lid on top of the Ninja Foodi Steam Fryer. Move the Lid Slider to the "Air Fry/Stovetop". Select the "Air Fry" mode for cooking. Adjust the cooking temperature to 350°F/175°C. 7. Cook for around 8 minutes, until the cheese has melted and browned. Transfer the prepared pizza to a cutting board and drizzle with the honey. Slice and serve.
Per serving: Calories: 354; Fat: 10.9g; Sodium: 454mg; Carbs: 10g; Fiber: 3.1g; Sugar 5.2g; Protein 10g

Strawberry Morning Toast

Prep Time: 10 minutes. | Cook Time: 8 minutes. | Serves: 4

4 slices bread, ½-inch thick Butter-flavored cooking spray
1 cup sliced strawberries
1 teaspoon sugar

1. Place the Cook & Crisp Basket in your Pressure Cooker Steam Fryer. 2. Grease one side of each bread slice with butter-flavored cooking spray. Lay slices sprayed side down. 3. Divide the strawberries among the bread slices. 4. Sprinkle evenly with the sugar and place in the Ninja Foodi Pressure Steam Fryer basket in a single layer. 5. Put on the Smart Lid on top of the Ninja Foodi Steam Fryer. 6. Move the Lid Slider to the "Air Fry/Stovetop". Select the "Air Fry" mode for cooking. 7. Air Fry toast at 390°F/200°C for 8 minutes. The bottom should look brown and crisp and the top should look glazed.
Per serving: Calories: 282; Fat: 19g; Sodium: 354mg; Carbs: 15g; Fiber: 5.1g; Sugar 8.2g; Protein 12g

Pepper Bread

Prep Time: 10 minutes. | Cook Time: 7 minutes. | Serves: 8

7-inch round bread boule	½ teaspoon dried oregano
Olive oil	½ cup black olives, sliced
½ cup mayonnaise	½ cup green olives, sliced
2 tablespoons butter, melted	½ cup coarsely chopped roasted
1 cup grated mozzarella or Fontina	red peppers
cheese	2 tablespoons minced red onion
¼ cup grated Parmesan cheese	Black pepper, to taste

1. Place the Cook & Crisp Basket in your Pressure Cooker Steam Fryer. 2. Cut the bread boule in half horizontally. If your bread boule has a rounded top, trim the top of the boule so that the top half will lie flat with the cut side facing up. Brush both sides of the boule halves with olive oil. 3. Place one half of the boule into the Ninja Foodi Pressure Steam Fryer basket with the center cut side facing down. 4. Put on the Smart Lid on top of the Ninja Foodi Steam Fryer. Move the Lid Slider to the "Air Fry/Stovetop". Select the "Air Fry" mode for cooking. 5. Air-fry at 370°F/185°C for around 2 minutes to toast the bread. Repeat with the other half of the bread boule. 6. Mix the mayonnaise, butter, mozzarella cheese, Parmesan cheese and dried oregano in a suitable bowl. Fold in the black and green olives, roasted red peppers and red onion and season with black pepper. Spread the cheese mixture over the untoasted side of the bread, covering the entire surface. 7. Put on the Smart Lid on top of the Ninja Foodi Steam Fryer. 8. Move the Lid Slider to the "Air Fry/Stovetop". Select the "Air Fry" mode for cooking. 9. Air Fry bread at 350°F/175°C for 5 minutes until the cheese is melted and browned. Repeat with the other half. Cut into slices and serve warm.
Per serving: Calories: 389; Fat: 11g; Sodium: 501mg; Carbs: 28.9g; Fiber: 4.6g; Sugar 8g; Protein 6g

Peach Vanilla Fritters

Prep Time: 10 minutes. | Cook Time: 6 minutes. | Serves: 8

1½ cups bread flour	2 cups small diced peaches
1 teaspoon active dry yeast	1 tablespoon butter
¼ cup sugar	1 teaspoon cinnamon
¼ teaspoon salt	1 to 2 tablespoons sugar
½ cup warm milk	Glaze
½ teaspoon vanilla extract	¾ cup powdered sugar
2 egg yolks	4 teaspoons milk
2 tablespoons melted butter	

1. Mix the flour, yeast, sugar and salt in a suitable bowl. Add the milk, vanilla, egg yolks and melted butter and mix until the prepared dough starts to come together. Transfer the prepared dough to a floured surface and knead it by hand for around 2 minutes. Shape the prepared dough into a ball, place it in a suitable oiled bowl, cover with a clean kitchen towel and let the prepared dough rise in a warm place for around 1 to 1½ hours, or until the prepared dough has doubled in size. 2. While the prepared dough is rising, melt one tablespoon of butter in a suitable saucepan on the stovetop. Add the diced peaches, cinnamon and sugar to taste. Cook the peaches for about 5 minutes, or until they soften. Set the peaches aside to cool. 3. Place the Cook & Crisp Basket in your Pressure Cooker Steam Fryer. 4. When the prepared dough has risen, transfer it to a floured surface and shape it into a 12-inch circle. Spread the peaches over half of the circle and fold the other half of the prepared dough over the top. With a knife or a board scraper, score the prepared dough by making slits in the prepared dough in a diamond shape. Push the knife straight down into the prepared dough and peaches, rather than slicing through. You should cut through the top layer of dough, but not the bottom. Roll the prepared dough up into a log from one short end to the other. It should be 8 inches long. Some of the peaches will be sticking out of the prepared dough – don't worry, these are supposed to be a little random. Cut the log into 8 equal slices. Place the prepared dough disks on a floured cookie sheet, cover with a clean kitchen towel and let rise in a warm place for around 30 minutes. 5. Put on the Smart Lid on top of the Ninja Foodi Steam Fryer. 6. Move the Lid Slider to the "Air Fry/Stovetop". Select the "Air Fry" mode for cooking. 7. Air-fry 2 or 3 fritters at a time at 370°F/185°C, for around 3 minutes. Flip them over and continue to air-fry for another 2 to 3 minutes, until they are golden brown. 8. Mix the powdered sugar and milk in a suitable bowl. Mix vigorously until smooth. Allow the fritters to cool for at least 10 minutes and then brush the glaze over both the bottom

and top of each one. Serve warm or at room temperature.
Per serving: Calories: 334; Fat: 7.9g; Sodium: 704mg; Carbs: 6g; Fiber: 3.6g; Sugar 6g; Protein 18g

Turkey Sausage Roll-Ups

Prep Time: 10 minutes. | Cook Time: 24 minutes. | Serves: 3

6 links turkey sausage	½ teaspoon cinnamon
6 slices of white bread, crusts	½ teaspoon vanilla extract
removed	1 tablespoon butter, melted
2 eggs	Powdered sugar (optional)
½ cup milk	Maple syrup

1. Place the Cook & Crisp Basket in your Pressure Cooker Steam Fryer. 2. Place the sausage links in the Ninja Steam Fryer. 3. Put on the Smart Lid on top of the Ninja Foodi Steam Fryer. 4. Move the Lid Slider to the "Air Fry/Stovetop". Select the "Air Fry" mode for cooking. 5. Air-fry the sausage links at 380°F/195°C for 8 to 10 minutes, turning them a couple of times during the cooking process. 6. Roll each sausage link in a piece of bread, pressing the finished seam tightly to seal shut. 7. Mix the eggs, milk, cinnamon, and vanilla in a shallow dish. Dip the sausage rolls in the egg mixture and let them soak in the egg for around 30 seconds. Grease the bottom of the "cook & crisp basket" with oil and transfer the sausage rolls to the basket, seam side down. 8. Put on the Smart Lid on top of the Ninja Foodi Steam Fryer. 9. Move the Lid Slider to the "Air Fry/Stovetop". Select the "Air Fry" mode for cooking. 10. Air-fry the rolls at 370°F/185°C for around 9 minutes. Brush melted butter over the bread, flip the rolls over. Cook on the "Air Fry" mode for an additional 5 minutes. Remove the French toast roll-ups from the basket and dust with powdered sugar, if using. Serve with maple syrup and enjoy.
Per serving: Calories: 284; Fat: 9g; Sodium: 441mg; Carbs: 7g; Fiber: 4.6g; Sugar 5g; Protein 19g

Hush Puffs

Prep Time: 10 minutes. | Cook Time: 8 minutes. | Serves: 20

1 cup buttermilk	⅓ cup sugar
¼ cup butter, melted	1 teaspoon baking soda
2 eggs	1 teaspoon salt
1½ cups all-purpose flour	4 scallions, minced
1½ cups cornmeal	Vegetable oil

1. Place the Cook & Crisp Basket in your Pressure Cooker Steam Fryer. 2. Mix the buttermilk, butter and eggs in a suitable mixing bowl. In a second bowl mix the flour, cornmeal, sugar, baking soda and salt. Add the dry recipe ingredients to the wet recipe ingredients, stirring just to mix. Stir in the minced scallions and refrigerate the prepared batter for around 30 minutes. 3. Shape the prepared batter into 2-inch balls. Brush or grease the balls with oil. 4. Put on the Smart Lid on top of the Ninja Foodi Steam Fryer. 5. Move the Lid Slider to the "Air Fry/Stovetop". Select the "Air Fry" mode for cooking. 6. Air-fry the hush puffins in two batches at 360°F/180°C for around 8 minutes, turning them over after 6 minutes of the cooking process. 7. Serve warm with butter.
Per serving: Calories: 349; Fat: 2.9g; Sodium: 511mg; Carbs: 12g; Fiber: 3g; Sugar 8g; Protein 17g

Sweet Potato Toast

Prep Time: 5 minutes. | Cook Time: 8 minutes. | Serves: 8

1 small sweet potato, cut into	Oil for misting
⅜-inch slices	Cinnamon

1. Place the Cook & Crisp Basket in your Pressure Cooker Steam Fryer. 2. Spray both sides of sweet potato slices with oil. Sprinkle both sides with cinnamon to taste. 3. Place potato slices in "cook & crisp basket" in a single layer. 4. Put on the Smart Lid on top of the Ninja Foodi Steam Fryer. 5. Move the Lid Slider to the "Air Fry/Stovetop". Select the "Air Fry" mode for cooking. 6. Cook at 390°F/200°C for around 4 minutes. Turn and cook for around 4 more minutes until potato slices are barely fork tender.
Per serving: Calories: 284; Fat: 9g; Sodium: 441mg; Carbs: 7g; Fiber: 4.6g; Sugar 5g; Protein 19g

Chocolate Rolls

Prep Time: 10 minutes. | Cook Time: 8 minutes. | Serves: 6

1 (8-ounce) tube of crescent roll dough	1 egg white, beaten
⅔ cup semi-sweet or bittersweet chocolate chunks	¼ cup sliced almonds
	Powdered sugar, for dusting
	Butter or oil

1. Unwrap the thawed crescent roll dough and separate it into triangles with the points facing away from you. Place a row of chocolate chunks along the bottom edge of the prepared dough. 2. Roll the prepared dough up around the chocolate and then place another row of chunks on the prepared dough. Roll again and finish with one or two chocolate chunks. Be sure to leave the end free of chocolate so that it can adhere to the rest of the roll. 3. Brush the tops of the crescent rolls with the beaten egg white and sprinkle the almonds on top, pressing them into the crescent dough so they adhere. 4. Place the Cook & Crisp Basket in your Pressure Cooker Steam Fryer. 5. Brush the bottom of the Ninja Foodi Pressure Steam Fryer basket with butter or oil and transfer the crescent rolls to the basket. 6. Put on the Smart Lid on top of the Ninja Foodi Steam Fryer. 7. Move the Lid Slider to the "Air Fry/Stovetop". Select the "Air Fry" mode for cooking. 8. Air-fry rolls at 350°F/175°C for 8 minutes. 9. Remove and let the crescent rolls cool before dusting with powdered sugar and serving.
Per serving: Calories: 372; Fat: 20g; Sodium: 891mg; Carbs: 29g; Fiber: 3g; Sugar 8g; Protein 17g

Baked Eggs

Prep Time: 10 minutes. | Cook Time: 12 minutes. | Serves: 1

1 teaspoon olive oil	Salt and black pepper
2 tablespoons finely chopped onion	2 slices of bacon, chopped
1 teaspoon chopped fresh oregano	2 large eggs
Pinch crushed red pepper flakes	¼ cup grated Cheddar cheese
1 (14-ounce) can crushed or diced tomatoes	Fresh parsley, chopped

1. Start by making the tomato sauce. Preheat a suitable saucepan over medium heat on the stovetop. Add the olive oil and sauté the onion, oregano and pepper flakes for around 5 minutes. Add the tomatoes and bring to a simmer. Season with salt and black pepper. Cook for on a simmer for around 10 minutes. 2. Place the Cook & Crisp Basket in your Pressure Cooker Steam Fryer. 3. Meanwhile, place the prepared bacon in the "cook & crisp basket". 4. Put on the Smart Lid on top of the Ninja Foodi Steam Fryer. 5. Move the Lid Slider to the "Air Fry/Stovetop". Select the "Air Fry" mode for cooking. 6. Cook on the "Air Fry" mode at 400°F/200°C for 5 minutes, shaking the basket every once in a while. 7. When the bacon is almost crispy, remove it to a paper-towel lined plate and rinse out the Ninja Foodi Steam Fryer, draining away the bacon grease. 8. Transfer the tomato sauce to a shallow 7-inch pie dish. Crack the eggs on top of the sauce and scatter the cooked bacon back on top. Season with salt and black pepper and transfer the pie dish into the Ninja Foodi Pressure Steam Fryer basket. 9. Air-fry eggs at 400°F/200°C for 5 minutes until the eggs are almost cooked to your liking. Sprinkle cheese on top. Cook on the "Air Fry" mode for 2 minutes. Sprinkle with a little chopped parsley and let the eggs cool for a few minutes.
Per serving: Calories: 289; Fat: 14g; Sodium: 791mg; Carbs: 8.9g; Fiber: 4.6g; Sugar 8g; Protein 16g

Walnut Apple Muffins

Prep Time: 10 minutes. | Cook Time: 11 minutes. | Serves: 8

1 cup flour	1 egg
⅓ cup sugar	4 tablespoons pancake syrup
1 teaspoon baking powder	4 tablespoons melted butter
¼ teaspoon baking soda	¾ cup unsweetened applesauce
¼ teaspoon salt	½ teaspoon vanilla extract
1 teaspoon cinnamon	¼ cup chopped walnuts
¼ teaspoon ginger	¼ cup diced apple
¼ teaspoon nutmeg	

1. In a suitable bowl, stir flour, sugar, baking powder, baking soda, salt, cinnamon, ginger, and nutmeg. 2. In a suitable bowl, beat egg until frothy. Add syrup, butter, applesauce, and vanilla and mix well. 3.

Place the Cook & Crisp Basket in your Pressure Cooker Steam Fryer. 4. Pour the prepared egg mixture into dry recipe ingredients and stir just until moistened. 5. Gently stir in nuts and diced apple. 6. Divide batter among the 8 muffin cups. 7. Place 4 muffin cups in "cook & crisp basket". 8. Put on the Smart Lid on top of the Ninja Foodi Steam Fryer. 9. Move the Lid Slider to the "Air Fry/Stovetop". Select the "Air Fry" mode for cooking. 10. Air fry at 330°F/165°C for around 9 to 11 minutes. 11. Repeat with remaining 4 muffins or until toothpick inserted in center comes out clean.
Per serving: Calories: 289; Fat: 14g; Sodium: 791mg; Carbs: 8.9g; Fiber: 4.6g; Sugar 8g; Protein 16g

Bacon Knots

Prep Time: 10 minutes. | Cook Time: 8 minutes. | Serves: 6

1-pound maple smoked center-cut bacon	¼ cup brown sugar
	Cracked black peppercorns
¼ cup maple syrup	

1. Place the Cook & Crisp Basket in your Pressure Cooker Steam Fryer. 2. Tie each bacon strip in a loose knot and place them on a suitable the Cook & Crisp Basket. 3. Mix the maple syrup and sugar in a suitable bowl. Brush each knot generously with this mixture and sprinkle with coarsely cracked black pepper. 4. Put on the Smart Lid on top of the Ninja Foodi Steam Fryer. 5. Move the Lid Slider to the "Air Fry/Stovetop". Select the "Air Fry" mode for cooking. 6. Air-fry the bacon knots in batches. Place one layer of knots in the Ninja Foodi Pressure Steam Fryer basket. Cook on the "Air Fry" mode at 390°F/200°C for around 5 minutes. Turn the bacon knots over. Cook on the "Air Fry" mode for 2 to 3 minutes. 7. Serve warm.
Per serving: Calories: 282; Fat: 19g; Sodium: 354mg; Carbs: 15g; Fiber: 5.1g; Sugar 8.2g; Protein 12g

Air Fried Grapefruit

Prep Time: 10 minutes. | Cook Time: 4 minutes. | Serves: 2

1 grapefruit	2 to 4 teaspoons brown sugar

1. Cut the grapefruit in half. 2. Slice the bottom of the grapefruit to help it sit flat on the counter if necessary. Using a sharp paring knife, cut around the grapefruit between the flesh of the fruit and the peel. 3. Then, cut each segment away from the membrane so that it is sitting freely in the fruit. 4. Place the Cook & Crisp Basket in your Pressure Cooker Steam Fryer. 5. Sprinkle 2 teaspoons of brown sugar on each half of the prepared grapefruit. 6. Transfer the grapefruit half to the "cook & crisp basket". 7. Put on the Smart Lid on top of the Ninja Foodi Steam Fryer. 8. Move the Lid Slider to the "Air Fry/Stovetop". Select the "Air Fry" mode for cooking. 9. Air-fry at 400°F/200°C for 4 minutes. 10. Remove and let it cool for just a minute before enjoying.
Per serving: Calories: 82; Fat: 10.9g; Sodium: 354mg; Carbs: 20.5g; Fiber: 4.1g; Sugar 8.2g; Protein 6g

Broccoli Quiche

Prep Time: 10 minutes. | Cook Time: 4 minutes. | Serves: 4

1 cup broccoli florets	¾ cup heavy cream
¾ cup chopped roasted red peppers	½ teaspoon salt
1¼ cups grated Fontina cheese	Black pepper
6 eggs	

1. Place the Cook & Crisp Basket in your Pressure Cooker Steam Fryer. 2. Grease the Cook & Crisp Basket. Place the broccoli florets and roasted red peppers in the Cook & Crisp Basket and top with the grated Fontina cheese. 3. Mix the eggs and heavy cream in a suitable bowl. Season the beaten eggs with salt and black pepper. Pour the egg mixture over the cheese and vegetables and cover the basket with aluminum foil. Transfer the basket to the Ninja Foodi Pressure Steam Fryer. 4. Put on the Smart Lid on top of the Ninja Foodi Steam Fryer. 5. Move the Lid Slider to the "Air Fry/Stovetop". Select the "Air Fry" mode for cooking. 6. Air-fry at 360°F/180°C for around 60 minutes. Remove the aluminum foil for the last two minutes of cooking time. 7. Unmold the quiche onto a platter and cut it into slices to serve with a side salad or perhaps some air-fried potatoes.
Per serving: Calories: 221; Fat: 7.9g; Sodium: 704mg; Carbs: 6g; Fiber: 3.6g; Sugar 6g; Protein 18g

Blueberry Morning Muffins

Prep Time: 10 minutes. | Cook Time: 14 minutes. | Serves: 8

1⅓ cups flour	1 egg
½ cup sugar	½ cup milk
2 teaspoons baking powder	⅔ cup blueberries, fresh or frozen
¼ teaspoon salt	and thawed
⅓ cup canola oil	

1. In a suitable bowl, stir flour, sugar, baking powder, and salt. 2. In a separate bowl, mix cooking oil with egg, and milk and mix well. 3. Add egg mixture to dry recipe ingredients and stir just until moistened. 4. Gently stir in blueberries. 5. Spoon batter evenly into muffin cups. 6. Place the Cook & Crisp Basket in your Pressure Cooker Steam Fryer. 7. Place 4 muffin cups in "cook & crisp basket". 8. Put on the Smart Lid on top of the Ninja Foodi Steam Fryer. 9. Move the Lid Slider to the "Air Fry/Stovetop". Select the "Air Fry" mode for cooking. 10. Air fry at 330°F/165°C for around 12 to 14 minutes or until tops spring back when touched lightly. 11. Repeat previous step to cook remaining muffins.
Per serving: Calories: 219; Fat: 10g; Sodium: 891mg; Carbs: 22.9g; Fiber: 4g; Sugar 4g; Protein 13g

Ham Cornmeal Muffins

Prep Time: 10 minutes. | Cook Time: 8 minutes. | Serves: 8

¾ cup yellow cornmeal	2 tablespoons canola oil
¼ cup flour	½ cup milk
1½ teaspoons baking powder	½ cup shredded sharp Cheddar
¼ teaspoon salt	cheese
1 egg, beaten	½ cup diced ham

1. Place the Cook & Crisp Basket in your Pressure Cooker Steam Fryer. 2. In a suitable bowl, stir the cornmeal, flour, baking powder, and salt. 3. Add egg, oil, and milk to dry recipe ingredients and mix well. 4. Stir in shredded cheese and diced ham. 5. Divide batter among the muffin cups. 6. Place 4 filled muffin cups in "cook & crisp basket". Put on the Smart Lid on top of the Ninja Foodi Steam Fryer. Move the Lid Slider to the "Air Fry/Stovetop". Select the "Air Fry" mode for cooking. Air-fry 390°F/200°C for around 5 minutes. 7. Reduce temperature to 330°F/165°C and cook for around 1 to 2 minutes or until toothpick inserted in center of muffin comes out clean. 8. Repeat to cook remaining muffins.
Per serving: Calories: 284; Fat: 9g; Sodium: 441mg; Carbs: 7g; Fiber: 4.6g; Sugar 5g; Protein 19g

Toast Sticks

Prep Time: 5 minutes. | Cook Time: 5–7 minutes. | Serves: 4

2 eggs	6 slices sandwich bread, each slice
½ cup milk	cut into 4 strips
⅛ teaspoon salt	Oil for misting or cooking spray
½ teaspoon pure vanilla extract	Maple syrup or honey
¾ cup crushed cornflakes	

1. Place the Cook & Crisp Basket in your Pressure Cooker Steam Fryer. 2. In a suitable bowl, beat eggs, milk, salt, and vanilla. 3. Place crushed cornflakes on a plate or in a shallow dish. 4. Dip bread strips in egg mixture, shake off excess, and roll in cornflake crumbs. 5. Spray both sides of bread strips with oil. 6. Place bread strips in "cook & crisp basket" in single layer. 7. Put on the Smart Lid on top of the Ninja Foodi Steam Fryer. 8. Move the Lid Slider to the "Air Fry/Stovetop". Select the "Air Fry" mode for cooking. 9. Air Fry the strips at 390°F/200°C for 5 to 7 minutes or until they're dark golden brown. 10. Repeat to cook remaining toast sticks. 11. Serve with maple syrup or honey for dipping.
Per serving: Calories: 282; Fat: 19g; Sodium: 354mg; Carbs: 15g; Fiber: 5.1g; Sugar 8.2g; Protein 12g

Oat Muffins

Prep Time: 10 minutes. | Cook Time: 12 minutes. | Serves: 8

⅔ cup oat bran	¼ cup brown sugar
½ cup flour	1 teaspoon baking powder

½ teaspoon baking soda	½ cup chopped dates, raisins, or
⅛ teaspoon salt	dried cranberries
½ cup buttermilk	24 paper muffin cups
1 egg	Cooking spray
2 tablespoons canola oil	

1. Place the Cook & Crisp Basket in your Pressure Cooker Steam Fryer. 2. In a suitable bowl, mix the oat bran, flour, brown sugar, baking powder, baking soda, and salt. 3. In a suitable bowl, beat the buttermilk, egg, and oil. 4. Pour the prepared buttermilk mixture into bowl with dry recipe ingredients and stir just until moistened. Do not beat. 5. Gently stir in dried fruit. 6. Use baking cups to help muffins hold shape during baking. Grease them with cooking spray, place 4 sets of cups in "cook & crisp basket" at a time, and fill each one ¾ full of batter. 7. Put on the Smart Lid on top of the Ninja Foodi Steam Fryer. 8. Move the Lid Slider to the "Air Fry/Stovetop". Select the "Air Fry" mode for cooking. 9. Cook at 330°F/165°C for around 12 minutes, until top springs back when touched and toothpick inserted in center comes out clean. 10. Repeat for remaining muffins.
Per serving: Calories: 334; Fat: 10.9g; Sodium: 454mg; Carbs: 10g; Fiber: 3.1g; Sugar 5.2g; Protein 10g

Orange Creamy Rolls

Prep Time: 15 minutes. | Cook Time: 8–10 minutes. | Serves: 8

3 ounces low-fat cream cheese	¼ cup dried cranberries
1 tablespoon low-fat sour cream or	¼ cup shredded, sweetened
plain yogurt	coconut
2 teaspoons sugar	Butter-flavored cooking spray
¼ teaspoon pure vanilla extract	Orange Glaze
¼ teaspoon orange extract	½ cup powdered sugar
1 can (8 count) organic crescent	1 tablespoon orange juice
roll dough	¼ teaspoon orange extract
¼ cup chopped walnuts	Dash of salt

1. Cut a circular piece of parchment paper smaller than the bottom of your Ninja Foodi Pressure Steam Fryer basket. Set aside. 2. In a suitable bowl, mix the cream cheese, sour cream or yogurt, sugar, and vanilla and orange extracts. Stir until smooth. 3. Divide crescent roll dough into 8 triangles and divide cream cheese mixture among them. Starting at wide end, spread cheese mixture to within 1 inch of point. 4. Sprinkle nuts and cranberries evenly over cheese mixture. 5. Place the Cook & Crisp Basket in your Pressure Cooker Steam Fryer. 6. Starting at wide end, roll up triangles, then sprinkle with coconut, pressing in to make it stick. Spray tops of rolls with butter-flavored cooking spray. 7. Place parchment paper in "cook & crisp basket", and place 4 rolls on top, spaced evenly. 8. Put on the Smart Lid on top of the Ninja Foodi Steam Fryer. 9. Move the Lid Slider to the "Air Fry/Stovetop". Select the "Air Fry" mode for cooking. 10. Cook at 300°F/150°C for 10 minutes. Repeat to cook remaining 4 rolls. 11. In a suitable bowl, stir ingredients for glaze and drizzle over warm rolls.
Per serving: Calories: 284; Fat: 9g; Sodium: 441mg; Carbs: 7g; Fiber: 4.6g; Sugar 5g; Protein 19g

Breakfast Scotch Eggs

Prep Time: 10 minutes. | Cook Time: 20–25 minutes. | Serves: 4

2 tablespoons flour, extra for	1 tablespoon water
coating	oil for misting or cooking spray
1-pound breakfast sausage	Crumb Coating
4 hardboiled eggs, peeled	¾ cup panko breadcrumbs
1 raw egg	¾ cup flour

1. Mix flour with sausage and mix thoroughly. 2. Divide into 4 equal portions and mold each around a hardboiled egg so the sausage completely covers the egg. 3. In a suitable bowl, beat the raw egg and water. 4. Dip sausage-covered eggs in the remaining flour, then the egg mixture, then roll in the crumb coating. 5. Place the Cook & Crisp Basket in your Pressure Cooker Steam Fryer. 6. Put on the Smart Lid on top of the Ninja Foodi Steam Fryer. 7. Move the Lid Slider to the "Air Fry/Stovetop". Select the "Air Fry" mode for cooking. 8. Air Fry at 360°F/180°C for around 10 minutes. Spray eggs, turn, and spray other side. 9. Continue air frying for another 15 minutes or until sausage is well done.
Per serving: Calories: 289; Fat: 14g; Sodium: 791mg; Carbs: 8.9g; Fiber: 4.6g; Sugar 8g; Protein 16g

Cheesy Bacon Muffins

Prep Time: 10 minutes. | Cook Time: 9 minutes. | Serves: 4

4 eggs
Black pepper and salt
Olive oil

4 English muffins, split
1 cup shredded Colby Jack cheese
4 slices ham or Canadian bacon

1. Place the Cook & Crisp Basket in your Pressure Cooker Steam Fryer. 2. Beat eggs and add black pepper and salt to taste. Spray the Cook & Crisp Basket with oil and add eggs. Put on the Smart Lid on top of the Ninja Foodi Steam Fryer. 3. Move the Lid Slider to the "Air Fry/Stovetop". Select the "Air Fry" mode for cooking. Cook at 390°F/200°C for around 2 minutes, stir, and continue cooking for around 3 or 4 minutes, stirring every minute, until eggs are scrambled to your preference. Remove the Cook & Crisp Basket. 4. Place bottom halves of English muffins in "cook & crisp basket". Take half of the shredded cheese and divide it among the muffins. Top each with a slice of ham and one-quarter of the eggs. Sprinkle remaining cheese on top of the eggs. Use a fork to press the cheese into the egg a little so it doesn't slip off before it melts. Transfer the basket to Pressure Cooker Steam Fryer. 5. Put on the Smart Lid on top of the Ninja Foodi Steam Fryer. 6. Move the Lid Slider to the "Air Fry/Stovetop". Select the "Air Fry" mode for cooking. 7. Air Fry at 360°F/180°C for around 1 minute. Add English muffin tops. Cook for around 2 to 4 minutes to heat through and toast the muffins.
Per serving: Calories: 221; Fat: 7.9g; Sodium: 704mg; Carbs: 6g; Fiber: 3.6g; Sugar 6g; Protein 18g

Jelly stuffed Muffins

Prep Time: 10 minutes. | Cook Time: 7–8 minutes. | Serves: 4

1 cup flour
2 tablespoons sugar (optional)
½ teaspoon baking soda
1 teaspoon baking powder
¼ teaspoon salt
1 egg, beaten
1 cup buttermilk
2 tablespoons melted butter
1 teaspoon pure vanilla extract
24 foil muffin cups
Cooking spray

Suggested Fillings
1 teaspoon of jelly or fruit preserves
1 tablespoon or less fresh blueberries; chopped fresh strawberries; chopped frozen cherries; dark chocolate chips; chopped walnuts, pecans, or other nuts; cooked, crumbled bacon or sausage

1. In a suitable bowl, stir flour, optional sugar, baking soda, baking powder, and salt. 2. In a suitable bowl, mix egg, buttermilk, butter, and vanilla. Mix well. 3. Pour egg mixture into dry recipe ingredients and stir to mix well but don't over beat. 4. Place the Cook & Crisp Basket in your Pressure Cooker Steam Fryer. 5. Double up the muffin cups and remove the paper liners from the top cups. Grease the foil cups with cooking spray. 6. Place 6 sets of muffin cups in "cook & crisp basket". Pour just enough batter into each cup to cover the bottom. Sprinkle with desired filling. Pour the prepared batter to cover the filling and fill the cups about ¾ full. 7. Put on the Smart Lid on top of the Ninja Foodi Steam Fryer. 8. Move the Lid Slider to the "Air Fry/Stovetop". Select the "Air Fry" mode for cooking. 9. Air Fry at 330°F/165°C for around7 to 8 minutes. 10. Repeat to cook the remaining 6 pancake muffins.
Per serving: Calories: 219; Fat: 10g; Sodium: 891mg; Carbs: 22.9g; Fiber: 4g; Sugar 4g; Protein 13g

Egg Quesadillas

Prep Time: 10 minutes. | Cook Time: 12 minutes. | Serves: 4

4 eggs
2 tablespoons skim milk
Black pepper and salt
Oil for misting or cooking spray

4 flour tortillas
4 tablespoons salsa
2 ounces Cheddar cheese, grated
½ small avocado, peeled and sliced

1. Beat eggs, milk, salt, and pepper. 2. Place the Cook & Crisp Basket in your Pressure Cooker Steam Fryer. 3. Spray the Cook & Crisp Basket with cooking spray and add egg mixture. 4. Put on the Smart Lid on top of the Ninja Foodi Steam Fryer. 5. Move the Lid Slider to the "Air Fry/Stovetop". Select the "Air Fry" mode for cooking. 6. Cook at 270°F/132°C for 8 to 9 minutes, stirring every 1 to 2 minutes, until eggs are scrambled to your liking. Remove and set aside. 7. Spray one side of each tortilla with oil or cooking spray. Flip over. 8. Divide eggs, salsa, cheese, and avocado among the tortillas, covering only half of each tortilla. 9. Fold tortilla in half and press down lightly. 10. Place 2 tortillas in "cook & crisp basket". 11. Put on the Smart Lid on top of the Ninja Foodi Steam Fryer. 12. Move the Lid Slider to the "Air Fry/Stovetop". Select the "Air Fry" mode for cooking. 13. Air fry at 390°F/200°C for 3 minutes or until cheese melts and outside feels crispy. Repeat with remaining two tortillas. 14. Cut each cooked tortilla into halves or thirds.
Per serving: Calories: 382; Fat: 10.9g; Sodium: 354mg; Carbs: 20.5g; Fiber: 4.1g; Sugar 8.2g; Protein 06g

Pork Quiche Cups

Prep Time: 15 minutes. | Cook Time: 20 minutes. | Serves: 10

¼ pound pork sausage
3 eggs
¾ cup milk
20 foil muffin cups

Cooking spray
4 ounces sharp Cheddar cheese, grated

1. Divide sausage into 3 portions and shape each into a thin patty. 2. Place the Cook & Crisp Basket in your Pressure Cooker Steam Fryer. 3. Place patties in "cook & crisp basket". Put on the Smart Lid on top of the Ninja Foodi Steam Fryer. Move the Lid Slider to the "Air Fry/Stovetop". Select the "Air Fry" mode for cooking. Cook at 390°F/200°C for 6 minutes. 4. While sausage is cooking, prepare the egg mixture. A suitable measuring cup or bowl with a pouring lip works best. Mix the eggs and milk and mix until well blended. Set aside. 5. When sausage has cooked fully, remove patties from basket, drain well, and use a fork to crumble the meat into small pieces. 6. Double the foil cups into 10 sets. Remove paper liners from the top muffin cups and grease the foil cups with cooking spray. 7. Divide crumbled sausage among the 10 muffin cup sets. 8. Top each with grated cheese evenly among the cups. 9. Place 5 cups in "cook & crisp basket". 10. Pour egg mixture into each cup, filling until each cup is at least ⅔ full. 11. Put on the Smart Lid on top of the Ninja Foodi Steam Fryer. 12. Move the Lid Slider to the "Air Fry/Stovetop". Select the "Air Fry" mode for cooking. 13. Cook at 390°F/200°C for around 8 minutes and test for doneness. A knife inserted into the center shouldn't have any raw egg on it when removed. 14. If needed, cook 1 to 2 more minutes, until egg completely sets. 15. Repeat to cook the remaining quiches.
Per serving: Calories: 351; Fat: 7.9g; Sodium: 704mg; Carbs: 6g; Fiber: 3.6g; Sugar 6g; Protein 18g

Mushroom Boat Eggs

Prep Time: 10 minutes. | Cook Time: 10 minutes. | Serves: 4

4 postulate rolls
1 teaspoon butter
¼ cup diced fresh mushrooms
½ teaspoon dried onion flakes
4 eggs

½ teaspoon salt
¼ teaspoon dried dill weed
¼ teaspoon dried parsley
1 tablespoon milk

1. Place the Cook & Crisp Basket in your Pressure Cooker Steam Fryer. 2. Cut a small rectangle in the top of each roll and scoop out center, leaving ½-inch shell on the sides and bottom. 3. Place butter, mushrooms, and dried onion in the Cook & Crisp Basket . 4 . Put on the Smart Lid on top of the Ninja Foodi Steam Fryer. Move the Lid Slider to the "Air Fry/Stovetop". Select the "Air Fry" mode for cooking. Cook at 390°F/200°C for around 1 minute. Stir and cook for 3 more minutes. 5. In a suitable bowl, beat the eggs, salt, dill, parsley, and milk. Pour mixture into basket with mushrooms. 6. Put on the Smart Lid on top of the Ninja Foodi Steam Fryer. 7. Move the Lid Slider to the "Air Fry/Stovetop". Select the "Air Fry" mode for cooking. 8. Air Fry the eggs at 390°F/200°C for 2 minutes. Stir. Continue cooking for around 3 or 4 minutes, stirring every minute, until eggs are scrambled to your liking.9. Remove basket from Pressure Cooker Steam Fryer and fill rolls with scrambled egg mixture. 10. Place filled rolls in "cook & crisp basket". Put on the Smart Lid on top of the Ninja Foodi Steam Fryer. Move the Lid Slider to the "Air Fry/Stovetop". Select the "Air Fry" mode for cooking. Air Fry at 390°F/200°C for 2 to 3 minutes or until rolls are browned.
Per serving: Calories: 334; Fat: 12.9g; Sodium: 414mg; Carbs: 11g; Fiber: 5g; Sugar 9g; Protein 11g

Fried PB&J Sandwich

Prep Time: 10 minutes. | Cook Time: 6–8 minutes. | Serves: 4

½ cup cornflakes, crushed
¼ cup shredded coconut
8 slices oat nut bread or any whole-grain, oversize bread
6 tablespoons peanut butter
2 medium bananas, cut into ½-inch-thick slices
6 tablespoons pineapple preserves
1 egg, beaten
Oil for misting or cooking spray

1. Place the Cook & Crisp Basket in your Pressure Cooker Steam Fryer. 2. In a shallow dish, mix the coconut and cornflake crumbs. 3. For each sandwich, spread one bread slice with 1½ tablespoons of peanut butter. Top with banana slices. Spread another bread slice with 1½ tablespoons of preserves. 4. Using a pastry brush, brush top of sandwich with beaten egg. Sprinkle with about 1½ tablespoons of crumb coating, pressing it in to make it stick. Grease with oil. 5. Turn sandwich over and repeat to coat and grease the other side. 6. Put on the Smart Lid on top of the Ninja Foodi Steam Fryer. 7. Move the Lid Slider to the "Air Fry/Stovetop". Select the "Air Fry" mode for cooking. 8. Cook at 360°F/180°C for around 6 to 7 minutes or until coating is golden brown and crispy. If sandwich doesn't brown enough, spray with a little more oil and cook for another minutes. 9. Cut cooked sandwiches in half and serve warm.
Per serving: Calories: 372; Fat: 20g; Sodium: 891mg; Carbs: 29g; Fiber: 3g; Sugar 8g; Protein 7g

Spinach- Rollups

Prep Time: 5 minutes. | Cook Time: 8–9 minutes. | Serves: 4

4 flour tortillas (6- or 7-inch size)
4 slices Swiss cheese
1 cup baby spinach leaves
4 slices turkey bacon

1. Place the Cook & Crisp Basket in your Pressure Cooker Steam Fryer. 2. On each tortilla, add one slice of cheese and ¼ cup of spinach. 3. Roll up tortillas and wrap each with a strip of bacon. Secure each end with a toothpick. 4. Place rollups in "cook & crisp basket", leaving a little space in between them. 5. Put on the Smart Lid on top of the Ninja Foodi Steam Fryer. 6. Move the Lid Slider to the "Air Fry/Stovetop". Select the "Air Fry" mode for cooking. 7.Cook at 390°F/200°C for around 4 minutes. Turn and rearrange rollups (for more even cooking). Cook for around 4 to 5 minutes longer, until bacon is crisp.
Per serving: Calories: 372; Fat: 12.9g; Sodium: 414mg; Carbs: 11g; Fiber: 5g; Sugar 9g; Protein 11g

Ham Eggs

Prep Time: 5 minutes. | Cook Time: 6–7 minutes. | Serves: 1

1 slice bread
1 teaspoon soft butter
1 egg
Black pepper and salt
1 tablespoon shredded Cheddar cheese
2 teaspoons diced ham

1. Place the Cook & Crisp Basket in your Pressure Cooker Steam Fryer. 2. Using a 2½-inch-diameter biscuit cutter, cut a hole in center of bread slice. 3. Spread softened butter on both sides of bread. 4. Lay bread slice in the Cook & Crisp Basket and crack egg into the hole. Top egg with black pepper and salt to taste. 5. Put on the Smart Lid on top of the Ninja Foodi Steam Fryer. 6. Move the Lid Slider to the "Air Fry/Stovetop". Select the "Air Fry" mode for cooking. 7. Cook at 330°F/165°C for 5 minutes. 8. Turn toast over and top it with shredded cheese and diced ham. 9. Cook for around 1 to 2 more minutes or until yolk is done to your liking.
Per serving: Calories: 372; Fat: 20g; Sodium: 891mg; Carbs: 29g; Fiber: 3g; Sugar 8g; Protein 7g

Flaxseed Muffins

Prep Time: 15 minutes. | Cook Time: 11 minutes. | Serves: 8

½ cup 2 tablespoons whole-wheat flour
¼ cup oat bran
2 tablespoons flaxseed meal
¼ cup brown sugar
½ teaspoon baking soda
½ teaspoon baking powder
¼ teaspoon salt
½ teaspoon cinnamon
½ cup buttermilk
2 tablespoons melted butter
1 egg
½ teaspoon pure vanilla extract
½ cup grated carrots
¼ cup chopped pecans
¼ cup chopped walnuts
1 tablespoon pumpkin seeds
1 tablespoon sunflower seeds
16 foil muffin cups, paper liners removed
Cooking spray

1. Place the Cook & Crisp Basket in your Pressure Cooker Steam Fryer. 2. In a suitable bowl, stir the flour, bran, flaxseed meal, sugar, baking soda, baking powder, salt, and cinnamon. 3. In a suitable bowl, beat the buttermilk, butter, egg, and vanilla. Pour into the prepared flour mixture and stir just until dry recipe ingredients moisten. Do not beat. 4. Gently stir in carrots, pecans, nuts, and seeds. 5. Double up the foil cups so you have 8 total and spray with cooking spray. 6. Place 4 foil cups in "cook & crisp basket" and divide half the prepared batter among them. 7. Put on the Smart Lid on top of the Ninja Foodi Steam Fryer. 8. Move the Lid Slider to the "Air Fry/Stovetop". Select the "Air Fry" mode for cooking. 9. Air-fry at 330°F/165°C for around 9 to 11 minutes or until toothpick inserted in center comes out clean. 10. Repeat to cook remaining 4 muffins.
Per serving: Calories: 349; Fat: 2.9g; Sodium: 511mg; Carbs: 12g; Fiber: 3g; Sugar 8g; Protein 7g

Walnut Vanilla Pancake

Prep Time: 5 minutes. | Cook Time: 20 minutes. | Serves: 4

3 tablespoons butter into thirds
1 cup flour
1½ teaspoons baking powder
¼ teaspoon salt
2 tablespoons sugar
¾ cup milk
1 egg, beaten
1 teaspoon pure vanilla extract
½ cup walnuts, chopped
Maple syrup, for serving

1. Place the Cook & Crisp Basket in your Pressure Cooker Steam Fryer. 2. Place 1 tablespoon of the butter in the Cook & Crisp Basket. Put on the Smart Lid on top of the Ninja Foodi Steam Fryer. Move the Lid Slider to the "Air Fry/Stovetop". Select the "Air Fry" mode for cooking. Air Fry at 330°F/165°C for around 3 minutes to melt. 3. In a suitable dish or pan, melt the remaining 2 tablespoons of butter either in the microwave or on the stove. 4. In a suitable bowl, stir the flour, baking powder, salt, and sugar. Add milk, beaten egg, the 2 tablespoons of melted butter, and vanilla. Stir until mixed but do not beat. Batter may be lumpy. 5. Pour batter over the melted butter in the Cook & Crisp Basket. Sprinkle nuts evenly over top. 6. Put on the Smart Lid on top of the Ninja Foodi Steam Fryer. 7. Move the Lid Slider to the "Air Fry/Stovetop". Select the "Air Fry" mode for cooking. 8. Cook at 330°F/165°C for around 20 minutes or cook until toothpick inserted in center comes out clean. Let pancake rest for around 2 minutes. 9. Remove pancake from pan, slice, and serve with syrup or fresh fruit.
Per serving: Calories: 351; Fat: 7.9g; Sodium: 704mg; Carbs: 6g; Fiber: 3.6g; Sugar 6g; Protein 18g

Western Cheese Omelet

Prep Time: 5 minutes. | Cook Time: 22 minutes. | Serves: 2

¼ cup chopped onion
¼ cup chopped bell pepper, green or red
¼ cup diced ham
1 teaspoon butter
4 large eggs
2 tablespoons milk
⅛ teaspoon salt
¾ cup grated sharp Cheddar cheese

1. Place the Cook & Crisp Basket in your Pressure Cooker Steam Fryer. 2. Place onion, bell pepper, ham, and butter in the Cook & Crisp Basket. 3. Put on the Smart Lid on top of the Ninja Foodi Steam Fryer. 4. Move the Lid Slider to the "Air Fry/Stovetop". Select the "Air Fry" mode for cooking. 5. Air Fry omelet at 390°F/200°C for 1 minute and stir. Continue cooking 4 to 5 minutes, until vegetables are tender. 6. Beat eggs, milk, and salt. Pour over vegetables and ham in the Cook & Crisp Basket. Put on the Smart Lid on top of the Ninja Foodi Steam Fryer. Move the Lid Slider to the "Air Fry/Stovetop". Select the "Air Fry" mode for cooking. Air Fry at 360°F/180°C for around 13 to 15 minutes or until eggs set and top has browned slightly. 7. Sprinkle grated cheese on top of omelet. Cook 1 minute or just long enough to melt the cheese.
Per serving: Calories: 221; Fat: 7.9g; Sodium: 704mg; Carbs: 6g; Fiber: 3.6g; Sugar 6g; Protein 18g

Chicken Hash

Prep Time: 10 minutes. | Cook Time: 14 minutes. | Serves: 3

6-ounces of cauliflower, chopped	½ yellow onion, diced
7-ounce chicken fillet	1 teaspoon black pepper
1 tablespoon water	3 tablespoons butter
1 green pepper, chopped	1 tablespoon cream

1. Place the Cook & Crisp Basket in your Pressure Cooker Steam Fryer. 2. Chop the cauliflower and place in the blender and blend it until you get cauliflower rice. Chop the chicken fillet into small pieces. Sprinkle the chicken fillet with black pepper and stir.. In a suitable mixing bowl, mix the ingredients, then add mixture to Cook & Crisp Basket. 3. Put on the Smart Lid on top of the Ninja Foodi Steam Fryer. 4. Move the Lid Slider to the "Air Fry/Stovetop". Select the "Air Fry" mode for cooking. 5. Cook at 380°F/195°C for 14 minutes. Then serve chicken hash warm!
Per serving: Calories: 312; Fat: 7.9g; Sodium: 704mg; Carbs: 6g; Fiber: 3.6g; Sugar 6g; Protein 18g

Breakfast Eggs with Cream

Prep Time: 10 minutes. | Cook Time: 17 minutes. | Serves: 2

4 eggs	1 tablespoon chives, chopped
1 teaspoon oregano	1 tablespoon cream
1 teaspoon parsley, dried	1 teaspoon paprika
½ teaspoon sea salt	

1. Place the Cook & Crisp Basket in your Pressure Cooker Steam Fryer. 2. Place the eggs in the Ninja Foodi Pressure Steam Fryer basket. 3. Put on the Smart Lid on top of the Ninja Foodi Steam Fryer. 4. Move the Lid Slider to the "Air Fry/Stovetop". Select the "Air Fry" mode for cooking. 5. Cook them for around 17 minutes at 320°F/160°C. Meanwhile, mix the parsley, oregano, cream, parpkia, and salt in shallow bowl. Chop the chives and add them to cream mixture. When the eggs are cooked, place them in cold water and allow them to chill. After this, peel the eggs and cut them into halves. Remove the egg yolks and add yolks to cream mixture and mash to blend well with a fork. Then fill the egg whites with the cream-egg yolk mixture. Serve immediately.
Per serving: Calories: 219; Fat: 10g; Sodium: 891mg; Carbs: 22.9g; Fiber: 4g; Sugar 4g; Protein 13g

Sesame Flax Meal Porridge

Prep Time: 10 minutes. | Cook Time: 8 minutes. | Serves: 4

2 tablespoons sesame seeds	3 tablespoons flax meal
½ teaspoon vanilla extract	1 cup almond milk
1 tablespoon butter	4 tablespoons chia seeds
1 tablespoon liquid Stevia	

1. Place the Cook & Crisp Basket in your Pressure Cooker Steam Fryer. 2. Put the sesame seeds, chia seeds, almond milk, flax meal, liquid Stevia and butter into the Ninja Foodi Pressure Steam Fryer basket tray. Add the vanilla extract. Put on the Smart Lid on top of the Ninja Foodi Steam Fryer. Move the Lid Slider to the "Air Fry/Stovetop". Select the "Air Fry" mode for cooking. 3. Adjust the cooking temperature to 375°F/190°C. 4. Cook porridge at 375°F/190°C for around 8 minutes. When porridge is cooked stir it carefully then allow it to rest for around 5 minutes before serving.
Per serving: Calories: 289; Fat: 14g; Sodium: 791mg; Carbs: 8.9g; Fiber: 4.6g; Sugar 8g; Protein 16g

Pancake Hash

Prep Time: 10 minutes. | Cook Time: 9 minutes. | Serves: 7

1 egg	1 teaspoon ginger
¼ cup heavy cream	1 teaspoon salt
5 tablespoons butter	1 tablespoon apple cider vinegar
1 cup coconut flour	1 teaspoon baking soda

1. Place the Cook & Crisp Basket in your Pressure Cooker Steam Fryer. Mix the salt, baking soda, ginger and flour in a suitable mixing bowl. In a separate bowl crack, the egg into it. Add butter and heavy cream. Mix well using a hand mixer. Mix the liquid and dry mixtures and stir until smooth. Pour the pancake mixture into the Ninja Foodi Pressure Steam Fryer basket. Put on the Smart Lid on top of the Ninja Foodi Steam Fryer. 2. Move the Lid Slider to the "Air Fry/Stovetop". Select the "Air Fry" mode for cooking. 3. Cook the pancake hash at 400°F/200°C for around 4 minutes. After this, scramble the pancake hash well and continue to cook for another 5 minutes more. When dish is cooked, transfer it to serving plates, and serve hot!
Per serving: Calories: 224; Fat: 7.9g; Sodium: 704mg; Carbs: 6g; Fiber: 3.6g; Sugar 6g; Protein 18g

Creamy Seed Porridge

Prep Time: 10 minutes. | Cook Time: 12 minutes. | Serves: 3

1 tablespoon butter	¼ teaspoon salt
¼ teaspoon nutmeg	3 tablespoons sesame seeds
⅓ cup heavy cream	3 tablespoons chia seeds
1 egg	

1. Place the Cook & Crisp Basket in your Pressure Cooker Steam Fryer. 2. Place the butter in the Cook & Crisp Basket . Add the chia seeds, sesame seeds, heavy cream, nutmeg, and salt. Stir gently. Beat the egg in a cup and mix it with a fork. Add the whisked egg to cook & crisp basket. Stir the mixture with a wooden spatula. Place the Cook & Crisp Basket into Pressure Cooker Steam Fryer. Put on the Smart Lid on top of the Ninja Foodi Steam Fryer. Move the Lid Slider to the "Air Fry/Stovetop". Select the "Air Fry" mode for cooking. Cook the porridge at 375°F/190°C for around 12 minutes. Stir it about 3 times during the cooking process. Remove the porridge from cook & crisp Basket immediately and serve hot!
Per serving: Calories: 382; Fat: 10.9g; Sodium: 354mg; Carbs: 20.5g; Fiber: 4.1g; Sugar 8.2g; Protein 06g

Breakfast Chicken Sandwich

Prep Time: 10 minutes. | Cook Time: 10 minutes. | Serves: 2

6-ounces chicken	½ teaspoon sea salt
2 slices of cheddar cheese	1 egg
2 lettuce leaves	1 teaspoon cayenne pepper
1 tablespoon dill, dried	1 teaspoon tomato puree

1. Place the Cook & Crisp Basket in your Pressure Cooker Steam Fryer. 2. Mix the chicken with the pepper and sea salt. Add the dried dill and stir. Beat the egg into the chicken mixture. Make 2 medium-sized burgers from the chicken mixture. Grease the Ninja Foodi Pressure Steam Fryer basket with olive oil and place the chicken burgers inside of it. 3. Put on the Smart Lid on top of the Ninja Foodi Steam Fryer. Move the Lid Slider to the "Air Fry/Stovetop". Select the "Air Fry" mode for cooking. 4. Adjust the cooking temperature to 380°F/195°C. 5. Cook the chicken burgers at 380°F/195°C for around 10 minutes. 6. Flip the burgers. Cook for 6minutes. 7. When the burgers are cooked, transfer them to the lettuce leaves. Sprinkle the top of them with tomato puree and with a slice of cheddar cheese. Serve immediately!
Per serving: Calories: 251; Fat: 19g; Sodium: 354mg; Carbs: 15g; Fiber: 5.1g; Sugar 8.2g; Protein 12g

Rice Paper Breakfast

Prep Time: 10 minutes. | Cook Time: 30 minutes. | Serves: 4

4 pieces white rice paper, cut into 1-inch thick strips	2 tablespoons liquid smoke
	2 tablespoons cashew butter
2 tablespoons water	3 tablespoons soy sauce or tamari

1. Place the Cook & Crisp Basket in your Pressure Cooker Steam Fryer. 2. In a suitable mixing bowl, add soy sauce, cashew butter, liquid smoke, and water, mix well. Soak the rice paper in this mixture for around 5 minutes. Place the rice paper the Cook & Crisp Basket and do not overlap pieces. Put on the Smart Lid on top of the Ninja Foodi Steam Fryer. Move the Lid Slider to the "Air Fry/Stovetop". Select the "Air Fry" mode for cooking. Adjust the cooking temperature to 350°F/175°C. Air Fry for around 15 minutes or until crispy. Serve with steamed vegetables!
Per serving: Calories: 382; Fat: 10.9g; Sodium: 354mg; Carbs: 20.5g; Fiber: 4.1g; Sugar 8.2g; Protein 06g

Parmesan Omelet

Prep Time: 10 minutes. | Cook Time: 10 minutes. | Serves: 4

1 green pepper	1 teaspoon oregano, dried
5 eggs	1 teaspoon cilantro, dried
½ yellow onion, diced	1 teaspoon olive oil
3-ounces Parmesan cheese, shredded	3 tablespoons cream cheese, softened
1 teaspoon butter	

1. Place the Cook & Crisp Basket in your Pressure Cooker Steam Fryer. 2. In a suitable bowl, add the eggs and mix them. Sprinkle the cilantro, oregano, and cream cheese into the eggs. Add the shredded parmesan and mix the egg mixture well. Pour the egg mixture into the Cook & Crisp Basket and place it into the Pressure Cooker Steam Fryer. Put on the Smart Lid on top of the Ninja Foodi Steam Fryer. 3. Move the Lid Slider to the "Air Fry/Stovetop". Select the "Air Fry" mode for cooking. 4. Cook the omelet at 360°F/180°C for around 10 minutes. Meanwhile, chop the green pepper and dice the onion. Pour olive oil into a suitable skillet. preheat well over medium heat. Add the chopped green pepper and onion to skillet and cook for around 8 minutes. Stir veggies often. Remove the omelet from "cook & crisp basket" and place it on a serving plate. Add the roasted vegetables and serve warm.
Per serving: Calories: 214; Fat: 10.9g; Sodium: 454mg; Carbs: 10g; Fiber: 3.1g; Sugar 5.2g; Protein 10g

Almond Egg Bread

Prep Time: 10 minutes. | Cook Time: 25 minutes. | Serves: 19

1 cup almond flour	¼ cup butter
¼ sea salt	3 eggs
1 teaspoon baking powder	

1. Place the Cook & Crisp Basket in your Pressure Cooker Steam Fryer. 2. Crack the eggs into a suitable bowl then using a hand blender mix them up. Melt the butter at room temperature. Take the melted butter and add it to the egg mixture. Add the salt, baking powder and almond flour to egg mixture and knead the prepared dough. Cover the prepared dough with a towel for around 10 minutes to rest. Place the prepared dough in the Cook & Crisp Basket. 3. Put on the Smart Lid on top of the Ninja Foodi Steam Fryer. 4. Move the Lid Slider to the "Air Fry/Stovetop". Select the "Air Fry" mode for cooking. 5. Cook the bread at 360°F/180°C for around 10 minutes. Then reduce its heat to 350°F/175°C. Cook the bread for an additional 15 minutes. You can use a toothpick to check to make sure the bread is cooked. Transfer the bread to a wooden board to allow it to chill. Once the bread has chilled, then slice and serve it.
Per serving: Calories: 82; Fat: 7.9g; Sodium: 704mg; Carbs: 6g; Fiber: 3.6g; Sugar 6g; Protein 18g

Kale Fritters

Prep Time: 10 minutes. | Cook Time: 8 minutes. | Serves: 8

12-ounces kale, chopped	2 tablespoons almond flour
1 teaspoon oil	1 egg
1 tablespoon cream	1 tablespoon butter
1 teaspoon paprika	½ yellow onion, diced
½ teaspoon sea salt	

1. Place the Cook & Crisp Basket in your Pressure Cooker Steam Fryer. 2. Wash and chop the kale. Add the chopped kale to blender and blend it until smooth. Dice up the yellow onion. Beat the egg and mix it in a suitable mixing bowl. Add the almond flour, paprika, cream and salt into bowl with whisked egg and stir. Add the diced onion and blended kale to mixing bowl and mix until you get fritter dough. Grease the inside of the Ninja Foodi Pressure Steam Fryer basket with olive oil. Make medium-sized fritters with prepared mixture and place them into "cook & crisp basket". 3. Put on the Smart Lid on top of the Ninja Foodi Steam Fryer. 4. Move the Lid Slider to the "Air Fry/Stovetop". Select the "Air Fry" mode for cooking. 5. Cook the kale fritters on each side at 360°F/180°C for 4 minutes. 6. Once they are cooked, allow them to chill then serve.
Per serving: Calories: 219; Fat: 10g; Sodium: 891mg; Carbs: 22.9g; Fiber: 4g; Sugar 4g; Protein 13g

Morning Sausages

Prep Time: 10 minutes. | Cook Time: 12 minutes. | Serves: 6

7-ounces chicken	1 teaspoon minced garlic
7-ounces pork	1 tablespoon coconut flour
1 teaspoon coriander	1 egg
1 teaspoon basil, dried	1 teaspoon soy sauce
½ teaspoon nutmeg	1 teaspoon sea salt
1 teaspoon olive oil	½ teaspoon black pepper

1. Place the Cook & Crisp Basket in your 2. Mix the pork, chicken, soy sauce, black pepper, garlic, basil, coriander, nutmeg, sea salt, and egg. Add the coconut flour and mix the mixture well to mix. Make medium-sized sausages with the meat mixture. Grease the inside of the Ninja Foodi Pressure Steam Fryer basket with the olive oil. Place prepared sausages into the "cook & crisp basket" and place inside of Pressure Cooker Steam Fryer. Put on the Smart Lid on top of the Ninja Foodi Steam Fryer. Move the Lid Slider to the "Air Fry/Stovetop". Select the "Air Fry" mode for cooking. 3. Cook the sausages at 360°F/180°C for around 6 minutes. Turn the sausages over. 4. Cook for around 6 minutes more. Serve warm.
Per serving: Calories: 184; Fat: 5g; Sodium: 441mg; Carbs: 17g; Fiber: 4.6g; Sugar 5g; Protein 9g

Bacon Egg Cups

Prep Time: 10 minutes. | Cook Time: 12 minutes. | Serves: 2

2 eggs	½ teaspoon butter
1 tablespoon chives, fresh, chopped	¼ teaspoon salt
½ teaspoon paprika	4-ounces bacon, cut into tiny
½ teaspoon cayenne pepper	pieces
3-ounces cheddar cheese, shredded	

1. Place the Cook & Crisp Basket in your Pressure Cooker Steam Fryer. 2. Sprinkle the bacon with cayenne pepper, salt, and paprika. Mix the chopped bacon. Spread butter in bottom of ramekin dishes and beat the eggs there. Add the chives and shredded cheese. Add the chopped bacon over egg mixture in ramekin dishes. Place the ramekins in your Ninja Foodi Pressure Steam Fryer basket. Place the Cook & Crisp Basket in your Ninja Foodi Pressure Steam Fryer . Put on the Smart Lid on top of the Ninja Foodi Steam Fryer. Move the Lid Slider to the "Air Fry/Stovetop". Select the "Air Fry" mode for cooking. 3. Cook at 360°F/180°C for around 12 minutes. Serve.
Per serving: Calories: 334; Fat: 7.9g; Sodium: 704mg; Carbs: 6g; Fiber: 3.6g; Sugar 6g; Protein 18g

Spinach Cheddar Quiche

Prep Time: 10 minutes. | Cook Time: 21 minutes. | Serves: 6

6-ounces cheddar cheese, shredded	¼ cup cream cheese
1 teaspoon olive oil	1 cup spinach
3 eggs	1 teaspoon sea salt
1 teaspoon black pepper	4 tablespoons water, boiled
½ yellow onion, diced	½ cup almond flour

1. Place the Cook & Crisp Basket in your Pressure Cooker Steam Fryer. 2. Mix the almond flour, water, and salt. Mix and knead the prepared dough. Grease inside of the fryer basket with olive oil. Roll the prepared dough and place it in your Ninja Foodi Pressure Steam Fryer basket tray in the shape of the crust. Place "cook & crisp basket" in your Pressure Cooker Steam Fryer. 3. Put on the Smart Lid on top of the Ninja Foodi Steam Fryer. 4. Move the Lid Slider to the "Air Fry/Stovetop". Select the "Air Fry" mode for cooking. 5. Cook at 375°F/190°C for around 5 minutes. Chop the spinach leaves and mix it with the cream cheese and black pepper. Dice the yellow onion and add it to the spinach mixture and stir. Mix eggs in a suitable bowl. When the quiche crust is cooked—transfer the spinach filling. Sprinkle the filling top with shredded cheese and pour the whisked eggs over the top. Put on the Smart Lid on top of the Ninja Foodi Steam Fryer. Move the Lid Slider to the "Air Fry/Stovetop". Select the "Air Fry" mode for cooking. Cook the quiche at 350°F/175°C for around 7 minutes. Reduce its heat to 300°F/150°C Cook for the quiche for an additional 9 minutes. Allow the quiche to chill and then cut it into pieces for serving.
Per serving: Calories: 284; Fat: 9g; Sodium: 441mg; Carbs: 7g; Fiber: 4.6g; Sugar 5g; Protein 19g

Zucchini Hash

Prep Time: 10 minutes. | Cook Time: 8 minutes. | Serves: 4

7-ounces bacon, cooked	1 teaspoon cilantro
1 zucchini, cubed into small pieces	1 teaspoon paprika
4-ounces cheddar cheese, shredded	1 teaspoon black pepper
2 tablespoons butter	1 teaspoon salt
1 teaspoon thyme	

1. Place the Cook & Crisp Basket in your Pressure Cooker Steam Fryer. 2. Chop the zucchini into small cubes and sprinkle with black pepper, salt, paprika, cilantro and thyme. Add butter to the Cook & Crisp Basket. Melt the butter and add the zucchini cubes. Put on the Smart Lid on top of the Ninja Foodi Steam Fryer. Move the Lid Slider to the "Air Fry/Stovetop". Select the "Air Fry" mode for cooking. Cook the zucchini cubes at 400°F/200°C for around 5 minutes. Meanwhile, shred the cheddar cheese. Add the bacon to the zucchini cubes. Sprinkle the zucchini mixture with shredded cheese. Cook for around 3 minutes more. When cooking is completed, transfer the breakfast hash into serving bowls.
Per serving: Calories: 372; Fat: 20g; Sodium: 891mg; Carbs: 29g; Fiber: 3g; Sugar 8g; Protein 7g

Coconut Porridge

Prep Time: 10 minutes. | Cook Time: 7 minutes. | Serves: 4

1 cup coconut milk	1 teaspoon cinnamon
3 tablespoons blackberries	5 tablespoons chia seeds
2 tablespoons walnuts	3 tablespoons coconut flakes
1 teaspoon butter	¼ teaspoon salt

1. Place the Cook & Crisp Basket in your Pressure Cooker Steam Fryer. 2. Pour the coconut milk into the "cook & crisp basket" . Add the coconut, salt, chia seeds, cinnamon, and butter. up the walnuts and add them to the "cook & crisp basket". Sprinkle the mixture with salt. Mash the blackberries with a fork and add them also to the Ninja Foodi Pressure Steam Fryer basket. Put on the Smart Lid on top of the Ninja Foodi Steam Fryer. 3. Move the Lid Slider to the "Air Fry/Stovetop". Select the "Air Fry" mode for cooking. 4. Cook the porridge at 375°F/190°C for around 7 minutes. Stir porridge with a wooden spoon and serve warm.
Per serving: Calories: 282; Fat: 7.9g; Sodium: 704mg; Carbs: 6g; Fiber: 3.6g; Sugar 6g; Protein 18g

Egg Scramble

Prep Time: 10 minutes. | Cook Time: 17 minutes | Serves: 4

4 eggs	1 teaspoon salt
4 tablespoons butter	

1. Place the Cook & Crisp Basket in your Pressure Cooker Steam Fryer. 2. Cover the Ninja Foodi Pressure Steam Fryer basket with foil and place the eggs there. Transfer the basket into the Pressure Cooker Steam Fryer. Put on the Smart Lid on top of the Ninja Foodi Steam Fryer. Move the Lid Slider to the "Air Fry/Stovetop". Select the "Air Fry" mode for cooking. Put on the Smart Lid on top of the Ninja Foodi Steam Fryer. 3. Move the Lid Slider to the "Air Fry/Stovetop". Select the "Air Fry" mode for cooking. 4. Cook for the eggs for around 17 minutes at 320°F/160°C. When the time is over, remove the eggs from the "cook & crisp basket" and put them in cold water to chill them. After this, peel the eggs and chop them up finely. Mix the chopped eggs with butter and add salt. Mix it until you get the spread texture. Serve the egg butter with the keto almond bread.
Per serving: Calories: 284; Fat: 9g; Sodium: 441mg; Carbs: 7g; Fiber: 4.6g; Sugar 5g; Protein 19g

Liver Pate

Prep Time: 10 minutes. | Cook Time: 10 minutes. | Serves: 7

1 lb. chicken liver	1 teaspoon black pepper
1 teaspoon salt	1 cup water
½ teaspoon cilantro, dried	4 tablespoons butter
1 yellow onion, diced	

1. Place the Cook & Crisp Basket in your Pressure Cooker Steam Fryer. 2. Chop the chicken liver and place it in the Cook & Crisp Basket . Add water and diced onion. Put on the Smart Lid on top of the Ninja Foodi Steam Fryer. Move the Lid Slider to the "Air Fry/Stovetop". Select the "Air Fry" mode for cooking. 3. Cook the chicken liver at 360°F/180°C for around 10 minutes. When it is finished cooking, drain the chicken liver. Transfer the chicken liver to blender, add butter, black pepper and dried cilantro and blend. Once you get a pate texture, transfer to liver pate bowl and serve immediately or keep in the fridge for later.
Per serving: Calories: 221; Fat: 7.9g; Sodium: 704mg; Carbs: 6g; Fiber: 3.6g; Sugar 6g; Protein 18g

Meatloaf Slices

Prep Time: 10 minutes. | Cook Time: 20 minutes. | Serves: 6

8-ounces pork	1 teaspoon salt
7-ounces beef	1 tablespoon chives
1 teaspoon olive oil	1 tablespoon almond flour
1 teaspoon butter	1 egg
1 tablespoon oregano, dried	1 onion, diced
1 teaspoon cayenne pepper	

1. Place the Cook & Crisp Basket in your Pressure Cooker Steam Fryer. 2. Beat egg in a suitable bowl. Add the beef and pork. Add the chives, almond flour, cayenne pepper, salt, dried oregano, and butter. Add diced onion to beef mixture. Use hands to shape a meatloaf mixture. Grease the inside of the "cook & crisp basket" with olive oil and place the meatloaf inside it. Put on the Smart Lid on top of the Ninja Foodi Steam Fryer. 3. Move the Lid Slider to the "Air Fry/Stovetop". Select the "Air Fry" mode for cooking. 4. Cook the meatloaf at 350°F/175°C for around 20 minutes. When the meatloaf has cooked, allow it to chill for a bit. Slice and serve it.
Per serving: Calories: 312; Fat: 12.9g; Sodium: 414mg; Carbs: 11g; Fiber: 5g; Sugar 9g; Protein 11g

Spinach Parsley Omelet

Prep Time: 10 minutes. | Cook Time: 10 minutes. | Serves: 1

1 teaspoon olive oil	1 tablespoon parsley, chopped
3 eggs	¼ cup spinach, chopped
3 tablespoons ricotta cheese	Black pepper and salt to taste

1. Place the Cook & Crisp Basket in your Pressure Cooker Steam Fryer. 2. Pour olive oil on the Cook & Crisp Basket. 3. Mix eggs adding black pepper and salt as seasoning. Stir in the ricotta, spinach, and parsley with eggs. Pour the egg mixture into the Cook & Crisp Basket. Put on the Smart Lid on top of the Ninja Foodi Steam Fryer. Move the Lid Slider to the "Air Fry/Stovetop". Select the "Air Fry" mode for cooking. Adjust the cooking temperature to 330°F/165°C. Cook for around 10 minutes. Serve warm.
Per serving: Calories: 219; Fat: 10g; Sodium: 891mg; Carbs: 22.9g; Fiber: 4g; Sugar 4g; Protein 13g

Minced Beef Sandwich

Prep Time: 10 minutes. | Cook Time: 16 minutes. | Serves: 2

6-ounces minced beef	½ teaspoon chili flakes
4 lettuce leaves	½ tomato, sliced
1 teaspoon flax seeds	½ avocado, pitted, sliced
1 teaspoon olive oil	Salt, to taste
½ teaspoon black pepper	

1. Place the Cook & Crisp Basket in your Pressure Cooker Steam Fryer. 2. Mix the chili flakes with the minced beef and salt. Add the flax seeds and stir the meat mixture using a fork. Pour the olive oil into the Ninja Foodi Pressure Steam Fryer basket. Make 2 burgers from the beef mixture and place them in the "cook & crisp basket". Put on the Smart Lid on top of the Ninja Foodi Steam Fryer. 3. Move the Lid Slider to the "Air Fry/Stovetop". Select the "Air Fry" mode for cooking. 4. Adjust the cooking temperature to 370°F/185°C Cook the burgers for around 8 minutes on each side. Meanwhile, slice the avocado and tomato. Place the avocado and tomato onto 2 lettuce leaves. Add the cooked minced beef burgers and serve them hot!
Per serving: Calories: 289; Fat: 14g; Sodium: 791mg; Carbs: 8.9g; Fiber: 4.6g; Sugar 8g; Protein 6g

Beef Chili

Prep Time: 10 minutes. | Cook Time: 10 minutes. | Serves: 4

8-ounces beef	1 teaspoon cilantro, dried
½ yellow onion, diced	1 teaspoon oregano, dried
1 teaspoon tomato puree	1 tablespoon dill weed
6-ounces cheddar cheese, shredded	1 teaspoon mustard
1 teaspoon parsley, dried	1 tablespoon butter

1. Place the Cook & Crisp Basket in your Pressure Cooker Steam Fryer. 2. Mix beef with diced onion in a suitable bowl. Sprinkle the mixture with tomato puree, cilantro, parsley, oregano and dried dill. Then add the butter and mustard and mix well. Add beef mixture to "cook & crisp basket" . Put on the Smart Lid on top of the Ninja Foodi Steam Fryer. Move the Lid Slider to the "Air Fry/Stovetop". Select the "Air Fry" mode for cooking. Put on the Smart Lid on top of the Ninja Foodi Steam Fryer. 3. Move the Lid Slider to the "Air Fry/Stovetop". Select the "Air Fry" mode for cooking. 4. Adjust the cooking temperature to 380°F/190°C. Cook for the chili for around 9 minutes. After about 6 minutes of cooking stir the chili. When the chili is cooked, sprinkle the top with shredded cheddar cheese and stir carefully. Transfer chili mixture into serving bowls. Serve warm.
Per serving: Calories: 334; Fat: 7.9g; Sodium: 704mg; Carbs: 6g; Fiber: 3.6g; Sugar 6g; Protein 18g

Bacon Burger

Prep Time: 10 minutes. | Cook Time: 8 minutes. | Serves: 2

8-ounces beef	1 teaspoon butter
2-ounces lettuce leaves	4-ounces bacon, cooked
½ teaspoon minced garlic	1 egg
1 teaspoon olive oil	½ yellow onion, diced
½ teaspoon sea salt	½ cucumber, slice finely
1 teaspoon black pepper	½ tomato, slice finely

1. Place the Cook & Crisp Basket in your Pressure Cooker Steam Fryer. 2. Begin by whisking the egg in a suitable bowl, then add the beef and mix well. Add cooked, chopped bacon to the beef mixture. Add butter, black pepper, minced garlic, and salt. Mix and make burgers. Grease the Ninja Foodi Pressure Steam Fryer basket with olive oil and place the burgers inside of it. Put on the Smart Lid on top of the Ninja Foodi Steam Fryer. 3. Move the Lid Slider to the "Air Fry/Stovetop". Select the "Air Fry" mode for cooking. 4. Adjust the cooking temperature to 370°F/185°C Cook the burgers for around 8-minutes on each side. Meanwhile, slice the cucumber, onion, and tomato finely. Place the tomato, onion, and cucumber onto the lettuce leaves. When the burgers are cooked, allow them to chill at room temperature, and place them over the vegetables and serve.
Per serving: Calories: 282; Fat: 10.9g; Sodium: 354mg; Carbs: 20.5g; Fiber: 4.1g; Sugar 8.2g; Protein 06g

English Bacon Breakfast

Prep Time: 10 minutes. | Cook Time: 20 minutes. | Serves: 4

8 medium sausages	2 tomatoes, sliced, sauté
8 slices of back bacon	½ cup mushrooms, finely sliced,
4 eggs	sauté
8 slices of toast	1 tablespoon olive oil
1 can baked beans	

1. Place the Cook & Crisp Basket in your Pressure Cooker Steam Fryer. 2. Heat olive oil in suitable saucepan over medium-high heat. Add mushrooms to pan and sauté for a few minutes. Remove mushrooms from pan and set aside, add tomatoes to pan and sauté for a few minutes then set aside. Place your sausages and bacon into the Cook & Crisp Basket . Put on the Smart Lid on top of the Ninja Foodi Steam Fryer. Move the Lid Slider to the "Air Fry/Stovetop". Select the "Air Fry" mode for cooking. Adjust the cooking temperature to 320°F/160°C. Cook for around 10 minutes. Place the baked beans into a ramekin and your eggs in another ramekin. Transfer to the Cook & Crisp Basket. Put on the Smart Lid on top of the Ninja Foodi Steam Fryer. Move the Lid Slider to the "Air Fry/Stovetop". Select the "Air Fry" mode for cooking. Cook for an additional 10 minutes at 390°F/200°C. Serve warm.
Per serving: Calories: 234; Fat: 19g; Sodium: 354mg; Carbs: 15g; Fiber: 5.1g; Sugar 8.2g; Protein 12g

Italian Frittata

Prep Time: 10 minutes. | Cook Time: 10 minutes. | Serves: 2

4 cherry tomatoes, sliced into halves	3 eggs
	1 tablespoon parsley, chopped
½ Italian sausage, sliced	Black pepper and salt to taste
½ teaspoon Italian seasoning	

1. Place the Cook & Crisp Basket in your Pressure Cooker Steam Fryer. 2. Put the sausage and cherry tomatoes into the Cook & Crisp Basket . Put on the Smart Lid on top of the Ninja Foodi Steam Fryer. Move the Lid Slider to the "Air Fry/Stovetop". Select the "Air Fry" mode for cooking. Adjust the cooking temperature to 360°F/180°C Cook for around 5 minutes. Crack eggs into small bowl, add parsley, Italian seasoning and mix well by whisking. Pour egg mixture over sausage and cherry tomatoes and place back into Pressure Cooker Steam Fryer and cook for an additional 5 minutes. Serve warm.
Per serving: Calories: 372; Fat: 20g; Sodium: 891mg; Carbs: 29g; Fiber: 3g; Sugar 8g; Protein 7g

Broccoli Tofu Scramble

Prep Time: 10 minutes. | Cook Time: 30 minutes. | Serves: 3

4 cups broccoli florets	1 teaspoon turmeric powder
1 block tofu, chopped finely	½ teaspoon garlic powder
2 ½ cups red potatoes, chopped	½ teaspoon onion powder
2 tablespoons olive oil	½ cup onion, chopped
2 tablespoons tamari	

1. Place the Cook & Crisp Basket in your Pressure Cooker Steam Fryer. 2. Mix the potatoes in a suitable bowl with half of the olive oil. Place the potatoes into the Cook & Crisp Basket. Put on the Smart Lid on top of the Ninja Foodi Steam Fryer. Move the Lid Slider to the "Air Fry/Stovetop". Select the "Air Fry" mode for cooking. Adjust the cooking temperature to 400°F/200°C . Cook for them for around 15 minutes. Mix the remaining olive oil, tofu, tamari, turmeric, garlic powder and onion powder. Stir in the chopped onions. Add the broccoli florets. Pour this mixture on top of the air-fried potatoes. Put on the Smart Lid on top of the Ninja Foodi Steam Fryer. Move the Lid Slider to the "Air Fry/Stovetop". Select the "Air Fry" mode for cooking. Cook for an additional 15 minutes. Serve warm.
Per serving: Calories: 282; Fat: 7.9g; Sodium: 704mg; Carbs: 6g; Fiber: 3.6g; Sugar 6g; Protein 18g

Healthy Blueberry Oat Mini Muffins

Prep time: 12 minutes| Cook time: 10 minutes| Serves: 7

½ cup rolled oats	2 large eggs
¼ cup whole wheat pastry flour or white whole wheat flour	½ cup plain Greek yogurt
	2 tablespoons pure maple syrup
½ tablespoon baking powder	2 teaspoons extra-virgin olive oil
½ teaspoon ground cardamom or ground cinnamon	½ teaspoon vanilla extract
	½ cup frozen blueberries
⅛ teaspoon kosher salt	

1. In a large bowl, stir together the oats, flour, baking powder, cardamom, and salt. 2. In a medium bowl, whisk together the eggs, yogurt, maple syrup, oil, and vanilla. 3. Add the egg mixture to oat mixture and stir just until combined. Gently fold in the blueberries. 4. Scoop the batter into each cup of the egg bite mold. 5. Pour 1 cup of water into the Ninja Foodi XL Pressure Cooker Steam Fryer with SmartLid cooking pot. Place the egg in Deluxe Reversible Rack and lower it into the pot. 6. Lock lid; move slider towards PRESSURE. Adjust pressure release valve in the SEAL position. Close pressure-release valve. The cooking temperature will default to HIGH, which is accurate. Set time to 10 minutes. Select START/STOP and start cooking. When cooking is complete, let pressure release naturally for about 10 minutes, then quickly release any remaining pressure by turning it into VENT position. 7. Lift the rack out of the pot and place on a cooling rack for 5 minutes. Invert the mold onto the cooling rack to release the muffins. 8. Serve the muffins warm or refrigerate or freeze.
Per Serving: Calories 278; Fat 20.9g; Sodium 145mg; Carbs 1.5g; Fiber 0.3g; Sugar 0.1g; Protein 20g

Veggies on Toast

Prep Time: 10 minutes. | Cook Time: 11 minutes. | Serves: 4

1 tablespoon olive oil
½ cup soft goat cheese
2 tablespoons softened butter
4 slices French bread
2 green onions, sliced
1 small yellow squash, sliced
1 cup button mushrooms, sliced
1 red bell pepper, cut into strips

1. Place the Cook & Crisp Basket in your Pressure Cooker Steam Fryer. 2. Sprinkle the Cook & Crisp Basket with olive oil. Mix the red bell peppers, squash, mushrooms and green onions. 3. Put on the Smart Lid on top of the Ninja Foodi Steam Fryer. 4. Move the Lid Slider to the "Air Fry/Stovetop". Select the "Air Fry" mode for cooking. 5. Cook them at 350°F/175°C for around 7 minutes. Place vegetables on a plate and set aside. Spread the bread slices with butter and place into the Cook & Crisp Basket, with butter side up. Put on the Smart Lid on top of the Ninja Foodi Steam Fryer. 6. Move the Lid Slider to the "Air Fry/Stovetop". Select the "Air Fry" mode for cooking. 7. Adjust the cooking temperature to 350°F/175°C. Toast for around 4 minutes. Spread the cheese on toasted bread and top with veggies. Serve warm.
Per serving: Calories: 184; Fat: 5g; Sodium: 441mg; Carbs: 17g; Fiber: 4.6g; Sugar 5g; Protein 9g

Tropical Oats

Prep time: 5 minutes| Cook time: 5 minutes| Serves: 4

1 cup steel cut oats
1 cup unsweetened almond milk
2 cups coconut water or water
¾ cup frozen chopped peaches
¾ cup frozen mango chunks
1 (2-inch) vanilla bean, scraped (seeds and pod)
Ground cinnamon
¼ cup chopped unsalted macadamia nuts

1. In the Ninja Foodi XL Pressure Cooker Steam Fryer with SmartLid cooking pot, combine the oats, almond milk, coconut water, peaches, mango chunks, and vanilla bean seeds and pod. Stir well. 2. Lock lid; move slider towards PRESSURE. Adjust pressure release valve in the SEAL position. Close pressure-release valve. The cooking temperature will default to HIGH, which is accurate. Set time to 3 minutes. Select START/STOP and start cooking. 3. When cooking is complete, let pressure release naturally for about 10 minutes, then release quickly any remaining pressure by turning it into VENT position. Unlock and remove the lid. 4. Discard the vanilla bean pod and stir well. 5. Spoon the oats into 4 bowls. Top each serving with a sprinkle of cinnamon and 1 tablespoon of the macadamia nuts.
Per Serving: Calories 220; Fat 14g; Sodium 211mg; Carbs 5g; Fiber 2g; Sugar 1g; Protein 11g

Farro with Berries and Walnuts

Prep time: 8 minutes| Cook time: 10 minutes| Serves: 6

1 cup farro, rinsed and drained
1 cup unsweetened almond milk
¼ teaspoon kosher salt
½ teaspoon pure vanilla extract
1 teaspoon ground cinnamon
1 tablespoon pure maple syrup
1½ cups fresh blueberries, raspberries, or strawberries
6 tablespoons chopped walnuts

1. In the Ninja Foodi XL Pressure Cooker Steam Fryer with SmartLid cooking pot, combine the farro, almond milk, 1 cup of water, salt, vanilla, cinnamon, and maple syrup. 2. Lock lid; move slider towards PRESSURE. Adjust pressure release valve in the SEAL position. Close pressure-release valve. The cooking temperature will default to HIGH, which is accurate. Set time to 10 minutes. Select START/STOP and start cooking. When cooking is complete, let pressure release naturally for about 10 minutes, then quickly release any remaining pressure by turning it into VENT position. 3. unlock and remove the lid. 4. Stir the farro. Spoon into bowls and top each serving with ¼ cup of berries and 1 tablespoon of walnuts.
Per Serving: Calories 241; Fat 11g; Sodium 266mg; Carbs 5g; Fiber 4g; Sugar 2g; Protein 12g

Eggs and Sausage Muffins

Prep Time: 10 minutes. | Cook Time: 20 minutes. | Serves: 2

3 eggs
¼ cup cream
2 sausages, boiled
Chopped fresh herbs
Sea salt to taste
4 tablespoons cheese, grated
1 piece of bread, sliced lengthwise

1. Place the Cook & Crisp Basket in your Pressure Cooker Steam Fryer. 2. Break the eggs in a suitable bowl, add cream, and scramble. Grease 3 muffin cups with cooking spray. Add equal amounts of egg mixture into each. Arrange sliced sausages and bread slices into muffin cups, sinking into egg mixture. Sprinkle the tops with cheese, and salt to taste. Put on the Smart Lid on top of the Ninja Foodi Steam Fryer. 3. Move the Lid Slider to the "Air Fry/Stovetop". Select the "Air Fry" mode for cooking. 4. Adjust the cooking temperature to 360°F/180°C. 5. Cook the muffins for around 20 minutes. Season with fresh herbs and serve warm.
Per serving: Calories: 361; Fat: 7.9g; Sodium: 704mg; Carbs: 6g; Fiber: 3.6g; Sugar 6g; Protein 18g

Mexican Casserole

Prep time: 5 minutes| Cook time: 45 minutes| Serves: 2

½ teaspoon olive oil
1 large red onion, chopped
1 lb. mild sausages, ground
8 large eggs, beaten
½ cup flour
1 can black beans, rinsed
1 cup Cotija cheese
1 cup mozzarella cheese
Sour cream, optional to garnish
Cilantro, optional to garnish
½ cup green onions

1. Move the slider towards "AIR FRY/STOVETOP" and set Ninja Foodi XL Pressure Cooker Steam Fryer with SmartLid to SEAR/SAUTÉ mode. Adjust the temperature to "Hi5" by using up arrow. Press START/STOP to begin cooking and heat the oil. Add the onion and sauté for 2-3 minutes. Add the sausages and cook until starting to brown on all sides. 2. In another bowl, combine the eggs and flour. Pour the mixture into the cooking pot and stir well. Add the beans, Cotija cheese and mozzarella cheese to the pot. Press the START/STOP button to reset the cooking program. 3. Lock lid; move slider towards PRESSURE. Adjust pressure release valve in the SEAL position. Close pressure-release valve. The cooking temperature will default to HIGH, which is accurate. Set the time to 20 minutes. Select START/STOP and start cooking. 4. When cooking is complete, let pressure release naturally for 10 minutes, then quick-release any remaining pressure by turning it into VENT position. 5. Uncover the pot. Top with sour cream, cilantro and green onion. Chill for a while and serve.
Per Serving: Calories 228; Fat 11.2g; Sodium 541mg; Carbs 10.3g; Fiber 4g; Sugar 2g; Protein 13.2g

Cheesy Bacon Quiche

Prep time: 5 minutes| Cook time: 45 minutes| Serves: 2

1 cup water
6 large eggs, beaten
½ cup almond or coconut milk
¼ teaspoon salt
⅛ teaspoon black pepper, ground
½ cup diced ham
1 cup ground sausage, cooked
4 slices cooked and crumbled bacon
1 cup parmesan cheese
2 large green onions, chopped

1. Pour the water into the Ninja Foodi XL Pressure Cooker Steam Fryer with SmartLid cooking pot and insert the Deluxe Reversible Rack. In a bowl, whisk together the eggs, milk, salt and pepper until combined. Add the ham, sausage, bacon, cheese and green onion and stir well. Cover the dish with foil and place on the Deluxe Reversible Rack. 2. Lock lid; move slider towards PRESSURE. Adjust pressure release valve in the SEAL position. Close pressure-release valve. The cooking temperature will default to HIGH, which is accurate. Set the time for 30 minutes. Select START/STOP and start cooking. 3. When cooking is complete, let pressure release naturally for 10 minutes, then quick-release any remaining pressure by turning it into VENT position. Remove the foil. 4. Serve. If you like a crisp top, you can sprinkle the dish with some additional cheese then slide under the broiler for a few minutes at the end.
Per Serving: Calories 224; Fat 12.3g; Sodium 458mg; Carbs 11.2g; Fiber 2g; Sugar 1g; Protein 14.2g

Porridge

Prep time: 5 minutes| **Cook time:** 20 minutes| **Serves:** 7

½ cup steel cut oats
½ cup short-grain brown rice
½ cup millet
½ cup barley
⅓ cup wild rice
¼ cup corn grits or polenta
3 tablespoons ground flaxseed
½ teaspoon salt
Ground cinnamon
Unsweetened almond milk
Berries
Sliced almonds or chopped walnuts

1. In the Ninja Foodi XL Pressure Cooker Steam Fryer with SmartLid cooking pot, combine the oats, brown rice, millet, barley, wild rice, grits, flaxseed, salt, and 8 cups of water. 2. Lock lid; move slider towards PRESSURE. Adjust pressure release valve in the SEAL position. Close pressure-release valve. The cooking temperature will default to HIGH, which is accurate. Set time to 20 minutes. Select START/STOP and start cooking. 3. When cooking is complete, let pressure release naturally for about 10 minutes, then quickly release any remaining pressure by turning it into VENT position. 4. Once the pin drops, unlock and remove the lid. Stir. 5. Serve with any combination of cinnamon, almond milk, berries, and nuts.
Per Serving: Calories 251; Fat 16g; Sodium 235mg; Carbs 6g; Fiber 3g; Sugar 2g; Protein 11g

Bell Pepper Cups

Prep time: 5 minutes| **Cook time:** 15 minutes| **Serves:** 4

4 bell peppers
4 eggs
Salt and ground black pepper to taste
⅔ cup water
2 tablespoons mozzarella cheese, grated freshly
Chopped fresh herbs

1. Cut the bell peppers ends to form about 1½-inch high cup. Remove the seeds. Crack 1 egg into each pepper. Season with salt and black pepper. Cover each bell pepper with a piece of foil. 2. Pour the water into the Ninja Foodi XL Pressure Cooker Steam Fryer with SmartLid cooking pot and insert a Cook & Crisp Basket. Place the bell peppers in the basket. 3. Lock lid; move slider towards PRESSURE. Adjust pressure release valve in the SEAL position. Close pressure-release valve. The cooking temperature will default to HIGH, which is accurate. Set the time for 4 minutes at HIGH pressure. Select START/STOP and start cooking. 4. When cooking is complete, let pressure release quickly by turning it into VENT position. Carefully unlock the lid. Transfer the bell pepper cups onto serving plates. 5. Sprinkle with mozzarella cheese and chopped fresh herbs of your choice. Serve.
Per Serving: Calories 226; Fat 9.3g; Sodium 324mg; Carbs 8.7g; Fiber 3g; Sugar 2g; Protein 12.6g

Tomato and Spinach Healthy Breakfast

Prep time: 5 minutes| **Cook time:** 30 minutes| **Serves:** 6

1½ cups water
12 beaten eggs
Salt and ground black pepper to the taste
½ cup milk
1 cup tomato, diced
3 cups baby spinach, chopped
3 green onions, sliced
4 tomatoes, sliced
¼ cup parmesan, grated

1. Prepare the Ninja Foodi XL Pressure Cooker Steam Fryer with SmartLid by adding the water to the cooking pot and placing the Deluxe Reversible Rack in it. 2. In a bowl, mix the eggs with salt, pepper and milk. Stir to combine. In a baking dish, mix diced tomato, spinach, and green onions. Pour the eggs mix over veggies, spread tomato slices on top. Sprinkle with parmesan. Place the dish on the Deluxe Reversible Rack. 3. Lock lid; move slider towards PRESSURE. Adjust pressure release valve in the SEAL position. Close pressure-release valve. The cooking temperature will default to HIGH, which is accurate. Set the time for 20 minutes at HIGH pressure. Select START/STOP and start cooking. 4. When cooking is complete, let pressure release quickly by turning it into VENT position. Carefully uncover the pot. 5. If you want a crisp top, slide under the broiler for a few minutes at the end.
Per Serving: Calories 191; Fat 6g; Sodium 298mg; Carbs 1.4g; Fiber 0.3g; Sugar 0.1g; Protein 31.2g

Eggs Dish

Prep time: 5 minutes| **Cook time:** 15 minutes| **Serves:** 6

1 cup water
8 eggs
¼ cup cream
1 teaspoon mayo sauce
1 tablespoon mustard
1 teaspoon ground white pepper
1 teaspoon minced garlic
½ teaspoon sea salt
¼ cup dill, chopped

1. Pour the water into the Ninja Foodi XL Pressure Cooker Steam Fryer with SmartLid cooking pot and insert a Cook & Crisp Basket. Place the eggs in the basket. 2. Lock lid; move slider towards PRESSURE. Adjust pressure release valve in the SEAL position. Close pressure-release valve. The cooking temperature will default to HIGH, which is accurate. Set the time for 5 minutes at HIGH pressure. Select START/STOP and start cooking. 3. When cooking is complete, let pressure release quickly by turning it into VENT position. Carefully unlock the lid. Transfer the eggs to the bowl of cold water and cool for 2-3 minutes. Peel the eggs, remove the egg yolks and mash them. 4. In a medium bowl, combine the cream, mayo sauce, mustard, pepper, garlic, salt and mashed egg yolks. Sprinkle the mixture with the dill. Mix well. Transfer the egg yolk mixture to the pastry bag. Fill the egg whites with the yolk mixture. 5. Serve.
Per Serving: Calories 142; Fat 10.2g; Sodium 269mg; Carbs 4.9g; Fiber 2.7g; Sugar 2g; Protein 8.8g

Omelet Cups

Prep time: 5 minutes| **Cook time:** 15 minutes| **Serves:** 2

½ teaspoon olive oil
3 eggs, beaten
1 cup water
Salt and freshly ground black
pepper to taste
1 onion, chopped
1 jalapeño pepper, chopped

1. Prepare two ramekins by adding a drop of olive oil in each and rubbing the bottom and sides. In a medium bowl, whisk together the eggs, water, salt and black pepper until combined. Add the onion and jalapeño, stir. 2. Transfer egg mixture to the ramekins. Prepare the Ninja Foodi XL Pressure Cooker Steam Fryer with SmartLid by adding the water to the pot and placing the Deluxe Reversible Rack in it. Place the ramekins on the Deluxe Reversible Rack. 3. Lock lid; move slider towards PRESSURE. Adjust pressure release valve in the SEAL position. Close pressure-release valve. The cooking temperature will default to HIGH, which is accurate. Set the time for 5 minutes at HIGH pressure. Select START/STOP and start cooking. 4. When cooking is complete, let pressure release quickly by turning it into VENT position. 5. Carefully unlock the lid. Serve hot.
Per Serving: Calories 220; Fat 13g; Sodium 321mg; Carbs 6g; Fiber 4g; Sugar 2g; Protein 12g

Spinach-Feta Cups

Prep time: 5 minutes| **Cook time:** 15 minutes| **Serves:** 4

1 cup water
1 cup chopped baby spinach
6 beaten eggs
1 chopped tomato
½ cup mozzarella cheese, shredded
¼ cup feta cheese, cubed
1 teaspoon black pepper
½ teaspoon salt

1. Pour the water into the Ninja Foodi XL Pressure Cooker Steam Fryer with SmartLid cooking pot and insert a Deluxe Reversible Rack. Lay the spinach in two heatproof cups. 2. In a bowl, whisk together the eggs, mozzarella cheese, feta cheese, tomato, salt and pepper until combined. Pour the mixture into the cups, leaving ¼-inch of head room. Place the cups on the Deluxe Reversible Rack. 3. Lock lid; move slider towards PRESSURE. Adjust pressure release valve in the SEAL position. Close pressure-release valve. The cooking temperature will default to HIGH, which is accurate. Set the time for 8 minutes at HIGH pressure. Select START/STOP and start cooking. 4. When cooking is complete, let pressure release quickly by turning it into VENT position. Carefully unlock the lid. 5. Serve the dish warm.
Per Serving: Calories 175; Fat 8g; Sodium 326mg; Carbs 5g; Fiber 0.2g; Sugar 0.3g; Protein 1g

Ham Casserole

Prep time: 5 minutes| Cook time: 30 minutes| Serves: 4

6 beaten eggs	¼ cup chives, chopped
½ cup plain Greek yogurt	½ teaspoon black pepper
1 cup cheddar cheese, shredded	1 cup water
1 cup ham, diced	

1. In a medium bowl, whisk together eggs and yogurt until combined. Add the cheese, ham, chives, and pepper. Stir well. 2. Prepare the Ninja Foodi XL Pressure Cooker Steam Fryer with SmartLid by adding the water to the cooking pot and placing the Deluxe Reversible Rack in it. Pour the mixture into the heatproof bowl or cup. Place the bowl on the Deluxe Reversible Rack. 3. Lock lid; move slider towards PRESSURE. Adjust pressure release valve in the SEAL position. Close pressure-release valve. The cooking temperature will default to HIGH, which is accurate. Set the time to 20 minutes. Select START/STOP and start cooking. 4. When cooking is complete, let pressure release quickly by turning it into VENT position. Carefully unlock the lid. 5. Serve the dish warm.
Per Serving: Calories 221; Fat 9.4g; Sodium 321mg; Carbs 8.6g; Fiber 2g; Sugar 1g; Protein 14.2g

Soft Eggs

Prep time: 5 minutes| Cook time: 5 minutes| Serves: 2

4 eggs	Salt and ground black pepper to
1 cup water	taste
2 English muffins, toasted	

1. Prepare the Ninja Foodi XL Pressure Cooker Steam Fryer with SmartLid cooking pot by adding the water to the pot and insert the Cook & Crisp Basket. Put the eggs in the basket. 2. Lock lid; move slider towards STEAMCRISP. Select STEAM & BAKE, set temperature to 400°F/200°C, and set time to 4 minutes. Press START/STOP to begin cooking. 3. When cooking is complete, transfer the eggs to the bowl of cold water. Wait 2 to 3 minutes. Peel the eggs. 4. Serve one egg per half of toasted English muffin. Sprinkle with salt and pepper to taste.
Per Serving: Calories 160; Fat 11.8g; Sodium 255mg; Carbs 9.6g; Fiber 3.9g; Sugar 2g; Protein 7.6g

Garlic Toast

Prep Time: 10 minutes. | Cook Time: 10 minutes. | Serves: 2

1 vegan bread loaf, large	2 tablespoons garlic puree
2 teaspoons chives	2 tablespoons olive oil
2 tablespoons nutritional yeast	Black pepper and salt to taste

1. Place the Cook & Crisp Basket in your Pressure Cooker Steam Fryer. 2. Slice the bread loaf (not all the way through). In a suitable bowl, mix the garlic puree, olive oil, and nutritional yeast. Add this mixture on top of the bread loaf. Sprinkle loaf with chives and season with black pepper and salt. Place loaf inside of the Cook & Crisp Basket. Put on the Smart Lid on top of the Ninja Foodi Steam Fryer. Move the Lid Slider to the "Air Fry/Stovetop". Select the "Air Fry" mode for cooking. Adjust the cooking temperature to 375°F/190°C. Cook for around 10 minutes.
Per serving: Calories: 234; Fat: 12.9g; Sodium: 414mg; Carbs: 11g; Fiber: 5g; Sugar 9g; Protein 11g

Classical Hard-Boiled Eggs

Prep time: 5 minutes| Cook time: 10 minutes| Serves: 4

5-15 eggs	1 cup water

1. Pour the water into the Ninja Foodi XL Pressure Cooker Steam Fryer with SmartLid cooking pot and insert a Cook & Crisp Basket. Put the eggs in the basket. 2. Lock lid; move slider towards PRESSURE. Adjust pressure release valve in the SEAL position. Close pressure-release valve. The cooking temperature will default to HIGH, which is accurate. Set time to 5 minutes. Select START/STOP and start cooking. 3. When cooking is complete, let pressure release naturally for 5 minutes, then quick-release any remaining pressure by turning it into VENT position.
4. Transfer the eggs to the bowl of cold water. Wait 2-3 minutes. If you like, you can peel immediately.
Per Serving: Calories 116; Fat 8.4g; Sodium 542mg; Carbs 0.9g; Fiber 0.2g; Sugar 0.1g; Protein 9.1g

Traditional French Eggs

Prep time: 5 minutes| Cook time: 15 minutes| Serves: 4

½ teaspoon olive oil	Salt to taste
4 eggs	4 tablespoon chives, chopped
4 slices bacon	1 cup water

1. Prepare the ramekins by adding a drop of olive oil in each and rubbing the bottom and sides. Crack an egg in each, add a bacon slice on top, season with salt and top each with chives. 2. Pour the water into the Ninja Foodi XL Pressure Cooker Steam Fryer with SmartLid cooking pot and insert a Cook & Crisp Basket. Place the ramekins in the basket. 3. Lock lid; move slider towards PRESSURE. Adjust pressure release valve in the SEAL position. Close pressure-release valve. The cooking temperature will default to HIGH, which is accurate. Set QUICK RELEASE and time to 8 minutes. Select START/STOP and start cooking. 4. When cooking is complete, let pressure release quickly by turning it into VENT position. 5. Serve immediately.
Per Serving: Calories 200; Fat 5g; Sodium 269mg; Carbs 4g; Fiber 1g; Sugar 1g; Protein 5g

Delightful Eggs

Prep time: 5 minutes| Cook time: 5 minutes| Serves: 4

3 eggs	1 cup water
1 teaspoon salt	6 oz. ham
½ teaspoon ground white pepper	2 tablespoon chives
1 teaspoon paprika	¼ teaspoon ground ginger

1. Beat the eggs into the small ramekins. Season with the salt, pepper, and paprika. Prepare the Ninja Foodi XL Pressure Cooker Steam Fryer with SmartLid cooking pot by adding the water to the pot and placing the Deluxe Reversible Rack on top. Place the ramekins on the Deluxe Reversible Rack. 2. Lock lid; move slider towards STEAMCRISP. Select STEAM & BAKE, set temperature to 350°F/175°C, and set time to 4 minutes. Press START/STOP to begin cooking. Meanwhile, chop the ham and chives and combine the ingredients together. Add ground ginger and stir the mixture. Transfer the mixture to the serving plates. 3. When cooking is complete, carefully unlock the lid. 4. Serve the eggs over the ham mixture.
Per Serving: Calories 221; Fat 14g; Sodium 221mg; Carbs 6g; Fiber 4g; Sugar 1g; Protein 11g

Healthy Egg Muffins

Prep time: 5 minutes| Cook time: 15 minutes| Serves: 2

4 beaten eggs	shredded
4 bacon slices, cooked and	1 green onion, chopped
crumbled	A pinch of salt
4 tablespoons cheddar cheese,	1½ cups water

1. In a medium bowl, whisk together eggs, bacon, cheese, onion and salt until combined. Divide the mixture into muffin cups. 2. Pour the water into the Ninja Foodi XL Pressure Cooker Steam Fryer with SmartLid cooking pot and insert the Cook & Crisp Basket. Place the muffin cups in the basket. 3. Lock lid; move slider towards PRESSURE. Adjust pressure release valve in the SEAL position. Close pressure-release valve. The cooking temperature will default to HIGH, which is accurate. Set the time for 8 minutes at HIGH pressure. Select START/STOP and start cooking. 4. When cooking is complete, let pressure release quickly by turning it into VENT position. Carefully unlock the lid. 5. Remove the Cook & Crisp Basket with muffins from the pot. Serve.
Per Serving: Calories 93; Fat 6.6g; Sodium 277mg; Carbs 1g; Fiber 0.2g; Sugar 0g; Protein 7.7g

Cranberry Nutty Grits

Prep time: 10 minutes| Cook time: 10 minutes| Serves: 5

¾ cup stone-ground grits or polenta
½ cup unsweetened dried cranberries
Pinch kosher salt
1 tablespoon unsalted butter or ghee
1 tablespoon half-and-half
¼ cup sliced almonds, toasted

1.In the Ninja Foodi XL Pressure Cooker Steam Fryer with SmartLid cooking pot, stir together the grits, cranberries, salt, and 3 cups of water. 2. Lock lid; move slider towards PRESSURE. Adjust pressure release valve in the SEAL position. Close pressure-release valve. The cooking temperature will default to HIGH, which is accurate. 3. Set QUICK RELEASE and time to 10 minutes. Select START/STOP and start cooking. 4. When cooking is complete, let pressure release quickly by turning it into VENT position. 5. unlock and remove the lid. 6. Add the butter and half-and-half. Stir until the mixture is creamy, adding more half-and-half if necessary. 7. Spoon into serving bowls and sprinkle with almonds.
Per Serving: Calories 107; Fat 10.9g; Sodium 471mg; Carbs 2.7g; Fiber 1.3g; Sugar 1g; Protein 1.2g

Tasty Tomato Spinach Quiche

Prep time: 5 minutes| Cook time: 40 minutes| Serves: 6

10-12 large eggs, beaten
½ cup milk
½ teaspoon kosher salt
Ground black pepper to taste
2½ cups baby spinach, diced
1 cup tomato, deseeded and
roughly chopped
4 medium green onions, chopped
3 tomato slices
⅓ cup parmesan cheese, shredded
2 cups water

1. In a large bowl, whisk together eggs, milk, salt, and pepper until combined. In a baking dish that can fit into the pot, combine the spinach, tomato and green onions. Add the egg mixture to the baking dish and stir well. Place 3 tomato slices on top and sprinkle with cheese. 2. Prepare the Ninja Foodi XL Pressure Cooker Steam Fryer with SmartLid cooking pot by adding the water to the pot and placing the Deluxe Reversible Rack in it. Put the baking dish on the rack. 3. Lock lid; move slider towards PRESSURE. Adjust pressure release valve in the SEAL position. Close pressure-release valve. The cooking temperature will default to HIGH, which is accurate. Set the time for 20 minutes. Select START/STOP and start cooking. 4. When cooking is complete, let pressure release naturally for 5 minutes, then quick-release any remaining pressure by turning it into VENT position. 5. Uncover the pot. Remove the dish from the pot. If desired, broil in the oven for a few minutes for a browned top. Serve.
Per Serving: Calories 242; Fat 13.1g; Sodium 269mg; Carbs 9.6g; Fiber 2g; Sugar 1g; Protein 14.2g

Mayo Egg Salad

Prep time: 5 minutes| Cook time: 15 minutes| Serves: 2

1½ cups water
6 russet potatoes, peeled and diced
4 large eggs
1 cup mayonnaise
2 tablespoons fresh parsley, chopped
¼ cup onion, chopped
1 tablespoon dill pickle juice
1 tablespoon mustard
Pinch of salt
Pinch of ground black pepper

1. Pour the water into the Ninja Foodi XL Pressure Cooker Steam Fryer with SmartLid cooking pot and insert a Cook & Crisp Basket. Place the potatoes and eggs in the basket. 2. Lock lid; move slider towards PRESSURE. Adjust pressure release valve in the SEAL position. Close pressure-release valve. The cooking temperature will default to HIGH, which is accurate. Set the time for 5 minutes at HIGH pressure. Select START/STOP and start cooking. 3. When cooking is complete, let pressure release quickly by turning it into VENT position. Carefully unlock the lid. 4. Transfer the eggs to the bowl of cold water and cool for 2-3 minutes. In a medium bowl, combine the mayonnaise, parsley, onion, dill pickle juice, and mustard. Mix well. 5. Add salt and pepper. Peel and slice the eggs. Toss the potatoes and eggs in the bowl. Stir and serve.
Per Serving: Calories 271; Fat 14g; Sodium 288mg; Carbs 5g; Fiber 3g; Sugar 5g; Protein 11g

Cheesy Meaty Sausage Frittata

Prep time: 5 minutes| Cook time: 35 minutes| Serves: 2

1½ cups water
1 tablespoon butter
4 beaten eggs
2 tablespoons sour cream
¼ cup cheddar cheese, grated
½ cup cooked ground sausage
Salt and ground black pepper to taste

1. Prepare the Ninja Foodi XL Pressure Cooker Steam Fryer with SmartLid by adding the water to the pot and placing the Deluxe Reversible Rack on top. 2. Grease 6-7-inch soufflé dish with butter. In a bowl, whisk together the eggs and sour cream until combined. 3. Add the cheese, sausage, salt and pepper, stir well. Pour into the dish and wrap tightly with foil all over. 4. Place the dish on the Deluxe Reversible Rack, close and secure the lid. 5. Lock lid; move slider towards PRESSURE. Adjust pressure release valve in the SEAL position. Close pressure-release valve. The cooking temperature will default to HIGH, which is accurate. Set the time for 17 minutes at LOW pressure. Select START/STOP and start cooking. 6. When cooking is complete, let pressure release quickly by turning it into VENT position. 7. Carefully unlock the lid. Serve.
Per Serving: Calories 374; Fat 31.7g; Sodium 287mg; Carbs 7g; Fiber 3g; Sugar 1g; Protein 18.7g

Baked Egg

Prep time: 5 minutes| Cook time: 20 minutes| Serves: 4

1 teaspoon olive oil
6 slices of turkey bacon, cubed
2 cups frozen hash browns
1 cup cheddar cheese, shredded
8 beaten eggs
½ cup half and half or milk
Salt to taste

1. Move the slider towards "AIR FRY/STOVETOP" and set Ninja Foodi XL Pressure Cooker Steam Fryer with SmartLid to SEAR/SAUTÉ mode. Adjust the temperature to "Hi5" by using up arrow. 2. Press START/STOP to begin cooking and heat the oil. Add the slices of turkey bacon. Sauté for about 1-2 minutes until the bacon is browned. Press the START/STOP button to stop the cooking program. Layer the hash brown potatoes over the top of the bacon. 3. Sprinkle one half of the cheddar cheese over the potatoes. In a medium bowl, whisk together the eggs, milk and salt until well combined. Pour the mixture into the Ninja Foodi XL Pressure Cooker Steam Fryer with SmartLid cooking pot and sprinkle with the remaining half of the cheddar cheese. 4. Lock lid; move slider towards PRESSURE. Adjust pressure release valve in the SEAL position. Close pressure-release valve. The cooking temperature will default to HIGH, which is accurate. Set the time for 7 minutes at HIGH pressure. Select START/STOP and start cooking. 5. When cooking is complete, let pressure release quickly by turning it into VENT position. Carefully unlock the lid. 6. Taste and season more if necessary.
Per Serving: Calories 216; Fat 11g; Sodium 230mg; Carbs 5g; Fiber 3g; Sugar 1g; Protein 9g

Baked Cheesy Hash Brown Bake

Prep time: 5 minutes| Cook time: 10 minutes| Serves: 4

6 slices bacon, chopped
2 cups frozen hash browns
8 beaten eggs
1 cup shredded cheddar cheese
¼ cup milk
½ teaspoon salt
½ teaspoon ground black pepper

1. Move the slider towards "AIR FRY/STOVETOP" and set Ninja Foodi XL Pressure Cooker Steam Fryer with SmartLid to SEAR/SAUTÉ mode. Adjust the temperature to "Hi5" by using up arrow. Press START/STOP to begin cooking. Sauté the bacon until lightly crispy. 2. Add hash brown. Cook, stirring occasionally, for 2 minutes or until they start to thaw. Press the START/STOP button to stop the cooking program. In a medium bowl, whisk together the eggs, cheese, milk, salt and pepper. Pour the mixture over the hash browns. 3. Lock lid; move slider towards PRESSURE. Adjust pressure release valve in the SEAL position. Close pressure-release valve. The cooking temperature will default to HIGH, which is accurate. Set the time for 5 minutes at HIGH pressure. Select START/STOP and start cooking. 4. When cooking is complete, let pressure release quickly by turning it into VENT position. 5. Slice and serve.
Per Serving: Calories 230; Fat 15.9g; Sodium 300mg; Carbs 15.9g; Fiber 9.3g; Sugar 3g; Protein 10g

Bacon and Sausage Omelet

Prep time: 5 minutes| Cook time: 55 minutes| Serves: 6

6-12 beaten eggs
½ cup milk
6 sausage links, sliced
1 onion, diced
Garlic powder
Salt and ground black pepper to
Equipment:
1½ quart ceramic baking dish or

taste
Olive oil cooking spray
2 cup water
6 bacon slices, cooked
Dried oregano, optional

Pyrex glass bowl

1. In a medium bowl, whisk together the eggs and milk, until well combined. 2. Add the sausages and onion. Season with garlic powder, salt, and pepper. Stir well. 3. Grease Pyrex glass bowl with cooking spray. 4. Pour the egg mixture into the Pyrex and wrap tightly with foil all over. 5. Prepare the Ninja Foodi XL Pressure Cooker Steam Fryer with SmartLid cooking pot by adding the water to the pot and placing the Deluxe Reversible Rack in it. 6. Place the bowl on the Deluxe Reversible Rack and secure the lid. 7. Lock lid; move slider towards PRESSURE. Adjust pressure release valve in the SEAL position. Close pressure-release valve. The cooking temperature will default to HIGH, which is accurate. Set the time for 25 minutes. Select START/STOP and start cooking. 8. When cooking is complete, let pressure naturally release for 10 minutes by turning it into VENT position. Open the lid. Remove the foil. The egg may pop-out of the bowl; just push it back. 9. Lay the cooked bacon on top and cover with shredded cheese. 10. Lock lid; move slider towards PRESSURE. Adjust pressure release valve in the SEAL position. Set the cooking time for 5 minutes at HIGH pressure. Press START/STOP to begin cooking. 11. When the timer beeps, use a Quick Release by turning it into VENT position. Carefully unlock the lid. 12. Take the dish out from the Ninja Foodi XL Pressure Cooker Steam Fryer with SmartLid. If you like, top with dried oregano and serve.
Per Serving: Calories 270; Fat 15g; Sodium 411mg; Carbs 5g; Fiber 3g; Sugar 2g; Protein 9g

Delicious Mushroom Frittata

Prep time: 5 minutes| Cook time: 15 minutes| Serves: 2

4 beaten eggs
1 cup fresh mushrooms, chopped
¼ cup half-and-half
Salt and freshly ground black

pepper to taste
1 cup sharp cheddar cheese, shredded and divided
1 cup water

1. In a medium bowl, combine the eggs, mushrooms, half-and-half, salt and pepper, and ½ cup cheese. Mix well. Divide mixture into ½-pint wide mouth jars evenly and sprinkle with remaining cheese. 2. Cover the jars with lids loosely. Pour the water into the Ninja Foodi XL Pressure Cooker Steam Fryer with SmartLid cooking pot and insert a Deluxe reversible rack. Place the jars on top of Deluxe reversible rack. 3. Lock lid; move slider towards PRESSURE. Adjust pressure release valve in the SEAL position. Close pressure-release valve. The cooking temperature will default to HIGH, which is accurate. Set the time for 3 minutes at HIGH pressure. Select START/STOP and start cooking. 4. When cooking is complete, let pressure release quickly by turning it into VENT position. Carefully unlock the lid. 5. Serve.
Per Serving: Calories 222; Fat 11g; Sodium 314mg; Carbs 6g; Fiber 4g; Sugar 1g; Protein 12g

Chapter 2 Vegetable and Sides Recipes

32 Delicious Sweet Potatoes
32 Refreshing Quinoa and Pomegranate Salad
32 Colorful Steamed Vegetables
32 Refresh Steamed Broccoli
32 Pomegranate Brussels Sprouts
32 Colorful Vegetable Buddha Bowl
32 Jacket Potatoes
33 Spanish Paella
33 Sweet Potatoes with nuts
33 Creamy Mashed Sweet Potatoes
33 Spicy Potato Wedges
33 Air Fried Olives
33 Oregano Cauliflower Florets
34 Potatoes and Brussels Sprouts
34 Refreshing Vegetable Dish
34 Broccoli with Mushrooms
34 Traditional Ratatouille
34 Traditional Broccoli Salad
34 Crispy Brussels Sprouts
35 Cauliflower Mash
35 Creamy Garlicky Artichoke, Zucchini
35 Delicious Pumpkin Stew
35 Crunchy Kale
35 Coconut Cauliflower Curry
35 Easy Cauliflower Patties
35 Roasted Mushroom
36 Lemony Steamed Artichokes
36 Cheesy Asparagus
36 Delicious Prosciutto Wrapped Asparagus
36 Tasty Steamed Asparagus
36 Corn Cob
36 Orange Pumpkin Puree
36 Broccoli Feta Balls
37 Bacon Brussels Sprouts
37 Taco Broccoli
37 Bacon Brussels Sprouts with Orange Zest
37 Cinnamon Garlic
37 Fried Celery
37 Buffalo Cauliflower Florets
37 Bacon with Brussels Sprouts
37 crusted Okra
38 Herbed Olives
38 Cauliflower Coconut Balls
38 Cajun Spiced Okra
38 Roasted Artichoke
38 Cajusn Eggplants
38 Creamy Macadamia Spinach
38 Egg with Green Beans
38 Seasoned Artichoke

38 Air Fried Bell Peppers
39 Avocado Wedges
39 Pita Chips
39 Cheesy Parsley Zucchini
39 Cheese Zucchini Skewers
39 Greek Olives
39 Crispy Zucchini Patties
39 Brussel Sprouts With Feta
39 Cabbage Egg Fritters
40 Broccoli Cheese Gnocchi
40 Lemony Peppers
40 Air-Fried Portobello Steak
40 Bacon-Wrapped Onion
40 Smoked BBQ Sausages
40 Fat Air Fried Eggplant
40 Cheese Flatbread
40 Buffalo Ranch Cauliflower
41 Pizza Crust
41 Crisp Brussels Sprout Chips
41 Parmesan Zucchini Bites
41 Cauliflower Cheese Tots
41 Mushroom Puff Pastry
41 Herbed Radishes
41 Spicy Jicama Fries
42 Salmon Jerky
42 Carrot Leek Croquettes
42 Air-Fried Green Beans
42 Crumbed Wax Beans
42 Potato Patties
42 Herbed Green Beans
42 Corn Broccoli
43 Corn Fritters
43 Turkey Potatoes
43 Cheese Potato Gratin
43 Ricotta Cheese Potatoes
43 Air-Fried Brown Mushrooms
43 Roasted Country-Style Vegetables
43 Stuffed Mushrooms
44 Air-Fried Cheese Lings
44 FatPotato Bites
44 Potatoes & Cheese
44 Vegetable Cheese Omelet
44 Scrambled Spinach Eggs
44 Zucchini with Sweet Potatoes
44 Cornbread
45 Curried Sweet Potato Fries
45 Roasted Bell Peppers
45 Parmesan Cauliflower
45 Szechuan Beans
45 Grilled Cheese
45 Spicy Potatoes
45 Air-Fried Vegetables

45 Roasted Broccoli
46 Crispy Sweet Potatoes
46 Green Beans Salad
46 Corn on The Cob
46 Air-Fried Brussels Sprouts
46 Crusted Eggplant
46 Cayenne Parsnip Burgers
46 Parsnips Meal
46 Crusted Portobello Mushrooms
47 Cheese Stuffed Peppers
47 Garlicky Roasted Cauliflower
47 Cheese Broccoli Pizza
47 Artichoke Stuffed Eggplant
47 Broccoli Cranberry Salad
47 Horseradish Gorgonzola Mushrooms
47 Sesame Carrots
48 Crispy Parmesan Artichokes
48 Parmesan Green Bean Casserole
48 Paprika Cabbage Steaks
48 Broccoli with Parmesan
48 Roasted Corn
48 Parmesan Zucchini Gratin
48 Parmesan Kale
48 Lemony Broccoli Salad
49 Creamy Spaghetti Squash
49 Roasted Garlic Asparagus
49 Parmesan Potatoes
49 Lemony Brussels Sprout Salad
49 Honey Carrots
49 Fried Cabbage
49 Buffalo Cauliflower
50 Sweet Potato Fries
50 Feta Stuffed Portobellos
50 Potatoes Fries
50 Hasselback Potatoes
50 Rosemary Potatoes
50 Mexican Corn
51 Bacon-Wrapped Asparagus
51 Sesame Green Beans
51 Baked Potatoes with Yogurt
51 Mushroom Cheese Loaf
51 Roasted Sweet Potatoes
51 Honey Cornbread
51 Spicy Acorn Squash
52 Tostones With Green Sauce
52 Broccoli Gratin
52 Bread-crumbed Onion Rings
52 Fried Eggplant
52 Bacon Brussels Sprouts
52 Cauliflower Nuggets

Delicious Sweet Potatoes

Prep time: 5 minutes| Cook time: 40 minutes| Serves: 6

4 sweet potatoes, cut in half	Cinnamon, for garnish
2 cups water	Sea salt, for garnish
Butter, for garnish	Black pepper, for garnish

1. Add 2 cups of water to the Ninja Foodi XL Pressure Cooker Steam Fryer with SmartLid cooking pot. 2. Add sweet potatoes to the Deluxe Reversible Rack, and place inside the pot. 3. Lock lid; move slider to AIR FRY/STOVETOP. Select STEAM. Set time to 30 minutes. Press START/STOP to begin cooking. Cook 5 minutes more. Garnish with butter, cinnamon, sea salt and black pepper.
Per Serving: Calories 280; Fat 13g; Sodium 3mg; Carbs 6g; Fiber 3g; Sugar 6g; Protein 14g

Refreshing Quinoa and Pomegranate Salad

Prep time: 10 minutes| Cook time: 45 minutes| Serves: 8

2 cups quinoa, rinsed	1 teaspoon honey
4 cups water	1 teaspoon balsamic vinegar
Pinch of sea salt	1 cup pomegranate seeds
½ lemon, juiced	½ cup chopped fresh mint
2 teaspoons olive oil	Manchego cheese, chopped,
⅛ teaspoon coarse ground black pepper	optional garnish

1. Add quinoa, water, and a pinch of salt to the Ninja Foodi XL Pressure Cooker Steam Fryer with SmartLid cooking pot. 2. Lock lid; move slider to AIR FRY/STOVETOP. Select STEAM, set time to 20 minutes. Press START/STOP to begin cooking. 3. Open the lid and transfer quinoa to a large mixing bowl. Add everything except mint and cheese; stir well to combine. 4. Gently fold in mint and cheese and enjoy!
Per Serving: Calories 214; Fat 9g; Sodium 123mg; Carbs 0.6g; Fiber 0.2g; Sugar 0g; Protein 30.9g

Colorful Steamed Vegetables

Prep time: 5 minutes| Cook time: 10 minutes| Serves: 4

1 cup water	½ cup garlic, peeled and minced
3 small zucchinis, sliced (1 inch thick)	1 tablespoon Italian herb mix
	Salt to taste
2 bell peppers, sliced (1 inch thick)	2 tablespoons olive oil

1. Prepare the Ninja Foodi XL Pressure Cooker Steam Fryer with SmartLid cooking pot by adding the water to the pot and placing the Deluxe Reversible Rack in it. 2. In a large bowl, combine the zucchinis, peppers, and garlic. Season the veggies with Italian herb mix, salt and oil. Stir well. Place the vegetables on the rack. 3. Lock lid; move slider to AIR FRY/STOVETOP. Select STEAM. Press START/STOP to begin cooking. Set time to 7 minutes. 4. Carefully unlock the lid. Serve.
Per Serving: Calories 230; Fat 13g; Sodium 456mg; Carbs 6g; Fiber 4g; Sugar 2g; Protein 16g

Refresh Steamed Broccoli

Prep time: 10 minutes| Cook time: 0 minutes| Serves: 2

¼ cup water	Salt and ground black pepper to
3 cups broccoli florets	taste
Bowl with iced water	

1. Prepare the Ninja Foodi XL Pressure Cooker Steam Fryer with SmartLid cooking pot by adding the water to the pot and placing the Cook & Crisp Basket in it. 2. Put the broccoli in the basket. 3. Lock lid; move slider towards PRESSURE. Adjust pressure release valve in the SEAL position. Close pressure-release valve. The cooking temperature will default to HIGH, which is accurate. Cook at HIGH pressure for 0 minutes. Press START/STOP to begin cooking. 4. Prepare the bowl with very cold water. When cooking is complete, let pressure release quickly by turning it into VENT position. 5. Carefully open the lid. Immediately transfer the broccoli to the bowl with cold water to keep bright green color. 6. Season the chilled broccoli with salt and pepper and serve.
Per Serving: Calories 105; Fat 6.9g; Sodium 147mg; Carbs 0.8g; Fiber 0.2g; Sugar 0.1g; Protein 9.2g

Pomegranate Brussels Sprouts

Prep time: 5 minutes| Cook time: 15 minutes| Serves: 2

1 cup water	taste
1 lb. Brussels sprouts, trimmed and cut into half	¼ cup pine nuts, toasted
	1 pomegranate, seeds separated
Salt and ground black pepper to	1 teaspoon olive oil

1. Pour the water into the Ninja Foodi XL Pressure Cooker Steam Fryer with SmartLid cooking pot and insert a Cook & Crisp Basket. 2. Place the Brussels sprouts in the basket. 3. Lock lid; move slider towards PRESSURE. Adjust pressure release valve in the SEAL position. Close pressure-release valve. The cooking temperature will default to HIGH, which is accurate. Set time to 4 minutes. Select START/STOP and start cooking. 4. When cooking is complete, let pressure release quickly by turning it into VENT position. Carefully unlock the lid. 5. Transfer the sprouts to a serving plate. 6. Season with salt, pepper and pine nuts. Add the pomegranate seeds and stir. 7. Drizzle with oil and stir well. Serve.
Per Serving: Calories 189; Fat 8g; Sodium 489mg; Carbs 1.1g; Fiber 0.6g; Sugar 0g; Protein 26.7g

Colorful Vegetable Buddha Bowl

Prep time: 8 minutes| Cook time: 40 minutes| Serves: 4

4 tablespoons extra-virgin olive oil, divided	1 stalk Chinese broccoli
	4 cups chopped kale
1 large sweet potato, peeled and cut into 1-inch pieces	2 cups water
	1 tablespoon lime juice
1 cup quinoa, rinsed and drained	1 (15 oz.) can chickpeas, drained and rinsed for garnish
1 large clove garlic, minced	
½ teaspoon sea salt	Unsalted pistachios, for garnish
2 small carrots, peeled and cut in half	1 whole avocado, sliced for garnish

1. Heat 2 tablespoons of olive oil over medium heat in a large frying pan. Add sweet potato, broccoli, carrots, quinoa, garlic and sea salt. Cook, while stirring, until the garlic is fragrant; about 3 minutes. 2. Add the quinoa mixture to the Ninja Foodi XL Pressure Cooker Steam Fryer with SmartLid cooking pot. Stir in kale and water. 3. Lock lid; move slider to AIR FRY/STOVETOP. Select STEAM. Press START/STOP to begin cooking. 4. Remove the lid and let stand for 5 minutes. Combine the remaining 2 tablespoons of olive oil, and lime juice in a small mixing bowl. 5. Divide the quinoa mixture among 2 to 4 bowls. 6. Top each portion with vegetables, chickpeas, pistachios and sliced avocado. Drizzle with the lime dressing and serve!
Per Serving: Calories 254; Fat 14g; Sodium 129mg; Carbs 6g; Fiber 4g; Sugar 1g; Protein 15g

Jacket Potatoes

Prep time: 5 minutes| Cook time: 21 minutes| Serves: 4

4 medium baking potatoes	Sour cream, for serving
1 cup of water	Additional toppings as desired:
Butter, for serving	Crumbled bacon, black beans,
Sea salt, for serving	tuna, baby spinach
Black pepper, for serving	

1. Fill the Ninja Foodi XL Pressure Cooker Steam Fryer with SmartLid cooking pot, add 1 cup of water. 2. Prick the potatoes, all over, with a fork. Place them in the Cook & Crisp Basket. 3. Lock lid; move slider to AIR FRY/STOVETOP. Select STEAM, and set time to 20 minutes. Press START/STOP to begin cooking. 4. Serve with sea salt, black pepper, butter and sour cream. Add any additional toppings to create a fancier
Per Serving: Calories 265; Fat 23.9g; Sodium 189mg; Carbs 0.1g; Fiber 0.1g; Sugar 0g; Protein 11.6g

Spanish Paella

Prep time: 15 minutes| Cook time: 40 minutes| Serves: 6

2 tablespoons olive oil, divided
1 yellow onion, diced
1 red bell pepper, diced
1 green bell pepper, diced
2 cloves garlic, minced
2 teaspoons smoked paprika
2 teaspoons dried oregano
1 pinch saffron
¾ teaspoon sea salt
½ teaspoon crushed red pepper flakes
Coarse ground black pepper
1 bay leaf
1 (15 oz.) can diced tomatoes
3 cups low-sodium vegetable or chicken broth
1-½ cups brown rice
3 boneless skinless chicken thighs, cut into 1-inch pieces
12 large shrimp or tiger prawns, deveined and peeled
¼ cup chorizo
½ cup frozen peas, defrosted
¼ cup sliced black olives
Hot sauce, for garnish
Freshly chopped parsley, for garnish

1. Move the slider towards "AIR FRY/STOVETOP" and set Ninja Foodi XL Pressure Cooker Steam Fryer with SmartLid to SEAR/SAUTÉ mode. Adjust the temperature to "Hi5" by using up arrow. Press START/STOP to begin cooking. 2. Heat 1 tablespoon olive oil in the cooking pot for 3 minutes. Add onion and bell peppers. Cook until soft, about 7 minutes. Add garlic to cooker and sauté for 1 minute or until fragrant. 3. Add the broth, then fold in smoked paprika, oregano, sea salt, crushed red pepper, black pepper, bay leaf, diced tomatoes, and rice. 4. Lock lid; move slider to AIR FRY/STOVETOP. Select STEAM, set time to 10 minutes. Press START/STOP to begin cooking. 5. Heat remaining olive oil in a frying pan over medium-high heat. Add chicken thighs and chorizo. 6. Cook until browned and no pink shows in the chicken; about 10 to 12 minutes. 7. Fold cooked chicken and sausage into the rice. Add saffron, peas, and black olives to the pot. Steam for 5 minutes to combine flavors. 8. Serve garnished with hot sauce and chopped parsley.
Per Serving: Calories 250; Fat 12g; Sodium 178mg; Carbs 6g; Fiber 4g; Sugar 1g; Protein 14g

Sweet Potatoes with nuts

Prep time: 5 minutes| Cook time: 25 minutes| Serves: 6

½ cup brown sugar
1 tablespoon lemon zest
½ teaspoon sea salt
1¼ cup water
4 large sweet potatoes, peeled and sliced
¼ cup butter
¼ cup maple syrup
1 tablespoon cornstarch
1 cup pecans, chopped

1. In the Ninja Foodi XL Pressure Cooker Steam Fryer with SmartLid cooking pot, combine the sugar, lemon zest, salt and water. Stir well. 2. Add the potatoes to the pot. Close and lock the lid. 3. Lock lid; move slider towards PRESSURE. Adjust pressure release valve in the SEAL position. Close pressure-release valve. The cooking temperature will default to HIGH, which is accurate. Set time to 15 minutes. Select START/STOP and start cooking. 4. When cooking is complete, let pressure release quickly by turning it into VENT position. 5. Carefully unlock the lid. Transfer the potatoes to a serving bowl. 6. Move the slider towards "AIR FRY/STOVETOP" and set Ninja Foodi XL Pressure Cooker Steam Fryer with SmartLid to SEAR/SAUTÉ mode. Adjust the temperature to "Hi5" by using up arrow. Press START/STOP to begin cooking, add the butter and melt it. Add the maple syrup, cornstarch, and chopped pecans. Stir to combine and sauté the sauce for 2 minutes. 7. Serve the potatoes with sauce and whole pecans.
Per Serving: Calories 247; Fat 11.9g; Sodium 112mg; Carbs 0g; Fiber 0g; Sugar 0g; Protein 32.8g

Creamy Mashed Sweet Potatoes

Prep time: 5 minutes| Cook time: 25 minutes| Serves: 6

1 cup water
1 lb. sweet potatoes, peeled and cubed
2 cloves garlic
¼ teaspoon dried thyme
¼ teaspoon dried sage
¼ teaspoon dried rosemary
½ teaspoon dried parsley
¼ cup milk
2 tablespoon butter
½ cup parmesan cheese, grated
Salt and ground black pepper to taste

1. Pour the water into the Ninja Foodi XL Pressure Cooker Steam Fryer with SmartLid cooking pot and insert a Cook & Crisp Basket. 2. Put the sweet potatoes and garlic in the basket. 3. Lock lid; move slider towards PRESSURE. Adjust pressure release valve in the SEAL position. Close pressure-release valve. The cooking temperature will default to HIGH, which is accurate. Set time to 15 minutes. Select START/STOP and start cooking. 4. When cooking is complete, let pressure release quickly by turning it into VENT position. Carefully unlock the lid. Transfer the potatoes to a serving bowl. 5. Add the thyme, sage, rosemary, and parsley. Stir well. 6. Using a potato masher or electric beater, slowly blend milk and butter into potatoes until smooth and creamy. 7. Add cheese and season with salt and pepper, stir well. Serve.
Per Serving: Calories 271; Fat 12g; Sodium 510mg; Carbs 6g; Fiber 4g; Sugar g; Protein 13g

Spicy Potato Wedges

Prep time: 5 minutes| Cook time: 20 minutes| Serves: 4

3 large sweet potatoes, peeled
1 cup water
2 tablespoon vegetable oil
½ teaspoon kosher salt
1 teaspoon paprika
1 tablespoon dry mango powder

1. Cut the potatoes into medium-sized wedges. Prepare the Ninja Foodi XL Pressure Cooker Steam Fryer with SmartLid cooking by adding the water to the pot and placing the Deluxe Reversible Rack in it. 2. Place the sweet potatoes on the rack. 3. Lock lid; move slider towards PRESSURE. Adjust pressure release valve in the SEAL position. Close pressure-release valve. The cooking temperature will default to HIGH, which is accurate. Set time to 15 minutes. Select START/STOP and start cooking. When cooking is complete, let pressure release quickly by turning it into VENT position. 4. Carefully unlock the lid. Drain the liquid from the pot and remove the rack as well. Add the potatoes to cooking pot. 5. Move the slider towards "AIR FRY/STOVETOP" and set Ninja Foodi XL Pressure Cooker Steam Fryer with SmartLid to SEAR/SAUTÉ mode. Adjust the temperature to "Hi5" by using up arrow. Press START/STOP to begin cooking. 6. Add and heat the oil. Add the cooked sweet potatoes and sauté the wedges for 3-5 minutes, until they turn brown. 7. Season with salt, paprika, and mango powder. Stir well. Serve.
Per Serving: Calories 200; Fat 9.7g; Sodium 321mg; Carbs 0.5g; Fiber 0.3g; Sugar 0.2g; Protein 26.4g

Air Fried Olives

Prep Time: 5 minutes. | Cook Time: 2 minutes. | Serves: 4

8 ounce olives, pitted
1 teaspoon olive oil

1. Place the Cook & Crisp Basket in your Ninja Foodi Pressure Cooker Steam Fryer. 2. Sprinkle olives with olive oil and put in your Ninja Foodi Pressure Cooker Steam Fryer. 3. Put on the Smart Lid on top of the Ninja Foodi Steam Fryer. 4. Move the Lid Slider to the "Air Fry/Stovetop". 5. Cook on "Air Fry" Mode for about 2 minutes per side at 400°F/200°C. 6. Serve.
Per Serving: Calories 157; Fat 10.1 g; Sodium 423 mg; Carbs 1.6g; Fiber 0.5g; Sugar 0.4g; Protein 14.9g

Oregano Cauliflower Florets

Prep Time: 10 minutes. | Cook Time: 25 minutes. | Serves: 4

16-ounce cauliflower head
1 tablespoon dried oregano
1 tablespoon coconut oil, melted
3 eggs, beaten
3 tablespoons coconut flour

1. Place the Cook & Crisp Basket in your Ninja Foodi Pressure Cooker Steam Fryer. 2. Rub the cauliflower head with dried oregano, coconut oil, and coconut flour. 3. Then sprinkle it with eggs and put in your Ninja Foodi Pressure Cooker Steam Fryer. 4. Put on the Smart Lid on top of the Ninja Foodi Steam Fryer. 5. Move the Lid Slider to the "Air Fry/Stovetop". 6. Cook the cauliflower head at 365°F/185°C on "Air Fry" Mode for about 25 minutes.
Per Serving: Calories 273; Fat 24 g; Sodium 1181 mg; Carbs 12.8g; Fiber 1g; Sugar 1.4g; Protein 20g

Potatoes and Brussels Sprouts

Prep time: 5 minutes| Cook time: 15 minutes| Serves: 4

1½ lbs. Brussels sprouts
1 cup new potatoes cut into 1 inch cubes
½ cup chicken stock
Salt and ground black pepper to taste
1½ tablespoon butter
1½ tablespoon bread crumbs

1. Wash the Brussels sprouts and remove the outer leaves, then cut into halves. 2. In the Ninja Foodi XL Pressure Cooker Steam Fryer with SmartLid cooking pot, combine the potatoes, sprouts, stock, salt and pepper. 3. Lock lid; move slider towards PRESSURE. Adjust pressure release valve in the SEAL position. Close pressure-release valve. The cooking temperature will default to HIGH, which is accurate. Set time to 5 minutes. Select START/STOP and start cooking. 4. When cooking is complete, let pressure release quickly by turning it into VENT position. Carefully open the lid. 5. Move the slider towards "AIR FRY/STOVETOP" and set Ninja Foodi XL Pressure Cooker Steam Fryer with SmartLid to SEAR/SAUTÉ mode. Adjust the temperature to "Hi5" by using up arrow. Press START/STOP to begin cooking, add the butter and bread crumbs to the pot. 6. Mix well and serve.
Per Serving: Calories 236; Fat 12g; Sodium 321mg; Carbs 6g; Fiber 4g; Sugar 2g; Protein 15g

Refreshing Vegetable Dish

Prep time: 5 minutes| Cook time: 20 minutes| Serves: 4

1 tablespoon extra-virgin olive oil
1 red onion, sliced
2 red bell peppers, sliced thinly
2 green bell pepper, sliced thinly
1 yellow bell peppers, sliced thinly
2 tomatoes, chopped
Salt and ground black pepper to taste
2 cloves garlic, chopped
1 bunch parsley, finely chopped

1. Move the slider towards "AIR FRY/STOVETOP" and set Ninja Foodi XL Pressure Cooker Steam Fryer with SmartLid to SEAR/SAUTÉ mode. Adjust the temperature to "Hi5" by using up arrow. Press START/STOP to begin cooking and heat the oil. 2. Add the onion and sauté for 3 minutes. 3. Add the bell peppers, stir and sauté for another 5 minutes. 4. Add the tomatoes and sprinkle with salt and pepper. Mix well. Close and lock the lid. Press the STOP button to reset the cooking program. 5. Lock lid; move slider towards PRESSURE. Adjust pressure release valve in the SEAL position. Close pressure-release valve. The cooking temperature will default to HIGH, which is accurate. Set time to 6 minutes. Select START/STOP and start cooking. 6. When cooking is complete, let pressure release quickly by turning it into VENT position. 7. Carefully unlock the lid. Transfer the veggies to a serving bowl and add the garlic and parsley. Stir well. Serve.
Per Serving: Calories 437; Fat 30.8g; Sodium 698mg; Carbs 1.2g; Fiber 0.1g; Sugar 0g; Protein 36.5g

Broccoli with Mushrooms

Prep time: 5 minutes| Cook time: 15 minutes| Serves: 2

2 tablespoon coconut oil
1 cup mushrooms, sliced
1 tablespoon soy sauce
2 cups broccoli florets
1 cup vegetable broth

1. Move the slider towards "AIR FRY/STOVETOP" and set Ninja Foodi XL Pressure Cooker Steam Fryer with SmartLid to SEAR/SAUTÉ mode. Adjust the temperature to "Hi5" by using up arrow. Press START/STOP to begin cooking. 2. Once hot, add the coconut oil to the pot. Add the mushrooms and sauté for 5 minutes. 3. Add the soy sauce and broccoli and cook for another 1 minute. 4. Pour in the broth and stir. Press the START/STOP button to reset the cooking program. 5. Lock lid; move slider towards PRESSURE. Adjust pressure release valve in the SEAL position. Close pressure-release valve. The cooking temperature will default to HIGH, which is accurate. Set time to 2 minutes. Select START/STOP and start cooking. 6. When cooking is complete, let pressure release quickly by turning it into VENT position. 7. Carefully unlock the lid. Let it cool a few minutes before serving.
Per Serving: Calories 89; Fat 3.6g; Sodium 411mg; Carbs 0.7g; Fiber 0.1g; Sugar 0.1g; Protein 12.8g

Traditional Ratatouille

Prep time: 15 minutes| Cook time: 15 minutes| Serves: 6

1 tablespoon olive oil
1 medium onion, sliced
2 cloves garlic, chopped
2 small eggplants, peeled and sliced thin
4 small zucchinis, sliced thin
1 jar (12 oz.) roasted red bell peppers, drained and sliced
1 can (28 oz.) tomatoes, chopped
½ cup water
1 teaspoon kosher salt

1. Move the slider towards "AIR FRY/STOVETOP" and set Ninja Foodi XL Pressure Cooker Steam Fryer with SmartLid to SEAR/SAUTÉ mode. Adjust the temperature to "Hi5" by using up arrow. Press START/STOP to begin cooking and heat the oil. 2. Add the onion, garlic, eggplant, zucchini, and bell peppers. Sauté for 3-4 minutes until softened. 3. Add the tomatoes and water and sprinkle with salt, stir well. Press the START/STOP button to stop the SAUTE function. 4. Lock lid; move slider towards PRESSURE. Adjust pressure release valve in the SEAL position. Close pressure-release valve. The cooking temperature will default to HIGH, which is accurate. Set time to 4 minutes. Select START/STOP and start cooking. 5. When cooking is complete, let pressure release quickly by turning it into VENT position. 6. Carefully unlock the lid. Serve warm or chilled.
Per Serving: Calories 284; Fat 14g; Sodium 477mg; Carbs 6g; Fiber 2g; Sugar 2g; Protein 20g

Traditional Broccoli Salad

Prep time: 5 minutes| Cook time: 20 minutes| Serves: 2

½ cup chicken stock
1 lb. broccoli florets
1 onion, sliced
1 tablespoon lemon juice
1 teaspoon oregano
1 teaspoon garlic powder
3 tablespoon raisins
2 tablespoon walnuts, crushed
1 teaspoon olive oil
1 tablespoon kosher salt
Bowl with iced water

1. Pour the stock into the Ninja Foodi XL Pressure Cooker Steam Fryer with SmartLid cooking pot and insert a Cook & Crisp Basket. 2. Put the broccoli in the basket. 3. Lock lid; move slider towards PRESSURE. Adjust pressure release valve in the SEAL position. Close pressure-release valve. The cooking temperature will default to HIGH, which is accurate. Cook at HIGH pressure for 0 minutes. Select START/STOP and start cooking. 4. When cooking is complete, let pressure release quickly by turning it into VENT position. 5. Carefully unlock the lid. Immediately transfer the broccoli to the bowl with cold water to keep bright green color. 6. Transfer the chilled broccoli to a serving bowl. 7. Add the onion, raisins, crushed walnuts and season with lemon juice, oregano, garlic powder, salt and oil. Gently stir to combine. 8. Serve.
Per Serving: Calories 250; Fat 12g; Sodium 663mg; Carbs 6g; Fiber 4g; Sugar 1g; Protein 15g

Crispy Brussels Sprouts

Prep time: 5 minutes| Cook time: 5 minutes| Serves: 2

1 lb. Brussels sprouts
1 cup water
Salt and ground black pepper to
taste
1 teaspoon extra virgin olive oil
¼ cup pine nuts

1. Wash the Brussels sprouts and remove the outer leaves, then cut into halves. 2. Prepare the Ninja Foodi XL Pressure Cooker Steam Fryer with SmartLid cooking pot by adding the water to the pot and placing the Cook & Crisp Basket in it. 3. Place the Brussels sprouts in the basket. 4. Lock lid; move slider towards PRESSURE. Adjust pressure release valve in the SEAL position. Close pressure-release valve. The cooking temperature will default to HIGH, which is accurate. Set time to 4 minutes. Select START/STOP and start cooking. 5. When cooking is complete, let pressure release quickly by turning it into VENT position. Carefully unlock the lid. 6. Transfer the Brussels sprouts to a serving bowl. 7. Season with salt, pepper and drizzle with oil. Top with the pine nuts and serve.
Per Serving: Calories 219; Fat 8.5g; Sodium 548mg; Carbs 0.7g; Fiber 0.2g; Sugar 0g; Protein 32.9g

Cauliflower Mash

Prep time: 5 minutes| Cook time: 15 minutes| Serves: 4

1½ cups water
1 cauliflower, florets separated
Salt and ground black pepper to taste

1 tablespoon butter
½ teaspoon turmeric
2 chives, finely chopped

1. Prepare the Ninja Foodi XL Pressure Cooker Steam Fryer with SmartLid cooking pot by adding the water to the pot and placing the Cook & Crisp Basket in it. 2. Put the cauliflower in the basket. 3. Lock lid; move slider towards PRESSURE. Adjust pressure release valve in the SEAL position. Close pressure-release valve. The cooking temperature will default to HIGH, which is accurate. Set time to 6 minutes. Select START/STOP and start cooking. 4. When cooking is complete, let pressure release naturally for 5 minutes by turning it into VENT position, then quick-release any remaining pressure. Uncover the pot. 5. Using a potato masher or fork, mash the cauliflower. 6. Season with salt and pepper. Add in the butter and turmeric and mix well. 7. Top with chopped chives and serve.
Per Serving: Calories 240; Fat 12g; Sodium 268mg; Carbs 6g; Fiber 4g; Sugar 2g; Protein 15g

Creamy Garlicky Artichoke, Zucchini

Prep time: 5 minutes| Cook time: 20 minutes| Serves: 8

2 tablespoons olive oil
8 cloves garlic, minced
2 medium zucchinis, sliced thin
1 large artichoke hearts, cleaned and sliced

½ cup whipping cream
½ cup vegetable broth
Salt and ground black pepper to taste

1. Move the slider towards "AIR FRY/STOVETOP" and set Ninja Foodi XL Pressure Cooker Steam Fryer with SmartLid to SEAR/SAUTÉ mode. Adjust the temperature to "Hi5" by using up arrow. Press START/STOP to begin cooking and heat the oil. 2. Add the garlic and sauté for 2 minutes, until fragrant. 3. Add the zucchinis, artichoke hearts, broth, and cream. Season with salt and pepper. Stir well. Close and lock the lid. 4. Press the START/STOP button to stop the SAUTE function. 5. Lock lid; move slider towards PRESSURE. Adjust pressure release valve in the SEAL position. Close pressure-release valve. The cooking temperature will default to HIGH, which is accurate. Set time to 10 minutes. Select START/STOP and start cooking. 6. When cooking is complete, let pressure release quickly by turning it into VENT position. 7. Carefully unlock the lid. Serve.
Per Serving: Calories 95; Fat 4.4g; Sodium 430mg; Carbs 0.3g; Fiber 0.2g; Sugar 0g; Protein 12.7g

Delicious Pumpkin Stew

Prep time: 5 minutes| Cook time: 20 minutes| Serves: 4

3 cups pumpkin, peeled and cubed (1 inch thick)
1 large can diced tomatoes
5 cups vegetable stock

3 cups mixed greens
Salt and ground black pepper to taste

1. Combine all of the ingredients in the Ninja Foodi XL Pressure Cooker Steam Fryer with SmartLid cooking pot and stir to mix. 2. Lock lid; move slider towards PRESSURE. Adjust pressure release valve in the SEAL position. Close pressure-release valve. The cooking temperature will default to HIGH, which is accurate. Set time to 10 minutes. Select START/STOP and start cooking. 3. When cooking is complete, let pressure release quickly by turning it into VENT position. 4. Carefully unlock the lid. Taste for seasoning and add more salt if needed. Serve.
Per Serving: Calories 267; Fat 13g; Sodium 520mg; Carbs 6g; Fiber 4g; Sugar 2g; Protein 16g

Crunchy Kale

Prep Time: 10 minutes. | Cook Time: 12 minutes. | Serves: 6

1 egg, beaten
1 teaspoon nutritional yeast

1 teaspoon sesame oil
3 cups kale leaves, chopped

1. Place the Cook & Crisp Basket in your Ninja Foodi Pressure Cooker Steam Fryer. 2. Sprinkle the kale leaves with sesame oil, nutritional yeast, and egg. 3. Carefully shake the leaves and put in your Ninja Foodi Pressure Cooker Steam Fryer. 4. Put on the Smart Lid on top of the Ninja Foodi Steam Fryer. 5. Move the Lid Slider to the "Air Fry/Stovetop". 6. Cook on "Air Fry" Mode at 400°F/200°C for about 12 minutes. Shake the leaves every 2 minutes to avoid burning.
Per Serving: Calories 379; Fat 20.9 g; Sodium 1598 mg; Carbs 10g; Fiber 2.2g; Sugar 2.1g; Protein 37g

Coconut Cauliflower Curry

Prep time: 5 minutes| Cook time: 5 minutes| Serves: 4

16 oz. cauliflower florets
1 can full-fat coconut milk
6 teaspoon garam masala

2 cups water
Salt and ground black pepper to taste

1. In the Ninja Foodi XL Pressure Cooker Steam Fryer with SmartLid cooking pot, combine the cauliflower, coconut milk, garam masala, and water. 2. Season with salt and pepper, stir well. 3. Lock lid; move slider towards PRESSURE. Adjust pressure release valve in the SEAL position. Close pressure-release valve. The cooking temperature will default to HIGH, which is accurate. Set time to 4 minutes. Select START/STOP and start cooking. 4. When cooking is complete, let pressure release quickly by turning it into VENT position. Carefully open the lid. 5. Serve.
Per Serving: Calories 227; Fat 20.4g; Sodium 365mg; Carbs 1.8g; Fiber 0.5g; Sugar 0g; Protein 9.9g

Easy Cauliflower Patties

Prep time: 15 minutes| Cook time: 15 minutes| Serves: 4

1½ cups water
1 cauliflower head, chopped
1 cup ground almonds
1 cup vegan cheese, shredded

Salt and ground black pepper to taste
2 tablespoons olive oil

1. Pour the water into the Ninja Foodi XL Pressure Cooker Steam Fryer with SmartLid cooking pot and insert a Cook & Crisp Basket. 2. Put the cauliflower in to the basket. 3. Lock lid; move slider towards PRESSURE. Adjust pressure release valve in the SEAL position. Close pressure-release valve. The cooking temperature will default to HIGH, which is accurate. Set time to 5 minutes. Select START/STOP and start cooking. 4. When cooking is complete, let pressure release quickly by turning it into VENT position. Carefully unlock the lid. 5. Place the cauliflower in a food processor and ground it. 6. Add the almonds and cheese. Season with salt and pepper. Mix well. 7. Shape the mixture into oval patties each ½ inch thick. 8. Carefully pour the water out of the pot and completely dry the pot before replacing it. 9. Move the slider towards "AIR FRY/STOVETOP" and set Ninja Foodi XL Pressure Cooker Steam Fryer with SmartLid to SEAR/SAUTÉ mode. Adjust the temperature to "Hi5" by using up arrow. Press START/STOP to begin cooking and heat the oil. 10. Add the patties and cook on both sides until golden. You may have to do it in two batches. Serve.
Per Serving: Calories 283; Fat 12g; Sodium 322mg; Carbs 5g; Fiber 3g; Sugar 1g; Protein 15g

Roasted Mushroom

Prep Time: 5 minutes. | Cook Time: 15 minutes. | Serves: 4

2-pounds mushroom caps
1 tablespoon avocado oil

1 teaspoon coriander

1. Place the Cook & Crisp Basket in your Ninja Foodi Pressure Cooker Steam Fryer. 2. Put the mushrooms caps in your Ninja Foodi Pressure Cooker Steam Fryer in one layer and sprinkle with avocado oil and coriander. 3. Put on the Smart Lid on top of the Ninja Foodi Steam Fryer. 4. Move the Lid Slider to the "Air Fry/Stovetop". 5. Cook the meal at 360°F/180°C on "Air Fry" Mode for about 15 minutes. 6. Serve.
Per Serving: Calories 380; Fat 7.7g; Sodium 403 mg; Carbs 7.6g; Fiber 0.1g; Sugar 5.4g; Protein 65.7g

Lemony Steamed Artichokes

Prep time: 10 minutes| Cook time: 30 minutes| Serves: 4

2 medium whole artichokes (about   1 lemon wedge
6 oz. each)   1 cup water

1. Wash the artichokes and remove any damaged outer leaves. 2. Trim off the stem and top edge. Rub the top with lemon wedge. 3. Prepare the Ninja Foodi XL Pressure Cooker Steam Fryer with SmartLid cooking pot by adding the water to the pot and placing the Cook & Crisp Basket in it. 4. Lock lid; move slider towards PRESSURE. Adjust pressure release valve in the SEAL position. Close pressure-release valve. The cooking temperature will default to HIGH, which is accurate. Set time to 20 minutes. Select START/STOP and start cooking. 5. When cooking is complete, let pressure release naturally for 10 minutes, then quick-release any remaining pressure by turning it into VENT position.
6. Uncover the pot. Transfer the artichokes to a serving plate and serve warm with your favorite sauce.
Per Serving: Calories 284; Fat 13g; Sodium 423mg; Carbs 5g; Fiber 3g; Sugar 2g; Protein 15g

Cheesy Asparagus

Prep time: 5 minutes| Cook time: 15 minutes| Serves: 4

1 cup water   Salt and ground black pepper to
1 lb. asparagus, trimmed (1 inch of   taste
the bottom)   3 tablespoons parmesan cheese,
3 tablespoons butter   grated
2 cloves garlic, chopped

1. Pour the water into the Ninja Foodi XL Pressure Cooker Steam Fryer with SmartLid cooking pot and set a Deluxe Reversible Rack in the pot. 2. Place the asparagus on a tin foil, add butter and garlic. Sprinkle with salt and pepper. 3. Fold over the foil and seal the asparagus inside so the foil doesn't come open. 4. Put the asparagus on the rack. 5. Lock lid; move slider towards PRESSURE. Adjust pressure release valve in the SEAL position. Close pressure-release valve. The cooking temperature will default to HIGH, which is accurate. Set time to 8 minutes. Select START/STOP and start cooking. 6. When cooking is complete, let pressure release quickly by turning it into VENT position. Carefully unlock the lid. 7. Unwrap the foil packet and transfer the asparagus to a serving plate. Sprinkle with cheese and serve.
Per Serving: Calories 274; Fat 12g; Sodium 402mg; Carbs 5g; Fiber 3g; Sugar 1g; Protein 14g

Delicious Prosciutto Wrapped Asparagus

Prep time: 5 minutes| Cook time: 10 minutes| Serves: 4

1½ cups water   10 oz. prosciutto, sliced
1 lb. asparagus

1. Wash asparagus and trim off bottom of stems by about 1 inch. 2. Prepare the Ninja Foodi XL Pressure Cooker Steam Fryer with SmartLid cooking pot by adding the water to the pot and placing the Deluxe Reversible Rack in it. 3. Wrap the prosciutto slices around the asparagus spears. 4. Place the un-wrapped asparagus on the rack, and then place the prosciutto-wrapped spears on top. 5. Lock lid; move slider towards PRESSURE. Adjust pressure release valve in the SEAL position. Close pressure-release valve. The cooking temperature will default to HIGH, which is accurate. Set time to 3 minutes. Select START/STOP and start cooking. 6. When cooking is complete, let pressure release naturally for 5 minutes, then quick-release any remaining pressure by turning it into VENT position. 7. Open the lid. Serve.
Per Serving: Calories 293; Fat 15.4g; Sodium 222mg; Carbs 0.4g; Fiber 0.1g; Sugar 0.1g; Protein 36.4g

Tasty Steamed Asparagus

Prep time: 5 minutes| Cook time: 15 minutes| Serves: 4

1 lb. asparagus   1 tablespoon onion, chopped
1 cup water   Salt and fresh ground pepper to
4 teaspoons olive oil   taste

1. Wash asparagus and trim off bottom of stems by about 1½ inches. 2. Prepare the Ninja Foodi XL Pressure Cooker Steam Fryer with SmartLid cooking pot by adding the water to the pot and placing the Deluxe Reversible Rack in it. 3. Place the asparagus on the Rack. Brush the asparagus with the olive oil. 4.Sprinkle with the onion. 5. Lock lid; move slider to AIR FRY/STOVETOP then select STEAM, set time to 2 minutes. Press START/STOP to begin cooking. 6. Carefully unlock the lid. 7. Season with salt and pepper and serve.
Per Serving: Calories 171; Fat 8.8g; Sodium 336mg; Carbs 1.8g; Fiber 0.8g; Sugar 0g; Protein 20.8g

Corn Cob

Prep time: 5 minutes| Cook time: 9 minutes| Serves: 6

6 ears corn   6 tablespoon butter
1 cup water   Salt to taste

1. Shuck the corn husks and rinse off the corn. Cut off the pointy ends. 2. Add the water to the Ninja Foodi XL Pressure Cooker Steam Fryer with SmartLid cooking pot. 3. Arrange the corn vertically, with the larger end in the water. If the ear is too tall break it in half. 4. Lock lid; move slider towards PRESSURE. Adjust pressure release valve in the SEAL position. Close pressure-release valve. The cooking temperature will default to HIGH, which is accurate. Set QUICK RELEASE and time to 3 minutes. Select START/STOP and start cooking. 5. When cooking is complete, let pressure release quickly by turning it into VENT position. 6. Carefully unlock the lid. Transfer the corn to a serving bowl. 7. Serve with butter and salt.
Per Serving: Calories 257; Fat 12g; Sodium 620mg; Carbs 5g; Fiber 4g; Sugar 1g; Protein 14g

Orange Pumpkin Puree

Prep time: 5 minutes| Cook time: 25 minutes| Serves: 6

2 lbs. small-sized sugar pumpkin,   1 + ¼ cup water
halved and seeds scooped out   Salt to taste, optional

1. Prepare the Ninja Foodi XL Pressure Cooker Steam Fryer with SmartLid cooking pot by adding 1 cup of water to the pot and placing the Deluxe Reversible Rack in it. 2. Place the pumpkin halves on the rack. 3. Lock lid; move slider towards PRESSURE. Adjust pressure release valve in the SEAL position. Close pressure-release valve. The cooking temperature will default to HIGH, which is accurate. Set time to 14 minutes. Select START/STOP and start cooking. 4. When cooking is complete, let pressure release quickly by turning it into VENT position. Carefully open the lid. 5. Transfer the pumpkin to a plate and let it cool. Then scoop out the flesh into a bowl. 6. Add ¼ cup of water. Using an immersion blender or food processor, blend until puree. 7. Season with salt and serve.
Per Serving: Calories 130; Fat 8.3g; Sodium 130mg; Carbs 1g; Fiber 0.1g; Sugar 0g; Protein 12.2g

Broccoli Feta Balls

Prep Time: 15 minutes. | Cook Time: 5 minute | Serves: 2

1 cup broccoli, shredded   ½ teaspoon white pepper
3 ounces Feta, crumbled   1 teaspoon mascarpone
1 egg, beaten   1 teaspoon avocado oil
1 tablespoon almond flour

1. Place the Cook & Crisp Basket in your Ninja Foodi Pressure Cooker Steam Fryer. 2. Brush the Ninja Foodi Cook & Crisp Basket with avocado oil. 3. Then mix all the remaining recipe ingredients and make the balls. 4. Put the balls in your Ninja Foodi Pressure Cooker Steam Fryer in one layer. 5. Put on the Smart Lid on top of the Ninja Foodi Steam Fryer. 6. Move the Lid Slider to the "Air Fry/Stovetop". 7. Cook on "Air Fry" Mode at 400°F/200°C for about 5 minutes.
Per Serving: Calories 197; Fat 8.6g; Sodium 510mg; Total Carbs 22.2g; Fiber 1.4g; Sugar 13g; Protein 7.6g

Bacon Brussels Sprouts

Prep time: 5 minutes| Cook time: 10 minutes| Serves: 4

1 lb. Brussels sprouts, trimmed and cut into halves
½ cup bacon, chopped
1 tablespoon mustard
1 cup chicken broth
Salt and ground black pepper to taste
1 tablespoon butter
2 tablespoon dill, chopped

1. Move the slider towards "AIR FRY/STOVETOP" and set Ninja Foodi XL Pressure Cooker Steam Fryer with SmartLid to SEAR/SAUTÉ mode. Adjust the temperature to "Hi5" by using up arrow. Press START/STOP to begin cooking. And add the bacon. Sauté until it is crispy. 2. Add the Brussels sprouts and cook, stirring occasionally, for 2 minutes more. 3. Add the mustard and broth. Season with salt and pepper, stir. 4. Press the START/STOP key to stop the SAUTÉ function. 5. Lock lid; move slider towards PRESSURE. Adjust pressure release valve in the SEAL position. Close pressure-release valve. The cooking temperature will default to HIGH, which is accurate. Set time to 4 minutes. Select START/STOP and start cooking. 6. When cooking is complete, let pressure release quickly by turning it into VENT position. 7. Carefully unlock the lid. Add the butter and sprinkle with dill, stir. 8. Select SAUTÉ again and cook for 1 minute more. Serve.
Per Serving: Calories 236; Fat 12g; Sodium 297mg; Carbs 6g; Fiber 4g; Sugar 3g; Protein 13g

Taco Broccoli

Prep Time: 10 minutes. | Cook Time: 12 minutes. | Serves: 4

1-pound broccoli florets
1 tablespoon taco seasonings
2 tablespoons olive oil

1. Place the Cook & Crisp Basket in your Ninja Foodi Pressure Cooker Steam Fryer. 2. Mix broccoli florets with taco seasonings and olive oil. 3. Put on the Smart Lid on top of the Ninja Foodi Steam Fryer. 4. Move the Lid Slider to the "Air Fry/Stovetop". 5. Cook on "Air Fry" Mode at 375°F/190°C for about 12 minutes. Shake the vegetables after 6 minutes of cooking.
Per Serving: Calories 210; Fat 5.4 g; Sodium 110 mg; Carbs 18.5g; Fiber 2.4g; Sugar 13.1g; Protein 23.5g

Bacon Brussels Sprouts with Orange Zest

Prep time: 5 minutes| 8 Cook time: minutes| Serves: 4

1 tablespoon avocado oil
2 slices bacon, diced
½ cup freshly squeezed orange juice
½ cup water
1 pound Brussels sprouts, trimmed and halved
2 teaspoons orange zest

1. Move the slider towards "AIR FRY/STOVETOP" and set Ninja Foodi XL Pressure Cooker Steam Fryer with SmartLid to SEAR/SAUTÉ mode. Adjust the temperature to "Hi5" by using up arrow. Press START/STOP to begin cooking. And heat avocado oil. Add bacon. Stir-fry 3–5 minutes or until bacon is almost crisp and the fat is rendered. Add the orange juice and water and deglaze the pot by scraping the bits from the sides and bottom. 2. Add Brussels sprouts. 3. Lock lid; move slider towards PRESSURE. Adjust pressure release valve in the SEAL position. Close pressure-release valve. The cooking temperature will default to HIGH, which is accurate. Set time to 3 minutes. Select START/STOP and start cooking. When cooking is complete, let pressure release quickly by turning it into VENT position. Unlock lid. 4. Using a slotted spoon, transfer Brussels sprouts to a serving dish. Garnish with orange zest and serve warm.
Per Serving: Calories 195; Fat 18.3g; Sodium 278mg; Carbs 5.4g; Fiber 1g; Sugar 2g; Protein 5.8g

Cinnamon Garlic

Prep Time: 5 minutes. | Cook Time: 10 minutes. | Serves: 4

8 garlic cloves, peeled
2 tablespoons olive oil
¼ teaspoon dried thyme

1. Place the Cook & Crisp Basket in your Ninja Foodi Pressure Cooker Steam Fryer. 2. Sprinkle the garlic cloves with olive oil and dried thyme and put in your Ninja Foodi Pressure Cooker Steam Fryer. 3. Put on the Smart Lid on top of the Ninja Foodi Steam Fryer. 4. Move the Lid Slider to the "Air Fry/Stovetop". 5. Cook the garlic at 350°F/175°C on "Air Fry" Mode for about 10 minutes. 6. Serve.
Per Serving: Calories 97; Fat 18.4 g; Sodium 1151 mg; Carbs 11.6g; Fiber 0.6g; Sugar 10.9g; Protein 2.5g

Fried Celery

Prep Time: 5 minutes. | Cook Time: 10 minutes. | Serves: 4

1-pound celery stalks, chopped
½ cup coconut cream
1-ounce Parmesan, grated
1 teaspoon white pepper

1. Place the Cook & Crisp Basket in your Ninja Foodi Pressure Cooker Steam Fryer. 2. Mix celery stalks with white pepper, Parmesan, and coconut cream. 3. Put on the Smart Lid on top of the Ninja Foodi Steam Fryer. 4. Move the Lid Slider to the "Air Fry/Stovetop". 5. Put the vegetables in your Ninja Foodi Pressure Cooker Steam Fryer. Cook on "Air Fry" Mode at 350°F/175°C for about 10 minutes.
Per Serving: Calories 384; Fat 20.5g; Sodium 449 mg; Carbs 5.1g; Fiber 2.1g; Sugar 0.7g; Protein 45g

Buffalo Cauliflower Florets

Prep Time: 10 minutes. | Cook Time: 6 minutes. | Serves: 4

2 cups cauliflower florets
¼ cup coconut cream
2 tablespoons buffalo sauce
1 teaspoon olive oil

1. Place the Cook & Crisp Basket in your Ninja Foodi Pressure Cooker Steam Fryer. 2. Mix cauliflower florets with coconut cream, buffalo sauce, and olive oil. 3. Put on the Smart Lid on top of the Ninja Foodi Steam Fryer. 4. Move the Lid Slider to the "Air Fry/Stovetop". 5. Put them in your Ninja Foodi Pressure Cooker Steam Fryer. Cook on "Air Fry" Mode at 400°F/200°C for about 3 minutes per side.
Per Serving: Calories 328; Fat 28.7 g; Sodium 95 mg; Carbs 7.4g; Fiber 2.8g; Sugar 0.7g; Protein 13g

Bacon with Brussels Sprouts

Prep Time: 10 minutes. | Cook Time: 15 minutes. | Serves: 8

1 pound Brussels sprouts, trimmed
3 ounces bacon, chopped
1 tablespoon coconut oil, melted
1 teaspoon salt

1. Place the Cook & Crisp Basket in your Ninja Foodi Pressure Cooker Steam Fryer. 2. Mix Brussel sprouts with coconut oil and salt and put in your Ninja Foodi Pressure Cooker Steam Fryer. 3. Top the vegetables with bacon. 4. Put on the Smart Lid on top of the Ninja Foodi Steam Fryer. 5. Move the Lid Slider to the "Air Fry/Stovetop". 6. Cook on "Air Fry" Mode at 360°F/180°C for about 15 minutes. Stir the vegetables from time to time to avoid burning.
Per Serving: Calories 370; Fat 10.5 g; Sodium 503 mg; Carbs 21.4g; Fiber 3.1g; Sugar 1.9g; Protein 6.6g

crusted Okra

Prep Time: 15 minutes. | Cook Time: 8 minutes. | Serves: 4

1-pound okra, trimmed
½ cup coconut flour
3 eggs, beaten
1 teaspoon chili powder

1. Place the Cook & Crisp Basket in your Ninja Foodi Pressure Cooker Steam Fryer. 2. Mix coconut flour with chili powder. 3. Then dip the okra in the eggs and coat in the coconut flour mixture. 4. Put the okra in your Ninja Foodi Pressure Cooker Steam Fryer. 5. Put on the Smart Lid on top of the Ninja Foodi Steam Fryer. 6. Move the Lid Slider to the "Air Fry/Stovetop". 7. Cook on "Air Fry" Mode at 385°F/195°C for about 4 minutes per side.
Per Serving: Calories 206; Fat 6.4 g; Sodium 911 mg; Carbs 28.9g; Fiber 3.6g; Sugar 20.4g; Protein 11g

Herbed Olives

Prep Time: 5 minutes. | Cook Time: 8 minutes. | Serves: 4

8 Kalamata Olives, pitted   1 tablespoon olive oil
1 teaspoon Italian seasonings   1 teaspoon coconut aminos

1. Place the Cook & Crisp Basket in your Ninja Foodi Pressure Cooker Steam Fryer. 2. Sprinkle olives with Italian seasonings, olive oil, and coconut aminos. 3. Put the olives in your Ninja Foodi Pressure Cooker Steam Fryer. 4. Put on the Smart Lid on top of the Ninja Foodi Steam Fryer. 5. Move the Lid Slider to the "Air Fry/Stovetop". 6. Cook on "Air Fry" Mode at 360°F/180°C on "Air Fry" Mode for about 8 minutes.
Per Serving: Calories 122; Fat 1.8g; Sodium 794mg; Total Carbs 17g; Fiber 8.9g; Sugar 1.6g; Protein 14.9g

Cauliflower Coconut Balls

Prep Time: 15 minutes. | Cook Time: 12 minutes. | Serves: 4

2 cups cauliflower, shredded   1 teaspoon salt
3 tablespoons coconut flour   1 teaspoon coriander
1 teaspoon cumin   1 teaspoon dried basil
2 tablespoons coconut oil   Cooking spray
1 egg, beaten

1. Place the Cook & Crisp Basket in your Ninja Foodi Pressure Cooker Steam Fryer. 2. Mix shredded cauliflower with coconut flour, cumin, coconut oil, egg, salt, coriander, and dried basil. 3. Make the balls from the mixture and put it in your Ninja Foodi Pressure Cooker Steam Fryer. 4. Spray the cauliflower balls with cooking spray. 5. Put on the Smart Lid on top of the Ninja Foodi Steam Fryer. 6. Move the Lid Slider to the "Air Fry/Stovetop". 7. Cook on "Air Fry" Mode at 385°F/195°C for about 6 minutes per side until they are golden brown.
Per Serving: Calories 163; Fat 11.5g; Sodium 918mg; Total Carbs 8.3g; Fiber 4.2g; Sugar 0.2g; Protein 7.4g

Cajun Spiced Okra

Prep Time: 10 minutes. | Cook Time: 10 minutes. | Serves: 3

12 ounces okra, chopped   1 tablespoon sesame oil
1 teaspoon Cajun seasonings

1. Place the Cook & Crisp Basket in your Ninja Foodi Pressure Cooker Steam Fryer. 2. Mix okra with Cajun seasonings and sesame oil. 3. Put the vegetables in your Ninja Foodi Pressure Cooker Steam Fryer. 4. Put on the Smart Lid on top of the Ninja Foodi Steam Fryer. 5. Move the Lid Slider to the "Air Fry/Stovetop". 6. Cook on "Air Fry" Mode at 360°F/180°C for about 5 minutes. 7. Then shake the vegetables. Cook on "Air Fry" Mode for about 5 minutes more.
Per Serving: Calories 180; Fat 3.2g; Sodium 133mg; Total Carbs 32g; Fiber 1.1g; Sugar 1.8g; Protein 9g

Roasted Artichoke

Prep Time: 5 minutes. | Cook Time: 15 minutes. | Serves: 4

4 artichoke hearts, canned   1 tablespoon lemon juice
1 teaspoon olive oil   1 teaspoon black pepper

1. Place the Cook & Crisp Basket in your Ninja Foodi Pressure Cooker Steam Fryer. 2. Move the Lid Slider to the "Air Fry/Stovetop". 3. Sprinkle the artichoke hearts with olive oil, lemon juice, and black pepper. 4. Put them in your Ninja Foodi Pressure Cooker Steam Fryer. 5. Cook on "Air Fry" Mode for about 15 minutes at 350°F/175°C.
Per Serving: Calories 322; Fat 14 g; Sodium 679 mg; Carbs 1.1g; Fiber 0.2g; Sugar 0.7g; Protein 45.5g

Cajusn Eggplants

Prep Time: 10 minutes. | Cook Time: 15 minutes. | Serves: 2

2 eggplants, chopped   1 tablespoon sesame oil
1 teaspoon Cajun seasonings

1. Place the Cook & Crisp Basket in your Ninja Foodi Pressure Cooker Steam Fryer. 2. Sprinkle the eggplants with Cajun seasonings and sesame oil. 3. Put the vegetables in your Ninja Foodi Pressure Cooker Steam Fryer. 4. Move the Lid Slider to the "Air Fry/Stovetop". 5. Cook on "Air Fry" Mode at 360°F/180°C for about 15 minutes.
Per Serving: Calories 360; Fat 30.8 g; Sodium 584 mg; Carbs 1.3g; Fiber 0.5g; Sugar 0.2g; Protein 18.6g

Creamy Macadamia Spinach

Prep Time: 5 minutes. | Cook Time: 15 minutes. | Serves: 4

3 cups fresh spinach, chopped   1 tablespoon butter
1 cup heavy cream   1 teaspoon salt
1-ounce macadamia nuts, chopped

1. Place the Cook & Crisp Basket in your Ninja Foodi Pressure Cooker Steam Fryer and place a reversible rack in it. 2. Mix spinach with heavy cream, nuts, butter, and salt. 3. Put the spinach mixture in the ramekin and place the ramekin in your Ninja Foodi Pressure Cooker Steam Fryer. 4. Put on the Smart Lid on top of the Ninja Foodi Steam Fryer. 5. Move the Lid Slider to the "Air Fry/Stovetop". 6. Cook the spinach at 350°F/175°C on "Air Fry" Mode for about 15 minutes.
Per Serving: Calories 512; Fat 7.1 g; Sodium 42 mg; Carbs 28.5g; Fiber 2.1g; Sugar 13.4g; Protein 1.2g

Egg with Green Beans

Prep Time: 15 minutes. | Cook Time: 5 minutes. | Serves: 2

10 ounce green beans   1 teaspoon turmeric
2 eggs, beaten   Cooking spray
2 tablespoons coconut shred

1. Place the Cook & Crisp Basket in your Ninja Foodi Pressure Cooker Steam Fryer. 2. Sprinkle the green beans with eggs and turmeric. 3. Then sprinkle them with coconut shred and put in your Ninja Foodi Pressure Cooker Steam Fryer. 4. Spray the green beans with cooking spray. 5. Put on the Smart Lid on top of the Ninja Foodi Steam Fryer. 6. Move the Lid Slider to the "Air Fry/Stovetop". 7. Cook on "Air Fry" Mode at 400°F/200°C for about 5 minutes.
Per Serving: Calories 404; Fat 20.3 g; Sodium 8 mg; Carbs 3.4g; Fiber 1g; Sugar 1.2g; Protein 53.4g

Seasoned Artichoke

Prep Time: 5 minutes. | Cook Time: 15 minutes. | Serves: 2

2 artichokes, trimmed   1 teaspoon onion powder
1 tablespoon olive oil

1. Place the Cook & Crisp Basket in your Ninja Foodi Pressure Cooker Steam Fryer. 2. Put artichokes in your Ninja Foodi Pressure Cooker Steam Fryer and sprinkle with onion powder and olive oil. 3. Put on the Smart Lid on top of the Ninja Foodi Steam Fryer. 4. Move the Lid Slider to the "Air Fry/Stovetop". 5. Cook the artichokes at 355°F/180°C on "Air Fry" Mode for about 15 minutes.
Per Serving: Calories 100; Fat 2g; Sodium 480mg; Total Carbs 4g; Fiber 2g; Sugar 0g; Protein 18g

Air Fried Bell Peppers

Prep Time: 10 minutes. | Cook Time: 5 minutes. | Serves: 4

4 bell peppers, trimmed   1 teaspoon minced garlic
1 tablespoon olive oil   1 tablespoon apple cider vinegar

1. Place the Cook & Crisp Basket in your Ninja Foodi Pressure Cooker Steam Fryer. 2. Sprinkle the bell peppers with olive oil and put in your Ninja Foodi Pressure Cooker Steam Fryer. 3. Put on the Smart Lid on top of the Ninja Foodi Steam Fryer. 4. Move the Lid Slider to the "Air Fry/Stovetop". 5. Cook the bell peppers at 400°F/200°C on "Air Fry" Mode for about 5 minutes. 6. Then chop the bell peppers and sprinkle with minced garlic and apple cider vinegar.
Per Serving: Calories 229; Fat 1.9 |Sodium 567mg; Total Carbs 1.9g; Fiber 0.4g; Sugar 0.6g; Protein 11.8g

Avocado Wedges

Prep Time: 10 minutes. | Cook Time: 6 minutes. | Serves: 4

1 avocado, pitted, cut into 4 wedges
4 teaspoons coconut shred
1 egg, beaten
½ teaspoon nutmeg

1. Place the Cook & Crisp Basket in your Ninja Foodi Pressure Cooker Steam Fryer. 2. Dip the avocado wedges in the egg and sprinkle with nutmeg. 3. Then sprinkle the avocado with coconut shred and put it in your Ninja Foodi Pressure Cooker Steam Fryer. 4. Put on the Smart Lid on top of the Ninja Foodi Steam Fryer. 5. Move the Lid Slider to the "Air Fry/Stovetop". 6. Cook the meal at 400°F/200°C on "Air Fry" Mode for about 3 minutes per side.
Per Serving: Calories 185; Fat 11g; Sodium 355mg; Total Carbs 21g; Fiber 5.8g; Sugar 3g; Protein 4.7g

Pita Chips

Prep Time: 10 minutes. | Cook Time: 15 minutes. | Serves: 1

1 cup Mozarella cheese, shredded
1 egg
¼ cup blanched flour
½ ounce pork rinds, ground

1. Place the Cook & Crisp Basket in your Ninja Foodi Pressure Cooker Steam Fryer. 2. Melt the Mozarella in the microwave. Add the egg, flour, and pork rinds and mix together to form a smooth paste. Microwave the cheese again if it begins to set. Between two sheets of parchment paper, put the dough and use a rolling pin to flatten it out into a rectangle. The thickness is up to you. With a sharp knife, cut into the dough to form triangles. It may be necessary to complete this step-in multiple batches. 4. Place the chips in the Pressure Cooker Steam Fryer. 5. Put on the Smart Lid on top of the Ninja Foodi Steam Fryer. 6. Move the Lid Slider to the "Air Fry/Stovetop". 7. Cook on "Air Fry" Mode for 5 minutes at 350°F/175°C. Turn them over. Cook on the other side for another 5 minutes, until the chips are golden and firm. 8. Allow the chips to cool and harden further. They can also be stored in an airtight container.
Per Serving: Calories 288; Fat 6.9g; Sodium 761mg; Total Carbs 46g; Fiber 4g; Sugar 12g; Protein 9.6g

Cheesy Parsley Zucchini

Prep Time: 5 minutes. | Cook Time: 12 minutes. | Serves: 2

1 large zucchini, trimmed, halved
1 teaspoon black pepper
1 cup Cheddar cheese, shredded
1 tablespoon olive oil
½ teaspoon dried parsley

1. Place the Cook & Crisp Basket in your Ninja Foodi Pressure Cooker Steam Fryer. 2. Brush the Ninja Foodi Cook & Crisp Basket with olive oil. 3. Put the zucchini inside and sprinkle with black pepper. 4. Then top the zucchini with Cheddar cheese and dried parsley. 5. Put on the Smart Lid on top of the Ninja Foodi Steam Fryer. 6. Move the Lid Slider to the "Air Fry/Stovetop". 7. Cook the meal at 375°F/190°C on "Air Fry" Mode for about 12 minutes.
Per Serving: Calories 413; Fat 30.8 g; Sodium 1279 mg; Carbs 2.4g; Fiber 0.5g; Sugar 1.3g; Protein 31.6g

Cheese Zucchini Skewers

Prep Time: 15 minutes. | Cook Time: 14 minutes. | Serves: 4

10-ounce halloumi cheese, chopped
1 zucchini, chopped
1 jalapeno, chopped
1 tomato, cut into 4 pieces
1 tablespoon olive oil
½ teaspoon dried rosemary

1. Place the Cook & Crisp Basket in your Ninja Foodi Pressure Cooker Steam Fryer. 2. Sting the cheese, zucchini, jalapeno, and tomato into the skewers and sprinkle with olive oil and dried rosemary. 3. Then put the vegetable skewers in your Ninja Foodi Pressure Cooker Steam Fryer. 4. Put on the Smart Lid on top of the Ninja Foodi Steam Fryer. 5. Move the Lid Slider to the "Air Fry/Stovetop". 6. Cook on "Air Fry" Mode at 375°F/190°C for about 14 minutes.

Per Serving: Calories 183; Fat 0.4 g; Sodium 4347 mg; Carbs 5.6g; Fiber 0.6g; Sugar 8.4g; Protein 40.2g

Greek Olives

Prep Time: 5 minutes. | Cook Time: 12 minutes. | Serves: 4

6-ounce Feta cheese, crumbled
8 ounce black olives, pitted
1 tablespoon coconut oil, melted
1 teaspoon dried thyme

1. Place the Cook & Crisp Basket in your Ninja Foodi Pressure Cooker Steam Fryer. 2. Put olives in your Ninja Foodi Pressure Cooker Steam Fryer and sprinkle with coconut oil and dried thyme. 3. Put on the Smart Lid on top of the Ninja Foodi Steam Fryer. 4. Move the Lid Slider to the "Air Fry/Stovetop". 5. Cook on "Air Fry" Mode at 350°F/175°C for about 12 minutes. 6. Sprinkle the cooked olives with crumbled Feta cheese.
Per Serving: Calories 134; Fat 5.9g; Sodium 343mg; Total Carbs 9.5g; Fiber 0.5g; Sugar 1.1g; Protein 10.4g

Crispy Zucchini Patties

Prep Time: 15 minutes. | Cook Time: 8 minutes. | Serves: 4

2 zucchinis, grated
1 tablespoon dried dill
1 teaspoon cream cheese
1 cup almond flour
1 teaspoon salt
Cooking spray

1. Place the Cook & Crisp Basket in your Ninja Foodi Pressure Cooker Steam Fryer. 2. Mix zucchini with dried dill, cream cheese, almond flour, and salt 3. Make the patties from the zucchini mixture and put it in your Ninja Foodi Pressure Cooker Steam Fryer. 4. Sprinkle the patties with cooking spray. 5. Put on the Smart Lid on top of the Ninja Foodi Steam Fryer. 6. Move the Lid Slider to the "Air Fry/Stovetop". 7. Cook on "Air Fry" Mode at 375°F/190°C for about 4 minutes per side.
Per Serving: Calories 186; Fat 3g; Sodium 223mg; Total Carbs 31g; Fiber 8.7g; Sugar 5.5g; Protein 9.7g

Brussel Sprouts With Feta

Prep Time: 5 minutes. | Cook Time: 12 minutes. | Serves: 4

1-pound Brussel sprouts, halved
1 tablespoon olive oil
1 teaspoon dried dill
2 ounces Feta, crumbled

1. Place the Cook & Crisp Basket in your Ninja Foodi Pressure Cooker Steam Fryer. 2. Mix Brussel sprouts with olive oil and dried dill. 3. Put the vegetables in your Ninja Foodi Pressure Cooker Steam Fryer. 4. Put on the Smart Lid on top of the Ninja Foodi Steam Fryer. 5. Move the Lid Slider to the "Air Fry/Stovetop". 6. Cook on "Air Fry" Mode at 375°F/190°C for about 6 minutes per side. 7. Top the cooked vegetables with crumbled feta.
Per Serving: Calories 103; Fat 8.4g; Sodium 117mg; Total Carbs 3.5g; Fiber 0.9g; Sugar 1.5g; Protein 5.1g

Cabbage Egg Fritters

Prep Time: 10 minutes. | Cook Time: 12 minutes. | Serves: 4

1 cup white cabbage, shredded
3 eggs, beaten
1 ounce scallions, chopped
⅓ cup coconut flour
1 teaspoon cream cheese
Cooking spray

1. Place the Cook & Crisp Basket in your Ninja Foodi Pressure Cooker Steam Fryer. 2. Spray the Ninja Foodi Cook & Crisp Basket with cooking spray from inside. 3. Then mix all the remaining recipe ingredients in the bowl. 4. Make the fritters from the cabbage mixture put in the Ninja Foodi Cook & Crisp Basket in one layer. 5. Put on the Smart Lid on top of the Ninja Foodi Steam Fryer. 6. Move the Lid Slider to the "Air Fry/Stovetop". 7. Cook the fritters at 375°F/190°C on "Air Fry" Mode for 6 minutes per side.
Per Serving: Calories 284; Fat 7.9g; Sodium 704mg; Total Carbs 38.1g; Fiber 1.9g; Sugar 1.9g; Protein 14.8g

Broccoli Cheese Gnocchi

Prep Time: 15 minutes. | Cook Time: 4 minutes. | Serves: 4

2 cups broccoli, chopped, boiled	1 teaspoon mascarpone
2 ounces provolone cheese, grated	3 tablespoons almond flour
1 egg, beaten	1 tablespoon coconut oil
1 teaspoon white pepper	1 teaspoon dried parsley

1. Place the Cook & Crisp Basket in your Ninja Foodi Pressure Cooker Steam Fryer. 2. Mix all the recipe ingredients in a suitable mixing bowl until smooth. 3. Then make the gnocchi and put them in your Ninja Foodi Pressure Cooker Steam Fryer in one layer. 4. Put on the Smart Lid on top of the Ninja Foodi Steam Fryer. 5. Move the Lid Slider to the "Air Fry/Stovetop". 6. Cook the gnocchi at 400°F/200°C on "Air Fry" Mode for about 2 minutes per side.
Per Serving: Calories 212; Fat 11.8g; Sodium 321mg; Total Carbs 24.6g; Fiber 4.4g; Sugar 8g; Protein 7.3g

Lemony Peppers

Prep Time: 5 minutes. | Cook Time: 15 minutes. | Serves: 4

2 cups bell peppers, chopped	1 garlic clove, diced
2 tablespoons lemon juice	1 teaspoon clove
1 teaspoon butter, softened	

1. Place the Cook & Crisp Basket in your Ninja Foodi Pressure Cooker Steam Fryer. 2. Put the bell peppers in the Ninja Foodi Cook & Crisp Basket and sprinkle with butter, garlic clove, and clove. 3. Put on the Smart Lid on top of the Ninja Foodi Steam Fryer. 4. Move the Lid Slider to the "Air Fry/Stovetop". 5. Cook the bell peppers for about 15 minutes at 350°F/175°C. Stir the peppers every 5 minutes to avoid burning. 6. Then transfer the cooked peppers in the bowl and sprinkle with lemon juice.
Per Serving: Calories 206; Fat 3.4g; Sodium 174mg; Total Carbs 35g; Fiber 9.4g; Sugar 5.9g; Protein 10.6g

Air-Fried Portobello Steak

Prep Time: 10 minutes. | Cook Time: 5 minute | Serves: 4

1-pound Portobello mushrooms	4 teaspoons butter
1 teaspoon coriander	½ teaspoon salt

1. Place the Cook & Crisp Basket in your Ninja Foodi Pressure Cooker Steam Fryer. 2. Sprinkle the mushrooms with coriander, salt, and butter. 3. Put the mushrooms in your Ninja Foodi Pressure Cooker Steam Fryer. 4. Put on the Smart Lid on top of the Ninja Foodi Steam Fryer. 5. Move the Lid Slider to the "Air Fry/Stovetop". 6. Cook on "Air Fry" Mode for about 5 minutes at 400°F/200°C.
Per Serving: Calories 131; Fat 0.1g; Sodium 271mg; Total Carbs 32.8g; Fiber 6.4g; Sugar 7g; Protein 6.3g

Bacon-Wrapped Onion

Prep Time: 10 minutes. | Cook Time: 15 minutes. | Serves: 8

1 large onion, peeled	1 tablespoon sriracha
8 slices sugar-free bacon	

1. Place the Cook & Crisp Basket in your Ninja Foodi Pressure Cooker Steam Fryer. 2. Chop up the onion into slices a quarter-inch thick. Gently pull apart the rings. Take a slice of bacon and wrap it around an onion ring. Repeat with the rest of the ingredients. Place each onion ring in your fryer. 3. Put on the Smart Lid on top of the Ninja Foodi Steam Fryer. 4. Move the Lid Slider to the "Air Fry/Stovetop". 5. Cook the onion rings at 350°F/175°C on "Air Fry" Mode for 10 minutes, turning them halfway through to ensure the bacon crisps up. 6. Serve hot with the sriracha.
Per Serving: Calories 350; Fat 2.6g; Sodium 358mg; Total Carbs 64.6g; Fiber 14.4g; Sugar 3.3g; Protein 19.9g

Smoked BBQ Sausages

Prep Time: 10 minutes. | Cook Time: 10 minutes. | Serves: 1

2 teaspoon coconut oil, melted	¼ teaspoon cumin
¼ teaspoon smoked paprika	1 cup raw sausages
1 teaspoon chili powder	

1. Place the Cook & Crisp Basket in your Ninja Foodi Pressure Cooker Steam Fryer. 2. Mix the melted coconut oil with the paprika, chili powder, and cumin. Place the sausage in a suitable bowl and pour the coconut oil over them, tossing them to cover them evenly. 3. Place the sausage in the basket of your fryer and spread them out across the base. 4. Put on the Smart Lid on top of the Ninja Foodi Steam Fryer. 5. Move the Lid Slider to the "Air Fry/Stovetop". 6. Cook on "Air Fry" Mode for 6 minutes at 320°F/160°C, giving the basket an occasional shake to make sure everything is cooked evenly. 7. Leave to cool and serve.
Per Serving: Calories 166; Fat 3.2g; Sodium 437mg; Total Carbs 28.8g; Fiber 1.8g; Sugar 2.7g; Protein 5.8g

Fat Air Fried Eggplant

Prep Time: 10 minutes. | Cook Time: 15 minutes. | Serves: 1

1 large eggplant, sliced	¼ teaspoon salt
2 tablespoons olive oil	½ teaspoon garlic powder

1. Place the Cook & Crisp Basket in your Ninja Foodi Pressure Cooker Steam Fryer. 2. Prepare the eggplant by slicing off the top and bottom and cutting it into slices around a quarter-inch thick. 3. Apply olive oil to the eggplant slices with a brush, coating both sides. Season each side with sprinklings of salt and garlic powder. 4. Place the slices in the fryer. 5. Put on the Smart Lid on top of the Ninja Foodi Steam Fryer. 6. Move the Lid Slider to the "Air Fry/Stovetop". 7. Cook on "Air Fry" Mode for fifteen minutes at 390°F/200°C. 8. Serve right away.
Per Serving: Calories 193; Fat 1g; Sodium 395mg; Total Carbs 38.7g; Fiber 1.6g; Sugar 0.9g; Protein 6.6g

Cheese Flatbread

Prep Time: 10 minutes. | Cook Time: 7 minutes. | Serves: 1

1 cup Mozzarella cheese, shredded	1 ounce full-fat cream cheese, softened
¼ cup blanched flour	

1. Place the Cook & Crisp Basket in your Ninja Foodi Pressure Cooker Steam Fryer. 2. Microwave the Mozzarella for half a minute until melted. Mix with the flour to achieve a smooth consistency, before adding the cream cheese. Keep mixing to create a dough, microwaving the mixture again if the cheese begins to harden. 3. Divide the dough into two equal pieces. Roll out the dough through two sheets of parchment paper, until it is about a quarter-inch thick. Cover the bottom of your fryer with another sheet of parchment. 4. Transfer the dough into the Cook & Crisp Basket. 5. Put on the Smart Lid on top of the Ninja Foodi Steam Fryer. 6. Move the Lid Slider to the "Air Fry/Stovetop". 7. Cook on "Air Fry" Mode at 320°F/160°C for 7 minutes. You may need to complete this step in two batches. Make sure to turn the flatbread halfway through cooking. Take care when removing it from the fryer and serve warm.
Per Serving: Calories 113; Fat 3g; Sodium 152mg; Total Carbs 20g; Fiber 3g; Sugar 1.1g; Protein 3.5g

Buffalo Ranch Cauliflower

Prep Time: 10 minutes. | Cook Time: 5 minutes. | Serves: 1

½ packet dry ranch seasoning	Cauliflower florets
2 tablespoon salted butter, melted	¼ cup buffalo sauce

1. Place the Cook & Crisp Basket in your Ninja Foodi Pressure Cooker Steam Fryer. 2. In a suitable bowl, mix the dry ranch seasoning and butter. Toss with the cauliflower florets to coat and transfer them to the fryer. 3. Put on the Smart Lid on top of the Ninja Foodi Steam Fryer. 4. Move the Lid Slider to the "Air Fry/Stovetop". 5. Cook on "Air Fry" Mode at 400°F/200°C for five minutes, shaking the basket occasionally to ensure the florets cook evenly. 6. Remove the cauliflower from the fryer, pour the buffalo sauce over it, and enjoy.
Per Serving: Calories 260; Fat 16g; Sodium 585mg; Total Carbs 3.1g; Fiber 1.3g; Sugar 0.2g; Protein 5.5g

Pizza Crust

Prep Time: 10 minutes. | Cook Time: 10 minutes. | Serves: 4

1 tablespoon full-fat cream cheese
½ cup whole-milk Mozzarella cheese, shredded
2 tablespoon flour
1 egg white

1. Place the Cook & Crisp Basket in your Ninja Foodi Pressure Cooker Steam Fryer. 2. In a microwave-safe bowl, mix the cream cheese, Mozzarella, and flour and heat in the microwave for half a minute. Mix well to create a smooth consistency. Add in the egg white and stir to form a soft ball of dough. 3. With slightly wet hands, press the dough into a pizza crust about six inches in diameter. 4. Place a sheet of parchment paper in the bottom of your fryer and lay the crust on top. 5. Put on the Smart Lid on top of the Ninja Foodi Steam Fryer. 6. Move the Lid Slider to the "Air Fry/Stovetop". 7. Cook on "Air Fry" Mode for ten minutes at 350°F/175°C, turning the crust over halfway through the cooking time. 8. Top the pizza base with the toppings of your choice and enjoy!
Per Serving: Calories 208; Fat 5g; Sodium 1205mg; Total Carbs 34.1g; Fiber 7.8g; Sugar 2.5g; Protein 5.9g

Crisp Brussels Sprout Chips

Prep Time: 10 minutes. | Cook Time: 10 minutes. | Serves: 1

1 lb. Brussels sprouts, cut in half
1 tablespoon coconut oil, melted
1 tablespoon unsalted butter, melted

1. Place the Cook & Crisp Basket in your Ninja Foodi Pressure Cooker Steam Fryer. 2. Toss the Brussel sprouts with coconut oil and transfer to your Ninja Foodi Pressure Cooker Steam Fryer. 3. Put on the Smart Lid on top of the Ninja Foodi Steam Fryer. 4. Move the Lid Slider to the "Air Fry/Stovetop". 5. Cook on "Air Fry" Mode at 400°F/200°C for 10 minutes, giving the basket a good shake throughout the cooking time to brown them up if desired. 6. Remove them from the fryer and serve with a topping of melted butter before serving.
Per Serving: Calories 266; Fat 6.3g; Sodium 193mg; Total Carbs 39.1g; Fiber 7.2g; Sugar 5.2g; Protein 14.8g

Parmesan Zucchini Bites

Prep Time: 10 minutes. | Cook Time: 10 minutes. | Serves: 4

4 zucchinis
1 egg
½ cup parmesan cheese, grated
1 tablespoon Italian herbs
1 cup coconut, grated

1. Place the Cook & Crisp Basket in your Ninja Foodi Pressure Cooker Steam Fryer. 2. Thinly grate the zucchini and dry with a cheesecloth, ensuring to remove all of the moisture. 3. In a suitable bowl, mix the zucchini with the egg, parmesan, Italian herbs, and grated coconut, mixing well to incorporate everything. Using your hands, mold the mixture into balls. 4. Place a rack inside. Lay the zucchini balls on the rack. 5. Put on the Smart Lid on top of the Ninja Foodi Steam Fryer. 6. Move the Lid Slider to the "Air Fry/Stovetop". 7. Cook on "Air Fry" Mode at 370°F/185°C for 10 minutes. Serve hot.
Per Serving: Calories 155; Fat 4.2g; Sodium 963mg; Total Carbs 21.5g; Fiber 0.8g; Sugar 5.7g; Protein 8.1g

Cauliflower Cheese Tots

Prep Time: 10 minutes. | Cook Time: 20 minutes. | Serves: 8

1 large head cauliflower
½ cup parmesan cheese, grated
1 cup Mozzarella cheese, shredded
1 teaspoon seasoned salt
1 egg

1. Place a steamer basket over a suitable pot of boiling water, ensuring the water is not high enough to enter the basket. 2. Cut up the cauliflower into florets and transfer to the steamer basket. Cover the pot with a lid and leave to steam for 7 minutes, making sure the cauliflower softens. 3. Place the florets on a cheesecloth and leave to cool. Remove as much moisture as possible. This is crucial as it ensures the cauliflower will harden. 4. In a suitable bowl, break up the cauliflower with a fork. 5. Stir in the parmesan, Mozzarella, seasoned salt, and egg, incorporating the cauliflower well with all of the other

ingredients. 6. Using your hand, mold about two tablespoons of the mixture into tots and repeat until you have used up all of the mixture. Put each tot into your Ninja Foodi Cook & Crisp Basket. They may need to be cooked in multiple batches. 7. Put on the Smart Lid on top of the Ninja Foodi Steam Fryer. 8. Move the Lid Slider to the "Air Fry/Stovetop". 9. Cook on "Air Fry" Mode at 320°F/160°C for twelve minutes, turning them halfway through. Ensure they are brown in color before serving.
Per Serving: Calories 297; Fat 1g; Sodium 291mg; Total Carbs 35g; Fiber 1g; Sugar 9g; Protein 2g

Mushroom Puff Pastry

Prep Time: 10 minutes. | Cook Time: 25 minutes. | Serves: 4

1 ½ tablespoon sesame oil
1 cup white mushrooms, sliced
2 cloves garlic, minced
1 bell pepper, seeded and chopped
¼ teaspoon salt
¼ teaspoon dried rosemary
½ teaspoon black pepper
11-ounce puff pastry sheets
½ cup crème fraiche
1 egg, well whisked
½ cup parmesan cheese, preferably freshly grated

1. Place the Cook & Crisp Basket in your Ninja Foodi Pressure Cooker Steam Fryer. 2. In a suitable skillet, heat the sesame oil over a Moderate heat and fry the mushrooms, garlic, and pepper until soft and fragrant. 3. Sprinkle on the salt, rosemary, and pepper. 4. In the meantime, unroll the puff pastry and slice it into 4-inch squares. 5. Spread the crème fraiche across each square. 6. Spoon equal amounts of the vegetables into the puff pastry squares. Enclose each square around the filling in a triangle shape, pressing the edges with your fingertips. 7. Brush each triangle with some whisked egg and cover with grated Parmesan. 8. Put on the Smart Lid on top of the Ninja Foodi Steam Fryer. 9. Move the Lid Slider to the "Air Fry/Stovetop". 10. Cook on "Air Fry" Mode at 400°F/200°C for about 22-25 minutes.
Per Serving: Calories 275; Fat 1.4g; Sodium 582mg; Total Carbs 31.5g; Fiber 1.1g; Sugar 0.1g; Protein 2.8g

Herbed Radishes

Prep Time: 10 minutes. | Cook Time: 10 minutes. | Serves: 2

1 lb. radishes
2 tablespoons unsalted butter, melted
¼ teaspoon dried oregano
½ teaspoon dried parsley
½ teaspoon garlic powder

1. Place the Cook & Crisp Basket in your Ninja Foodi Pressure Cooker Steam Fryer. 2. Prepare the radishes by cutting off their tops and bottoms and quartering them. 3. In a suitable bowl, mix the butter, dried oregano, dried parsley, and garlic powder. Toss with the radishes to coat. 4. Transfer the radishes to your Ninja Foodi Pressure Cooker Steam Fryer. 5. Put on the Smart Lid on top of the Ninja Foodi Steam Fryer. 6. Move the Lid Slider to the "Air Fry/Stovetop". 7. Cook on "Air Fry" Mode at 350°F/175°C for 10 minutes, shaking the basket at the halfway point to ensure the radishes cook evenly through. The radishes are ready when they begin to turn brown.
Per Serving: Calories 248; Fat 30g; Sodium 660mg; Total Carbs 5g; Fiber 0g; Sugar 0g; Protein 4g

Spicy Jicama Fries

Prep Time: 10 minutes. | Cook Time: 20 minutes. | Serves: 1

1 small jicama, peeled
¼ teaspoon onion powder
¾ teaspoon chili powder
¼ teaspoon garlic powder
¼ teaspoon black pepper

1. Place the Cook & Crisp Basket in your Ninja Foodi Pressure Cooker Steam Fryer. 2. To make the fries, cut the jicama into matchsticks of your desired thickness. 3. In a suitable bowl, toss them with the onion powder, chili powder, garlic powder, and black pepper to coat. Transfer the fries into the basket of your Ninja Foodi Pressure Cooker Steam Fryer. 4. Put on the Smart Lid on top of the Ninja Foodi Steam Fryer. 5. Move the Lid Slider to the "Air Fry/Stovetop". 6. Cook on "Air Fry" Mode at 350°F/175°C for twenty minutes, giving the basket an occasional shake throughout the cooking process. The fries are ready when they are hot and golden in color. Enjoy!
Per Serving: Calories 257; Fat 10.4g; Sodium 431mg; Total Carbs 20g; Fiber 0g; Sugar 1.6g; Protein 2g

Salmon Jerky

Prep Time: 10 minutes. | Cook Time: 4 hours | Serves: 2

1 lb. boneless skinless salmon
½ teaspoon liquid smoke
½ teaspoon ginger

¼ cup soy sauce
¼ teaspoon red pepper flakes

1. Place the Cook & Crisp Basket in your Ninja Foodi Pressure Cooker Steam Fryer. 2. Cut the salmon into strips about four inches long and a quarter-inch thick. 3. Put the salmon in an airtight container or bag along with the liquid smoke, ginger, soy sauce, and red pepper flakes, combining everything to coat the salmon completely. Leave the salmon in the refrigerator for at least two hours. 4. Transfer the salmon slices in the fryer, taking care not to overlap any pieces. 5. Put on the Smart Lid on top of the Ninja Foodi Steam Fryer. 6. Move the Lid Slider to the "Air Fry/Stovetop". 7. Cook on "Air Fry" Mode at 140°F/60°C for four hours. 8. Take care when removing the salmon from the fryer and leave it to cool. This jerky makes a good snack and can be stored in an airtight container.
Per Serving: Calories 399; Fat 16g; Sodium 537mg; Total Carbs 28g; Fiber 3g; Sugar 10g; Protein 5g

Carrot Leek Croquettes

Prep Time: 10 minutes. | Cook Time: 6 minutes. | Serves: 4

2 medium-sized carrots, trimmed and grated
2 medium-sized celery stalks, trimmed and grated
½ cup of leek, chopped
1 tablespoon garlic paste
¼ teaspoon freshly cracked black pepper

1 teaspoon fine salt
1 tablespoon fresh dill, chopped
1 egg, lightly whisked
¼ cup flour
¼ teaspoon baking powder
½ cup bread crumbs [seasoned or regular]
Chive mayo to serve

1. Place the Cook & Crisp Basket in your Ninja Foodi Pressure Cooker Steam Fryer. 2. Drain any excess liquid from the carrots and celery by placing them on a paper towel. 3. Stir together the vegetables with all of the other ingredients, save for the bread crumbs and chive mayo. 4. Use your hands to mold 1 tablespoon of the vegetable mixture into a ball and repeat until all of the mixture has been used up. 5. Press down on each vegetable ball with your hand. Cover completely with bread crumbs. Spritz the croquettes with a non-stick cooking spray. 6. Arrange the croquettes in a single layer in your Ninja Foodi Pressure Cooker Steam Fryer. 7. Put on the Smart Lid on top of the Ninja Foodi Steam Fryer. 8. Move the Lid Slider to the "Air Fry/Stovetop". 9. Air fry for about 6 minutes at 360°F/180°C. 10. Serve warm with the chive mayo on the side.
Per Serving: Calories 275; Fat 1.4g; Sodium 582mg; Total Carbs 31.5g; Fiber 1.1g; Sugar 0.1g; Protein 2.8g

Air-Fried Green Beans

Prep Time: 10 minutes. | Cook Time: 12 minutes. | Serves: 4

¾ lb. green beans, cleaned
1 tablespoon balsamic vinegar
¼ teaspoon kosher salt
½ teaspoon mixed peppercorns,

freshly cracked
1 tablespoon butter
Sesame seeds to serve

1. Place the Cook & Crisp Basket in your Ninja Foodi Pressure Cooker Steam Fryer. 2. Mix the green beans with the rest of the ingredients, except for the sesame seeds. Transfer to the fryer. 3. Put on the Smart Lid on top of the Ninja Foodi Steam Fryer. 4. Move the Lid Slider to the "Air Fry/Stovetop". 5. Cook on "Air Fry" Mode at 390°F/200°C for about 10 minutes. 6. In the meantime, heat the sesame seeds in a small skillet to toast all over, stirring constantly to prevent burning. 7. Serve the green beans accompanied by the toasted sesame seeds.
Per Serving: Calories 268; Fat 10.4g; Sodium 411mg; Total Carbs 0.4g; Fiber 0.1g; Sugar 0.1g; Protein 4.6

Crumbed Wax Beans

Prep Time: 10 minutes. | Cook Time: 6 minutes. | Serves: 4

½ cup flour

1 teaspoon smoky chipotle powder

½ teaspoon black pepper
1 teaspoon salt flakes
2 eggs, beaten

½ cup crushed saltines
10-ounce wax beans
Cooking spray

1. Place the Cook & Crisp Basket in your Ninja Foodi Pressure Cooker Steam Fryer. 2. Mix the flour, chipotle powder, black pepper, and salt in a suitable bowl. Put the eggs in a second bowl. Place the crushed saltines in a third bowl. 3. Wash the beans with cold water and discard any tough strings. 4. Coat the beans with the flour mixture, before dipping them into the beaten egg. Lastly cover them with the crushed saltines. 5. Spritz the beans with cooking spray. 6. Put on the Smart Lid on top of the Ninja Foodi Steam Fryer. 7. Move the Lid Slider to the "Air Fry/Stovetop". 8. Cook on "Air Fry" Mode at 360°F/180°C for about 4 minutes. Give the cooking basket a good shake and continue to cook for about 3 minutes. Serve hot.
Per Serving: Calories 346; Fat 16.1g; Sodium 882mg; Total Carbs 1.3g; Fiber 0.5g; Sugar 0.5g; Protein 4.2g

Potato Patties

Prep Time: 10 minutes. | Cook Time: 15 minutes. | Serves: 8

2 lb. white potatoes, peeled and grated
½ cup scallions, chopped
½ teaspoon black pepper
1 tablespoon fine salt

½ teaspoon hot paprika
2 cups Colby cheese, shredded
¼ cup canola oil
1 cup crushed crackers

1. Place the Cook & Crisp Basket in your Ninja Foodi Pressure Cooker Steam Fryer. 2. Boil the potatoes until soft. Dry them off and peel them before mashing thoroughly, leaving no lumps. 3. Mix the mashed potatoes with scallions, pepper, salt, paprika, and cheese. 4. Mold the mixture into balls with your hands and press with your palm to flatten them into patties. 5. In a shallow dish, mix the canola oil and crushed crackers. Coat the patties in the crumb mixture. 6. Put on the Smart Lid on top of the Ninja Foodi Steam Fryer. 7. Move the Lid Slider to the "Air Fry/Stovetop". 8. Cook the patties at 360°F/180°C on "Air Fry" Mode for about 10 minutes, in multiple batches if necessary. 9. Serve with tabasco mayo or the sauce of your choice.
Per Serving: Calories 223; Fat 11.7g; Sodium 721mg; Total Carbs 13.6g; Fiber 0.7g; Sugar 8g; Protein 5.7g

Herbed Green Beans

Prep Time: 10 minutes. | Cook Time: 5 minutes. | Serves: 1

1 tablespoon butter, melted
2 tablespoon rosemary
½ teaspoon salt

3 cloves garlic, minced
¾ cup green beans, chopped

1. Place the Cook & Crisp Basket in your Ninja Foodi Pressure Cooker Steam Fryer. 2. Mix the melted butter with the rosemary, salt, and minced garlic. Toss in the green beans, making sure to coat them well. 3. Put on the Smart Lid on top of the Ninja Foodi Steam Fryer. 4. Move the Lid Slider to the "Air Fry/Stovetop". 5. Cook in the fryer on Air Fry Mode at 390°F/200°C for five minutes.
Per Serving: Calories 275; Fat 1.4g; Sodium 582mg; Total Carbs 31.5g; Fiber 1.1g; Sugar 0.1g; Protein 9.8g

Corn Broccoli

Prep Time: 10 minutes. | Cook Time: 12 minutes. | Serves: 1

4 egg yolks
¼ cup butter, melted
2 cups coconut flower

Salt and pepper
2 cups broccoli florets

1. Place the Cook & Crisp Basket in your Ninja Foodi Pressure Cooker Steam Fryer. 2. In a suitable bowl, whisk the egg yolks and melted butter together. Throw in the coconut flour, salt and pepper, then stir again to mix well. 3. Dip each broccoli floret into the mixture and place in the fryer. 4. Put on the Smart Lid on top of the Ninja Foodi Steam Fryer. 5. Move the Lid Slider to the "Air Fry/Stovetop". 6. Cook on "Air Fry" Mode at 400°F/200°C for 6 minutes, in multiple batches if necessary. Take care when removing them from the fryer and enjoy!
Per Serving: Calories 196; Fat 7.1g; Sodium 492mg; Total Carbs 21.6g; Fiber 2.9g; Sugar 0.8g; Protein 13.4g

Corn Fritters

Prep Time: 10 minutes. | Cook Time: 11 minutes. | Serves: 4

1 carrot, grated
1 yellow onion, chopped
4 ounce canned sweet corn kernels, drained
1 teaspoon salt flakes
1 heaping tablespoon fresh cilantro, chopped
1 medium-sized egg, whisked
2 tablespoons plain milk
1 cup of Parmesan cheese, grated
¼ cup flour
⅓ teaspoon baking powder
⅓ teaspoon sugar

1. Place the Cook & Crisp Basket in your Ninja Foodi Pressure Cooker Steam Fryer. 2. Place the grated carrot in a colander and press down to squeeze out any excess moisture. Dry it with a paper towel. 3. Mix the carrots with the remaining ingredients. 4. Mold 1 tablespoon of the mixture into a ball and press it down with your hand or a spoon to flatten it. Repeat until the rest of the mixture is used up. 5. Spritz the balls with cooking spray. 6. Arrange in the basket of your Ninja Foodi Pressure Cooker Steam Fryer, taking care not to overlap any balls. 7. Put on the Smart Lid on top of the Ninja Foodi Steam Fryer. 8. Move the Lid Slider to the "Air Fry/Stovetop". 9. Cook on "Air Fry" Mode at 350°F/175°C for about 8 to 11 minutes until they're firm. 10. Serve warm.
Per Serving: Calories 209; Fat 7.5g; Sodium 321mg; Total Carbs 34.1g; Fiber 4g; Sugar 3.8g; Protein 4.3g

Turkey Potatoes

Prep Time: 10 minutes. | Cook Time: 20 minutes. | Serves: 2

3 unsmoked turkey strips
6 small potatoes
1 teaspoon garlic, minced
2 teaspoons olive oil
Salt to taste
Pepper to taste

1. Place the Cook & Crisp Basket in your Ninja Foodi Pressure Cooker Steam Fryer. 2. Peel the potatoes and cube them finely. 3. Coat in 1 teaspoon of oil. Cook in your Ninja Foodi. 4. Put on the Smart Lid on top of the Ninja Foodi Steam Fryer. 5. Move the Lid Slider to the "Air Fry/Stovetop". 6. Cook on "Air Fry" Mode for about 10 minutes at 350°F/175°C. 7. In a separate bowl, slice the turkey and mix with the garlic, oil, salt and pepper. Pour the potatoes into the bowl and mix well. 8. Lay the mixture on some silver aluminum foil, transfer to the fryer. Cook on "Air Fry" Mode for about 10 minutes. 9. Serve with raita.
Per Serving: Calories 256; Fat 16.4g; Sodium 1321mg; Total Carbs 19.2g; Fiber 2.2g; Sugar 4.2g; Protein 5.2g

Cheese Potato Gratin

Prep Time: 10 minutes. | Cook Time: 35 minutes. | Serves: 6

½ cup milk
7 medium russet potatoes, peeled
1 teaspoon black pepper
½ cup cream
½ cup semi-mature cheese, grated
½ teaspoon nutmeg

Salt, as desired.
1. Place the Cook & Crisp Basket in your Ninja Foodi Pressure Cooker Steam Fryer. 2. Cut the potatoes into wafer-thin slices. 3. In a bowl, mix the milk and cream and sprinkle with salt, pepper, and nutmeg as desired. 4. Use the milk mixture to coat the slices of potatoes. Place in Cook & Crisp Basket. Top the potatoes with the rest of the cream mixture. 5. Put the Cook & Crisp Basket into the basket of the fryer. 6. Put on the Smart Lid on top of the Ninja Foodi Steam Fryer. 7. Move the Lid Slider to the "Air Fry/Stovetop". 8. Cook on "Air Fry" Mode at 390°F/200°C for about 25 minutes. 9. Pour the cheese over the potatoes. 10. Put on the Smart Lid on top of the Ninja Foodi Steam Fryer. 11. Move the Lid Slider to the "Air Fry/Stovetop". 12. Cook on "Air Fry" Mode at 350°F/175°C for an additional 10 minutes, ensuring the top is nicely browned before serving.
Per Serving: Calories 229; Fat 1.9 |Sodium 567mg; Total Carbs 1.9g; Fiber 0.4g; Sugar 0.6g; Protein 11.8g

Ricotta Cheese Potatoes

Prep Time: 10 minutes. | Cook Time: 6 minutes. | Serves: 4

4 baking potatoes
2 tablespoons olive oil
½ cup Ricotta cheese, room temperature
2 tablespoon scallions, chopped
1 heaped tablespoon fresh parsley, chopped
1 heaped tablespoon coriander, minced
2 ounces Cheddar cheese, preferably freshly grated
1 teaspoon celery seeds
½ teaspoon salt
½ teaspoon garlic pepper

1. Place the Cook & Crisp Basket in your Ninja Foodi Pressure Cooker Steam Fryer. 2. Put the potatoes in the Ninja Foodi Cook & Crisp Basket. 3. Put on the Smart Lid on top of the Ninja Foodi Steam Fryer. 4. Move the Lid Slider to the "Air Fry/Stovetop". 5. Cook on "Air Fry" Mode for 13 minutes at 350°F/175°C. If they are not cooked through by this time, leave for about 2 – 3 minutes longer. 6. In the meantime, make the stuffing by combining all the other ingredients. 7. Cut halfway into the cooked potatoes to open them. 8. Divide equal amounts of the stuffing into each potato and serve hot.
Per Serving: Calories 353; Fat 5g; Sodium 818mg; Total Carbs 53.2g; Fiber 4.4g; Sugar 8g; Protein 1.3g

Air-Fried Brown Mushrooms

Prep Time: 10 minutes. | Cook Time: 9 minutes. | Serves: 4

1-pound brown mushrooms, quartered
2 tablespoons sesame oil
1 tablespoon tamari sauce
1 garlic clove, pressed
Sea salt and black pepper, to taste

1. Place the Cook & Crisp Basket in your Pressure Cooker Steam Fryer. 2. Toss the mushrooms with the remaining ingredients. Toss until coated on all sides. 3. Arrange the mushrooms in the Ninja Foodi Pressure Steam Fryer basket. 4. Put on the Smart Lid on top of the Ninja Foodi Steam Fryer. 5. Move the Lid Slider to the "Air Fry/Stovetop". Select the "Air Fry" mode for cooking. 6. Cook your mushrooms at 400°F/200°C for about 7 minutes, shaking the basket halfway through the cooking time. 7. Serve.
Per serving: Calories: 349; Fat: 2.9g; Sodium: 511mg; Carbs: 12g; Fiber: 3g; Sugar 8g; Protein 7g

Roasted Country-Style Vegetables

Prep Time: 10 minutes. | Cook Time: 20 minutes. | Serves: 4

1 carrot, trimmed and sliced
1 parsnip, trimmed and sliced
1 celery stalk, trimmed and sliced
1 onion, peeled and diced
2 tablespoons olive oil
Sea salt and black pepper, to taste
1 teaspoon red pepper flakes, crushed

1. Place the Cook & Crisp Basket in your Pressure Cooker Steam Fryer. 2. Toss all the recipe ingredients in the Ninja Foodi Pressure Steam Fryer basket. 3. Put on the Smart Lid on top of the Ninja Foodi Steam Fryer. 4. Move the Lid Slider to the "Air Fry/Stovetop". Select the "Air Fry" mode for cooking. 5. Cook your mushrooms at 380°F/195°C for about 15 minutes, shaking the basket halfway through the cooking time. 6. Serve.
Per serving: Calories: 281; Fat: 7.9g; Sodium: 704mg; Carbs: 6g; Fiber: 3.6g; Sugar 6g; Protein 18g

Stuffed Mushrooms

Prep Time: 10 minutes. | Cook Time: 10 minutes. | Serves: 4

6 small mushrooms
1-ounce onion, peeled and diced
1 tablespoon friendly bread crumbs
1 tablespoon olive oil
1 teaspoon garlic, pureed
1 teaspoon parsley
Salt and pepper to taste

1. Place the Cook & Crisp Basket in your Ninja Foodi Pressure Cooker Steam Fryer. 2. Mix the bread crumbs, oil, onion, parsley, salt, pepper and garlic in a bowl. Cut out the mushrooms' stalks and stuff each cap with the crumb mixture. 3. Put on the Smart Lid on top of the Ninja Foodi Steam Fryer. 4. Move the Lid Slider to the "Air Fry/Stovetop". 5. Cook in your Ninja Foodi Cook on "Air Fry" Mode for about 10 minutes at 350°F/175°C. 6. Serve with a side of mayo dip.
Per Serving: Calories 190; Fat 18g; Sodium 150mg; Total Carbs 0.6g; Fiber 0.4g; Sugar 0.4g; Protein 7.2g

Air-Fried Cheese Lings

Prep Time: 10 minutes. | Cook Time: 15 minutes. | Serves: 6

1 cup flour	1 teaspoon butter
4 small cubes cheese, grated	Salt to taste
¼ teaspoon chili powder	1 teaspoon baking powder

1. Place the Cook & Crisp Basket in your Ninja Foodi Pressure Cooker Steam Fryer. 2. Mix all the recipe ingredients to form a dough, along with a small amount water as necessary. 3. Divide the prepared cheese dough into equal portions and roll each one into a ball. 4. Put on the Smart Lid on top of the Ninja Foodi Steam Fryer. 5. Move the Lid Slider to the "Air Fry/Stovetop". 6. Transfer the balls to the fryer. Cook on "Air Fry" Mode at 360°F/180°C for about 15 minutes, stirring periodically. 7. Serve.

Per Serving: Calories 183; Fat 15g; Sodium 402mg; Total Carbs 2.5g; Fiber 0.4g; Sugar 1.1g; Protein 10g

FatPotato Bites

Prep Time: 10 minutes. | Cook Time: 15 minutes. | Serves: 2

2 medium potatoes	1 teaspoon chives
1 teaspoon butter	1 ½ tablespoon cheese, grated
3 tablespoons sour cream	Salt and pepper to taste

1. Place the Cook & Crisp Basket in your Ninja Foodi Pressure Cooker Steam Fryer. 2. Pierce the potatoes skin with a fork and boil them in water until they are cooked. 3. Transfer to your Ninja Foodi Pressure Cooker Steam Fryer. 4. Put on the Smart Lid on top of the Ninja Foodi Steam Fryer. 5. Move the Lid Slider to the "Air Fry/Stovetop". 6. Cook on "Air Fry" Mode for about 15 minutes at 350°F/175°C. 7. In the meantime, mix the sour cream, cheese and chives in a bowl. Cut the potatoes halfway to open them up and fill with the butter and toppings. 8. Serve with salad.

Per Serving: Calories 73; Fat 22g; Sodium 517mg; Total Carbs 3.3g; Fiber 0.2g; Sugar 1.4g; Protein 1.1g

Potatoes & Cheese

Prep Time: 10 minutes. | Cook Time: 23 minutes. | Serves: 4

4 medium potatoes	⅓ cup low-fat crème fraiche
1 asparagus bunch	1 tablespoon wholegrain mustard
⅓ cup cottage cheese	Salt and pepper

1. Place the Cook & Crisp Basket in your Ninja Foodi Pressure Cooker Steam Fryer. 2. Place the potatoes in the fryer and pour oil on top. 3. Put on the Smart Lid on top of the Ninja Foodi Steam Fryer. 4. Move the Lid Slider to the "Air Fry/Stovetop". 5. Cook potatoes on Air Fry Mode at 390°F/200°C for about 20 minutes. 6. Boil the asparagus in salted water for about 3 minutes. 7. Remove the potatoes and mash them with rest of ingredients. Sprinkle on salt and pepper. 8. Serve with rice.

Per Serving: Calories 102; Fat 7.6g; Sodium 545mg; Total Carbs 1.5g; Fiber 0.4g; Sugar 0.7g; Protein 7.1g

Vegetable Cheese Omelet

Prep Time: 10 minutes. | Cook Time: 13 minutes. | Serves: 2

3 tablespoons plain milk	1 green bell pepper, deveined and chopped
4 eggs, whisked	1 white onion, chopped
1 teaspoon melted butter	½ cup baby spinach leaves, chopped
Kosher salt and black pepper, to taste	½ cup Halloumi cheese, shaved
1 red bell pepper, deveined and chopped	Canola oil

1. Place the cooker's pot in your Pressure Cooker Steam Fryer and set a reversible rack inside. 2. Grease your baking pan with some canola oil. 3. Place all of the ingredients in the baking pan and stir well. Put the baking pan on the rack. 4. Transfer to the Ninja Foodi Steam Fryer. 5. Put on the Smart Lid on top of the Ninja Foodi Steam Fryer. 6. Move the Lid Slider to the "Air Fry/Stovetop". 7. Cook on "Air Fry" Mode at 350°F/175°C for about 13 minutes. 8. Serve warm.

Per Serving: Calories 282; Fat 15g; Sodium 526mg; Total Carbs 20g; Fiber 0.6g; Sugar 3.3g; Protein 16g

Scrambled Spinach Eggs

Prep Time: 10 minutes. | Cook Time: 12 minutes. | Serves: 2

2 tablespoons olive oil, melted	1 teaspoon fresh lemon juice
4 eggs, whisked	½ teaspoon coarse salt
5-ounce fresh spinach, chopped	½ teaspoon black pepper
1 medium-sized tomato, chopped	½ cup of fresh basil, chopped

1. Place the Cook & Crisp Basket in your Ninja Foodi Pressure Cooker Steam Fryer. 2. Grease your Cook & Crisp Basket with the oil, tilting it to spread the oil around. 3. Mix the remaining ingredients, apart from the basil leaves, whisking well until everything is completely mixed. 4. Place the Cook & Crisp Basket inside the Ninja Foodi Steam Fryer. 5. Put on the Smart Lid on top of the Ninja Foodi Steam Fryer. 6. Move the Lid Slider to the "Air Fry/Stovetop". 7. Cook on "Air Fry" Mode 280°F/140°C, for about 8 - 12 minutes. 8. Top with fresh basil leaves before serving with a little sour cream if desired.

Per Serving: Calories 147; Fat 1g; Sodium 518mg; Total Carbs 7g; Fiber 1.5g; Sugar 3.4g; Protein 12g

Zucchini with Sweet Potatoes

Prep Time: 10 minutes. | Cook Time: 15 minutes. | Serves: 4

2 large-sized sweet potatoes, peeled and quartered	1 ½ tablespoon maple syrup
1 medium-sized zucchini, sliced	½ teaspoon porcini powder
1 Serrano pepper, deveined and thinly sliced	¼ teaspoon mustard powder
1 bell pepper, deveined and thinly sliced	½ teaspoon fennel seeds
1 – 2 carrots, cut into matchsticks	1 tablespoon garlic powder
¼ cup olive oil	½ teaspoon fine salt
	¼ teaspoon black pepper
	Tomato ketchup to serve

1. Place the Cook & Crisp Basket in your Ninja Foodi Pressure Cooker Steam Fryer. 2. Put the sweet potatoes, zucchini, peppers, and the carrot into the basket of your Ninja Foodi Pressure Cooker Steam Fryer. Coat with a drizzling of olive oil. 3. Put on the Smart Lid on top of the Ninja Foodi Steam Fryer. 4. Move the Lid Slider to the "Air Fry/Stovetop". 5. Cook the vegetables at 350°F/175°C on "Air Fry" Mode for about 15 minutes. 6. In the meantime, prepare the sauce by vigorously combining the other ingredients, save for the tomato ketchup, with a whisk. 7. Lightly grease Cook & Crisp Basket Move the cooked vegetables to the Cook & Crisp Basket, pour over the sauce and make sure to coat the vegetables well. 8. Raise the temperature to 390°F/200°C. Cook the vegetables for an additional 5 minutes. 9. Serve warm with a side of ketchup.

Per Serving: Calories 267; Fat 12g; Sodium 165mg; Total Carbs 39g; Fiber 1.4g; Sugar 22g; Protein 3.3g

Cornbread

Prep Time: 10 minutes. | Cook Time: 1 hr. | Serves: 6

1 cup cornmeal	¼ teaspoon garlic powder
1 ½ cups flour	2 tablespoon sugar
½ teaspoon baking soda	2 eggs
½ teaspoon baking powder	¼ cup melted butter
¼ teaspoon kosher salt	1 cup buttermilk
1 teaspoon dried rosemary	½ cup corn kernels

1. Place the Cook & Crisp Basket in your Pressure Cooker Steam Fryer and set a reversible rack inside. 2. In a bowl, mix all the dry ingredients. 3. In a separate suitable bowl, mix together all the wet recipe ingredients. Mix the two bowls. 4. Fold in the corn kernels and stir vigorously. 5. Pour the batter into a lightly greased Cook & Crisp Basket. 6. Put on the Smart Lid on top of the Ninja Foodi Steam Fryer. 7. Move the Lid Slider to the "Air Fry/Stovetop". 8. Cook on "Air Fry" Mode for about 1 hour at 380°F/195°C.

Per Serving: Calories 99; Fat 11.1g; Sodium 297mg; Total Carbs 14.9g; Fiber 1g; Sugar 2.5g; Protein 9.9g

Curried Sweet Potato Fries

Prep Time: 10 minutes. | Cook Time: 25 minutes. | Serves: 4

2 lb. sweet potatoes
1 teaspoon curry powder

2 tablespoons olive oil
Salt to taste

1. Place the Cook & Crisp Basket in your Ninja Foodi Pressure Cooker Steam Fryer. 2. Wash the sweet potatoes before slicing them into matchsticks. 3. Drizzle the oil in the Cook & Crisp Basket and place inside. 4. Put on the Smart Lid on top of the Ninja Foodi Steam Fryer. 5. Move the Lid Slider to the "Air Fry/Stovetop". 6. Cook on "Air Fry" Mode at 390°F/200°C for about 25 minutes. 7. Sprinkle with curry and salt before serving with ketchup if desired.
Per Serving: Calories 122; Fat 1.8g; Sodium 794mg; Total Carbs 17g; Fiber 8.9g; Sugar 1.6g; Protein 14.9g

Roasted Bell Peppers

Prep Time: 10 minutes. | Cook Time: 15 minutes. | Serves: 3

1-pound bell peppers, seeded and halved
1 chili pepper, seeded

2 tablespoons olive oil
Salt and black pepper, to taste
1 teaspoon granulated garlic

1. Place the Cook & Crisp Basket in your Pressure Cooker Steam Fryer. 2. Toss the peppers with the remaining ingredients; place them in the cook and crisp basket. 3. Put on the Smart Lid on top of the Ninja Foodi Steam Fryer. 4. Move the Lid Slider to the "Air Fry/Stovetop". Select the "Air Fry" mode for cooking. 5. Cook the peppers at 400°F/200°C for about 15 minutes, shaking the basket halfway through the cooking time. 6. Taste, adjust the seasonings and serve at room temperature. Serve.
Per serving: Calories: 270; Fat: 10.9g; Sodium: 454mg; Carbs: 10g; Fiber: 3.1g; Sugar 5.2g; Protein 10g

Parmesan Cauliflower

Prep Time: 10 minutes. | Cook Time: 15 minutes. | Serves: 4

1-pound cauliflower florets
2 tablespoons olive oil
1 teaspoon smoked paprika

Sea salt and black pepper, to taste
4 ounces parmesan cheese, grated

1. Place the Cook & Crisp Basket in your Pressure Cooker Steam Fryer. 2. Mix the cauliflower florets with the olive oil and spices. Mix until they are well coated on all sides. 3. Arrange the cauliflower florets in the Ninja Foodi Pressure Steam Fryer basket. 4. Put on the Smart Lid on top of the Ninja Foodi Steam Fryer. 5. Move the Lid Slider to the "Air Fry/Stovetop". Select the "Air Fry" mode for cooking. 6. Cook the cauliflower florets at 400°F/200°C for about 13 minutes, shaking the basket halfway through the cooking time. 7. Toss the warm cauliflower florets with cheese. Serve.
Per serving: Calories: 295; Fat: 10.9g; Sodium: 354mg; Carbs: 20.5g; Fiber: 4.1g; Sugar 8.2g; Protein 06g

Szechuan Beans

Prep Time: 10 minutes. | Cook Time: 9 minutes. | Serves: 4

1 pound fresh green beans, trimmed
1 tablespoon sesame oil
½ teaspoon garlic powder
1 tablespoon soy sauce

Sea salt and Szechuan pepper, to taste
2 tablespoons sesame seeds, toasted

1. Place the Cook & Crisp Basket in your Pressure Cooker Steam Fryer. 2. Mix the green beans with the sesame oil and garlic powder; then, arrange them in the Ninja Foodi Pressure Steam Fryer basket. 3. Put on the Smart Lid on top of the Ninja Foodi Steam Fryer. 4. Move the Lid Slider to the "Air Fry/Stovetop". Select the "Air Fry" mode for cooking. 5. Cook the green beans at 380°F/195°C for around 7 minutes; make sure to check the green beans halfway through the cooking time. 6. Toss the green beans with the remaining recipe ingredients and stir to mix well. Enjoy!
Per serving: Calories: 334; Fat: 7.9g; Sodium: 704mg; Carbs: 6g; Fiber: 3.6g; Sugar 6g; Protein 18g

Grilled Cheese

Prep Time: 10 minutes. | Cook Time: 7 minutes. | Serves: 2

4 slices bread
½ cup sharp cheddar cheese

¼ cup butter, melted

1. Place the Cook & Crisp Basket in your Ninja Foodi Pressure Cooker Steam Fryer. 2. Put cheese and butter in separate bowls. 3. Apply the butter to each side of the bread slices with a brush. 4. Spread the cheese across two of the slices of bread and make two sandwiches. Transfer both to the fryer. 5. Put on the Smart Lid on top of the Ninja Foodi Steam Fryer. 6. Move the Lid Slider to the "Air Fry/Stovetop". 7. Cook on "Air Fry" Mode at 360°F/180°C for about 5 – 7 minutes until a golden brown color is achieved and the cheese is melted.
Per Serving: Calories 180; Fat 3.2g; Sodium 133mg; Total Carbs 32g; Fiber 1.1g; Sugar 1.8g; Protein 9g

Spicy Potatoes

Prep Time: 10 minutes. | Cook Time: 20 minutes. | Serves: 4

1 pound potatoes, diced into bite-sized chunks
1 tablespoon olive oil

Sea salt and black pepper, to taste
1 teaspoon chili powder

1. Place the Cook & Crisp Basket in your Pressure Cooker Steam Fryer. 2. Toss the potatoes with the remaining recipe ingredients until well coated on all sides. 3. Arrange the potatoes in the Ninja Foodi Pressure Steam Fryer basket. 4. Put on the Smart Lid on top of the Ninja Foodi Steam Fryer. 5. Move the Lid Slider to the "Air Fry/Stovetop". Select the "Air Fry" mode for cooking. 6. Cook the potatoes at 400°F/200°C for about 13 minutes, shaking the basket halfway through the cooking time. 7. Serve.
Per serving: Calories: 289; Fat: 14g; Sodium: 791mg; Carbs: 18.9g; Fiber: 4.6g; Sugar 8g; Protein 6g

Air-Fried Vegetables

Prep Time: 10 minutes. | Cook Time: 20 minutes. | Serves: 6

1 ⅓ cup small parsnips
1 ⅓ cup celery
2 red onions
1 ⅓ cup small butternut squash

1 tablespoon fresh thyme needles
1 tablespoon olive oil
Salt and pepper to taste

1. Place the Cook & Crisp Basket in your Ninja Foodi Pressure Cooker Steam Fryer. 2. Peel the parsnips and onions and cut them into 2-cm cubes. Slice the onions into wedges. 3. Do not peel the butternut squash. Cut it in half, deseed it, and cube. 4. Mix the cut vegetables with the thyme, olive oil, salt and pepper. 5. Put the vegetables in the Cook & Crisp Basket and transfer to your Ninja Foodi Pressure Cooker Steam Fryer. 6. Put on the Smart Lid on top of the Ninja Foodi Steam Fryer. 7. Move the Lid Slider to the "Air Fry/Stovetop". 8. Cook on "Air Fry" Mode at 390°F/200°C for about 20 minutes, stirring once throughout the cooking time, until the vegetables are nicely browned. Cooked through.
Per Serving: Calories 185; Fat 11g; Sodium 355mg; Total Carbs 21g; Fiber 5.8g; Sugar 3g; Protein 4.7g

Roasted Broccoli

Prep Time: 10 minutes. | Cook Time: 8 minutes. | Serves: 3

¾-pound broccoli florets
1 ½ tablespoons olive oil
1 teaspoon garlic powder
½ teaspoon onion powder

½ teaspoon mustard seeds
Sea salt and black pepper, to taste
2 tablespoons pepitas, roasted

1. Place the Cook & Crisp Basket in your Pressure Cooker Steam Fryer. 2. Toss the broccoli florets with the olive oil, garlic powder, onion powder, mustard seeds, salt, and black pepper. 3. Put on the Smart Lid on top of the Ninja Foodi Steam Fryer. 4. Move the Lid Slider to the "Air Fry/Stovetop". Select the "Air Fry" mode for cooking. 5. Cook the broccoli florets at 395°F/200°C for around 6 minutes, shaking the basket halfway through the cooking time. 6. Top with roasted pepitas and serve warm. Serve.
Per serving: Calories: 334; Fat: 7.9g; Sodium: 704mg; Carbs: 6g; Fiber: 3.6g; Sugar 6g; Protein 18g

Crispy Sweet Potatoes

Prep Time: 10 minutes. | Cook Time: 40 minutes. | Serves: 4

1 pound sweet potatoes, scrubbed and halved
3 tablespoons olive oil
1 teaspoon paprika
Sea salt and black pepper, to taste

1. Place the Cook & Crisp Basket in your Pressure Cooker Steam Fryer. 2. Toss the halved sweet potatoes with the olive oil, paprika, salt, and black pepper. 3. Put on the Smart Lid on top of the Ninja Foodi Steam Fryer. 4. Move the Lid Slider to the "Air Fry/Stovetop". Select the "Air Fry" mode for cooking. 5. Cook the sweet potatoes at 380°F/195°C for around 35 minutes, shaking the basket halfway through the cooking time. 6. Taste and adjust the seasonings. Serve.
Per serving: Calories: 372; Fat: 20g; Sodium: 891mg; Carbs: 29g; Fiber: 3g; Sugar 8g; Protein 7g

Green Beans Salad

Prep Time: 10 minutes. | Cook Time: 10 minutes. | Serves: 3

¾ pound fresh green beans, washed and trimmed
2 tablespoons olive oil
½ cup green onions, sliced
2 cups baby spinach
1 tablespoon fresh basil, chopped
1 green pepper, sliced
2 tablespoons fresh lemon juice
Sea salt and black pepper, to taste

1. Place the Cook & Crisp Basket in your Pressure Cooker Steam Fryer. 2. Toss the green beans with 1 tablespoon of the olive oil. Arrange the green beans in the Ninja Foodi Pressure Steam Fryer basket. 3. Put on the Smart Lid on top of the Ninja Foodi Steam Fryer. 4. Move the Lid Slider to the "Air Fry/Stovetop". Select the "Air Fry" mode for cooking. 5. Cook the green beans at 375°F/190°C for around 7 minutes; make sure to check the green beans halfway through the cooking time. 6. Add the green beans to a salad bowl; add in the remaining recipe ingredients and stir to mix well. Enjoy!
Per serving: Calories: 312; Fat: 19g; Sodium: 354mg; Carbs: 15g; Fiber: 5.1g; Sugar 8.2g; Protein 12g

Corn on The Cob

Prep Time: 10 minutes. | Cook Time: 10 minutes. | Serves: 2

2 ears of corn, husked and halved
2 tablespoons Chinese chili oil
Sea salt and red pepper, to taste
2 tablespoons fresh cilantro, chopped

1. Place the Cook & Crisp Basket in your Pressure Cooker Steam Fryer. 2. Toss the ears of corn with the oil, salt, and red pepper. Arrange the ears of corn in the Cook and crisp basket. 3. Put on the Smart Lid on top of the Ninja Foodi Steam Fryer. 4. Move the Lid Slider to the "Air Fry/Stovetop". Select the "Air Fry" mode for cooking. 5. Cook the ears of Corn at 390°F/200°C for about 6 minutes, tossing them halfway through the cooking time. 6. Garnish the ears of Corn with the fresh cilantro. Serve.
Per serving: Calories: 382; Fat: 7.9g; Sodium: 704mg; Carbs: 6g; Fiber: 3.6g; Sugar 6g; Protein 38g

Air-Fried Brussels Sprouts

Prep Time: 10 minutes. | Cook Time: 15 minutes. | Serves: 3

¾ pound Brussels sprouts, trimmed
1 tablespoon butter, melted
1 teaspoon red pepper flakes,
crushed
Salt and black pepper, to taste

1. Place the Cook & Crisp Basket in your Pressure Cooker Steam Fryer. 2. Toss the trimmed Brussels sprouts with the butter and spices until they are well coated on all sides; then, arrange the Brussels sprouts in the Ninja Foodi Pressure Steam Fryer basket. 3. Put on the Smart Lid on top of the Ninja Foodi Steam Fryer. 4. Move the Lid Slider to the "Air Fry/Stovetop". Select the "Air Fry" mode for cooking. 5. Cook the Brussels sprouts at 380°F/195°C for around 10 minutes, shaking the basket halfway through the cooking time. 6. Serve warm and enjoy!
Per serving: Calories: 184; Fat: 5g; Sodium: 441mg; Carbs: 17g; Fiber: 4.6g; Sugar 5g; Protein 9g

Crusted Eggplant

Prep Time: 10 minutes. | Cook Time: 13 minutes. | Serves: 3

Salt and black pepper, to taste
½ cup all-purpose flour
2 eggs
¾-pound eggplant, sliced
½ cup bread crumbs

1. Place the Cook & Crisp Basket in your Pressure Cooker Steam Fryer. 2. In a shallow bowl, mix the salt, black pepper, and flour. Mix the eggs in the second bowl, and place the breadcrumbs in the third bowl. 3. Dip the eggplant slices in the flour mixture, then in the whisked eggs; finally, roll the eggplant slices over the breadcrumbs until they are well coated on all sides. 4. Arrange the eggplant in the Ninja Foodi Pressure Steam Fryer basket. 5. Put on the Smart Lid on top of the Ninja Foodi Steam Fryer. 6. Move the Lid Slider to the "Air Fry/Stovetop". Select the "Air Fry" mode for cooking. 7. Cook the eggplant at 400°F/200°C for about 13 minutes, shaking the basket halfway through the cooking time. 8. Serve.
Per serving: Calories: 219; Fat: 10g; Sodium: 891mg; Carbs: 22.9g; Fiber: 4g; Sugar 4g; Protein 13g

Cayenne Parsnip Burgers

Prep Time: 10 minutes. | Cook Time: 20 minutes. | Serves: 3

¾ pound peeled parsnips, shredded
¼ cup all-purpose flour
¼ cup corn flour
1 egg, beaten
1 teaspoon cayenne pepper
Sea salt and black pepper, to taste

1. Place the Cook & Crisp Basket in your Pressure Cooker Steam Fryer. 2. Mix all the recipe ingredients until everything is well mixed. Form the mixture into three patties. 3. Put on the Smart Lid on top of the Ninja Foodi Steam Fryer. 4. Move the Lid Slider to the "Air Fry/Stovetop". Select the "Air Fry" mode for cooking. 5. Cook the burgers at 380°F/195°C for about 15 minutes or until cooked through. Serve.
Per serving: Calories: 184; Fat: 5g; Sodium: 441mg; Carbs: 17g; Fiber: 4.6g; Sugar 5g; Protein 9g

Parsnips Meal

Prep Time: 10 minutes. | Cook Time: 10 minutes. | Serves: 4

1 pound parsnips, trimmed
1 tablespoon olive oil
1 teaspoon Herbs de province
1 teaspoon cayenne pepper
Sea salt and black pepper, to taste

1. Place the Cook & Crisp Basket in your Pressure Cooker Steam Fryer. 2. Toss the parsnip with the olive oil and spices until they are well coated on all sides; then, arrange the parsnip in the Ninja Foodi Pressure Steam Fryer basket. 3. Put on the Smart Lid on top of the Ninja Foodi Steam Fryer. 4. Move the Lid Slider to the "Air Fry/Stovetop". Select the "Air Fry" mode for cooking. 5. Cook the parsnip at 380°F/195°C for around 10 minutes, shaking the basket halfway through the cooking time. 6. Serve.
Per serving: Calories: 282; Fat: 7.9g; Sodium: 704mg; Carbs: 6g; Fiber: 3.6g; Sugar 6g; Protein 18g

Crusted Portobello Mushrooms

Prep Time: 10 minutes. | Cook Time: 10 minutes. | Serves: 3

½ cup flour
2 eggs
1 cup seasoned breadcrumbs
1 teaspoon smoked paprika
Sea salt and black pepper, to taste
¾ pound Portobello mushrooms, sliced

1. Place the Cook & Crisp Basket in your Pressure Cooker Steam Fryer. 2. Place the flour in a plate. Mix the eggs in a shallow bowl. In a third bowl, whisk the breadcrumbs, paprika, salt, and black pepper. 3. Dip your mushrooms in the flour, then dunk them in the whisked eggs, and finally toss them in the breadcrumb mixture. Toss until well coated on all sides. 4. Put on the Smart Lid on top of the Ninja Foodi Steam Fryer. 5. Move the Lid Slider to the "Air Fry/Stovetop". Select the "Air Fry" mode for cooking. 6. Cook the mushrooms at 400°F/200°C for about 7 minutes, turning them halfway through the cooking time. 7. Serve.
Per serving: Calories: 221; Fat: 12.9g; Sodium: 414mg; Carbs: 11g; Fiber: 5g; Sugar 9g; Protein 11g

Cheese Stuffed Peppers

Prep Time: 10 minutes. | Cook Time: 13 minutes. | Serves: 3

3 bell peppers, seeded and halved
1 tablespoon olive oil
1 small onion, chopped
2 garlic cloves, minced
Sea salt and black pepper, to taste
1 cup tomato sauce
2 ounces cheddar cheese, shredded

1. Place the Cook & Crisp Basket in your Pressure Cooker Steam Fryer. 2. Toss the peppers with the oil; place them in the cook and crisp basket. 3. Mix the onion, garlic, salt, black pepper, and tomato sauce. Spoon the sauce into the pepper halves. 4. Put on the Smart Lid on top of the Ninja Foodi Steam Fryer. 5. Move the Lid Slider to the "Air Fry/Stovetop". Select the "Air Fry" mode for cooking. 6. Cook the peppers at 400°F/200°C for about 10 minutes. Top the peppers with the cheese. Continue to cook for around 5 minutes more. 7. Serve.
Per serving: Calories: 289; Fat: 14g; Sodium: 791mg; Carbs: 18.9g; Fiber: 4.6g; Sugar 8g; Protein 6g

Garlicky Roasted Cauliflower

Prep Time: 10 minutes. | Cook Time: 20 minutes. | Serves: 2

1 medium head cauliflower
2 tablespoon salted butter, melted
1 medium lemon
1 teaspoon dried parsley
½ teaspoon garlic powder

1. Place the Cook & Crisp Basket in your Pressure Cooker Steam Fryer. 2. Having removed the leaves from the cauliflower head, brush it with the melted butter. Grate the rind of the lemon over it and then drizzle some juice. Finally add the parsley and garlic powder on top. 3. Transfer the cauliflower to the basket of the Pressure Cooker Steam Fryer . 4. Put on the Smart Lid on top of the Ninja Foodi Steam Fryer. 5. Move the Lid Slider to the "Air Fry/Stovetop". Select the "Air Fry" mode for cooking. 6. Cook for fifteen minutes at 350°F/175°C, checking regularly to ensure it doesn't overcook. The cauliflower is ready when it is hot and fork tender. 7. Take care when removing it from the fryer, cut up and serve.
Per serving: Calories: 219; Fat: 10g; Sodium: 891mg; Carbs: 22.9g; Fiber: 4g; Sugar 4g; Protein 13g

Cheese Broccoli Pizza

Prep Time: 10 minutes. | Cook Time: 30 minutes. | Serves: 1

3 cups broccoli rice, steamed
½ cup parmesan cheese, grated
1 egg
3 tablespoon low-carb Alfredo sauce
½ cup mozzarella cheese, grated

1. Place the Cook & Crisp Basket in your Pressure Cooker Steam Fryer. 2. Drain the broccoli rice and mix with the parmesan cheese and egg in a suitable bowl, mixing well. 3. Cut a piece of parchment paper the size of the base of the basket. Using a spoon, place four equal-sized amounts of the broccoli mixture on the paper. And press each part into the shape of a pizza crust. You may have to complete this part in two batches. Transfer the parchment to the Cook & Crisp Basket . 4. Put on the Smart Lid on top of the Ninja Foodi Steam Fryer. 5. Move the Lid Slider to the "Air Fry/Stovetop". Select the "Air Fry" mode for cooking. 6. Air Fry broccoli at 370°F/185°C. Cook for 5 minutes. When the crust is firm, flip over. Cook for an additional 2 minutes. 7. Pour the sauce and mozzarella cheese on top of the crusts. Cook for an additional 7 minutes until the sauce and cheese melt. Serve hot.
Per serving: Calories: 295; Fat: 12.9g; Sodium: 414mg; Carbs: 11g; Fiber: 5g; Sugar 9g; Protein 11g

Artichoke Stuffed Eggplant

Prep Time: 10 minutes. | Cook Time: 35 minutes. | Serves: 2

1 large eggplant
¼ medium yellow onion, diced
2 tablespoons red bell pepper, diced
1 cup spinach
¼ cup artichoke hearts, chopped
Cooking spray

1. Place the Cook & Crisp Basket in your Pressure Cooker Steam Fryer. 2. Slice the eggplant lengthwise and scoop out the flesh with a spoon, leaving a shell about a half-inch thick. Chop it up and set aside. 3. Set a suitable skillet over a suitable heat and spritz with cooking spray. Cook the onions for about 3 to 5 minutes to soften. Then add the pepper, spinach, artichokes, and the flesh of eggplant. Fry for a further 5 minutes, then remove from the heat. 4. Scoop this mixture in equal parts into the eggplant shells and place each one in the basket. 5. Put on the Smart Lid on top of the Ninja Foodi Steam Fryer. 6. Move the Lid Slider to the "Air Fry/Stovetop". Select the "Air Fry" mode for cooking. 7. Cook for 20 minutes at 320°F/160°C until the eggplant shells are soft. Serve warm.
Per serving: Calories: 122; Fat: 7.9g; Sodium: 704mg; Carbs: 6g; Fiber: 3.6g; Sugar 6g; Protein 18g

Broccoli Cranberry Salad

Prep Time: 10 minutes. | Cook Time: 8 minutes. | Serves: 3

¾-pound broccoli florets
¼ cup raw sunflower seeds
1 clove garlic, peeled and minced
1 small red onion, sliced
¼ cup dried cranberries
¼ cup extra-virgin olive oil
2 tablespoons fresh lemon juice
1 tablespoon Dijon mustard
Sea salt and black pepper, to taste

1. Place the Cook & Crisp Basket in your Pressure Cooker Steam Fryer. 2. Place the broccoli florets in the greased "cook & crisp basket". 3. Put on the Smart Lid on top of the Ninja Foodi Steam Fryer. 4. Move the Lid Slider to the "Air Fry/Stovetop". Select the "Air Fry" mode for cooking. 5. Cook the broccoli florets at 395°F/200°C for around 6 minutes, shaking the basket halfway through the cooking time. 6. Toss the broccoli florets with the remaining ingredients. Serve at room temperature. 7. Serve.
Per serving: Calories: 122; Fat: 7.9g; Sodium: 704mg; Carbs: 6g; Fiber: 3.6g; Sugar 6g; Protein 18g

Horseradish Gorgonzola Mushrooms

Prep Time: 10 minutes. | Cook Time: 12 minutes. | Serves: 5

½ cup of bread crumbs
2 cloves garlic, pressed
2 tablespoons fresh coriander, chopped
⅓ teaspoon kosher salt
½ teaspoon crushed red pepper flakes
1 ½ tablespoon olive oil
20 medium-sized mushrooms, stems removed
½ cup Gorgonzola cheese, grated
¼ cup low-fat mayo
1 teaspoon prepared horseradish, well-drained
1 tablespoon fresh parsley, chopped

1. Place the Cook & Crisp Basket in your Pressure Cooker Steam Fryer and set a reversible rack inside. 2. Mix the bread crumbs together with the garlic, coriander, salt, red pepper, and the olive oil. 3. Take equal-sized amounts of the bread crumb mixture and use them to stuff the mushroom caps. Add the grated Gorgonzola on top of each. 4. Put the mushrooms in the Cook & Crisp Basket and transfer to the cook. 5. Put on the Smart Lid on top of the Ninja Foodi Steam Fryer. 6. Move the Lid Slider to the "Air Fry/Stovetop". 7. Grill them at 380°F/195°C on "Air Fry" Mode for about 8-12 minutes, ensuring the stuffing is warm throughout. 8. In the meantime, prepare the horseradish and mayo. Mix together the mayo, horseradish and parsley. 9. When the mushrooms are ready, serve with the mayo.
Per Serving: Calories 220; Fat 13g; Sodium 542mg; Total Carbs 0.9g; Fiber 0.3g; Sugar 0.2g; Protein 5.6g

Sesame Carrots

Prep Time: 10 minutes. | Cook Time: 20 minutes. | Serves: 3

¾ pound carrots, trimmed and cut into sticks
2 tablespoons butter, melted
Salt and white pepper, to taste
1 tablespoon sesame seeds, toasted

1. Place the Cook & Crisp Basket in your Pressure Cooker Steam Fryer. 2. Toss the carrots with the butter, salt, and white pepper; then, arrange them in the Ninja Foodi Pressure Steam Fryer basket. 3. Put on the Smart Lid on top of the Ninja Foodi Steam Fryer. 4. Move the Lid Slider to the "Air Fry/Stovetop". Select the "Air Fry" mode for cooking. 5. Cook the carrots at 380°F/195°C for around 15 minutes; make sure to check the carrots halfway through the cooking time. 6. Top the carrots with the sesame seeds. Serve.
Per serving: Calories: 382; Fat: 7.9g; Sodium: 704mg; Carbs: 6g; Fiber: 3.6g; Sugar 6g; Protein 18g

Crispy Parmesan Artichokes

Prep Time: 10 minutes. | Cook Time: 35 minutes. | Serves: 4

2 medium artichokes, with the centers removed	1 egg, beaten
2 tablespoon coconut oil, melted	½ cup parmesan cheese, grated
	¼ cup blanched, finely flour

1. Place the Cook & Crisp Basket in your Pressure Cooker Steam Fryer. 2. Place the artichokes in a suitable bowl with the coconut oil and stir well, then dip the artichokes into a suitable bowl of beaten egg. 3. In another bowl, mix the parmesan cheese and the flour. Mix with artichoke, making 4. sure to coat each piece well. Transfer the artichoke to the basket. 5. Put on the Smart Lid on top of the Ninja Foodi Steam Fryer. 6. Move the Lid Slider to the "Air Fry/Stovetop". Select the "Air Fry" mode for cooking. 7. Air Fry artichoke at 400°F/200°C. Cook for 10 minutes, shaking occasionally throughout the cooking time. Serve hot.
Per serving: Calories: 372; Fat: 20g; Sodium: 891mg; Carbs: 29g; Fiber: 3g; Sugar 8g; Protein 7g

Parmesan Green Bean Casserole

Prep Time: 10 minutes. | Cook Time: 10 minutes. | Serves: 2

1 tablespoon butter, melted	7 ounces parmesan cheese, shredded
1 cup green beans	
6 ounces cheddar cheese, shredded	¼ cup heavy cream

1. Place the Cook & Crisp Basket in your Pressure Cooker Steam Fryer. 2. Cover the Cook & Crisp Basket with melted butter. Throw in the green beans, cheddar cheese, and any seasoning as desired, then give it a stir. Add the parmesan on top and finally the heavy cream. 3. Put on the Smart Lid on top of the Ninja Foodi Steam Fryer. 4. Move the Lid Slider to the "Air Fry/Stovetop". Select the "Air Fry" mode for cooking. 5. Adjust the cooking temperature to 400°F/200°C. 6. Cook for 6 minutes. Allow to cool before serving.
Per serving: Calories: 184; Fat: 5g; Sodium: 441mg; Carbs: 17g; Fiber: 4.6g; Sugar 5g; Protein 9g

Paprika Cabbage Steaks

Prep Time: 10 minutes. | Cook Time: 5 minutes. | Serves: 2

1 small head cabbage	1 teaspoon paprika
1 teaspoon butter, butter	1 teaspoon olive oil

1. Place the Cook & Crisp Basket in your Pressure Cooker Steam Fryer. 2. Halve the cabbage. 3. In a suitable bowl, mix the melted butter, paprika, and olive oil. Massage into the cabbage slices, making sure to coat it well. Season as desired with black pepper and salt or any other seasonings of your choosing. 4. Put the cabbage in the Cook & Crisp Basket . Put on the Smart Lid on top of the Ninja Foodi Steam Fryer. Move the Lid Slider to the "Air Fry/Stovetop". Select the "Air Fry" mode for cooking. 5. Adjust the cooking temperature to 400°F/200°C. 6. and cook for 3 minutes. Flip it. Cook for on the other side for another 2 minutes. Enjoy!
Per serving: Calories: 314; Fat: 7.9g; Sodium: 704mg; Carbs: 6g; Fiber: 3.6g; Sugar 6g; Protein 18g

Broccoli with Parmesan

Prep Time: 5 minutes. | Cook Time: 4 minutes. | Serves: 4

1-pound broccoli florets	¼ cup grated or shaved Parmesan cheese
2 teaspoons minced garlic	
2 tablespoons olive oil	

1. Place the Cook & Crisp Basket in your Pressure Cooker Steam Fryer. 2. In a suitable mixing bowl, mix the broccoli florets, garlic, olive oil, and Parmesan cheese. 3. Place the broccoli in the Ninja Foodi Pressure Steam Fryer basket in a single layer. 4. Put on the Smart Lid on top of the Ninja Foodi Steam Fryer. 5. Move the Lid Slider to the "Air Fry/Stovetop". Select the "Air Fry" mode for cooking. 6. Adjust the cooking temperature to 360°F/180°C. 7. Set the timer and steam for around 4 minutes.
Per serving: Calories: 219; Fat: 10g; Sodium: 891mg; Carbs: 22.9g; Fiber: 4g; Sugar 4g; Protein 13g

Roasted Corn

Prep Time: 5 minutes. | Cook Time: 10 minutes. | Serves: 4

1 tablespoon vegetable oil	Unsalted butter, for topping
4 ears of corn, husks and silk removed	Salt, for topping
	Black pepper, for topping

1. Place the Cook & Crisp Basket in your Pressure Cooker Steam Fryer. 2. Rub the vegetable oil onto the corn, coating it thoroughly. 3. Adjust the Ninja Foodi Pressure Steam Fryer temperature to 400°F/200°C. Set the timer. Put on the Smart Lid on top of the Ninja Foodi Steam Fryer. Move the Lid Slider to the "Air Fry/Stovetop". Select the "Air Fry" mode for cooking. Cook the corn at 400°F/200°C for around 5 minutes. 4. Using tongs, flip or rotate the Corn. 5. Reset the timer. Air Fry for around 5 minutes more. 6. Serve with a pat of butter and a generous sprinkle of black pepper and salt.
Per serving: Calories: 282; Fat: 12.9g; Sodium: 414mg; Carbs: 11g; Fiber: 5g; Sugar 9g; Protein 11g

Parmesan Zucchini Gratin

Prep Time: 10 minutes. | Cook Time: 15 minutes. | Serves: 2

5 ounces parmesan cheese, shredded	1 tablespoon dried parsley
	2 zucchinis
1 tablespoon coconut flour	1 teaspoon butter, melted

1. Place the Cook & Crisp Basket in your Pressure Cooker Steam Fryer. 2. Mix the parmesan and coconut flour in a suitable bowl, seasoning with parsley to taste. 3. Cut the zucchini in half lengthwise and chop the halves into four slices. 4. Pour the melted butter over the zucchini and then dip the zucchini into the parmesan-flour mixture, coating it all over. 5. Put on the Smart Lid on top of the Ninja Foodi Steam Fryer. 6. Move the Lid Slider to the "Air Fry/Stovetop". Select the "Air Fry" mode for cooking. 7. Adjust the cooking temperature to 400°F/200°C. 8. Cook the zucchini for 13 minutes.
Per serving: Calories: 382; Fat: 10.9g; Sodium: 354mg; Carbs: 20.5g; Fiber: 4.1g; Sugar 8.2g; Protein 06g

Parmesan Kale

Prep Time: 10 minutes. | Cook Time: 15 minutes. | Serves: 2

1 lb. kale	1 onion, diced
8 ounces parmesan cheese, shredded	1 teaspoon butter
	1 cup heavy cream

1. Place the deluxe reversible rack in your Pressure Cooker Steam Fryer. 2. Dice up the kale, discarding any hard stems. In a suitable baking dish small enough to fit inside the Pressure Cooker Steam Fryer, mix the kale with the parmesan, onion, butter and cream. 3. Put the baking dish on the rack . Put on the Smart Lid on top of the Ninja Foodi Steam Fryer. Move the Lid Slider to the "Air Fry/Stovetop". Select the "Air Fry" mode for cooking. Adjust the cooking temperature to 250°F/120°C. 4. Cook for 12 minutes. Make sure to give it a good stir before serving.
Per serving: Calories: 372; Fat: 20g; Sodium: 891mg; Carbs: 29g; Fiber: 3g; Sugar 8g; Protein 7g

Lemony Broccoli Salad

Prep Time: 10 minutes. | Cook Time: 15 minutes. | Serves: 2

3 cups fresh broccoli florets	¼ cup sliced scallion
2 tablespoon coconut oil, melted	½ medium lemon, juiced

1. Place the Cook & Crisp Basket in your Pressure Cooker Steam Fryer. 2. Fill the broccoli florets on the Cook & Crisp Basket. Pour the melted coconut oil over the broccoli and add in the sliced scallion. Toss together. Put the basket in the Ninja Foodi Pressure Steam Fryer. 3. Put on the Smart Lid on top of the Ninja Foodi Steam Fryer. 4. Move the Lid Slider to the "Air Fry/Stovetop". Select the "Air Fry" mode for cooking. 5. Air Fry at 380°F/195°C for 7 minutes, stirring at the halfway point. 6. Place the broccoli in a suitable bowl and drizzle the lemon juice over it.
Per serving: Calories: 221; Fat: 19g; Sodium: 354mg; Carbs: 15g; Fiber: 5.1g; Sugar 8.2g; Protein 12g

Creamy Spaghetti Squash

Prep Time: 10 minutes. | Cook Time: 45 minutes. | Serves: 2

1 spaghetti squash
1 teaspoon olive oil
Salt and black pepper, to taste
4 tablespoons heavy cream
1 teaspoon butter
Black pepper and salt, to taste

1. Place the Cook & Crisp Basket in your Pressure Cooker Steam Fryer. 2. Cut and de-seed the spaghetti squash. Brush with the olive oil and season with black pepper and salt to taste. 3. Put the squash inside the Cook & Crisp Basket, placing it cut-side-down. 4. Put on the Smart Lid on top of the Ninja Foodi Steam Fryer. 5. Move the Lid Slider to the "Air Fry/Stovetop". Select the "Air Fry" mode for cooking. 6. Adjust the cooking temperature to 360°F/180°C. 7. Cook for 30 minutes. Halfway through cooking, fluff the spaghetti inside the squash with a fork. 8. When the squash is ready, fluff the spaghetti some more, then pour some heavy cream and butter over it and give it a good stir. Serve with the low-carb tomato sauce of your choice.
Per serving: Calories: 349; Fat: 2.9g; Sodium: 511mg; Carbs: 12g; Fiber: 3g; Sugar 8g; Protein 7g

Roasted Garlic Asparagus

Prep Time: 5 minutes. | Cook Time: 10 minutes. | Serves: 4

1-pound asparagus
2 tablespoons olive oil
1 tablespoon balsamic vinegar
2 teaspoons minced garlic
Salt
Black pepper

1. Place the Cook & Crisp Basket in your Pressure Cooker Steam Fryer. 2. Cut or snap off the white end of the asparagus. 3. In a suitable bowl, mix the asparagus, olive oil, vinegar, garlic, salt, and pepper. 4. Using your hands, gently mix all the recipe ingredients together, making sure that the asparagus is coated. 5. Lay out the asparagus in the Ninja Foodi Pressure Steam Fryer basket. 6. Put on the Smart Lid on top of the Ninja Foodi Steam Fryer. 7. Move the Lid Slider to the "Air Fry/Stovetop". Select the "Air Fry" mode for cooking. 8. Adjust the air fryer temperature to 400°F/200°C. Set the timer and cook for around 5 minutes. 9. Using tongs, flip the asparagus. 10. Reset the timer and cook for around 5 minutes more.
Per serving: Calories: 172; Fat: 20g; Sodium: 191mg; Carbs: 9g; Fiber: 3g; Sugar 8g; Protein 7g

Parmesan Potatoes

Prep Time: 10 minutes. | Cook Time: 20 minutes. | Serves: 3

¾ pound potatoes, diced
1 tablespoon olive oil
1 teaspoon smoked paprika
1 teaspoon red pepper flakes,
crushed
Sea salt and black pepper, to taste
2 ounces parmesan cheese, grated

1. Place the Cook & Crisp Basket in your Pressure Cooker Steam Fryer. 2. Mix the potatoes with the olive oil and spices until well coated on all sides. 3. Arrange the potatoes in the Ninja Foodi Pressure Steam Fryer basket. 4. Put on the Smart Lid on top of the Ninja Foodi Steam Fryer. 5. Move the Lid Slider to the "Air Fry/Stovetop". Select the "Air Fry" mode for cooking. 6. Cook the potatoes at 400°F/200°C for about 15 minutes, shaking the basket halfway through the cooking time. 7. Top the warm potatoes with cheese and serve immediately. Enjoy!
Per serving: Calories: 361; Fat: 10.9g; Sodium: 454mg; Carbs: 10g; Fiber: 3.1g; Sugar 5.2g; Protein 10g

Lemony Brussels Sprout Salad

Prep Time: 10 minutes. | Cook Time: 12 minutes. | Serves: 3

¾ pound Brussels sprouts, trimmed
2 tablespoons olive oil
Sea salt and black pepper, to taste
½ teaspoon dried dill weed
1 tablespoon fresh lemon juice
1 tablespoon rice vinegar

1. Place the Cook & Crisp Basket in your Pressure Cooker Steam Fryer. 2. Mix the Brussels sprouts with the oil and spices until they are well coated on all sides; then, arrange the Brussels sprouts in the Ninja Foodi Pressure Steam Fryer basket. 3. Put on the Smart Lid on

top of the Ninja Foodi Steam Fryer. 4. Move the Lid Slider to the "Air Fry/Stovetop". Select the "Air Fry" mode for cooking. 5. Cook the Brussels sprouts at 380°F/195°C for around 10 minutes, shaking the basket halfway through the cooking time. 6. Mix the Brussels sprouts with lemon juice and vinegar. Enjoy!
Per serving: Calories: 184; Fat: 5g; Sodium: 441mg; Carbs: 17g; Fiber: 4.6g; Sugar 5g; Protein 9g

Honey Carrots

Prep Time: 5 minutes. | Cook Time: 12 minutes. | Serves: 4

3 cups baby carrots
1 tablespoon extra-virgin olive oil
1 tablespoon honey
Salt
Black pepper
Fresh dill

1. Place the Cook & Crisp Basket in your Pressure Cooker Steam Fryer. 2. In a suitable bowl, mix the carrots, olive oil, honey, salt, and pepper. Make sure that the carrots are coated with oil. 3. Place the carrots in the Ninja Foodi Pressure Steam Fryer basket. 4. Put on the Smart Lid on top of the Ninja Foodi Steam Fryer. 5. Move the Lid Slider to the "Air Fry/Stovetop". Select the "Air Fry" mode for cooking. 6. Adjust the Ninja Foodi Pressure Steam Fryer temperature to 390°F/200°C. Set the timer and cook for around 12 minutes, or until fork-tender. 7. Pour the carrots into a suitable bowl, sprinkle with dill, if desired, and serve.
Per serving: Calories: 80; Fat: 14g; Sodium: 101mg; Carbs: 8.9g; Fiber: 4.6g; Sugar 8g; Protein 6g

Fried Cabbage

Prep time: 5 minutes. | Cook Time: 7 minutes. | Serves: 4

1 head cabbage, sliced in 1-inch-thick ribbons
1 tablespoon olive oil
1 teaspoon salt
1 teaspoon black pepper
1 teaspoon garlic powder
1 teaspoon red pepper flakes

1. Place the Cook & Crisp Basket in your Pressure Cooker Steam Fryer. 2. In a suitable bowl, mix the cabbage, olive oil, salt, pepper, garlic powder, and red pepper flakes. Make sure that the cabbage is coated with oil. 3. Place the cabbage in the Ninja Foodi Pressure Steam Fryer basket. 4. Put on the Smart Lid on top of the Ninja Foodi Steam Fryer. 5. Move the Lid Slider to the "Air Fry/Stovetop". Select the "Air Fry" mode for cooking. 6. Adjust the Ninja Foodi Pressure Steam Fryer temperature to 350°F/175°C. Set the timer and cook for around 4 minutes. 7. Using tongs, flip the cabbage. 8. Reset the timer and cook for around 3 minutes more. 9. Serve with additional salt, pepper, or red pepper flakes, if desired.
Per serving: Calories: 78; Fat: 7.9g; Sodium: 704mg; Carbs: 6g; Fiber: 3.6g; Sugar 6g; Protein 8g

Buffalo Cauliflower

prep time: 5 minutes. | Cook Time: 13 minutes. | Serves: 4

4 tablespoons (½ stick) unsalted butter, melted
¼ cup buffalo wing sauce
4 cups cauliflower florets
1 cup panko bread crumbs
Olive oil

1. Place the Cook & Crisp Basket in your Pressure Cooker Steam Fryer. 2. Grease the Ninja Foodi Pressure Steam Fryer basket with olive oil. 3. In a suitable bowl, mix the melted butter with the buffalo wing sauce. 4. Put the panko bread crumbs in a separate small bowl. 5. Dip the cauliflower in the sauce, making sure to coat the top of the cauliflower, then dip the cauliflower in the panko. 6. Place the cauliflower into the greased "cook & crisp basket", being careful not to overcrowd them. Grease the cauliflower generously with olive oil. 7. Put on the Smart Lid on top of the Ninja Foodi Steam Fryer. 8. Move the Lid Slider to the "Air Fry/Stovetop". Select the "Air Fry" mode for cooking. 9. Adjust the Ninja Foodi Pressure Steam Fryer temperature to 350°F/175°C. Set the timer and cook for around 7 minutes. 10. Using tongs, flip the cauliflower. Spray generously with olive oil. 11. Reset the timer and cook for another 6 minutes.
Per serving: Calories: 212; Fat: 10.9g; Sodium: 454mg; Carbs: 10g; Fiber: 3.1g; Sugar 5.2g; Protein 10g

Sweet Potato Fries

Prep Time: 5 Minutes. | Cook Time: 20 to 22 Minutes. | Serves: 4

2 sweet potatoes	½ teaspoon black pepper
1 teaspoon salt	2 teaspoons olive oil

1. Place the Cook & Crisp Basket in your Pressure Cooker Steam Fryer. 2. Cut the sweet potatoes lengthwise into ½-inch-thick slices. Then cut each slice into ½-inch-thick fries. 3. In a suitable mixing bowl, toss the sweet potato with the salt, pepper, and olive oil, making sure that all the potatoes are coated with oil. Add more oil as needed. 4. Place the potatoes in the Ninja Foodi Pressure Steam Fryer basket. 5. Put on the Smart Lid on top of the Ninja Foodi Steam Fryer. 6. Move the Lid Slider to the "Air Fry/Stovetop". Select the "Air Fry" mode for cooking. 7. Adjust the cooking temperature to 385°F/195°C. 8. Set the timer and cook for around 20 minutes. Shake the basket several times during cooking so that the fries will be evenly cooked and crisp. 9. Pour the potatoes into a serving bowl and toss with additional black pepper and salt, if desired.
Per serving: Calories: 221; Fat: 7.9g; Sodium: 704mg; Carbs: 6g; Fiber: 3.6g; Sugar 6g; Protein 18g

Feta Stuffed Portobellos

prep time: 10 minutes. | Cook Time: 12 minutes. | Serves: 4

4 large portobello mushroom caps (about 3 ounces each)	2 tablespoons panko bread crumbs, regular or gluten-free
Olive oil spray	1 tablespoon chopped fresh oregano
Salt	
2 medium plum tomatoes, chopped	1 tablespoon freshly grated
1 cup baby spinach, chopped	Parmesan cheese
¾ cup crumbled feta cheese	⅛ teaspoon black pepper
1 shallot, chopped	1 tablespoon olive oil
1 large garlic clove, minced	Balsamic glaze, for drizzling
¼ cup chopped fresh basil	(Optional)

1. Place the Cook & Crisp Basket in your Pressure Cooker Steam Fryer. 2. Use a suitable metal spoon to carefully scrape the black gills out of each mushroom cap. Grease both sides of the mushrooms with olive oil and season with a dash of salt. 3. In a suitable bowl, mix the tomatoes, spinach, feta, shallot, garlic, basil, panko, oregano, Parmesan, ¼ teaspoon salt, pepper, and olive oil and mix well. Carefully fill the inside of each mushroom cap with the mixture. 4. Spread a single layer of the stuffed mushrooms in the Ninja Foodi Pressure Steam Fryer basket. Put on the Smart Lid on top of the Ninja Foodi Steam Fryer. Move the Lid Slider to the "Air Fry/Stovetop". Select the "Air Fry" mode for cooking. Adjust the cooking temperature to 370°F/185°C. 5. Air Fry mushrooms for around 10 to 12 minutes, until mushrooms become tender and the top is golden. Use a flexible spatula to carefully remove the mushrooms from the basket and transfer to a serving dish. Drizzle the balsamic glaze (if using) over the mushrooms and serve.
Per serving: Calories: 334; Fat: 7.9g; Sodium: 704mg; Carbs: 6g; Fiber: 3.6g; Sugar 6g; Protein 18g

Potatoes Fries

Prep Time: 10 minutes. | Cook Time: 15 minutes. | Serves: 2

2 (6-ounce) Yukon Gold or russet potatoes, washed and dried	¼ teaspoon salt
	¼ teaspoon garlic powder
2 teaspoons olive oil	Black pepper

1. Place the Cook & Crisp Basket in your Pressure Cooker Steam Fryer. 2. Slice the potatoes lengthwise into ¼-inch-thick slices, then cut each slice into ¼-inch-thick fries. 3. In a suitable bowl, toss the potatoes with the oil. Season with the salt, garlic powder, and pepper to taste, tossing to coat. 4. Working in batches, arrange a single layer (no overlapping) of the potatoes in the Ninja Foodi Pressure Steam Fryer basket. 5. Put on the Smart Lid on top of the Ninja Foodi Steam Fryer. 6. Move the Lid Slider to the "Air Fry/Stovetop". Select the "Air Fry" mode for cooking. 7. Adjust the cooking temperature to 385°F/195°C. 8. Cook for around 12 to 15 minutes, flipping halfway, until the potatoes are golden and crisp. Serve immediately.

Per serving: Calories: 226; Fat: 10.9g; Sodium: 354mg; Carbs: 20.5g; Fiber: 4.1g; Sugar 8.2g; Protein 06g

Hasselback Potatoes

prep time: 10 minutes. | Cook Time: 35 minutes. | Serves: 4

4 russet potatoes	½ teaspoon black pepper
2 tablespoons olive oil	¼ cup grated Parmesan cheese
1 teaspoon salt	

1. Place the Cook & Crisp Basket in your Pressure Cooker Steam Fryer. 2. Without slicing all the way through the bottom of the potato (so the slices stay connected), cut each potato into ½-inch-wide horizontal slices. 3. Brush the potatoes with olive oil, being careful to brush in between all the slices. Season with black pepper and salt. 4. Place the potatoes in the Ninja Foodi Pressure Steam Fryer basket. 5. Put on the Smart Lid on top of the Ninja Foodi Steam Fryer. 6. Move the Lid Slider to the "Air Fry/Stovetop". Select the "Air Fry" mode for cooking. 7. Adjust the Ninja Foodi Pressure Steam Fryer temperature to 350°F/175°C. Set the timer. Air Fry for around 20 minutes. 8. Brush more olive oil onto the potatoes. 9. Reset the timer. Air Fry for around 15 minutes more. Remove the potatoes when they are fork-tender. 10. Sprinkle the cooked potatoes with salt, pepper, and Parmesan cheese.
Per serving: Calories: 220; Fat: 10.9g; Sodium: 354mg; Carbs: 20.5g; Fiber: 4.1g; Sugar 8.2g; Protein 06g

Rosemary Potatoes

Prep Time: 5 minutes. | Cook Time: 22 minutes. | Serves: 4

1½ pounds small red potatoes, cut into 1-inch cubes	½ teaspoon black pepper
	1 tablespoon minced garlic
2 tablespoons olive oil	2 tablespoons minced fresh
1 teaspoon salt	rosemary

1. Place the Cook & Crisp Basket in your Pressure Cooker Steam Fryer. 2. In a suitable mixing bowl, mix the diced potatoes, olive oil, salt, pepper, minced garlic, and rosemary and mix well, so the potatoes are coated with olive oil. 3. Place the potatoes into the Ninja Foodi Pressure Steam Fryer basket in a single layer. 4. Put on the Smart Lid on top of the Ninja Foodi Steam Fryer. 5. Move the Lid Slider to the "Air Fry/Stovetop". Select the "Air Fry" mode for cooking. 6. Adjust the cooking temperature to 400°F/200°C. 7. Set the timer and cook for around 20 to 22 minutes. Every 5 minutes, shake the basket, so the potatoes redistribute in the basket for even cooking. 8. Pour the potatoes into a suitable serving bowl, toss with additional black pepper and salt, and serve.
Per serving: Calories: 282; Fat: 12.9g; Sodium: 414mg; Carbs: 11g; Fiber: 5g; Sugar 9g; Protein 11g

Mexican Corn

prep time: 10 minutes. | Cook Time: 7 minutes. | Serves: 4

4 medium ears corn, husked	¼ teaspoon salt
Olive oil spray	2 ounces crumbled Cotija or feta
2 tablespoons mayonnaise	cheese
1 tablespoon fresh lime juice	2 tablespoons chopped fresh
½ teaspoon ancho chile powder	cilantro

1. Place the Cook & Crisp Basket in your Pressure Cooker Steam Fryer. 2. Spritz the corn with olive oil. Working in batches, arrange the ears of corn in the Ninja Foodi Pressure Steam Fryer basket in a single layer. 3. Put on the Smart Lid on top of the Ninja Foodi Steam Fryer. 4. Move the Lid Slider to the "Air Fry/Stovetop". Select the "Air Fry" mode for cooking. 5. Adjust the cooking temperature to 375°F/190°C. 6. Cook for about 7 minutes, flipping halfway, until the kernels are tender when pierced with a paring knife. When cool enough to handle, cut the corn kernels off the cob. 7. In a suitable bowl, mix mayonnaise, lime juice, ancho powder, and salt. Add the corn kernels and mix to mix. Transfer this mixture to a serving dish and top with the Cotija and cilantro. Serve immediately.
Per serving: Calories: 361; Fat: 7.9g; Sodium: 704mg; Carbs: 6g; Fiber: 3.6g; Sugar 6g; Protein 18g

Bacon-Wrapped Asparagus

Prep Time: 10 minutes. | Cook Time: 10 minutes. | Serves: 4

20 asparagus spears (12 ounces), tough ends trimmed
Olive oil spray
½ teaspoon grated lemon zest
⅛ teaspoon salt
Black pepper
4 slices center-cut bacon

1. Place the Cook & Crisp Basket in your Pressure Cooker Steam Fryer. 2. Place the asparagus on a suitable sheet pan and spritz with olive oil. Season with the lemon zest, salt, and pepper to taste, tossing to coat. Group the asparagus into 4 bundles of 5 spears and wrap the center of each bundle with a slice of bacon. 3. Working in batches, place the asparagus bundles in the "cook & crisp basket". Put on the Smart Lid on top of the Ninja Foodi Steam Fryer. Move the Lid Slider to the "Air Fry/Stovetop". Select the "Air Fry" mode for cooking. 4. Adjust the cooking temperature to 400°F/200°C. 5. Air Fry until the bacon is browned and the asparagus is charred on the edges, 8 to 10 minutes, depending on the thickness of the spears. Serve immediately.
Per serving: Calories: 226; Fat: 10.9g; Sodium: 354mg; Carbs: 20.5g; Fiber: 4.1g; Sugar 8.2g; Protein 06g

Sesame Green Beans

prep time: 10 minutes. | Cook Time: 8 minutes. | Serves: 4

1 tablespoon soy sauce or tamari
½ tablespoon Sriracha sauce
4 teaspoons toasted sesame oil
12 ounces trimmed green beans
½ tablespoon toasted sesame seeds

1. Place the Cook & Crisp Basket in your Pressure Cooker Steam Fryer. 2. In a suitable bowl, mix well the soy sauce, Sriracha, and 1 teaspoon of the sesame oil. 3. In a suitable bowl, mix the green beans with the remaining 3 teaspoons sesame oil and toss to coat. 4. Working in batches, spread a single layer of the green beans in the Ninja Foodi Pressure Steam Fryer basket. Put on the Smart Lid on top of the Ninja Foodi Steam Fryer. Move the Lid Slider to the "Air Fry/Stovetop". Select the "Air Fry" mode for cooking. 5. Adjust the cooking temperature to 375°F/190°C. 6. Air Fry for about 8 minutes, shaking the basket halfway, until charred and tender. Transfer to a serving dish. Toss with the sauce and sesame seeds and serve.
Per serving: Calories: 77; Fat: 14g; Sodium: 791mg; Carbs: 8.9g; Fiber: 4.6g; Sugar 1g; Protein 2g

Baked Potatoes with Yogurt

Prep Time: 10 minutes. | Cook Time: 35 minutes. | Serves: 4

4 (7-ounce) russet potatoes, washed and dried
Olive oil spray
½ teaspoon salt
½ cup 2% Greek yogurt
¼ cup minced fresh chives
Black pepper

1. Place the Cook & Crisp Basket in your Pressure Cooker Steam Fryer. 2. Using any fork, pierce the potatoes all over. Spray each potato with a few spritzes of oil. Season the potatoes with ¼ teaspoon of the salt. 3. Place the potatoes in the Ninja Foodi Pressure Steam Fryer basket. 4. Put on the Smart Lid on top of the Ninja Foodi Steam Fryer. 5. Move the Lid Slider to the "Air Fry/Stovetop". Select the "Air Fry" mode for cooking. 6. Adjust the cooking temperature to 400°F/200°C. 7. Cook for about 35 minutes, flipping halfway through, until a knife can easily be inserted into the center of each potato. 8. Split open the potatoes and serve topped with the yogurt, chives, the remaining ¼ teaspoon salt, and pepper to taste.
Per serving: Calories: 120; Fat: 19g; Sodium: 354mg; Carbs: 15g; Fiber: 5.1g; Sugar 8.2g; Protein 12g

Mushroom Cheese Loaf

Prep Time: 10 minutes. | Cook Time: 20 minutes. | Serves: 2

2 cups mushrooms, chopped
½ cups cheddar cheese, shredded
¾ cup flour
2 tablespoons butter, melted
2 eggs
Black pepper and salt, if desired

1. Place the deluxe reversible rack in your Pressure Cooker Steam Fryer. 2. In a food processor, pulse the mushrooms, cheese, flour, melted butter, and eggs, along with some black pepper and salt if desired, until a uniform consistency is achieved. 3. Transfer into a silicone loaf pan, spreading and levelling with a palette knife. 4. Set the loaf pan on the rack. Put on the Smart Lid on top of the Ninja Foodi Steam Fryer. Move the Lid Slider to the "Air Fry/Stovetop". Select the "Air Fry" mode for cooking. Adjust the cooking temperature to 375°F/190°C and cook for 15 minutes. 5. Take care when removing the pan from the Pressure Cooker Steam Fryer. 6. and leave it to cool. Then slice and serve.
Per serving: Calories: 334; Fat: 7.9g; Sodium: 704mg; Carbs: 6g; Fiber: 3.6g; Sugar 6g; Protein 18g

Roasted Sweet Potatoes

Prep Time: 10 Minutes. | Cook Time: 45 Minutes. | Serves: 4

4 sweet potatoes
¼ cup olive oil
2 teaspoons salt
½ teaspoon black pepper

1. Place the Cook & Crisp Basket in your Pressure Cooker Steam Fryer. 2. Use any fork to poke a few holes in each of the sweet potatoes. 3. Rub the skins of the sweet potatoes with olive oil, salt, and pepper. 4. Place the coated sweet potatoes in the Ninja Foodi Pressure Steam Fryer basket. 5. Put on the Smart Lid on top of the Ninja Foodi Steam Fryer. 6. Move the Lid Slider to the "Air Fry/Stovetop". Select the "Air Fry" mode for cooking. 7. Adjust the Ninja Foodi Pressure Steam Fryer temperature to 400°F/200°C. Set the timer and cook for around 15 minutes. 8. Using tongs, flip or rotate the potatoes. 9. Reset the timer and cook for another 15 minutes. Check to see if the sweet potatoes are fork-tender. If not, add up to 15 minutes more.
Per serving: Calories: 289; Fat: 14g; Sodium: 791mg; Carbs: 18.9g; Fiber: 4.6g; Sugar 8g; Protein 6g

Honey Cornbread

Prep Time: 10 minutes. | Cook Time: 20 minutes. | Serves: 4

1 cup all-purpose flour
1 cup yellow cornmeal
½ cup sugar
1 teaspoon salt
2 teaspoons baking powder
1 large egg
1 cup milk
⅓ cup vegetable oil
¼ cup honey

1. Place the Cook & Crisp Basket in your Pressure Cooker Steam Fryer. 2. Spray the Cook & Crisp Basket with oil or cooking spray. 3. In a suitable mixing bowl, mix the flour, cornmeal, sugar, salt, baking powder, egg, milk, oil, and honey and mix lightly. 4. Pour the cornbread batter into the basket. 5. Put on the Smart Lid on top of the Ninja Foodi Steam Fryer. Move the Lid Slider to the "Air Fry/Stovetop". Select the "Air Fry" mode for cooking. Adjust the Ninja Foodi Pressure Steam Fryer temperature to 360°F/180°C. Set the timer. Air Fry for around 20 minutes. 6. Insert a toothpick into the center of cornbread to make sure the middle is cooked; if not, air fry for another 3 to 4 minutes. 7. Using silicone oven mitts, remove the basket from the Ninja Foodi Pressure Steam Fryer and let cool slightly. Serve warm.
Per serving: Calories: 302; Fat: 19g; Sodium: 354mg; Carbs: 15g; Fiber: 5.1g; Sugar 8.2g; Protein 12g

Spicy Acorn Squash

prep time: 10 minutes. | Cook Time: 15 minutes. | Serves: 2

1 teaspoon coconut oil
1 medium acorn squash, halved crosswise and seeded
1 teaspoon light brown sugar
Few dashes of nutmeg
Few dashes of cinnamon

1. Place the Cook & Crisp Basket in your Pressure Cooker Steam Fryer. 2. Rub the coconut oil on the cut sides of the squash. Sprinkle with the brown sugar, nutmeg, and cinnamon. 3. Place the squash halves, cut sides up, in the Ninja Foodi Pressure Steam Fryer basket. 4. Put on the Smart Lid on top of the Ninja Foodi Steam Fryer. 5. Move the Lid Slider to the "Air Fry/Stovetop". Select the "Air Fry" mode for cooking. 6. Adjust the cooking temperature to 325°F/160°C. 7. Cook for around 15 minutes, until soft in the center when pierced with a paring knife. Serve immediately.
Per serving: Calories: 212; Fat: 7.9g; Sodium: 704mg; Carbs: 6g; Fiber: 3.6g; Sugar 6g; Protein 18g

Tostones With Green Sauce

prep time: 10 minutes. | Cook Time: 24 minutes. | Serves: 2

1 large green plantain, peeled and sliced	¾ teaspoon garlic powder
Salt	Olive oil spray
	Peruvian Green Sauce, for serving

1. Place the Cook & Crisp Basket in your Pressure Cooker Steam Fryer. 2. In a suitable bowl, mix 1 cup water with 1 teaspoon salt and the garlic powder. 3. Spritz the plantain all over with olive oil and transfer to the Ninja Foodi Pressure Steam Fryer basket. 4. Put on the Smart Lid on top of the Ninja Foodi Steam Fryer. 5. Move the Lid Slider to the "Air Fry/Stovetop". Select the "Air Fry" mode for cooking. 6. Cook at 400°F/200°C for around 6 minutes, shaking halfway, until soft. Immediately transfer to a work surface. 7. Dip each piece, one at a time, in the seasoned water, then transfer to the work surface. Generously spray both sides of the plantain with oil. 8. Working in batches, spread in a single layer of the plantain in the "cook & crisp basket". Put on the Smart Lid on top of the Ninja Foodi Steam Fryer. 9. Move the Lid Slider to the "Air Fry/Stovetop". Select the "Air Fry" mode for cooking. 10.Cook at 400°F/200°C for about 10 minutes, turning halfway, until golden and crisp. Transfer to a serving dish. While still hot, spray with olive oil and season with ⅛ teaspoon salt. Serve immediately with the green sauce on the side.
Per serving: Calories: 349; Fat: 2.9g; Sodium: 511mg; Carbs: 12g; Fiber: 3g; Sugar 8g; Protein 7g

Broccoli Gratin

Prep Time: 10 minutes. | Cook Time: 14 minutes. | Serves: 2

Olive oil spray	chopped
½ tablespoon olive oil	6 tablespoons (1½ ounces)
1 tablespoon all-purpose or gluten-free flour	shredded extra-sharp cheddar cheese
⅓ cup fat-free milk	2 tablespoons panko bread crumbs,
½ teaspoon sage	regular or gluten-free
¼ teaspoon salt	1 tablespoon freshly grated
⅛ teaspoon black pepper	Parmesan cheese
2 cups (5 ounces) broccoli florets,	

1. Place the Cook & Crisp Basket in your Pressure Cooker Steam Fryer. 2. Spray the Cook & Crisp Basket with oil. 3. In a suitable bowl, mix the olive oil, flour, milk, sage, salt, and pepper. Add the broccoli, cheddar, panko, and Parmesan and mix well. 4. Place the mixture in the Ninja Foodi Pressure Steam Fryer basket. 5. Put on the Smart Lid on top of the Ninja Foodi Steam Fryer. 6. Move the Lid Slider to the "Air Fry/Stovetop". Select the "Air Fry" mode for cooking. 7. Adjust the cooking temperature to 330°F/165°C. 8. Cook for around 12 to 14 minutes, until the broccoli is crisp-tender and the cheese is golden brown on top. Serve immediately.
Per serving: Calories: 184; Fat: 5g; Sodium: 441mg; Carbs: 17g; Fiber: 4.6g; Sugar 5g; Protein 9g

Bread-crumbed Onion Rings

Prep Time: 10 minutes. | Cook Time: 10 minutes. | Serves: 4

1 medium Vidalia onion (about 9 ounces)	½ cup 1% buttermilk
1½ cups (1½ ounces) cornflakes	1 large egg
½ cup seasoned bread crumbs	¼ cup all-purpose flour
½ teaspoon sweet paprika	½ teaspoon salt
	Olive oil spray

1. Place the Cook & Crisp Basket in your Pressure Cooker Steam Fryer. 2. Trim the ends off the onion, then quarter the onion crosswise (about ⅓-inch-thick slices) and separate into rings. 3. In a food processor, pulse the cornflakes until fine. Transfer to a suitable bowl and stir in the bread crumbs and paprika. In another medium bowl, mix the buttermilk, egg, flour, and ½ teaspoon salt until mixed. 4. Dip the onion rings in the buttermilk batter, then into the cornflake mixture to coat. Set aside on a work surface and spray both sides with oil. 5. Working in batches, spread a single layer of the onion rings in the Ninja Foodi Pressure Steam Fryer basket. Put on the Smart Lid on top of the Ninja Foodi Steam Fryer. Move the Lid Slider to the "Air Fry/Stovetop". Select the "Air Fry" mode for cooking. Adjust the cooking temperature to 340°F/170°C. 6. Air Fry the rings for about 10 minutes, flipping halfway, until golden brown. Serve immediately.

Per serving: Calories: 219; Fat: 10g; Sodium: 891mg; Carbs: 22.9g; Fiber: 4g; Sugar 4g; Protein 13g

Fried Eggplant

Prep Time: 10 minutes. | Cook Time: 24 minutes. | Serves: 8

1 large eggplant (about 1½ pounds)	1⅔ cups seasoned bread crumbs,
¾ teaspoon salt	whole wheat or gluten-free
Black pepper	Olive oil spray
3 large eggs	Marinara sauce, for dipping

1. Place the Cook & Crisp Basket in your Pressure Cooker Steam Fryer. 2. Slice the ends off the eggplant and cut into ¼-inch-thick rounds, 40 to 42 slices. Season both sides with the black pepper and salt to taste. 3. On a shallow plate, beat the eggs with 1 teaspoon water. Place the bread crumbs on another plate. Dip the eggplant slice in the egg, then in the bread crumbs, pressing gently to adhere. Remove the excess bread crumbs and place on a work surface. Generously spray both sides of the eggplant with oil. 4. Air frying in batches, arrange a single layer of the eggplant in the Ninja Foodi Pressure Steam Fryer basket. 5. Put on the Smart Lid on top of the Ninja Foodi Steam Fryer. Move the Lid Slider to the "Air Fry/Stovetop". Select the "Air Fry" mode for cooking. 6. Adjust the cooking temperature to 385°F/195°C. 7. Air Fry for about 8 minutes, flipping halfway, until crisp, golden, and cooked through in the center. Serve.
Per serving: Calories: 116; Fat: 1.9g; Sodium: 224mg; Carbs: 18g; Fiber: 3.6g; Sugar 3g; Protein 2g

Bacon Brussels Sprouts

prep time: 10 minutes. | Cook Time: 25 minutes. | Serves: 4

3 slices center-cut bacon, halved	oil
1 pound Brussels sprouts, trimmed and halved	¼ teaspoon salt
1½ tablespoons extra-virgin olive	¼ teaspoon dried thyme

1. Place the Cook & Crisp Basket in your Pressure Cooker Steam Fryer. 2. Spread the bacon in a single layer in the basket. 3. Put on the Smart Lid on top of the Ninja Foodi Steam Fryer. 4. Move the Lid Slider to the "Air Fry/Stovetop". Select the "Air Fry" mode for cooking. 5. Adjust the cooking temperature to 350°F/175°C. 6. Air fry them for 10 minutes until crispy then transfer to a bowl. 7. Toss Brussel sprouts with oil, salt and thyme then add to the Ninja Foodi Pressure Steam Fryer. 8. Put on the Smart Lid on top of the Ninja Foodi Steam Fryer. 9. Move the Lid Slider to the "Air Fry/Stovetop". Select the "Air Fry" mode for cooking. 10. Adjust the cooking temperature to 350°F/175°C. Air fry the sprouts for 15 minutes until crispy. 11. Add the sprouts to the bacon and mix well. 12. Serve.
Per serving: Calories: 221; Fat: 7.9g; Sodium: 704mg; Carbs: 6g; Fiber: 3.6g; Sugar 6g; Protein 6g

Cauliflower Nuggets

prep time: 10 minutes. | Cook Time: 9 minutes. | Serves: 4

3 large eggs, beaten	sauce
½ cup all-purpose or gluten-free flour	1 tablespoon unsalted butter, melted
28 bite-size (about 1½-inch) cauliflower florets (16 ounces)	Blue cheese dip, homemade or store-bought (optional)
Olive oil spray	Carrot sticks and celery sticks, for
6 tablespoons Frank's Red-hot	serving (optional)

1. Place the Cook & Crisp Basket in your Pressure Cooker Steam Fryer. 2. Place the eggs in a suitable bowl. Place the flour in a separate bowl. 3. Dip the cauliflower in the egg, then in the flour to coat, shaking off the excess. Place on a work surface and spray both sides with olive oil. 4. Working in batches, spread a single layer of the cauliflower in the Ninja Foodi Pressure Steam Fryer basket. Put on the Smart Lid on top of the Ninja Foodi Steam Fryer. 5. Move the Lid Slider to the "Air Fry/Stovetop". Select the "Air Fry" mode for cooking. 6. Adjust the cooking temperature to 385°F/195°C. 7. Cook for around 7 to 8 minutes. When all the batches are done, return all the cauliflower to the air fryer. Cook for around 1 minute to heat through. Transfer to a suitable bowl and toss with the hot sauce and melted butter. Serve.
Per serving: Calories: 382; Fat: 7.9g; Sodium: 704mg; Carbs: 6g; Fiber: 3.6g; Sugar 6g; Protein 18g

Chapter 3 Poultry Recipes

54 Saucy Chicken Wings
54 Lemon Chicken
54 Sweet Chicken Wings
54 Curried Chicken Wings
54 Herbed Chicken Drumsticks
54 Sage Rubbed Turkey Breast
54 Broccoli- Chicken
54 Scallions Chicken
55 Air-Fried Turkey
55 Chicken Roll
55 Turkey With Sweet Sauce
55 Bacon Wrapped Chicken
55 Mustard Chicken Bites
55 Easy Chicken Pate
55 Turkey Cream Spread
55 Tomato Drumsticks
56 Saucy Turkey Leg
56 Tasty Chicken Meatballs
56 Air-Fried Meatballs
56 Dill Chicken
56 Chicken Strips
56 Fried Cheese Chicken
56 Chicken Sausages
56 Turkey Cheese Cups
57 Crusted Chicken
57 Gingered Turkey
57 Paprika Chicken Breast
57 Air-Fried Turkey Mash
57 Italian Chicken Parmesan
57 Basil Chicken Breast
57 Chicken Beans Bowl
57 Celery Chicken
58 Turkey Cheese Pockets
58 Mozarella Chicken
58 Chicken Cabbage Pan
58 Pepper Chicken Halves
58 Lemon-Dijon Chicken
58 Spiced Turkey Breast
58 Buffalo Chicken
59 Nashville Chicken
59 Chicken Tenders
59 Turkey Meatballs
59 Mushroom Stuffed Turkey
59 Stuffed Chicken Kiev
60 Crusted Chicken Chunks
60 Chicken Filling
60 Fried Buffalo Chicken Wings
60 Homemade turkey Pot Pie
60 Smoky Chicken Quarters
60 Easy Chicken Paillard
61 Chicken Roll-Ups
61 Jalapeño Chicken
61 Chicken Egg Rolls
61 Fried Drumsticks

61 Chicken with Chimichangas Sauce
62 Chicken Ham Cordon Bleu
62 Chicken Pies
62 Basic Chicken Nuggets
62 Chicken Parmesan with Spaghetti
62 Crispy Turkey Burgers
62 Air Fried Turkey Breast
63 Chicken Hot Dogs
63 Chicken with Apricot-Ginger Sauce
63 Barbeque Sauce Chicken
63 Fiesta Chicken
63 Easy Nacho Chicken Fries
64 Cornish Hens With Honey-Glaze
64 Peachy Chicken With Cherries
64 Fried Chicken Strips
64 Turkey Cutlets
64 Poblano Turkey Bake
64 Southern Chicken Livers
65 Turkey Wraps
65 Chicken and Cheese Taquitos
65 Simple Teriyaki Chicken
65 Korean Wings
65 Spicy Buffalo Chicken Wings
65 Turkey With Mustard Glaze
66 Chicken BBQ Burgers
66 Fajita Rollups
66 Crispy Honey Chicken Wings
66 Mexican Burgers
66 Asian-Spiced Duck
66 Mayo Chicken Salad
66 Spiced Chicken Thighs
67 Crispy Fried Chicken
67 KFC Chicken
67 Chicken Ham Rochambeau
67 Chicken Fritters
67 Chicken Wing Stir-Fry
68 Chicken Parmesan
68 Jerk-Spiced Chicken Wings
68 Crusted Chicken Fingers
68 Air-Fried Chicken Breasts
68 Chicken Taquitos
68 Air-Fried Chicken Legs
68 Thanksgiving Turkey
69 Paprika Chicken Cutlets
69 Hawaiian Roll Sliders
69 Mustard Chicken Thighs
69 Roasted Turkey
69 Mediterranean Chicken Fillets
69 Chicken with Pineapple
69 Chicken Pepper Fajitas
70 Air-Fried Turkey Wings
70 Limey Duck Breast
70 Fried Chicken
70 Crusted Chicken Schnitzel

70 Cheese Stuffed Chicken
70 Chicken Omelet
70 Turkey Sandwiches
71 Chicken Wings with Piri Piri Sauce
71 Turkey Pepper Meatballs
71 Italian Turkey Sausage
71 Ricotta Chicken Wraps
71 Cajun- Turkey Fingers
71 Honey Turkey Breast
72 Chicken Turnip Curry
72 Chicken Mushroom Kabobs
72 Buttered Marjoram Chicken
72 Hoisin Glazed Drumsticks
72 Stuffed Roulade
72 Chicken Nuggets
72 Balsamic Drumettes
73 Turkey Sliders
73 Spicy Turkey Wings
73 Turkey Meatloaf
73 Crusted Chicken Drumsticks
73 Bacon Chicken
73 Holiday Chicken Wings
73 Lemon Garlic Chicken
74 Cajun Chicken
74 Italian Chicken Fillets
74 Chicken Parsley Nuggets
74 Crusted Chicken Tenders
74 Rosemary Spiced Chicken
74 Tuscan Chicken
75 Lemon Chicken with Herbed Potatoes
75 Delicious Sesame Chicken
75 Lo Mein
75 Refreshing Chicken Tacos
75 Breaded Chicken
76 Chicken Egg Roll
76 Herbed Chicken Wings
76 Turkey with Gravy
76 Stuffed Turkey Breast with Gravy
77 Indian Chicken Marsala
77 Spicy Teriyaki Chicken
77 Roasted Chicken
77 Spicy Chicken Alfredo
77 Burrito Bowls with Chicken And Beans
78 Pesto Turkey Meatballs with Pasta
78 Spicy Buffalo Wings
78 Shredded Greek-Style Chicken
78 Chicken with Broccoli Stir-Fry
78 Delicious Teriyaki Chicken
79 Chicken with Marinara Sauce
79 Smoky Barbecue Chicken
79 Thai Chicken Rice

Saucy Chicken Wings

Prep Time: 10 minutes. | Cook Time: 30 minutes. | Serves:5

3-pounds chicken wings   1 tablespoon coconut oil, melted
¼ cup marinara sauce

1. Place the Cook & Crisp Basket in your Ninja Foodi Pressure Cooker Steam Fryer. 2. Mix marinara sauce with coconut oil. 3. Then put the chicken wings in the Ninja Foodi Cook & Crisp Basket and add marinara sauce mixture. 4. Put on the Smart Lid on top of the Ninja Foodi Steam Fryer. 5. Move the Lid Slider to the "Air Fry/Stovetop". 6. Cook the meal at 360°F/180°C on "Air Fry" Mode for about 30 minutes.
Per Serving: Calories 382; Fat 32.5 g; Sodium 1363 mg; Carbs 3.2g; Fiber 0.2g; Sugar 1.9g; Protein 19.1g

Lemon Chicken

Prep Time: 5 minutes. | Cook Time: 20 minutes. | Serves: 4

2-pounds chicken tenders   2 tablespoons lemon juice
1 teaspoon lemon zest, grated   1 tablespoon avocado oil

1. Place the Cook & Crisp Basket in your Ninja Foodi Pressure Cooker Steam Fryer. 2. Mix avocado oil with lemon juice and lemon zest. 3. Then mix chicken tenders with lemon mixture and put in your Ninja Foodi Pressure Cooker Steam Fryer. 4. Put on the Smart Lid on top of the Ninja Foodi Steam Fryer. 5. Move the Lid Slider to the "Air Fry/Stovetop". 6. Cook the chicken tenders at 365°F/185°C on "Air Fry" Mode for about 10 minutes per side.
Per Serving: Calories 324; Fat 17.8 g; Sodium 363 mg; Carbs 8.9g; Fiber 0.5g; Sugar 1.9g; Protein 36.6g

Sweet Chicken Wings

Prep Time: 15 minutes. | Cook Time: 15 minutes. | Serves: 8

4-pounds chicken wings   1 tablespoon avocado oil
1 tablespoon Splenda   ½ teaspoon coriander

1. Place the Cook & Crisp Basket in your Ninja Foodi Pressure Cooker Steam Fryer. 2. Rub the chicken wings with Splenda, avocado oil, and coriander. 3. Put the chicken wings in the Ninja Foodi Cook & Crisp Basket. 4. Put on the Smart Lid on top of the Ninja Foodi Steam Fryer. 5. Move the Lid Slider to the "Air Fry/Stovetop". 6. Cook on "Air Fry" Mode at 385°F/195°C for about 15 minutes.
Per Serving: Calories 398; Fat 37.8 g; Sodium 1463 mg; Carbs 2.5g; Fiber 0.2g; Sugar 0.5g; Protein 13.6g

Curried Chicken Wings

Prep Time: 10 minutes. | Cook Time: 25 minutes. | Serves: 4

2 pounds chicken wings, boneless   3 tablespoons heavy cream
1 teaspoon curry powder   1 tablespoon avocado oil

1. Place the Cook & Crisp Basket in your Ninja Foodi Pressure Cooker Steam Fryer. 2. Mix heavy cream with curry powder. 3. Then mix chicken wings with curry mixture and put in your Ninja Foodi Pressure Cooker Steam Fryer. 4. Sprinkle the chicken wings with avocado oil. 5. Put on the Smart Lid on top of the Ninja Foodi Steam Fryer. 6. Move the Lid Slider to the "Air Fry/Stovetop". 7. Cook on "Air Fry" Mode for about 25 minutes at 375°F/190°C.
Per Serving: Calories 368; Fat 32.8 g; Sodium 507 mg; Carbs 0.6g; Fiber 0.1g; Sugar 1.1g; Protein 18.5g

Herbed Chicken Drumsticks

Prep Time: 10 minutes. | Cook Time: 21 minutes. | Serves: 4

2-pounds chicken drumsticks   1 tablespoon coconut oil, melted
1 tablespoon dried thyme   1 teaspoon salt

1. Place the Cook & Crisp Basket in your Ninja Foodi Pressure Cooker Steam Fryer. 2. Mix chicken drumsticks with dried thyme, coconut oil, and salt. 3. Put the chicken drumsticks in the Ninja Foodi

Cook & Crisp Basket. Put on the Smart Lid on top of the Ninja Foodi Steam Fryer. 4. Move the Lid Slider to the "Air Fry/Stovetop". 5. Cook on "Air Fry" Mode at 385°F/195°C for about 21 minutes.
Per Serving: Calories 267; Fat 15.2 g; Sodium 479 mg; Carbs 13.9g; Fiber 0.1g; Sugar 12.9g; Protein 20.6g

Sage Rubbed Turkey Breast

Prep Time: 10 minutes. | Cook Time: 25 minutes. | Serves: 4

2-pounds turkey breast, skinless,   1 teaspoon salt
boneless   2 tablespoons avocado oil
1 tablespoon dried sage

1. Place the Cook & Crisp Basket in your Ninja Foodi Pressure Cooker Steam Fryer. 2. Put the turkey breast in the Ninja Foodi Cook & Crisp Basket and sprinkle with dried sage, salt, and avocado oil. 3. Put on the Smart Lid on top of the Ninja Foodi Steam Fryer. 4. Move the Lid Slider to the "Air Fry/Stovetop". 5. Cook it at 385°F/195°C on "Air Fry" Mode for about 12 minutes per side. 6. Then cook the turkey breast for about 1 minute more at 400°F/200°C.
Per Serving: Calories 257; Fat 17 g; Sodium 674 mg; Carbs 13.9g; Fiber 4.2; Sugar 5.9g; Protein 13.6g

Broccoli- Chicken

Prep time: 10 minutes. | Cook Time: 24 minutes. | Serves: 6

1 tablespoon avocado oil   seasoning
¼ cup chopped onion   ¼ black pepper, plus additional for
½ cup chopped broccoli   seasoning
4 ounces cream cheese   2 pounds boneless, skinless
2 ounces Cheddar cheese, shredded   chicken breasts
1 teaspoon garlic powder   1 teaspoon smoked paprika
½ teaspoon salt, plus additional for

1. Place the Cook & Crisp Basket in your Ninja Foodi Pressure Cooker Steam Fryer. 2. Heat a suitable skillet over medium-high heat and pour in the avocado oil. Add the onion and broccoli. Cook, stirring occasionally, for about 5 to 8 minutes, until the onion is tender. 3. Transfer to a suitable bowl and stir in the cream cheese, Cheddar cheese, and garlic powder, and season to taste with salt and pepper. 4. Hold a sharp knife parallel to the chicken breast and cut a long pocket into one side. Stuff the chicken pockets with the broccoli mixture, using toothpicks to secure the pockets around the filling. 5. In a small dish, mix the paprika, ½ teaspoon salt, and ¼ teaspoon pepper. Sprinkle this over the outside of the chicken. 6. Place the chicken in a single layer in your Ninja Foodi Cook & Crisp Basket, cooking in batches if necessary. 7. Put on the Smart Lid on top of the Ninja Foodi Steam Fryer. 8. Move the Lid Slider to the "Air Fry/Stovetop". 9. Cook on "Air Fry" Mode at 400°F/200°C for about 14 to 16 minutes, until an instant-read thermometer reads 160°F/70°C. Place the chicken on a plate and tent a piece of aluminum foil over the chicken. Allow to rest for about 10 minutes before serving.
Per Serving: Calories 260; Fat 16g; Sodium 585mg; Total Carbs 3.1g; Fiber 1.3g; Sugar 0.2g; Protein 25.5g

Scallions Chicken

Prep Time: 15 minutes. | Cook Time: 10 minutes. | Serves: 2

8-ounce chicken fillet   1 teaspoon salt
2 ounces scallions, chopped   ½ teaspoon black pepper
2 tablespoons olive oil

1. Place the Cook & Crisp Basket in your Ninja Foodi Pressure Cooker Steam Fryer. 2. Cut the chicken into the tenders and sprinkle with olive oil, salt, and black pepper. 3. Put the chicken tenders in the Ninja Foodi Cook & Crisp Basket in one layer. 4. Put on the Smart Lid on top of the Ninja Foodi Steam Fryer. 5. Move the Lid Slider to the "Air Fry/Stovetop". 6. Cook on "Air Fry" Mode at 390°F/200°C for about 4 minutes per side. 7. Then top the chicken tenders with scallions. Cook it for about 2 minutes more.
Per Serving: Calories 341; Fat 24.6 g; Sodium 401 mg; Carbs 12g; Fiber 0.1g; Sugar 11.9g; Protein 18.6g

Air-Fried Turkey

Prep Time: 5 minutes. | Cook Time: 24 minutes. | Serves: 4

3 tablespoons butter	1 teaspoon black pepper
1-pound turkey	½ teaspoon dried rosemary
1 teaspoon olive oil	

1. Place the Cook & Crisp Basket in your Ninja Foodi Pressure Cooker Steam Fryer. 2. In a suitable mixing bowl, mix butter with turkey, olive oil, black pepper, and dried rosemary. 3. Put the mixture in your Ninja Foodi Pressure Cooker Steam Fryer. Put on the Smart Lid on top of the Ninja Foodi Steam Fryer. 4. Move the Lid Slider to the "Air Fry/Stovetop". 5. Cook it for about 24 minutes at 355°F/180°C. Stir the mixture from time to time to avoid burning. 6. Blend the cooked turkey mixture and put it in the serving bowl.
Per Serving: Calories 634; Fat 19.6 g; Sodium 1263 mg; Carbs 13.1g; Fiber 1.5g; Sugar 8.6g; Protein 96g

Chicken Roll

Prep Time: 15 minutes. | Cook Time: 25 minutes. | Serves:5

1-pound chicken fillet	½ teaspoon dried basil
1 teaspoon cayenne pepper	½ teaspoon olive oil
1 ounce scallions, chopped	½ teaspoon chili powder
1-ounce Parmesan, grated	

1. Place the Cook & Crisp Basket in your Ninja Foodi Pressure Cooker Steam Fryer. 2. Beat the chicken fillet with the help of the kitchen hammer to get the flat cutlet. 3. Then rub it with cayenne pepper, dried basil, olive oil, and chili powder. 4. Top the chicken fillet with Parmesan and scallions and roll into a roll. 5. Put it in the Ninja Foodi Cook & Crisp Basket. Put on the Smart Lid on top of the Ninja Foodi Steam Fryer. 6. Move the Lid Slider to the "Air Fry/Stovetop". 7. Cook it for about 25 minutes at 385°F/195°C.
Per Serving: Calories 324; Fat 17.8 g; Sodium 363 mg; Carbs 8.9g; Fiber 0.5g; Sugar 1.9g; Protein 36.6g

Turkey With Sweet Sauce

Prep Time: 10 minutes. | Cook Time: 30 minutes. | Serves: 4

1-pound turkey breast, skinless, boneless, chopped	1 tablespoon sugar
	1 jalapeno pepper, chopped
1 tablespoon coconut oil	1 teaspoon paprika

1. Place the Cook & Crisp Basket in your Ninja Foodi Pressure Cooker Steam Fryer. 2. Grease the Ninja Foodi Cook & Crisp Basket with coconut oil. 3. Rub the turkey breast with sugar and paprika. Put the turkey breast in your Ninja Foodi Pressure Cooker Steam Fryer and add jalapeno pepper. 4. Put on the Smart Lid on top of the Ninja Foodi Steam Fryer. 5. Move the Lid Slider to the "Air Fry/Stovetop". 6. Cook the meal at 365°F/185°C on "Air Fry" Mode for about 30 minutes. Flip the half-cooked turkey after 15 minutes of cooking. 7. Slice the turkey breast and sprinkle it with sweet liquid (sauce) from your Ninja Foodi Cook & Crisp Basket.
Per Serving: Calories 539; Fat 17.5 g; Sodium 1875 mg; Carbs 79.2g; Fiber 4.5g; Sugar 26.9g; Protein 15.6g

Bacon Wrapped Chicken

Prep Time: 15 minutes. | Cook Time: 25 minutes. | Serves: 2

4 chicken drumsticks	1 teaspoon nutmeg
4 bacon slices	¼ teaspoon salt

1. Place the Cook & Crisp Basket in your Ninja Foodi Pressure Cooker Steam Fryer. 2. Rub the chicken drumsticks with nutmeg and salt. 3. Then wrap the chicken in bacon slices and put in your Ninja Foodi Pressure Cooker Steam Fryer. 4. Put on the Smart Lid on top of the Ninja Foodi Steam Fryer. 5. Move the Lid Slider to the "Air Fry/Stovetop". 6. Cook the meal at 375°F/190°C on "Air Fry" Mode for about 25 minutes.
Per Serving: Calories 398; Fat 27 g; Sodium 416mg; Carbs 34.9g; Fiber 6.5g; Sugar 6.9g; Protein 11.6g

Mustard Chicken Bites

Prep Time: 5 minutes. | Cook Time: 20 minutes. | Serves: 4

16-ounce chicken breast, skinless, boneless, cubed	1 teaspoon mustard
	1 teaspoon cream cheese
1 tablespoon avocado oil	

1. Place the Cook & Crisp Basket in your Ninja Foodi Pressure Cooker Steam Fryer. 2. In a suitable mixing bowl, mix avocado oil with mustard and cream cheese. 3. When the mixture is smooth, add chicken cubes and mix well. 4. Transfer the chicken cubes in the Ninja Foodi Cook & Crisp Basket. Put on the Smart Lid on top of the Ninja Foodi Steam Fryer. 5. Move the Lid Slider to the "Air Fry/Stovetop". 6. Cook on "Air Fry" Mode at 360°F/180°C for about 20 minutes.
Per Serving: Calories 116; Fat 2.3 g; Sodium 15 mg; Carbs 18.9g; Fiber 4.5g; Sugar 2.2g; Protein 6g

Easy Chicken Pate

Prep Time: 15 minutes. | Cook Time: 10 minutes. | Serves: 6

½ cup coconut oil, softened	1 teaspoon onion powder
2-pounds chicken fillet	1 teaspoon salt
1 tablespoon avocado oil	

1. Place the Cook & Crisp Basket in your Ninja Foodi Pressure Cooker Steam Fryer. 2. Mix chicken fillet with avocado oil and put it in your Ninja Foodi Pressure Cooker Steam Fryer. 3. Put on the Smart Lid on top of the Ninja Foodi Steam Fryer. 4. Move the Lid Slider to the "Air Fry/Stovetop". 5. Cook it at 395°F/200°C on "Air Fry" Mode for about 10 minutes. 6. Then chop the chicken and put it in the blender. 7. Add remaining ingredients and blend until smooth.
Per Serving: Calories 213; Fat 4.1 g; Sodium 303 mg; Carbs 37.9g; Fiber 1.5g; Sugar 1.9g; Protein 6.6g

Turkey Cream Spread

Prep Time: 5 minutes. | Cook Time: 30 minutes. | Serves: 4

1-pound turkey breast, skinless, boneless, chopped	1 teaspoon cayenne pepper
	½ teaspoon dried oregano
1 tablespoon coconut oil	1 teaspoon salt
3 tablespoons cream cheese	

1. Place the Cook & Crisp Basket in your Ninja Foodi Pressure Cooker Steam Fryer. 2. Mix turkey breast with cayenne pepper, dried oregano, and salt. 3. Put it in your Ninja Foodi Pressure Cooker Steam Fryer. Put on the Smart Lid on top of the Ninja Foodi Steam Fryer. 4. Move the Lid Slider to the "Air Fry/Stovetop". 5. Cook on "Air Fry" Mode at 350°F/175°C for about 15 minutes per side. 6. Then transfer the cooked turkey in the blender and blend until smooth. 7. Mix the blended turkey with remaining ingredients and transfer it in the serving bowl.
Per Serving: Calories 685; Fat 18.3 g; Sodium 865 mg; Carbs99.3g; Fiber 6.5g; Sugar 7.9g; Protein 27.6g

Tomato Drumsticks

Prep Time: 15 minutes. | Cook Time: 18 minutes. | Serves: 8

8 chicken drumsticks	2 tablespoons apple cider vinegar
1 tablespoon tomato paste	1 tablespoon avocado oil
1 teaspoon cayenne pepper	

1. Place the Cook & Crisp Basket in your Ninja Foodi Pressure Cooker Steam Fryer. 2. Mix tomato paste with cayenne pepper, apple cider vinegar, and avocado oil. 3. Then rub the chicken drumsticks with the tomato paste mixture and marinate for about 8 hours. 4. Put the chicken drumsticks in your Ninja Foodi Pressure Cooker Steam Fryer. Put on the Smart Lid on top of the Ninja Foodi Steam Fryer. 5. Move the Lid Slider to the "Air Fry/Stovetop". 6. Cook on "Air Fry" Mode at 360°F/180°C for about 18 minutes.
Per Serving: Calories 249; Fat 5.7 g; Sodium 574 mg; Carbs 23.9g; Fiber 0.9g; Sugar 1.9g; Protein 3.6g

Saucy Turkey Leg

Prep Time: 10 minutes. | Cook Time: 40 minutes. | Serves: 4

2-pounds turkey leg	1 tablespoon coconut oil, melted
¼ cup marinara sauce	½ teaspoon dried thyme
1 teaspoon nutmeg	

1. Place the Cook & Crisp Basket in your Ninja Foodi Pressure Cooker Steam Fryer. 2. Mix the turkey leg with all the remaining recipe ingredients and put it in your Ninja Foodi Pressure Cooker Steam Fryer. 3. Put on the Smart Lid on top of the Ninja Foodi Steam Fryer. 4. Move the Lid Slider to the "Air Fry/Stovetop". 5. Cook it at 355°F/180°C on "Air Fry" Mode for about 40 minutes. Flip it from time to time to avoid burning.
Per Serving: Calories 351; Fat 20.3 g; Sodium 298 mg; Carbs 40.9g; Fiber 0.5g; Sugar 35.5g; Protein3.6g

Tasty Chicken Meatballs

Prep Time: 20 minutes. | Cook Time: 11 minutes. | Serves: 6

3-pounds chicken	1 teaspoon garlic powder
1 teaspoon cream cheese	Cooking spray
1 teaspoon dried cilantro	

1. Place the Cook & Crisp Basket in your Ninja Foodi Pressure Cooker Steam Fryer. 2. Mix the chicken with cream cheese, dried cilantro, and garlic powder. 3. Make the meatballs from the chicken mixture and put them in your Ninja Foodi Cook & Crisp Basket. 4. Spray the Ninja Foodi Cook & Crisp Basket with cooking spray and put the meatballs inside. 5. Put on the Smart Lid on top of the Ninja Foodi Steam Fryer. 6. Move the Lid Slider to the "Air Fry/Stovetop". 7. Cook the meatballs at 360°F/180°C on "Air Fry" Mode for about 11 minutes.
Per Serving: Calories 416; Fat 8.3 g; Sodium 208 mg; Carbs 22.9g; Fiber 0.5g; Sugar 19g; Protein 60.6g

Air-Fried Meatballs

Prep Time: 15 minutes. | Cook Time: 24 minutes. | Serves: 2

2 cups chicken	1 teaspoon coconut cream
2 ounces scallions, minced	½ teaspoon salt
½ teaspoon black pepper	1 teaspoon olive oil

1. Place the Cook & Crisp Basket in your Ninja Foodi Pressure Cooker Steam Fryer. 2. Mix chicken with minced scallions, black pepper, coconut cream, and salt. 3. Make the meatballs and put them in your Ninja Foodi Pressure Cooker Steam Fryer. 4. Sprinkle the meatballs with olive oil. Put on the Smart Lid on top of the Ninja Foodi Steam Fryer. 5. Move the Lid Slider to the "Air Fry/Stovetop". 6. Cook on "Air Fry" Mode at 360°F/180°C for about 12 minutes per side.
Per Serving: Calories 386; Fat 10.3 g; Sodium 238 mg; Carbs 72.9g; Fiber 4.5g; Sugar 59g; Protein 2.6g

Dill Chicken

Prep Time: 15 minutes. | Cook Time: 14 minutes. | Serves: 2

12 ounces chicken fillets	1 tablespoon avocado oil
1 tablespoon dried dill	

1. Place the Cook & Crisp Basket in your Ninja Foodi Pressure Cooker Steam Fryer. 2. Cut the chicken fillet into servings and sprinkle with dried dill and avocado oil. 3. Put the chicken fillets in the Ninja Foodi Cook & Crisp Basket. Put on the Smart Lid on top of the Ninja Foodi Steam Fryer. 4. Move the Lid Slider to the "Air Fry/Stovetop". 5. Cook on "Air Fry" Mode at 360°F/180°C for about 7 minutes per side.
Per Serving: Calories 426; Fat 36.3 g; Sodium 248 mg; Carbs 22.1g; Fiber 2g; Sugar 10.9g; Protein 6.6g

Chicken Strips

Prep Time: 10 minutes. | Cook Time: 30 minutes. | Serves: 4

2-pound chicken fillet, cut into strips	¼ cup heavy cream
1 tablespoon sugar	½ teaspoon white pepper
	Cooking spray

1. Place the Cook & Crisp Basket in your Ninja Foodi Pressure Cooker Steam Fryer. 2. Mix the chicken strips with sugar, heavy cream, and white pepper. 3. Spray the Ninja Foodi Cook & Crisp Basket with cooking spray and put the chicken strips inside. 4. Cook the chicken strips at 350°F/175°C on "Air Fry" Mode for about 30 minutes.
Per Serving: Calories 148; Fat 0.3 g; Sodium 3 mg; Carbs 38.9g; Fiber 0.5g; Sugar 33.9g; Protein 0.6g

Fried Cheese Chicken

Prep Time: 10 Minutes. | Cook Time: 14 Minutes. | Serves: 4

1 pound boneless, skinless chicken breasts	½ teaspoon salt
¾ cup dill pickle juice	½ teaspoon black pepper
¾ cup blanched almond flour	2 large eggs
¾ cup grated Parmesan cheese	Avocado oil spray

1. Place the Cook & Crisp Basket in your Ninja Foodi Pressure Cooker Steam Fryer. 2. Place the boneless chicken breasts in a zip-top bag or between two pieces of plastic sheet. Using any meat mallet or heavy skillet, pound the chicken to a uniform ½-inch thickness. 3. Place the chicken in a suitable bowl with the pickle juice. Cover and allow to brine in the refrigerator for up to 2 hours. 4. In a shallow dish, mix well the almond flour, Parmesan cheese, salt, and pepper. 5. In an another, shallow bowl, beat the eggs. 6. Drain the chicken and pat it dry with paper towels. Dip in the eggs and then in the flour mixture, making sure to press the coating into the chicken. Spray both sides of the coated breasts with oil. 7. Spray the Ninja Foodi Cook & Crisp Basket with oil and put the chicken inside. 8. Put on the Smart Lid on top of the Ninja Foodi Steam Fryer. 9. Move the Lid Slider to the "Air Fry/Stovetop". 10. Set the air fryer temperature to 400°F/200°C. Cook on "Air Fry" Mode at 350°F/175°C for about 6 to 7 minutes. 11. Carefully flip the half-cooked breasts with a spatula. Spray the breasts again with oil and continue cooking for about 6 to 7 minutes more, until golden and crispy.
Per Serving: Calories 209; Fat 7.5g; Sodium 321mg; Total Carbs 34.1g; Fiber 4g; Sugar 3.8g; Protein 4.3g

Chicken Sausages

Prep Time: 20 minutes. | Cook Time: 10 minutes. | Serves: 5

2-pound chicken sausages	1 teaspoon dried mint
1 tablespoon olive oil	¼ teaspoon salt

1. Place the Cook & Crisp Basket in your Ninja Foodi Pressure Cooker Steam Fryer. 2. Sprinkle the chicken sausages with dried mint and salt. 3. Then put the chicken sausages in your Ninja Foodi Pressure Cooker Steam Fryer and sprinkle with olive oil. 4. Put on the Smart Lid on top of the Ninja Foodi Steam Fryer. 5. Move the Lid Slider to the "Air Fry/Stovetop". 6. Cook the meal at 390°F/200°C on "Air Fry" Mode for about 5 minutes per side.
Per Serving: Calories 326; Fat 2.1 g; Sodium 18 mg; Carbs 10g; Fiber 4.5g; Sugar 9g; Protein 20.6g

Turkey Cheese Cups

Prep Time: 5 minutes. | Cook Time: 25 minutes. | Serves: 4

17-ounce turkey	1 teaspoon Italian seasonings
¼ cup cream cheese	1 teaspoon coconut oil

1. Place the Cook & Crisp Basket in your Ninja Foodi Pressure Cooker Steam Fryer and place a reversible rack in it. 2. Grease the ramekins with coconut oil. 3. Then mix turkey with cream cheese and Italian seasonings. 4. Put the turkey mixture in the ramekins. Put on the Smart Lid on top of the Ninja Foodi Steam Fryer. 5. Move the Lid Slider to the "Air Fry/Stovetop". 6. Cook in your Ninja Foodi Pressure Cooker Steam Fryer at 375°F/190°C on "Air Fry" Mode for about 25 minutes.
Per Serving: Calories 477; Fat 13.3 g; Sodium 128 mg; Carbs 89.5g; Fiber 6.5g; Sugar 59.2g; Protein 5.4g

Crusted Chicken

Prep Time: 15 minutes. | Cook Time: 14 minutes. | Serves: 6

2-pound chicken breast, skinless, boneless
4 eggs, beaten
½ cup coconut flour
1 teaspoon Italian seasonings

1. Place the Cook & Crisp Basket in your Ninja Foodi Pressure Cooker Steam Fryer. 2. Cut the chicken breast into the strips and sprinkle with Italian seasonings. 3. Then dip the chicken strips in the egg and coat in the coconut flour. 4. Put on the Smart Lid on top of the Ninja Foodi Steam Fryer. 5. Move the Lid Slider to the "Air Fry/Stovetop". 6. Cook the chicken strips in your Ninja Foodi Pressure Cooker Steam Fryer at 375°F/190°C on "Air Fry" Mode for about 7 minutes per side.
Per Serving: Calories 551; Fat 29.3 g; Sodium 74 mg; Carbs 73.9g; Fiber 3.5g; Sugar 55.9g; Protein 5g

Gingered Turkey

Prep Time: 5 minutes. | Cook Time: 15 minutes. | Serves: 4

2-pound turkey breast, skinless, boneless, chopped
1 tablespoon ginger powder
½ teaspoon salt
1 tablespoon olive oil

1. Place the Cook & Crisp Basket in your Ninja Foodi Pressure Cooker Steam Fryer. 2. Mix turkey breast with ginger powder, salt, and olive oil. 3. Put on the Smart Lid on top of the Ninja Foodi Steam Fryer. 4. Move the Lid Slider to the "Air Fry/Stovetop". 5. Cook the turkey at 385°F/195°C on "Air Fry" Mode for about 15 minutes.
Per Serving: Calories 416; Fat 8.3 g; Sodium 208 mg; Carbs 22.9g; Fiber 0.5g; Sugar 19g; Protein 60.6g

Paprika Chicken Breast

Prep Time: 10 minutes. | Cook Time: 30 minutes. | Serves: 3

1-pound chicken breast, skinless, boneless
1 tablespoon paprika
1 teaspoon salt
1 teaspoon turmeric
1 tablespoon avocado oil

1. Place the Cook & Crisp Basket in your Ninja Foodi Pressure Cooker Steam Fryer. 2. Rub the chicken with all the remaining recipe ingredients and put in your Ninja Foodi Cook & Crisp Basket. 3. Put on the Smart Lid on top of the Ninja Foodi Steam Fryer. 4. Move the Lid Slider to the "Air Fry/Stovetop". 5. Cook the chicken breast at 360°F/180°C on "Air Fry" Mode for about 30 minutes.
Per Serving: Calories 305; Fat 25g; Sodium 532mg; Total Carbs 2.3g; Fiber 0.4g; Sugar 2g; Protein 18.3g

Air-Fried Turkey Mash

Prep Time: 5 minutes. | Cook Time: 35 minutes. | Serves: 4

1-pound turkey breast, skinless, boneless, chopped
2 tablespoons mascarpone
1 teaspoon garlic powder
1 tablespoon dried parsley
Cooking spray

1. Place the Cook & Crisp Basket in your Ninja Foodi Pressure Cooker Steam Fryer. 2. Spray the Ninja Foodi Cook & Crisp Basket with cooking spray from inside. 3. Then put all the remaining recipe ingredients in the Ninja Foodi Cook & Crisp Basket and carefully mix. 4. Put on the Smart Lid on top of the Ninja Foodi Steam Fryer. 5. Move the Lid Slider to the "Air Fry/Stovetop". 6. Cook the turkey mash at 355°F/180°C on "Air Fry" Mode for about 35 minutes.
Per Serving: Calories 190; Fat 18g; Sodium 150mg; Total Carbs 0.6g; Fiber 0.4g; Sugar 0.4g; Protein 7.2g

Italian Chicken Parmesan

Prep Time: 25 Minutes. | Cook Time: 20 Minutes. | Serves 8

2 pounds boneless chicken breasts
1 cup blanched almond flour
1 cup grated Parmesan cheese
1 teaspoon Italian seasoning
Salt
Black pepper
2 large eggs
Avocado oil spray
⅓ cup sugar-free marinara sauce
4 ounces fresh Mozarella cheese, sliced or shredded

1. Place the Cook & Crisp Basket in your Ninja Foodi Pressure Cooker Steam Fryer. 2. Place the boneless chicken in a zip-top bag. 3. Use any meat mallet or heavy skillet to pound the chicken to a uniform ½-inch thickness. 4. Place the almond flour, Parmesan cheese, Italian seasoning, and salt and pepper to taste in a large shallow bowl. 5. In a separate shallow bowl, beat the eggs. 6. Dip each boneless chicken breast in the egg, then coat it in the almond flour mixture, making sure to press the coating onto the chicken gently. Repeat with the remaining chicken. 7. Spray both sides of the chicken well with oil and place the pieces in a single layer in your Ninja Foodi Cook & Crisp Basket, working in batches if necessary. Put on the Smart Lid on top of the Ninja Foodi Steam Fryer. 8. Move the Lid Slider to the "Air Fry/Stovetop". 9. Cook on "Air Fry" Mode at 400°F/200°C for about 10 minutes. 10. Flip the half-cooked chicken with a spatula. Spray each piece with more oil and continue cooking for about 5 minutes more. 11. Top each chicken piece with the marinara sauce and Mozarella. Return to your Ninja Foodi Pressure Cooker Steam Fryer. Cook on "Air Fry" Mode at 400°F/200°C for about 3 to 5 minutes, until the cheese is melted and an instant-read thermometer reads 160°F/70°C. 12. Allow the chicken to rest for about 5 minutes, then serve.
Per Serving: Calories 266; Fat 6.3g; Sodium 193mg; Total Carbs 39.1g; Fiber 7.2g; Sugar 5.2g; Protein 14.8g

Basil Chicken Breast

Prep Time: 25 minutes. | Cook Time: 30 minutes. | Serves: 5

2-pounds chicken breast, skinless, boneless, chopped
2 teaspoons dried basil
3 tablespoons apple cider vinegar
2 tablespoons avocado oil
1 teaspoon salt
1 teaspoon black pepper

1. Place the Cook & Crisp Basket in your Ninja Foodi Pressure Cooker Steam Fryer. 2. Mix chicken breast with dried basil, apple cider vinegar, avocado oil, salt, and black pepper. 3. Then leave the chicken for about 20 minutes to marinate. 4. Put the marinated chicken in your Ninja Foodi Pressure Cooker Steam Fryer. Put on the Smart Lid on top of the Ninja Foodi Steam Fryer. 5. Move the Lid Slider to the "Air Fry/Stovetop". 6. Cook on "Air Fry" Mode for about 30 minutes at 370°F/185°C.
Per Serving: Calories 267; Fat 12g; Sodium 165mg; Total Carbs 39g; Fiber 1.4g; Sugar 22g; Protein 3.3g

Chicken Beans Bowl

Prep Time: 10 minutes. | Cook Time: 35 minutes. | Serves: 4

1-pound chicken
2 cups green beans, chopped
1 cup chicken broth
1 teaspoon Italian seasonings
1 teaspoon salt
1 cup Cheddar cheese, shredded
1 teaspoon avocado oil

1. Place the Cook & Crisp Basket in your Ninja Foodi Pressure Cooker Steam Fryer. 2. Mix chicken with Italian seasonings, salt, and avocado oil. 3. Put the mixture in your Ninja Foodi Cook & Crisp Basket. 4. Add chicken broth, green beans, and cheddar cheese. 5. Put on the Smart Lid on top of the Ninja Foodi Steam Fryer. 6. Move the Lid Slider to the "Air Fry/Stovetop". 7. Cook the meal at 365°F/185°C on "Air Fry" Mode for about 35 minutes.
Per Serving: Calories 183; Fat 15g; Sodium 402mg; Total Carbs 2.5g; Fiber 0.4g; Sugar 1.1g; Protein 10g

Celery Chicken

Prep Time: 5 minutes. | Cook Time: 30 minutes. | Serves: 4

1 teaspoon onion powder
1 teaspoon garlic powder
2-pounds chicken breast, skinless, boneless
2 tablespoons celery root
1 tablespoon avocado oil

1. Place the Cook & Crisp Basket in your Ninja Foodi Pressure Cooker Steam Fryer. 2. In the shallow bowl, mix onion powder with garlic powder, and celery root. 3. Mix the chicken breast with the spice mixture and sprinkle with avocado oil. 4. Put on the Smart Lid on top of the Ninja Foodi Steam Fryer. 5. Move the Lid Slider to the "Air Fry/Stovetop". 6. Cook the chicken breast at 360°F/180°C on "Air Fry" Mode for about 15 minutes per side.
Per Serving: Calories 276; Fat 2.1 g; Sodium 18 mg; Carbs 65.9g; Fiber 4.5g; Sugar 59g; Protein 2.6g

Turkey Cheese Pockets

Prep Time: 15 minutes. | Cook Time: 4 minutes. | Serves: 4

4 tortillas
1 bell pepper, chopped
3 ounces Provolone cheese, grated

1 teaspoon dried parsley
1-pound turkey breast, boiled, chopped

1. Place the Cook & Crisp Basket in your Ninja Foodi Pressure Cooker Steam Fryer. 2. Mix the bell pepper with cheese, dried parsley, and turkey breast. 3. Then top the tortillas with turkey mixture and fold in the shape of pockets. 4. Put on the Smart Lid on top of the Ninja Foodi Steam Fryer. 5. Move the Lid Slider to the "Air Fry/Stovetop". 6. Cook the turkey pockets at 400°F/200°C on "Air Fry" Mode for about 4 minutes.
Per Serving: Calories 416; Fat 8.3 g; Sodium 208 mg; Carbs 22.9g; Fiber 0.5g; Sugar 19g; Protein 60.6g

Mozarella Chicken

Prep Time: 15 minutes. | Cook Time: 30 minutes. | Serves: 4

1 cup Mozzarella, shredded
1 teaspoon dried basil
1 teaspoon coconut oil

1 teaspoon black pepper
2-pounds chicken breast, skinless, boneless, sliced

1. Place the Cook & Crisp Basket in your Ninja Foodi Pressure Cooker Steam Fryer. 2. Grease the Ninja Foodi Cook & Crisp Basket with coconut oil. 3. Then mix chicken breast with black pepper and dried basil. 4. Put it in the Ninja Foodi Cook & Crisp Basket and flatten gently. 5. Then top the chicken breast with Mozzarella. Put on the Smart Lid on top of the Ninja Foodi Steam Fryer. 6. Move the Lid Slider to the "Air Fry/Stovetop". 7. Cook the meal at 365°F/185°C on "Air Fry" Mode for about 30 minutes.
Per Serving: Calories 273; Fat 22g; Sodium 517mg; Total Carbs 3.3g; Fiber 0.2g; Sugar 1.4g; Protein 16.1g

Chicken Cabbage Pan

Prep Time: 10 minutes. | Cook Time: 35 minutes. | Serves: 4

1 cup white cabbage, shredded
1-pound chicken fillet, chopped
1 teaspoon chili powder
1 teaspoon dried cilantro

1 tablespoon coconut oil, melted
½ teaspoon salt
½ cup heavy cream

1. Place the Cook & Crisp Basket in your Ninja Foodi Pressure Cooker Steam Fryer. 2. Put all the recipe ingredients in the Ninja Foodi Cook & Crisp Basket and carefully mix the mixture. 3. Put on the Smart Lid on top of the Ninja Foodi Steam Fryer. 4. Move the Lid Slider to the "Air Fry/Stovetop". 5. Cook the meal at 360°F/180°C on "Air Fry" Mode for about 35 minutes.
Per Serving: Calories 282; Fat 15g; Sodium 526mg; Total Carbs 20g; Fiber 0.6g; Sugar 3.3g; Protein 16g

Pepper Chicken Halves

Prep Time: 10 minutes. | Cook Time: 30 minutes. | Serves: 4

2-pounds chicken, halved
1 tablespoon cayenne pepper

1 tablespoon apple cider vinegar
1 tablespoon avocado oil

1. Place the Cook & Crisp Basket in your Ninja Foodi Pressure Cooker Steam Fryer. 2. Rub the chicken halves with cayenne pepper, apple cider vinegar, and avocado oil. 3. Put the chicken halves in your Ninja Foodi Pressure Cooker Steam Fryer. Put on the Smart Lid on top of the Ninja Foodi Steam Fryer. 4. Move the Lid Slider to the "Air Fry/Stovetop". 5. Cook on "Air Fry" Mode at 360°F/180°C for about 30 minutes per side.
Per Serving: Calories 237; Fat 19g; Sodium 518mg; Total Carbs 7g; Fiber 1.5g; Sugar 3.4g; Protein 12g

Lemon-Dijon Chicken

Prep Time: 5 Minutes. | Cook Time: 16 Minutes. | Serves: 6

½ cup sugar-free mayo
1 tablespoon Dijon mustard
1 tablespoon freshly squeezed

lemon juice (optional)
1 tablespoon coconut aminos
1 teaspoon Italian seasoning

1 teaspoon salt
½ teaspoon black pepper
¼ teaspoon cayenne pepper

1½ pounds boneless, skinless chicken breasts or thighs

1. Place the Cook & Crisp Basket in your Ninja Foodi Pressure Cooker Steam Fryer. 2. In a suitable bowl, mix the mayo, mustard, lemon juice (if using), coconut aminos, Italian seasoning, salt, black pepper, and cayenne pepper. 3. Place the boneless chicken in a large zip-top plastic bag. 4. Add the prepared marinade, making sure all the pieces are coated. 5. Cover and refrigerate the chicken for at least 30 minutes. 6. Set the Ninja Foodi Pressure Cooker Steam Fryer to 400°F/200°C. Arrange the chicken in a single layer in your Ninja Foodi Cook & Crisp Basket, working in batches if necessary. Put on the Smart Lid on top of the Ninja Foodi Steam Fryer. 7. Move the Lid Slider to the "Air Fry/Stovetop". 8. Cook on "Air Fry" Mode at 400°F/200°C for about 7 minutes. 9. Flip the half-cooked chicken and continue cooking for about 6 to 9 minutes more. 10. Serve.
Per Serving: Calories 297; Fat 1g; Sodium 291mg; Total Carbs 35g; Fiber 1g; Sugar 9g; Protein 29g

Spiced Turkey Breast

Prep time: 5 minutes. | Cook Time: 55 minutes. | Serves: 10

1 tablespoon salt
1 teaspoon paprika
1 teaspoon onion powder
1 teaspoon garlic powder
½ teaspoon black pepper

4 pounds bone-in, skin-on turkey breast
2 tablespoons unsalted butter, melted

1. Place the Cook & Crisp Basket in your Ninja Foodi Pressure Cooker Steam Fryer. 2. In a suitable bowl, mix the salt, paprika, onion powder, garlic powder, and pepper. 3. Sprinkle the seasonings all over the turkey. Brush the seasoned turkey with some of the melted butter. 4. Place the turkey in your Ninja Foodi Cook & Crisp Basket, skin-side down. 5. Put on the Smart Lid on top of the Ninja Foodi Steam Fryer. 6. Move the Lid Slider to the "Air Fry/Stovetop". 7. Cook on "Air Fry" Mode at 350°F/175°C for about 25 minutes. 8. Flip the half-cooked turkey and brush it with the remaining butter. Continue cooking this turkey for another 20 to 30 minutes, until an instant-read thermometer reads 160°F/70°C. 9. Remove the turkey breast from your Ninja Foodi Pressure Cooker Steam Fryer. Tent a piece of aluminum foil over the turkey, and allow it to rest for about 5 minutes before serving.
Per Serving: Calories 348; Fat 30g; Sodium 660mg; Total Carbs 5g; Fiber 0g; Sugar 0g; Protein 14g

Buffalo Chicken

prep time: 15 minutes. | Cook Time: 10 minutes. | Serves: 4

½ cup blanched almond flour
½ cup grated Parmesan cheese
1 teaspoon smoked paprika
¼ teaspoon cayenne pepper
½ teaspoon salt, plus additional for seasoning
black pepper
2 large eggs
1-pound chicken tenders

Avocado oil spray
⅓ cup hot sauce, such as Frank's Red-hot
2 tablespoons unsalted butter
2 tablespoons white vinegar
1 garlic clove, minced
Blue cheese crumbles, for serving
Blue cheese dressing, for serving

1. Place the Cook & Crisp Basket in your Ninja Foodi Pressure Cooker Steam Fryer. 2. In any shallow bowl, mix the almond flour, Parmesan cheese, smoked paprika, and cayenne pepper and season with salt and pepper to taste. In a separate shallow bowl, beat the eggs. 3. One at a time, dip the chicken tenders in the eggs, then coat them with the almond flour mixture, making sure to press the coating into the chicken gently. 4. Place the chicken tenders in a single layer in the Ninja Foodi Cook & Crisp Basket and spray them with oil. 5. Put on the Smart Lid on top of the Ninja Foodi Steam Fryer. 6. Move the Lid Slider to the "Air Fry/Stovetop". 7. Cook on "Air Fry" Mode at 400°F/200°C for about 4 minutes. Flip the half-cooked tenders and spray them with more oil. Cook on "Air Fry" Mode for about 6 minutes more until an instant-read thermometer reads 165°F/75°C. 8. While the chicken is cooking, mix the hot sauce, butter, vinegar, garlic, and ½ teaspoon of salt in a small saucepan over medium-low heat. Heat until the butter is melted, whisking to mix. 9. Toss the chicken tenders with the sauce. Serve warm with blue cheese dressing and blue cheese crumbles.
Per Serving: Calories 257; Fat 10.4g; Sodium 431mg; Total Carbs 20g; Fiber 0g; Sugar 1.6g; Protein 21g

Nashville Chicken

prep time: 20 minutes | Cook Time: 28 minutes. | Serves: 8

3 pounds bone-in, skin-on chicken pieces, breasts halved crosswise	2 large eggs, beaten
1 tablespoon salt	1 tablespoon hot sauce
1 tablespoon black pepper	Avocado oil spray
1½ cups blanched almond flour	½ cup (1 stick) unsalted butter
1½ cups grated Parmesan cheese	½ cup avocado oil
1 tablespoon baking powder	1 tablespoon cayenne pepper
2 teaspoons garlic powder	2 tablespoons brown sugar
½ cup heavy cream	substitute, such as Sukrin Gold

1. Place the Cook & Crisp Basket in your Ninja Foodi Pressure Cooker Steam Fryer. 2. Season the chicken with the black pepper and salt. 3. In a suitable shallow bowl, mix well the almond flour, Parmesan cheese, baking powder, and 1 teaspoon of the garlic powder. 4. In a separate bowl, mix well the heavy cream, eggs, and hot sauce. 5. Dip the cut chicken pieces in the beat egg mixture, then coat each with the dry almond flour mixture, pressing the mixture into the chicken to coat well. Allow to sit for almost 15 minutes to let the breading set. 6. Place the chicken in a single layer in your Ninja Foodi Cook & Crisp Basket, being careful not to overcrowd the pieces, working in batches if necessary. Spray the prepared chicken with oil. 7. Put on the Smart Lid on top of the Ninja Foodi Steam Fryer. 8. Move the Lid Slider to the "Air Fry/Stovetop". 9. Cook on "Air Fry" Mode at 400°F/200°C for about 13 minutes. 10. Carefully flip the half-cooked chicken and spray it with more oil. Reduce your Ninja Foodi Pressure Cooker Steam Fryer temperature to 350°F/175°C. Cook on "Air Fry" Mode at 350°F/175°C for another 11 to 15 minutes, until an instant-read thermometer reads 160°F/70°C. 11. Meanwhile heat the butter with avocado oil, cayenne pepper, brown sugar substitute, and remaining 1 teaspoon of garlic powder in a suitable saucepan over medium heat. 12. Cook on a simmer until the butter is melted. 13. Remove the chicken from your Ninja Foodi Pressure Cooker Steam Fryer. 14. Dip the prepared chicken in the sauce. 15. Then transfer the coated chicken on a rack over a baking sheet, and allow it to rest for about 5 minutes before serving.
Per Serving: Calories 399; Fat 16g; Sodium 537mg; Total Carbs 28g; Fiber 3g; Sugar 10g; Protein 35g

Chicken Tenders

Prep Time: 10 minutes. | Cook Time: 15 minutes. | Serves: 4-6

½ cup coconut flour	2 beaten eggs
1 tablespoon spicy brown mustard	1 pound of chicken tenders

1. Place the Cook & Crisp Basket in your Pressure Cooker Steam Fryer. 2. Season tenders with pepper and salt. 3. Place a thin layer of mustard onto tenders and then dredge in flour and dip in egg. 4. Place tenders in the Cook & Crisp Basket. Put on the Smart Lid on top of the Ninja Foodi Steam Fryer. Move the Lid Slider to the "Air Fry/Stovetop". Select the "Air Fry" mode for cooking. Cook for 10 to 15 minutes at 390°F/200°C till crispy.
Per serving: Calories: 478; Fat: 12.9g; Sodium: 414mg; Carbs: 11g; Fiber: 5g; Sugar 9g; Protein 11g

Turkey Meatballs

prep time: 20 minutes. | Cook Time: 12 minutes. | Serves: 4

1-pound turkey	2 teaspoons garlic powder
½ teaspoon salt	Avocado oil spray
Black pepper	¾ cup sugar-free ketchup
1 large egg, beaten	1 tablespoon yellow mustard
1 teaspoon gelatin	1 tablespoon apple cider vinegar
½ cup almond meal	2 tablespoons brown sugar
½ tablespoon chili powder	substitute, such as Swerve
2½ teaspoons smoked paprika	1 teaspoon liquid smoke
1 teaspoon onion powder	

1. Place the Cook & Crisp Basket in your Ninja Foodi Pressure Cooker Steam Fryer. 2. Place the turkey in a suitable bowl and season with salt and pepper. 3. Place the beaten egg in a suitable bowl and sprinkle with the gelatin. Allow to sit for about 5 minutes, then whisk to mix. 4. Pour the prepared gelatin mixture over the turkey and add the almond meal, chili powder, 1 teaspoon of smoked paprika,

onion powder, and 1 teaspoon of garlic powder. Mix gently with your hands until mixed. 5. Form the mixture into 1½-inch balls. 6. Spray the meatballs with oil and place in the Ninja Foodi Cook & Crisp Basket in a single layer. 7. Put on the Smart Lid on top of the Ninja Foodi Steam Fryer. 8. Move the Lid Slider to the "Air Fry/Stovetop". 9. Cook on "Air Fry" Mode at 400°F/200°C for about 5 minutes. Flip the half-cooked meatballs and spray them with more oil. Cook for about 4 to 7 minutes more, until an instant-read thermometer reads 165°F/75°C. 10. While the meatballs cook, place the ketchup, mustard, apple cider vinegar, and brown sugar substitute in a small saucepan over medium heat. Bring to a simmer and cook for 5 minutes. Reduce its heat to low and add the remaining 1½ teaspoons of smoked paprika, liquid smoke, remaining 1 teaspoon of garlic powder, and ½ teaspoon of salt. Cook for about 5 minutes more, stirring occasionally, until thickened. Remove meatballs from the Ninja Foodi Steam Fryer. 11. Toss the meatballs with the sauce and serve warm. 12. Cooking tip: I like to use a cookie scoop to form the meatballs. This helps keep them uniform in size, which ensures that they will cook evenly.
Per Serving: Calories 305; Fat 15g; Sodium 482mg; Total Carbs 17g; Fiber 3g; Sugar 2g; Protein 35g

Mushroom Stuffed Turkey

Prep Time: 15 minutes. | Cook Time: 30 minutes. | Serves: 4

2-pound turkey fillet	1 tablespoon coconut oil
1 cup mushrooms, chopped	1 teaspoon olive oil
1 teaspoon garlic powder	1 teaspoon chili powder
2 ounces scallions, chopped	

1. Place the Cook & Crisp Basket in your Ninja Foodi Pressure Cooker Steam Fryer. 2. Mix chili powder with mushrooms, garlic powder, olive oil, coconut oil and scallions. 3. Then make the cut in the shape of pocket in the turkey fillet. Fill it with mushroom mixture and secure the cut with the help of the toothpick. 4. Grease the Ninja Foodi Cook & Crisp Basket with coconut oil and put the stuffed turkey inside. 5. Put on the Smart Lid on top of the Ninja Foodi Steam Fryer. 6. Move the Lid Slider to the "Air Fry/Stovetop". 7. Cook it at 380°F/195°C on "Air Fry" Mode for about 30 minutes.
Per Serving: Calories 506; Fat 48.3 g; Sodium 608 mg; Carbs 158.9g; Fiber 6.5g; Sugar 83.9g; Protein 12.6g

Stuffed Chicken Kiev

prep time: 25 minutes | Cook Time: 18 minutes. | serves 8

½ cup (1 stick) unsalted butter	Salt
1 teaspoon minced garlic	¾ cup blanched almond flour
2 tablespoons chopped fresh parsley	¾ cup grated Parmesan cheese
½ teaspoon black pepper	⅛ teaspoon cayenne pepper
2 pounds boneless, skinless chicken breasts	2 large eggs
	Avocado oil spray

1. Place the Cook & Crisp Basket in your Ninja Foodi Pressure Cooker Steam Fryer. 2. In a suitable bowl, mix the butter, garlic, parsley, and black pepper. Allow to harden. 3. Form the butter garlic mixture into a log and wrap it tightly with parchment paper or plastic wrap. 4. Refrigerate this butter for at least 2 hours, until firm. 5. Place the chicken breasts in a zip-top bag or between two pieces of plastic wrap. Pound the chicken with any meat mallet or heavy skillet to an even ¼-inch thickness. 6. Place a pat of unsalted butter in the center of each chicken breast and wrap the chicken tightly around the butter from the long side, tucking in the short sides as you go. Secure with toothpicks. Season the outside of the chicken with some salt. Wrap the stuffed chicken tightly with plastic wrap. Refrigerate at least 2 hours or overnight. 7. In any shallow bowl, mix the almond flour, Parmesan cheese, and cayenne pepper. 8. In another shallow bowl, beat the eggs. 9. Dip each piece of chicken in the eggs, then coat it in the almond flour mixture, using your fingers to press the breading gently into the chicken. 10. Spray the chicken with oil and place it in a single layer in your Ninja Foodi Cook & Crisp Basket, working in batches if necessary. 11. Put on the Smart Lid on top of the Ninja Foodi Steam Fryer. 12. Move the Lid Slider to the "Air Fry/Stovetop". 13. Cook on "Air Fry" Mode at 350°F/175°C for about 8 minutes. Flip the half-cooked chicken, then spray it again with oil. Cook for about 6 to 10 minutes more, until the instant-read thermometer reads 165°F/75°C.
Per Serving: Calories 336; Fat 6g; Sodium 181mg; Total Carbs 1.3g; Fiber 0.2g; Sugar 0.4g; Protein 69.2g

Crusted Chicken Chunks

Prep Time: 10 minutes. | Cook Time: 8-10 minutes | Serves: 4

1-pound chicken tenders cut in large chunks, about 1½ inches	2 eggs, beaten
Salt and pepper	1 cup panko breadcrumbs
½ cup cornstarch	Oil for misting or cooking spray

1. Place the Cook & Crisp Basket in your Ninja Foodi Pressure Cooker Steam Fryer. 2. Season chicken chunks to your liking with salt and pepper. 3. Dip chicken chunks in cornstarch. Then dip in egg and shake off excess. Then roll in panko crumbs to coat well. 4. Spray all sides of chicken chunks with oil or cooking spray. 5. Place chicken in Cook & Crisp Basket in single layer. 6. Put on the Smart Lid on top of the Ninja Foodi Steam Fryer. 7. Move the Lid Slider to the "Air Fry/Stovetop". 8. Cook on "Air Fry" Mode at 390°F/200°C for about 5 minutes. Spray with oil, turn chunks over, and spray other side. 9. Cook for 5 minutes more until chicken juices run clear and outside is golden brown. 10. Cook remaining chicken in the same way.
Per Serving: Calories 220; Fat 13g; Sodium 542mg; Total Carbs 0.9g; Fiber 0.3g; Sugar 0.2g; Protein 25.6g

Chicken Filling

Prep Time: 5 minutes. | Cook Time: 8 minutes. | Serves: 2

½ cups	½ teaspoon garlic powder
1-pound chicken tenders boneless	Cooking spray
½ teaspoon cumin	

1. Place the Cook & Crisp Basket in your Ninja Foodi Pressure Cooker Steam Fryer. 2. Sprinkle raw chicken tenders with seasonings. 3. Spray Cook & Crisp Basket lightly with cooking spray to prevent sticking. 4. Place chicken in Cook & Crisp Basket in single layer. 5. Put on the Smart Lid on top of the Ninja Foodi Steam Fryer. 6. Move the Lid Slider to the "Air Fry/Stovetop". 7. Cook on "Air Fry" Mode at 390°F/200°C for about 4 minutes, turn chicken strips over. Cook for an additional 4 minutes. 8. Test for doneness. Thick tenders may require an additional minute or two.
Per Serving: Calories 374; Fat 13g; Sodium 552mg; Total Carbs 25g; Fiber 1.2g; Sugar 1.2g; Protein 37.7g

Fried Buffalo Chicken Wings

Prep time: 10 minutes. | Cook Time: 25 minutes. | Serves: 4

2 tablespoons baking powder	½ cup Buffalo hot sauce
1 teaspoon smoked paprika	¼ cup unsalted butter
Salt	2 tablespoons apple cider vinegar
Black pepper	1 teaspoon minced garlic
2 pounds chicken wings	Blue Cheese Dressing or Garlic
Avocado oil spray	Ranch Dressing, for serving
⅓ cup avocado oil	

1. Place the Cook & Crisp Basket in your Ninja Foodi Pressure Cooker Steam Fryer. 2. In a suitable bowl, mix the smoked paprika, baking powder, and salt and black pepper to taste. 3. Now add the chicken wings to this bowl and toss to coat. 4. Spray the wings with oil. 5. Place the wings in the Cook & Crisp Basket in a single layer. 6. Put on the Smart Lid on top of the Ninja Foodi Steam Fryer. 7. Move the Lid Slider to the "Air Fry/Stovetop". 8. Cook on "Air Fry" Mode at 400°F/200°C for about 25 minutes. 9. Meanwhile mix hot sauce, butter, avocado oil, vinegar, and garlic in a small saucepan over medium-low heat until warm. 10. Toss the cooked wings with the Buffalo sauce. Serve warm with the dressing.
Per Serving: Calories 199; Fat 11.1g; Sodium 297mg; Total Carbs 14.9g; Fiber 1g; Sugar 2.5g; Protein 9.9g

Homemade turkey Pot Pie

prep time: 20 minutes. | Cook Time: 35 minutes. | Serves: 8

¼ cup (4 tablespoons) unsalted butter	1 teaspoon minced garlic
	1 teaspoon salt
2 shallots, minced	¼ teaspoon black pepper
1 cup mushrooms, chopped	1¾ cups turkey broth or chicken
2 celery stalks, chopped	broth
⅔ cup heavy (whipping) cream	3 cups chopped cooked turkey
2 ounces cream cheese	½ cup frozen baby peas (optional)
½ teaspoon xanthan gum	1 recipe Fathead Pizza Dough

1. Place the Cook & Crisp Basket in your Ninja Foodi Pressure Cooker Steam Fryer and place a reversible rack in it. 2. Melt the unsalted butter in a suitable saucepan over medium heat. Add the shallots, mushrooms, and celery stalks. Cook for 5 minutes, stirring frequently. Add the garlic, salt, and pepper and cook for 1 minute more. 3. Mode Stir in the broth, heavy cream, cream cheese, and xanthan gum. Bring to a simmer. Cook for about 1 minute, stirring constantly. Reduce the heat to low. Cook for about 5 minutes, stirring often, until thickened. 4. Stir in the turkey and peas (if using). 5. Divide the mixture among 8 individual ramekins. 6. Roll out the pizza dough between two sheets of parchment paper. 7. Cut the prepared dough into pieces large enough to cover each ramekin, and place them over the filling. Using a sharp knife, cut a slit or two in the top of each crust to vent. 8. Place the ramekins in the Ninja Foodi Cook & Crisp Basket. 9. Put on the Smart Lid on top of the Ninja Foodi Steam Fryer. 10. Move the Lid Slider to the "Air Fry/Stovetop". 11. Cook on "Air Fry" Mode at 325°F/160°C for about 18 to 23 minutes, until the crusts are golden brown.
Per Serving: Calories 255; Fat 4.2g; Sodium 963mg; Total Carbs 21.5g; Fiber 0.8g; Sugar 5.7g; Protein 8.1g

Smoky Chicken Quarters

prep time: 5 minutes. | Cook Time: 27 minutes. | Serves: 6

½ cup avocado oil	½ teaspoon dried thyme
2 teaspoons smoked paprika	½ teaspoon black pepper
1 teaspoon salt	2 pounds bone-in, skin-on chicken
1 teaspoon garlic powder	leg quarters
½ teaspoon dried rosemary	

1. Place the Cook & Crisp Basket in your Ninja Foodi Pressure Cooker Steam Fryer. 2. In a blender or small bowl, mix the avocado oil, smoked paprika, salt, garlic powder, rosemary, thyme, and black pepper. 3. Place the bone-in chicken leg quarters in a shallow dish. 4. Pour the prepared marinade over the chicken to coat well. Cover and marinate this chicken for at least 2 hours or overnight. 5. Place the prepared chicken in a single layer in your Ninja Foodi Cook & Crisp Basket, working in batches if necessary. 6. Put on the Smart Lid on top of the Ninja Foodi Steam Fryer. 7. Move the Lid Slider to the "Air Fry/Stovetop". 8. Cook on "Air Fry" Mode at 400°F/200°C for about 15 minutes. Flip the half-cooked chicken legs, then reduce the temperature to 350°F/175°C. Cook for about 8 to 12 minutes more, until an instant-read thermometer reads 160°F/70°C when inserted into the chicken. 9. Serve warm.
Per Serving: Calories 308; Fat 24g; Sodium 715mg; Total Carbs 0.8g; Fiber 0.1g; Sugar 0.1g; Protein 21.9g

Easy Chicken Paillard

prep time: 20 minutes. | Cook Time: 10 minutes. | Serves: 4

1-pound boneless chicken breasts	1 teaspoon chopped fresh oregano
2 tablespoons avocado oil	½ teaspoon garlic powder
1 tablespoon freshly squeezed	Salt
lemon juice	black pepper

1. Place the Cook & Crisp Basket in your Ninja Foodi Pressure Cooker Steam Fryer. 2. Place the boneless chicken in a zip-top bag or between two pieces of plastic wrap. Using any meat mallet or a heavy skillet, pound the chicken until it is very thin, about ¼ inch thick. 3. In a suitable bowl, mix the avocado oil, lemon juice, oregano, garlic powder, salt, and pepper. Place the prepared chicken in a dish and pour the marinade on it. Toss to coat all the chicken, and let it rest at room temperature for about 10 to 15 minutes. 4. Place the chicken in the Ninja Foodi Cook & Crisp Basket. Put on the Smart Lid on top of the Ninja Foodi Steam Fryer. 5. Move the Lid Slider to the "Air Fry/Stovetop". 6. Cook on "Air Fry" Mode at 400°F/200°C for about 5 minutes. 7. Flip and cook on "Air Fry" Mode for another 2 to 5 minutes, until an instant-read thermometer reads 160°F/70°C. Allow to rest for about 5 minutes before serving.
Per Serving: Calories 275; Fat 1.4g; Sodium 582mg; Total Carbs 31.5g; Fiber 1.1g; Sugar 0.1g; Protein 29.8g

Chicken Roll-Ups

prep time: 10 minutes. | Cook Time: 17 minutes. | Serves: 8

2 pounds boneless chicken breasts	Black pepper
1 teaspoon chili powder	6 ounces Monterey Jack cheese,
½ teaspoon smoked paprika	shredded
½ teaspoon cumin	4 ounces canned diced green chiles
Salt	Avocado oil spray

1. Place the Cook & Crisp Basket in your Ninja Foodi Pressure Cooker Steam Fryer. 2. Place the boneless chicken in a large zip-top bag or between two pieces of plastic wrap. Using any meat mallet or heavy skillet, pound the chicken until it is about ¼ inch thick. 3. In a suitable bowl, mix the chili powder, smoked paprika, cumin, and salt and pepper to taste. Sprinkle the boneless chicken with the seasonings. 4. Sprinkle the chicken with the Monterey Jack cheese, then the diced green chiles. 5. Roll up each piece of pounded chicken from the long side, tucking in the ends as you go. Secure the roll-up with a toothpick. 6. Spray the outside of the chicken with avocado oil. Spread the prepared chicken in a single layer in the basket, working in batches if necessary. Put on the Smart Lid on top of the Ninja Foodi Steam Fryer. 7. Move the Lid Slider to the "Air Fry/Stovetop". 8. Cook on "Air Fry" Mode at 350°F/175°C for about 7 minutes. Flip and cook for another 7 to 10 minutes, until an instant-read thermometer reads 160°F/70°C. 9. Remove the chicken from your Ninja Foodi Pressure Cooker Steam Fryer and rest for about 5 minutes before serving.
Per Serving: Calories 275; Fat 1.4g; Sodium 582mg; Total Carbs 31.5g; Fiber 1.1g; Sugar 0.1g; Protein 29.8g

Jalapeño Chicken

Prep time: 10 minutes. | Cook Time: 17 minutes. | Serves: 8

2 pounds boneless chicken breasts	4 ounces Cheddar cheese, shredded
Salt, to taste	2 jalapeños, seeded and diced
Black pepper, to taste	1 teaspoon minced garlic
8 ounces cream cheese	Avocado oil spray

1. Place the Cook & Crisp Basket in your Ninja Foodi Pressure Cooker Steam Fryer. 2. Place the boneless chicken in a large zip-top bag. Using any meat mallet or heavy skillet, pound the chicken until it is about ¼-inch thick. Season the chicken with salt and pepper. 3. In a suitable bowl, mix the cream cheese, Cheddar cheese, jalapeños, and garlic. Divide the mixture among the chicken pieces. Roll up each piece from the long side, tucking in the ends as you go. Secure with toothpicks. 4. Spray the chicken with oil. 5. Spread the prepared chicken in a single layer in your Ninja Foodi Cook & Crisp Basket, working in batches if necessary. 6. Put on the Smart Lid on top of the Ninja Foodi Steam Fryer. 7. Move the Lid Slider to the "Air Fry/Stovetop". 8. Cook on "Air Fry" Mode at 350°F/175°C for about 7 minutes. Flip the half-cooked chicken. Cook for 7 to 10 minutes more, until an instant-read thermometer reads 160°F/70°C.
Per Serving: Calories 220; Fat 1.7g; Sodium 178mg; Total Carbs 1.7g; Fiber 0.2g; Sugar 0.2g; Protein 32.9g

Chicken Egg Rolls

Prep Time: 20 minutes. | Cook Time: 9 minutes | Serves: 8

1 teaspoon water	Oil for misting or cooking spray
1 tablespoon cornstarch	Blue Cheese Dip
1 egg	3 ounces cream cheese, softened
2½ cups cooked chicken, diced	⅓ cup blue cheese, crumbled
⅓ cup chopped green onion	1 teaspoon Worcestershire sauce
⅓ cup diced celery	¼ teaspoon garlic powder
⅓ cup buffalo wing sauce	¼ cup buttermilk (or sour cream)
8 egg roll wraps	

1. Place the Cook & Crisp Basket in your Ninja Foodi Pressure Cooker Steam Fryer. 2. Mix water and cornstarch in a suitable bowl until dissolved. Add egg, beat well, and set aside. 3. In a medium size bowl, mix together chicken, green onion, celery, and buffalo wing sauce. 4. Divide chicken mixture evenly among 8 egg roll wraps, spooning ½ inch from one edge. 5. Moisten all edges of each wrap with beaten egg wash. 6. Fold the short ends over filling, then roll up tightly and press to seal edges. 7. Brush outside of wraps with egg wash, then spritz with oil or cooking spray. 8. Place 4 egg rolls in Cook & Crisp Basket. 9. Put on the Smart Lid on top of the Ninja Foodi Steam Fryer. 10. Move the Lid Slider to the "Air Fry/Stovetop". 11. Cook on "Air Fry" Mode at 390°F/200°C for about 9 minutes until outside is brown and crispy. 12. While the rolls are cooking, prepare the Blue Cheese Dip. With a fork, mash together cream cheese and blue cheese. 13. Stir in remaining ingredients. 14. Dip should be just thick enough to slightly cling to egg rolls. If too thick, stir in buttermilk or milk. Take1 tablespoon at a time until you reach the desired consistency. 15. Cook remaining 4 egg rolls in the same way. 16. Serve while hot with Blue Cheese Dip, more buffalo wing sauce, or both.
Per Serving: Calories 380; Fat 29g; Sodium 821mg; Total Carbs 34.6g; Fiber 0g; Sugar 0g; Protein 30g

Fried Drumsticks

Prep Time: 10 minutes. | Cook Time: 25 minutes. | Serves: 2

1 egg	1 teaspoon salt
½ cup buttermilk	¼ teaspoon black pepper (to mix
¾ cup self-rising flour	into coating)
¾ cup seasoned panko	4 chicken drumsticks, skin on
breadcrumbs	Oil for misting or cooking spray

1. Place the Cook & Crisp Basket in your Ninja Foodi Pressure Cooker Steam Fryer. 2. Beat egg and buttermilk in any shallow dish. 3. In another shallow dish, mix the flour, panko crumbs, salt, and pepper. 4. Sprinkle chicken legs with additional salt and black pepper to taste. 5. Dip the chicken legs in buttermilk mixture, then roll in panko mixture, pressing in crumbs to make coating stick. Mist with oil or cooking spray. 6. Spray Cook & Crisp Basket with cooking spray. 7. Put on the Smart Lid on top of the Ninja Foodi Steam Fryer. 8. Move the Lid Slider to the "Air Fry/Stovetop". 9. Cook drumsticks at 360°F/180°C on "Air Fry" Mode for about 10 minutes. Flip those pieces over. Cook an additional 10 minutes. 10. If you have any white spots that haven't begun to brown, spritz them with oil or cooking spray. Continue cooking the chicken for about 5 more minutes until golden brown.
Per Serving: Calories 351; Fat 16g; Sodium 777mg; Total Carbs 26g; Fiber 4g; Sugar 5g; Protein 28g

Chicken with Chimichangas Sauce

Prep Time: 20 minutes. | Cook Time: 8–10 minutes. | Serves: 4

2 cups cooked chicken, shredded	Oil for misting or cooking spray
2 tablespoons chopped green chiles	Chimichanga Sauce
½ teaspoon oregano	2 tablespoons butter
½ teaspoon cumin	2 tablespoons flour
½ teaspoon onion powder	1 cup chicken broth
¼ teaspoon garlic powder	¼ cup light sour cream
Salt and pepper	¼ teaspoon salt
8 flour tortillas (6- or 7-inch	2 ounces Pepper Jack or Monterey
diameter)	Jack cheese, shredded

1. Place the Cook & Crisp Basket in your Ninja Foodi Pressure Cooker Steam Fryer. 2. Make the sauce by melting butter in a suitable saucepan over medium-low heat. Stir in flour until smooth and slightly bubbly. Gradually add broth, stirring constantly until smooth. Cook and stir 1 minute, until the mixture slightly thickens. Remove from the heat and stir in sour cream and salt. Set aside. 3. In a suitable bowl, mix together the chicken, chiles, oregano, cumin, onion powder, garlic, salt, and pepper. Stir in 3 to 4 tablespoons of the sauce, using just enough to make the filling moist but not soupy. 4. Divide filling among the 8 tortillas. Place filling down the center of tortilla, stopping about 1 inch from edges. Fold one side of tortilla over filling, fold the two sides in, and then roll up. Mist all sides with oil or cooking spray. 5. Place chimichangas in Cook & Crisp Basket seam side down. To fit more into the basket, you can stand them on their sides with the seams against the sides of the basket. 6. Put on the Smart Lid on top of the Ninja Foodi Steam Fryer. 7. Move the Lid Slider to the "Air Fry/Stovetop". 8. Cook on "Air Fry" Mode at 360°F/180°C for about 8 to 10 minutes until heated through and crispy brown outside. 9. Add the shredded cheese to the remaining sauce. Stir over low heat, warming just until the cheese melts. Don't boil or sour cream may curdle. 10. Drizzle the sauce over the chimichangas.
Per Serving: Calories 268; Fat 10.4g; Sodium 411mg; Total Carbs 0.4g; Fiber 0.1g; Sugar 0.1g; Protein 40.6g

Chicken Ham Cordon Bleu

Prep Time: 20 minutes. | Cook Time: 15–20 minutes. | Serves: 4

4 small boneless, skinless chicken breasts	4 slices deli Swiss cheese
Salt and pepper	2 tablespoons olive oil
4 slices deli ham	2 teaspoons marjoram
	¼ teaspoon paprika

1. Place the Cook & Crisp Basket in your Ninja Foodi Pressure Cooker Steam Fryer. 2. Split each chicken breast horizontally almost in two, leaving one edge intact. 3. Lay breasts open flat and sprinkle with salt and pepper to taste. 4. Place a ham slice on top of each chicken breast. 5. Cut cheese slices in half and place one half atop each breast. Set aside remaining halves of cheese slices. 6. Roll up chicken breasts to enclose cheese and ham and secure with toothpicks. 7. Mix together the olive oil, marjoram, and paprika. Rub all over outsides of chicken breasts. 8. Place chicken in Cook & Crisp Basket. 9. Put on the Smart Lid on top of the Ninja Foodi Steam Fryer. 10. Move the Lid Slider to the "Air Fry/Stovetop". 11. Cook on "Air Fry" Mode at 360°F/180°C for about 15 to 20 minutes, until well done and juices run clear. 12. Remove all toothpicks. To avoid burns, place chicken breasts on a plate to remove toothpicks, then immediately return them to your Ninja Foodi Cook & Crisp Basket. 13. Place a half slice of cheese on top of each chicken breast. Cook on "Air Fry" Mode at 350°F/175°C for a minute or so just to melt cheese.
Per Serving: Calories 353; Fat 5g; Sodium 818mg; Total Carbs 53.2g; Fiber 4.4g; Sugar 8g; Protein 7.3g

Chicken Pies

Prep Time: 30 minutes. | Cook Time: 10 minutes | Serves: 8 pies

¾ cup chicken broth	1 tablespoon milk
¾ cup frozen mixed peas and carrots	Salt and pepper
1 cup cooked chicken, chopped	1 8-count can organic flaky biscuits
1 tablespoon cornstarch	Oil for misting or cooking spray

1. Place the Cook & Crisp Basket in your Ninja Foodi Pressure Cooker Steam Fryer. 2. In a suitable saucepan, bring chicken broth to a boil. Stir in the frozen peas and carrots. Stir in chicken. 3. Mix the cornstarch into the milk until it dissolves. Stir it into the simmering chicken broth mixture. Cook just until thickened. 4. Remove from heat, add salt and pepper to taste, and let cool slightly. 5. Lay biscuits out on wax paper. Peel each biscuit apart in the middle to make 2 rounds so you have 16 rounds total. Using your hands or a rolling pin, flatten each biscuit round slightly to make it larger and thinner. 6. Divide chicken filling among 8 of the biscuit rounds. Place remaining biscuit rounds on top and press edges all around. Use the tines of a fork to crimp biscuit edges and make sure they are sealed well. 7. Spray both sides lightly with oil or cooking spray. Place in Cook & Crisp Basket. 8. Put on the Smart Lid on top of the Ninja Foodi Steam Fryer. 9. Move the Lid Slider to the "Air Fry/Stovetop". 10. Cook in a single layer, 4 at a time, at 330°F/165°C on "Air Fry" Mode for about 10 minutes until biscuit dough is cooked through and golden brown.
Per Serving: Calories 346; Fat 16.1g; Sodium 882mg; Total Carbs 1.3g; Fiber 0.5g; Sugar 0.5g; Protein 48.2g

Basic Chicken Nuggets

Prep Time: 20 minutes. | Cook Time: 10–14 minutes | Serves: 24 nuggets

1-pound boneless chicken thighs, diced	½ cup flour
¾ teaspoon salt	2 eggs, beaten
½ teaspoon black pepper	½ cup panko breadcrumbs
½ teaspoon garlic powder	3 tablespoons plain breadcrumbs
½ teaspoon onion powder	Oil for misting or cooking spray

1. Place the Cook & Crisp Basket in your Ninja Foodi Pressure Cooker Steam Fryer. 2. In the bowl of your food processor, blend chicken, ½ teaspoon salt, pepper, garlic powder, and onion powder. Process in short pulses until chicken is very chopped and well blended. 3. Place flour in one shallow dish and beaten eggs in another. In a third dish or plastic bag, mix together the panko crumbs, plain breadcrumbs, and ¼ teaspoon salt. 4. Shape chicken mixture into small nuggets. Dip nuggets in flour, then eggs, then panko crumb mixture. 5. Spray nuggets on both sides with oil or cooking spray and place in Cook & Crisp Basket in a single layer, close but not overlapping. 6. Put on the Smart Lid on top of the Ninja Foodi Steam Fryer. 7. Move the Lid Slider to the "Air Fry/Stovetop". 8. Cook on "Air Fry" Mode at 360°F/180°C for about 10 minutes. Spray with oil. Cook 3 to 4 minutes, until chicken is done and coating is golden brown. 9. In the same way, cook remaining nuggets.
Per Serving: Calories 502; Fat 25g; Sodium 230mg; Total Carbs 1.5g; Fiber 0.2g; Sugar 0.4g; Protein 64.1g

Chicken Parmesan with Spaghetti

Prep Time: 15 minutes. | Cook Time: 11 minutes. | Serves: 4

4 chicken tenders	¼ cup panko breadcrumbs
Italian seasoning	¼ cup grated Parmesan cheese
Salt	Oil for misting or cooking spray
¼ cup cornstarch	8 ounces spaghetti, cooked
½ cup Italian salad dressing	1 24-ounce jar marinara sauce

1. Place the Cook & Crisp Basket in your Ninja Foodi Pressure Cooker Steam Fryer. 2. Pound chicken tenders with meat mallet or rolling pin until about ¼-inch thick. 3. Sprinkle both sides with Italian seasoning and salt to taste. 4. Place cornstarch and salad dressing in 2 separate shallow dishes. 5. In a third shallow dish, mix the panko crumbs and Parmesan cheese. 6. Dip flattened chicken in cornstarch, then salad dressing. Dip in the panko mixture, pressing into the chicken so the coating sticks well. 7. Spray both chicken sides with oil or cooking spray. Place in Cook & Crisp Basket in single layer. 8. Put on the Smart Lid on top of the Ninja Foodi Steam Fryer. 9. Move the Lid Slider to the "Air Fry/Stovetop". 10. Cook on "Air Fry" Mode at 390°F/200°C for about 5 minutes. Spray with oil again, turning chicken to coat both sides. 11. Cook on "Air Fry" Mode for an additional 4 to 6 minutes until chicken juices run clear and outside is browned. 12. While chicken is cooking, heat marinara sauce and stir into cooked spaghetti. 13. To serve, divide spaghetti with sauce among 4 dinner plates, and top each with a fried chicken tender. Pass additional Parmesan at the table for those who want extra cheese.
Per Serving: Calories 223; Fat 11.7g; Sodium 721mg; Total Carbs 13.6g; Fiber 0.7g; Sugar 8g; Protein 15.7g

Crispy Turkey Burgers

Prep Time: 5 minutes. | Cook Time: 10–13 minutes. | Serves: 4

1-pound turkey	½ teaspoon salt
¼ cup diced red onion	4 slices provolone cheese
1 tablespoon grilled chicken seasoning	4 whole-grain sandwich buns
½ teaspoon dried parsley	Toppings: lettuce, sliced tomatoes, dill pickles, and mustard

1. Place the Cook & Crisp Basket in your Ninja Foodi Pressure Cooker Steam Fryer. 2. Mix the turkey, onion, chicken seasoning, parsley, and salt and mix well. 3. Shape into 4 patties. 4. Put on the Smart Lid on top of the Ninja Foodi Steam Fryer. 5. Move the Lid Slider to the "Air Fry/Stovetop". 6. Cook on "Air Fry" Mode at 360°F/180°C for about 9 to 11 minutes until turkey is well done and juices run clear. 7. Put a slice of cheese on each burger. Cook 1 to 2 minutes to melt. 8. Serve on buns with your favorite toppings.
Per Serving: Calories 264; Fat 17g; Sodium 129mg; Total Carbs 0.9g; Fiber 0.3g; Sugar 0g; Protein 27g

Air Fried Turkey Breast

Prep Time: 10 minutes. | Cook Time: 60 minutes. | Serves: 6-8

Pepper and salt	Turkey seasonings of choice
1 oven-ready turkey breast	

1. Place the Cook & Crisp Basket in your Pressure Cooker Steam Fryer. 2. Season turkey with pepper, salt, and other desired seasonings. 3. Place turkey in "cook & crisp basket". 4. Put on the Smart Lid on top of the Ninja Foodi Steam Fryer. 5. Move the Lid Slider to the "Air Fry/Stovetop". Select the "Air Fry" mode for cooking. 6. Adjust the cooking temperature to 350°F/175°C. 7. Cook 60 minutes. The meat should be at 165°F/75°C when done. 8. Allow to rest 10 to 15 minutes before slicing. Enjoy!
Per serving: Calories: 237; Fat: 10.9g; Sodium: 354mg; Carbs: 20.5g; Fiber: 4.1g; Sugar 8.2g; Protein 26g

Chicken Hot Dogs

Prep Time: 15 minutes. | Cook Time: 8–10 minutes. | Serves: 4

½ cup flour
½ teaspoon salt
1 teaspoon marjoram
1 teaspoon dried parsley flakes
½ teaspoon thyme
1 egg
1 teaspoon lemon juice
1 teaspoon water
1 cup breadcrumbs

4 chicken tenders, pounded thin
Oil for misting or cooking spray
4 whole-grain hotdog buns
4 slices Gouda cheese
1 small Granny Smith apple, thinly sliced
½ cup shredded Napa cabbage
Coleslaw dressing

1. Place the Cook & Crisp Basket in your Ninja Foodi Pressure Cooker Steam Fryer. 2. In any shallow dish, mix the flour, salt, marjoram, parsley, and thyme. 3. In another shallow dish, beat together egg, lemon juice, and water. 4. Place breadcrumbs in a third shallow dish. 5. Cut each of the flattened chicken tenders in half lengthwise. 6. Dip flattened chicken strips in flour mixture, then egg wash. Let extra egg drip off and roll in breadcrumbs. Spray both the chicken sides with oil or cooking spray. 7. Put on the Smart Lid on top of the Ninja Foodi Steam Fryer. 8. Move the Lid Slider to the "Air Fry/Stovetop". 9. Cook on "Air Fry" Mode at 390°F/200°C for about 5 minutes. Spray with oil, turn over, and spray other side. 10. Cook for about 3 to 5 minutes more, until well done and crispy brown. 11. To serve, place 2 schnitzel strips on bottom of each hotdog bun. Top with cheese, sliced apple, and cabbage. Drizzle with coleslaw dressing and top with other half of bun.
Per Serving: Calories 379; Fat 19g; Sodium 184mg; Total Carbs 12.3g; Fiber 0.6g; Sugar 2g; Protein 37.7g

Chicken with Apricot-Ginger Sauce

Prep Time: 20 minutes. | Cook Time: 7–8 minutes. | Serves: 4

1½ pounds boneless, skinless chicken tenders, cut in large chunks
Salt and pepper
½ cup cornstarch
2 eggs
1 tablespoon milk
3 cups shredded coconut

Oil for misting or cooking spray
Apricot-Ginger Sauce
½ cup apricot preserves
2 tablespoons white vinegar
¼ teaspoon ginger
¼ teaspoon low-sodium soy sauce
2 teaspoons white or yellow onion, grated or minced

1. Place the Cook & Crisp Basket in your Ninja Foodi Pressure Cooker Steam Fryer. 2. Mix all the recipe ingredients for the Apricot-Ginger Sauce well and let sit for flavors to blend while you cook the chicken. 3. Season chicken chunks with salt and pepper to taste. 4. Place cornstarch in a shallow dish. 5. In another shallow dish, beat together eggs and milk. 6. Place coconut in a third shallow dish. (If also using panko breadcrumbs, as suggested below, stir them to mix well.) 7. Spray Cook & Crisp Basket with oil or cooking spray. 8. Dip each chicken chunk into cornstarch, shake off excess, and dip in egg mixture. 9. Shake off excess egg mixture and roll lightly in coconut or coconut mixture. Spray with oil. 10. Place coated chicken chunks in Cook & Crisp Basket in a single layer, close together but without sides touching. 11. Put on the Smart Lid on top of the Ninja Foodi Steam Fryer. 12. Move the Lid Slider to the "Air Fry/Stovetop". 13. Cook at 360°F/180°C on "Air Fry" Mode for about 4 minutes, stop, and turn chunks over. 14. Cook an additional 3 to 4 minutes until chicken is done inside and coating is crispy brown. 15. In the same way, cook the remaining chicken chunks.
Per Serving: Calories 400; Fat 32g; Sodium 721mg; Total Carbs 2.6g; Fiber 0g; Sugar 0g; Protein 27.4g

Barbeque Sauce Chicken

Prep Time: 40 minutes. | Cook Time: 20 minutes. | Serves: 4

1 pound boneless, skinless chicken thighs
Salt and pepper
1 large orange
½ cup barbeque sauce

2 tablespoons smooth peanut butter
2 tablespoons chopped peanuts for garnish (optional)
Cooking spray

1. Place the Cook & Crisp Basket in your Ninja Foodi Pressure Cooker Steam Fryer. 2. Season the boneless chicken with salt and pepper to taste. Place in a shallow dish or plastic bag. 3. Grate orange peel, squeeze orange and reserve 1 tablespoon of juice for the sauce. 4. Pour remaining juice over chicken and marinate for about 30 minutes. 5. Mix together the reserved 1 tablespoon of orange juice, barbeque sauce, peanut butter, and 1 teaspoon grated orange peel. 6. Place ¼ cup of sauce mixture in a suitable bowl for basting. Set remaining sauce aside to serve with cooked chicken. 7. Spray basket with nonstick cooking spray. 8. Remove the chicken from marinade, letting excess drip off. 9. Place the marinated chicken in Cook & Crisp Basket. 10. Put on the Smart Lid on top of the Ninja Foodi Steam Fryer. 11. Move the Lid Slider to the "Air Fry/Stovetop". 12. Cook on "Air Fry" Mode at 350°F/175°C for about 5 minutes. Flip this chicken over. Cook 5 minutes longer. 13. Brush both sides of chicken lightly with sauce. 14. Cook chicken 5 minutes, then turn thighs one more time, again brushing both sides lightly with sauce. Cook for about 5 more minutes until chicken is done and juices run clear. 15. Serve this chicken with remaining sauce on the side and garnish with chopped peanuts if you like.
Per Serving: Calories 396; Fat 23.2g; Sodium 622mg; Total Carbs 0.7g; Fiber 0g; Sugar 0g; Protein 45.6g

Fiesta Chicken

Prep Time: 15 minutes. | Cook Time: 12–15 minutes. | Serves: 4

1-pound boneless chicken breasts (2 large breasts)
2 tablespoons lime juice
1 teaspoon cumin
½ teaspoon salt
½ cup grated Pepper Jack cheese
1 16-ounce can refried beans

½ cup salsa
2 cups shredded lettuce
1 medium tomato, chopped
2 avocados, peeled and sliced
1 small onion, sliced into thin rings
Sour cream
Tortilla chips (optional)

1. Place the Cook & Crisp Basket in your Ninja Foodi Pressure Cooker Steam Fryer. 2. Split each chicken breast in half lengthwise. 3. Mix cumin, lime juice, and salt together and brush on all surfaces of chicken breasts. 4. Place those chicken breasts in the Cook & Crisp Basket. 5. Put on the Smart Lid on top of the Ninja Foodi Steam Fryer. 6. Move the Lid Slider to the "Air Fry/Stovetop". 7. Cook on "Air Fry" Mode at 390°F/200°C for about 12 to 15 minutes, until well done. 8. Divide the grated cheese evenly over chicken breasts. Cook on "Air Fry" Mode for an additional minute to melt cheese. 9. Meanwhile heat the refried beans on stovetop or in microwave. 10. Divide the prepared beans among 4 serving plates. 11. Add chicken breasts on top of beans and spoon salsa over. 12. Spread the lettuce, tomatoes, and avocados on each plate and scatter with the onion rings. 13. Serve with sour cream and tortilla chips.
Per Serving: Calories 336; Fat 27.1g; Sodium 66mg; Total Carbs 1.1g; Fiber 0.4g; Sugar 0.2g; Protein 19.7g

Easy Nacho Chicken Fries

Prep Time: 20 minutes. | Cook Time: 6–7 minutes. | Serves: 4–6

1-pound chicken tenders
Salt
¼ cup flour
2 eggs
¾ cup panko breadcrumbs
¾ cup crushed organic nacho cheese tortilla chips

oil for misting or cooking spray
Seasoning Mix
1 tablespoon chili powder
1 teaspoon cumin
½ teaspoon garlic powder
½ teaspoon onion powder

1. Place the Cook & Crisp Basket in your Ninja Foodi Pressure Cooker Steam Fryer. 2. Stir all the nacho seasonings in a small cup and set aside. 3. Cut boneless chicken tenders in half crosswise, then cut into strips no wider than about ½ inch. 4. Season the chicken tenders with salt to taste. Place the tender strips in large bowl and sprinkle with 1 tablespoon of the prepared seasoning mix. Mix well to coat. 5. Add flour to boneless chicken and stir well to coat all sides. 6. Beat eggs together in a shallow dish. 7. In the second shallow dish, mix the panko, crushed chips, and the remaining 2 teaspoons of seasoning mix. 8. Dip prepared chicken strips in beaten eggs, then roll them in dry crumbs. Lightly coat them with oil or cooking spray. 9. Chicken strips in two batches to avoid overcrowding. Place the chicken strips in basket. 10. Put on the Smart Lid on top of the Ninja Foodi Steam Fryer. 11. Move the Lid Slider to the "Air Fry/Stovetop". 12. Cook on "Air Fry" Mode at 390°F/200°C for about 4 minutes. 13. Shake the Cook & Crisp Basket, mist them with more oil. Cook for another 2 to 3 more minutes, until chicken juices run clear and outside is crispy. 14. Serve warm.
Per Serving: Calories 351; Fat 31g; Sodium 1329mg; Total Carbs 1.5g; Fiber 0.8g; Sugar 0.4g; Protein 24g

Cornish Hens With Honey-Glaze

Prep Time: 15 minutes. | Cook Time: 25–30 minutes. | Serves: 2–3

1 Cornish game hen (1½–2 pounds)
1 tablespoon honey
1 tablespoon lime juice
1 teaspoon poultry seasoning
Salt and pepper
Cooking spray

1. Place the Cook & Crisp Basket in your Ninja Foodi Pressure Cooker Steam Fryer. 2. To split the hen into halves, cut through breast bone and down one side of the backbone. 3. Mix the honey, lime juice, and poultry seasoning together and brush or rub onto all sides of the hen. Season to taste with salt and pepper. 4. Spray Ninja Foody Cook & Crisp Basket with cooking spray and place hen halves in the basket, skin-side down. 5. Put on the Smart Lid on top of the Ninja Foodi Steam Fryer. 6. Move the Lid Slider to the "Air Fry/Stovetop". 7. Cook on "Air Fry" Mode at 330°F/165°C for about 25 to 30 minutes. Hen will be done when juices run clear when pierced at leg joint with a fork. Let hen rest for about 5 to 10 minutes before cutting.
Per Serving: Calories 316; Fat 12.2g; Sodium 587mg; Total Carbs 12.2g; Fiber 1g; Sugar 1.8g; Protein 25.8g

Peachy Chicken With Cherries

Prep Time: 8 minutes. | Cook Time: 14–16 minutes. | Serves: 4

⅓ cup peach preserves
1 teaspoon rosemary
½ teaspoon black pepper
½ teaspoon salt
½ teaspoon marjoram
1 teaspoon light olive oil
1-pound boneless chicken breasts, diced
Oil for misting or cooking spray
10-ounce package frozen unsweetened dark cherries, thawed and drained

1. Place the Cook & Crisp Basket in your Ninja Foodi Pressure Cooker Steam Fryer. 2. In a suitable bowl, mix peach preserves, rosemary, pepper, salt, marjoram, and olive oil. 3. Stir in chicken chunks and toss to coat well with the preserve mixture. 4. Spray Cook & Crisp Basket with oil or cooking spray and lay chicken chunks in basket. 5. Put on the Smart Lid on top of the Ninja Foodi Steam Fryer. 6. Move the Lid Slider to the "Air Fry/Stovetop". 7. Cook on "Air Fry" Mode at 390°F/200°C for about 7 minutes. Stir. Cook for about 6 to 8 more minutes until chicken juices run clear. 8. When chicken has cooked through, scatter the cherries over. Cook for additional minute to heat cherries.
Per Serving: Calories 410; Fat 17.8g; Sodium 619mg; Total Carbs 21g; Fiber 1.4g; Sugar 1.8g; Protein 38.4g

Fried Chicken Strips

Prep Time: 40 minutes. | Cook Time: 6–8 minutes | Serves: 4

1-pound chicken tenders
Marinade
¼ cup olive oil
2 tablespoons water
2 tablespoons honey
2 tablespoons white vinegar
½ teaspoon salt
½ teaspoon crushed red pepper
1 teaspoon garlic powder
1 teaspoon onion powder
½ teaspoon paprika

1. Place the Cook & Crisp Basket in your Ninja Foodi Pressure Cooker Steam Fryer. 2. Mix all the marinade recipe ingredients then mix well. 3. Add chicken tenders and stir to coat. 4. Cover these tenders tightly and let them marinate in refrigerator for about 30 minutes. 5. Remove tenders from marinade and place them in a single layer in your Ninja Foodi Cook & Crisp Basket. 6. Put on the Smart Lid on top of the Ninja Foodi Steam Fryer. 7. Move the Lid Slider to the "Air Fry/Stovetop". 8. Cook on "Air Fry" Mode at 390°F/200°C for about 3 minutes. Turn tenders over. Cook for about 3 to 5 minutes longer until chicken is done and juices run clear. 9. In the same way, cook remaining tenders.
Per Serving: Calories 351; Fat 11g; Sodium 150mg; Total Carbs 3.3g; Fiber 0.2g; Sugar 1g; Protein 33.2g

Turkey Cutlets

Prep Time: 10 minutes. | Cook Time: 10–12 minutes. | Serves: 4

¾ cup panko breadcrumbs
¼ teaspoon salt
¼ teaspoon pepper
¼ teaspoon dry mustard
¼ teaspoon poultry seasoning
½ cup pecans
¼ cup cornstarch
1 egg, beaten
1-pound turkey cutlets, ½-inch thick
Salt and pepper
Oil for misting or cooking spray

1. Place the Cook & Crisp Basket in your Ninja Foodi Pressure Cooker Steam Fryer. 2. Place the panko crumbs, ¼ teaspoon salt, ¼ teaspoon pepper, mustard, and poultry seasoning in food processor. Process until crumbs are crushed. Add pecans and process in short pulses just until nuts are chopped. Go easy so you don't overdo it! 3. Place cornstarch in one shallow dish and beaten egg in another. Transfer coating mixture from food processor into a third shallow dish. 4. Sprinkle turkey cutlets with salt and pepper to taste. 5. Dip cutlets in cornstarch and shake off excess. Then dip in beaten egg and roll in crumbs, pressing to coat well. Spray both sides with oil or cooking spray. 6. Place 2 cutlets in Cook & Crisp Basket in a single layer. 7. Put on the Smart Lid on top of the Ninja Foodi Steam Fryer. 8. Move the Lid Slider to the "Air Fry/Stovetop". 9. Cook on "Air Fry" Mode at 360°F/180°C for about 10 to 12 minutes until juices run clear. 10. In the same way, cook remaining cutlets.
Per Serving: Calories 437; Fat 28g; Sodium 1221mg; Total Carbs 22.3g; Fiber 0.9g; Sugar 8g; Protein 30.3g

Poblano Turkey Bake

Prep Time: 15 minutes. | Cook Time: 11 minutes. | Serves: 4

2 large poblano peppers
¾ pound turkey, raw
¾ cup cooked brown rice
1 teaspoon chile powder
½ teaspoon cumin
½ teaspoon garlic powder
4 ounces sharp Cheddar cheese, grated
1 8-ounce jar salsa, warmed

1. Place the Cook & Crisp Basket in your Ninja Foodi Pressure Cooker Steam Fryer. 2. Slice each pepper in half lengthwise so that you have four wide, flat pepper halves. 3. Remove seeds and membrane and discard. Rinse inside and out. 4. In a suitable bowl, mix turkey, rice, chile powder, cumin, and garlic powder. Mix well. 5. Divide turkey filling into 4 portions and stuff one into each of the 4 pepper halves. Press lightly to pack down. 6. Place 2 pepper halves in Cook & Crisp Basket. 7. Put on the Smart Lid on top of the Ninja Foodi Steam Fryer. 8. Move the Lid Slider to the "Air Fry/Stovetop". 9. Cook on "Air Fry" Mode at 390°F/200°C for about 10 minutes until turkey is well done. 10. Top each pepper half with ¼ of the grated cheese. 11. Cook for a minute more until cheese melts. 12. In the same way, cook remaining pepper halves. 13. To serve, place each pepper half on a plate and top with ¼ cup warm salsa.
Per Serving: Calories 352; Fat 9.1g; Sodium 1294mg; Total Carbs 3.9g; Fiber 1g; Sugar 1g; Protein 61g

Southern Chicken Livers

Prep Time: 10 minutes. | Cook Time: 10–12 minutes. | Serves: 4

2 eggs
2 tablespoons water
¾ cup flour
1½ cups panko breadcrumbs
½ cup plain breadcrumbs
1 teaspoon salt
½ teaspoon black pepper
20 ounces chicken livers, salted to taste
Oil for misting or cooking spray

1. Place the Cook & Crisp Basket in your Ninja Foodi Pressure Cooker Steam Fryer. 2. Beat together eggs and water in a shallow dish. Place the flour in a separate shallow dish. 3. In the bowl of your food processor, mix the panko, plain breadcrumbs, salt, and pepper. Process until well mixed and panko crumbs are crushed. Place crumbs in a third shallow dish. 4. Dip livers in flour, then egg wash, and then roll in panko mixture to coat well with crumbs. 5. Spray both sides of livers with oil or cooking spray. Cooking in two batches, place livers in Cook & Crisp Basket in single layer. 6. Put on the Smart Lid on top of the Ninja Foodi Steam Fryer. 7. Move the Lid Slider to the "Air Fry/Stovetop". 8. Cook on "Air Fry" Mode at 390°F/200°C for about 7 minutes. Spray livers, turn over, and spray again. Cook for about 3 to 5 more minutes, until done inside and coating is golden brown. 9. Repeat to cook remaining livers.
Per Serving: Calories 374; Fat 25g; Sodium 275mg; Total Carbs 7.3g; Fiber 0g; Sugar 6g; Protein 12.3g

Turkey Wraps

Prep Time: 10 minutes. | Cook Time: 3–7 minutes. | Serves: 4

4 large whole wheat wraps
½ cup hummus
16 thin slices deli turkey

8 slices provolone cheese
1 cup fresh baby spinach

1. Place the Cook & Crisp Basket in your Ninja Foodi Pressure Cooker Steam Fryer. 2. To assemble, place 2 tablespoons of hummus on each wrap and spread to within about a half inch from edges. Top with 4 slices of turkey and 2 slices of provolone. Finish with ¼ cup of baby spinach—or pile on as much as you like. 3. Roll up each wrap. You don't need to fold or seal the ends. 4. Place 2 wraps in Cook & Crisp Basket, seam side down. 5. Put on the Smart Lid on top of the Ninja Foodi Steam Fryer. 6. Move the Lid Slider to the "Air Fry/Stovetop". 7. Cook on "Air Fry" Mode at 360°F/180°C for about 3 to 4 minutes to warm filling and melt cheese. If you like, you can continue cooking for about 2 or 3 more minutes, until the wrap is slightly crispy. 8. Repeat to cook remaining wraps.
Per Serving: Calories 449; Fat 26.1 g; Sodium 3255 mg; Carbs 37.5g; Fiber 5.4g; Sugar 27.4g; Protein 19.2g

Chicken and Cheese Taquitos

Prep Time: 15 minutes. | Cook Time: 4–6 minutes. | Serves: 12 taquitos

1 teaspoon butter
2 tablespoons chopped green onions
1 cup cooked chicken, shredded
2 tablespoons chopped green chiles
2 ounces Pepper Jack cheese, shredded

4 tablespoons salsa
½ teaspoon lime juice
¼ teaspoon cumin
½ teaspoon chile powder
⅛ teaspoon garlic powder
12 corn tortillas
Oil for misting or cooking spray

1. Place the Cook & Crisp Basket in your Ninja Foodi Pressure Cooker Steam Fryer. 2. Melt butter in a suitable saucepan over medium heat. Add green onions and sauté a minute or two, until tender. 3. Remove from heat and stir in the chicken, green chiles, cheese, salsa, lime juice, and seasonings. 4. To soften refrigerated tortillas, wrap in damp paper towels and microwave for about 30 to 60 seconds, until slightly warmed. 5. Remove one tortilla at a time, keeping others covered with the damp paper towels. Place a heaping tablespoon of filling into tortilla, roll up and secure with toothpick. Spray all sides with oil or cooking spray. 6. Place taquitos in Cook & Crisp Basket, either in a single layer or stacked. To stack, leave plenty of space between taquitos and alternate the direction of the layers, 4 on the bottom lengthwise, then 4 more on top crosswise. 7. Put on the Smart Lid on top of the Ninja Foodi Steam Fryer. 8. Move the Lid Slider to the "Air Fry/Stovetop". 9. Cook on "Air Fry" Mode at 390°F/200°C for about 4 to 6 minutes until brown and crispy. 10. Repeat to cook remaining taquitos. 11. Serve hot with guacamole, sour cream, salsa.
Per Serving: Calories 316; Fat 17g; Sodium 271mg; Total Carbs 4.3g; Fiber 0.9g; Sugar 2.1g; Protein 35g

Simple Teriyaki Chicken

Prep Time: 12 minutes. | Cook Time: 18–20 minutes. | Serves: 2

4 tablespoons teriyaki sauce
1 tablespoon orange juice
1 teaspoon smoked paprika

4 chicken legs
Cooking spray

1. Place the Cook & Crisp Basket in your Ninja Foodi Pressure Cooker Steam Fryer. 2. Mix together the teriyaki sauce, orange juice, and smoked paprika. Brush on all sides of chicken legs. 3. Spray the Ninja Foody Cook & Crisp Basket with nonstick cooking spray and place chicken in basket. 4. Put on the Smart Lid on top of the Ninja Foodi Steam Fryer. 5. Move the Lid Slider to the "Air Fry/Stovetop". 6. Cook on "Air Fry" Mode at 360°F/180°C for about 6 minutes. Turn and baste with sauce. Cook for about 6 more minutes, turn and baste. Cook for about 6 to 8 minutes more, until juices run clear when chicken is pierced with a fork.
Per Serving: Calories 459; Fat 17.7g; Sodium 1516mg; Total Carbs 1.7g; Fiber 0.5g; Sugar 0.4g; Protein 69.2g

Korean Wings

Prep Time: 10 minutes. | Cook Time: 45 minutes. | Serves: 4

Wings:
1 teaspoon pepper
1 teaspoon salt
2 pounds chicken wings
Sauce:
2 packets Splenda
1 tablespoon minced garlic
Finishing:
¼ cup chopped green onions

1 tablespoon minced ginger
1 tablespoon sesame oil
1 teaspoon agave nectar
1 tablespoon mayo
2 tablespoon gochujang

2 teaspoon sesame seeds

1. Place the Cook & Crisp Basket in your Pressure Cooker Steam Fryer. 2. Line the Cook & Crisp Basket with foil. 3. Season the chicken wings with black pepper and salt and place in the Cook & Crisp Basket. 4. Put on the Smart Lid on top of the Ninja Foodi Steam Fryer. 5. Move the Lid Slider to the "Air Fry/Stovetop". Select the "Air Fry" mode for cooking. 6. Adjust the cooking temperature to 400°F/200°C. 7. Air fry the seasoned chicken wings for around 20 minutes, turning at 10 minutes. 8. As chicken wings air fries, mix all the sauce components. 9. Once a thermometer says that the chicken has reached 160°F/70°C, take out wings and place into a suitable bowl. 10. Add half of the prepared sauce mixture over wings, tossing well to coat. 11. Put coated wings back into Pressure Cooker Steam Fryer for around 5 minutes or till they reach 165°F/75°C. 12. Remove and sprinkle with green onions and sesame seeds. Dip into extra sauce.
Per serving: Calories: 489; Fat: 11g; Sodium: 501mg; Carbs: 8.9g; Fiber: 4.6g; Sugar 8g; Protein 26g

Spicy Buffalo Chicken Wings

Prep Time: 10 minutes. | Cook Time: 25 minutes. | Serves: 6-8

1 teaspoon salt
1-2 tablespoon brown sugar
1 tablespoon Worcestershire sauce

½ cup vegan butter
½ cup cayenne pepper sauce
4 pounds chicken wings

1. Place the Cook & Crisp Basket in your Pressure Cooker Steam Fryer. 2. Mix salt, brown sugar, Worcestershire sauce, butter, and hot sauce and set to the side. 3. Dry wings and add to "cook & crisp basket". 4. Put on the Smart Lid on top of the Ninja Foodi Steam Fryer. 5. Move the Lid Slider to the "Air Fry/Stovetop". Select the "Air Fry" mode for cooking. 6. Cook 25 minutes at 380°F/195°C, tossing halfway through. 7. When timer sounds, shake wings and bump up the temperature to 400°F/200°C . Cook for another 5 minutes. 8. Take out wings and place into a big bowl. Add sauce and toss well. 9. Serve alongside celery sticks!
Per serving: Calories: 221; Fat: 7.9g; Sodium: 704mg; Carbs: 6g; Fiber: 3.6g; Sugar 6g; Protein 18g

Turkey With Mustard Glaze

Prep Time: 10 minutes. | Cook Time: 30 minutes. | Serves: 5-7

1 tablespoon vegan butter
1 tablespoon stone-brown mustard
¼ cup pure maple syrup
1 teaspoon crushed pepper
2 teaspoon salt

½ teaspoon dried rosemary
2 minced garlic cloves
¼ cup olive oil
2.5 pounds turkey breast loin

1. Place the Cook & Crisp Basket in your Pressure Cooker Steam Fryer. 2. Mix pepper, salt, rosemary, garlic, and olive oil together. Spread herb mixture over turkey breast. Cover and chill 2 hours or overnight to marinade. 3. Make sure to remove from fridge about half an hour before cooking. 4. Place loin into the basket . Put on the Smart Lid on top of the Ninja Foodi Steam Fryer. Move the Lid Slider to the "Air Fry/Stovetop". Select the "Air Fry" mode for cooking. 5. Adjust the cooking temperature to 400°F/200°C. Cook for 20 minutes. 6. While turkey cooks, melt butter in the microwave. Then add brown mustard and maple syrup. 7. Spoon on butter mixture over turkey. Cook another 10 minutes. 8. Remove turkey from the Pressure Cooker Steam Fryer and let rest 5 to 10 minutes before attempting to slice. 9. Slice against the grain and enjoy!
Per serving: Calories: 372; Fat: 20g; Sodium: 891mg; Carbs: 29g; Fiber: 3g; Sugar 8g; Protein 27g

Chicken BBQ Burgers

Prep Time: 10 minutes. | Cook Time: 17 minutes. | Serves: 3

¾-pound chicken, ground
¼ cup tortilla chips, crushed
¼ cup Parmesan cheese, grated
1 egg, beaten

2 tablespoons onion, minced
2 garlic cloves, minced
1 tablespoon BBQ sauce

1. Place the Cook & Crisp Basket in your Pressure Cooker Steam Fryer. 2. Mix all the recipe ingredients until everything is well mixed. Form the mixture into three patties. 3. Put on the Smart Lid on top of the Ninja Foodi Steam Fryer. 4. Move the Lid Slider to the "Air Fry/Stovetop". Select the "Air Fry" mode for cooking. 5. Cook the burgers at 380°F/195°C for about 17 minutes or until cooked through; make sure to turn them over halfway through the cooking time. 6. Serve.
Per serving: Calories: 373; Fat:23.8g; Carbs: 7g; Proteins: 27g; Sugars: 0.7g; Fiber: 0.9g

Fajita Rollups

Prep Time: 10 minutes. | Cook Time: 12 minutes. | Serves: 6-8

½ teaspoon oregano
½ teaspoon cayenne pepper
1 teaspoon cumin
1 teaspoon garlic powder
2 teaspoons paprika
½ sliced red onion

½ yellow bell pepper, sliced into strips
½ green bell pepper, sliced into strips
½ red bell pepper, sliced into strips
3 chicken breasts

1. Place the Cook & Crisp Basket in your Pressure Cooker Steam Fryer. 2. Mix oregano, cayenne pepper, garlic powder, cumin and paprika along with a pinch or two of pepper and salt. Set to the side. 3. Slice chicken breasts lengthwise into 2 slices. 4. Between two pieces of parchment paper, add breast slices and pound till they are ¼-inch thick. With seasoning, liberally season both sides of chicken slices. 5. Put 2 strips of each color of bell pepper and a few onion slices onto chicken pieces. 6. Roll up tightly and secure with toothpicks. 7. Repeat with remaining ingredients and sprinkle and rub mixture that is left over the chicken rolls. 8. Grease your Ninja Foodi Pressure Steam Fryer basket and place 3 rollups into the fryer. 9. Put on the Smart Lid on top of the Ninja Foodi Steam Fryer. 10. Move the Lid Slider to the "Air Fry/Stovetop". Select the "Air Fry" mode for cooking. 11. Cook 12 minutes at 400°F/200°C. 12. Repeat with remaining rollups. 13. Serve with salad!
Per serving: Calories: 372; Fat: 20g; Sodium: 891mg; Carbs: 29g; Fiber: 3g; Sugar 8g; Protein 7g

Crispy Honey Chicken Wings

Prep Time: 10 minutes. | Cook Time: 35 minutes. | Serves: 8

⅛ cup water
½ teaspoon salt
4 tablespoon minced garlic
¼ cup vegan butter

¼ cup raw honey
¾ cup almond flour
16 chicken wings

1. Place the Cook & Crisp Basket in your Pressure Cooker Steam Fryer. 2. Grease your Ninja Foodi "cook & crisp basket" with olive oil. 3. Coat chicken wings with almond flour and add coated wings to basket. 4. Put on the Smart Lid on top of the Ninja Foodi Steam Fryer. 5. Move the Lid Slider to the "Air Fry/Stovetop". Select the "Air Fry" mode for cooking. 6. Cook 25 minutes at 380°F/195°C. 7. Then cook 5 to 10 minutes at 400°F/200°C till skin becomes crispy and dry. 8. As chicken cooks, melt butter in a suitable saucepan and add garlic. Sauté garlic 5 minutes. Add salt and honey, simmering 20 minutes. 9. Add a bit of water after 15 minutes to ensure sauce does not harden. 10. Take out chicken wings from Pressure Cooker Steam Fryer and coat in sauce. Enjoy!
Per serving: Calories: 289; Fat: 14g; Sodium: 791mg; Carbs: 18.9g; Fiber: 4.6g; Sugar 8g; Protein 26g

Mexican Burgers

Prep Time: 10 minutes. | Cook Time: 20 minutes. | Serves: 6-8

1 jalapeno pepper

1 teaspoon cayenne pepper

1 tablespoon mustard powder
1 tablespoon oregano
1 tablespoon thyme
3 tablespoon smoked paprika

1 beaten egg
1 small head of cauliflower
4 chicken breasts

1. Place the Cook & Crisp Basket in your Pressure Cooker Steam Fryer. 2. Add seasonings to a blender. Slice cauliflower into florets and add to blender. 3. Pulse till mixture resembles that of breadcrumbs. 4. Take out ¾ of cauliflower mixture and add to a suitable bowl. Set to the side. In another bowl, beat your egg and set to the side. 5. Remove skin and bones from chicken breasts and add to blender with remaining cauliflower mixture. Season with pepper and salt. 6. Take out mixture and form into burger shapes. Roll each patty in cauliflower crumbs, then the egg, and back into crumbs again. 7. Put on the Smart Lid on top of the Ninja Foodi Steam Fryer. 8. Move the Lid Slider to the "Air Fry/Stovetop". Select the "Air Fry" mode for cooking. 9. Adjust the cooking temperature to 350°F/175°C. 10. Place coated patties into the Ninja Foodi Pressure Steam Fryer, cooking 20 minutes. 11. Flip over at 10 minute mark. They are done when crispy!
Per serving: Calories: 184; Fat: 5g; Sodium: 441mg; Carbs: 17g; Fiber: 4.6g; Sugar 5g; Protein 29g

Asian-Spiced Duck

Prep Time: 10 minutes. | Cook Time: 30 minutes. | Serves: 3

1-pound duck breast
1 tablespoon Hoisin sauce
1 tablespoon Five-spice powder

Sea salt and black pepper, to taste
¼ teaspoon cinnamon

1. Place the Cook & Crisp Basket in your Pressure Cooker Steam Fryer. 2. Toss the duck breast with the remaining ingredients. 3. Put on the Smart Lid on top of the Ninja Foodi Steam Fryer. 4. Move the Lid Slider to the "Air Fry/Stovetop". Select the "Air Fry" mode for cooking. 5. Cook the duck breast at 330°F/165°C for around 15 minutes, turning them over halfway through the cooking time. 6. Turn the heat to 350°F/175°C; continue to cook for about 15 minutes or until cooked through. 7. Serve.
Per serving: Calories: 345; Fat:23.2g; Carbs: 5.7g; Proteins: 27.1g; Sugars: 2.3g; Fiber: 0.8g

Mayo Chicken Salad

Prep Time: 10 minutes. | Cook Time: 12 minutes. | Serves: 3

1 pound chicken breast
2 tablespoons scallions, chopped
1 carrot, shredded
½ cup mayonnaise

1 tablespoon mustard
Sea salt and black pepper, to taste
Oil

1. Place the Cook & Crisp Basket in your Pressure Cooker Steam Fryer. 2. Pat the chicken dry with kitchen towels. Brush the oil on the Cook & Crisp Basket and place the chicken in it.. 3. Put on the Smart Lid on top of the Ninja Foodi Steam Fryer. 4. Move the Lid Slider to the "Air Fry/Stovetop". Select the "Air Fry" mode for cooking. 5. Cook the prepared chicken at 380°F/195°C for around 12 minutes, turning them over halfway through the cooking time. 6. Chop the chicken breasts and transfer it to a salad bowl; add in the remaining recipe ingredients and toss to mix well. Serve.
Per serving: Calories: 373; Fat:23.8g; Carbs: 7g; Proteins: 27g; Sugars: 0.7g; Fiber: 0.9g

Spiced Chicken Thighs

Prep Time: 10 minutes. | Cook Time: 22 minutes. | Serves: 4

1-pound chicken thighs, bone-in
Sea salt and black pepper, to taste
2 tablespoons olive oil

1 teaspoon stone-mustard
¼ cup hot sauce

1. Place the Cook & Crisp Basket in your Pressure Cooker Steam Fryer. 2. Pat the chicken dry with kitchen towels. Toss the chicken with the remaining ingredients. 3. Put on the Smart Lid on top of the Ninja Foodi Steam Fryer. 4. Move the Lid Slider to the "Air Fry/Stovetop". Select the "Air Fry" mode for cooking. 5. Cook the prepared chicken at 380°F/195°C for around 22 minutes, turning them over halfway through the cooking time. 6. Serve.
Per serving: Calories: 317; Fat:25.4g; Carbs: 1.5g; Proteins: 19.1g; Sugars: 0.6g; Fiber: 1g

Crispy Fried Chicken

Prep Time: 10 minutes. | Cook Time: 20 minutes. | Serves: 4

1 teaspoon cayenne pepper	1 beaten egg
2 tablespoon mustard powder	¼ cup cauliflower
2 tablespoon oregano	¼ cup gluten-free oats
2 tablespoon thyme	8 chicken drumsticks
3 tablespoon coconut milk	

1. Place the Cook & Crisp Basket in your Pressure Cooker Steam Fryer. 2. Lay out chicken and season with pepper and salt on all sides. 3. Add all other ingredients to a blender, blending till a smooth-like breadcrumb mixture is created. Place in a suitable bowl and add a beaten egg to another bowl. 4. Dip chicken into breadcrumbs, then into egg, and breadcrumbs once more. 5. Place coated drumsticks into basket. Put on the Smart Lid on top of the Ninja Foodi Steam Fryer. Move the Lid Slider to the "Air Fry/Stovetop". Select the "Air Fry" mode for cooking. 6. Adjust the cooking temperature to 350°F/175°C. 7. Cook for 20 minutes. Bump up the temperature to 390°F/200°C . Cook for another 5 minutes till crispy.

Per serving: Calories: 489; Fat: 11g; Sodium: 501mg; Carbs: 8.9g; Fiber: 4.6g; Sugar 8g; Protein 26g

KFC Chicken

Prep Time: 10 minutes. | Cook Time: 20 minutes. | Serves: 6

1 teaspoon chili flakes	⅓ teaspoon oregano
1 teaspoon curcumin	½ tablespoon basil
1 teaspoon white pepper	½ teaspoon thyme
1 teaspoon ginger powder	2 garlic cloves
1 teaspoon garlic powder	1 egg
1 teaspoon paprika	6 boneless, skinless chicken thighs
1 teaspoon powdered mustard	2 tablespoons unsweetened almond
1 teaspoon pepper	milk
1 tablespoon celery salt	¼ cup whey protein isolate powder

1. Place the Cook & Crisp Basket in your Pressure Cooker Steam Fryer. 2. Wash and pat dry chicken thighs. Slice into small chunks. 3. Mash cloves and add them along with all spices in a blender. Blend until smooth and pour over chicken, adding milk and egg. Mix thoroughly. 4. Cover chicken and chill for around 1 hour. 5. Add whey protein to a suitable bowl and dredge coated chicken pieces. Shake excess powder. Place coated chicken in the Cook & Crisp Basket. Put on the Smart Lid on top of the Ninja Foodi Steam Fryer. Move the Lid Slider to the "Air Fry/Stovetop". Select the "Air Fry" mode for cooking. Adjust the cooking temperature to 390°F/200°C. Cook for 20 minutes till crispy, making sure to turn halfway through cooking.

Per serving: Calories: 184; Fat: 5g; Sodium: 441mg; Carbs: 17g; Fiber: 4.6g; Sugar 5g; Protein 9g

Chicken Ham Rochambeau

Prep Time: 15 minutes. | Cook Time: 20 minutes. | Serves: 4

1 tablespoon melted butter	Sauce
4 chicken tenders, cut in half	2 tablespoons butter
crosswise	½ cup chopped green onions
Salt and pepper	½ cup chopped mushrooms
¼ cup flour	2 tablespoons flour
Oil for misting	1 cup chicken broth
4 slices ham	¼ teaspoon garlic powder
2 English muffins, split	1½ teaspoons Worcestershire sauce

1. Place the Cook & Crisp Basket in your Ninja Foodi Pressure Cooker Steam Fryer. 2. Add 1 tablespoon of melted butter to a shallow bowl. 3. Sprinkle chicken tenders with salt and pepper to taste, then roll in the ¼ cup of flour. 4. Place chicken in bowl, turning pieces to coat with melted butter. 5. Place the coated chicken in the Cook & Crisp Basket and put on the Smart Lid on top of the Ninja Foodi Steam Fryer. 6. Move the Lid Slider to the "Air Fry/Stovetop". 7. Cook on "Air Fry" Mode at 390°F/200°C for about 5 minutes. Turn chicken pieces over, and spray tops lightly with olive oil. Cook 5 minutes longer until juices run clear. The chicken will not brown. 8. While chicken is cooking, make the sauce: In a medium saucepan, melt the 2 tablespoons of butter. 9. Add onions and mushrooms and sauté until tender, about 3 minutes. 10. Stir in the flour. Gradually

add broth, stirring constantly until you have a smooth gravy. 11. Add garlic powder and Worcestershire sauce and simmer on low heat until sauce thickens, about 5 minutes. 12. When chicken is cooked, remove baking pan from the Ninja Foodi Steam Fryer, and set aside. 13. Place ham slices directly into Cook & Crisp Basket. 14. Put on the Smart Lid on top of the Ninja Foodi Steam Fryer. 15. Move the Lid Slider to the "Air Fry/Stovetop". 16. Cook on "Air Fry" Mode at 390°F/200°C for about 5 minutes until hot and beginning to sizzle a little. Remove and set aside on top of the chicken for now. 17. Place the English muffin halves in Cook & Crisp Basket. Cook on "Air Fry" Mode at 390°F/200°C for about 1 minute. 18. Open your Pressure Cooker Steam Fryer and place a ham slice on top of each English muffin half. Stack 2 pieces of chicken on top of each ham slice. Cook at chicken at 390°F/200°C on "Air Fry" Mode for about 1 to 2 minutes to heat through. 19. Place each English muffin stack on a serving plate and top with plenty of sauce.

Per Serving: Calories 456; Fat 16.4g; Sodium 1321mg; Total Carbs 19.2g; Fiber 2.2g; Sugar 4.2g; Protein 55.2g

Chicken Fritters

Prep Time: 10 minutes. | Cook Time: 20 minutes. | Serve: 16-18 fritters

Chicken Fritters:

½ teaspoon salt	⅓ cup coconut flour
⅛ teaspoon pepper	⅓ cup vegan mayo
1 ½ tablespoon fresh dill	2 eggs
1 ⅓ cup shredded mozzarella	1 ½ pounds chicken breasts
cheese	

Garlic Dip:

⅛ teaspoon pepper	1 pressed garlic cloves
¼ teaspoon salt	⅓ cup vegan mayo
½ tablespoon lemon juice	

1. Place the Cook & Crisp Basket in your Pressure Cooker Steam Fryer. 2. Slice chicken breasts into ⅓ pieces and place in a suitable bowl. Add all remaining fritter ingredients to the bowl and stir well. Cover and chill 2 hours or overnight. 3. Spray "cook & crisp basket" with a bit of olive oil. 4. Add marinated chicken to basket. Put on the Smart Lid on top of the Ninja Foodi Steam Fryer. Move the Lid Slider to the "Air Fry/Stovetop". Select the "Air Fry" mode for cooking. 5. Adjust the cooking temperature to 350°F/175°C. 6. Cook for 20 minutes, making sure to turn halfway through cooking process. 7. To make the dipping sauce, mix all the dip ingredients until smooth.

Per serving: Calories: 334; Fat: 12.9g; Sodium: 414mg; Carbs: 11g; Fiber: 5g; Sugar 9g; Protein 31g

Chicken Wing Stir-Fry

Prep Time: 10 minutes. | Cook Time: 25 minutes. | Serves: 14-20 wings

¾ cup potato starch	1 egg white
¼ teaspoon pepper	14-20 chicken wing pieces
½ teaspoon salt	
Stir-fry:	
¼ teaspoon pepper	2 trimmed scallions
1 teaspoon sea salt	2 jalapeno peppers
2 tablespoons avocado oil	

1. Place the Cook & Crisp Basket in your Pressure Cooker Steam Fryer. 2. Coat the Cook & Crisp Basket with oil. 3. Mix pepper, salt, and egg white till foamy. 4. Pat wings dry and add to the bowl of egg white mixture. Coat well. Let marinate at least 20 minutes. 5. Place coated wings in a big bowl and add starch. Dredge wings well. Shake off and add to "cook & crisp basket". 6. Put on the Smart Lid on top of the Ninja Foodi Steam Fryer. 7. Move the Lid Slider to the "Air Fry/Stovetop". Select the "Air Fry" mode for cooking. 8. Cook 25 minutes at 380°F/195°C. When timer sounds, bump up the temperature to 400°F/200°C . Cook for an additional 5 minutes till browned. 9. For stir fry, remove seeds from jalapenos and chop up scallions. Add both to bowl and set to the side. Heat a wok with oil and add pepper, salt, scallions, and jalapenos. Cook 1 minute. Add air fried chicken to skillet and toss with stir-fried veggies. Cook 1 minute and devour!

Per serving: Calories: 489; Fat: 11g; Sodium: 501mg; Carbs: 8.9g; Fiber: 4.6g; Sugar 8g; Protein 26g

Chicken Parmesan

Prep Time: 10 minutes. | Cook Time: 9 minutes. | Serves: 4

½ cup keto marinara
6 tablespoon mozzarella cheese
1 tablespoon melted ghee
2 tablespoon grated parmesan cheese

6 tablespoon gluten-free seasoned breadcrumbs
2 (8-ounce) chicken breasts
Olive oil

1. Place the Cook & Crisp Basket in your Pressure Cooker Steam Fryer. 2. Grease the "cook & crisp basket" with olive oil. 3. Mix parmesan cheese and breadcrumbs together. 4. Brush melted ghee onto the chicken and dip into breadcrumb mixture. 5. Place the coated chicken in the basket and top with olive oil. 6. Put on the Smart Lid on top of the Ninja Foodi Steam Fryer. 7. Move the Lid Slider to the "Air Fry/Stovetop". Select the "Air Fry" mode for cooking. 8. Adjust the cooking temperature to 360°F/180°C. 9. Cook 2 breasts for around 6 minutes and top each breast with a tablespoon of sauce and 1 ½ tablespoons of mozzarella cheese. Cook another 3 minutes to melt cheese. 10. Keep cooked pieces warm as you repeat the process with remaining breasts.
Per serving: Calories: 584; Fat: 15g; Sodium: 441mg; Carbs: 17g; Fiber: 4.6g; Sugar 5g; Protein 29g

Jerk-Spiced Chicken Wings

Prep Time: 10 minutes. | Cook Time: 16 minutes. | Serves: 8

1 teaspoon salt
½ cup red wine vinegar
5 tablespoon lime juice
4 chopped scallions
1 tablespoon grated ginger
2 tablespoon brown sugar
1 tablespoon chopped thyme
1 teaspoon white pepper
1 teaspoon cayenne pepper

1 teaspoon cinnamon
1 tablespoon allspice
1 Habanero pepper, chopped
6 chopped garlic cloves
2 tablespoon low-sodium soy sauce
2 tablespoons olive oil
4 pounds of chicken wings

1. Place the Cook & Crisp Basket in your Pressure Cooker Steam Fryer. 2. Mix all the recipe ingredients except wings in a suitable bowl. 3. Pour the prepared marinade into a gallon bag and add chicken wings. Chill 2 to 24 hours to marinate. 4. Place all the chicken wings into a strainer to drain excess liquids. 5. Pour half of the wings into your Ninja Foodi Pressure Steam Fryer. 6. Put on the Smart Lid on top of the Ninja Foodi Steam Fryer. 7. Move the Lid Slider to the "Air Fry/Stovetop". Select the "Air Fry" mode for cooking. 8. Adjust the cooking temperature to 390°F/200°C. 9. Cook for 14 to 16 minutes, making sure to shake halfway through the cooking process. 10. Remove and repeat the process with remaining wings.
Per serving: Calories: 483; Fat: 7.9g; Sodium: 704mg; Carbs: 6g; Fiber: 3.6g; Sugar 6g; Protein 21g

Crusted Chicken Fingers

Prep Time: 10 minutes. | Cook Time: 10 minutes. | Serves: 4

1 ½ pounds chicken tenders
1 tablespoon olive oil
1 egg, whisked
1 teaspoon fresh parsley, minced

1 teaspoon garlic, minced
Sea salt and black pepper, to taste
1 cup breadcrumbs

1. Place the Cook & Crisp Basket in your Pressure Cooker Steam Fryer. 2. Pat the chicken dry with kitchen towels. 3. In a suitable bowl, mix the oil, egg, parsley, garlic, salt, and black pepper. 4. Dip the prepared chicken tenders into the egg mixture. Then, roll the chicken over the breadcrumbs. 5. Put on the Smart Lid on top of the Ninja Foodi Steam Fryer. 6. Move the Lid Slider to the "Air Fry/Stovetop". Select the "Air Fry" mode for cooking. 7. Cook the chicken tenders at 360°F/180°C for around 10 minutes, shaking the "cook & crisp basket" halfway through the cooking time. 8. Serve.
Per serving: Calories: 302; Fat: 7g; Sodium: 224mg; Carbs: 6g; Fiber: 6g; Sugar 2g; Protein 22g

Air-Fried Chicken Breasts

Prep Time: 10 minutes. | Cook Time: 12 minutes. | Serves: 4

1-pound chicken breasts raw, boneless and skinless
1 tablespoon butter, room temperature
1 teaspoon garlic powder

Salt and black pepper, to taste
1 teaspoon dried parsley flakes
1 teaspoon smoked paprika
½ teaspoon dried oregano

1. Place the Cook & Crisp Basket in your Pressure Cooker Steam Fryer. 2. Pat the chicken dry with kitchen towels. Toss the chicken breasts with the remaining ingredients. 3. Put on the Smart Lid on top of the Ninja Foodi Steam Fryer. 4. Move the Lid Slider to the "Air Fry/Stovetop". Select the "Air Fry" mode for cooking. 5. Cook the prepared chicken at 380°F/195°C for around 12 minutes, turning them over halfway through the cooking time. Serve.
Per serving: Calories: 227; Fat:13.4g; Carbs: 0.2g; Proteins: 23.4g; Sugars: 0.2g; Fiber: 1g

Chicken Taquitos

Prep Time: 10 minutes. | Cook Time: 18 minutes. | Serves: 5

¾-pound chicken breasts, boneless and skinless
Salt and black pepper, to taste

½ teaspoon red chili powder
5 small corn tortillas
5 ounces Cotija cheese, crumbled

1. Place the Cook & Crisp Basket in your Pressure Cooker Steam Fryer. 2. Pat the chicken dry with kitchen towels. Toss the boneless chicken breasts with the salt, pepper, and red chili powder. 3. Put on the Smart Lid on top of the Ninja Foodi Steam Fryer. 4. Move the Lid Slider to the "Air Fry/Stovetop". Select the "Air Fry" mode for cooking. 5. Cook the prepared chicken at 380°F/195°C for around 12 minutes, turning them over halfway through the cooking time. 6. Place the shredded chicken and cheese on one end of each tortilla. Roll them up tightly and transfer them to an oiled "cook & crisp basket". 7. Air fry your taquitos at 360°F/180°C for around 6 minutes. 8. Serve.
Per serving: Calories: 256; Fat:13g; Carbs: 14.2g; Proteins: 20.4g; Sugars: 2.7g; Fiber: 1.7g

Air-Fried Chicken Legs

Prep Time: 10 minutes. | Cook Time: 30 minutes. | Serves: 4

4 chicken legs, bone-in
2 tablespoons sesame oil
Salt and black pepper, to taste
½ teaspoon mustard seeds

1 teaspoon cayenne pepper
½ teaspoon onion powder
½ teaspoon garlic powder

1. Place the Cook & Crisp Basket in your Pressure Cooker Steam Fryer. 2. Pat the chicken dry with paper towels. Toss the bone-in chicken legs with the remaining ingredients. 3. Put on the Smart Lid on top of the Ninja Foodi Steam Fryer. 4. Move the Lid Slider to the "Air Fry/Stovetop". Select the "Air Fry" mode for cooking. 5. Cook the prepared chicken at 380°F/195°C for around 30 minutes, turning them over halfway through the cooking time. 6. Serve.
Per serving: Calories: 387; Fat:18.1g; Carbs: 1.9g; Proteins: 51.1g; Sugars: 0.6g; Fiber: 0.4g

Thanksgiving Turkey

Prep Time: 10 minutes. | Cook Time: 1 hour. | Serves: 4

1 tablespoon butter
Salt and black pepper, to taste
1 teaspoon cayenne pepper

1 teaspoon Italian herb mix
1-pound turkey breast, bone-in

1. Place the Cook & Crisp Basket in your Pressure Cooker Steam Fryer. 2. In a suitable mixing bowl, mix the butter, salt, black pepper, cayenne pepper, and herb mix. 3. Rub the mixture all over the turkey breast. 4. Put on the Smart Lid on top of the Ninja Foodi Steam Fryer. 5. Move the Lid Slider to the "Air Fry/Stovetop". Select the "Air Fry" mode for cooking. 6. Cook the turkey breast at 350°F/175°C for around 1 hour, turning them over every 20 minutes. 7. Serve.
Per serving: Calories: 210; Fat:10.1g; Carbs: 1.3g; Proteins: 25.1g; Sugars: 0.6g; Fiber: 0.4g

Paprika Chicken Cutlets

Prep Time: 10 minutes. | Cook Time: 12 minutes. | Serves: 4

1-pound chicken breasts, boneless, skinless, cut into 4 pieces	1 teaspoon smoked paprika
1 tablespoon butter, melted	Salt and black pepper, to taste
	1 teaspoon garlic powder

1. Place the Cook & Crisp Basket in your Pressure Cooker Steam Fryer. 2. Flatten the chicken breasts to ¼-inch thickness. 3. Toss the chicken breasts with the remaining ingredients. 4. Put on the Smart Lid on top of the Ninja Foodi Steam Fryer. 5. Move the Lid Slider to the "Air Fry/Stovetop". Select the "Air Fry" mode for cooking. 6. Cook the prepared chicken at 380°F/195°C for around 12 minutes, turning them over halfway through the cooking time. 7. Serve.
Per serving: Calories: 229; Fat:13.8g; Carbs: 1.9g; Proteins: 24.1g; Sugars: 0.6g; Fiber: 0.4g

Hawaiian Roll Sliders

Prep Time: 10 minutes. | Cook Time: 17 minutes. | Serves: 3

¾-pound chicken,	½ teaspoon mustard seeds
1 teaspoon garlic, minced	½ teaspoon cumin
1 small onion, minced	½ teaspoon paprika
2 tablespoons fresh parsley, minced	Sea salt and black pepper, to taste
2 tablespoons fresh cilantro, minced	2 tablespoons olive oil
	6 Hawaiian rolls

1. Place the Cook & Crisp Basket in your Pressure Cooker Steam Fryer. 2. Mix all the recipe ingredients , except for the Hawaiian rolls, until everything is well mixed. Shape the mixture into six patties. 3. Put on the Smart Lid on top of the Ninja Foodi Steam Fryer. 4. Move the Lid Slider to the "Air Fry/Stovetop". Select the "Air Fry" mode for cooking. 5. Cook the burgers at 380°F/195°C for about 17 minutes or until cooked through; make sure to turn them over halfway through the cooking time. 6. Serve your burgers over Hawaiian rolls and garnish with toppings of choice. Serve.
Per serving: Calories: 490; Fat:21.8g; Carbs: 46.7g; Proteins: 28g; Sugars: 7g; Fiber: 2.7g

Mustard Chicken Thighs

Prep Time: 10 minutes. | Cook Time: 15 minutes. | Serves: 6

1 large egg, well whisked	1 teaspoon fine sea salt
2 tablespoon whole-grain Dijon mustard	½ teaspoon black pepper, or more to taste
¼ cup of mayonnaise	½ teaspoon turmeric powder
¼ cup of chili sauce	10 chicken thighs
½ teaspoon sugar	2 cups crushed saltines

1. Place the Cook & Crisp Basket in your Pressure Cooker Steam Fryer. 2. In a suitable bowl, mix the egg, mustard, mayonnaise, chili sauce, sugar, salt, pepper, and turmeric, incorporating everything well. 3. Coat the chicken thighs with the mixture. Place a layer of aluminum foil over the bowl, transfer it to the refrigerator and allow the chicken to marinate for at least 5 hours or overnight. 4. Separate the chicken from the marinade. 5. Put the crushed saltines into a shallow dish and use them to coat the chicken. 6. Place the chicken in the basket. Put on the Smart Lid on top of the Ninja Foodi Steam Fryer. Move the Lid Slider to the "Air Fry/Stovetop". Select the "Air Fry" mode for cooking. Adjust the cooking temperature to 360°F/180°C. 7. Cook for around 15 minutes, ensuring the thighs are cooked through. 8. Serve with the rest of the marinade as a sauce.
Per serving: Calories: 471; Fat: 7.9g; Sodium: 704mg; Carbs: 6g; Fiber: 3.6g; Sugar 6g; Protein 18g

Roasted Turkey

Prep Time: 10 minutes. | Cook Time: 45 minute | Serves: 4

1 red onion, cut into wedges	1 tablespoon apple cider vinegar
1 carrot, trimmed and sliced	1 teaspoon maple syrup
1 celery stalk, trimmed and sliced	2 turkey thighs
1 cup Brussels sprouts, trimmed and halved	½ teaspoon mixed peppercorns, freshly cracked
1 cup roasted vegetable broth	1 teaspoon fine sea salt

1 teaspoon cayenne pepper	½ teaspoon garlic powder
1 teaspoon onion powder	⅓ teaspoon mustard seeds

1. Place the Cook & Crisp Basket in your Pressure Cooker Steam Fryer. 2. Put the vegetables into the Cook & Crisp Basket and add in the roasted vegetable broth. 3. In a large bowl, pour in the rest of the ingredients, and set aside for around 30 minutes. 4. Put on the Smart Lid on top of the Ninja Foodi Steam Fryer. 5. Move the Lid Slider to the "Air Fry/Stovetop". Select the "Air Fry" mode for cooking. 6. Place them on the top of the vegetables. 7. Cook at 330°F/165°C for around 40 to 45 minutes.
Per serving: Calories 289; Fat: 14g; Sodium: 791mg; Carbs: 18.9g; Fiber: 4.6g; Sugar 8g; Protein 6g

Mediterranean Chicken Fillets

Prep Time: 10 minutes. | Cook Time: 12 minutes. | Serves: 4

1 ½ pounds chicken fillets	½ teaspoon red pepper flakes, crushed
1 tablespoon olive oil	
1 teaspoon garlic, minced	Sea salt and black pepper, to taste
1 tablespoon Greek seasoning mix	

1. Place the Cook & Crisp Basket in your Pressure Cooker Steam Fryer. 2. Pat the chicken dry with paper towels. Toss the chicken with the remaining ingredients. 3. Put on the Smart Lid on top of the Ninja Foodi Steam Fryer. 4. Move the Lid Slider to the "Air Fry/Stovetop". Select the "Air Fry" mode for cooking. 5. Cook the chicken fillets at 380°F/195°C for around 12 minutes, turning them over halfway through the cooking time. 6. Serve.
Per serving: Calories: 227; Fat:13.4g; Carbs: 0.2g; Proteins: 23.4g; Sugars: 0.2g; Fiber: 1g

Chicken with Pineapple

Prep Time: 10 minutes. | Cook Time: 35 minutes. | Serves: 4

1-pound chicken legs, boneless	1 cup pineapple, peeled and diced
Salt and black pepper, to taste	1 tablespoon fresh cilantro, chopped
2 tablespoons tamari sauce	
1 tablespoon hot sauce	

1. Place the Cook & Crisp Basket in your Pressure Cooker Steam Fryer. 2. Pat the chicken dry with paper towels. Toss the chicken legs with the salt, black pepper, tamari sauce, and hot sauce. 3. Put on the Smart Lid on top of the Ninja Foodi Steam Fryer. 4. Move the Lid Slider to the "Air Fry/Stovetop". Select the "Air Fry" mode for cooking. 5. Cook the prepared chicken at 380°F/195°C for around 30 minutes, turning them over halfway through the cooking time. 6. Top the chicken with the pineapple and continue to cook for around 5 minutes more. Serve warm, garnished with the fresh cilantro. 7. Serve.
Per serving: Calories: 267; Fat:18.1g; Carbs: 6.5g; Proteins: 19g; Sugars: 4.6g; Fiber: 0.8g

Chicken Pepper Fajitas

Prep Time: 10 minutes. | Cook Time: 30 minutes. | Serves: 4

1-pound chicken legs, boneless, skinless, cut into pieces	1 jalapeno pepper, sliced
	1 onion, sliced
2 tablespoons canola oil	½ teaspoon onion powder
1 red bell pepper, sliced	½ teaspoon garlic powder
1 yellow bell pepper, sliced	Sea salt and black pepper, to taste

1. Place the Cook & Crisp Basket in your Pressure Cooker Steam Fryer. 2. Pat the chicken dry with paper towels. Toss the chicken legs with 1 tablespoon of the canola oil. 3. Put on the Smart Lid on top of the Ninja Foodi Steam Fryer. 4. Move the Lid Slider to the "Air Fry/Stovetop". Select the "Air Fry" mode for cooking. 5. Cook the prepared chicken at 380°F/195°C for around 15 minutes, shaking the "cook & crisp basket" halfway through the cooking time. 6. Add the remaining recipe ingredients to the Ninja Foodi Pressure Steam Fryer "cook & crisp basket" and turn the heat to 400°F/200°C. Let it cook for around 15 minutes more or until cooked through. 7. Serve.
Per serving: Calories: 330; Fat:25.1g; Carbs: 6.1g; Proteins: 19.6g; Sugars: 1.4g; Fiber: 1g

Air-Fried Turkey Wings

Prep Time: 10 minutes. | Cook Time: 40 minutes. | Serves: 5

2 pounds turkey wings, bone-in	½ cup red wine
2 garlic cloves, minced	Sea salt and black pepper, to taste
1 small onion, chopped	1 teaspoon poultry seasoning
1 tablespoon Dijon mustard	

1. Place the Cook & Crisp Basket in your Pressure Cooker Steam Fryer. 2. Place the turkey wings, garlic, onion, mustard, and wine in a ceramic bowl. Cover the bowl and let the turkey marinate in your refrigerator overnight. 3. Discard the marinade and toss the turkey wings with the salt, black pepper, and poultry seasoning. 4. Put on the Smart Lid on top of the Ninja Foodi Steam Fryer. 5. Move the Lid Slider to the "Air Fry/Stovetop". Select the "Air Fry" mode for cooking. 6. Cook the turkey wings at 400°F/200°C for around 40 minutes, turning them over halfway through the cooking time. 7. Serve.
Per serving: Calories: 377; Fat:22.5g; Carbs: 3.2g; Proteins: 37.4g; Sugars: 1.3g; Fiber: 0.6g

Limey Duck Breast

Prep Time: 10 minutes. | Cook Time: 30 minutes. | Serves: 4

2 tablespoons fresh lime juice	1 teaspoon cayenne pepper
1 ½ pounds duck breast	Salt and black pepper, to taste
2 tablespoons olive oil	

1. Place the Cook & Crisp Basket in your Pressure Cooker Steam Fryer. 2. Toss the duck breast with the remaining ingredients. 3. Put on the Smart Lid on top of the Ninja Foodi Steam Fryer. 4. Move the Lid Slider to the "Air Fry/Stovetop". Select the "Air Fry" mode for cooking. 5. Cook the duck breast at 330°F/165°C for around 15 minutes, turning them over halfway through the cooking time. 6. Turn the heat to 350°F/175°C; continue to cook for about 15 minutes or until cooked through. 7. Let the duck breasts rest for around 10 minutes before serving.
Per serving: Calories: 295; Fat:16.4g; Carbs: 2.2g; Proteins: 31.4g; Sugars: 0.1g; Fiber: 0.1g

Fried Chicken

Prep Time: 10 minutes. | Cook Time: 12 minutes. | Serves: 4

1-pound chicken fillets	1 tablespoon fresh parsley, minced
1 egg	Sea salt and black pepper, to taste
1 tablespoon olive oil	¼ teaspoon cumin
1 cup crackers, crushed	¼ teaspoon mustard seeds
1 tablespoon fresh coriander, minced	1 teaspoon celery seeds

1. Place the Cook & Crisp Basket in your Pressure Cooker Steam Fryer. 2. Mix the egg in a shallow bowl. 3. Mix the remaining recipe ingredients in a separate shallow bowl. 4. Dip the dry chicken breasts into the egg mixture. Then, roll the chicken breasts over the cracker crumb mixture. 5. Put on the Smart Lid on top of the Ninja Foodi Steam Fryer. 6. Move the Lid Slider to the "Air Fry/Stovetop". Select the "Air Fry" mode for cooking. 7. Cook the prepared chicken at 380°F/195°C for around 12 minutes, turning them over halfway through the cooking time. 8. Serve.
Per serving: Calories: 318; Fat:23.3g; Carbs: 2.1g; Proteins: 23.7g; Sugars: 0.8g; Fiber: 0.3g

Crusted Chicken Schnitzel

Prep Time: 10 minutes. | Cook Time: 20 minutes. | Serves: 3

3 chicken legs, boneless and skinless	1 teaspoon dried sage
2 tablespoons olive oil	Sea salt and freshly cracked black pepper
1 teaspoon dried basil	½ cup breadcrumbs
1 teaspoon dried oregano	

1. Place the Cook & Crisp Basket in your Pressure Cooker Steam Fryer. 2. Pat the chicken dry with paper towels. Toss the chicken legs with the remaining recipe ingredients. 3. Put on the Smart Lid on top of the Ninja Foodi Steam Fryer. 4. Move the Lid Slider to the "Air Fry/Stovetop". Select the "Air Fry" mode for cooking. 5. Cook the chicken at 370°F/185°C for around 20 minutes, turning them over halfway through the cooking time. 6. Serve.
Per serving: Calories: 477; Fat:21.2g; Carbs: 14.8g; Proteins: 53.3g; Sugars: 1.9g; Fiber: 1.4g

Cheese Stuffed Chicken

Prep Time: 10 minutes. | Cook Time: 20 minutes. | Serves: 4

1-pound chicken breasts, boneless, skinless, cut into four pieces	2 ounces mozzarella cheese, crumbled
2 tablespoons sundried tomatoes, chopped	Sea salt and black pepper, to taste
1 garlic clove, minced	1 tablespoon olive oil

1. Place the Cook & Crisp Basket in your Pressure Cooker Steam Fryer. 2. Flatten the chicken breasts with a mallet. 3. Stuff each piece of chicken with the sundried tomatoes, garlic, and cheese. Roll them up and secure with toothpicks. 4. Season the chicken with the black pepper and salt and drizzle the olive oil over them. 5. Place the stuffed chicken in the Cook and crisp basket. 6. Put on the Smart Lid on top of the Ninja Foodi Steam Fryer. 7. Move the Lid Slider to the "Air Fry/Stovetop". Select the "Air Fry" mode for cooking. 8. Cook the chicken at 400°F/200°C for about 20 minutes, turning them over halfway through the cooking time. 9. Serve.
Per serving: Calories: 257; Fat:13.9g; Carbs: 2.7g; Proteins: 28.3g; Sugars: 1.4g; Fiber: 0.6g

Chicken Omelet

Prep Time: 10 minutes. | Cook Time: 13 minutes. | Serves: 2

4 eggs, whisked	½ teaspoon black pepper
4 ounces chicken	½ teaspoon paprika
½ cup scallions, finely chopped	1 teaspoon dried thyme
2 cloves garlic, finely minced	Dash of hot sauce
½ teaspoon salt	

1. Place the Cook & Crisp Basket in your Pressure Cooker Steam Fryer. 2. Mix all the recipe ingredients in a bowl, ensuring to incorporate everything well. 3. Grease the Cook & Crisp Basket with vegetable oil. 4. Transfer the mixture to the Ninja Foodi Pressure Steam Fryer. Put on the Smart Lid on top of the Ninja Foodi Steam Fryer. Move the Lid Slider to the "Air Fry/Stovetop". Select the "Air Fry" mode for cooking. Air Fry at 350°F/175°C for 13 minutes. 5. Ensure they are cooked through and serve immediately.
Per serving: Calories 489; Fat: 11g; Sodium: 501mg; Carbs: 8.9g; Fiber: 4.6g; Sugar 8g; Protein 26g

Turkey Sandwiches

Prep Time: 10 minutes. | Cook Time: 20 minutes. | Serves: 4

1 cup leftover turkey, cut into bite-sized chunks	1 teaspoon hot paprika
2 bell peppers, deveined and chopped	¾ teaspoon salt
1 Serrano pepper, deveined and chopped	½ teaspoon black pepper
1 leek, sliced	1 heaping tablespoon fresh cilantro, chopped
½ cup sour cream	Dash of Tabasco sauce
	4 hamburger buns

1. Place the Cook & Crisp Basket in your Pressure Cooker Steam Fryer. 2. Mix all of the recipe ingredients except for the hamburger buns, ensuring to coat the turkey well. 3. Place in the Cook & Crisp Basket. 4. Put on the Smart Lid on top of the Ninja Foodi Steam Fryer. 5. Move the Lid Slider to the "Air Fry/Stovetop". Select the "Air Fry" mode for cooking. 6. cook for around 20 minutes at 385°F/195°C. 7. Top the hamburger buns with the turkey, and serve with mustard or sour cream as desired.
Per serving: Calories 334; Fat: 19g; Sodium: 354mg; Carbs: 15g; Fiber: 5.1g; Sugar 8.2g; Protein 12g

Chicken Wings with Piri Piri Sauce

Prep Time: 10 minutes. | Cook Time: 1 hr. 30 minutes. | Serves: 6

12 chicken wings
1 ½ ounces butter, melted
1 teaspoon onion powder
For the Sauce:
2 ounces Piri Piri peppers, stemmed and chopped
1 tablespoon pimiento, deveined and minced
1 garlic clove, chopped

½ teaspoon cumin powder
1 teaspoon garlic paste

2 tablespoons fresh lemon juice
⅓ teaspoon sea salt
½ teaspoon tarragon
¾ teaspoon sugar

1. Place the Cook & Crisp Basket in your Pressure Cooker Steam Fryer. 2. Place the chicken wings in a steamer basket over a suitable saucepan of boiling water. Lower the temperature and steam the chicken for around 10 minutes over a medium heat. 3. Coat the wings with the butter, onion powder, cumin powder, and garlic paste. 4. Allow the chicken wings to cool slightly. Place them in the refrigerator for around 45 to 50 minutes. Then transfer the chicken wings to the Cook & Crisp Basket 5. Put on the Smart Lid on top of the Ninja Foodi Steam Fryer. 6. Move the Lid Slider to the "Air Fry/Stovetop". Select the "Air Fry" mode for cooking. 7. Adjust the cooking temperature to 330°F/165°C. 8. Cook the chicken wings for around 25 to 30 minutes, turning them once halfway through the cooking time. 9. In the meantime, make the Piri Piri sauce. Blend all of the sauce ingredients in a food processor. 10. Coat the chicken wings in the sauce before serving.
Per serving: Calories 382; Fat: 12.9g; Sodium: 414mg; Carbs: 11g; Fiber: 5g; Sugar 9g; Protein 31g

Turkey Pepper Meatballs

Prep Time: 10 minutes. | Cook Time: 7 minutes. | Serves: 6

1 lb. turkey
1 tablespoon fresh mint leaves, finely chopped
1 teaspoon onion powder
1 ½ teaspoons garlic paste

1 teaspoon crushed red pepper flakes
¼ cup melted butter
¾ teaspoon fine sea salt
¼ cup grated Pecorino Romano

1. Place the Cook & Crisp Basket in your Pressure Cooker Steam Fryer. 2. In a suitable bowl, mix all of the recipe ingredients well. Using an ice cream scoop, mold the meat into balls. 3. Put on the Smart Lid on top of the Ninja Foodi Steam Fryer. 4. Move the Lid Slider to the "Air Fry/Stovetop". Select the "Air Fry" mode for cooking. 5. Air fry the meatballs at 380°F/195°C for about 7 minutes, in batches if necessary. Shake the "cook & crisp basket" frequently throughout the cooking time for even results. 6. Serve with basil leaves and tomato sauce if desired.
Per serving: Calories 372; Fat: 20g; Sodium: 891mg; Carbs: 29g; Fiber: 3g; Sugar 8g; Protein 27g

Italian Turkey Sausage

Prep Time: 10 minutes. | Cook Time: 37 minutes. | Serves: 4

1 onion, cut into wedges
2 carrots, trimmed and sliced
1 parsnip, trimmed and sliced
2 potatoes, peeled and diced
1 teaspoon dried thyme
½ teaspoon dried marjoram

1 teaspoon dried basil
½ teaspoon celery seeds
Sea salt and black pepper to taste
1 tablespoon melted butter
¾ lb. sweet Italian turkey sausage

1. Place the Cook & Crisp Basket in your Pressure Cooker Steam Fryer. 2. Cover the vegetables with all of the seasonings and the melted butter. 3. Place the vegetables in the Ninja Foodi Pressure Steam Fryer basket. 4. Add the sausage on top. 5. Put on the Smart Lid on top of the Ninja Foodi Steam Fryer. 6. Move the Lid Slider to the "Air Fry/Stovetop". Select the "Air Fry" mode for cooking. 7. Cook at 360°F/180°C for around 33 to 37 minutes, ensuring the sausages are no longer pink, giving the "cook & crisp basket" a good shake halfway through the cooking time. You may need to cook everything in batches.
Per serving: Calories 584; Fat: 15g; Sodium: 441mg; Carbs: 17g; Fiber: 4.6g; Sugar 5g; Protein 29g

Ricotta Chicken Wraps

Prep Time: 10 minutes. | Cook Time: 10 minutes. | Serves: 12

2 large-sized chicken breasts, cooked and shredded
⅓ teaspoon sea salt
¼ teaspoon black pepper, or more to taste
2 spring onions, chopped
¼ cup soy sauce

1 tablespoon molasses
1 tablespoon rice vinegar
10 ounces Ricotta cheese
1 teaspoon grated fresh ginger
50 wonton wrappers
Cooking spray

1. Place the Cook & Crisp Basket in your Pressure Cooker Steam Fryer. 2. In a suitable bowl, mix all of the ingredients, minus the wonton wrappers. 3. Unroll the wrappers and spritz with cooking spray. 4. Fill each of the wonton wrappers with equal amounts of the mixture. 5. Dampen the edges with a little water as an adhesive and roll up the wrappers, fully enclosing the filling. 6. Put on the Smart Lid on top of the Ninja Foodi Steam Fryer. 7. Move the Lid Slider to the "Air Fry/Stovetop". Select the "Air Fry" mode for cooking. 8. Cook the rolls in the Ninja Foodi Pressure Steam Fryer for around 5 minutes at 375°F/190°C. You will need to do this step in batches. 9. Serve with your preferred sauce.
Per serving: Calories 334; Fat: 7.9g; Sodium: 704mg; Carbs: 6g; Fiber: 3.6g; Sugar 6g; Protein 18g

Cajun- Turkey Fingers

Prep Time: 10 minutes. | Cook Time: 15 minutes. | Serves: 4

½ cup cornmeal mix
½ cup flour
1 ½ tablespoon Cajun seasoning
1 ½ tablespoon whole-grain mustard

1 ½ cups buttermilk
1 teaspoon soy sauce
¾ lb. turkey tenderloins, cut into finger-sized strips
Salt and black pepper to taste

1. Place the Cook & Crisp Basket in your Pressure Cooker Steam Fryer. 2. In a suitable bowl, mix the cornmeal, flour, and Cajun seasoning. 3. In a separate bowl, mix the whole-grain mustard, buttermilk and soy sauce. 4. Sprinkle some black pepper and salt on the turkey fingers. 5. Dredge each finger in the buttermilk mixture, before coating them completely with the cornmeal mixture. 6. Place the prepared turkey fingers in the Ninja Foodi Pressure Steam Fryer basket. Put on the Smart Lid on top of the Ninja Foodi Steam Fryer. Move the Lid Slider to the "Air Fry/Stovetop". Select the "Air Fry" mode for cooking. Cook for around 15 minutes at 360°F/180°C. 7. Serve immediately, with ketchup if desired.
Per serving: Calories 472; Fat: 10.9g; Sodium: 354mg; Carbs: 10.5g; Fiber: 4.1g; Sugar 8.2g; Protein 26g

Honey Turkey Breast

Prep Time: 10 minutes. | Cook Time: 28 minutes. | Serves: 6

2 teaspoon butter, softened
1 teaspoon dried sage
2 sprigs rosemary, chopped
1 teaspoon salt
¼ teaspoon black pepper, or more if desired

1 whole turkey breast
2 tablespoon turkey broth
¼ cup honey
2 tablespoon whole-grain mustard
1 tablespoon butter

1. Place the Cook & Crisp Basket in your Pressure Cooker Steam Fryer. 2. Mix the 2 tablespoon of butter, sage, rosemary, salt, and pepper. 3. Rub the turkey breast with this mixture. 4. Place the turkey in your fryer's cooking "cook & crisp basket". Put on the Smart Lid on top of the Ninja Foodi Steam Fryer. Move the Lid Slider to the "Air Fry/Stovetop". Select the "Air Fry" mode for cooking. Adjust the cooking temperature to 360°F/180°C and cook for around 20 minutes. 5. Turn the turkey breast over and allow to cook for another 15 to 16 minutes. 6. Finally turn it once more and cook for another 12 minutes. 7. In the meantime, mix the remaining recipe ingredients in a saucepan using a whisk. 8. Coat the turkey breast with the glaze. 9. Cook for an additional 5 minutes. Remove it from the Pressure Cooker Steam Fryer, let it rest, and carve before serving.
Per serving: Calories 521; Fat: 7.9g; Sodium: 704mg; Carbs: 6g; Fiber: 3.6g; Sugar 6g; Protein 18g

Chicken Turnip Curry

Prep Time: 10 minutes. | Cook Time: 30 minutes. | Serves: 2

2 chicken thighs	1 tablespoon whole pistachios
1 small zucchini	1 tablespoon raisin soup
2 cloves garlic	1 tablespoon olive oil
6 dried apricots	1 large pinch salt
3 ½ ounces long turnip	Pinch of pepper
6 basil leaves	1 teaspoon curry powder

1. Place the Cook & Crisp Basket in your Pressure Cooker Steam Fryer. 2. Cut the chicken into 2 thin slices and chop up the vegetables into bite-sized pieces. 3. In a dish, mix all of the ingredients, incorporating everything well. 4. Place in the basket. Put on the Smart Lid on top of the Ninja Foodi Steam Fryer. Move the Lid Slider to the "Air Fry/Stovetop". Select the "Air Fry" mode for cooking. 5. Adjust the cooking temperature to 320°F/160°C. 6. Cook for a minimum of 30 minutes. 7. Serve with rice if desired.
Per serving: Calories 219; Fat: 10g; Sodium: 891mg; Carbs: 22.9g; Fiber: 4g; Sugar 4g; Protein 13g

Chicken Mushroom Kabobs

Prep Time: 10 minutes. | Cook Time: 20 minutes. | Serves: 4

2 diced chicken breasts	⅓ cup low-sodium soy sauce
3 bell peppers	⅓ cup raw honey
6 mushrooms	Olive oil
Sesame seeds	Salt and pepper, to taste

1. Place the Cook & Crisp Basket in your Pressure Cooker Steam Fryer. 2. Chop up chicken into cubes, seasoning with a few sprays of olive oil, pepper, and salt. 3. Dice up bell peppers and cut mushrooms in half. 4. Mix soy sauce and honey till well mixed. Add sesame seeds and stir. 5. Skewer chicken, peppers, and mushrooms onto wooden skewers. 6. Coat kabobs with honey-soy sauce. 7. Place coated kabobs in "cook & crisp basket". Put on the Smart Lid on top of the Ninja Foodi Steam Fryer. Move the Lid Slider to the "Air Fry/Stovetop". Select the "Air Fry" mode for cooking. 8. Adjust the cooking temperature to 390°F/200°C. Cook for 15 to 20 minutes.
Per serving: Calories: 219; Fat: 10g; Sodium: 891mg; Carbs: 22.9g; Fiber: 4g; Sugar 4g; Protein 13g

Buttered Marjoram Chicken

Prep Time: 10 minutes. | Cook Time: 20 minutes. | Serves: 2

2 skinless, boneless small chicken breasts	½ teaspoon red pepper flakes, crushed
2 tablespoon butter	2 teaspoon marjoram
1 teaspoon sea salt	¼ teaspoon lemon pepper

1. Place the Cook & Crisp Basket in your Pressure Cooker Steam Fryer. 2. In a suitable bowl, coat the chicken breasts with all of the other ingredients. Set aside to marinate for around 30 to 60 minutes. 3. Put on the Smart Lid on top of the Ninja Foodi Steam Fryer. 4. Move the Lid Slider to the "Air Fry/Stovetop". Select the "Air Fry" mode for cooking. 5. Adjust the cooking temperature to 400°F/200°C. 6. Cook for around 20 minutes, turning halfway through cooking time. 7. Check for doneness using an instant-read thermometer. Serve over jasmine rice.
Per serving: Calories 585; Fat: 39.5g; Sodium 1687mg; Carbs: 10.4g; Fiber: 2.7g; Sugars 3.1g; Protein 43.2g

Hoisin Glazed Drumsticks

Prep Time: 10 minutes. | Cook Time: 40 minutes. | Serves: 4

2 turkey drumsticks	1 sprig rosemary, chopped
2 tablespoons balsamic vinegar	Salt and black pepper, to taste
2 tablespoons dry white wine	2 ½ tablespoon butter, melted
1 tablespoon extra-virgin olive oil	
For the Hoisin Glaze:	
2 tablespoon hoisin sauce	1 tablespoon honey mustard
1 tablespoon honey	

1. Place the Cook & Crisp Basket in your Pressure Cooker Steam

Fryer. 2. In a suitable bowl, coat the turkey drumsticks with the vinegar, wine, olive oil, and rosemary. Allow to marinate for around 3 hours. 3. Sprinkle the turkey drumsticks with salt and black pepper. Cover the surface of each drumstick with the butter. 4. Place the turkey in the basket. Put on the Smart Lid on top of the Ninja Foodi Steam Fryer. Move the Lid Slider to the "Air Fry/Stovetop". Select the "Air Fry" mode for cooking. Air Fry at 350°F/175°C for 30 to 35 minutes, flipping it occasionally through the cooking time. Work in batches. 5. In the meantime, make the Hoisin glaze by combining all the glaze ingredients. 6. Pour the glaze over the turkey, and cook for another 5 minutes. 7. Allow the drumsticks to rest for about 10 minutes before carving.
Per serving: Calories 596; Fat: 24.6g; Sodium 316mg; Carbs: 36.8g; Fiber: 15.6g; Sugars 9.5g; Protein 58.8g

Stuffed Roulade

Prep Time: 10 minutes. | Cook Time: 50 minutes. | Serves: 4

1 turkey fillet	½ teaspoon fennel seeds
Salt and garlic pepper to taste	2 tablespoon melted butter
⅓ teaspoon onion powder	3 tablespoon coriander, finely chopped
½ teaspoon dried basil	
⅓ teaspoon red chipotle pepper	½ cup scallions, finely chopped
1 ½ tablespoon mustard seeds	2 cloves garlic, finely minced

1. Place the Cook & Crisp Basket in your Pressure Cooker Steam Fryer. 2. Flatten out the turkey fillets with a mallet, until they are about a half-inch thick. 3. Season each one with salt, garlic pepper, and onion powder. 4. In a suitable bowl, mix the basil, chipotle pepper, mustard seeds, fennel seeds and butter. 5. Use a pallet knife to spread the mixture over the fillets, leaving the edges uncovered. 6. Add the coriander, scallions and garlic on top. 7. Roll up the fillets into a log and wrap a piece of twine around them to hold them in place. 8. Place them in the Cook and crisp basket. 9. Put on the Smart Lid on top of the Ninja Foodi Steam Fryer. 10. Move the Lid Slider to the "Air Fry/Stovetop". Select the "Air Fry" mode for cooking. 11. Cook at 350°F/175°C for about 50 minutes, flipping it at the halfway point. Cook for longer if necessary. Serve warm.
Per serving: Calories 372; Fat: 16.3g; Sodium 742mg; Carbs: 6.8g; Fiber: 0.8g; Sugars 1.8g; Protein 42.3g

Chicken Nuggets

Prep Time: 10 minutes. | Cook Time: 10 minutes. | Serves: 4

2 slices friendly breadcrumbs	1 tablespoon olive oil
9 ounces chicken breast, chopped	1 teaspoon paprika
1 teaspoon garlic, minced	1 teaspoon parsley
1 teaspoon tomato ketchup	Black pepper and salt to taste
2 medium egg	

1. Place the Cook & Crisp Basket in your Pressure Cooker Steam Fryer. 2. Mix the breadcrumbs, paprika, salt, pepper and oil into a thick batter. 3. Coat the chopped chicken with the parsley, one egg and ketchup. 4. Shape the mixture into several nuggets and dredge each one in the other egg. Roll the nuggets into the breadcrumbs. 5. Put on the Smart Lid on top of the Ninja Foodi Steam Fryer. 6. Move the Lid Slider to the "Air Fry/Stovetop". Select the "Air Fry" mode for cooking. 7. Air Fry at 390°F/200°C for 10 minutes in the Ninja Foodi Pressure Steam Fryer. 8. Serve the nuggets with a side of mayo dip if desired.
Per serving: Calories 326; Fat: 12g; Sodium 779mg; Carbs: 8.3g; Fiber: 2.9g; Sugars 1.3g; Protein 46.9g

Balsamic Drumettes

Prep Time: 10 minutes. | Cook Time: 22 minutes. | Serves: 4

1 ½ pounds chicken drumettes	2 tablespoons balsamic vinegar
2 tablespoons olive oil	Salt and black pepper, to taste

1. Place the Cook & Crisp Basket in your Pressure Cooker Steam Fryer. 2. Toss the chicken drumettes with the remaining ingredients. 3. Put on the Smart Lid on top of the Ninja Foodi Steam Fryer. 4. Move the Lid Slider to the "Air Fry/Stovetop". Select the "Air Fry" mode for cooking. 5. Cook the chicken drumettes at 380°F/195°C for around 22 minutes, turning them over halfway through the cooking time. 6. Serve.
Per serving: Calories: 265; Fat:4g; Carbs: 2.4g; Proteins: 34.4g; Sugars: 1.7g; Fiber: 0.2g

Turkey Sliders

Prep Time: 10 minutes. | Cook Time: 15 minutes. | Serves: 6

For the Turkey Sliders:
¾ lb. turkey mince
¼ cup pickled jalapeno, chopped
1 tablespoon oyster sauce
1 – 2 cloves garlic, minced
1 tablespoon chopped fresh cilantro
2 tablespoon chopped scallions
Sea salt and black pepper to taste

For the Chive Mayo:
1 cup mayonnaise
1 tablespoon chives
1 teaspoon salt
Zest of 1 lime

1. Place the Cook & Crisp Basket in your Pressure Cooker Steam Fryer. 2. In a bowl, mix all of the recipe ingredients for the turkey sliders. Use your hands to shape 6 equal amounts of the mixture into slider patties. 3. Transfer the patties to the Ninja Foodi Pressure Steam Fryer. 4. Put on the Smart Lid on top of the Ninja Foodi Steam Fryer. 5. Move the Lid Slider to the "Air Fry/Stovetop". Select the "Air Fry" mode for cooking. 6. fry them at 365°F/185°C for around 15 minutes. 7. In the meantime, prepare the Chive Mayo by combining the rest of the ingredients. 8. Make sandwiches by placing each patty between two burger buns and serve with the mayo.
Per serving: Calories 343; Fat: 20.1g; Sodium 903mg; Carbs: 0.2g; Fiber: 0.1g; Sugars 0.2g; Protein 37.1g

Spicy Turkey Wings

Prep Time: 10 minutes. | Cook Time: 40 minutes. | Serves: 4

¾ lb. turkey wings, cut into pieces
1 teaspoon ginger powder
1 teaspoon garlic powder
¾ teaspoon paprika
2 tablespoon soy sauce
1 handful minced lemongrass
Sea salt flakes and black pepper to taste
2 tablespoon rice wine vinegar
¼ cup peanut butter
1 tablespoon sesame oil
½ cup Thai sweet chili sauce

1. Place the Cook & Crisp Basket in your Pressure Cooker Steam Fryer. 2. Boil the turkey wings in a suitable saucepan full of water for around 20 minutes. 3. Put the turkey wings in a large bowl and cover them with the remaining ingredients, minus the Thai sweet chili sauce. 4. Transfer to the Ninja Foodi Pressure Steam Fryer. 5. Put on the Smart Lid on top of the Ninja Foodi Steam Fryer. 6. Move the Lid Slider to the "Air Fry/Stovetop". Select the "Air Fry" mode for cooking. 7. Cook for around 20 minutes at 350°F/175°C, turning once halfway through the cooking time. Ensure they are cooked through before serving with the Thai sweet chili sauce, as well as some lemon wedges if desired.
Per serving: Calories 416; Fat: 23.6g; Sodium 934mg; Carbs: 6g; Fiber: 2g; Sugars 0.6g; Protein 37.9g

Turkey Meatloaf

Prep Time: 10 minutes. | Cook Time: 50 minutes. | Serves: 6

1 lb. turkey mince
½ cup scallions, finely chopped
2 garlic cloves, finely minced
1 teaspoon dried thyme
½ teaspoon dried basil
¾ cup Colby cheese, shredded
¾ cup crushed saltines
1 tablespoon tamari sauce
Salt and black pepper, to taste
¼ cup roasted red pepper tomato sauce
1 teaspoon sugar
¾ tablespoon olive oil
1 medium egg, well beaten

1. Place the Cook & Crisp Basket in your Pressure Cooker Steam Fryer. 2. Over a suitable heat, fry up the turkey mince, scallions, garlic, thyme, and basil until soft and fragrant. 3. Mix the mixture with the cheese, saltines and tamari sauce, before shaping it into a loaf. 4. Stir the remaining items and top the meatloaf with them. 5. Place in the Ninja Foodi Pressure Steam Fryer basket. 6. Put on the Smart Lid on top of the Ninja Foodi Steam Fryer. 7. Move the Lid Slider to the "Air Fry/Stovetop". Select the "Air Fry" mode for cooking. 8. Adjust the cooking temperature to 360°F/180°C. 9. Allow to cook for around 45 to 47 minutes.
Per serving: Calories 618; Fat: 13.5g; Sodium 96mg; Carbs: 98.7g; Fiber: 5.3g; Sugars 0.5g; Protein 24.4g

Crusted Chicken Drumsticks

Prep Time: 10 minutes. | Cook Time: 35 minutes. | Serves: 4

8 chicken drumsticks
1 teaspoon cayenne pepper
2 tablespoon mustard powder
2 tablespoon oregano
2 tablespoon thyme
3 tablespoon coconut milk
1 large egg, beaten
⅓ cup cauliflower
⅓ cup oats
Pepper and salt to taste

1. Place the Cook & Crisp Basket in your Pressure Cooker Steam Fryer. 2. Sprinkle black pepper and salt over the chicken drumsticks and massage the coconut milk into them. 3. Put all the recipe ingredients except the egg into the food processor and pulse to create a bread crumb-like mixture. 4. Transfer to a suitable bowl. 5. In a separate bowl, put the beaten egg. Coat each chicken drumstick in the bread crumb mixture before dredging it in the egg. Roll it in the bread crumbs once more. 6. Put the coated chicken drumsticks in "cook & crisp basket". Put on the Smart Lid on top of the Ninja Foodi Steam Fryer. Move the Lid Slider to the "Air Fry/Stovetop". Select the "Air Fry" mode for cooking. 7. Adjust the cooking temperature to 350°F/175°C. 8. Cook for around 20 minutes. Serve hot.
Per serving: Calories 412; Fat: 23.6g; Sodium 1495mg; Carbs: 4.8g; Fiber: 1.3g; Sugars 1.7g; Protein 37.9g

Bacon Chicken

Prep Time: 10 minutes. | Cook Time: 20 minutes. | Serves: 6

1 chicken breast, cut into 6 pieces
6 rashers back bacon
1 tablespoon soft cheese

1. Place the Cook & Crisp Basket in your Pressure Cooker Steam Fryer. 2. Put the bacon rashers on a flat surface and cover one side with the soft cheese. 3. Lay the chicken pieces on each bacon rasher. Wrap the bacon around the chicken and use a toothpick stick to hold each one in place. Put them in "cook & crisp basket". 4. Put on the Smart Lid on top of the Ninja Foodi Steam Fryer. 5. Move the Lid Slider to the "Air Fry/Stovetop". Select the "Air Fry" mode for cooking. 6. Air fry at 350°F/175°C for 15 minutes.
Per serving: Calories 413; Fat: 24.5g; Sodium 962mg; Carbs: 6.9g; Fiber: 1.1g; Sugars 2.9g; Protein 39.1g

Holiday Chicken Wings

Prep Time: 10 minutes. | Cook Time: 20 minutes. | Serves: 6

6 chicken wings
1 tablespoon honey
2 cloves garlic, chopped
1 teaspoon red chili flakes
2 tablespoon Worcestershire sauce
Pepper and salt to taste
Cooking spray

1. Place the Cook & Crisp Basket in your Pressure Cooker Steam Fryer. 2. Place all the recipe ingredients, except for the chicken wings, in a suitable bowl and mix well. 3. Coat the chicken with the mixture and refrigerate for around 1 hour. 4. Put the marinated chicken wings in the Ninja Foodi Pressure Steam Fryer basket and spritz with cooking spray. 5. Put on the Smart Lid on top of the Ninja Foodi Steam Fryer. 6. Move the Lid Slider to the "Air Fry/Stovetop". Select the "Air Fry" mode for cooking. 7. Air fry the chicken wings at 320°F/160°C for around 8 minutes. Raise the temperature to 350°F/175°C. Cook for an additional 4 minutes. Serve hot.
Per serving: Calories 612; Fat: 38.2g; Sodium 76mg; Carbs: 39.1g; Fiber: 5.8g; Sugars 1.6g; Protein 30.6g

Lemon Garlic Chicken

Prep Time: 10 minutes. | Cook Time: 15 minutes. | Serves: 1

1 chicken breast
1 teaspoon garlic, minced
1 tablespoon chicken seasoning
1 lemon juice
Handful black peppercorns
Pepper and salt to taste

1. Place the Cook & Crisp Basket in your Pressure Cooker Steam Fryer. 2. Sprinkle the chicken with pepper and salt. Massage the chicken seasoning into the chicken breast, coating it well, and lay the seasoned chicken on a sheet of aluminum foil. 3. Top the chicken with the garlic, lemon juice, and black peppercorns. Wrap the foil to seal the chicken tightly. 4. Put on the Smart Lid on top of the Ninja Foodi Steam Fryer. 5. Move the Lid Slider to the "Air Fry/Stovetop". Select the "Air Fry" mode for cooking. 6. Adjust the cooking temperature to 350°F/175°C. 7. Cook the chicken for around 15 minutes.
Per serving: Calories 347; Fat: 15.7g; Sodium 999mg; Carbs: 11.8g; Fiber: 1.1g; Sugars 7g; Protein 39.6g

Cajun Chicken

Prep Time: 10 minutes. | Cook Time: 10 minutes. | Serves: 2

2 boneless chicken breasts   3 tablespoon Cajun spice

1. Place the Cook & Crisp Basket in your Pressure Cooker Steam Fryer. 2. Coat both sides of the chicken breasts with Cajun spice. 3. Put the seasoned chicken in "cook & crisp basket". 4. Put on the Smart Lid on top of the Ninja Foodi Steam Fryer. 5. Move the Lid Slider to the "Air Fry/Stovetop". Select the "Air Fry" mode for cooking. 6. Air fry at 350°F/175°C for 10 minutes, ensuring they are cooked through before slicing up and serving.
Per serving: Calories 236; Fat: 10.4g; Sodium 713mg; Carbs: 9.8g; Fiber: 0.5g; Sugars 0.1g; Protein 25.7g

Italian Chicken Fillets

Prep Time: 10 minutes. | Cook Time: 6 minutes. | Serves: 3

8 pieces of chicken fillet	1 teaspoon garlic powder
1 egg	½ cup parmesan cheese
1 ounces salted butter, melted	1 teaspoon Italian herbs
1 cup friendly bread crumbs	

1. Place the Cook & Crisp Basket in your Pressure Cooker Steam Fryer. 2. Cover the chicken pieces in the whisked egg, melted butter, garlic powder, and Italian herbs. Allow to marinate for about 10 minutes. 3. In a suitable bowl, mix the bread crumbs and parmesan. Use this mixture to coat the marinated chicken. 4. Put the aluminum foil in your Ninja Foodi Pressure Steam Fryer basket. 5. Place 4 pieces of the chicken in the basket. 6. Put on the Smart Lid on top of the Ninja Foodi Steam Fryer. 7. Move the Lid Slider to the "Air Fry/Stovetop". Select the "Air Fry" mode for cooking. 8. Cook at 390°F/200°C for around 6 minutes until golden brown. Don't turn the chicken over. 9. Repeat with the rest of the chicken pieces. 10. Serve the chicken fillets hot.
Per serving: Calories 427; Fat: 18.1g; Sodium 676mg; Carbs: 13.7g; Fiber: 7.5g; Sugars 1.7g; Protein 51.2g

Chicken Parsley Nuggets

Prep Time: 10 minutes. | Cook Time: 10 minutes. | Serves: 4

½ lb. chicken breast, cut into pieces	2 eggs, beaten
1 teaspoon parsley	1 teaspoon tomato ketchup
1 teaspoon paprika	1 teaspoon garlic, minced
1 tablespoon olive oil	½ cup friendly bread crumbs
	Pepper and salt to taste

1. Place the Cook & Crisp Basket in your Pressure Cooker Steam Fryer. 2. In a bowl, mix the bread crumbs, olive oil, paprika, pepper, and salt. 3. Place the chicken, ketchup, one egg, garlic, and parsley in a food processor and pulse together. 4. Put the other egg in a suitable bowl. 5. Shape equal amounts of the pureed chicken into nuggets. Dredge each one in the egg before coating it in bread crumbs. 6. Put the coated chicken nuggets in the Ninja Foodi Pressure Steam Fryer basket. Put on the Smart Lid on top of the Ninja Foodi Steam Fryer. Move the Lid Slider to the "Air Fry/Stovetop". Select the "Air Fry" mode for cooking. Air Fry at 390°F/200°C for 10 minutes. 7. Serve the nuggets hot.
Per serving: Calories 227; Fat: 8.8g; Sodium 302mg; Carbs: 8.9g; Fiber: 2.1g; Sugars 3.3g; Protein 28.5g

Crusted Chicken Tenders

Prep Time: 10 minutes. | Cook Time: 15 minutes. | Serves: 4

2 lb. skinless and boneless chicken tenders	1 cup friendly bread crumbs
3 large eggs	¼ teaspoon black pepper
6 tablespoon skimmed milk	1 teaspoon salt
½ cup flour	2 tablespoons olive oil

1. Place the Cook & Crisp Basket in your Pressure Cooker Steam Fryer. 2. In a suitable bowl, mix the bread crumbs and olive oil. 3. In a separate bowl, stir the eggs and milk using a whisk. Sprinkle in the salt and black pepper. 4. Put the flour in a third bowl. 5. Slice up the chicken tenders into 1-inch strips. Coat each piece of chicken in the flour, before dipping it into the egg mixture, followed by the bread crumbs. 6. Put on the Smart Lid on top of the Ninja Foodi Steam Fryer. 7. Move the Lid Slider to the "Air Fry/Stovetop". Select the "Air Fry" mode for cooking. 8. Adjust the cooking temperature to 385°F/195°C. 9. Cook the coated chicken tenders for about 13 to 15 minutes, shaking the basket a few times to ensure they turn crispy. Serve hot, with mashed potatoes and a dipping sauce if desired.
Per serving: Calories 232; Fat: 8.4g; Sodium 300mg; Carbs: 8.6g; Fiber: 0.9g; Sugars 0.1g; Protein 30.1g

Rosemary Spiced Chicken

Prep Time: 10 minutes. | Cook Time: 20 minutes. | Serves: 2

¾ lb. chicken	3 tablespoon sugar
½ tablespoon olive oil	1 tablespoon fresh rosemary, chopped
1 tablespoon soy sauce	
1 teaspoon fresh ginger, minced	½ fresh lemon, cut into wedges
1 tablespoon oyster sauce	

1. Place the Cook & Crisp Basket in your Pressure Cooker Steam Fryer. 2. In a suitable bowl, mix the chicken, oil, soy sauce, and ginger, coating the chicken well. 3. Refrigerate for around 30 minutes. 4. Place the chicken in the Cook & Crisp Basket, transfer to the Pressure Cooker Steam Fryer. Put on the Smart Lid on top of the Ninja Foodi Steam Fryer. Move the Lid Slider to the "Air Fry/Stovetop". Select the "Air Fry" mode for cooking. 5. Adjust the cooking temperature to 390°F/200°C. 6. Cook for around 6 minutes. 7. In the meantime, put the rosemary, sugar, and oyster sauce in a suitable bowl and mix together. 8. Add the rosemary mixture in the Pressure Cooker Steam Fryer over the chicken and top the chicken with the lemon wedges. 9. Resume cooking for another 13 minutes, turning the chicken halfway through.
Per serving: Calories 344; Fat: 10g; Sodium 251mg; Carbs: 4.7g; Fiber: 0.5g; Sugars 2.2g; Protein 55.7g

Tuscan Chicken

Prep time: 10 minutes| Cook time: 23 minutes| Serves: 4

2 pounds boneless, skinless chicken breasts	¾ cup low-sodium chicken broth
1 tablespoon Italian seasoning	¾ cup heavy cream
½ teaspoon fine sea salt	¾ cup grated Parmesan cheese
4 garlic cloves, minced	½ cup oil-packed sun-dried tomatoes, drained
2 tablespoons olive oil	2 cups chopped fresh spinach

1. Cut the chicken breasts in half lengthwise. One at a time, place the chicken breasts between two pieces of plastic wrap. On top of a protected surface, like a cutting board on the counter, use a pan or rolling pin to pound the meat to about ½ inch thick. Season the chicken with the Italian seasoning, salt, and garlic, pressing the seasonings into the chicken with your fingertips. 2. Move the slider towards "AIR FRY/STOVETOP" and set Ninja Foodi XL Pressure Cooker Steam Fryer with SmartLid to SEAR/SAUTÉ mode. Adjust the temperature to "Hi5" by using up arrow. Press START/STOP to begin cooking. Add the oil to the cooking pot. When the oil is hot, add the chicken and brown for 2 minutes on each side. Remove the chicken and add the broth, stirring to loosen any chicken pieces that may have stuck to the bottom. Return the chicken to the pot. 3. Lock lid; move slider towards PRESSURE. Adjust pressure release valve in the SEAL position. Close pressure-release valve. The cooking temperature will default to HIGH, which is accurate. Set time to 3 minutes. Select START/STOP and start cooking. When cooking is complete, let pressure release quickly by turning it into VENT position. 4. Unlock and remove the lid. Use tongs to transfer the chicken pieces to a plate. Move the slider towards "AIR FRY/STOVETOP" and set Ninja Foodi XL Pressure Cooker Steam Fryer with SmartLid to SEAR/SAUTÉ mode. Adjust the temperature to "Hi5" by using up arrow. Press START/STOP to begin cooking and whisk the cream into the broth, stirring to combine. Bring to a simmer and cook, stirring occasionally, for 5 minutes. 5. Add the cheese and sun-dried tomatoes and stir until the cheese melts. Add the spinach and stir just until the spinach wilts.
Per Serving: Calories 282; Fat 12.6g; Sodium 269mg; Carbs 11.5g; Fiber 2g; Sugar 2g; Protein 17.3g

Lemon Chicken with Herbed Potatoes

Prep time: 5 minutes| Cook time: 25 minutes| Serves: 4

2 pounds chicken thighs	juice
1 teaspoon fine sea salt	2 to 3 tablespoons Dijon mustard
½ teaspoon ground black pepper	2 tablespoons Italian seasoning
2 tablespoons olive oil	2 to 3 pounds red potatoes,
¾ cup low-sodium chicken broth	quartered
¼ cup freshly squeezed lemon	

1. Season the chicken with the salt and pepper. 2. Move the slider towards "AIR FRY/STOVETOP" and set Ninja Foodi XL Pressure Cooker Steam Fryer with SmartLid to SEAR/SAUTÉ mode. Adjust the temperature to "Hi5" by using up arrow. Press START/STOP to begin cooking. Add the oil to the cooking pot. Add the chicken and brown for 3 minutes on each side. 3. In a medium mixing bowl, combine the chicken broth, lemon juice, mustard, and Italian seasoning and mix well. Pour over the chicken. Add the potatoes. 4. Lock lid; move slider towards PRESSURE. Adjust pressure release valve in the SEAL position. Close pressure-release valve. The cooking temperature will default to HIGH, which is accurate. Set time to 15 minutes. Select START/STOP and start cooking. 5. When cooking is complete, let pressure release quickly by turning it into VENT position. Carefully open it and serve hot.
Per Serving: Calories 284; Fat 12.5g; Sodium 412mg; Carbs 11.2g; Fiber 3g; Sugar 3g; Protein 16.5g

Delicious Sesame Chicken

Prep time: 5 minutes| Cook time: 15 minutes| Serves: 4

2 tablespoons cornstarch, divided	¼ cup soy sauce
¼ teaspoon fine sea salt	2 tablespoons ketchup
1-pound chicken tenders, cut into	¼ teaspoon red pepper flakes
1-inch pieces	¼ cup honey
2 tablespoons toasted sesame oil,	2 tablespoons water
divided	2 teaspoons sesame seeds

1. In a small bowl, combine 1 tablespoon of cornstarch with the salt. Toss the chicken pieces in the cornstarch mixture until it is coated evenly. Move the slider towards "AIR FRY/STOVETOP" and set Ninja Foodi XL Pressure Cooker Steam Fryer with SmartLid to SEAR/SAUTÉ mode. Adjust the temperature to "Hi5" by using up arrow. Press START/STOP to begin cooking. Add 1 tablespoon of sesame oil. When the oil is hot, add the chicken and cook for about 4 minutes, turning occasionally, or until golden brown. 2. In another small bowl, combine the soy sauce, ketchup, and red pepper flakes and stir until well combined. Pour this sauce over the chicken. 3. Lock lid; move slider towards PRESSURE. Adjust pressure release valve in the SEAL position. Close pressure-release valve. The cooking temperature will default to HIGH, which is accurate. Set time to 3 minutes. Select START/STOP and start cooking. When cooking is complete, let pressure release quickly by turning it into VENT position. 4. Unlock and remove the lid. Add the remaining 1 tablespoon of sesame oil and the honey and stir quickly to combine. Move the slider towards "AIR FRY/STOVETOP" and set Ninja Foodi XL Pressure Cooker Steam Fryer with SmartLid to SEAR/SAUTÉ mode. Adjust the temperature to "Hi5" by using up arrow. Press START/STOP to begin cooking. 5. In a clean small bowl, whisk the remaining 1 tablespoon of cornstarch into the water until it is smooth. Stir this slurry into the chicken, stirring constantly for 2 minutes, or until sauce reaches the desired consistency. 6. Sprinkle with the sesame seeds.
Per Serving: Calories 287; Fat 12.4g; Sodium 333mg; Carbs 11.6g; Fiber 7g; Sugar 2g; Protein 16.5g

Lo Mein

Prep time: 10 minutes| Cook time: 30 minutes| Serves: 4

1 tablespoon toasted sesame oil	1 cup snow peas
1½ pounds boneless, skinless	1 cup broccoli florets
chicken breast, cut into bite-size	1 carrot, peeled and thinly sliced
pieces	1½ cups low-sodium chicken broth
1 garlic clove, minced	1 tablespoon soy sauce
8 ounces dried linguine, broken in	1 tablespoon fish sauce
half	1 tablespoon Shaoxing rice wine

1 teaspoon grated fresh ginger	1 tablespoon brown sugar

1. Move the slider towards "AIR FRY/STOVETOP" and set Ninja Foodi XL Pressure Cooker Steam Fryer with SmartLid to SEAR/SAUTÉ mode. Adjust the temperature to "Hi5" by using up arrow. Press START/STOP to begin cooking. Add the sesame oil. When the oil is hot, add the chicken and garlic and cook until the garlic is light brown and chicken is opaque, about 5 minutes. Fan the noodles across the bottom of the pot. Add the snow peas, broccoli, and carrot on top of the noodles. 2. In a medium bowl, combine the broth, soy sauce, fish sauce, rice wine, ginger, and brown sugar. Stir until the sugar is dissolved. Pour the sauce over the vegetables in the pot. 3. Lock lid; move slider towards PRESSURE. Adjust pressure release valve in the SEAL position. Close pressure-release valve. The cooking temperature will default to HIGH, which is accurate. Set time to 5 minutes. Select START/STOP and start cooking. When cooking is complete, let pressure release quickly by turning it into VENT position. 4. Unlock and remove the lid. Stir the noodles, breaking up any clumps, until the liquid is absorbed.
Per Serving: Calories 287; Fat 12.5g; Sodium 364mg; Carbs 11.5g; Fiber 3g; Sugar 2g; Protein 16.2g

Refreshing Chicken Tacos

Prep time: 5 minutes| Cook time: 25 minutes| Serves: 2

½ cup salsa	chicken breasts
½ cup chicken broth	4 (8-inch) corn tortillas
1 tablespoon olive oil	Optional toppings: shredded
½ teaspoon salt	cheddar cheese, sliced onion, sliced
2 (5- to 6-ounce) boneless, skinless	avocado, chopped fresh cilantro

1. Combine the salsa, broth, olive oil, and salt in the Ninja Foodi XL Pressure Cooker Steam Fryer. 2. Lock lid; move slider towards PRESSURE. Adjust pressure release valve in the SEAL position. Close pressure-release valve. The cooking temperature will default to HIGH, which is accurate. Set time to 15 minutes. Select START/STOP and start cooking. 3. When cooking is complete, let pressure release naturally for about 5 minutes, then quickly release any remaining pressure by turning it into VENT position. Open the lid and transfer the chicken to a plate or cutting board. 4. Shred the chicken with two forks, then return the meat to the salsa mixture and stir it in. 5. Serve the chicken warm on corn tortillas with your favorite toppings.
Per Serving: Calories 286; Fat 12.7g; Sodium 444mg; Carbs 11.5g; Fiber 3g; Sugar 3g; Protein 16.4g

Breaded Chicken

Prep Time: 10 minutes. | Cook Time: 52 minutes. | Serves: 2

2 chicken breasts, boneless and	1 teaspoon smoked paprika
skinless	1 teaspoon salt
2 large eggs	¼ teaspoon black pepper
½ cup skimmed milk	½ teaspoon garlic powder
6 tablespoon soy sauce	1 tablespoon olive oil
1 cup flour	4 hamburger buns

1. Place the Cook & Crisp Basket in your Pressure Cooker Steam Fryer. 2. Slice the chicken breast into 2 to 3 pieces. 3. Place in a large bowl and drizzle with the soy sauce. Sprinkle on the smoked paprika, black pepper, salt, and garlic powder and mix well. 4. Allow to marinate for around 30 to 40 minutes. 5. In the meantime, mix the eggs with the milk in a bowl. Put the flour in a separate bowl. 6. Dip the marinated chicken into the egg mixture before coating it with the flour. Cover each piece of chicken evenly. 7. Drizzle on the olive oil and put chicken pieces in the Cook & Crisp Basket . 8. Put on the Smart Lid on top of the Ninja Foodi Steam Fryer. 9. Move the Lid Slider to the "Air Fry/Stovetop". Select the "Air Fry" mode for cooking. 10. Adjust the cooking temperature to 380°F/195°C. 11. Cook for around 10 to 12 minutes. Flip the chicken once throughout the cooking process. 12. Toast the hamburger buns and put each slice of chicken between two buns to make a sandwich. Serve with ketchup or any other sauce of your choice.
Per serving: Calories 408; Fat: 23.1g; Sodium 412mg; Carbs: 27.7g; Fiber: 7.2g; Sugars 19.2g; Protein 24.4g

Chicken Egg Roll

Prep time: 10 minutes| Cook time: 14 minutes| Serves: 4

3 tablespoons soy sauce
1 tablespoon rice vinegar, white wine vinegar, or lime juice
1 teaspoon granulated sugar
4 cups shredded cabbage or coleslaw mix
1 large carrot, shredded (about ½ cup)
½ cup chopped mushrooms

3 scallions, chopped
2 teaspoons minced garlic
1 teaspoon grated fresh ginger
1 tablespoon toasted sesame oil
12 ounces chicken tenders or chicken breast, cut into 1-inch strips
4 to 6 flour tortillas or other wraps, warmed

1. Combine the soy sauce, vinegar, and sugar in the cooking pot. Add the cabbage, carrot, mushrooms, scallions, garlic, ginger, and sesame oil and stir. Lay the chicken tenders on top. 2. Lock lid; move slider towards PRESSURE. Adjust pressure release valve in the SEAL position. Close pressure-release valve. The cooking temperature will default to HIGH, which is accurate. Set time to 2 minutes. Select START/STOP and start cooking. When cooking is complete, let pressure release quickly by turning it into VENT position. 3. Unlock and remove the lid. Use tongs to transfer the chicken to a plate. When the chicken is cool enough to handle, shred it with two forks or cut it into bite-size pieces. Stir the chicken back into the vegetables. Move the slider towards "AIR FRY/STOVETOP" and set Ninja Foodi XL Pressure Cooker Steam Fryer with SmartLid to SEAR/SAUTÉ mode. Adjust the temperature to "Hi5" by using up arrow. Press START/STOP to begin cooking. Bring the mixture to a boil for a minute or so, just to reduce the liquid by about half and finish cooking the chicken if necessary. 4. Using a slotted spoon, scoop out the filling onto the wraps, leaving most of the liquid behind so the wraps don't get soggy. Fold the wraps around the filling, tucking in the edges.
Per Serving: Calories 286; Fat 12.6g; Sodium 399mg; Carbs 11.4g; Fiber 5g; Sugar 6g; Protein 16.6g

Herbed Chicken Wings

Prep Time: 10 minutes. | Cook Time: 15 minutes. | Serves: 6

4 lb. chicken wings
6 tablespoons red wine vinegar
6 tablespoons lime juice
1 teaspoon fresh ginger, minced
1 tablespoon sugar
1 teaspoon thyme, chopped
½ teaspoon white pepper

¼ teaspoon cinnamon
1 habanero pepper, chopped
6 garlic cloves, chopped
2 tablespoon soy sauce
2 ½ tablespoon olive oil
¼ teaspoon salt

1. Place the Cook & Crisp Basket in your Pressure Cooker Steam Fryer. 2. Place all of the recipe ingredients in a suitable bowl and mix well, ensuring to coat the chicken entirely. 3. Put the chicken in the refrigerator to marinate for around 1 hour. 4. Put half of the marinated chicken in the "cook & crisp basket". Put on the Smart Lid on top of the Ninja Foodi Steam Fryer. Move the Lid Slider to the "Air Fry/Stovetop". Select the "Air Fry" mode for cooking. 5. Adjust the cooking temperature to 390°F/200°C. 6. Cook for around 15 minutes, shaking the basket once throughout the cooking process. 7. Repeat with the other half of the chicken. 8. Serve hot.
Per serving: Calories 347; Fat: 18.8g; Sodium 137mg; Carbs: 13.4g; Fiber: 8.5g; Sugars 1g; Protein 36.3g

Turkey with Gravy

Prep time: 25 minutes| Cook time: 60 minutes| Serves: 4

1 (4½- to 5-pound) bone-in turkey breast
4 teaspoons poultry seasoning
¾ teaspoon fine sea salt
1 cup low-sodium chicken broth

2 tablespoons unsalted butter, melted
2 tablespoons all-purpose flour
2 tablespoons heavy cream

1. Prepare the turkey: Pat the turkey breast dry. Mix together the poultry seasoning and salt. Rub about half of the mixture on the skin and in the cavity on the underside of the breast; reserve the rest. 2. Pour the chicken broth into the cooking pot. Place a Deluxe reversible rack in the pot. Lock lid; move slider towards PRESSURE. Adjust pressure release valve in the SEAL position. Close pressure-

release valve. The cooking temperature will default to HIGH, which is accurate. Set time to 8 minutes. Select START/STOP and start cooking. When cooking is complete, let pressure release naturally for about 8 minutes, then quickly release any remaining pressure by turning it into VENT position. Unlock and remove the lid. 3. Mix the remaining seasoning mixture with the butter. When the turkey is ready, remove it from the pot and place it, skin-side up, on a rack set over a rimmed baking sheet. Brush the turkey skin with the seasoned butter. 4. Lock lid; move slider to STEAMCRISP. Select STEAM & CRISP, set temperature to 400°F/200°C, and set time to 15 minutes. Press START/STOP to begin cooking. Roast the turkey for 10 to 15 minutes, until the skin is browned and the interior temperature reaches at least 155°F/70°C. 5. While the turkey roasts, remove the Deluxe reversible rack from the cooking pot. Remove about ½ cup of the cooking liquid and leave the rest in the pot. Move the slider towards "AIR FRY/STOVETOP" and set Ninja Foodi XL Pressure Cooker Steam Fryer with SmartLid to SEAR/SAUTÉ mode. Adjust the temperature to "3" by using up arrow. Press START/STOP to begin cooking. In a small bowl, stir together the flour and the ½ cup cooking liquid. When the liquid in the pot is simmering, gradually stir in the flour mixture. Cook for 3 to 5 minutes, until the gravy comes to a boil and is thickened. For a creamier gravy, stir in the optional cream. 6. When the turkey is done, remove it from the oven and let it rest for about 10 minutes before slicing.
Per Serving: Calories 286; Fat 12.5g; Sodium 711mg; Carbs 11.6g; Fiber 3g; Sugar 1.3g; Protein 16.3g

Stuffed Turkey Breast with Gravy

Prep time: 25 minutes| Cook time: 60 minutes| Serves: 4

5 tablespoons unsalted butter
1 small yellow onion, chopped
2 celery ribs, chopped
4 cups dry sage stuffing mix (such as Pepperidge Farm; 7 ounces)
2¾ cups store-bought chicken broth, or homemade

1 (2½- to 2¾-pound) boneless, skin-on turkey breast half or tied turkey breast roast
Salt and freshly ground black pepper
1 tablespoon olive oil
2½ tablespoons all-purpose flour

1. Smear 1 tablespoon of the butter in the Cook & Crisp Basket. 2. Put 1 tablespoon of the butter in the pot, move the slider towards "AIR FRY/STOVETOP" and set Ninja Foodi XL Pressure Cooker Steam Fryer with SmartLid to SEAR/SAUTÉ mode. Adjust the temperature to "Hi5" by using up arrow. Press START/STOP to begin cooking. When the butter has melted, add the onion and celery and cook, stirring frequently, until tender, 4 minutes. Press START/STOP. Pour the vegetables into a bowl, add the stuffing mix and 1¼ cups of the broth, and stir to moisten. Pour into the Cook & Crisp Basket and cover tightly with foil. set aside. 3. Season the turkey breast all over with salt and pepper and drizzle with the oil. Select SAUTÉ like before. When the pot is hot, place the turkey breast skin-side down in the pot and cook until golden brown, 3 minutes. Press START/STOP. Remove the turkey breast from the pot. 4. Add the remaining 1½ cups broth to the pot and scrape up any browned bits on the bottom. 5. Place a Deluxe reversible rack with handles into the pot and place the turkey breast skin-side up on the Deluxe reversible rack. Place the stuffing in the Cook & Crisp Basket on top of the turkey breast. 6. Lock lid; move slider towards PRESSURE. Adjust pressure release valve in the SEAL position. Close pressure-release valve. The cooking temperature will default to HIGH, which is accurate. Set time to 35 minutes. Select START/STOP and start cooking. When cooking is complete, let pressure release naturally for about 10 minutes, then quickly release any remaining pressure by turning it into VENT position. Remove the stuffing from the pot. 7. Insert an instant-read thermometer into the thickest part of the breast; it should read 160°F/70°C. If it doesn't, cover the pot with a regular pot lid, select SEAR/SAUTÉ again and simmer briefly until 160°F/70°C is reached. Press START/STOP. Transfer the turkey breast to a cutting board and cover loosely with foil; leave the cooking liquid in the pot. 8. In a medium bowl, combine the remaining 3 tablespoons butter with the flour and stir until smooth. Select SEAR/SAUTÉ gradually whisk the flour mixture into the cooking liquid and cook until bubbly, 3 minutes. Season with salt and pepper. Press START/STOP. 9. Slice the turkey roast crosswise. Serve with the gravy and stuffing.
Per Serving: Calories 282; Fat 11.3g; Sodium 113mg; Carbs 10.3g; Fiber 3g; Sugar 4g; Protein 16.2g

Indian Chicken Marsala

Prep time: 10minutes| Cook time: 28 minutes| Serves: 2

1 tablespoon olive oil	½ cup water, plus 2 tablespoons, divided
¼ cup all-purpose flour, divided	
2 (5- to 6-ounce) boneless, skinless chicken breasts	1 cup sliced mushrooms
¼ teaspoon salt	½ cup marsala wine
⅛ teaspoon black pepper	2 tablespoons heavy cream

1. Move the slider towards "AIR FRY/STOVETOP" and set Ninja Foodi XL Pressure Cooker Steam Fryer with SmartLid to SEAR/SAUTÉ mode. Adjust the temperature to "Hi5" by using up arrow. Press START/STOP to begin cooking and pour in the olive oil. 2. Set aside 1 tablespoon of flour for use later. Put the rest of the flour in a shallow dish. Season the chicken breasts with the salt and pepper, then dredge them in the flour. Once the oil is shimmering, add the chicken and cook until golden brown, 3 to 4 minutes per side. Press START/STOP to turn off the pot and transfer the chicken to a plate. 3. Pour the water into the Ninja Foodi XL Pressure Cooker Steam Fryer and scrape up any bits from the bottom of the pot. 4. Return the chicken to the pot and top with the mushrooms and wine. 5. Lock lid; move slider towards PRESSURE. Adjust pressure release valve in the SEAL position. Close pressure-release valve. The cooking temperature will default to HIGH, which is accurate. Set time to 8 minutes. Select START/STOP and start cooking. When cooking is complete, let the pressure release naturally for about 5 minutes, then quickly release any remaining pressure by turning it into VENT position. 6. Transfer the chicken breasts to a clean plate. 7. Move the slider towards "AIR FRY/STOVETOP" and set Ninja Foodi XL Pressure Cooker Steam Fryer with SmartLid to SEAR/SAUTÉ mode. Adjust the temperature to "Hi5" by using up arrow. Press START/STOP to begin cooking. 8. In a small bowl, whisk together the reserved 1 tablespoon of flour and the remaining 2 tablespoons of water until completely dissolved. Pour the flour slurry into the pot while whisking the sauce. 9. Allow to cook for 2 to 3 minutes, stirring occasionally, until the sauce has thickened. Stir in the heavy cream. Press START/STOP to turn off. 10. Serve the chicken breasts warm, topped with the mushroom sauce.
Per Serving: Calories 279; Fat 11.6g; Sodium 741mg; Carbs 9.3g; Fiber 2g; Sugar 2g; Protein 16.2g

Spicy Teriyaki Chicken

Prep time: 15 minutes| Cook time: 30 minutes| Serves: 4

4 to 6 bone-in, skin-on chicken thighs	sauce, divided (see tip to make your own)
½ teaspoon kosher salt	1 large red bell pepper, seeded and cut into 1-inch chunks
2 tablespoons olive oil	
¼ cup low-sodium chicken broth	1 (8-ounce) can unsweetened pineapple chunks, drained
¼ cup plus 2 tablespoons teriyaki	

1. Season the chicken thighs on both sides with the salt. Move the slider towards "AIR FRY/STOVETOP" and set Ninja Foodi XL Pressure Cooker Steam Fryer with SmartLid to SEAR/SAUTÉ mode. Adjust the temperature to "Hi5" by using up arrow. Press START/STOP to begin cooking. Add the oil to the pot and heat until it shimmers and flows like water. Add the chicken thighs, skin-side down, and let them cook, undisturbed, for about 4 minutes, until the skin is golden brown. Transfer the thighs to a plate. 2. Pour out the fat. Add the broth and scrape the bottom of the pan to release the browned bits. Add 2 tablespoons of teriyaki sauce and stir to combine. Add the bell pepper chunks and chicken thighs, skin-side up. 3. Lock lid; move slider towards PRESSURE. Adjust pressure release valve in the SEAL position. Close pressure-release valve. The cooking temperature will default to HIGH, which is accurate. Set time to 8 minutes. Select START/STOP and start cooking. When cooking is complete, let pressure release naturally for about 5 minutes, then quickly release any remaining pressure by turning it into VENT position. 4. Lock lid; move slider to STEAMCRISP. Select STEAM & CRISP, set temperature to 400°F/200°C, and set time to 5 minutes. Press START/STOP to begin cooking. Remove the chicken thighs from the pan and place them on a rack set over a rimmed baking sheet. Brush with the remaining ¼ cup of teriyaki sauce. Crisp the chicken thighs for 3 to 5 minutes, until browned. 5. While the chicken broils, add the pineapple chunks to the pot. Select Sauté again and adjust the heat to Medium. Bring to a simmer to thicken the sauce and warm the pineapple through. 6. When the chicken is done, top it with the peppers and pineapple, and drizzle with the sauce.

Per Serving: Calories 283; Fat 12.3g; Sodium 444mg; Carbs 11.5g; Fiber 2g; Sugar 2g; Protein 16.7g

Roasted Chicken

Prep Time: 10 minutes. | Cook Time: 55 minutes. | Serves: 4

5 – 7 lbs. whole chicken with skin	½ teaspoon dried rosemary
1 teaspoon garlic powder	½ teaspoon black pepper
1 teaspoon onion powder	2 teaspoons salt
½ teaspoon dried thyme	2 tablespoon olive oil
½ teaspoon dried basil	

1. Place the Cook & Crisp Basket in your Pressure Cooker Steam Fryer. 2. Massage the salt, pepper, herbs, and olive oil into the chicken. Allow to marinade for a minimum of 20 to 30 minutes. 3. Place the chicken in the basket. Put on the Smart Lid on top of the Ninja Foodi Steam Fryer. Move the Lid Slider to the "Air Fry/Stovetop". Select the "Air Fry" mode for cooking. Cook at 340°F/170°C for around 18 to 20 minutes. 4. Flip the chicken over. 5. Cook for an additional 20 minutes. 6. Leave the chicken to rest for about 10 minutes before carving and serving.
Per serving: Calories 314; Fat: 8.7g; Sodium 337mg; Carbs: 21.2g; Fiber: 4.1g; Sugars 16g; Protein 37.9g

Spicy Chicken Alfredo

Prep time: 10 minutes| Cook time: 20 minutes| Serves: 2

1 tablespoon olive oil	1 cup chicken broth
1 (5- to 6-ounce) boneless, skinless chicken breast, cut into 1-inch pieces	1 cup heavy cream
	4 ounces fettuccine noodles, broken in half
¼ teaspoon salt	1 cup grated Parmesan cheese
¼ teaspoon black pepper	

1. Move the slider towards "AIR FRY/STOVETOP" and set Ninja Foodi XL Pressure Cooker Steam Fryer with SmartLid to SEAR/SAUTÉ mode. Adjust the temperature to "Hi5" by using up arrow. Press START/STOP to begin cooking and pour in the olive oil. 2. Season the chicken with the salt and pepper. Once the oil is shimmering, add the chicken and cook until golden brown, 3 to 4 minutes. Press START/STOP to turn off the pot and transfer the chicken to a plate. 3. Add the broth to the pot and scrape up any bits from the bottom of the pot. 4. Add the heavy cream and fettuccine to the pot and stir, then top with the chicken. 5. Lock lid; move slider towards PRESSURE. Adjust pressure release valve in the SEAL position. Close pressure-release valve. The cooking temperature will default to HIGH, which is accurate. Set time to 6 minutes. Select START/STOP and start cooking. When cooking is complete, let pressure release quickly by turning it into VENT position. 6. Open the lid. Stir the pasta and chicken, and slowly add the Parmesan cheese until melted. Serve warm.
Per Serving: Calories 494; Fat 24.3g; Sodium 257mg; Carbs 43.8g; Fiber 8.3g; Sugar 3.7g; Protein 28.8g

Burrito Bowls with Chicken And Beans

Prep time: 10 minutes| Cook time: 15 minutes| Serves: 2

1 (5- to 6-ounce) boneless, skinless chicken breast, cut into 1-inch pieces	and rinsed
	1 cup water
	¾ cup salsa
1 tablespoon taco seasoning	Optional toppings: shredded cheddar cheese, sliced tomatoes, chopped fresh cilantro
½ cup long-grain rice	
½ cup canned black beans, drained	

1. Combine the chicken, taco seasoning, rice, beans, and water to the Ninja Foodi XL Pressure Cooker Steam Fryer with SmartLid cooking pot and stir. 2. Top with the salsa, but do not stir. 3. Lock lid; move slider towards PRESSURE. Adjust pressure release valve in the SEAL position. Close pressure-release valve. The cooking temperature will default to HIGH, which is accurate. Set time to 10 minutes. Select START/STOP and start cooking. 4. When cooking is complete, let pressure release quickly by turning it into VENT position. 5. Open the lid. Stir the mixture. If using shredded cheese, add it now and put the lid back on until the cheese is melted, 2 to 3 minutes. 6. Serve warm, with cheese, tomatoes and cilantro, if using.
Per Serving: Calories 494; Fat 24.3g; Sodium 257mg; Carbs 43.8g; Fiber 8.3g; Sugar 3.7g; Protein 28.8g

Pesto Turkey Meatballs with Pasta

Prep time: 15 minutes| Cook time: 20 minutes| Serves: 4

1 pound Italian turkey sausage, casings removed and discarded	or homemade
¼ cup dry Italian breadcrumbs	1 cup fresh prepared basil pesto
1 large egg	Salt and freshly ground black pepper
12 ounces dry gemelli pasta, medium shells, or rotini	1 cup fresh basil leaves, torn into small pieces
3 cups store-bought chicken broth,	

1. In a medium bowl, mix the sausage meat, breadcrumbs, and egg. Divide the mixture into 20 portions, about 1 heaping tablespoon each. Set aside. 2. Place the pasta, broth, pesto, 1 cup water, ½ teaspoon salt, and several grinds of pepper in the pot and stir to combine. Place the meatballs on top of the pasta mixture. Lock lid; move slider towards PRESSURE. Adjust pressure release valve in the SEAL position. Close pressure-release valve. The cooking temperature will default to HIGH, which is accurate. Adjust to low pressure and set time to 5 minutes. Select START/STOP and start cooking. When cooking is complete, let pressure release quickly by turning it into VENT position. 3. Gently stir the fresh basil into the pasta mixture and season with salt and pepper, taking care not to break up the meatballs.

Per Serving: Calories 288; Fat 12.2g; Sodium 339mg; Carbs 11.6g; Fiber 3g; Sugar 2g; Protein 16.5g

Spicy Buffalo Wings

Prep time: 5 minutes| Cook time: 20 minutes| Serves: 2

2 pounds chicken wings (10 to 12 wings)	¼ teaspoon black pepper
1 teaspoon garlic powder	4 tablespoons butter
¼ teaspoon salt	½ cup Buffalo sauce

1. Place a Deluxe reversible rack in the bottom of the Ninja Foodi XL Pressure Cooker Steam Fryer with SmartLid cooking pot, then pour in ¾ cup water. 2. Season the wings with the garlic powder, salt, and pepper, and place on top of the Deluxe reversible rack. 3. Lock lid; move slider towards PRESSURE. Adjust pressure release valve in the SEAL position. Close pressure-release valve. The cooking temperature will default to HIGH, which is accurate. Set time to 10 minutes. Select START/STOP and start cooking. When cooking is complete, let pressure release quickly by turning it into VENT position. 4. Open the lid and carefully transfer the wings to a plate. Press START/STOP to turn off the Ninja Foodi XL Pressure Cooker Steam Fryer and wipe out the cooking pot. 5. Move the slider towards "AIR FRY/STOVETOP" and set Ninja Foodi XL Pressure Cooker Steam Fryer with SmartLid to SEAR/SAUTÉ mode. Adjust the temperature to "Hi5" by using up arrow. Press START/STOP to begin cooking add butter to the cooking pot. Once melted, whisk in the hot sauce. 6. Return the wings to the pot and toss until coated with sauce. Serve warm.

Per Serving: Calories 404; Fat 10.3g; Sodium 347mg; Carbs 37.2g; Fiber 1.7g; Sugar 0.7g; Protein 39g

Shredded Greek-Style Chicken

Prep time: 5 minutes| Cook time: 15 minutes| Serves: 8

2 pounds boneless, skinless chicken breasts	3 tablespoons red wine vinegar
1 cup plain Greek yogurt	2 tablespoons olive oil
½ cup diced red onion	2 tablespoons Greek seasoning
3 tablespoons freshly squeezed lemon juice	2 tablespoons dried dill
	1 or 2 garlic cloves, minced
	1 teaspoon dried oregano

1. In the cooking pot, combine the chicken, yogurt, onion, lemon juice, vinegar, olive oil, Greek seasoning, dried dill, garlic, and oregano. 2. Lock lid; move slider towards PRESSURE. Adjust pressure release valve in the SEAL position. Close pressure-release valve. The cooking temperature will default to HIGH, which is accurate. Set time to 15 minutes. Select START/STOP and start cooking. When cooking is complete, let pressure release quickly by turning it into VENT position. 3. Remove the chicken from the pot, place it in a medium bowl, and shred it using two forks. Return the

chicken to the juices and serve warm.

Per Serving: Calories 230; Fat 14.3g; Sodium 258mg; Carbs 0.8g; Fiber 0.2g; Sugar 0.2g; Protein 22.3g

Chicken with Broccoli Stir-Fry

Prep time: 10 minutes| Cook time: 20 minutes| Serves: 2

2 (5- to 6-ounce) boneless, skinless chicken breasts, cut into 1-inch pieces	1 teaspoon sesame oil
	1 cup water, divided
	1 tablespoon cornstarch
1 tablespoon packed light brown sugar	1 cup frozen broccoli florets
¼ cup soy sauce	Sesame seeds, for garnish

1. Combine the chicken, brown sugar, soy sauce, sesame oil, and ¾ cup of water in the Ninja Foodi XL Pressure Cooker Steam Fryer with SmartLid cooking pot and stir. 2. Lock lid; move slider towards PRESSURE. Adjust pressure release valve in the SEAL position. Close pressure-release valve. The cooking temperature will default to HIGH, which is accurate. Set time to 4 minutes. Select START/STOP and start cooking. When cooking is complete, let pressure release quickly by turning it into VENT position. 3. Open the lid. Press START/STOP to turn off the pot, then move the slider towards "AIR FRY/STOVETOP" and set Ninja Foodi XL Pressure Cooker Steam Fryer with SmartLid to SEAR/SAUTÉ mode. Adjust the temperature to "Hi5" by using up arrow. Select START/STOP and start cooking. 4. In a small bowl, whisk together the cornstarch and remaining ¼ cup of water until completely dissolved. Pour the cornstarch slurry into the pot while whisking the sauce. 5. Add the broccoli and stir until the broccoli cooks through and the sauce thickens, 2 to 3 minutes. Press START/STOP to turn off the Ninja Foodi XL Pressure Cooker Steam Fryer. 6. Serve warm, garnished with sesame seeds if you like.

Per Serving: Calories 283; Fat 12.3g; Sodium 432mg; Carbs 11.5g; Fiber 3g; Sugar 3g; Protein 16.5g

Delicious Teriyaki Chicken

Prep time: 10 minutes| Cook time: 25 minutes| Serves: 2

1 tablespoon sesame oil	½ cup water, divided
3 (4- to 5-ounce) boneless, skinless chicken thighs	2 teaspoons minced garlic
	¼ cup soy sauce
¼ teaspoon salt	¼ cup packed light brown sugar
⅛ teaspoon black pepper	1 tablespoon cornstarch

1. Move the slider towards "AIR FRY/STOVETOP" and set Ninja Foodi XL Pressure Cooker Steam Fryer with SmartLid to SEAR/SAUTÉ mode. Adjust the temperature to "Hi5" by using up arrow. Press START/STOP to begin cooking and pour in the sesame oil. 2. Season the chicken thighs with the salt and pepper. Once the oil is shimmering, put the thighs into the Ninja Foodi XL Pressure Cooker Steam Fryer with SmartLid cooking pot and allow them to sear for 2 minutes on each side. Press START/STOP to turn off the Ninja Foodi XL Pressure Cooker Steam Fryer. Transfer the thighs to a plate. 3. Pour ¼ cup of water into the Ninja Foodi XL Pressure Cooker Steam Fryer and scrape up any brown bits from the bottom of the pot. 4. Add the garlic, soy sauce, and brown sugar and stir. Return the chicken thighs to the pot and stir to coat. 5. Lock lid; move slider towards PRESSURE. Adjust pressure release valve in the SEAL position. Close pressure-release valve. The cooking temperature will default to HIGH, which is accurate. Set time to 8 minutes. Select START/STOP and start cooking. When cooking is complete, let pressure release naturally for about 5 minutes, then quickly release any remaining pressure by turning it into VENT position. 6. Open the lid. Transfer the chicken thighs to a clean plate. Then set Ninja Foodi XL Pressure Cooker Steam Fryer with SmartLid to SEAR/SAUTÉ mode. Adjust the temperature to "Hi5" by using up arrow. Press START/STOP to begin cooking. 7. In a small bowl, whisk together the cornstarch and remaining ¼ cup of water until completely dissolved. Pour the cornstarch slurry into the pot while whisking the sauce. Allow to cook for 2 to 3 minutes, stirring occasionally, until the sauce has thickened. Press START/STOP to turn off the pot. 8. Serve the chicken thighs warm, topped with the thickened sauce.

Per Serving: Calories 279; Fat 12.3g; Sodium 520mg; Carbs 10.4g; Fiber 2g; Sugar 2g; Protein 15.2g

Chicken with Marinara Sauce

Prep time: 10 minutes| Cook time: 28 minutes| Serves: 2

1 tablespoon olive oil
2 (5- to 6-ounce) boneless, skinless chicken breasts
2 teaspoons Italian seasoning
¼ teaspoon salt
⅛ teaspoon black pepper
½ cup water
1 cup marinara sauce
1 cup shredded mozzarella cheese

1. Move the slider towards "AIR FRY/STOVETOP" and set Ninja Foodi XL Pressure Cooker Steam Fryer with SmartLid to SEAR/ SAUTÉ mode. Adjust the temperature to "Hi5" by using up arrow. Press START/STOP to begin cooking. and pour in the olive oil. 2. Season the chicken breasts with the Italian seasoning, salt, and pepper. Once the oil is shimmering, add the chicken and cook until golden brown, 3 to 4 minutes per side. Press START/STOP to turn off the pot and transfer the chicken to a plate. 3. Pour the water into the pot and scrape up any bits from the bottom of the pot. 4. Transfer the chicken breasts to the pot and top with the marinara sauce. 5. Lock lid; move slider towards PRESSURE. Adjust pressure release valve in the SEAL position. Close pressure-release valve. The cooking temperature will default to HIGH, which is accurate. Set time to 8 minutes. Select START/STOP and start cooking. When cooking is complete, let pressure release naturally for about 5 minutes, then quickly release any remaining pressure by turning it into VENT position. 6. Scatter the cheese over the top, put the lid back on, and let stand until the cheese is melted, 2 to 3 minutes. Serve warm.
Per Serving: Calories 218; Fat 6.8g; Sodium 268mg; Carbs 2.3g; Fiber 0.3g; Sugar 0.7g; Protein 34.6g

Smoky Barbecue Chicken

Prep time: 5 minutes| Cook time: 15 minutes| Serves: 8

2 pounds boneless, skinless chicken breasts
1 small red onion, diced
1 cup Sweet and Smoky Barbecue Sauce or store-bought
2 tablespoons olive oil

1. In the Ninja Foodi XL Pressure Cooker Steam Fryer with SmartLid cooking pot combine the chicken, onion, barbecue sauce, and oil. 2. Lock lid; move slider towards PRESSURE. Adjust pressure release valve in the SEAL position. Close pressure-release valve. The cooking temperature will default to HIGH, which is accurate. Set time to 15 minutes. Select START/STOP and start cooking. 3. When cooking is complete, let pressure release quickly by turning it into VENT position. 4. Remove the chicken from the pot, place it in a medium bowl, and shred it using two forks. Return the chicken to the juices and serve warm.
Per Serving: Calories 243; Fat 13.3g; Sodium 269mg; Carbs 5.5g; Fiber 1.2g; Sugar 2g; Protein 24.4g

Thai Chicken Rice

Prep time: 7 minutes| Cook time: 25 minutes| Serves: 4

2 tablespoons toasted sesame oil
2 pounds boneless, skinless chicken breast
½ cup Thai sweet chili sauce
3 tablespoons soy sauce
1½ teaspoons fish sauce
1½ teaspoons minced fresh ginger
1 garlic clove, minced
1 teaspoon freshly squeezed lime juice
1 teaspoon hot sauce
1 tablespoon peanut butter
1 cup long-grain white rice
2 cups low-sodium chicken broth

1. Move the slider towards "AIR FRY/STOVETOP" and set Ninja Foodi XL Pressure Cooker Steam Fryer with SmartLid to SEAR/ SAUTÉ mode. Adjust the temperature to "Hi5" by using up arrow. Press START/STOP to begin cooking. Add the oil to the cooking pot. When the oil is hot, add the chicken and brown, about 3 minutes per side. Transfer the chicken to a plate. 2. In a medium bowl, whisk the sweet chili sauce, soy sauce, fish sauce, ginger, garlic, lime juice, hot sauce, and peanut butter until well combined. 3. Add the rice to the pot. Place the chicken breasts on top of the rice. Pour the sauce over the chicken and rice. Pour in the broth. 4. Lock lid; move slider towards PRESSURE. Adjust pressure release valve in the SEAL position. Close pressure-release valve. The cooking temperature will default to HIGH, which is accurate. Set time to 10 minutes. Select START/STOP and start cooking. When cooking is complete, let pressure release naturally. 5. Unlock and remove the lid. Transfer the chicken to a clean plate. Using a hand mixer or two forks, shred the chicken. Stir the rice, divide it between four serving bowls, and top with the chicken.
Per Serving: Calories 267; Fat 12.3g; Sodium 432mg; Carbs 11.6g; Fiber 2g; Sugar 3g; Protein 16.4g

Chapter 4 Beef, Pork, and Lamb Recipes

81 Beef, Red Pepper and Paprika Stew
81 Spicy Beef Stew with Olives
81 Spicy Beef Stew with Caraway
81 Cola Pulled Pork
82 French Meat and Vegetable Stew with Tarragon
82 Delicious Chili Con Carne
82 Beef and Bean Stew with Tomatoes and Dill
82 beef and Chickpea Stew with Cilantro
83 Sesame-Ginger Tenderloin
83 Greek Beef Stew with Tomatoes
83 Meatballs in Spicy Tomato Sauce
83 Delicious Beef Picadillo
84 Indonesian Nutty Beef
84 Korean Braised Ribs
84 Salsa Pulled Pork
84 Mexican Brisket Salad
85 Braised Beef with Pancettaand Red Wine
85 Rib Ragu with Pappardelle
85 Pork Tenderloin with Pepper Glaze
85 Herbes de Provence Chops
86 Smoky Ribs
86 Delicious Ropa Vieja
86 Austrian Beef with Root Vegetables
86 Smoky Barbecue Pork Chop Sandwiches
87 Pork Ragu
87 Apple Cider Pulled Pork
87 Savory-Sweet Braised Beef
87 Cinnamon Applesauce Chops
87 Sausage with Peppers
88 Sweet Tangy Ham
88 Stewed Lamb
88 Garlic Beef Meatballs
88 Parmesan Meatballs
88 Beef Greens Bowl
88 Beef Bites
88 Lamb Chops With Olive Spread
88 Coconut Cream Beef
89 Baked Beef
89 Oregano Beef
89 Mongolian Beef
89 Beef Cabbage Rolls
89 Beef Steak
89 Garlic Beef Bread
89 Pork With Herbs and Onions
89 Lamb Chops with Mint Sauce
90 Onion Beef Delights
90 Italian Beef
90 Eggplant Beef Sauté
90 Beef Roll
90 Garlicky Beef Steak

90 Za'Atar Chops
90 Fried Rib Eye Steaks
90 Lamb Cauliflower Fritters
91 Mustard Glazed Beef Loin
91 Curried Beef
91 Rosemary Meatballs
91 Saucy BBQ Beef
91 Minced Beef Sauté
91 Tender Beef Salad
91 Pork Kebab With Dill Sauce
91 Basil Beef Steak
92 Beef Provolone Casserole
92 Easy Burgers
92 Pork with Vegetables
92 Beef Artichoke Sauté
92 Vinegar Glazed Beef Shank
92 Chives Mixed Beef
92 Thymed Beef
92 Spicy Pork Gratin
93 Crusted Pork Cutlets
93 Marinated Beef Loin
93 Fried Lamb Steak
93 Beef Marinara Wraps
93 Fried Lamb Chops
93 Lemony Lamb Chops
93 Lamb Skewers
93 Air Fried Rack Of Lamb
94 Spicy Lamb Steak
94 Lamb Avocado Bowl
94 Fried Pork Loin Chops
94 Pork Sausage With Cauliflower
94 Bacon Hot Dogs
94 Lamb Meatballs
94 Parmesan Cheeseburger Meatballs
94 Beef Brisket with BBQ Sauce
95 Worcester Pork Meatballs
95 Hoisin Pork Steak
95 Pork Kebabs With Pepper
95 Pork Tenderloin with Herbs
95 Pork Steak With Herbs
95 German Roulade
95 Herbed Pork Casserole
96 Mexican Meatloaf
96 BBQ Cheeseburgers
96 Garlic London Broil
96 Mexican Carnitas
96 Herbed Filet Mignon
96 Beef Meatloaf Cups
96 Meatball Lettuce Wraps
97 Coulotte Roast
97 Soy Dipped Beef Tenderloin
97 Beefy Poppers
97 Herbed Lamb Chops

97 Beef With Carrots
97 Rump Roast
97 Cheese Ribeye Steak
98 Sriracha Glazed Ribs
98 Flank Steak
98 Mushroom Beef Patties
98 Mustard Tender Filet Mignon
98 Beef Shoulder
98 BBQ Ribs
98 Pork Skewers
98 Pork Bun Thit Nuong
99 Peppery Beef
99 Italian Pork Cut
99 Sausage with Fennel
99 Meatloaf
99 Pork Burgers
99 Beef Dinner Rolls
99 Steak Salad
99 Pork Cutlets
100 Pork Roast with Applesauce
100 Bacon with Cauliflower
100 Glazed Ham
100 Sausage Patties
100 Pork Chops with Peppers
100 Country Style Ribs
100 Steak Bulgogi
100 Crackled Pork Loin
101 Muffin Burgers
101 Honey Bratwurst with Brussels Sprouts
101 Dijon Glazed Pork Loin
101 Citrus-Glazed Pork Chops
101 Easy Pork Chops
101 Indian Lamb Steaks
101 Stuffed Venison Tenderloin
102 Salisbury Steak with Mushroom Gravy
102 Spicy Bacon Pieces
102 Swedish Beef Meatloaf
102 Beef Carne Asada
102 Air-Fried Bacon Slices
103 Beef Reuben Fritters
103 Hamburgers
103 Mushroom Burgers
103 Beef Steak Nuggets
103 Air Fried Bacon Slices
104 Bacon Cups
104 Beef Meat Loaf
104 Italian Pork Loin
104 Taco Seasoned Meatballs
104 BBQ Baby Ribs
104 Crusted Lamb Chops
105 Crispy Pork Bites
105 Madeira Glazed Ham

Beef, Red Pepper and Paprika Stew

Prep time: 5 minutes| Cook time: 25 minutes| Serves: 4

1 tablespoon extra-virgin olive oil	4 teaspoons finely chopped fresh rosemary, divided
10 medium garlic cloves, smashed and peeled	1 tablespoon sweet paprika
1 large shallot, halved and thickly sliced	3 pounds boneless beef chuck roast, trimmed, cut into 2-inch chunks
1 plum tomato, cored, seeded and chopped	2 tablespoons all-purpose flour
½ cup jarred roasted red peppers, patted dry, finely chopped	1 teaspoon lemon juice
4 ounces prosciutto or pancetta, chopped	Kosher salt and ground black pepper

1. Move the slider towards "AIR FRY/STOVETOP" and set Ninja Foodi XL Pressure Cooker Steam Fryer with SmartLid to SEAR/SAUTÉ mode. Adjust the temperature to "Hi5" by using up arrow. Press START/STOP to begin cooking. 2. Add the oil and pancetta and cook, stirring occasionally, until the pancetta is depleted of fat but not yet crisp, 3 to 5 minutes. Stir in the mushrooms and ½ teaspoon of salt and pepper. Cook, stirring occasionally, until the liquid released from the mushrooms has evaporated and the mushrooms begin to brown, 6 to 8 minutes. Add the garlic and cook, stirring, until fragrant, 1 to 2 minutes. 3. Using a slotted spoon, transfer the mixture to a bowl and set aside. To the remaining fat in the pan, add the tomato paste and cook, stirring occasionally, until browned, 1 to 2 minutes. Add the wine and ¼ cup water, scraping up any brown bits. 4. Lock lid; move slider to PRESSURE. Make sure the pressure release valve is in the SEAL position. The cooking temperature will default to HIGH, which is accurate. Set time to 35 minutes. Press START/STOP to cooking. 5. When pressure cooking is complete, let the pressure release naturally for 15 minutes, then quickly release the remaining steam by turning it into VENT position. Then carefully open the lid. 6. Using a large spoon, skim and discard the fat from the surface of the cooking liquid. In a small bowl, whisk the flour with 6 tablespoons of the cooking liquid until smooth, then stir the mixture into the pot along with the remaining 1 teaspoon rosemary. 7. Select SEAR/SAUTÉ mode again. Bring the stew to a simmer and cook, stirring often, until thickened, 2 to 3 minutes. Press START/STOP to turn off the pot. Stir in the lemon juice, then taste and sprinkle with salt and pepper.

Per Serving: Calories 134; Fat 2.8g; Sodium 64mg; Carbs 26g; Fiber 4g; Sugar 8g; Protein 3g

Spicy Beef Stew with Olives

Prep time: 5 minutes| Cook time: 25 minutes| Serves: 4

2½ pounds boneless beef short ribs, trimmed, cut into 1-inch chunks	3 or 4 Fresno or serrano chilies, stemmed, seeded and thinly sliced, divided
⅓ cup Worcestershire sauce	½ cup brandy
Kosher salt and ground black pepper	4 bay leaves
2 tablespoons salted butter	½ cup pitted Kalamata olives, halved lengthwise
2 medium yellow onions, chopped	3 tablespoons all-purpose flour
4 medium garlic cloves, smashed and peeled	Chopped fresh flat-leaf parsley, to serve

1. In a large bowl, stir together the beef, Worcestershire sauce, 1½ teaspoons salt and 1 teaspoon pepper. Set aside. Move the slider towards "AIR FRY/STOVETOP" and set Ninja Foodi XL Pressure Cooker Steam Fryer with SmartLid to SEAR/SAUTÉ mode. Adjust the temperature to "Hi5" by using up arrow. Press START/STOP to begin cooking. 2. Add butter and let melt, then add the onions and garlic. Cook, stirring often, until the onions are browned, about 8 to 10 minutes. Add half of the chilies and cook, stirring, until fragrant, for about 1 minute. Pour in the brandy and cook, scraping up any browned bits. Then add the bay and beef with its marinade; stir to mix, then distribute in an even layer. 3. Lock lid; move slider to PRESSURE. Make sure the pressure release valve is in the SEAL position. The cooking temperature will default to HIGH, which is accurate. Set time to 25 minutes. Press START/STOP to cooking. 4. When pressure cooking is complete, let the pressure release naturally for 15 minutes, then quickly release the remaining steam by turning it into VENT position. Then carefully open the lid. 5. Using a large spoon, skim off and discard any fat from the surface of the cooking liquid. Remove and discard the bay, then stir in the olives and remaining chilies. 6. In a small bowl, whisk the flour with 6 tablespoons of the cooking liquid until smooth, then stir into the pot. Select SEAR/SAUTÉ mode again. Bring the stew to a simmer, stirring often, and cook until lightly thickened, 2 to 3 minutes. Press START/STOP to turn off the pot. 7. Taste and season with salt and pepper. Serve sprinkled with parsley.

Per Serving: Calories 153; Fat 2.8g; Sodium 28mg; Carbs 26g; Fiber 1g; Sugar 1g; Protein 6g

Spicy Beef Stew with Caraway

Prep time: 5 minutes| Cook time: 25 minutes| Serves: 6

4 pounds boneless beef chuck roast, trimmed and cut into 1½-inch chunks	2 tablespoons caraway seeds, lightly crushed
6 tablespoons sweet paprika, divided	1 tablespoon hot paprika
4 tablespoons (½ stick) salted butter	2 cups low-sodium beef broth
	¼ cup tomato paste
1 large yellow onion, finely chopped	3 bay leaves
	6 tablespoons all-purpose flour
Kosher salt and ground black pepper	¼ cup finely chopped fresh dill, plus dill sprigs to serve
	1 tablespoon cider vinegar
	Sour cream, to serve

1. In a large bowl, toss the beef with 2 tablespoons sweet paprika until evenly coated. 2. Move the slider towards "AIR FRY/STOVETOP" and set Ninja Foodi XL Pressure Cooker Steam Fryer with SmartLid to SEAR/SAUTÉ mode. Adjust the temperature to "Hi5" by using up arrow. Press START/STOP to begin cooking. 3. Add the butter and let melt. Add the onion and 1 teaspoon salt, then cook, stirring occasionally, until the onion is lightly browned, about 8 minutes. Add the caraway and cook, stirring, until fragrant, about 30 seconds. 4. Add the remaining 4 tablespoons sweet paprika and the hot paprika, then cook, stirring, until fragrant, about 30 seconds. Whisk in the broth and tomato paste, scraping up any browned bits. Add the bay and beef; stir to combine, then distribute in an even layer. 5. Lock lid; move slider to PRESSURE. Make sure the pressure release valve is in the SEAL position. The cooking temperature will default to HIGH, which is accurate. Set time to 25 minutes. Press START/STOP to cooking. 6. When the cooking is complete, let the pressure release naturally for 15 minutes, then release quickly the remaining steam by turning it into VENT position. Then carefully open the lid. Using a large spoon, skim and discard the fat from the surface of cooking liquid. 7. In a medium bowl, whisk the flour with 1 cup of the cooking liquid until smooth, then whisk the mixture into the pot. 8. Select SEAR/SAUTÉ mode again. Bring the stew to a simmer and cook, stirring often, until thickened, about 2 minutes. Press START/STOP to turn off the pot. 9. Stir in the dill and vinegar, then taste and sprinkle with salt and pepper. Serve garnished with dill sprigs and with sour cream on the side.

Per Serving: Calories 292; Fat 24.3g; Sodium 660mg; Carbs 5g; Fiber 0g; Sugar 3g; Protein 14g

Cola Pulled Pork

Prep time: 5 minutes| Cook time: 45 minutes| Serves: 6

2 pounds boneless pork loin roast	1 (12-ounce) can cola
Sea salt	1 onion, chopped
Freshly ground black pepper	2 garlic cloves, minced
1 cup Sweet and Smoky Barbecue Sauce	2 tablespoons Worcestershire sauce

1. Season the pork with salt and pepper. 2. In the Ninja Foodi XL Pressure Cooker Steam Fryer with SmartLid cooking pot, combine the pork, barbecue sauce, cola, onion, garlic, and Worcestershire sauce. 3. Lock lid; move slider to PRESSURE. Make sure the pressure release valve is in the SEAL position. The cooking temperature will default to HIGH, which is accurate. Set time to 45 minutes. Press START/STOP to cooking. When pressure cooking is complete, let the pressure release naturally for at least 10 minutes. 4. Remove the lid, transfer the pork to a medium bowl, and shred it using two forks. Return the pork to the juices and serve.

Per Serving: Calories 295; Fat 21.2g; Sodium 94mg; Carbs 3g; Fiber 1g; Sugar 1g; Protein 23g

French Meat and Vegetable Stew with Tarragon

Prep time: 5 minutes| Cook time: 30 minutes| Serves: 4

2 tablespoons salted butter
8 ounces (about 2 cups) peeled pearl onions
8 medium garlic cloves, peeled and smashed
1 tablespoon fennel seeds
1 cup dry white wine
Kosher salt and ground black pepper
2½ pounds boneless lamb shoulder
or boneless beef chuck, trimmed and cut into 1½-inch chunks
6 ounces green beans, trimmed and cut into 1-inch pieces
1 cup cherry or grape tomatoes, halved
2 tablespoons lemon juice
½ cup lightly packed fresh tarragon, roughly chopped

1. Move the slider towards "AIR FRY/STOVETOP" and set Ninja Foodi XL Pressure Cooker Steam Fryer with SmartLid to SEAR/ SAUTÉ mode. Adjust the temperature to "Hi5" by using up arrow. Press START/STOP to begin cooking. 2. Add the butter and melt. Add the onions, garlic and fennel seeds, then cook, stirring occasionally, until the onions are lightly browned, 3 to 4 minutes. Add the wine, ½ cup water, 2 teaspoons salt and ½ teaspoon pepper, then bring to a simmer. Add the lamb or beef and stir to combine, then distribute in an even layer. 3. Lock lid; move slider to PRESSURE. Make sure the pressure release valve is in the SEAL position. The cooking temperature will default to HIGH, which is accurate. Set time to 25 minutes. Press START/STOP to cooking. 4. When pressure cooking is complete, let the pressure release naturally for 15 minutes, then quickly release the remaining steam by turning it into VENT position. Then carefully open the lid. 5. Using a large spoon, skim off and discard the fat from the surface of the cooking liquid. Select SEAR/SAUTÉ mode again and bring to a simmer. Add the green beans and tomatoes, then cook, stirring occasionally, until the beans are tender, 7 to 10 minutes. Press START/STOP to turn off the pot. 6. Stir in the lemon juice, then taste and season with salt and pepper. Serve sprinkled with the tarragon.
Per Serving: Calories 147; Fat 7.3g; Sodium 56mg; Carbs 20g; Fiber 5g; Sugar 11g; Protein 4g

Delicious Chili Con Carne

Prep time: 5 minutes| Cook time: 35 minutes| Serves: 6

3 tablespoons ancho chili powder
2 tablespoons chili powder
2 tablespoons packed light or dark brown sugar
2 tablespoons ground cumin
1 tablespoon dried oregano
Kosher salt
4 pounds boneless beef chuck roast, trimmed and cut into 1- to 1½-inch chunks
3 tablespoons grapeseed or other neutral oil
1 large yellow onion, finely chopped
6 medium garlic cloves, finely chopped
3 tablespoons tomato paste
14½-ounce can diced fire-roasted tomatoes
4 chipotle chilies in adobo sauce, finely chopped, plus 3 tablespoons adobo sauce
3 ounces (2 cups) tortilla chips, finely crushed (about 1 cup)

1. In a large bowl, stir together both chili powders, the sugar, cumin, oregano and 2 teaspoons salt. Add the beef and toss until evenly coated; set aside. 2. Move the slider towards "AIR FRY/STOVETOP" and set Ninja Foodi XL Pressure Cooker Steam Fryer with SmartLid to SEAR/SAUTÉ mode. Adjust the temperature to "Hi5" by using up arrow. Press START/STOP to begin cooking. Add the oil and heat until shimmering. 3. Add the onion and cook, stirring occasionally, until lightly browned, about 5 minutes. Add the garlic and cook, stirring, until fragrant, about 30 seconds. Stir in the tomato paste and cook, stirring, until the tomato paste is well browned, about 3 minutes. Stir in the tomatoes with their juice, the chipotle chilies and adobo sauce and 1 cup water, scraping up any browned bits. Add the beef; stir to combine, then distribute in an even layer. 4. Lock lid; move slider to PRESSURE. Make sure the pressure release valve is in the SEAL position. The cooking temperature will default to HIGH, which is accurate. Set time to 50 minutes. Press START/STOP to cooking. 5. When pressure cooking is complete, let the pressure release naturally for 15 minutes, then quickly release the remaining steam by turning it into VENT position. Then carefully open the lid. 6. Using a large spoon, skim off and discard the fat from the surface of the cooking liquid. Stir the crushed tortilla chips into the chili. 7. Select SEAR/ SAUTÉ mode again and cook, stirring occasionally, until the chili is lightly thickened, about 5 minutes. Press START/STOP to turn off the

pot. 8. Let stand for 10 minutes, then taste and sprinkle with salt.
Per Serving: Calories 409; Fat 18.9g; Sodium 214mg; Carbs 10g; Fiber 1g; Sugar 9g; Protein 48g

Beef and Bean Stew with Tomatoes and Dill

Prep time: 5 minutes| Cook time: 25 minutes| Serves: 6

2 tablespoons extra-virgin olive oil, plus more to serve
8 medium garlic cloves, smashed and peeled
3 tablespoons tomato paste
1 tablespoon sweet paprika
1 teaspoon red pepper flakes
1 large yellow onion, chopped
1-quart low-sodium chicken broth
Kosher salt and ground black pepper
2¾ to 3 pounds beef shanks (each about 1 inch thick), trimmed
2½ cups (1 pound) dried navy beans
14½-ounce can diced tomatoes, drained
½ cup finely chopped fresh dill, plus more to serve
2 tablespoons pomegranate molasses, plus more to serve

1. Move the slider towards "AIR FRY/STOVETOP" and set Ninja Foodi XL Pressure Cooker Steam Fryer with SmartLid to SEAR/ SAUTÉ mode. Adjust the temperature to "Hi5" by using up arrow. Press START/STOP to begin cooking. 2. Add the oil, heat until shimmering. Add the onion and cook, stirring, until lightly browned, about 8 minutes. Stir in the garlic, tomato paste, paprika and pepper flakes, then cook until fragrant, about 30 seconds. 3. Add the broth and 1 tablespoon salt, then stir in the beans and distribute in an even layer. Place the shanks in the pot in a single layer, submerging them in the liquid. 4. Lock lid; move slider to PRESSURE. Make sure the pressure release valve is in the SEAL position. The cooking temperature will default to HIGH, which is accurate. Set time to 45 minutes. Press START/STOP to cooking. 5. When pressure cooking is complete, let the pressure release naturally for 40 minutes, then quickly release the remaining steam by turning it into VENT position. 6. Then carefully open the lid. Remove and discard the shank bones; the meat should easily fall away from the bones. Stir in the tomatoes, dill and pomegranate molasses, breaking the meat into large bite-size pieces. 7. Taste and sprinkle with salt and black pepper. Serve sprinkled with additional dill and drizzled with additional oil and pomegranate molasses.
Per Serving: Calories 193; Fat 8.9g; Sodium 93mg; Carbs 2g; Fiber 1g; Sugar 0g; Protein 25g

beef and Chickpea Stew with Cilantro

Prep time: 5 minutes| Cook time: 25 minutes| Serves: 6

Kosher salt and ground black pepper
2 tablespoons salted butter
1 large yellow onion, chopped
2 medium carrots (about 8 ounces), peeled and shredded
8 medium garlic cloves, smashed and peeled
⅓ cup tomato paste
1 tablespoon sweet paprika
1 tablespoon ground cumin
1 teaspoon ground cardamom
1 teaspoon ground cinnamon
2 pounds boneless beef chuck roast, trimmed and cut into ¾-inch chunks
Two 15½-ounce cans chickpeas, rinsed and drained
2 cups lightly packed fresh cilantro, chopped
3 tablespoons lemon juice

1. Move the slider towards "AIR FRY/STOVETOP" and set Ninja Foodi XL Pressure Cooker Steam Fryer with SmartLid to SEAR/ SAUTÉ mode. Adjust the temperature to "Hi5" by using up arrow. Press START/STOP to begin cooking. 2. Add the butter and melt. Add the onion and carrots, then cook, stirring occasionally, until the vegetables are softened, for about 5 minutes. Stir in the garlic, tomato paste, paprika, cumin, cardamom, cinnamon and 1 teaspoon salt, then cook, stirring, until fragrant, about 1 minute. Add 1-quart water and scrape up any browned bits. Stir in the beef, then distribute in an even layer. 3. Lock lid; move slider to PRESSURE. Make sure the pressure release valve is in the SEAL position. The cooking temperature will default to HIGH, which is accurate. Set time to 30 minutes. Press START/STOP to cooking. 4. When pressure cooking is complete, let the pressure release naturally for 15 minutes, then quickly release the remaining steam by turning it into VENT position. Then carefully open the lid. 5. Stir in the chickpeas, cilantro and lemon juice, then taste and season with salt and pepper.
Per Serving: Calories 101; Fat 5.4g; Sodium 106mg; Carbs 8g; Fiber 3g; Sugar 3g; Protein 7g

Sesame-Ginger Tenderloin

Prep time: 10 minutes| Cook time: 23 minutes| Serves: 6

2 tablespoons light brown sugar	1½ pounds pork tenderloin
1 tablespoon sesame oil	Sea salt
1 tablespoon soy sauce	Freshly ground black pepper
1 tablespoon rice vinegar	1 cup water
2 teaspoons ground ginger	1 tablespoon cornstarch
2 garlic cloves, minced	

1. Move the slider towards "AIR FRY/STOVETOP" and set Ninja Foodi XL Pressure Cooker Steam Fryer with SmartLid to SEAR/SAUTÉ mode. Adjust the temperature to "Hi5" by using up arrow. Press START/STOP to begin cooking. Add the hoisin sauce, brown sugar, sesame oil, soy sauce, rice vinegar, ground ginger, and garlic. Whisk for about 3 minutes, until a sauce forms. 2. Season the pork tenderloin with salt and pepper. Add the pork tenderloin and water. 3. Lock lid; move slider to PRESSURE. Make sure the pressure release valve is in the SEAL position. The cooking temperature will default to HIGH, which is accurate. Set time to 15 minutes. Press START/STOP to cooking. When pressure cooking is complete, let the pressure release naturally for at least 10 minutes. 4. Remove the lid and transfer the pork to a cutting board. 5. Select SEAR/SAUTÉ. Whisk the cornstarch into the pot and whisk for about 5 minutes to thicken the sauce. 6. Slice the pork and serve with the sauce poured over it.
Per Serving: Calories 722; Fat 39g; Sodium 140mg; Carbs 7g; Fiber 2g; Sugar 4g; Protein 18g

Greek Beef Stew with Tomatoes

Prep time: 5 minutes| Cook time: 15 minutes| Serves: 4

2 tablespoons extra-virgin olive oil, plus more to serve	chunks
	8 ounces (about 2 cups) peeled
2 medium tomatoes (about 10 ounces), cored and chopped	pearl onions
	Kosher salt and ground black
2 cinnamon sticks	pepper
1 teaspoon ground allspice	1 tablespoon red wine vinegar, plus
1 teaspoon white sugar	more to serve
½ cup dry red wine	Feta cheese, crumbled, to serve
2 pounds boneless beef short ribs, trimmed and cut into 1½-inch	Chopped fresh flat-leaf parsley, to serve

1. Move the slider towards "AIR FRY/STOVETOP" and set Ninja Foodi XL Pressure Cooker Steam Fryer with SmartLid to SEAR/SAUTÉ mode. Adjust the temperature to "Hi5" by using up arrow. Press START/STOP to begin cooking. 2. Add the oil and heat until shimmering. Add the tomatoes and their juices, the cinnamon, allspice and sugar, then cook, stirring occasionally, until the juices evaporate and the tomatoes begin to brown, about 5 minutes. Add the wine and scrape up any browned bits. Add the beef, onions, 2 teaspoons salt and 1 teaspoon pepper; stir to combine, then distribute in an even layer. 3. Lock lid; move slider to PRESSURE. Make sure the pressure release valve is in the SEAL position. The cooking temperature will default to HIGH, which is accurate. Set time to 30 minutes. Press START/STOP to cooking. 4. When pressure cooking is complete, let the pressure release naturally for 15 minutes, then quickly release the remaining steam by turning it into VENT position. 5. Then carefully open the lid. Using a large spoon, skim off and discard the fat from the surface of the cooking liquid. Remove and discard the cinnamon sticks. 6. Select SEAR/SAUTÉ mode again. Bring the stew to a simmer, stir in the vinegar and cook, stirring occasionally, until slightly thickened, about 5 minutes. Press START/STOP to turn off the pot. 7. Taste and season with salt and pepper. Serve sprinkled with feta cheese and parsley and drizzled with oil; offer additional vinegar at the table.
Per Serving: Calories 162; Fat 9.4g; Sodium 68mg; Carbs 21g; Fiber 4g; Sugar 16g; Protein 1g

Meatballs in Spicy Tomato Sauce

Prep time: 5 minutes| Cook time: 15 minutes| Serves: 4

½ cup fine dry breadcrumbs	Two 28-ounce cans whole peeled
tomatoes, drained, juices reserved	4 tablespoons (½ stick) salted butter
2 teaspoons dried oregano	
2 teaspoons fennel seeds, finely ground	¾ teaspoon red pepper flakes
	3 tablespoons tomato paste
1 teaspoon granulated garlic	3 tablespoons finely chopped fresh basil
1 pound 85 percent lean ground beef	
	Grated Parmesan or pecorino
Kosher salt and ground black pepper	Romano cheese, to serve

1. In a large bowl, mix together the breadcrumbs, ½ cup tomato juices, the oregano, fennel seeds and garlic. Add the beef, 1½ teaspoons salt and 1 teaspoon black pepper. 2. Mix with your hands until no streaks of breadcrumbs remain. Divide into 10 portions and form each into a compact ball about 2 inches in diameter, placing the meatballs on a large plate. Refrigerate for 15 minutes. 3. Move the slider towards "AIR FRY/STOVETOP" and set Ninja Foodi XL Pressure Cooker Steam Fryer with SmartLid to SEAR/SAUTÉ mode. Adjust the temperature to "Hi5" by using up arrow. Press START/STOP to begin cooking. Add the tomatoes and their remaining juices, the butter and pepper flakes, then bring to a boil, stirring. Set the meatballs on top of the tomatoes in an even layer, gently pressing to submerge them. 4. Lock lid; move slider to PRESSURE. Make sure the pressure release valve is in the SEAL position. The cooking temperature will default to HIGH, which is accurate. Set time to 3 minutes. Press START/STOP to cooking. 5. When pressure cooking is complete, let the pressure release naturally for 10 minutes, then release the remaining steam by turning it into VENT position. Then carefully open the lid. 6. Using a slotted spoon, transfer the meatballs to a clean plate. Select SEAR/SAUTÉ mode again. Bring the tomato mixture to a boil, mashing with a potato masher to break up the tomatoes. Whisk in the tomato paste and cook, stirring occasionally, until slightly thickened, about 8 minutes. 7. Taste and season with salt and black pepper. Add the basil and return the meatballs to the pot, then gently stir. Press STOP to turn off the pot. 8. Let stand until the meatballs are heated through, about 10 minutes. Serve sprinkled with Parmesan.
Per Serving: Calories 271; Fat 9.3g; Sodium 15mg; Carbs 43g; Fiber 6g; Sugar 2g; Protein 5g

Delicious Beef Picadillo

Prep time: 5 minutes| Cook time: 15 minutes| Serves: 4

2 tablespoons salted butter	3 tablespoons tomato paste
1 large red onion, halved and thinly sliced	1½ pounds 85 percent lean ground beef
Kosher salt and ground black pepper	1 cup low-sodium beef broth
	¾ cup golden raisins, divided
1 tablespoon ground cumin	¾ cup pimiento-stuffed green olives, chopped
2 teaspoons dried oregano	
2 medium garlic cloves, finely chopped	¼ cup chopped fresh cilantro

1. Move the slider towards "AIR FRY/STOVETOP" and set Ninja Foodi XL Pressure Cooker Steam Fryer with SmartLid to SEAR/SAUTÉ mode. Adjust the temperature to "Hi5" by using up arrow. Press START/STOP to begin cooking. 2. Add the butter and let melt. Add the onion and 1 teaspoon salt, then cook, stirring often, until golden brown at the edges, 5 to 7 minutes. Stir in the cumin, oregano and garlic, then cook until fragrant, about 30 seconds. Stir in the tomato paste and cook until the paste begins to brown, about 1 minute. 3. Stir in the beef and broth, scraping up any browned bits and breaking the meat into smaller pieces. Stir in ¼ cup of raisins, then distribute the mixture in an even layer. 4. Lock lid; move slider to PRESSURE. Make sure the pressure release valve is in the SEAL position. The cooking temperature will default to HIGH, which is accurate. Set time to 12 minutes. Press START/STOP to cooking. 5. When pressure cooking is complete, let the pressure release naturally for 10 minutes, then quickly release the remaining steam by turning it into VENT position. 6. Then carefully open the lid. Using a large spoon, skim off and discard the fat from the surface. Select SEAR/SAUTÉ mode again. Stir in the olives and the remaining ½ cup raisins, then cook, breaking up large clumps of beef with a wooden spoon, until most of the liquid has evaporated and the mixture begins to sizzle, 5 to 7 minutes. 7. Press START/STOP to turn off the pot. Taste and season with salt and pepper, then stir in the cilantro.
Per Serving: Calories 139; Fat 3.2g; Sodium 45mg; Carbs 26g; Fiber 4g; Sugar 8g; Protein 3g

Indonesian Nutty Beef

Prep time: 5 minutes| Cook time: 25 minutes| Serves: 4

½ cup unsweetened shredded coconut
3 Fresno or serrano chilies, stemmed, seeded and roughly chopped, plus 1 chili, stemmed and thinly sliced
3 medium garlic cloves, smashed and peeled
1 lemon grass stalk, tough outer layers removed, trimmed to lower 6 inches and thinly sliced
1-inch piece fresh ginger, peeled and roughly chopped

1 medium shallot, roughly chopped
½ teaspoon ground turmeric
⅛ teaspoon ground cinnamon
1-star anise pod
1 tablespoon grated lime zest, plus 1 tablespoon juice
Kosher salt and ground black pepper
¾ cup coconut milk
2½ to 3 pounds boneless beef chuck roast, trimmed and cut into 1½- to 2-inch chunks
Fresh cilantro, to serve

1. Move the slider towards "AIR FRY/STOVETOP" and set Ninja Foodi XL Pressure Cooker Steam Fryer with SmartLid to SEAR/SAUTÉ mode. Adjust the temperature to "Hi5" by using up arrow. Press START/STOP to begin cooking. 2. Add the shredded coconut. Cook, stirring frequently, until the coconut is golden brown, about 5 minutes. Press START/STOP, then add the chopped chilies, garlic, lemon grass, ginger, shallot, turmeric, cinnamon, star anise, lime zest and 1½ teaspoons each salt and pepper. Using the pot's residual heat, cook the mixture, stirring, until fragrant, about 1 minute. Stir in the coconut milk and beef, scraping up any bits stuck to the bottom, then distribute in an even layer. 3. Lock lid; move slider to PRESSURE. Make sure the pressure release valve is in the SEAL position. The cooking temperature will default to HIGH, which is accurate. Set time to 25 minutes. Press START/STOP to cooking. 4. When pressure cooking is complete, let the pressure release naturally for 15 minutes, then quickly release the remaining steam by turning it into VENT position. Then carefully open the lid. 5. Using tongs, place the meat to a small bowl and set aside. Pour the cooking liquid into a fine mesh strainer set over a bowl. Add the solids in the strainer to a blender, then pour in ¼ cup of the strained liquid; discard the remaining liquid or reserve for another use. 6. Blend on high until very smooth, 1 to 2 minutes, scraping the sides as needed. Pour the puree back into the pot, then stir in the beef and lime juice. 7. Select SEAR/SAUTÉ mode again and cook, stirring often, until the sauce clinging to the bottom of the pot is golden brown, 3 to 5 minutes. Press START/STOP to turn off the pot. Taste and sprinkle with salt and pepper. 8. Serve garnished with sliced chilies and cilantro.
Per Serving: Calories 716; Fat 62.6g; Sodium 302mg; Carbs 18g; Fiber 8g; Sugar 2g; Protein 34g

Korean Braised Ribs

Prep time: 5 minutes| Cook time: 35 minutes| Serves: 6

2½ to 3 pounds bone-in beef short ribs
½ cup soy sauce
½ cup sake
8 medium garlic cloves, peeled
4-inch piece fresh ginger (about 3 ounces), peeled and roughly chopped
3 tablespoons packed light brown sugar
2 tablespoons sesame seeds, toasted, plus more to serve

1 ripe pear (about 8 ounces), cored and roughly chopped
10 dried shiitake mushrooms (about 1 ounce), broken in half
1 medium carrot, peeled and cut into 1-inch chunks
1 small daikon radish (about 8 ounces), peeled and cut into 1-inch chunks
scallions, thinly sliced on the diagonal

1. In a large bowl, cover the short ribs with cool water. Set aside at room temperature for at least 10 minutes or up to 1 hour. 2. In a blender, combine the soy sauce, sake, garlic, ginger, sugar, sesame seeds and pear, then puree until smooth, scraping down the sides as needed, about 1 minute. Pour the mixture into a Ninja Foodi XL Pressure Cooker Steam Fryer. 3. Drain the short ribs and briefly rinse under running water, then arrange them in an even layer in the pot and add the mushrooms. 4. Lock lid; move slider to PRESSURE. Make sure the pressure release valve is in the SEAL position. The cooking temperature will default to HIGH, which is accurate. Set time to 55 minutes. Press START/STOP to cooking. 5. When pressure cooking is complete, let the pressure release naturally for 15 minutes, then quickly release the remaining steam by turning it into VENT position.

Then carefully open the lid. 6. Using a large spoon, skim off and discard the fat from the surface of the cooking liquid. Select SEAR/SAUTÉ mode again, then add the carrot and daikon. Cook, stirring occasionally, until the vegetables are tender and the cooking liquid thickens to a light glaze, about 15 minutes. 7. Press START/STOP to turn off the pot. Remove and discard the beef bones, then stir in half of the scallions. 8. Serve sprinkled with the remaining scallions and additional sesame seeds.
Per Serving: Calories 427; Fat 18.3g; Sodium 603mg; Carbs 44g; Fiber 6g; Sugar 3g; Protein 23g

Salsa Pulled Pork

Prep time: 5 minutes| Cook time: 45 minutes| Serves: 6

1 tablespoon vegetable oil
2 pounds boneless pork loin roast
3½ cups Garden Salsa
1 (1-ounce) packet taco seasoning

1. In the Ninja Foodi XL Pressure Cooker Steam Fryer with SmartLid cooking pot, combine the vegetable oil, pork, salsa, and taco seasoning. 2. Lock lid; move slider to PRESSURE. Make sure the pressure release valve is in the SEAL position. The cooking temperature will default to HIGH, which is accurate. Set time to 45 minutes. Press START/STOP to cooking. When pressure cooking is complete, let the pressure release naturally for at least 10 minutes. 3. Remove the lid, transfer the pork to a medium bowl, and shred it using two forks. Return the pork to the juices and serve.
Per Serving: Calories 314; Fat 27.2g; Sodium 182mg; Carbs 0g; Fiber 0g; Sugar 0g; Protein 17g

Mexican Brisket Salad

Prep time: 5 minutes| Cook time: 25 minutes| Serves: 4

6 tablespoons extra-virgin olive oil, divided
1 medium yellow onion, halved and thinly sliced
5 medium garlic cloves, smashed and peeled
Kosher salt and ground black pepper
3 bay leaves
2 teaspoons dried oregano, divided
2 pounds beef brisket, trimmed and

cut into 2- to 2½-inch pieces
½ cup lime juice, plus lime wedges to serve
½ cup pitted green olives, chopped
1 medium head romaine lettuce, roughly chopped (6 to 7 cups)
6 radishes, halved and thinly sliced
1 cup lightly packed fresh cilantro, roughly chopped
1 ripe avocado, halved, pitted, peeled and diced

1. Move the slider towards "AIR FRY/STOVETOP" and set Ninja Foodi XL Pressure Cooker Steam Fryer with SmartLid to SEAR/SAUTÉ mode. Adjust the temperature to "Hi5" by using up arrow. Press START/STOP to begin cooking. 2. Add 1 tablespoon oil and heat until shimmering, then add the onion and cook, stirring occasionally, until softened, about 5 minutes. Add the garlic and cook, stirring often, until the onion is golden brown, another 2 to 3 minutes. 3. Stir in 1½ teaspoons salt, 1 teaspoon pepper, the bay, 1 teaspoon oregano and 1 cup water, scraping up any browned bits. Add the beef in an even layer, slightly overlapping the pieces if needed. 4. Lock lid; move slider to PRESSURE. Make sure the pressure release valve is in the SEAL position. The cooking temperature will default to HIGH, which is accurate. Set time to 45 minutes. Press START/STOP to cooking. 5. When pressure cooking is complete, let the pressure release naturally for 15 minutes, then quickly release the remaining steam by turning it into VENT position. Then carefully open the lid and let the contents cool for 5 to 10 minutes. 6. While the beef is cooking, in a large bowl whisk together the lime juice, the remaining 5 tablespoons oil, the remaining 1 teaspoon dried oregano and 1 teaspoon each salt and pepper. Set aside. 7. Once the meat is done, use a slotted spoon to transfer the meat and onion to a medium bowl; do not discard the liquid remaining in the pot. With two forks, shred the beef into bite-size pieces. Whisk the dressing to recombine. Add ½ cup of the dressing, the olives and ¼ cup of the reserved cooking liquid to the shredded meat, then toss to coat. Let cool to room temperature. 8. Whisk the remaining dressing once again. Add the lettuce, radishes and cilantro to it, then toss to coat. Transfer to a platter and top with the beef and the avocado. Serve with lime wedges.
Per Serving: Calories 162; Fat 5.3g; Sodium 1006mg; Carbs 3g; Fiber 2g; Sugar 0g; Protein 25g

Braised Beef with Pancetta and Red Wine

Prep time: 5 minutes| Cook time: 35 minutes| Serves: 6

4½- to 5-pound boneless beef chuck roast, pulled apart at the natural seams into 3 pieces, trimmed, each piece tied with twine at 1-inch intervals
1 teaspoon grated nutmeg
Kosher salt and ground black pepper
1 teaspoon extra-virgin olive oil
6 ounces pancetta, chopped
8 ounces cremini mushrooms, trimmed and quartered
3 medium garlic cloves, thinly sliced
2 tablespoons tomato paste
¼ cup dry red wine
3 tablespoons all-purpose flour
1 cup roughly chopped fresh flat-leaf parsley
¼ cup chopped fresh tarragon

1. In a small bowl, mix together the nutmeg, 2 teaspoons salt and 1 teaspoon pepper. 2. Use to season the beef on all sides. Move the slider towards "AIR FRY/STOVETOP" and set Ninja Foodi XL Pressure Cooker Steam Fryer with SmartLid to SEAR/SAUTÉ mode. Adjust the temperature to "Hi5" by using up arrow. Press START/STOP to begin cooking. 3. Add the oil and pancetta, then cook, stirring occasionally, until the pancetta has rendered its fat but is not yet crisp, 3 to 5 minutes. Stir in the mushrooms and ½ teaspoon each salt and pepper. Cook, stirring occasionally, until the liquid released by the mushrooms has evaporated and the mushrooms begin to brown, 6 to 8 minutes. 4. Add the garlic and cook, stirring, until fragrant, 1 to 2 minutes. Using a slotted spoon, transfer the mixture to a bowl and set aside. To the fat remaining in the pot, add the tomato paste and cook, stirring occasionally, until browned, 1 to 2 minutes. Add the wine and ¼ cup water, scraping up any browned bits. Nestle the beef in the pot. 5. Lock lid; move slider to PRESSURE. Make sure the pressure release valve is in the SEAL position. The cooking temperature will default to HIGH, which is accurate. Set time to 60 minutes. Press START/STOP to cooking. 6. When pressure cooking is complete, let the pressure release naturally for 25 minutes, then quickly release the remaining steam by turning it into VENT position. Then carefully open the lid. 7. Transfer the beef to a cutting board and tent with foil. Using a large spoon, skim off and discard the fat from the surface of the cooking liquid. In a small bowl, whisk the flour with about ¼ cup of the cooking liquid until smooth, then stir into the pot along with the mushroom mixture. 8. Select SEAR/SAUTÉ mode again. Bring the mixture to a simmer and cook, stirring often, until lightly thickened, 3 to 5 minutes. Press START/STOP to turn off the pot. 9. Stir in the parsley and tarragon, then taste and season with salt and pepper. Cut the beef into ½-inch slices against the grain, removing the twine as you go. Arrange the slices on a platter, then pour the sauce over the top.
Per Serving: Calories 203; Fat 10.9g; Sodium 402mg; Carbs 2g; Fiber 0g; Sugar 1g; Protein 23g

Rib Ragu with Pappardelle

Prep time: 5 minutes| Cook time: 35 minutes| Serves: 4

1 tablespoon extra-virgin olive oil
1 large yellow onion, finely chopped
1 large fennel bulb, trimmed, halved, cored and roughly chopped, divided
Kosher salt and ground black pepper
8 medium garlic cloves, smashed and peeled
2 tablespoons tomato paste
1 cup dry red wine
28-ounce can whole peeled tomatoes, crushed by hand
2-inch piece Parmesan cheese rind, plus finely grated Parmesan, to serve
2½ pounds boneless beef short ribs, trimmed and cut into ¾-inch chunks
3 medium carrots, peeled and finely chopped
½ cup heavy cream
3 tablespoons finely chopped fresh flat-leaf parsley
12 ounces dried pappardelle pasta, cooked until al dente and drained
5 cups of the ragu

1. Move the slider towards "AIR FRY/STOVETOP" and set Ninja Foodi XL Pressure Cooker Steam Fryer with SmartLid to SEAR/SAUTÉ mode. Adjust the temperature to "Hi5" by using up arrow. Press START/STOP to begin cooking. 2. Add the oil and heat until shimmering, then add the onion, half of the fennel and ½ teaspoon salt. Cook, stirring occasionally, until softened, about 5 minutes. Stir in the garlic and tomato paste and cook until fragrant, about 30 seconds. 3. Add the wine and cook, stirring occasionally, until the liquid has almost fully evaporated, about 4 minutes. Stir in the tomatoes with their juice, add the Parmesan rind and the beef, then distribute in an even layer. 4. Lock lid; move slider to PRESSURE. Make sure the pressure release valve is in the SEAL position. The cooking temperature will default to HIGH, which is accurate. Set time to 30 minutes. Press START/STOP to cooking. 5. When pressure cooking is complete, let the pressure reduce quickly by turning it into VENT position. Then carefully open the lid. Remove and discard the Parmesan rind. (Using a potato masher, mash the beef until shredded. Stir in the carrots, the remaining fennel and the cream. 6. Select SEAR/SAUTÉ mode again and cook, stirring occasionally, until the sauce thickens slightly and the carrots are tender, 10 to 15 minutes. Stir in the parsley, then taste and season with salt and pepper. 7. In a large warmed bowl or the pot used to cook the pasta, toss the pasta with about 5 cups of the ragu. Serve sprinkled with Parmesan and pass the remaining sauce at the table.
Per Serving: Calories 463; Fat 15.5g; Sodium 553mg; Carbs 366g; Fiber 3g; Sugar 3g; Protein 41g

Pork Tenderloin with Pepper Glaze

Prep time: 10 minutes| Cook time: 20 minutes| Serves: 6

½ cup apple juice
½ cup hot pepper jelly
2 tablespoons apple cider vinegar
1½ pounds pork tenderloin
Sea salt
Freshly ground black pepper
½ cup water
1½ teaspoons cornstarch

1. In the cooking pot, combine the apple juice, hot pepper jelly, and vinegar. Whisk together until a sauce forms. 2. Season the pork with salt and pepper and add the pork tenderloin and water to the pot. 3. Lock lid; move slider to PRESSURE. Make sure the pressure release valve is in the SEAL position. The cooking temperature will default to HIGH, which is accurate. Set time to 15 minutes. Press START/STOP to cooking. When pressure cooking is complete, let the pressure release naturally. 4. Remove the lid and transfer the pork to a cutting board. 5. Move the slider towards "AIR FRY/STOVETOP" and set Ninja Foodi XL Pressure Cooker Steam Fryer with SmartLid to SEAR/SAUTÉ mode. Adjust the temperature to "Hi5" by using up arrow. Press START/STOP to begin cooking. Add the cornstarch and whisk until the sauce thickens, about 5 minutes. 6. Slice the pork and serve with the sauce on top.
Per Serving: Calories 153; Fat 39g; Sodium 108mg; Carbs 25g; Fiber 6g; Sugar 2g; Protein 37g

Herbes de Provence Chops

Prep time: 10 minutes| Cook time: 14 minutes| Serves: 6

¼ cup freshly squeezed lemon juice
3 tablespoons Dijon mustard
2 tablespoons herbes de Provence
2 tablespoons olive oil
1 small onion, chopped
1 tablespoon minced garlic
4 to 6 (4-ounce) boneless pork chops (½ inch thick)
Sea salt
Freshly ground black pepper
1 cup water
1 tablespoon cornstarch

1. Move the slider towards "AIR FRY/STOVETOP" and set Ninja Foodi XL Pressure Cooker Steam Fryer with SmartLid to SEAR/SAUTÉ mode. Adjust the temperature to "Hi5" by using up arrow. Press START/STOP to begin cooking. Add the lemon juice, mustard, herbes de Provence, olive oil, onion, and garlic. Whisk for 1 minute, until well blended. 2. Season the pork chops with salt and pepper and add to the pot along with the water. 3. Lock lid; move slider to PRESSURE. Make sure the pressure release valve is in the SEAL position. The cooking temperature will default to HIGH, which is accurate. Set time to 8 minutes. Press START/STOP to cooking. When pressure cooking is complete, let the pressure release naturally. 4. Remove the lid and transfer the pork chops to a serving dish. 5. Select SEAR/SAUTÉ. Whisk the cornstarch into the pot and whisk for about 5 minutes to thicken the sauce. 6. Pour the sauce on top of the pork chops and serve.
Per Serving: Calories 365; Fat 12.4g; Sodium 717mg; Carbs 29g; Fiber 3g; Sugar 10g; Protein 19g

Smoky Ribs

Prep time: 10 minutes| Cook time: 30 minutes| Serves: 6

2 tablespoons light brown sugar
2 tablespoons smoked paprika
1 teaspoon cayenne pepper
1 (4-pound) rack pork back ribs, shiny membrane removed
1 cup water
1 cup Sweet and Smoky Barbecue Sauce or store-bought
1 onion, chopped
3 garlic cloves, minced
1 tablespoon Worcestershire sauce

1. In a small bowl, mix together the brown sugar, smoked paprika, and cayenne and rub the spice mixture all over the ribs. 2. In the cooking pot, combine the water, barbecue sauce, onion, garlic, and Worcestershire sauce. Fold the ribs into the pot. You can also cut them up if you like. 3. Lock lid; move slider to PRESSURE. Make sure the pressure release valve is in the SEAL position. The cooking temperature will default to HIGH, which is accurate. Set time to 25 minutes. Press START/STOP to cooking. When pressure cooking is complete, let the pressure release naturally. 4. Remove the lid and transfer the ribs to a serving platter. 5. Move the slider towards "AIR FRY/STOVETOP" and set Ninja Foodi XL Pressure Cooker Steam Fryer with SmartLid to SEAR/SAUTÉ mode. Adjust the temperature to "Hi5" by using up arrow. Press START/STOP to begin cooking. 6. Cook the sauce for 5 minutes to thicken. Brush the sauce on the ribs and serve.
Per Serving: Calories 300; Fat 24g; Sodium 117mg; Carbs 3g; Fiber 3g; Sugar 2g; Protein 18g

Delicious Ropa Vieja

Prep time: 5 minutes| Cook time: 35 minutes| Serves: 8

2 tablespoons extra-virgin olive oil
2 medium white onions, halved and thinly sliced
2 medium red bell peppers, stemmed, seeded and sliced ¼-inch thick
2 jalapeño chilies, stemmed and sliced into thin rounds
10 medium garlic cloves, smashed and peeled
Kosher salt and ground black pepper
2½ tablespoons ground cumin
2½ tablespoons ground coriander
28-ounce can whole peeled tomatoes, drained, ¼ cup juices reserved, tomatoes crushed by hand
3 pounds flank steak, halved lengthwise with the grain, then cut across the grain into 1½-inch-wide strips
1 cup pimiento-stuffed green olives, roughly chopped
3 tablespoons lime juice, plus lime wedges to serve

1. Move the slider towards "AIR FRY/STOVETOP" and set Ninja Foodi XL Pressure Cooker Steam Fryer with SmartLid to SEAR/SAUTÉ mode. Adjust the temperature to "Hi5" by using up arrow. Press START/STOP to begin cooking. 2. Add the oil and heat until shimmering. Add the onions, bell peppers, jalapeños, garlic and 2 teaspoons salt, then cook, stirring occasionally, until the vegetables are softened and beginning to brown, about 10 minutes. Stir in the cumin and coriander, then cook until fragrant, about 30 seconds. 3. Add the tomatoes and reserved juices, scraping up any browned bits. Add the meat and stir to combine, then distribute in an even layer. 4. Lock lid; move slider to PRESSURE. Make sure the pressure release valve is in the SEAL position. The cooking temperature will default to HIGH, which is accurate. Set time to 20 minutes. Press START/STOP to cooking. 5. When pressure cooking is complete, let the pressure release naturally for 25 minutes, then quickly release the remaining steam by turning it into VENT position. Then carefully open the lid. 6. Using a slotted spoon, place the beef and peppers to a large bowl. Select SEAR/SAUTÉ mode again. Bring the cooking liquid to a simmer and cook, stirring often, until reduced and slightly thickened, about 15 minutes. Press START/STOP to turn off the pot. 7. Pour off and discard any accumulated liquid in the bowl with the beef. Using 2 forks or your fingers, shred the meat. Stir the meat, olives and lime juice into the reduced cooking liquid in the pot. 8. Taste and sprinkle with salt and pepper. Serve with lime wedges.
Per Serving: Calories 387; Fat 26.3g; Sodium 602mg; Carbs 12g; Fiber 8g; Sugar 1g; Protein 26g

Austrian Beef with Root Vegetables

Prep time: 10 minutes| Cook time: 25 minutes| Serves: 6

2 tablespoons grapeseed or other neutral oil
1 large yellow onion, cut into 6 wedges

6 medium carrots, peeled and cut into 3-inch lengths, thicker pieces halved lengthwise
6 medium parsnips, peeled and cut into 6-inch lengths, thicker pieces halved lengthwise
4½- to 5-pound boneless beef chuck roast, pulled apart at the natural seams in 3 pieces, trimmed, each piece tied at 1-inch intervals
3 cups low-sodium beef broth
5 bay leaves
2 tablespoons caraway seeds
2 tablespoons allspice berries
2 thyme sprigs
Kosher salt and ground black pepper
2 pounds red potatoes (about 2 inches in diameter), halved
3 dill sprigs, plus ¼ cup chopped fresh dill
Prepared horseradish and/or Dijon mustard, to serve

1. Move the slider towards "AIR FRY/STOVETOP" and set Ninja Foodi XL Pressure Cooker Steam Fryer with SmartLid to SEAR/SAUTÉ mode. Adjust the temperature to "Hi5" by using up arrow. Press START/STOP to begin cooking. 2. Add the oil and heat until shimmering, then stir in the onion and cook, stirring, until softened and golden brown at the edges, 5 to 7 minutes. Add 4 pieces each of carrot and parsnip, then nestle in the beef. Add the broth, bay, caraway, allspice, thyme and 1 tablespoon pepper. 3. Lock lid; move slider to PRESSURE. Make sure the pressure release valve is in the SEAL position. The cooking temperature will default to HIGH, which is accurate. Set time to 60 minutes. Press START/STOP to cooking. 4. When pressure cooking is complete, let the pressure release naturally for 25 minutes, then quickly release the remaining steam by turning it into VENT position. Then carefully open the lid. 5. Place the beef to a cutting board and tent with foil. Using potholders, carefully remove the insert from the housing and pour the broth into a fine mesh strainer set over a medium bowl; discard the solids in the strainer. Use a wide spoon to skim off and discard the fat from the surface of the cooking liquid, then return the liquid to the pot. Add the remaining carrots, the remaining parsnips and the potatoes, distributing them evenly. 6. Lock the lid, move slider to PRESSURE. Make sure the pressure release valve is in the SEAL position. The cooking temperature will default to HIGH, which is accurate. Set time to 7 minutes. Press START/STOP to cooking. 7. When pressure cooking is complete, let the pressure reduce quickly by turning it into VENT position. Then carefully open the lid. Using a slotted spoon, transfer the vegetables to a large platter and tent with foil. 8. Add the dill sprigs to the cooking liquid. Cut the meat against the grain into ½-inch slices, removing the twine as you go. Place the slices on the platter with the vegetables. Taste the broth and season with salt and pepper. 9. Remove and discard the dill sprigs, then ladle about 1 cup of the broth over the meat and sprinkle with the chopped dill. 10. Serve with the remaining broth on the side and with horseradish and/or mustard.
Per Serving: Calories 494; Fat 36g; Sodium 690mg; Carbs 17g; Fiber 11g; Sugar 2g; Protein 28g

Smoky Barbecue Pork Chop Sandwiches

Prep time: 5 minutes| Cook time: 25 minutes| Serves: 10

For the pork
1 tablespoon butter
1 small onion, chopped
2 garlic cloves, minced
10 (8-ounce) boneless pork chops (1 inch thick)
1 cup Sweet and Smoky Barbecue
Sauce or store-bought
1 cup water
½ cup packed light brown sugar
1 tablespoon Worcestershire sauce
1 tablespoon apple cider vinegar
For the sandwiches
10 hamburger buns
1 head lettuce, separated into large lettuce leaves
3 tomatoes, sliced
½ cup yellow mustard
Sliced pickles

To make the pork: 1. Move the slider towards "AIR FRY/STOVETOP" and set Ninja Foodi XL Pressure Cooker Steam Fryer with SmartLid to SEAR/SAUTÉ mode. Adjust the temperature to "Hi5" by using up arrow. Press START/STOP to begin cooking and let the pot heat up for 2 minutes. 2. Add the butter, onion, and garlic and sauté for 2 minutes, or until the onion is translucent. 3. Add the pork chops, barbecue sauce, water, brown sugar, Worcestershire sauce, and vinegar. 4. Lock lid; move slider to PRESSURE. Make sure the pressure release valve is in the SEAL position. The cooking temperature will default to HIGH, which is accurate. Set time to 20 minutes. Press START/STOP to cooking. When pressure cooking is complete, let the pressure release naturally for at least 10 minutes.
To make the sandwiches: Set out the buns and all the fixings and let people assemble their own sandwiches.
Per Serving: Calories 143; Fat 7.5g; Sodium 5mg; Carbs 19g; Fiber 3g; Sugar 3g; Protein 3g

Pork Ragu

Prep time: 5 minutes| Cook time: 45 minutes| Serves: 6

1 tablespoon olive oil	3 carrots, cut into ½-inch chunks
1½ pounds pork tenderloin, cut into 3-inch chunks	3 shallots or 1 small onion, chopped
1 (28-ounce) can crushed tomatoes	3 garlic cloves, minced
½ cup water	1 tablespoon Italian seasoning

1. In the Ninja Foodi XL Pressure Cooker Steam Fryer with SmartLid cooking pot, combine the olive oil, pork, crushed tomatoes, water, carrots, shallots, garlic, and Italian seasoning. 2. Lock lid; move slider to PRESSURE. Make sure the pressure release valve is in the SEAL position. The cooking temperature will default to HIGH, which is accurate. Set time to 45 minutes. Press START/STOP to cooking. When pressure cooking is complete, let the pressure release naturally for at least 10 minutes. 3. Remove the lid, transfer the pork to a medium bowl, and shred it using two forks. Return the pork to the juices and serve.

Per Serving: Calories 144; Fat 6.6g; Sodium 171mg; Carbs 2g; Fiber 0g; Sugar 1g; Protein 19g

Apple Cider Pulled Pork

Prep time: 5 minutes| Cook time: 45 minutes| Serves: 6

2 pounds boneless pork loin roast	sliced
Sea salt	1 small onion, chopped
Freshly ground black pepper	1 tablespoon light brown sugar
1 tablespoon vegetable oil	1 teaspoon chili powder
2 cups apple cider	1 teaspoon smoked paprika
2 Honeycrisp apples, peeled and	

1. Season the pork with salt and pepper.2. In the Ninja Foodi XL Pressure Cooker Steam Fryer with SmartLid cooking pot, combine the vegetable oil, pork, apple cider, apples, onion, brown sugar, chili powder, and smoked paprika. 3. Lock lid; move slider to PRESSURE. Make sure the pressure release valve is in the SEAL position. The cooking temperature will default to HIGH, which is accurate. Set time to 45 minutes. Press START/STOP to cooking. When pressure cooking is complete, let the pressure release naturally for at least 10 minutes. 4. Remove the lid, transfer the pork to a medium bowl, and shred it using two forks. Return the pork to the juices and serve.

Per Serving: Calories 543; Fat 38.1g; Sodium 134mg; Carbs 27g; Fiber 1g; Sugar 0g; Protein 23g

Savory-Sweet Braised Beef

Prep time: 5 minutes| Cook time: 40 minutes| Serves: 6

4½- to 5-pound boneless beef chuck roast, pulled apart at the natural seams into 3 pieces, trimmed, each piece tied at 1-inch intervals	and peeled
	2 tablespoons tomato paste
	½ cup packed dark brown sugar
	2 cinnamon sticks
	1 tablespoon allspice berries
Kosher salt and ground black pepper	1 cup dry red wine
	¼ cup Worcestershire sauce
2 tablespoons grapeseed or other neutral oil	1 cup pitted prunes, roughly chopped
1 large yellow onion, chopped	1½ tablespoons cornstarch
10 medium garlic cloves, smashed	3 to 4 tablespoons red wine vinegar

1. Season the beef on all sides with salt and pepper. 2. Move the slider towards "AIR FRY/STOVETOP" and set Ninja Foodi XL Pressure Cooker Steam Fryer with SmartLid to SEAR/SAUTÉ mode. Adjust the temperature to "Hi5" by using up arrow. Press START/STOP to begin cooking. 3. Add the oil and heat until shimmering. Add the onion and ½ teaspoon salt, then cook, stirring occasionally, until the onion is well browned, about 9 minutes. Add the garlic and cook, stirring, until fragrant, about 30 seconds. 4. Add the tomato paste and cook, stirring constantly, until it begins to brown, about 1 minute. Stir in the sugar, cinnamon, allspice and 1 teaspoon pepper, then add the wine, scraping up any browned bits. Bring to a simmer and cook, stirring occasionally, until thick and syrupy, 3 to 5 minutes. Stir in the Worcestershire sauce, prunes and 1 cup water. Nestle the beef in the pot. 5. Lock lid; move slider to PRESSURE. Make sure the pressure release valve is in the SEAL position. The cooking temperature will default to HIGH, which is accurate. Set time to 60 minutes. Press START/STOP to cooking. 6. When pressure cooking is complete, let the pressure release naturally for 25 minutes, then quickly release the remaining steam by turning it into VENT position. Then carefully open the lid. 7. Place the beef to a cutting board and tent with foil. Set a fine mesh strainer over a medium bowl. Using potholders, carefully remove the insert from the housing and pour the contents of the pot into the strainer. 8. Press on the solids with a silicone spatula to extract as much liquid and pulp as possible; scrape the underside of the strainer to collect the pulp. Discard the solids. Let the liquid and pulp settle for about 5 minutes, then use a large spoon to skim off and discard the fat on the surface; you should have about 3 cups defatted liquid. Return the liquid to the pot. 9. Select SEAR/SAUTÉ mode again. Bring to a simmer and cook, stirring occasionally, until slightly reduced, about 10 minutes. In a small bowl, stir together the cornstarch and 3 tablespoons water. 10. Whisk into the simmering liquid and cook, stirring constantly, until lightly thickened, about 2 minutes. Press START/STOP to turn off the pot. Stir in the vinegar, then taste and season with salt and pepper. Cut the beef into ½-inch slices against the grain, removing the twine as you go. 11. Arrange the slices on a platter, then pour about 1 cup of the sauce over the top. Serve with the remaining sauce on the side.

Per Serving: Calories 184; Fat 7.4g; Sodium 103mg; Carbs 7g; Fiber 1g; Sugar 1g; Protein 22g

Cinnamon Applesauce Chops

Prep time: 10 minutes| Cook time: 12 minutes| Serves: 6

6 (6- to 8-ounce) boneless pork chops (1 inch thick)	1½ cups applesauce, store-bought or homemade
Sea salt	1 cup water
Freshly ground black pepper	1 teaspoon dried sage
1 tablespoon vegetable oil	1 cinnamon stick
1 small onion, chopped	

1. Season the pork chops with salt and pepper. 2. Move the slider towards "AIR FRY/STOVETOP" and set Ninja Foodi XL Pressure Cooker Steam Fryer with SmartLid to SEAR/SAUTÉ mode. Adjust the temperature to "Hi5" by using up arrow. Press START/STOP to begin cooking and let the pot heat up for 2 minutes. 3. Pour the oil into the pot, then add the onion and sauté for about 2 minutes, or until the onion is translucent. Add the pork chops and sear for 1 minute on each side. 4. Add the applesauce, water, sage, and cinnamon stick. 5. Lock lid; move slider to PRESSURE. Make sure the pressure release valve is in the SEAL position. The cooking temperature will default to HIGH, which is accurate. Set time to 10 minutes. Press START/STOP to cooking. When pressure cooking is complete, let the pressure release natural. 6. Remove the lid and transfer the pork chops to a serving dish. Discard the cinnamon stick, scoop the applesauce on top of the pork, and serve.

Per Serving: Calories 205; Fat 5.8g; Sodium 1481mg; Carbs 1g; Fiber 0g; Sugar 0g; Protein 35g

Sausage with Peppers

Prep time: 10 minutes| Cook time: 20 minutes| Serves: 4

1 (28-ounce) can crushed tomatoes	2 garlic cloves, minced
½ cup water	1 tablespoon Italian seasoning
5 links sweet Italian sausage, halved	4 bell peppers, any color, cut into strips
1 onion, sliced	

1. In the cooking pot, combine the crushed tomatoes, water, sausages, onion, garlic, and Italian seasoning. 2. Place the peppers in a vegetable Cook & Crisp Basket and add it to the pot on top of the sausage mixture. 3. Lock lid; move slider to PRESSURE. Make sure the pressure release valve is in the SEAL position. The cooking temperature will default to HIGH, which is accurate. Set time to 15 minutes. Press START/STOP to cooking. When cooking is complete, let pressure release quickly by turning it into VENT position. 4. Remove the Cook & Crisp Basket of bell peppers from the pot. 5. Move the slider towards "AIR FRY/STOVETOP" and set Ninja Foodi XL Pressure Cooker Steam Fryer with SmartLid to SEAR/SAUTÉ mode. Adjust the temperature to "Hi5" by using up arrow. Press START/STOP to begin cooking. Cook for about 5 minutes to thicken the sauce. 6. Return the bell peppers to the pot, stir them into the sauce, and serve.

Per Serving: Calories 605; Fat 31g; Sodium 833mg; Carbs 51g; Fiber 6g; Sugar 5g; Protein 74g

Sweet Tangy Ham

Prep time: 5 minutes| Cook time: 20 minutes| Serves: 6

1 cup orange juice	1 teaspoon ground cinnamon
½ cup water	1 teaspoon ground cloves
2 tablespoons butter	1 teaspoon ground nutmeg
1 (3- to 4-pound) spiral-cut ham	1 tablespoon cornstarch
½ cup packed light brown sugar	

1. In the cooking pot, combine the orange juice, water, and butter. 2. Rub the ham all over with the brown sugar, cinnamon, cloves, and nutmeg. 3. Place the Deluxe reversible rack in the Ninja Foodi XL Pressure Cooker Steam Fryer cooking pot and set the ham on the Deluxe reversible rack. 4. Lock lid; move slider to PRESSURE. Make sure the pressure release valve is in the SEAL position. The cooking temperature will default to HIGH, which is accurate. Set time to 15 minutes. Press START/STOP to cooking. When cooking is complete, let pressure release naturally. 5. Remove the lid and carefully lift out the ham and Deluxe reversible rack. Move the slider towards "AIR FRY/STOVETOP" and set Ninja Foodi XL Pressure Cooker Steam Fryer with SmartLid to SEAR/SAUTÉ mode. Adjust the temperature to "Hi5" by using up arrow. Press START/STOP to begin cooking. Whisk the cornstarch into the pot and whisk for about 5 minutes to thicken the sauce. 6. Serve the ham drizzled with the sauce.
Per Serving: Calories 218; Fat 2.4g; Sodium 641mg; Carbs 14g; Fiber 6g; Sugar 2g; Protein 19g

Stewed Lamb

Prep Time: 10 minutes. | Cook Time: 30 minutes. | Serves: 2

15-ounce lamb sirloin	½ teaspoon onion powder
1 tablespoon avocado oil	1 teaspoon tomato paste
1 teaspoon ginger powder	

1. Place the Cook & Crisp Basket in your Ninja Foodi Pressure Cooker Steam Fryer. 2. Rub the lamb sirloin with ginger powder and onion powder. 3. Then mix avocado oil with tomato paste. 4. Brush the lamb sirloin with tomato mixture and put it in your Ninja Foodi Cook & Crisp Basket. 5. Put on the Smart Lid on top of the Ninja Foodi Steam Fryer. 6. Move the Lid Slider to the "Air Fry/Stovetop". 7. Cook the meal at 360°F/180°C on "Air Fry" Mode for about 30 minutes.
Per Serving: Calories 720; Fat 50.1 g; Sodium 2142 mg; Carbs 44.5g; Fiber 8.2g; Sugar 33g; Protein 25.2g

Garlic Beef Meatballs

Prep Time: 20 minutes. | Cook Time: 10 minutes. | Serves: 4

2 cups beef	1 teaspoon dried cilantro
1 tablespoon garlic powder	1 tablespoon almond flour
1 teaspoon chili powder	Cooking spray

1. Place the Cook & Crisp Basket in your Ninja Foodi Pressure Cooker Steam Fryer. 2. In a suitable mixing bowl, mix beef with garlic powder, chili powder, dried cilantro, and almond flour. 3. Make the meatballs and put them in your Ninja Foodi Cook & Crisp Basket. 4. Spray the meatballs with cooking spray. 5. Put on the Smart Lid on top of the Ninja Foodi Steam Fryer. 6. Move the Lid Slider to the "Air Fry/Stovetop". 7. Cook on "Air Fry" Mode at 400°F/200°C for about 5 minutes per side.
Per Serving: Calories 283; Fat 6.6g; Sodium 693mg; Carbs 8.5g; Fiber 1.4g; Sugar 3.4g; Protein 45.2g

Parmesan Meatballs

Prep Time: 15 minutes. | Cook Time: 8 minutes. | Serves: 6

2-pounds beef	2 ounces Parmesan, grated
1 tablespoon taco seasonings	1 teaspoon olive oil

1. Place the Cook & Crisp Basket in your Ninja Foodi Pressure Cooker Steam Fryer. 2. Brush the Ninja Foodi Cook & Crisp Basket with olive oil. 3. Then mix all the remaining recipe ingredients and make the meatballs. 4. Put the meatballs in the Ninja Foodi Cook & Crisp Basket. 5. Put on the Smart Lid on top of the Ninja Foodi Steam

Fryer. 6. Move the Lid Slider to the "Air Fry/Stovetop". 7. Cook on "Air Fry" Mode at 390°F/200°C for about 4 minutes per side.
Per Serving: Calories 274; Fat 9.5 g; Sodium 3542 mg; Carbs 6.3g; Fiber 0.9g; Sugar 4.6g; Protein 40.5g

Beef Greens Bowl

Prep Time: 5 minutes. | Cook Time: 45 minutes. | Serves: 4

1-pound beef sirloin, chopped	1 teaspoon Italian seasonings
2 cups fresh spinach, chopped	1 teaspoon avocado oil
1 cup heavy cream	1 teaspoon turmeric

1. Place the Cook & Crisp Basket in your Ninja Foodi Pressure Cooker Steam Fryer. 2. Mix all the recipe ingredients in a suitable mixing bowl. 3. Then transfer the beef sirloin mixture in your Ninja Foodi Cook & Crisp Basket. 4. Put on the Smart Lid on top of the Ninja Foodi Steam Fryer. 5. Move the Lid Slider to the "Air Fry/Stovetop". 6. Cook the meat at 350°F/175°C on "Air Fry" Mode for about 45 minutes.
Per Serving: Calories 597; Fat 17.1 g; Sodium 723 mg; Carbs 66.5g; Fiber 9.3g; Sugar 45g; Protein 48.6g

Beef Bites

Prep Time: 10 minutes. | Cook Time: 25 minutes. | Serves: 4

2-pounds beef sirloin, cubed	1 teaspoon chili powder
2 eggs, beaten	½ teaspoon turmeric
3 tablespoons almond flour	1 teaspoon avocado oil

1. Place the Cook & Crisp Basket in your Ninja Foodi Pressure Cooker Steam Fryer. 2. Mix beef sirloins with eggs, almond flour, chili powder, and turmeric. 3. Then transfer the meat cubes in your Ninja Foodi Pressure Cooker Steam Fryer and sprinkle with avocado oil. 4. Put on the Smart Lid on top of the Ninja Foodi Steam Fryer. 5. Move the Lid Slider to the "Air Fry/Stovetop". 6. Cook the beef popcorn at 375°F/190°C on "Air Fry" Mode for about 25 minutes. Shake the meal every 5 minutes.
Per Serving: Calories 183; Fat 0.4 g; Sodium 4347 mg; Carbs 5.6g; Fiber 0.6g; Sugar 8.4g; Protein 40.2g

Lamb Chops With Olive Spread

Prep Time: 10 minutes. | Cook Time: 20 minutes. | Serves: 4

4 lamb chops	2 tablespoons olive oil
4 kalamata olives, diced	1 tablespoon lemon juice
1 teaspoon minced garlic	½ teaspoon black pepper
1 cup fresh spinach, chopped	

1. Place the Cook & Crisp Basket in your Ninja Foodi Pressure Cooker Steam Fryer. 2. Mix lamb chops with black pepper, lemon juice, and olive oil. 3. Put the lamb chops in your Ninja Foodi Pressure Cooker Steam Fryer. 4. Put on the Smart Lid on top of the Ninja Foodi Steam Fryer. 5. Move the Lid Slider to the "Air Fry/Stovetop". 6. Cook on "Air Fry" Mode for about 10 minutes per side at 360°F/180°C. 7. Meanwhile, blend all the remaining recipe ingredients until smooth. 8. Top the cooked lamb chops with olives spread.
Per Serving: Calories 386; Fat 9.8 g; Sodium 50mg; Carbs 6.2g; Fiber 1.7g; Sugar 3.1g; Protein 19.2g

Coconut Cream Beef

Prep Time: 10 minutes. | Cook Time: 35 minutes. | Serves: 2

16-ounce beef sirloin, sliced	½ teaspoon black pepper
½ cup coconut cream	½ teaspoon olive oil
1 teaspoon paprika	

1. Place the Cook & Crisp Basket in your Ninja Foodi Pressure Cooker Steam Fryer. 2. Mix beef sirloin with paprika, black pepper, and olive oil. 3. Transfer the mixture in the Ninja Foodi Cook & Crisp Basket and add coconut cream. 4. Put on the Smart Lid on top of the Ninja Foodi Steam Fryer. 5. Move the Lid Slider to the "Air Fry/Stovetop". 6. Cook the coconut beef at 365°F/185°C on "Air Fry" Mode for about 35 minutes.
Per Serving: Calories 445; Fat 28.2 g; Sodium 322 mg; Carbs 6.2g; Fiber 2.2g; Sugar 1.4g; Protein 43.7g

Baked Beef

Prep Time: 10 minutes. | Cook Time: 50 minutes. | Serves: 2

1-pound beef sirloin, chopped
1 teaspoon nutmeg
1 teaspoon salt
1 cup radish, chopped
1 tablespoon avocado oil
½ teaspoon dried basil
¼ cup of water

1. Place the Cook & Crisp Basket in your Ninja Foodi Pressure Cooker Steam Fryer. 2. Put all the recipe ingredients in the Ninja Foodi Cook & Crisp Basket and carefully mix. 3. Put on the Smart Lid on top of the Ninja Foodi Steam Fryer. 4. Move the Lid Slider to the "Air Fry/Stovetop". 5. Cook the beef meal at 355°F/180°C on "Air Fry" Mode for about 50 minutes.
Per Serving: Calories 210; Fat 5.4 g; Sodium 110 mg; Carbs 18.5g; Fiber 2.4g; Sugar 13.1g; Protein 23.5g

Oregano Beef

Prep Time: 5 minutes. | Cook Time: 30 minutes. | Serves: 4

2-pounds beef roast, chopped
1 teaspoon black pepper
1 teaspoon minced garlic
2 tablespoons avocado oil
1 teaspoon dried oregano
½ teaspoon cayenne pepper

1. Place the Cook & Crisp Basket in your Ninja Foodi Pressure Cooker Steam Fryer. 2. Rub the beef roast with black pepper, minced garlic, avocado oil, dried oregano, and cayenne pepper. 3. Put the beef in the Ninja Foodi Cook & Crisp Basket. 4. Put on the Smart Lid on top of the Ninja Foodi Steam Fryer. 5. Move the Lid Slider to the "Air Fry/Stovetop". 6. Cook on "Air Fry" Mode at 365°F/185°C for about 30 minutes.
Per Serving: Calories 319; Fat 14.7 g; Sodium 92 mg; Carbs 30.3g; Fiber 4g; Sugar 12.3g; Protein 24g

Mongolian Beef

Prep Time: 15 minutes. | Cook Time: 20 minutes. | Serves: 2

10-ounce beef steak, chopped
2 tablespoons almond flour
1 teaspoon avocado oil
½ teaspoon onion powder
4 tablespoons coconut aminos
1 teaspoon sugar

1. Place the Cook & Crisp Basket in your Ninja Foodi Pressure Cooker Steam Fryer. 2. Mix the beef steak with onion powder, coconut aminos, and sugar. 3. Then coat every beef steak piece with almond flour and put in your Ninja Foodi Cook & Crisp Basket. 4. Sprinkle the beef with avocado oil. 5. Put on the Smart Lid on top of the Ninja Foodi Steam Fryer. 6. Move the Lid Slider to the "Air Fry/Stovetop". 7. Cook on "Air Fry" Mode at 365°F/185°C for about 10 minutes per side.
Per Serving: Calories 362; Fat 22.6 g; Sodium 242 mg; Carbs 2.9g; Fiber 1.4g; Sugar 0.5g; Protein 37.4g

Beef Cabbage Rolls

Prep Time: 10 minutes. | Cook Time: 50 minutes. | Serves: 4

2-pounds beef sirloin, diced
1 cup white cabbage, shredded
½ cup beef broth
1 teaspoon taco seasonings
1 teaspoon coconut oil
1 teaspoon salt

1. Place the Cook & Crisp Basket in your Ninja Foodi Pressure Cooker Steam Fryer. 2. Mix beef sirloin with taco seasonings and salt. 3. Put the coconut oil in your Ninja Foodi Cook & Crisp Basket. Add beef sirloin and beef broth. 4. Then top the beef with white cabbage. 5. Put on the Smart Lid on top of the Ninja Foodi Steam Fryer. 6. Move the Lid Slider to the "Air Fry/Stovetop". 7. Cook the meal at 360°F/180°C on "Air Fry" Mode for about 50 minutes.
Per Serving: Calories 457; Fat 10.1 g; Sodium 423 mg; Carbs 1.6g; Fiber 0.5g; Sugar 0.4g; Protein 14.9g

Beef Steak

Prep Time: 10 minutes. | Cook Time: 16 minutes. | Serves: 4

2-pounds beef steak
3 tablespoons coconut oil
1 teaspoon coconut shred
1 teaspoon dried basil

1. Place the Cook & Crisp Basket in your Ninja Foodi Pressure Cooker Steam Fryer. 2. Rub the beef steak with coconut shred and dried basil. 3. Then brush the beef steak with coconut oil and put it in your Ninja Foodi Pressure Cooker Steam Fryer. 4. Put on the Smart Lid on top of the Ninja Foodi Steam Fryer. 5. Move the Lid Slider to the "Air Fry/Stovetop". 6. Cook the beef steak at 390°F/200°C on "Air Fry" Mode for about 8 minutes per side.
Per Serving: Calories 376; Fat 34.2 g; Sodium 635 mg; Carbs 2.4g; Fiber 0.5g; Sugar 0.3g; Protein 16.2g

Garlic Beef Bread

Prep Time: 10 minutes. | Cook Time: 25 minutes. | Serves: 4

2-pounds beef
1 teaspoon minced garlic
1 tablespoon dried parsley
1 teaspoon turmeric
¼ cup coconut flour
1 tablespoon coconut oil, softened

1. Place the Cook & Crisp Basket in your Ninja Foodi Pressure Cooker Steam Fryer. 2. In a suitable mixing bowl mix beef with minced garlic, dried parsley, turmeric, and coconut flour. 3. After this, grease the Ninja Foodi Cook & Crisp Basket with coconut oil from inside. 4. Put the beef mixture in the Ninja Foodi Cook & Crisp Basket and flatten gently. 5. Put on the Smart Lid on top of the Ninja Foodi Steam Fryer. 6. Move the Lid Slider to the "Air Fry/Stovetop". 7. Cook the beef bread at 370°F/185°C on "Air Fry" Mode for about 25 minutes.
Per Serving: Calories 487; Fat 15 g; Sodium 4856 mg; Carbs 0g; Fiber 0g; Sugar 0g; Protein 85.4g

Pork With Herbs and Onions

Prep Time: 10 minutes. | Cook Time: 1 hour | Serves: 4

1 rosemary sprig, chopped
1 thyme sprig, chopped
1 teaspoon dried sage, crushed
Salt and black pepper, to taste
1 teaspoon cayenne pepper
2 teaspoons sesame oil
2 pounds pork leg roast, scored
½-pound candy onions, peeled
2 chili peppers, minced
4 cloves garlic, chopped

1. Place the Cook & Crisp Basket in your Ninja Foodi Pressure Cooker Steam Fryer. 2. Then, mix the seasonings with the sesame oil. 3. Rub the seasoning mixture all over the pork leg. 4. Put on the Smart Lid on top of the Ninja Foodi Steam Fryer. 5. Move the Lid Slider to the "Air Fry/Stovetop". 6. Cook on "Air Fry" Mode at 400°F/200°C for about 40 minutes. 7. Add the candy onions, peppers and garlic. 8. Cook an additional 12 minutes. Slice the pork leg. Afterwards, spoon the pan juices over the meat and serve with the candy onions. Bon appétit!
Per Serving: Calories 244; Fat 13.3 g; Sodium 144 mg; Carbs 3g; Fiber 0.9g; Sugar 0.7g; Protein 32.2g

Lamb Chops with Mint Sauce

Prep Time: 5 minutes. | Cook Time: 24 minutes. | Serves: 4

8 lamb chops
1 teaspoon salt
1 tablespoon mint, chopped
1 teaspoon garlic powder
3 tablespoons lime juice
¼ cup of water
2 tablespoons avocado oil

1. Place the Cook & Crisp Basket in your Ninja Foodi Pressure Cooker Steam Fryer. 2. Sprinkle the lamb chops with salt and avocado oil and put in your Ninja Foodi Pressure Cooker Steam Fryer. 3. Add mint and garlic powder. 4. Then add water and lime juice. 5. Put on the Smart Lid on top of the Ninja Foodi Steam Fryer. 6. Move the Lid Slider to the "Air Fry/Stovetop". 7. Cook the lamb chops a 375°F/190°C on "Air Fry" Mode for about 24 minutes.
Per Serving: Calories 226; Fat 2.8 g; Sodium 2448 mg; Carbs 33.9g; Fiber 1.2g; Sugar 27.9g; Protein 16.2g

Onion Beef Delights

Prep Time: 10 minutes. | Cook Time: 30 minutes. | Serves: 4

2-pound beef fillet
1 tablespoon onion powder
¼ cup heavy cream

½ teaspoon salt
1 teaspoon olive oil

1. Place the Cook & Crisp Basket in your Ninja Foodi Pressure Cooker Steam Fryer. 2. Cut the beef fillet into bites and sprinkle with onion powder, salt and oil. 3. Then put the beef bites in your Ninja Foodi Pressure Cooker Steam Fryer and add heavy cream. 4. Put on the Smart Lid on top of the Ninja Foodi Steam Fryer. 5. Move the Lid Slider to the "Air Fry/Stovetop". 6. Cook the beef bites at 360°F/180°C on "Air Fry" Mode for about 15 minutes per side.
Per Serving: Calories 273; Fat 24 g; Sodium 1181 mg; Carbs 12.8g; Fiber 1g; Sugar 1.4g; Protein 20g

Italian Beef

Prep Time: 10 minutes. | Cook Time: 35 minutes. | Serves: 4

2-pounds beef steak, cut into strips
¼ cup plain yogurt
1 teaspoon lemon juice

1 teaspoon white pepper
½ teaspoon dried oregano
Cooking spray

1. Place the Cook & Crisp Basket in your Ninja Foodi Pressure Cooker Steam Fryer. 2. Mix plain yogurt with lemon juice, white pepper, and dried oregano. 3. Then put beef strips in the plain yogurt mixture. 4. Spray the Ninja Foodi Cook & Crisp Basket with cooking spray. 5. Put the beef strips mixture in your Ninja Foodi Pressure Cooker Steam Fryer. 6. Put on the Smart Lid on top of the Ninja Foodi Steam Fryer. 7. Move the Lid Slider to the "Air Fry/Stovetop". 8. Cook on "Air Fry" Mode for about 35 minutes at 360°F/180°C.
Per Serving: Calories 373; Fat 8.5 g; Sodium 4928 mg; Carbs 0.8g; Fiber 0.3g; Sugar 7.6g; Protein 74.5g

Eggplant Beef Sauté

Prep Time: 5 minutes. | Cook Time: 45 minutes. | Serves: 4

1-pound beef sirloin, chopped
1 eggplant, chopped
1 teaspoon salt

1 teaspoon black pepper
1 teaspoon dried cilantro
1 cup beef broth

1. Place the Cook & Crisp Basket in your Ninja Foodi Pressure Cooker Steam Fryer. 2. Put all the recipe ingredients in the Ninja Foodi Cook & Crisp Basket and carefully mix. 3. Put on the Smart Lid on top of the Ninja Foodi Steam Fryer. 4. Move the Lid Slider to the "Air Fry/Stovetop". 5. Cook the sauté at 360°F/180°C on "Air Fry" Mode for about 45 minutes.
Per Serving: Calories 379; Fat 20.9 g; Sodium 1598 mg; Carbs 10g; Fiber 2.2g; Sugar 2.1g; Protein 37g

Beef Roll

Prep Time: 20 minutes. | Cook Time: 40 minutes. | Serves: 4

1-pound beef loin
2 ounces mushrooms, chopped
1 teaspoon onion powder
1-ounce bacon, chopped, cooked

½ teaspoon dried dill
1 teaspoon chili powder
1 tablespoon avocado oil
½ teaspoon cream cheese

1. Place the Cook & Crisp Basket in your Ninja Foodi Pressure Cooker Steam Fryer. 2. Beat the beef loin with the help of the kitchen hammer to get the flat loin. 3. After this, mix mushrooms with onion powder, bacon, dried dill, chili powder, and cream cheese. 4. Put the mixture over the beef loin and roll it. 5. Secure the beef roll with toothpicks and brush with avocado oil. 6. Put on the Smart Lid on top of the Ninja Foodi Steam Fryer. 7. Move the Lid Slider to the "Air Fry/Stovetop". 8. Cook the beef roll at 370°F/185°C on "Air Fry" Mode for about 40 minutes.
Per Serving: Calories 467; Fat 18.1 g; Sodium 438 mg; Carbs 6.6g; Fiber 0.5g; Sugar 5.5g; Protein 66.1g

Garlicky Beef Steak

Prep Time: 10 minutes. | Cook Time: 14 minutes. | Serves: 4

4 beef steaks
1 teaspoon garlic powder

1 tablespoon coconut oil

1. Place the Cook & Crisp Basket in your Ninja Foodi Pressure Cooker Steam Fryer. 2. Mix beef steaks with garlic powder and coconut oil. 3. Put the beef steaks in your Ninja Foodi Pressure Cooker Steam Fryer. 4. Put on the Smart Lid on top of the Ninja Foodi Steam Fryer. 5. Move the Lid Slider to the "Air Fry/Stovetop". 6. Cook on "Air Fry" Mode for about 7 minutes per side at 400°F/200°C.
Per Serving: Calories 540; Fat 26.8 g; Sodium 309 mg; Carbs 2.6g; Fiber 0.4g; Sugar 1.2g; Protein 69.9g

Za'Atar Chops

Prep Time: 10 minutes. | Cook Time: 11 minutes. | Serves: 6

6 beef chops
1 tablespoon coconut oil, melted

1 tablespoon za'atar seasonings

1. Place the Cook & Crisp Basket in your Ninja Foodi Pressure Cooker Steam Fryer. 2. Mix za'atar seasonings with coconut oil. 3. Brush the beef chops with coconut oil mixture and put it in your Ninja Foodi Pressure Cooker Steam Fryer. 4. Put on the Smart Lid on top of the Ninja Foodi Steam Fryer. 5. Move the Lid Slider to the "Air Fry/Stovetop". 6. Cook the meal at 400°F/200°C on "Air Fry" Mode for about 11 minutes.
Per Serving: Calories 363; Fat 17.1 g; Sodium1065 mg; Carbs 19.8g; Fiber 3.4g; Sugar 12.9g; Protein 33.7g

Fried Rib Eye Steaks

Prep Time: 10 minutes. | Cook Time: 24 minutes. | Serves: 4

3-pound rib-eye steak
1 tablespoon tomato paste
1 tablespoon avocado oil

1 teaspoon salt
1 teaspoon cayenne pepper

1. Place the Cook & Crisp Basket in your Ninja Foodi Pressure Cooker Steam Fryer. 2. In the shallow bowl, mix tomato paste with avocado oil, salt, and cayenne pepper. 3. Then run the beef with tomato mixture and put it in your Ninja Foodi Pressure Cooker Steam Fryer. 4. Put on the Smart Lid on top of the Ninja Foodi Steam Fryer. 5. Move the Lid Slider to the "Air Fry/Stovetop". 6. Cook the meal at 380°F/195°C on "Air Fry" Mode for about 12 minutes per side.
Per Serving: Calories 297; Fat 18.4 g; Sodium 1151 mg; Carbs 11.6g; Fiber 0.6g; Sugar 10.9g; Protein 20.5g

Lamb Cauliflower Fritters

Prep Time: 15 minutes. | Cook Time: 20 minutes. | Serves: 8

1 teaspoon onion powder
1 teaspoon garlic powder
½ teaspoon coriander
1 teaspoon salt

2-pound lamb, minced
½ cup cauliflower, shredded
Cooking spray

1. Place the Cook & Crisp Basket in your Ninja Foodi Pressure Cooker Steam Fryer. 2. Spray the Ninja Foodi Cook & Crisp Basket with cooking spray from inside. 3. Then mix onion powder with garlic powder, coriander, salt, lamb, and cauliflower. 4. Make the fritters from the beef mixture and put them in your Ninja Foodi Pressure Cooker Steam Fryer. 5. Put on the Smart Lid on top of the Ninja Foodi Steam Fryer. 6. Move the Lid Slider to the "Air Fry/Stovetop". 7. Cook the fritters at 360°F/180°C on "Air Fry" Mode for about 10 minutes per side.
Per Serving: Calories 346; Fat 16.8 g; Sodium 1585 mg; Carbs 5.7g; Fiber 1g; Sugar 2.9g; Protein 42.2g

Mustard Glazed Beef Loin

Prep Time: 10 minutes. | Cook Time: 40 minutes. | Serves: 7

4-pounds beef loin
2 tablespoon Dijon mustard
1 tablespoon olive oil
½ tablespoon apple cider vinegar

1. Place the Cook & Crisp Basket in your Ninja Foodi Pressure Cooker Steam Fryer. 2. Mix mustard with olive oil and apple cider vinegar. 3. Then rub the beef loin with mustard mixture and put it in your Ninja Foodi Pressure Cooker Steam Fryer. 4. Put on the Smart Lid on top of the Ninja Foodi Steam Fryer. 5. Move the Lid Slider to the "Air Fry/Stovetop". 6. Cook the meal at 375°F/190°C on "Air Fry" Mode for about 20 minutes per side.
Per Serving: Calories 384; Fat 20.5g; Sodium 449 mg; Carbs 5.1g; Fiber 2.1g; Sugar 0.7g; Protein 45g

Curried Beef

Prep Time: 15 minutes. | Cook Time: 30 minutes. | Serves: 4

2-pounds beef tenderloin, chopped
¼ cup heavy cream
1 teaspoon curry paste
¼ teaspoon minced garlic
1 teaspoon coconut oil, melted

1. Place the Cook & Crisp Basket in your Ninja Foodi Pressure Cooker Steam Fryer. 2. Mix heavy cream with curry paste and minced garlic. 3. Then put the beef tenderloin in the curry mixture and leave for about 10 minutes to marinate. 4. Put the coconut oil in your Ninja Foodi Pressure Cooker Steam Fryer. 5. Add curry mixture. 6. Put on the Smart Lid on top of the Ninja Foodi Steam Fryer. 7. Move the Lid Slider to the "Air Fry/Stovetop". 8. Cook on "Air Fry" Mode at 370°F/185°C for about 30 minutes.
Per Serving: Calories 328; Fat 28.7 g; Sodium 95 mg; Carbs 7.4g; Fiber 2.8g; Sugar 0.7g; Protein 13g

Rosemary Meatballs

Prep Time: 5 minutes. | Cook Time: 25 minutes. | Serves: 4

2-pound beef
1 teaspoon dried rosemary
1 teaspoon onion powder
½ teaspoon salt
1 tablespoon olive oil

1. Place the Cook & Crisp Basket in your Ninja Foodi Pressure Cooker Steam Fryer. 2. Mix beef with dried rosemary, onion powder, and salt. 3. Make the meatballs and put them in your Ninja Foodi Pressure Cooker Steam Fryer. 4. Sprinkle the meatballs with olive oil. 5. Put on the Smart Lid on top of the Ninja Foodi Steam Fryer. 6. Move the Lid Slider to the "Air Fry/Stovetop". 7. Cook on "Air Fry" Mode at 360°F/180°C for about 25 minutes.
Per Serving: Calories 370; Fat 10.5 g; Sodium 503 mg; Carbs 21.4g; Fiber 3.1g; Sugar 1.9g; Protein 46.6g

Saucy BBQ Beef

Prep Time: 15 minutes. | Cook Time: 15 minutes. | Serves: 4

4 beef steaks
1 cup BBQ sauce
1 tablespoon olive oil

1. Place the Cook & Crisp Basket in your Ninja Foodi Pressure Cooker Steam Fryer. 2. Mix olive oil with BBQ sauce. 3. Then mix beef steaks with sauce mixture and put in your Ninja Foodi Pressure Cooker Steam Fryer. 4. Put on the Smart Lid on top of the Ninja Foodi Steam Fryer. 5. Move the Lid Slider to the "Air Fry/Stovetop". 6. Cook the beef at 400°F/200°C on "Air Fry" Mode for about 15 minutes.
Per Serving: Calories 596; Fat 10.8 g; Sodium 7429 mg; Carbs 14.9g; Fiber 1.9g; Sugar 21.9g; Protein 112.2g

Minced Beef Sauté

Prep Time: 5 minutes. | Cook Time: 30 minutes. | Serves: 4

1 cup bell pepper, diced
1-pound beef

1 garlic clove, diced
1 teaspoon dried oregano
1 teaspoon coconut oil
1 tablespoon cream cheese

1. Place the Cook & Crisp Basket in your Ninja Foodi Pressure Cooker Steam Fryer. 2. Mix all the recipe ingredients from the list above in a suitable mixing bowl. 3. Then transfer the mixture in the Ninja Foodi Cook & Crisp Basket. 4. Put on the Smart Lid on top of the Ninja Foodi Steam Fryer. 5. Move the Lid Slider to the "Air Fry/Stovetop". 6. Cook on "Air Fry" Mode at 365°F/185°C for about 30 minutes.
Per Serving: Calories 559; Fat 23.8 g; Sodium 430 mg; Carbs 18.3g; Fiber 0.3g; Sugar 17.6g; Protein 65.8g

Tender Beef Salad

Prep Time: 10 minutes. | Cook Time: 25 minutes. | Serves: 4

1-pound beef sirloin, sliced
1 teaspoon white pepper
½ teaspoon salt
1 teaspoon coconut oil, melted
1 cup lettuce, chopped
2 pecans, chopped
1 tablespoon avocado oil

1. Place the Cook & Crisp Basket in your Ninja Foodi Pressure Cooker Steam Fryer. 2. In a suitable mixing bowl, mix beef sirloin with white pepper, salt, and coconut oil. 3. Put the beef in the Ninja Foodi Cook & Crisp Basket. 4. Put on the Smart Lid on top of the Ninja Foodi Steam Fryer. 5. Move the Lid Slider to the "Air Fry/Stovetop". 6. Cook on "Air Fry" Mode at 365°F/185°C for about 25 minutes. 7. Then mix beef sirloin with lettuce, pecans, and avocado oil. 8. Shake the salad gently.
Per Serving: Calories 512; Fat 7.1 g; Sodium 42 mg; Carbs 28.5g; Fiber 2.1g; Sugar 13.4g; Protein 1.2g

Pork Kebab With Dill Sauce

Prep Time: 10 minutes. | Cook Time: 25 minutes. | Serves: 4

2 teaspoons olive oil
½-pound pork
½-pound beef
1 egg, whisked
Salt and black pepper, to taste
1 teaspoon paprika
2 garlic cloves, minced
1 teaspoon dried marjoram
1 teaspoon mustard seeds
½ teaspoon celery seeds
Yogurt Sauce:
2 tablespoons olive oil
2 tablespoons fresh lemon juice
Salt, to taste
¼ teaspoon red pepper flakes, crushed
½ cup full-fat yogurt
1 teaspoon dried dill weed

1. Place the Cook & Crisp Basket in your Ninja Foodi Pressure Cooker Steam Fryer. 2. Spritz the sides and bottom of the cooking basket with 2 teaspoons of olive oil. 3. In a mixing dish, mix the pork, beef, egg, salt, black pepper, paprika, garlic, marjoram, mustard seeds, and celery seeds. 4. Make kebabs from the prepared mixture and transfer them to the greased cooking basket. 5. Put on the Smart Lid on top of the Ninja Foodi Steam Fryer. 6. Move the Lid Slider to the "Air Fry/Stovetop". 7. Cook on "Air Fry" Mode at 365°F/185°C for about 12 minutes. 8. In the meantime, mix all the sauce recipe ingredients and place in the refrigerator until ready to serve. 9. Serve the pork kebabs with the yogurt sauce on the side. Enjoy!
Per Serving: Calories 391; Fat 12.3 g; Sodium 2031 mg; Carbs 23.9g; Fiber 3.7g; Sugar 13.9g; Protein 46.2g

Basil Beef Steak

Prep Time: 10 minutes. | Cook Time: 40 minutes. | Serves: 4

3-pounds beef steak
2 tablespoons coconut oil, melted
1 tablespoon dried basil
½ teaspoon salt

1. Place the Cook & Crisp Basket in your Ninja Foodi Pressure Cooker Steam Fryer. 2. Rub the beef steak with dried basil and salt. 3. Then put the steak in your Ninja Foodi Pressure Cooker Steam Fryer and sprinkle with coconut oil. 4. Put on the Smart Lid on top of the Ninja Foodi Steam Fryer. 5. Move the Lid Slider to the "Air Fry/Stovetop". 6. Cook the beef at 365°F/185°C on "Air Fry" Mode for about 20 minutes per side.
Per Serving: Calories 206; Fat 6.4 g; Sodium 911 mg; Carbs 28.9g; Fiber 3.6g; Sugar 20.4g; Protein 11g

Beef Provolone Casserole

Prep Time: 10 minutes. | Cook Time: 40 minutes. | Serves: 4

2 ounces Provolone cheese, grated
1 teaspoon coconut oil, softened
1 teaspoon dried cilantro
2-pounds beef
1 jalapeno pepper, sliced
1 teaspoon chili powder
¼ cup beef broth

1. Place the Cook & Crisp Basket in your Ninja Foodi Pressure Cooker Steam Fryer. 2. Grease the Ninja Foodi Cook & Crisp Basket with coconut oil. 3. Then mix beef with dried cilantro, jalapeno pepper, and chili powder. 4. Put the mixture in your Ninja Foodi Cook & Crisp Basket. 5. Add beef broth and Provolone cheese. 6. Put on the Smart Lid on top of the Ninja Foodi Steam Fryer. 7. Move the Lid Slider to the "Air Fry/Stovetop". 8. Cook the casserole at 360°F/180°C on "Air Fry" Mode for about 40 minutes.
Per Serving: Calories 546; Fat 40 g; Sodium 231 mg; Carbs 3.1g; Fiber 0.2g; Sugar 0.9g; Protein 40.4g

Easy Burgers

Prep Time: 15 minutes. | Cook Time: 15 minutes. | Serves: 4

2-pounds beef
1 teaspoon garlic powder
1 egg, beaten
1 teaspoon black pepper

1. Place the Cook & Crisp Basket in your Ninja Foodi Pressure Cooker Steam Fryer. 2. Mix beef with garlic powder, black pepper, and egg. 3. Make the burgers from the mixture and put them in your Ninja Foodi Pressure Cooker Steam Fryer in one layer. 4. Put on the Smart Lid on top of the Ninja Foodi Steam Fryer. 5. Move the Lid Slider to the "Air Fry/Stovetop". 6. Cook the burgers at 385°F/195°C on "Air Fry" Mode for about 15 minutes.
Per Serving: Calories 467; Fat 19.8 g; Sodium 958 mg; Carbs 2.6g; Fiber 0.1g; Sugar 2.2g; Protein 65.7g

Pork with Vegetables

Prep Time: 10 minutes. | Cook Time: 50 minutes. | Serves: 6

1½ pounds pork belly
2 bell peppers, sliced
2 cloves garlic, minced
4 green onions, quartered, white and green parts
¼ cup cooking wine
Kosher salt and black pepper, to taste
1 teaspoon cayenne pepper
1 tablespoon coriander
1 teaspoon celery seeds

1. Place the Cook & Crisp Basket in your Ninja Foodi Pressure Cooker Steam Fryer. 2. Add the pork belly to boiling water to blanch for approximately 15 minutes. Then, cut it into chunks. 3. Arrange the pork chunks, bell peppers, garlic, and green onions in your Ninja Foodi Cook & Crisp Basket. Drizzle everything with cooking wine of your choice. 4. Sprinkle with salt, black pepper, cayenne pepper, fresh coriander, and celery seeds. Toss to coat well. 5. Put on the Smart Lid on top of the Ninja Foodi Steam Fryer. 6. Move the Lid Slider to the "Air Fry/Stovetop". 7. Roast in the preheated Air Fryer at 330°F/165°C on "Air Fry" Mode for about 30 minutes. 8. Serve on individual serving plates. Bon appétit!
Per Serving: Calories 499; Fat 23.8 g; Sodium 197 mg; Carbs 0.9g; Fiber 0.3g; Sugar 0.1g; Protein 65.6g

Beef Artichoke Sauté

Prep Time: 10 minutes. | Cook Time: 65 minutes. | Serves: 4

1 and ½ pounds beef stew meat, cubed
6-ounce artichoke hearts, chopped
1 cup beef broth
1 teaspoon Italian seasonings
1 garlic clove, peeled
1 teaspoon nutmeg
1 teaspoon coconut oil

1. Place the Cook & Crisp Basket in your Ninja Foodi Pressure Cooker Steam Fryer. 2. Put all the recipe ingredients in the Ninja Foodi Cook & Crisp Basket and gently mix. 3. Put on the Smart Lid on top of the Ninja Foodi Steam Fryer. 4. Move the Lid Slider to the "Air Fry/Stovetop". 5. Cook on "Air Fry" Mode at 350°F/175°C for about 65 minutes.
Per Serving: Calories 322; Fat 14 g; Sodium 679 mg; Carbs 1.1g; Fiber 0.2g; Sugar 0.7g; Protein 45.5g

Vinegar Glazed Beef Shank

Prep Time: 15 minutes. | Cook Time: 40 minutes. | Serves: 6

3-pound beef shank
¼ cup apple cider vinegar
1 tablespoon avocado oil
1 teaspoon white pepper
½ teaspoon salt

1. Place the Cook & Crisp Basket in your Ninja Foodi Pressure Cooker Steam Fryer. 2. Mix avocado oil with apple cider vinegar, white pepper, and salt. 3. Then sprinkle the beef shank with apple cider vinegar mixture. 4. Put the beef shank in the Ninja Foodi Cook & Crisp Basket. 5. Put on the Smart Lid on top of the Ninja Foodi Steam Fryer. 6. Move the Lid Slider to the "Air Fry/Stovetop". 7. Cook it at 365°F/185°C on "Air Fry" Mode for about 40 minutes.
Per Serving: Calories 556; Fat 37.8 g; Sodium 1792 mg; Carbs 16.5g; Fiber 0.5g; Sugar 0g; Protein 29.8g

Chives Mixed Beef

Prep Time: 10 minutes. | Cook Time: 35 minutes. | Serves: 4

2 ounces chives, chopped
2-pound beef sirloin, chopped
3 tablespoons apple cider vinegar
1 tablespoon avocado oil
½ teaspoon minced garlic
1 teaspoon dried dill

1. Place the Cook & Crisp Basket in your Ninja Foodi Pressure Cooker Steam Fryer. 2. Sprinkle the beef sirloin in your Ninja Foodi Pressure Cooker Steam Fryer. 3. Add apple cider vinegar, avocado oil, minced garlic, dried dill, and chives. 4. Put on the Smart Lid on top of the Ninja Foodi Steam Fryer. 5. Move the Lid Slider to the "Air Fry/Stovetop". 6. Cook the meal at 365°F/185°C on "Air Fry" Mode for about 35 minutes. Shake the beef every 10 minutes.
Per Serving: Calories 556; Fat 37.8 g; Sodium 1792 mg; Carbs 16.5g; Fiber 0.5g; Sugar 0g; Protein 29.8g

Thymed Beef

Prep Time: 15 minutes. | Cook Time: 40 minutes. | Serves: 4

1-pound beef sirloin
2 tablespoons avocado oil
1 teaspoon dried thyme
1 teaspoon coconut aminos

1. Place the Cook & Crisp Basket in your Ninja Foodi Pressure Cooker Steam Fryer. 2. Mix beef sirloin with avocado oil, dried thyme, and coconut aminos. 3. Marinate the beef sirloin for about 10 minutes. 4. Then put the meat in the Ninja Foodi Cook & Crisp Basket. 5. Put on the Smart Lid on top of the Ninja Foodi Steam Fryer. 6. Move the Lid Slider to the "Air Fry/Stovetop". 7. Cook on "Air Fry" Mode for about 40 minutes at 360°F/180°C.
Per Serving: Calories 667; Fat 18.4 g; Sodium 1526 mg; Carbs 22.5g; Fiber 3.2g; Sugar 2.9g; Protein 101.2g

Spicy Pork Gratin

Prep Time: 10 minutes. | Cook Time: 25 minutes. | Serves: 4

2 tablespoons olive oil
2 pounds pork tenderloin, cut into serving-size pieces
1 teaspoon coarse salt
½ teaspoon pepper
¼ teaspoon chili powder
1 teaspoon dried marjoram
1 tablespoon mustard
1 cup Ricotta cheese
1 ½ cups chicken broth

1. Place the Cook & Crisp Basket in your Ninja Foodi Pressure Cooker Steam Fryer and place a reversible rack in it. 2. Preheat the olive oil in a suitable pan over medium-high heat. Once hot, cook the pork for about 6 to 7 minutes, flipping it to ensure even cooking. 3. Arrange the pork in a lightly greased Cook & Crisp Basket. Season with salt, black pepper, chili powder, and marjoram. 4. In a mixing dish, mix the mustard, cheese, and chicken broth. Pour the prepared mixture over the pork chops on the Cook & Crisp Basket. 5. Put on the Smart Lid on top of the Ninja Foodi Steam Fryer. 6. Move the Lid Slider to the "Air Fry/Stovetop". 7. Cook on "Air Fry" Mode at 350°F/175°C for another 15 minutes until bubbly and heated through. Bon appétit!
Per Serving: Calories 475; Fat 24.8 g; Sodium 508 mg; Carbs 4.1g; Fiber 0.9g; Sugar 1.9g; Protein 58g

Crusted Pork Cutlets

Prep Time: 10 minutes. | Cook Time: 1 hour 20 minutes. | Serves: 2

1 cup water	1 teaspoon shallot powder
1 cup red wine	½ teaspoon porcini powder
1 tablespoon salt	Salt and black pepper, to taste
2 pork cutlets	1 egg
¼ cup almond meal	¼ cup yogurt
¼ cup flaxseed meal	1 teaspoon brown mustard
½ teaspoon baking powder	⅓ cup parmesan cheese, grated

1. Place the Cook & Crisp Basket in your Ninja Foodi Pressure Cooker Steam Fryer. 2. In a large ceramic dish, mix the water, wine and salt. Add the pork cutlets and put for about 1 hour in the refrigerator. 3. In any shallow bowl, mix the almond meal, flaxseed meal, baking powder, shallot powder, porcini powder, salt, and pepper. In another bowl, whisk the eggs with yogurt and mustard. 4. In a third bowl, place the grated parmesan cheese. 5. Dip the pork cutlets in seasoned flour mixture and toss evenly; then, in the egg mixture. Finally, roll them over the grated parmesan cheese. 6. Spritz the bottom of the cooking basket with cooking oil. Add the breaded pork cutlets. 7. Put on the Smart Lid on top of the Ninja Foodi Steam Fryer. 8. Move the Lid Slider to the "Air Fry/Stovetop". 9. Cook on "Air Fry" Mode at 395°F/200°C and for about 10 minutes. 10. Flip. Cook for about 5 minutes more on the other side. Serve warm.
Per Serving: Calories 292; Fat 9.4 g; Sodium 349 mg; Carbs 2.5g; Fiber 0.4g; Sugar 1.6g; Protein 46.6g

Marinated Beef Loin

Prep Time: 5 minutes. | Cook Time: 75 minutes. | Serves: 4

¼ cup apple cider vinegar	1 garlic clove, crushed
1 teaspoon dried rosemary	1 tablespoon olive oil
½ teaspoon coriander	2-pounds beef loin, chopped

1. Place the Cook & Crisp Basket in your Ninja Foodi Pressure Cooker Steam Fryer. 2. Mix all the recipe ingredients in your Ninja Foodi Pressure Cooker Steam Fryer. 3. Put on the Smart Lid on top of the Ninja Foodi Steam Fryer. 4. Move the Lid Slider to the "Air Fry/Stovetop". 5. Cook the meal at 355°F/180°C on "Air Fry" Mode for about 75 minutes.
Per Serving: Calories 263; Fat 9.1 g; Sodium 110 mg; Carbs 8.3g; Fiber 2.6g; Sugar 3.6g; Protein 37.5g

Fried Lamb Steak

Prep Time: 10 minutes. | Cook Time: 12 minutes. | Serves: 2

14-ounce lamb steak	1 teaspoon garlic powder
1 teaspoon coriander	1 tablespoon olive oil

1. Place the Cook & Crisp Basket in your Ninja Foodi Pressure Cooker Steam Fryer. 2. Rub the lamb steak with coriander, garlic powder, and olive oil. 3. Put the lamb steaks in your Ninja Foodi Pressure Cooker Steam Fryer. 4. Put on the Smart Lid on top of the Ninja Foodi Steam Fryer. 5. Move the Lid Slider to the "Air Fry/Stovetop". 6. Cook on "Air Fry" Mode for about 6 minutes per side at 385°F/195°C.
Per Serving: Calories 199; Fat 7.8 g; Sodium 402 mg; Carbs 5.9g; Fiber 1.7g; Sugar 1.9g; Protein 25.9g

Beef Marinara Wraps

Prep Time: 10 minutes. | Cook Time: 4 minutes. | Serves: 5

5 wonton wraps	1 egg, beaten
1-pound beef loin, boiled, shredded	1 teaspoon olive oil
2 tablespoons marinara sauce	

1. Place the Cook & Crisp Basket in your Ninja Foodi Pressure Cooker Steam Fryer. 2. Mix shredded beef loin with marinara sauce and egg. 3. Then fill the wonton wraps with beef mixture and wrap them. 4. Brush every wrap with olive oil. 5. Put on the Smart Lid on top of the Ninja Foodi Steam Fryer. 6. Move the Lid Slider to the "Air Fry/Stovetop". 7. Cook in your Ninja Foodi Pressure Cooker Steam Fryer at 400°F/200°C on "Air Fry" Mode for about 4 minutes.
Per Serving: Calories 669; Fat 43.4 g; Sodium 156 mg; Carbs 36.2g; Fiber 14.9g; Sugar 4.3g; Protein 38.4g

Fried Lamb Chops

Prep Time: 10 minutes. | Cook Time: 16 minutes. | Serves: 4

8 lamb chops	1 teaspoon salt
1 teaspoon turmeric	3 tablespoons apple cider vinegar
1 tablespoon avocado oil	

1. Place the Cook & Crisp Basket in your Ninja Foodi Pressure Cooker Steam Fryer. 2. Sprinkle the lamb chops with turmeric, avocado oil, apple cider vinegar, and salt. 3. Put the lamb chops in your Ninja Foodi Pressure Cooker Steam Fryer. 4. Put on the Smart Lid on top of the Ninja Foodi Steam Fryer. 5. Move the Lid Slider to the "Air Fry/Stovetop". 6. Cook on "Air Fry" Mode for about 8 minutes per side at 375°F/190°C.
Per Serving: Calories 206; Fat 10.3 g; Sodium 171mg; Carbs 5.4g; Fiber 0.7g; Sugar 1g; Protein 26g

Lemony Lamb Chops

Prep Time: 15 minutes. | Cook Time: 12 minutes. | Serves: 4

16-ounce lamb chops	2 tablespoons avocado oil
1 teaspoon nutmeg	¼ teaspoon salt
2 tablespoons lemon juice	

1. Place the Cook & Crisp Basket in your Ninja Foodi Pressure Cooker Steam Fryer. 2. Rub the lamb chops with nutmeg, lemon juice, avocado oil, and salt. 3. Put the lamb chops in your Ninja Foodi Pressure Cooker Steam Fryer. 4. Put on the Smart Lid on top of the Ninja Foodi Steam Fryer. 5. Move the Lid Slider to the "Air Fry/Stovetop". 6. Cook on "Air Fry" Mode at 385°F/195°C for about 6 minutes per side.
Per Serving: Calories 407; Fat 11.5 g; Sodium 412 mg; Carbs 31.9g; Fiber 1.3g; Sugar 25.9g; Protein 42.2g

Lamb Skewers

Prep Time: 10 minutes. | Cook Time: 20 minutes. | Serves: 4

2-pounds lamb meat, cubed	1 teaspoon chili flakes
2 tablespoons avocado oil	1 teaspoon tomato paste
1 teaspoon smoked paprika	

1. Place the Cook & Crisp Basket in your Ninja Foodi Pressure Cooker Steam Fryer. 2. Mix lamb meat with avocado oil, smoked paprika, chili flakes, and tomato paste. 3. Then sting the meat into skewers and put in your Ninja Foodi Pressure Cooker Steam Fryer. 4. Put on the Smart Lid on top of the Ninja Foodi Steam Fryer. 5. Move the Lid Slider to the "Air Fry/Stovetop". Cook the lamb skewers at 385°F/195°C on "Air Fry" Mode for about 20 minutes.
Per Serving: Calories 562; Fat 31.2 g; Sodium 198 mg; Carbs 1.9g; Fiber 1.1g; Sugar 0.9g; Protein 66g

Air Fried Rack Of Lamb

Prep Time: 10 minutes. | Cook Time: 30 minutes. | Serves: 5

18-ounce rack of lamb	1 jalapeno pepper, minced
1 tablespoon fennel seeds	2 tablespoons coconut aminos
2 tablespoons olive oil	

1. Place the Cook & Crisp Basket in your Ninja Foodi Pressure Cooker Steam Fryer. 2. In the shallow bowl, mix fennel seeds with olive oil, minced jalapeno pepper, and coconut aminos. 3. Then rub the rack of lamb with jalapeno pepper mixture and put it in your Ninja Foodi Cook & Crisp Basket. 4. Put on the Smart Lid on top of the Ninja Foodi Steam Fryer. 5. Move the Lid Slider to the "Air Fry/Stovetop". 6. Cook the meal at 365°F/185°C on "Air Fry" Mode for about 30 minutes.
Per Serving: Calories 291; Fat 15.2 g; Sodium 544 mg; Carbs 13g; Fiber 0.9g; Sugar 10.9g; Protein 26.5g

Spicy Lamb Steak

Prep Time: 20 minutes. | Cook Time: 35 minutes. | Serves: 4

2-pounds lamb sirloin	1 teaspoon minced ginger
1 teaspoon chili powder	2 tablespoons avocado oil
1 teaspoon cayenne pepper	2 tablespoons coconut cream

1. Place the Cook & Crisp Basket in your Ninja Foodi Pressure Cooker Steam Fryer. 2. Sprinkle the lamb sirloin with chili powder, cayenne pepper, minced ginger, avocado oil, and coconut cream. 3. Leave the lamb sirloin to marinate for about 15 minutes. 4. Then transfer it in your Ninja Foodi Pressure Cooker Steam Fryer. 5. Put on the Smart Lid on top of the Ninja Foodi Steam Fryer. 6. Move the Lid Slider to the "Air Fry/Stovetop". 7. Cook on "Air Fry" Mode at 375°F/190°C for about 35 minutes.

Per Serving: Calories 722; Fat 40.8 g; Sodium 1229 mg; Carbs 7.2g; Fiber 0.9g; Sugar 5.9g; Protein 79.2g

Lamb Avocado Bowl

Prep Time: 15 minutes. | Cook Time: 35 minutes. | Serves: 4

1-pound lamb sirloin, chopped	1 tablespoon olive oil
½ teaspoon turmeric	4 tablespoons water
½ teaspoon paprika	1 avocado, pitted, chopped
½ teaspoon chili flakes	4 tablespoons heavy cream

1. Place the Cook & Crisp Basket in your Ninja Foodi Pressure Cooker Steam Fryer. 2. Mix lamb sirloin with turmeric, paprika, chili flakes, olive oil, and water. 3. Put the meat in your Ninja Foodi Pressure Cooker Steam Fryer. 4. Put on the Smart Lid on top of the Ninja Foodi Steam Fryer. 5. Move the Lid Slider to the "Air Fry/Stovetop". 6. Cook it for about 35 minutes at 365°F/185°C. 7. Then put the meat in the bowl, add avocado and top the meal with heavy cream.

Per Serving: Calories 186; Fat 5.8 g; Sodium 113 mg; Carbs 8.1g; Fiber 1.9g; Sugar 4.3g; Protein 25.2g

Fried Pork Loin Chops

Prep Time: 10 minutes. | Cook Time: 22 minutes. | Serves: 6)

2 tablespoons vermouth	⅓ teaspoon black pepper
6 center-cut loin pork chops	2 tablespoons whole grain mustard
½ tablespoon fresh basil, minced	1 teaspoon fine kosher salt

1. Place the Cook & Crisp Basket in your Ninja Foodi Pressure Cooker Steam Fryer. 2. Toss pork chops with other ingredients until they are well coated on both sides. 3. Put on the Smart Lid on top of the Ninja Foodi Steam Fryer. 4. Move the Lid Slider to the "Air Fry/Stovetop". 5. Cook on "Air Fry" Mode your chops for about 18 minutes at 400°F/200°C, turning once or twice. 6. Mound your favorite salad on a serving plate; top with pork chops and enjoy.

Per Serving: Calories 236; Fat 13.2 g; Sodium 502 mg; Carbs 6.3g; Fiber 0.9g; Sugar 4.4g; Protein 23.2g

Pork Sausage With Cauliflower

Prep Time: 10 minutes. | Cook Time: 30 minutes. | Serves: 6

1-pound cauliflower, chopped	1 teaspoon cumin powder
½ teaspoon tarragon	½ teaspoon salt
⅓ cup Colby cheese	3 beaten eggs
½ teaspoon black pepper	6 pork sausages, chopped
½ onion, peeled and sliced	

1. Place the Cook & Crisp Basket in your Ninja Foodi Pressure Cooker Steam Fryer and place a reversible rack in it. 2. Boil the cauliflower until tender. Then, purée the cauliflower in your blender. Transfer to a mixing dish along with the other ingredients. 3. Divide the prepared mixture among six lightly greased ramekins; now, place ramekins in your Ninja Foodi Pressure Cooker Steam Fryer. 4. Put on the Smart Lid on top of the Ninja Foodi Steam Fryer. 5. Move the Lid Slider to the "Air Fry/Stovetop". 6. Cook on "Air Fry" Mode for about 27 minutes at 365°F/185°C. Eat warm.

Per Serving: Calories 433; Fat 8.7 g; Sodium 364 mg; Carbs 4.9g; Fiber 1.1g; Sugar 1.9g; Protein 33.2g

Bacon Hot Dogs

Prep Time: 10 minutes. | Cook Time: 25 minutes. | Serves: 5

10 thin slices of bacon	¼ cup mayo
5 pork hot dogs, halved	4 tablespoons ketchup, low-carb
1 teaspoon cayenne pepper	1 teaspoon rice vinegar
Sauce:	1 teaspoon chili powder

1. Place the Cook & Crisp Basket in your Ninja Foodi Pressure Cooker Steam Fryer. 2. Lay the slices of bacon on your working surface. Place a hot dog on one end of each slice; sprinkle with cayenne pepper and roll them over. 3. Put on the Smart Lid on top of the Ninja Foodi Steam Fryer. 4. Move the Lid Slider to the "Air Fry/Stovetop". 5. Cook in the preheated Ninja Foody Air Fryer at 390°F/200°C on "Air Fry" Mode for about 10 to 12 minutes. 6. Whisk all the recipe ingredients for the sauce in a mixing bowl and store in your refrigerator, covered, until ready to serve. 7. Serve bacon-wrapped hot dogs with the sauce on the side. Enjoy!

Per Serving: Calories 237; Fat 12.8 g; Sodium 162 mg; Carbs 3.9g; Fiber 0.9g; Sugar 1.9g; Protein 31.7g

Lamb Meatballs

Prep Time: 15 minutes. | Cook Time: 35 minutes. | Serves: 4

2 pecans, grinded	1 teaspoon olive oil
1-ounce Provolone, grated	½ teaspoon white pepper
2-pound lamb, minced	

1. Place the Cook & Crisp Basket in your Ninja Foodi Pressure Cooker Steam Fryer. 2. Mix minced lamb with white pepper, grinded pecans, and Provolone. 3. Make the meatballs and put them in your Ninja Foodi Cook & Crisp Basket. 4. Sprinkle the meatballs with olive oil. 5. Put on the Smart Lid on top of the Ninja Foodi Steam Fryer. 6. Move the Lid Slider to the "Air Fry/Stovetop". 7. Cook on "Air Fry" Mode at 350°F/175°C for about 35 minutes.

Per Serving: Calories 286; Fat 9.8 g; Sodium 270 mg; Carbs 11.9g; Fiber 0.9g; Sugar 1.2g; Protein 36.2g

Parmesan Cheeseburger Meatballs

Prep Time: 10 minutes. | Cook Time: 10 minutes. | Serves: 3

1-pound pork	chopped
1 tablespoon coconut aminos	½ cup pork rinds
1 teaspoon garlic, minced	½ cup parmesan cheese, preferably
2 tablespoons spring onions,	freshly grated

1. Place the Cook & Crisp Basket in your Ninja Foodi Pressure Cooker Steam Fryer. 2. Mix the pork, coconut aminos, garlic, and spring onions in a mixing dish. Mix until everything is well incorporated. 3. Form the mixture into small meatballs. 4. In any shallow bowl, mix the pork rinds and grated parmesan cheese. Roll the meatballs over the parmesan mixture. 5. Put on the Smart Lid on top of the Ninja Foodi Steam Fryer. 6. Move the Lid Slider to the "Air Fry/Stovetop". 7. Cook on "Air Fry" Mode at 380°F/195°C for about 3 minutes; shake the basket. Cook an additional 4 minutes until meatballs are browned on all sides. Bon appétit!

Per Serving: Calories 291; Fat 14.8 g; Sodium 1363 mg; Carbs 5.2g; Fiber 0.5g; Sugar 4.9g; Protein 33.6g

Beef Brisket with BBQ Sauce

Prep Time: 10 minutes. | Cook Time: 1 hour 10 minutes. | Serves: 4

1 ½ pounds beef brisket	¼ cup barbecue sauce
	2 tablespoons soy sauce

1. Place the Cook & Crisp Basket in your Pressure Cooker Steam Fryer. 2. Toss the beef with the remaining ingredients; place the beef in the Cook & Crisp Basket. 3. Put on the Smart Lid on top of the Ninja Foodi Steam Fryer. 4. Move the Lid Slider to the "Air Fry/Stovetop". Select the "Air Fry" mode for cooking. 5. Cook the beef at 390°F/200°C for around 15 minutes, turn the beef over and turn the temperature to 360°F/180°C. 6. Continue to cook the beef for around 55 minutes more. Serve.

Per serving: Calories 319; Fat: 15.6g; Sodium 99mg; Carbs: 4.8g; Fiber: 0.7g; Sugars 2.9g; Protein 38.5g

Worcester Pork Meatballs

Prep Time: 10 minutes. | Cook Time: 20 minutes. | Serves: 4

1-pound pork
1 cup scallions, chopped
2 cloves garlic, minced
1 ½ tablespoons Worcester sauce

1 tablespoon oyster sauce
1 teaspoon turmeric powder
½ teaspoon ginger root
1 small sliced red chili, for garnish

1. Place the Cook & Crisp Basket in your Ninja Foodi Pressure Cooker Steam Fryer. 2. Mix all of the above ingredients, apart from the red chili. Knead with your hands to ensure an even mixture. 3. Roll into equal balls and transfer them to your Ninja Foodi Pressure Cooker Steam Fryer cooking basket. 4. Put on the Smart Lid on top of the Ninja Foodi Steam Fryer. 5. Move the Lid Slider to the "Air Fry/Stovetop". 6. Cook on "Air Fry" Mode at 350°F/175°C for 15 minutes. Sprinkle with sliced red chili; serve immediately with your favorite sauce for dipping. Enjoy!
Per Serving: Calories 457; Fat 28.8 g; Sodium 712 mg; Carbs 7.8g; Fiber 2.9g; Sugar 3.9g; Protein 42g

Hoisin Pork Steak

Prep Time: 10 minutes. | Cook Time: 30 minutes. | Serves: 4

2 tablespoons dry white wine
⅓ cup hoisin sauce
2 teaspoons smoked cayenne pepper
3 garlic cloves, pressed

½-pound pork loin steak, cut into strips
3 teaspoons fresh lime juice
Salt and black pepper, to taste

1. Place the Cook & Crisp Basket in your Ninja Foodi Pressure Cooker Steam Fryer. 2. Toss the pork with other ingredients; let it marinate at least 20 minutes in a fridge. 3. Put on the Smart Lid on top of the Ninja Foodi Steam Fryer. 4. Move the Lid Slider to the "Air Fry/Stovetop". 5. Then, cook on "Air Fry" Mode at 350°F/175°C for 5 minutes. Bon appétit!
Per Serving: Calories 642; Fat 34.3 g; Sodium 551 mg; Carbs 12.9g; Fiber 2.9g; Sugar 9.1g; Protein 70.8g

Pork Kebabs With Pepper

Prep Time: 10 minutes. | Cook Time: 22 minutes. | Serves: 3

2 tablespoons tomato puree
½ fresh serrano, minced
⅓ teaspoon paprika
1-pound pork,

½ cup green onions, chopped
3 cloves garlic, peeled and minced
1 teaspoon black pepper
1 teaspoon salt

1. Place the Cook & Crisp Basket in your Ninja Foodi Pressure Cooker Steam Fryer. 2. Mix all the recipe ingredients in a mixing dish. Then, form your mixture into sausage shapes. 3. Put on the Smart Lid on top of the Ninja Foodi Steam Fryer. 4. Move the Lid Slider to the "Air Fry/Stovetop". 5. Cook on "Air Fry" Mode for about 18 minutes at 355°F/180°C. Serve warm. Bon appétit!
Per Serving: Calories 301; Fat 11.2g; Sodium 413 mg; Carbs 4.7g; Fiber 0.3g; Sugar 3.5g; Protein 42.9g

Pork Tenderloin with Herbs

Prep Time: 10 minutes. | Cook Time: 17 minutes. | Serves: 4

1-pound pork tenderloin
4-5 garlic cloves, peeled and halved
1 teaspoon kosher salt
⅓ teaspoon black pepper

1 teaspoon dried basil
½ teaspoon dried oregano
½ teaspoon dried rosemary
½ teaspoon dried marjoram
2 tablespoons cooking wine

1. Place the Cook & Crisp Basket in your Ninja Foodi Pressure Cooker Steam Fryer. 2. Rub the pork with garlic halves; add the seasoning and drizzle with the cooking wine. Then, cut slits completely through pork tenderloin. Tuck the remaining garlic into the slits. 3. Wrap the pork tenderloin with foil; let it marinate overnight. 4. Put on the Smart Lid on top of the Ninja Foodi Steam Fryer. 5. Move the Lid Slider to the "Air Fry/Stovetop". 6. Roast at 360°F/180°C on "Air Fry" Mode for about 15 to 17 minutes. Serve warm with roasted potatoes. Bon appétit!
Per Serving: Calories 325; Fat 27 g; Sodium 58 mg; Carbs 2.2g;

Fiber 0.2g; Sugar 0.2g; Protein 18.3g

Pork Steak With Herbs

Prep Time: 10 minutes. | Cook Time: 20 minutes. | Serves: 2

1-pound porterhouse steak, cut meat from bones in 2 pieces
½ teaspoon black pepper
1 teaspoon cayenne pepper
½ teaspoon salt

1 teaspoon garlic powder
½ teaspoon dried thyme
½ teaspoon dried marjoram
1 teaspoon Dijon mustard
1 tablespoon butter, melted

1. Place the Cook & Crisp Basket in your Ninja Foodi Pressure Cooker Steam Fryer. 2. Sprinkle the porterhouse steak with all the seasonings. 3. Spread the mustard and butter evenly over the meat. 4. Put on the Smart Lid on top of the Ninja Foodi Steam Fryer. 5. Move the Lid Slider to the "Air Fry/Stovetop". 6. Cook in the Ninja Food Air Fryer at 390°F/200°C on "Air Fry" Mode for about 12 to 14 minutes. 7. Taste for doneness with a meat thermometer and serve immediately.
Per Serving: Calories 324; Fat 17.8 g; Sodium 363 mg; Carbs 8.9g; Fiber 0.5g; Sugar 1.9g; Protein 36.6g

German Roulade

Prep Time: 10 minutes. | Cook Time: 18 minutes. | Serves: 4

For the Sauce
¼ cup chopped dill pickles
½ cup sour cream
1 tablespoon tomato paste
1 teaspoon chopped parsley
For the Meat
¼ cup Dijon mustard
¼ cup chopped parsley
1-pound flank steak

2 cups diced onion
3 tablespoons avocado oil
Black pepper and salt, to taste

1 teaspoon black pepper
4 bacon slices

1. Place the Cook & Crisp Basket in your Pressure Cooker Steam Fryer. Brush the basket with oil. 2. Using a suitable mixing bowl, add in the pepper, salt, diced onions and incorporate together. 3. Put on the Smart Lid on top of the Ninja Foodi Steam Fryer. 4. Move the Lid Slider to the "Air Fry/Stovetop". Select the "Air Fry" mode for cooking. 5. Air fry the seasoned onions for around 6 minutes at 400°F/200°C. 6. Once fried, mix half of the onion with the chopped parsley, pickles, tomato paste, sour cream and add in a tablespoon of water you desire to thin out the sauce. 7. Cover the meat with the mustard then add on the slices of bacon, chopped parsley remaining fried onion and season with the pepper. 8. Tightly roll up the steak, holding it firm at the end then transfer into the Cook & Crisp Basket. 9. Air fry the meat wrap for around 10 minutes at 400°F/200°C, flipping the wrap halfway through. 10. Serve and enjoy with the sauce mixture.
Per serving: Calories: 254; Fat: 10.3g; Sodium 514mg; Carbs: 32.8g; Fiber: 3.3g; Sugars 5g; Protein 7.9g

Herbed Pork Casserole

Prep Time: 10 minutes. | Cook Time: 25 minutes. | Serves: 4

1-pound lean pork
1 teaspoon dried basil
1 teaspoon dried rosemary
½-pound beef
¼ cup tomato puree
½ teaspoon dried oregano

Salt and black pepper, to taste
1 teaspoon smoked paprika
2 eggs
1 cup Cottage cheese, crumbled
½ cup Cotija cheese, shredded

1. Place the Cook & Crisp Basket in your Ninja Foodi Pressure Cooker Steam Fryer. 2. Lightly grease any casserole dish with a nonstick cooking oil. 3. Add the meat to the bottom of your casserole dish. 4. Add the tomato puree. Sprinkle with paprika, oregano, basil, and rosemary. 5. In a mixing bowl, whisk the egg with cheese. Place on top of the meat mixture. Place a piece of foil on top. 6. Put on the Smart Lid on top of the Ninja Foodi Steam Fryer. 7. Move the Lid Slider to the "Air Fry/Stovetop". 8. Cook on "Air Fry" Mode at 350°F/175°C for about 10 minutes; remove the foil and cook an additional 6 minutes. Bon appétit!
Per Serving: Calories 467; Fat 20.6 g; Sodium 424 mg; Carbs 19.4g; Fiber 1.1g; Sugar 17.6g; Protein 50.4g

Mexican Meatloaf

Prep Time: 10 minutes. | Cook Time: 25 minutes. | Serves: 4

1 ½ pounds chuck	1 teaspoon garlic, minced
½ onion, chopped	Sea salt and black pepper, to taste
1 teaspoon habanero pepper, minced	2 tablespoons olive oil
¼ cup tortilla chips, crushed	1 egg, whisked

1. Place the Cook & Crisp Basket in your Pressure Cooker Steam Fryer. 2. Mix all the recipe ingredients until everything is well mixed. 3. Brush the Cook & Crisp Basket with oil and scrape the beef mixture into the Cook & Crisp Basket. 4. Put on the Smart Lid on top of the Ninja Foodi Steam Fryer. 5. Move the Lid Slider to the "Air Fry/Stovetop". Select the "Air Fry" mode for cooking. 6. Cook your meatloaf at 390°F/200°C for around 25 minutes. Serve.
Per serving: Calories: 368; Fat:22.4g; Carbs: 5.4g; Fiber: 0.7g; Sugars: 2g; Proteins: 36.5g

BBQ Cheeseburgers

Prep Time: 10 minutes. | Cook Time: 15 minutes. | Serves: 3

¾-pound chuck	Sea salt and black pepper, to taste
1 teaspoon garlic, minced	3 slices cheese
2 tablespoons BBQ sauce	3 hamburger buns

1. Place the Cook & Crisp Basket in your Pressure Cooker Steam Fryer. 2. Mix the chuck, garlic, BBQ sauce, salt, and black pepper until everything is well mixed. Form the mixture into four patties. 3. Put on the Smart Lid on top of the Ninja Foodi Steam Fryer. 4. Move the Lid Slider to the "Air Fry/Stovetop". Select the "Air Fry" mode for cooking. 5. Cook the burgers at 380°F/195°C for about 15 minutes or until cooked through; make sure to turn them over halfway through the cooking time. 6. Top each burger with cheese. Serve your burgers on the prepared buns and enjoy!
Per serving: Calories 182; Fat: 14.1g; Sodium 18mg; Carbs: 8.9g; Fiber: 4.1g; Sugars 4g; Protein 7.2g

Garlic London Broil

Prep Time: 10 minutes. | Cook Time: 28 minutes. | Serves: 4

1 ½ pounds London broil	1 tablespoon Dijon mustard
Salt and black pepper, to taste	1 teaspoon garlic, pressed
¼ teaspoon bay leaf	1 tablespoon fresh parsley, chopped
3 tablespoons butter, cold	

1. Place the Cook & Crisp Basket in your Pressure Cooker Steam Fryer. 2. Toss the beef with the salt and black pepper; brush the basket with oil and place the beef in it. 3. Put on the Smart Lid on top of the Ninja Foodi Steam Fryer. 4. Move the Lid Slider to the "Air Fry/Stovetop". Select the "Air Fry" mode for cooking. 5. Cook the beef at 400°F/200°C for around 28 minutes, turning over halfway through the cooking time. 6. In the meantime, mix the butter with the remaining recipe ingredients and place it in the refrigerator until well-chilled. 7. Serve warm beef with the chilled garlic butter on the side. Serve.
Per serving: Calories: 394; Fat:17.5g; Carbs: 26.5g; Fiber: 1.3g; Sugars: 6.4g; Proteins: 32.5g

Mexican Carnitas

Prep Time: 10 minutes. | Cook Time: 1 hour 10 minutes. | Serves: 4

1½ pounds beef brisket	1 teaspoon chili powder
2 tablespoons olive oil	4 medium-sized flour tortillas
Sea salt and black pepper, to taste	

1. Place the Cook & Crisp Basket in your Pressure Cooker Steam Fryer. 2. Toss the beef brisket with the olive oil, salt, black pepper, and chili powder; now, place the beef brisket in the Cook & Crisp Basket. 3. Put on the Smart Lid on top of the Ninja Foodi Steam Fryer. 4. Move the Lid Slider to the "Air Fry/Stovetop". Select the "Air Fry" mode for cooking. 5. Cook the beef brisket at 390°F/200°C for around 15 minutes, turn the beef over and reduce the temperature to 360°F/180°C. 6. Continue to cook the beef brisket for approximately

55 minutes or until cooked through. 7. Shred the beef with two forks and serve with tortillas and toppings of choice. Serve.
Per serving: Calories: 542; Fat:34.2g; Carbs: 25.6g; Fiber: 1.6g; Sugars: 2.1g Proteins: 29.1g

Herbed Filet Mignon

Prep Time: 10 minutes. | Cook Time: 14 minutes. | Serves: 4

1 ½ pounds filet mignon	1 teaspoon dried thyme
Sea salt and black pepper, to taste	1 teaspoon dried basil
2 tablespoons olive oil	2 cloves garlic, minced
1 teaspoon dried rosemary	

1. Place the Cook & Crisp Basket in your Pressure Cooker Steam Fryer. 2. Toss the beef with the remaining ingredients; place the beef in the Cook & Crisp Basket. 3. Put on the Smart Lid on top of the Ninja Foodi Steam Fryer. 4. Move the Lid Slider to the "Air Fry/Stovetop". Select the "Air Fry" mode for cooking. 5. Cook the beef at 400°F/200°C for around 14 minutes, turning it over halfway through the cooking time. 6. Enjoy!
Per serving: Calories: 385; Fat:26g; Carbs: 2.2g; Fiber: 0.3g; Sugars: 0.5g; Proteins: 36.2g

Beef Meatloaf Cups

Prep Time: 10 minutes. | Cook Time: 25 minutes. | Serves: 4

Meatloaves:

1-pound beef	2 garlic cloves, pressed
¼ cup seasoned breadcrumbs	1 egg, beaten
¼ cup parmesan cheese, grated	Sea salt and black pepper, to taste
1 small onion, minced	

Glaze:

4 tablespoons tomato sauce	1 tablespoon Dijon mustard
1 tablespoon brown sugar	

1. Place the Cook & Crisp Basket in your Pressure Cooker Steam Fryer. 2. Mix all the recipe ingredients for the meatloaves until everything is well mixed. 3. Scrape the beef mixture into oiled silicone cups and transfer them to the Cook & Crisp Basket. 4. Put on the Smart Lid on top of the Ninja Foodi Steam Fryer. 5. Move the Lid Slider to the "Air Fry/Stovetop". Select the "Air Fry" mode for cooking. 6. Cook the beef cups at 380°F/195°C for around 20 minutes. 7. In the meantime, mix the remaining recipe ingredients for the glaze. Then, spread the glaze on top of each muffin; continue to cook for another 5 minutes. 8. Serve.
Per serving: Calories: 355; Fat:18.6g; Carbs: 14.2g; Fiber: 2.3g; Sugars: 6.2g; Proteins: 27.5g

Meatball Lettuce Wraps

Prep Time: 10 minutes. | Cook Time: 10 minutes | Serves: 4

1-pound beef (85% lean)	½ teaspoon chili powder
½ cup salsa, more for serving if desired	½ teaspoon cumin
¼ cup chopped onions	1 clove garlic, minced
¼ cup diced green or red bell peppers	Avocado oil
1 large egg, beaten	For Serving (optional)
1 teaspoon fine sea salt	8 leaves Boston lettuce
	Pico De Gallo or salsa
	Lime slices

1. Place the Cook & Crisp Basket in your Pressure Cooker Steam Fryer. 2. Grease the Ninja Foodi Pressure Steam Fryer basket with avocado oil. 3. In a suitable bowl, mix all the recipe ingredients until well mixed. 4. Make the meat mixture into eight 1-inch balls. Put the meatballs in the "cook & crisp basket", leaving a little space between them. Put on the Smart Lid on top of the Ninja Foodi Steam Fryer. 5. Move the Lid Slider to the "Air Fry/Stovetop". Select the "Air Fry" mode for cooking. 6. Adjust the cooking temperature to 350°F/175°C. 7. Cook for around 10 minutes, or until cooked through and no longer pink inside and the internal temperature reaches 145°F/60°C. 8. Serve each meatball on a lettuce leaf, topped with Pico De Gallo or salsa, if desired. Serve with lime slices if desired. 9. Store the leftovers in an airtight container and then put in the fridge for around 3 days or in the freezer for up to a month. Reheat at 350°F/175°C for around 4 minutes in your Pressure Cooker Steam Fryer, or until heated through.
Per serving: Calories 499; Fat: 9.4g; Sodium 422mg; Carbs: 83.4g; Fiber: 17.2g; Sugars 1.6g; Protein 26.9g

Coulotte Roast

Prep Time: 10 minutes. | Cook Time: 55 minutes. | Serves: 5

2 pounds Coulotte roast
2 tablespoons olive oil
1 tablespoon fresh parsley, finely chopped

1 tablespoon fresh cilantro, finely chopped
2 garlic cloves, minced
Salt and black pepper, to taste

1. Place the Cook & Crisp Basket in your Pressure Cooker Steam Fryer. 2. Toss the roast beef with the remaining ingredients; place the roast beef in the Cook & Crisp Basket Put on the Smart Lid on top of the Ninja Foodi Steam Fryer. 3. Move the Lid Slider to the "Air Fry/Stovetop". Select the "Air Fry" mode for cooking. 4. Cook the roast beef at 390°F/200°C for around 55 minutes, turning over halfway through the cooking time. 5. Enjoy!

Per serving: Calories: 306; Fat:16.7g; Carbs: 1.3g; Fiber: 0.2g; Sugars: 0.4g; Proteins: 37.7g

Soy Dipped Beef Tenderloin

Prep Time: 10 minutes. | Cook Time: 20 minutes. | Serves: 4

1 ½ pounds beef tenderloin, sliced
2 tablespoons sesame oil
1 teaspoon Five-spice powder
2 garlic cloves, minced

1 teaspoon fresh ginger, peeled and grated
2 tablespoons soy sauce

1. Place the Cook & Crisp Basket in your Pressure Cooker Steam Fryer. 2. Toss the beef tenderloin with the remaining ingredients; place the beef tenderloin in the Cook & Crisp Basket Put on the Smart Lid on top of the Ninja Foodi Steam Fryer. 3. Move the Lid Slider to the "Air Fry/Stovetop". Select the "Air Fry" mode for cooking. 4. Cook the beef tenderloin at 400°F/200°C for around 20 minutes, turning it over halfway through the cooking time. 5. Enjoy!

Per serving: Calories: 326; Fat:18.7g; Carbs: 3g; Fiber: 0.3g; Sugars: 1.6g; Proteins: 35.7g

Beefy Poppers

Prep Time: 15 minutes. | Cook Time: 15 minutes. | Serves: 8 poppers

8 medium jalapeño peppers, stemmed, halved, and seeded
1 (8-ounce) package cream cheese
2 pounds beef (85% lean)
1 teaspoon fine sea salt

½ teaspoon black pepper
8 slices thin-cut bacon
Fresh cilantro leaves, for garnish
Avocado oil

1. Place the Cook & Crisp Basket in your Pressure Cooker Steam Fryer. 2. Grease the Ninja Foodi Pressure Steam Fryer basket with avocado oil. 3. Stuff each jalapeño half with a few tablespoons of cream cheese. Place the halves back again to form 8 jalapeños. 4. Season the beef with the black pepper and salt and mix with your hands to incorporate. Flatten about ¼ pound of beef in the palm of your hand and place a stuffed jalapeño in the center. Fold the beef around the jalapeño, forming an egg shape. Wrap the beef-covered jalapeño with a slice of bacon and secure it with a toothpick. 5. Place the jalapeños in the "cook & crisp basket", leaving space between them. 6. Put on the Smart Lid on top of the Ninja Foodi Steam Fryer. Move the Lid Slider to the "Air Fry/Stovetop". Select the "Air Fry" mode for cooking. 7. Adjust the cooking temperature to 400°F/200°C. 8. Cook for around 15 minutes, or until the beef is cooked through and the bacon is crispy. Garnish with cilantro before serving. 9. Store leftovers in an airtight container in the fridge for around 3 days or in the freezer for up to a month. Reheat in your Pressure Cooker Steam Fryer at350°F/175°C for around 4 minutes, or until heated through and the bacon is crispy.

Per serving: Calories: 396; Fat: 8.6g; Sodium 596mg; Carbs: 65.9g; Fiber: 3.4g; Sugars 3.8g; Protein 12.1g

Herbed Lamb Chops

Prep Time: 5 minutes| Cook Time: 5 minutes | Serves: 2

Marinade:
2 teaspoons grated lime zest
½ cup lime juice
¼ cup avocado oil

¼ cup chopped fresh mint leaves
4 cloves garlic, chopped
2 teaspoons fine sea salt

½ teaspoon black pepper
4 (1-inch-thick) lamb chops
Sprigs of fresh mint, for garnish

(optional)
Lime slices, for serving (optional)

1. Place the Cook & Crisp Basket in your Pressure Cooker Steam Fryer. 2. Make the marinade: Place all the recipe ingredients for the marinade in a food processor and puree until mostly smooth with a few small chunks. Transfer half of the marinade to a shallow dish and set the other half aside for serving. Add the lamb to the shallow dish, cover, and put in the refrigerator to marinate for at least 2 hours or overnight. 3. Grease the Ninja Foodi Pressure Steam Fryer basket with avocado oil. 4. Transfer the chops from the marinade and place them in the "cook & crisp basket". 5. Put on the Smart Lid on top of the Ninja Foodi Steam Fryer. 6. Move the Lid Slider to the "Air Fry/Stovetop". Select the "Air Fry" mode for cooking. 7. Adjust the cooking temperature to 390°F/200°C. 8. Cook for around 5 minutes, or until the internal temperature reaches 145°F/60°C for medium doneness. 9. Allow the chops to rest for around 10 minutes before serving with the rest of the marinade as a sauce. Garnish with fresh mint leaves and serve with lime slices, if desired. Best served fresh.

Per serving: Calories 128; Fat: 1.7g; Sodium 771mg; Carbs: 22.1g; Fiber: 4.5g; Sugars 3.9g; Protein 7.1g

Beef With Carrots

Prep Time: 10 minutes. | Cook Time: 55 minutes. | Serves: 5

2 pounds top sirloin roast
2 tablespoons olive oil
Sea salt and black pepper, to taste
2 carrots, sliced

1 tablespoon fresh coriander
1 tablespoon fresh thyme
1 tablespoon fresh rosemary

1. Place the Cook & Crisp Basket in your Pressure Cooker Steam Fryer. 2. Toss the beef with the olive oil, salt, and black pepper; place the beef in the Cook & Crisp Basket Put on the Smart Lid on top of the Ninja Foodi Steam Fryer. 3. Move the Lid Slider to the "Air Fry/Stovetop". Select the "Air Fry" mode for cooking. 4. Cook the beef eye round cook at 390°F/200°C for around 45 minutes, turning it over halfway through the cooking time. 5. Top the beef with the carrots and herbs. Continue to cook an additional 10 minutes. 6. Enjoy!

Per serving: Calories 349; Fat: 15.1g; Sodium 157mg; Carbs: 25.6g; Fiber: 2.6g; Sugars 22.5g; Protein 29.7g

Rump Roast

Prep Time: 10 minutes. | Cook Time: 50 minutes. | Serves: 4

1 ½ pounds rump roast
Black pepper and salt, to taste
1 teaspoon paprika

2 tablespoons olive oil
¼ cup brandy
2 tablespoons cold butter

1. Place the Cook & Crisp Basket in your Pressure Cooker Steam Fryer. 2. Brush the basket with oil. 3. Toss the rump roast with the black pepper, salt, paprika, olive oil, and brandy; place the rump roast in Cook & Crisp Basket. 4. Put on the Smart Lid on top of the Ninja Foodi Steam Fryer. 5. Move the Lid Slider to the "Air Fry/Stovetop". Select the "Air Fry" mode for cooking. 6. Cook the rump roast at 390°F/200°C for around 50 minutes, turning it over halfway through the cooking time. 7. Serve with the cold butter and enjoy!

Per serving: Calories: 390; Fat:22.4g; Carbs: 1.4g; Fiber: 0.4g; Sugars: 0.6g; Proteins: 35.2g;

Cheese Ribeye Steak

Prep Time: 10 minutes. | Cook Time: 15 minutes. | Serves: 4

1-pound ribeye steak, bone-in
Sea salt and black pepper, to taste
2 tablespoons olive oil

½ teaspoon onion powder
1 teaspoon garlic powder
1 cup blue cheese, crumbled

1. Place the Cook & Crisp Basket in your Pressure Cooker Steam Fryer. 2. Toss the ribeye steak with the salt, black pepper, olive oil, onion powder, and garlic powder; place the ribeye steak in the Cook & Crisp Basket. 3. Put on the Smart Lid on top of the Ninja Foodi Steam Fryer. 4. Move the Lid Slider to the "Air Fry/Stovetop". Select the "Air Fry" mode for cooking. 5. Cook the ribeye steak at 400°F/200°C for around 15 minutes, turning it over halfway through the cooking time. 6. Top the ribeye steak with the cheese and serve warm. Serve.

Per serving: Calories: 399; Fat:29.4g; Carbs: 4.6g; Fiber: 0.3g; Sugars: 0.7g; Proteins: 29.2g

Sriracha Glazed Ribs

Prep Time: 10 minutes. | Cook Time: 35 minutes. | Serves: 5

2 pounds Country-style ribs	1 tablespoon honey
¼ cup Sriracha sauce	1 teaspoon stone-ground mustard
2 tablespoons bourbon	

1. Toss all the recipe ingredients in a greased Cook & Crisp Basket. 2. Place the Cook & Crisp Basket in your Pressure Cooker Steam Fryer. 3. Put on the Smart Lid on top of the Ninja Foodi Steam Fryer. 4. Move the Lid Slider to the "Air Fry/Stovetop". Select the "Air Fry" mode for cooking. 5. Cook the pork ribs at 350°F/175°C for around 35 minutes, turning them over halfway through the cooking time. 6. Serve.
Per serving: Calories: 371; Fat:21.6g; Carbs: 4.4g; Fiber: 0.3g; Sugars: 3.9g; Proteins: 35.4g

Flank Steak

Prep Time: 10 minutes. | Cook Time: 12 minutes. | Serves: 5

2 pounds flank steak	1 teaspoon paprika
2 tablespoons olive oil	Sea salt and black pepper, to taste

1. Place the Cook & Crisp Basket in your Pressure Cooker Steam Fryer. 2. Toss the steak with the remaining ingredients; place the steak in the Cook & Crisp Basket. 3. Put on the Smart Lid on top of the Ninja Foodi Steam Fryer. 4. Move the Lid Slider to the "Air Fry/Stovetop". Select the "Air Fry" mode for cooking. 5. Cook the steak at 400°F/200°C for around 12 minutes, turning over halfway through the cooking time. 6. Serve.
Per serving: Calories: 299; Fat:14.5g; Carbs: 0.3g; Fiber: 0.2g; Sugars: 0g; Proteins: 38.5g

Mushroom Beef Patties

Prep Time: 10 minutes. | Cook Time: 15 minutes. | Serves: 4

1-pound chuck	1 teaspoon cayenne pepper
2 garlic cloves, minced	Sea salt and black pepper, to taste
1 small onion, chopped	4 brioche rolls
1 cup mushrooms, chopped	

1. Place the Cook & Crisp Basket in your Pressure Cooker Steam Fryer. 2. Mix the chuck, garlic, onion, mushrooms, cayenne pepper, salt, and black pepper until everything is well mixed. Form the mixture into four patties. 3. Put on the Smart Lid on top of the Ninja Foodi Steam Fryer. 4. Move the Lid Slider to the "Air Fry/Stovetop". Select the "Air Fry" mode for cooking. 5. Cook the patties at 380°F/195°C for about 15 minutes or until cooked through; make sure to turn them over halfway through the cooking time. 6. Serve your patties on the prepared brioche rolls and enjoy!
Per serving: Calories: 305; Fat:10.4g; Carbs: 25.3g; Fiber: 1.7g; Sugars: 4.5g; Proteins: 27.7g

Mustard Tender Filet Mignon

Prep Time: 10 minutes. | Cook Time: 14 minutes. | Serves: 4

1 ½ pounds filet mignon	1 teaspoon mustard powder
2 tablespoons soy sauce	1 teaspoon garlic powder
2 tablespoons butter, melted	Sea salt and black pepper, to taste

1. Place the Cook & Crisp Basket in your Pressure Cooker Steam Fryer. 2. Toss the filet mignon with the remaining ingredients; place the filet mignon in the Cook & Crisp Basket. 3. Put on the Smart Lid on top of the Ninja Foodi Steam Fryer. 4. Move the Lid Slider to the "Air Fry/Stovetop". Select the "Air Fry" mode for cooking. 5. Cook the filet mignon at 400°F/200°C for around 14 minutes, turning it over halfway through the cooking time. 6. Enjoy!
Per serving: Calories: 393; Fat:26.2g; Carbs: 2.7g; Fiber: 0.2g; Sugars: 1.5g; Proteins: 36.2g

Beef Shoulder

Prep Time: 10 minutes. | Cook Time: 55 minutes. | Serves: 4

1 ½ pounds beef shoulder	1 teaspoon cayenne pepper
Sea salt and black pepper, to taste	½ teaspoon cumin
2 tablespoons olive oil	1 teaspoon Dijon mustard
2 cloves garlic, minced	1 onion, cut into slices

1. Place the Cook & Crisp Basket in your Pressure Cooker Steam Fryer. 2. Toss the beef with the spices, garlic, mustard, and olive oil; brush the Cook & Crisp Basket with oil and place the beef in it. 3. Put on the Smart Lid on top of the Ninja Foodi Steam Fryer. 4. Move the Lid Slider to the "Air Fry/Stovetop". Select the "Air Fry" mode for cooking. 5. Cook the beef at 390°F/200°C for around 45 minutes, turning it over halfway through the cooking time. 6. Add in the onion and continue to cook an additional 10 minutes. 7. Serve.
Per serving: Calories: 309; Fat:16.2g; Carbs: 2.2g; Fiber: 0.4g; Sugars: 0.7g; Proteins: 36.2g

BBQ Ribs

Prep Time: 10 minutes. | Cook Time: 35 minutes. | Serves: 4

1 ½ pound baby back ribs	½ teaspoon cumin
2 tablespoons olive oil	1 teaspoon mustard powder
1 teaspoon smoked paprika	1 teaspoon dried thyme
1 teaspoon garlic powder	Coarse sea salt and freshly cracked
1 teaspoon onion powder	black pepper, to season

1. Toss all the recipe ingredients in a greased Cook & Crisp Basket. 2. Place the Cook & Crisp Basket in your Pressure Cooker Steam Fryer. 3. Put on the Smart Lid on top of the Ninja Foodi Steam Fryer. 4. Move the Lid Slider to the "Air Fry/Stovetop". Select the "Air Fry" mode for cooking. 5. Cook the pork ribs at 350°F/175°C for around 35 minutes, turning them over halfway through the cooking time. 6. Serve.
Per serving: Calories: 440; Fat:33.3g; Carbs: 1.8g; Fiber: 0.4g; Sugars: 0.1g;Proteins: 33.7g

Pork Skewers

Prep Time: 10 minutes. | Cook Time: 15 minutes. | Serves: 4

1-pound pork tenderloin, cubed	1 tablespoon parsley, chopped
1-pound bell peppers, diced	1 tablespoon cilantro, chopped
1-pound eggplant, diced	Sea salt and black pepper, to taste
1 tablespoon olive oil	

1. Place the Cook & Crisp Basket in your Pressure Cooker Steam Fryer. 2. Toss all the recipe ingredients in a suitable mixing bowl until well coated on all sides. 3. Thread the ingredients onto skewers and place them in the Cook & Crisp Basket. 4. Put on the Smart Lid on top of the Ninja Foodi Steam Fryer. 5. Move the Lid Slider to the "Air Fry/Stovetop". Select the "Air Fry" mode for cooking. 6. Then, cook the skewers at 400°F/200°C for approximately 15 minutes, turning them over halfway through the cooking time. 7. Serve.
Per serving: Calories: 344; Fat:16.3g; Carbs: 18g; Fiber: 5.3g; Sugars: 10.1g; Proteins: 32.6g

Pork Bun Thit Nuong

Prep Time: 40 minutes. | Cook Time: 10 minutes. | Serves: 4

For the pork
¼ cup diced onions	1 tablespoon minced lemongrass
½ teaspoon black pepper	paste
1 tablespoon fish sauce	2 tablespoons sugar
1 tablespoon minced garlic cloves	2 teaspoons soy sauce
1-pound pork shoulder, sliced thin	2 tablespoons avocado oil

To Garnish
¼ cup crushed roasted peanuts	2 tablespoons cilantro, chopped

1. Using a suitable mixing bowl, add in the black pepper, sugar, onions, avocado oil, soy sauce, fish sauce, garlic and lemongrass then mix together. 2. Cut the sliced pork shoulders crisscross ways into 4 pieces then add into the marinade and allow to marinate for around 2 hours. 3. Transfer the marinated pork into the "cook & crisp basket". 4. Put on the Smart Lid on top of the Ninja Foodi Steam Fryer. Move the Lid Slider to the "Air Fry/Stovetop". Select the "Air Fry" mode for cooking. 5. Cook for around 5 minutes at 400°F/200°C. 6. Flip the pork shoulders over. 7. Cook for an extra 5 minutes then transfer into serving platters. 8. Top with the cilantro, roasted peanuts, serve and enjoy as desired.
Per serving: Calories: 589; Fat: 18.2g; Sodium 513mg; Carbs: 85.6g; Fiber: 24.5g; Sugars 13.2g; Protein 26g

Peppery Beef

Prep Time: 10 minutes. | Cook Time: 14 minutes. | Serves: 4

1 ½ pounds Tomahawk steaks
2 bell peppers, sliced
2 tablespoons butter, melted
2 teaspoons Montreal steak
seasoning
2 tablespoons fish sauce
Sea salt and black pepper, to taste

1. Place the Cook & Crisp Basket in your Pressure Cooker Steam Fryer. 2. Toss all the recipe ingredients in the Cook & Crisp Basket. 3. Put on the Smart Lid on top of the Ninja Foodi Steam Fryer. 4. Move the Lid Slider to the "Air Fry/Stovetop". Select the "Air Fry" mode for cooking. 5. Cook the steak and peppers at 400°F/200°C for about 14 minutes, turning it over halfway through the cooking time. 6. Serve.
Per serving: Calories: 299; Fat:15.6g; Carbs: 4.3g; Fiber: 0.7g; Sugars: 2.2g; Proteins: 33.1g

Italian Pork Cut

Prep Time: 10 minutes. | Cook Time: 55 minutes. | Serves: 5

2 pounds pork center cut
2 tablespoons olive oil
1 tablespoon Italian herb mix
1 teaspoon red pepper flakes, crushed
Sea salt and black pepper, to taste

1. Toss all the recipe ingredients in a greased Cook & Crisp Basket. 2. Place the Cook & Crisp Basket in your Pressure Cooker Steam Fryer. 3. Put on the Smart Lid on top of the Ninja Foodi Steam Fryer. 4. Move the Lid Slider to the "Air Fry/Stovetop". Select the "Air Fry" mode for cooking. 5. Cook the pork at 360°F/180°C for around 55 minutes, turning it over halfway through the cooking time. 6. Serve warm and enjoy!
Per serving: Calories: 356; Fat:21.7g; Carbs: 0.1g; Fiber: 0.1g; Sugars: 0.1g Proteins: 37.5g

Sausage with Fennel

Prep Time: 10 minutes. | Cook Time: 15 minutes. | Serves: 4

1-pound pork sausage
1-pound fennel, quartered
1 teaspoon garlic powder
½ teaspoon onion powder
2 teaspoons mustard

1. Place all the recipe ingredients in a greased Cook & Crisp Basket. 2. Place the Cook & Crisp Basket in your Pressure Cooker Steam Fryer. 3. Put on the Smart Lid on top of the Ninja Foodi Steam Fryer. 4. Move the Lid Slider to the "Air Fry/Stovetop". Select the "Air Fry" mode for cooking. 5. Air fry the sausage and fennel at 370°F/185°C for approximately 15 minutes, tossing the basket halfway through the cooking time. 6. Serve.
Per serving: Calories: 433; Fat:35.7g; Carbs: 9.9g; Fiber: 3.7g; Sugars: 1g; Proteins: 17.8g

Meatloaf

Prep Time: 10 minutes. | Cook Time: 10 minutes. | Serves: 10

¼ cup ketchup
¼ cup diced onion
¼ cup coconut flour
½ teaspoon sea salt
½ teaspoon black pepper
½ teaspoon dried tarragon
½ cup blanched almond flour
1-pound beef
1 minced garlic clove
1 teaspoon Italian seasoning
1 tablespoon Worcestershire sauce
2 beaten eggs

1. Place the Cook & Crisp Basket in your Pressure Cooker Steam Fryer. 2. Using a suitable mixing bowl, add in all the recipe ingredients and incorporate until a batter is formed. 3. Mold 10 even loaves from the patties then transfer into the refrigerator to firm up for about 15 minutes. 4. Transfer the firm loaves into the Cook & Crisp Basket. Put on the Smart Lid on top of the Ninja Foodi Steam Fryer. Move the Lid Slider to the "Air Fry/Stovetop". Select the "Air Fry" mode for cooking. Air Fry at 360°F/180°C for around 10 minutes. 5. If cooking in batches, keep the cooked ones warm until done cooking. 6. Serve hot and enjoy as desired.
Per serving: Calories 390; Fat: 15.3g; Sodium 1086mg; Carbs: 50g; Fiber: 17.3g; Sugars 6.6g; Protein 18.2g

Pork Burgers

Prep Time: 10 minutes. | Cook Time: 15 minutes. | Serves: 4

1-pound pork
1 small onion, chopped
1 garlic clove, minced
4 tablespoons tortilla chips, crushed
1 teaspoon fresh sage, minced
1 teaspoon fresh coriander, minced
1 tablespoon fresh parsley, minced
1 egg, beaten
½ teaspoon smoked paprika
Sea salt and black pepper, to taste

1. Place the Cook & Crisp Basket in your Pressure Cooker Steam Fryer. 2. In a suitable mixing bowl, mix all the recipe ingredients. Form the mixture into four patties. 3. Put on the Smart Lid on top of the Ninja Foodi Steam Fryer. 4. Move the Lid Slider to the "Air Fry/Stovetop". Select the "Air Fry" mode for cooking. 5. Cook the burgers at 380°F/195°C for about 15 minutes or until cooked through; make sure to turn them over halfway through the cooking time. 6. Serve.
Per serving: Calories: 386; Fat:28.7g; Carbs: 9.2g; Fiber: 1.1g; Sugars: 1g;Proteins: 22.3g

Beef Dinner Rolls

Prep Time: 10 minutes. | Cook Time: 15 minutes. | Serves: 4

1-pound beef
½ teaspoon garlic powder
½ teaspoon onion powder
1 teaspoon paprika
Sea salt and black pepper, to taste
8 dinner rolls

1. Place the Cook & Crisp Basket in your Pressure Cooker Steam Fryer. 2. Mix all the recipe ingredients, except for the dinner rolls. Shape the mixture into four patties. 3. Put on the Smart Lid on top of the Ninja Foodi Steam Fryer. 4. Move the Lid Slider to the "Air Fry/Stovetop". Select the "Air Fry" mode for cooking. 5. Cook the burgers at 380°F/195°C for about 15 minutes or until cooked through; make sure to turn them over halfway through the cooking time. 6. Serve your burgers on the prepared dinner rolls and enjoy!
Per serving: Calories: 406; Fat:16.2g; Carbs: 27g; Fiber: 2.6g; Sugars: 1.5g; Proteins: 35.2g

Steak Salad

Prep Time: 10 minutes. | Cook Time: 12 minutes. | Serves: 5

2 pounds T-bone steak
1 teaspoon garlic powder
Sea salt and black pepper, to taste
2 tablespoons lime juice
¼ cup extra-virgin olive oil
1 bell pepper, seeded and sliced
1 red onion, sliced
1 tomato, diced

1. Place the Cook & Crisp Basket in your Pressure Cooker Steam Fryer. 2. Toss the steak with the garlic powder, salt, and black pepper; place the steak in the Cook & Crisp Basket. Put on the Smart Lid on top of the Ninja Foodi Steam Fryer. 3. Move the Lid Slider to the "Air Fry/Stovetop". Select the "Air Fry" mode for cooking. 4. Cook the steak at 400°F/200°C for around 12 minutes, turning it over halfway through the cooking time. 5. Cut the steak into slices and add in the remaining ingredients. Serve at room temperature or well-chilled. 6. Serve.
Per serving: Calories: 316; Fat:16g; Carbs: 3.7g; Fiber: 0.7g; Sugars: 1.7g; Proteins: 38.2g

Pork Cutlets

Prep Time: 10 minutes. | Cook Time: 15 minutes. | Serves: 4

1 ½ pounds pork cutlets
Seasoned salt and black pepper, to taste
1 cup tortilla chips, crushed
½ teaspoon cayenne pepper
2 tablespoons olive oil

1. Toss the pork cutlets with the remaining ingredients; brush the Cook & Crisp Basket with oil. 2. Place the Cook & Crisp Basket in your Pressure Cooker Steam Fryer. 3. Put on the Smart Lid on top of the Ninja Foodi Steam Fryer. 4. Move the Lid Slider to the "Air Fry/Stovetop". Select the "Air Fry" mode for cooking. 5. Cook the pork cutlets at 400°F/200°C for around 15 minutes, turning them over halfway through the cooking time. 6. Serve.
Per serving: Calories: 480; Fat:25.1g; Carbs: 18.2g; Fiber: 1.4g; Sugars: 0.9g; Proteins: 43.7g

Pork Roast with Applesauce

Prep Time: 10 minutes. | Cook Time: 1 hour | Serves: 5

1 tablespoon olive oil	2 cloves garlic, smashed
2 tablespoons soy sauce	2 sprigs fresh sage, chopped
2 pounds pork butt	1 cup applesauce
Salt and black pepper, to taste	

1. Toss all the recipe ingredients, except for the applesauce, in a greased Cook & Crisp Basket. 2. Place the Cook & Crisp Basket in your Pressure Cooker Steam Fryer. 3. Put on the Smart Lid on top of the Ninja Foodi Steam Fryer. 4. Move the Lid Slider to the "Air Fry/ Stovetop". Select the "Air Fry" mode for cooking. 5. Cook the pork butt at 360°F/180°C for around 45 minutes, turning it over halfway through the cooking time. 6. Top the pork butt with the applesauce and continue cooking for a further 10 minutes. 7. Let it rest for a few minutes before slicing and serving.
Per serving: Calories: 402; Fat:26.2g; Carbs: 7.4g; Fiber: 0.7g; Sugars: 5.8g; Proteins: 32.3g

Bacon with Cauliflower

Prep Time: 10 minutes. | Cook Time: 12 minutes. | Serves: 4

1-pound bacon, cut into thick slices	1 teaspoon paprika
1-pound cauliflower, cut into florets	Salt and black pepper, to taste
1 tablespoon maple syrup	2 cloves garlic, minced

1. Place the Cook & Crisp Basket in your Pressure Cooker Steam Fryer. 2. Toss all the recipe ingredients in the Cook & Crisp Basket. 3. Put on the Smart Lid on top of the Ninja Foodi Steam Fryer. 4. Move the Lid Slider to the "Air Fry/Stovetop". Select the "Air Fry" mode for cooking. 5. Then, cook the bacon and cauliflower at 400°F/200°C for approximately 12 minutes, turning them over halfway through the cooking time. 6. Serve immediately.
Per serving: Calories: 512; Fat:44.9g; Carbs: 8g; Fiber: 2.7g; Sugars: 6.7g; Proteins: 16.7g

Glazed Ham

Prep Time: 10 minutes. | Cook Time: 1 hour | Serves: 4

1 ½ pounds ham	1 tablespoon stone-mustard
¼ cup sherry wine	A pinch of grated nutmeg
2 tablespoons dark brown sugar	½ teaspoon cloves
2 tablespoons freshly squeezed lime juice	¼ teaspoon cardamom
	½ teaspoon black pepper, to taste

1. Place the Cook & Crisp Basket in your Pressure Cooker Steam Fryer. 2. In a suitable mixing bowl, mix all the remaining recipe ingredients to make the glaze. 3. Wrap the ham in a piece of aluminum foil and lower it into the Cook & Crisp Basket Put on the Smart Lid on top of the Ninja Foodi Steam Fryer. Move the Lid Slider to the "Air Fry/Stovetop". Select the "Air Fry" mode for cooking. Cook for the ham at 375°F/190°C for about 30 minutes. 4. Remove the foil, turn the temperature to 400°F/200°C, and continue to cook an additional 15 minutes, coating the ham with the glaze every 5 minutes. 5. Serve.
Per serving: Calories: 470; Fat:30.3g; Carbs: 1.6g; Fiber: 0.4g; Sugars: 0.4g;; Proteins:45.7g

Sausage Patties

Prep Time: 10 minutes. | Cook Time: 15 minutes. | Serves: 4

1-pound sausage patties	1 teaspoon jalapeno pepper, minced
1 tablespoon mustard	
1 teaspoon cayenne pepper	

1. Place all the recipe ingredients in a greased Cook & Crisp Basket. 2. Place the Cook & Crisp Basket in your Pressure Cooker Steam Fryer. 3. Put on the Smart Lid on top of the Ninja Foodi Steam Fryer. 4. Move the Lid Slider to the "Air Fry/Stovetop". Select the "Air Fry" mode for cooking. 5. Air fry the sausage at 370°F/185°C for approximately 15 minutes, tossing the basket halfway through the cooking time. 6. Serve.
Per serving: Calories: 392; Fat:35.7g; Carbs: 1.5g; Fiber: 0.4g;;

Sugars: 0.2g; Proteins: 16.3g

Pork Chops with Peppers

Prep Time: 10 minutes. | Cook Time: 15 minutes. | Serves: 4

1 ½ pounds center-cut rib chops	Salt and black pepper, to taste
2 bell peppers, seeded and sliced	1 teaspoon fresh rosemary, chopped
2 tablespoons olive oil	1 teaspoon fresh basil, chopped
½ teaspoon mustard powder	

1. Toss all the recipe ingredients in a greased Cook & Crisp Basket. 2. Place the Cook & Crisp Basket in your Pressure Cooker Steam Fryer. 3. Put on the Smart Lid on top of the Ninja Foodi Steam Fryer. 4. Move the Lid Slider to the "Air Fry/Stovetop". Select the "Air Fry" mode for cooking. 5. Cook the pork chops and bell peppers at 400°F/200°C for around 15 minutes, turning them over halfway through the cooking time. 6. Serve.
Per serving: Calories: 359; Fat:22.2g; Carbs: 2.3g; Fiber: 0.5g; Sugars: 1.1g; Proteins: 35.7g

Country Style Ribs

Prep Time: 10 minutes. | Cook Time: 35 minutes. | Serves: 5

2 pounds Country-style ribs	1 teaspoon mustard powder
Coarse sea salt and black pepper, to taste	1 tablespoon butter, melted
	1 teaspoon chili sauce
1 teaspoon smoked paprika	4 tablespoons dry red wine

1. Toss all the recipe ingredients in a greased Cook & Crisp Basket. 2. Place the Cook & Crisp Basket in your Pressure Cooker Steam Fryer. 3. Put on the Smart Lid on top of the Ninja Foodi Steam Fryer. 4. Move the Lid Slider to the "Air Fry/Stovetop". Select the "Air Fry" mode for cooking. 5. Cook the pork ribs at 350°F/175°C for around 35 minutes, turning them over halfway through the cooking time. 6. Serve.
Per serving: Calories: 374; Fat:23.8g; Carbs: 1.4g; Fiber: 0.4g; Sugars: 0.6g; Proteins: 35.4g

Steak Bulgogi

Prep Time: 10 minutes. | Cook Time: 12 minutes. | Serves: 6

½ teaspoon black pepper	2 tablespoons sesame seeds
1 cup diced carrots	2 teaspoons minced garlic cloves
1 ½ pounds sliced sirloin steak	3 tablespoons soy sauce
2 tablespoons coconut oil	3 chopped green scallions
2 tablespoons brown sugar	

1. Place the Cook & Crisp Basket in your Pressure Cooker Steam Fryer. 2. Using a suitable Ziploc bag, add in the green scallions , carrots and sirloin steak. 3. Pour in the pepper, garlic, sesame seeds, coconut oil, brown sugar, soy sauce and massage into the steak. 4. Set the Ziploc bag aside to marinate for an hour. 5. Transfer the veggies and marinated beef into the "cook & crisp basket". 6. Put on the Smart Lid on top of the Ninja Foodi Steam Fryer. 7. Move the Lid Slider to the "Air Fry/Stovetop". Select the "Air Fry" mode for cooking. 8. Air fry for around 6 minutes at 400°F/200°C 9. Shake the basket and flip the beef over then air fry for an extra 6 minutes. 10. Serve and enjoy as desired.
Per serving: Calories 253; Fat: 13.9g; Sodium 21mg; Carbs: 27g; Fiber: 9.3g; Sugars 3.8g; Protein 8.3g

Crackled Pork Loin

Prep Time: 10 minutes. | Cook Time: 55 minutes. | Serves: 5

4 tablespoons beer	Sea salt and black pepper, to taste
1 tablespoon garlic, crushed	2 pounds pork loin
1 teaspoon paprika	

1. Toss all the recipe ingredients in a greased Cook & Crisp Basket. 2. Place the Cook & Crisp Basket in your Pressure Cooker Steam Fryer. 3. Put on the Smart Lid on top of the Ninja Foodi Steam Fryer. 4. Move the Lid Slider to the "Air Fry/Stovetop". Select the "Air Fry" mode for cooking. 5. Cook the pork at 360°F/180°C for around 55 minutes, turning it over halfway through the cooking time. 6. Serve warm and enjoy!
Per serving: Calories: 315; Fat:15.2g; Carbs: 2.1g; Fiber: 0.3g; Sugars: 0.5g; Proteins: 39.1g

Muffin Burgers

Prep Time: 10 minutes. | Cook Time: 15 minutes. | Serves: 4

1-pound pork
1 egg
½ cup seasoned breadcrumbs
1 teaspoon dried oregano
½ teaspoon dried basil
Sea salt and black pepper, to taste
1 small red onion, chopped
1 teaspoon garlic, minced
1 tablespoon olive oil
4 English muffins

1. Place the Cook & Crisp Basket in your Pressure Cooker Steam Fryer. 2. In a suitable mixing bowl, mix the pork, egg, breadcrumbs, spices, onion, garlic, and 3. olive oil. Form the mixture into four patties. 4. Put on the Smart Lid on top of the Ninja Foodi Steam Fryer. 5. Move the Lid Slider to the "Air Fry/Stovetop". Select the "Air Fry" mode for cooking. 6. Cook the burgers at 380°F/195°C for about 15 minutes or until cooked through; make sure to turn them over halfway through the cooking time. 7. Serve your burgers with English muffins and enjoy!
Per serving: Calories: 479; Fat:48.1g; Carbs: 2.3g; Fiber: 0.1g; Sugars: 1.6g; Proteins: 8.6g

Honey Bratwurst with Brussels Sprouts

Prep Time: 10 minutes. | Cook Time: 15 minutes. | Serves: 4

1-pound bratwurst
1 pound Brussels sprouts
1 large onion, cut into wedges
1 teaspoon garlic, minced
1 tablespoon mustard
2 tablespoons honey

1. Toss all the recipe ingredients in a greased Cook & Crisp Basket. 2. Place the Cook & Crisp Basket in your Pressure Cooker Steam Fryer. 3. Put on the Smart Lid on top of the Ninja Foodi Steam Fryer. 4. Move the Lid Slider to the "Air Fry/Stovetop". Select the "Air Fry" mode for cooking. 5. Air fry the sausage at 380°F/195°C for approximately 15 minutes, tossing the basket halfway through the cooking time. 6. Serve.
Per serving: Calories: 438; Fat:30.3g; Carbs: 25g; Fiber: 5.1g; Sugars: 12g; Proteins: 18.7g

Dijon Glazed Pork Loin

Prep Time: 10 minutes. | Cook Time: 55 minutes. | Serves: 4

1 ½ pounds pork top loin
1 tablespoon olive oil
1 tablespoon Dijon mustard
2 cloves garlic, crushed
1 tablespoon parsley
1 tablespoon coriander
½ teaspoon red pepper flakes, crushed
Salt and black pepper, to taste

1. Toss all the recipe ingredients in a greased Cook & Crisp Basket. 2. Place the Cook & Crisp Basket in your Pressure Cooker Steam Fryer. 3. Put on the Smart Lid on top of the Ninja Foodi Steam Fryer. 4. Move the Lid Slider to the "Air Fry/Stovetop". Select the "Air Fry" mode for cooking. 5. Cook the pork at 360°F/180°C for around 55 minutes, turning it over halfway through the cooking time. 6. Serve warm and enjoy!
Per serving: Calories: 302; Fat:15.3g; Carbs: 1g; Fiber: 0.3g; Sugars: 0g; Proteins: 36.9g

Citrus-Glazed Pork Chops

Prep Time: 10 minutes. | Cook Time: 15 minutes. | Serves: 3

1-pound rib pork chops
1 ½ tablespoons butter, melted
2 tablespoons orange juice, freshly squeezed
1 teaspoon rosemary, chopped
Sea salt and cayenne pepper, to taste

1. Toss all the recipe ingredients in a greased Cook & Crisp Basket. 2. Place the Cook & Crisp Basket in your Pressure Cooker Steam Fryer. 3. Put on the Smart Lid on top of the Ninja Foodi Steam Fryer. 4. Move the Lid Slider to the "Air Fry/Stovetop". Select the "Air Fry" mode for cooking. 5. Cook the pork chops at 400°F/200°C for around 15 minutes, turning them over halfway through the cooking time. 6. Serve.
Per serving: Calories: 372; Fat:22.5g; Carbs: 1.3g; Fiber: 0.2g; Sugars: 1g; Proteins: 38.6g

Easy Pork Chops

Prep Time: 15 minutes. | Cook Time: 15 minutes. | Serves: 4

½ cup water
1 teaspoon sugar
4 pork chops
Melted butter
Salt, to taste

1. Place the Cook & Crisp Basket in your Pressure Cooker Steam Fryer. 2. Mix the water, sugar and salt into a suitable mixing bowl. 3. Add the pork chops into the water mixture and brine. 4. Pat dry the pork chops then coat with the melted butter. 5. Place the coated chops into the "cook & crisp basket". 6. Put on the Smart Lid on top of the Ninja Foodi Steam Fryer. 7. Move the Lid Slider to the "Air Fry/Stovetop". Select the "Air Fry" mode for cooking. 8. Air fry for around 15 minutes at 385°F/195°C. 9. Once done, serve and enjoy as desired.
Per serving: Calories 557; Fat: 10g; Sodium 2706mg; Carbs: 87.6g; Fiber: 17.8g; Sugars 5.6g; Protein 29.2g

Indian Lamb Steaks

Prep Time: 40 minutes. | Cook Time: 7 minutes. | Serves: 4

½ diced onion
½ teaspoon cardamom
1 teaspoon garam masala
1 teaspoon fennel
1 teaspoon cinnamon
1-pound lamb sirloin steaks, boneless
4 chopped ginger
5 minced garlic cloves
Salt and cayenne pepper, to taste

1. Place the Cook & Crisp Basket in your Pressure Cooker Steam Fryer. 2. Using a high speed blender, add in all the recipe ingredients (except the lamb steaks) and pulse until blended. 3. Make small incisions on the body of the lamb steaks then place into a suitable Ziploc bag. 4. Pour the blender marinade into the Ziploc bag and allow the steaks to marinate for an hour. 5. Transfer the marinated steaks into the basket. Put on the Smart Lid on top of the Ninja Foodi Steam Fryer. Move the Lid Slider to the "Air Fry/Stovetop". Select the "Air Fry" mode for cooking. Air Fry for around 8 minutes at 330°F/165°C. 6. Flip the lamb steaks and cook for another 7 minutes. 7. Serve hot and enjoy as desired.
Per serving: Calories 100; Fat: 1.1g; Sodium 741mg; Carbs: 19.4g; Fiber: 5.2g; Sugars 6.2g; Protein 4.3g

Stuffed Venison Tenderloin

Prep Time: 10 minutes. | Cook Time: 10 minutes. | Serves: 4

1½ pounds venison or beef tenderloin, pounded to ¼ inch thick
3 teaspoons fine sea salt
1 teaspoon black pepper
2 ounces creamy goat cheese
½ cup crumbled feta cheese (about 2 ounces)
¼ cup finely chopped onions
2 cloves garlic, minced
Avocado oil
For Garnish
Prepared yellow mustard
Halved cherry tomatoes
Extra-virgin olive oil
Sprigs of fresh rosemary
Lavender flowers

1. Place the Cook & Crisp Basket in your Pressure Cooker Steam Fryer. 2. Grease the Ninja Foodi Pressure Steam Fryer basket with avocado oil. 3. Season the tenderloin on all sides with the black pepper and salt. 4. In a suitable-sized mixing bowl, mix the goat cheese, feta, onions, and garlic. Place the mixture in the center of the tenderloin. Starting at the end closest to you, tightly roll the tenderloin like a jelly roll. Tie the rolled tenderloin tightly with kitchen twine. 5. Place the meat in the "cook & crisp basket". Put on the Smart Lid on top of the Ninja Foodi Steam Fryer. Move the Lid Slider to the "Air Fry/Stovetop". Select the "Air Fry" mode for cooking. 6. Adjust the cooking temperature to 400°F/200°C. 7. Cook for around 5 minutes. Flip the meat over. Cook for 5 minutes more, or until the internal temperature reaches 135°F/55°C for medium-rare. 8. To serve, smear a line of prepared yellow mustard on a platter, then place the meat next to it and add halved cherry tomatoes on the side, if desired. Drizzle with olive oil and garnish with rosemary sprigs and lavender flowers, if desired. 9. Best served fresh. Store leftovers in an airtight container and put in the fridge for around 3 days. Reheat them at 350°F/175°C for around 4 minutes in your Pressure Cooker Steam Fryer, or until heated through.
Per serving: Calories 231; Fat: 2.1g; Sodium 816mg; Carbs: 38.1g; Fiber: 14.4g; Sugars 4.5g; Protein 16.6g

Salisbury Steak with Mushroom Gravy

Prep Time: 10 minutes. | Cook Time: 33 minutes | Serves: 2

Mushroom Onion Gravy

¾ cup sliced button mushrooms	½ teaspoon fine sea salt
¼ cup sliced onions	¼ cup beef broth
¼ cup unsalted butter, melted	

Steaks:

½ pound beef (85% lean)	teaspoon garlic powder
¼ cup minced onions, or ½	½ teaspoon fine sea salt
teaspoon onion powder	¼ teaspoon black pepper, more for
2 tablespoons tomato paste	garnish if desired
1 tablespoon dry mustard	Chopped fresh thyme leaves, for
1 clove garlic, minced, or ¼	garnish (optional)

1. Place the Cook & Crisp Basket in your Pressure Cooker Steam Fryer. 2. Make the gravy: Place the mushrooms and onions in the Cook & Crisp Basket. Pour the melted butter over them and stir to coat, then season with the salt. Place the Cook & Crisp Basket in your Pressure Cooker Steam Fryer. 3. Put on the Smart Lid on top of the Ninja Foodi Steam Fryer. Move the Lid Slider to the "Air Fry/Stovetop". Select the "Air Fry" mode for cooking. 4. Adjust the cooking temperature to 390°F/200°C. 5. Cook for around 5 minutes, stir, then cook for another 3 minutes, or until the onions are soft and the mushrooms are browning. Add the broth. Cook for another 10 minutes. 6. While the gravy is cooking, prepare the steaks: In a suitable bowl, mix the beef, onions, tomato paste, dry mustard, garlic, salt, and pepper until well mixed. Form the mixture into 2 oval-shaped patties. 7. Place the patties on top of the mushroom gravy. Cook for around 10 minutes, gently flip the patties, then cook for another 2 to 5 minutes, until the beef is cooked through or the internal temperature reaches 145°F/60°C. 8. Remove the steaks to a serving platter and pour the gravy over them. Garnish with black pepper and chopped fresh thyme, if desired. Store leftovers in an airtight container and put in the fridge for around 3 days or in the freezer for up to a month. 9. Reheat at 350°F/175°C for around 4 minutes in your Pressure Cooker Steam Fryer, or until heated through.
Per serving: Calories 371; Fat: 4.9g; Sodium 1207mg; Carbs: 57.5g; Fiber: 25g; Sugars 7g; Protein 25.6g

Spicy Bacon Pieces

Prep Time: 5 minutes. | Cook Time: 10 minutes. | Serves: 3

¼ cup hot sauce	6 uncooked bacon strips
½ cup pork rinds, crushed	

1. Place the Cook & Crisp Basket in your Pressure Cooker Steam Fryer. 2. Slice the bacon strips into 6 pieces then transfer into a suitable mixing bowl. 3. Pour the hot sauce into the mixing bowl and ensure the bacon pieces are well coated. 4. Dredge the coated bacon pieces in the crushed pork rinds until well covered. 5. Transfer the covered pieces into the "cook & crisp basket". 6. Put on the Smart Lid on top of the Ninja Foodi Steam Fryer. 7. Move the Lid Slider to the "Air Fry/Stovetop". Select the "Air Fry" mode for cooking. 8. Air fry for around 10 minutes at 350°F/175°C. 9. Serve and enjoy as desired.
Per serving: Calories 483; Fat: 6g; Sodium 184mg; Carbs: 77.2g; Fiber: 31.2g; Sugars 6g; Protein 30.4g

Swedish Beef Meatloaf

Prep Time: 10 minutes. | Cook Time: 45 minutes | Serves: 8

1½ pounds beef (85% lean)	2 tablespoons dry mustard
¼ pound pork	2 cloves garlic, minced
1 large egg (omit for egg-free)	2 teaspoons fine sea salt
½ cup minced onions	1 teaspoon black pepper, more for
¼ cup tomato sauce	garnish

Sauce:

½ cup (1 stick) unsalted butter	⅓ cup beef broth
½ cup shredded Swiss or mild	⅛ teaspoon nutmeg
cheddar cheese (about 2 ounces)	Halved cherry tomatoes, for
2 ounces cream cheese (¼ cup),	serving (optional)
softened	

1. Place the Cook & Crisp Basket in your Pressure Cooker Steam Fryer. 2. In a suitable bowl, mix the beef, pork, egg, onions, tomato sauce, dry mustard, garlic, salt, and pepper. Using your hands, mix until well mixed. 3. Place the meatloaf mixture in the Cook & Crisp Basket. 4. Put on the Smart Lid on top of the Ninja Foodi Steam Fryer. 5. Move the Lid Slider to the "Air Fry/Stovetop". Select the "Air Fry" mode for cooking. 6. Adjust the cooking temperature to 390°F/200°C. 7. Cook for around 35 minutes, or until cooked through and the internal temperature reaches 145°F/60°C. Check the meatloaf after 25 minutes; if it's too brown on the top, you can cover it loosely with foil to prevent burning. 8. While the meatloaf cooks, make the sauce: Add the butter in a suitable saucepan over medium-high heat until it sizzles and brown flecks appear, with constant stirring to keep the butter from burning. Turn the heat to low and mix in the Swiss cheese, cream cheese, broth, and nutmeg. Cook on a simmer for at least 10 minutes. The longer it simmers, the more the flavors open up. 9. When the meatloaf is done, transfer it to a serving tray and pour the sauce over it. Garnish with black pepper and serve with cherry tomatoes, if desired. Allow the meatloaf to rest for around 10 minutes before slicing so it doesn't crumble apart. 10. Store leftovers in an airtight container, then put in the fridge for around 3 days or in the freezer for up to a month. Reheat at 350°F/175°C for around 4 minutes in your Pressure Cooker Steam Fryer, or until heated through.
Per serving: Calories 426; Fat: 8.6g; Sodium 588mg; Carbs: 67g; Fiber: 16.4g; Sugars 2.4g; Protein 23.2g

Beef Carne Asada

Prep Time: 5 minutes. | Cook Time: 8 minutes. | Serves: 8

Marinade:

1 cup fresh cilantro leaves and	1 teaspoon stevia glycerite, or ⅛
stems	teaspoon liquid stevia
1 jalapeño pepper, seeded and	2 teaspoons ancho chili powder
diced	2 teaspoons fine sea salt
½ cup lime juice	1 teaspoon coriander seeds
2 tablespoons avocado oil	1 teaspoon cumin seeds
2 tablespoons coconut vinegar or	1-pound skirt steak, cut into 4
apple cider vinegar	equal portions
2 teaspoons orange extract	

For Serving

Chopped avocado	Sliced radishes
Lime slices	

1. Place the Cook & Crisp Basket in your Pressure Cooker Steam Fryer. 2. Make the marinade: Place all the recipe ingredients for the marinade in a blender and puree until smooth. 3. Place the steak in a shallow dish and pour the marinade in it, making sure the meat is covered completely. Cover and place in the fridge for around 2 hours or overnight. 4. Grease the Ninja Foodi Pressure Steam Fryer basket with avocado oil. 5. Transfer the steak from the marinade and place it in the "cook & crisp basket" in one layer. 6. Put on the Smart Lid on top of the Ninja Foodi Steam Fryer. 7. Move the Lid Slider to the "Air Fry/Stovetop". Select the "Air Fry" mode for cooking. 8. Adjust the cooking temperature to 400°F/200°C. 9. Cook for around 8 minutes, or until the internal temperature is 145°F/60°C; do not overcook or it will become tough. 10. Remove the steak from the basket and place it on a cutting board, rest for around 10 minutes before slicing it against the grain. Garnish with cilantro, if need, and serve with chopped avocado, lime slices, sliced radishes, if desired. 11. Store leftovers in the airtight container and put in the fridge for around 3 days or in the freezer for up to a month. Reheat them at 350°F/175°C for around 4 minutes in your Pressure Cooker Steam Fryer, or until heated through.
Per serving: Calories 336; Fat: 9.9g; Sodium 1672mg; Carbs: 42.6g; Fiber: 1.7g; Sugars 2.1g; Protein 12.3g

Air-Fried Bacon Slices

Prep Time: 4 minutes. | Cook Time: 10 minutes. | Serves: 10

10 bacon slices	Beef seasoning

1. Place the Cook & Crisp Basket in your Pressure Cooker Steam Fryer. 2. Generously coat the bacon slices with the seasonings. 3. Place the seasoned slices into the Cook & Crisp Basket. 4. Put on the Smart Lid on top of the Ninja Foodi Steam Fryer. 5. Move the Lid Slider to the "Air Fry/Stovetop". Select the "Air Fry" mode for cooking. 6. Cook for around 10 minutes at 400°F/200°C until crispy to taste. 7. Serve and enjoy as desired.
Per serving: Calories 460; Fat: 10.1g; Sodium 332mg; Carbs: 73.9g; Fiber: 20.3g; Sugars 14.5g; Protein 21.7g

Beef Reuben Fritters

Prep Time: 10 minutes. | Cook Time: 16 minutes. | Serves: 12

2 cups finely diced cooked corned beef
1 (8-ounce) package cream cheese, softened
½ cup finely shredded Swiss cheese
¼ cup sauerkraut
1 cup pork dust
Chopped fresh thyme, for garnish
Thousand Island Dipping Sauce, for serving
Cornichons, for serving (optional)

1. Place the Cook & Crisp Basket in your Pressure Cooker Steam Fryer. 2. Grease the Ninja Foodi Pressure Steam Fryer basket with avocado oil. 3. In a suitable bowl, mix the corned beef, cream cheese, Swiss cheese, and sauerkraut until well mixed. Form the corned beef mixture into twelve 1½-inch balls. 4. Place the pork dust in a shallow bowl. Roll the corned beef balls in the pork dust and use your hands to form it into a thick crust around each ball. 5. Place 6 balls in the "cook & crisp basket", spaced about ½ inch apart. Put on the Smart Lid on top of the Ninja Foodi Steam Fryer. Move the Lid Slider to the "Air Fry/Stovetop". Select the "Air Fry" mode for cooking. 6. Adjust the cooking temperature to 390°F/200°C. 7. Cook for around 8 minutes, or until golden brown and crispy. Allow them to cool a bit before lifting them out of the Pressure Cooker Steam Fryer (the fritters are very soft when the cheese is melted; they're easier to handle once the cheese has hardened a bit). Repeat with the remaining fritters. 8. Garnish with chopped fresh thyme and serve with the dipping sauce and cornichons, if desired. Store the leftovers in an airtight container and then put in the fridge for around 3 days or in the freezer for up to a month. Reheat them at 350°F/175°C for around 4 minutes in your Pressure Cooker Steam Fryer, or until heated through.
Per serving: Calories 339; Fat: 14g; Sodium 556mg; Carbs: 44.6g; Fiber: 6.4g; Sugars 3.8g; Protein 10.5g

Hamburgers

Prep Time: 6 minutes. | Cook Time: 10 minutes | Serves: 2

½ teaspoon fine sea salt
¼ teaspoon black pepper
¼ teaspoon garlic powder
¼ teaspoon onion powder
¼ teaspoon smoked paprika
2 (¼-pound) hamburger patties, ½ inch thick
½ cup crumbled blue cheese
2 Hamburger Buns
2 tablespoons mayonnaise
6 red onion slices
2 Boston lettuce leaves
Avocado oil

1. Place the Cook & Crisp Basket in your Pressure Cooker Steam Fryer. 2. Grease the Ninja Foodi Pressure Steam Fryer basket with avocado oil. 3. In a suitable bowl, mix the salt, pepper, and seasonings. Season the patties well on both sides with the seasoning mixture. 4. Place the patties in the "cook & crisp basket". Put on the Smart Lid on top of the Ninja Foodi Steam Fryer. Move the Lid Slider to the "Air Fry/Stovetop". Select the "Air Fry" mode for cooking. Adjust the cooking temperature to 360°F/180°C. Cook for around 7 minutes, or until the internal temperature reaches 145°F/60°C for a suitable-done burger. Place the blue cheese on top of the patties. Cook for another minute to melt the cheese. Remove the burgers and allow to rest for around 5 minutes. 5. Slice the buns in half and smear 2 halves with a tablespoon of mayo each. Place the buns in the "cook & crisp basket" cut side up. Put on the Smart Lid on top of the Ninja Foodi Steam Fryer. Move the Lid Slider to the "Air Fry/Stovetop". Select the "Air Fry" mode for cooking. Toast the buns at 400°F/200°C for around 1 to 2 minutes, until golden brown. 6. Remove the buns from the Ninja Foodi Pressure Steam Fryer and place them on a serving plate. Put the burgers on the buns and top each burger with 3 red onion slices and a lettuce leaf. 7. Best served fresh. Store leftover patties in an airtight container and put in the fridge for around 3 days or in the freezer for up to a month. Reheat it at 350°F/175°C for around 4 minutes in your Pressure Cooker Steam Fryer, or until heated through.
Per serving: Calories 283; Fat: 3.6g; Sodium 381mg; Carbs: 55.4g; Fiber: 8.1g; Sugars 3.1g; Protein 8.7g

Mushroom Burgers

Prep Time: 5 minutes. | Cook Time: 16 minutes | Serves: 2

2 large portobello mushrooms
1 teaspoon fine sea salt
¼ teaspoon garlic powder
¼ teaspoon black pepper
¼ teaspoon onion powder
¼ teaspoon smoked paprika
2 (¼-pound) hamburger patties, ½ inch thick
2 slices Swiss cheese
Condiments of choice, such as Ranch Dressing, prepared yellow mustard, or mayonnaise, for serving

1. Place the Cook & Crisp Basket in your Pressure Cooker Steam Fryer. 2. Clean the portobello mushrooms and then remove the stems. Grease the mushrooms on all sides with avocado oil and season them with ½ teaspoon of the salt. Place the mushrooms in the Ninja Foodi Pressure Steam Fryer basket. Put on the Smart Lid on top of the Ninja Foodi Steam Fryer. Move the Lid Slider to the "Air Fry/Stovetop". Select the "Air Fry" mode for cooking. Adjust the cooking temperature to 360°F/180°C. 3. Cook for around 7 to 8 minutes, until fork-tender and soft to the touch. 4. While the mushrooms cook, in a suitable bowl mix the remaining ½ teaspoon of salt, the garlic powder, pepper, onion powder, and paprika. Sprinkle the hamburger patties with the seasoning mixture. 5. When the mushrooms are done cooking, remove them from the Pressure Cooker Steam Fryer and place them on a serving platter with the cap side down. 6. Place the hamburger patties in the Pressure Cooker Steam Fryer. Put on the Smart Lid on top of the Ninja Foodi Steam Fryer. Move the Lid Slider to the "Air Fry/Stovetop". Select the "Air Fry" mode for cooking. Cook at 360°F/180°C for around 7 minutes, or until the internal temperature reaches 145°F/60°C for a suitable-done burger. Place a slice of Swiss cheese on each patty. Cook for another minute to melt the cheese. 7. Place the burgers on top of the mushrooms and drizzle with condiments of your choice. Best served fresh.
Per serving: Calories 244; Fat: 9.1g; Sodium 199mg; Carbs: 34.3g; Fiber: 8.7g; Sugars 15.7g; Protein 8.3g

Beef Steak Nuggets

Prep Time: 10 minutes. | Cook Time: 35 minutes. | Serves: 4

1 large egg
1 pound diced beef steak
For the Breading
½ cup pork panko
½ teaspoon seasoned salt
For the Dip
¼ lemon juice
¼ cup sour cream
¼ cup mayonnaise
Cooking oil

½ cup shaved parmesan cheese

½ teaspoon dip mix and ranch dressing
1 teaspoon chipotle paste

1. Place the Cook & Crisp Basket in your Pressure Cooker Steam Fryer. 2. Using a suitable sized mixing bowl, add in all the dip ingredients and incorporate then refrigerate until ready to use. 3. Using a separate mixing bowl, add in the parmesan cheese, pork panko, salt then incorporate and set aside. 4. Break the egg into a suitable bowl and mix then dredge the diced beef steak in the egg mixture then the pork panko mix and transfer unto a paper lined plate. 5. Transfer the plate into a freezer and allow to set for around 30 minutes then Grease the "cook & crisp basket" with cooking oil . 6. Put on the Smart Lid on top of the Ninja Foodi Steam Fryer. 7. Move the Lid Slider to the "Air Fry/Stovetop". Select the "Air Fry" mode for cooking. 8. Heat the fryer up to 325°F/160°C then fry the steak nuggets for around 3 to 5 minutes until browned. 9. Season the fried nuggets with little salt then serve along with the dip and enjoy as desired.
Per serving: Calories 562; Fat: 2.1g; Sodium 238mg; Carbs: 108.8g; Fiber: 19g; Sugars 5.3g; Protein 28.6g

Air Fried Bacon Slices

Prep Time: 2 minutes. | Cook Time: 10 minutes. | Serves: 2

6 bacon slices

1. Place the Cook & Crisp Basket in your Pressure Cooker Steam Fryer. 2. Prepare the basket with a parchment paper then add in the bacon slices. 3. Put on the Smart Lid on top of the Ninja Foodi Steam Fryer. 4. Move the Lid Slider to the "Air Fry/Stovetop". Select the "Air Fry" mode for cooking. 5. Air fryer at 385°F/195°C for 10 minutes then open and check for desired doneness. 6. Once done and ready, serve and enjoy with any dipping sauce of choice.
Per serving: Calories 589; Fat: 22.7g; Sodium 266mg; Carbs: 76.5g; Fiber: 23.9g; Sugars 5.1g; Protein 25.5g

Bacon Cups

Prep Time: 10 minutes. | Cook Time: 15 minutes. | Serves: 8

¼ cup minced onions	2 tablespoons heavy whipping
¼ cup diced red peppers	cream
¼ cup diced green peppers	3 crumbled and cooked bacon
¼ cup chopped fresh spinach	slices
¼ cup shaved mozzarella cheese	6 large eggs
½ cup shaved cheddar cheese	Black pepper and salt, to taste

1. Place the Cook & Crisp Basket in your Pressure Cooker Steam Fryer. 2. Break the eggs into a suitable mixing bowl then add in the pepper, salt, whipping cream and mix until mixed. 3. Add in the cheeses, onions, red peppers, spinach, green peppers, bacon and mix until incorporated. 4. Pour the mixture into 8 silicone molds and sprinkle the top with the remaining veggies then place the molds in the Ninja Foodi Pressure Steam Fryer. 5. Put on the Smart Lid on top of the Ninja Foodi Steam Fryer. 6. Move the Lid Slider to the "Air Fry/Stovetop". Select the "Air Fry" mode for cooking. 7. Air Fry at 300°F/150°C for 15 minutes then check to confirm if the eggs have set and done as desired. 8. Serve warm and enjoy as desired.
Per serving: Calories 276; Fat: 11.8g; Sodium 888mg; Carbs: 33.1g; Fiber: 6.2g; Sugars 2.6g; Protein 14.4g

Beef Meat Loaf

Prep Time: 10 minutes. | Cook Time: 15 minutes. | Serves: 4

⅛ teaspoon cardamom	1 tablespoon minced ginger
¼ cup chopped cilantro	1 tablespoon minced garlic
½ teaspoon cinnamon	2 large eggs
1 cup diced onion	2 teaspoons garam masala
1 teaspoon turmeric	salt and cayenne pepper to taste
1-pound lean beef	

1. Place the Cook & Crisp Basket in your Pressure Cooker Steam Fryer. 2. Using a suitable mixing bowl, add in all the recipe ingredients and mix until incorporated. 3. Transfer the meat batter into the "cook & crisp basket". 4. Put on the Smart Lid on top of the Ninja Foodi Steam Fryer. 5. Move the Lid Slider to the "Air Fry/Stovetop". Select the "Air Fry" mode for cooking. 6. Air fry for around 15 minutes at 360°F/180°C. 7. Slice the fried meat loaf, serve and enjoy as desired.
Per serving: Calories 353; Fat: 28.2g; Sodium 472mg; Carbs: 14.9g; Fiber: 9.9g; Sugars 1.2g; Protein 14.6g

Italian Pork Loin

Prep Time: 5 minutes. | Cook Time: 40 minutes. | Serves: 8

¼ cup Italian vinaigrette	4 minced garlic cloves
½ teaspoon Italian Seasoning	4-pound boneless pork loin
1 teaspoon thyme	Black pepper and salt, to taste
1 teaspoon rosemary	

1. Place the Cook & Crisp Basket in your Pressure Cooker Steam Fryer. 2. Generously coat the pork loin with the Italian vinaigrette then sprinkle with the remaining seasoning. 3. Transfer the seasoned pork loin into a Ziploc bag and place in a refrigerator for around 2 hours to marinate. 4. Transfer the marinated pork loin into the "cook & crisp basket" lined with parchment paper. 5. Put on the Smart Lid on top of the Ninja Foodi Steam Fryer. 6. Move the Lid Slider to the "Air Fry/Stovetop". Select the "Air Fry" mode for cooking. 7. Air fry the pork loin at 360°F/180°C for around 25 minutes. 8. Open the Pressure Cooker Steam Fryer and flip the pork over then fry for an extra 15 minutes. 9. Allow the pork to cool off then slices into pieces, glaze with extra vinaigrette, serve and enjoy as desired.
Per serving: Calories 687; Fat: 17.1g; Sodium 495mg; Carbs: 112.7g; Fiber: 27.3g; Sugars 12.9g; Protein 26g

Taco Seasoned Meatballs

Prep Time: 10 minutes. | Cook Time: 10 minutes. | Serves: 4

¼ cup diced onions	1 large eggs
¼ cup chopped cilantro	1-pound lean beef
½ cup shredded cheese	1 tablespoon minced garlic
2 tablespoons taco seasoning	Salt and black pepper, to taste
For the Sauce	
¼ cup heavy cream	Hot sauce
½ cup salsa	

1. Place the Cook & Crisp Basket in your Pressure Cooker Steam Fryer. 2. Add all the recipe ingredients into a suitable mixing bowl then incorporate until a paste like texture is achieved. 3. Scoop bits from the mixture and mold out 15 even sized meatballs. 4. Arrange the meatballs in the "cook & crisp basket". 5. Put on the Smart Lid on top of the Ninja Foodi Steam Fryer. 6. Move the Lid Slider to the "Air Fry/Stovetop". Select the "Air Fry" mode for cooking. 7. Air fry for around 10 minutes at 400°F/200°C. 8. In the meantime, mix all the sauce ingredients together. 9. Serve the meatballs and enjoy along with the creamy sauce.
Per serving: Calories 448; Fat: 32.9g; Sodium 71mg; Carbs: 28.1g; Fiber: 9.4g; Sugars 6.3g; Protein 14.6g

BBQ Baby Ribs

Prep Time: 30 minutes. | Cook Time: 30 minutes. | Serves: 4

½ cup BBQ sauce	3 tablespoons pork rub
1 baby back rack ribs	Black pepper and salt, to taste
1 tablespoon liquid smoke	

1. Place the Cook & Crisp Basket in your Pressure Cooker Steam Fryer. 2. Take the membrane off from the ribs back then slice the rib in half. 3. Drizzle the two sides of the rib with the liquid smoke then generously season with salt, pepper and pork rub. 4. Set the ribs aside to marinate for an hour then transfer into the basket. 5. Put on the Smart Lid on top of the Ninja Foodi Steam Fryer. 6. Move the Lid Slider to the "Air Fry/Stovetop". Select the "Air Fry" mode for cooking. 7. Air fry at 360°F/180°C for around 15 minutes then flip over and fry for an extra 15 minutes. 8. Allow the ribs to cool for a few minutes then top with the sauce, serve and enjoy.
Per serving: Calories 280; Fat: 4.6g; Sodium 271mg; Carbs: 52.7g; Fiber: 7.4g; Sugars 6.3g; Protein 8g

Crusted Lamb Chops

Prep Time: 10 minutes. | Cook Time: 5 minutes. | Serves: 2

1 large egg	rosemary leaves
2 cloves garlic, minced	1 teaspoon chopped fresh thyme
¼ cup pork dust	leaves
¼ cup powdered Parmesan cheese	½ teaspoon black pepper
1 tablespoon chopped fresh	4 (1-inch-thick) lamb chops
oregano leaves	Avocado oil
1 tablespoon chopped fresh	
For Garnish	
Sprigs of fresh oregano	Lavender flowers
Sprigs of fresh rosemary	Lemon slices
Sprigs of fresh thyme	

1. Place the Cook & Crisp Basket in your Pressure Cooker Steam Fryer. 2. Grease the Ninja Foodi Pressure Steam Fryer basket with avocado oil. 3. Beat the egg in a shallow bowl, add the garlic, and stir well to mix. In another shallow bowl, mix the pork dust, Parmesan, herbs, and pepper. 4. One at a time, dip the lamb chops into the egg mixture, shake off the excess egg, and then dredge them in the Parmesan mixture. Use your hands to coat the chops well in the Parmesan mixture and form a nice crust on all sides; if necessary, dip the chops again in both the egg and the Parmesan mixture. 5. Place the lamb chops in the "cook & crisp basket", leaving space between them. Put on the Smart Lid on top of the Ninja Foodi Steam Fryer. Move the Lid Slider to the "Air Fry/Stovetop". Select the "Air Fry" mode for cooking. 6. Adjust the cooking temperature to 400°F/200°C. 7. Cook for around 5 minutes, or until the internal temperature reaches 145°F/60°C for medium doneness. Allow to rest for around 10 minutes before serving. 8. Garnish with sprigs of oregano, rosemary, and thyme, and lavender flowers, if desired. Serve with lemon slices, if desired. 9. Best served fresh. Store the leftovers in an airtight container, then put in the fridge for up to 4 days. Serve chilled over a salad, or reheat at 350°F/175°C for around 4 minutes in your Pressure Cooker Steam Fryer, or until heated through.
Per serving: Calories 373; Fat: 3.1g; Sodium 687mg; Carbs: 69.2g; Fiber: 9.6g; Sugars 3.4g; Protein 17.8g

Crispy Pork Bites

Prep Time: 10 minutes. | Cook Time: 17 minutes. | Serves: 5

1-pound pork belly, cut into cubes
1 teaspoon coarse sea salt
Black pepper, to taste
1 tablespoon granulated sugar
1 teaspoon onion powder
½ teaspoon garlic powder

1. Place the Cook & Crisp Basket in your Pressure Cooker Steam Fryer. 2. Toss all the recipe ingredients in your Cook and crisp basket. 3. Put on the Smart Lid on top of the Ninja Foodi Steam Fryer. 4. Move the Lid Slider to the "Air Fry/Stovetop". Select the "Air Fry" mode for cooking. 5. Cook the pork belly at 400°F/200°C for about 17 minutes, shaking the basket halfway through the cooking time. 6. Serve.
Per serving: Calories: 479; Fat:48.1g; Carbs: 2.3g; Fiber: 0.1g; Sugars: 1.6g; Proteins: 8.6g

Madeira Glazed Ham

Prep Time: 10 minutes. | Cook Time: 1 hour | Serves: 5

2 pounds cooked ham
1 apple, cored and chopped
¼ cup maple syrup
2 garlic cloves, crushed
¼ cup Madeira wine

1. Place the Cook & Crisp Basket in your Pressure Cooker Steam Fryer. 2. In a suitable mixing bowl, mix all the remaining recipe ingredients to make the glaze. 3. Wrap the ham in a piece of aluminum foil and lower it onto the Cook & Crisp Basket. Reduce the temperature to 375°F/190°C . Put on the Smart Lid on top of the Ninja Foodi Steam Fryer. Move the Lid Slider to the "Air Fry/Stovetop". Select the "Air Fry" mode for cooking. Cook for the ham for about 30 minutes. 4. Remove the foil, turn the temperature to 400°F/200°C, and continue to cook an additional 15 minutes, coating the ham with the glaze every 5 minutes. 5. Serve.
Per serving: Calories: 359; Fat:15.6g; Carbs: 23g; Fiber: 3.3g; Sugars: 13.4g; Proteins: 30.3g

Chapter 5 Fish and Seafood Recipes

107 Crab Cakes With Aioli
107 BBQ Shrimp With Butter Sauce
107 Shrimp Kebabs
107 Shrimp with Spicy Dipping Sauce
107 Sesame Salmon
107 Blackened Snapper
108 Breaded Salmon
108 Fish Sticks with Tartar Sauce
108 Scallops in Butter Sauce
108 Stuffed Flounder
108 Cucumber Salmon Salad
108 Crusted Flounder Fillets
109 Tuna Steaks with Tapenade
109 Tuna Patties with Sriracha Sauce
109 Fish Fillets With Dill Sauce
109 Shrimp Salad
109 Crab Meat Cakes
110 Scallops with Lemon Sauce
110 Swordfish Skewers
110 Coconut Crusted Shrimp
110 Almond-Coated Fish
110 Spicy Salmon
110 Fish for Kids
111 Garlicky Shrimp
111 Mayo Fish Sticks
111 Fish Tacos
111 Italian Tuna
111 Shrimp Po' Boys
112 Crispy Salmon Croquettes
112 Fish Cakes with Potatoes
112 Fish Nuggets
112 Crunchy Cod
112 Crumbed Fish Sticks
112 Easy Crab Cakes
113 Crisp Crawfish
113 Crusted Sea Scallops
113 Marinated Shrimp
113 Shrimp Grits
113 Pecan Crusted Striped Bass
114 Shrimp cakes
114 Crab Stuffed Shrimp
114 Tilapia Teriyaki with Rice
114 Tuna Nuggets with Hoisin Sauce

114 Red Snapper with Green Onions Salsa
114 Grilled Salmon
115 Cod with Grapes
115 Salmon with Zucchini
115 Fish Fingers
115 Asian Style Sea Bass
115 Shrimp Sliders
116 Horseradish Salmon
116 Shrimp Scampi
116 Grilled Salmon with Capers
116 Shrimp and Fingerling Potatoes
116 Crispy Fish Sticks
116 Vegetable with Salmon Fillets
117 Fish Capers Cakes
117 Parmesan Tilapia
117 Red Salmon Croquettes
117 Salmon with Veggies
117 Cajun Lemon Salmon
117 Salmon Potato Patties
117 Fried Shrimp
118 Buttery Shrimp Scampi
118 Miso Salmon Fillets
118 Creamy Scallops
118 Garlicky Salmon Fillets
118 Salmon Cakes
118 Delicious Fish Tacos
119 Parmesan Cod
119 Bacon Wrapped Scallops
119 Cod with Spring Onions
119 Salmon with Chives Sauce
119 Garlic Shrimp
119 Tilapia with Tomato Salsa
119 Crusted Salmon
119 Catfish With Avocado
120 Herbed Shrimp Skewers
120 Air-Fried Cod
120 Crab Muffins
120 Tilapia with Kale
120 Chili Crispy Haddock
120 Lime paprika Cod
120 Mackerel with Peppers
120 Ginger Lime Salmon
121 Crusted Sardine Cakes
121 Gingered Cod

121 Paprika Tilapia with Capers
121 Sesame Crusted Salmon
121 Parsley Coconut Shrimp
121 Bacon Halibut Steaks
121 Trout with Herb Sauce
122 Parmesan Salmon
122 Crusted Cheesy Shrimps
122 Salmon with Lime Sauce
122 Catfish Fillet Bites
122 Mustard Parmesan Cod
122 Turmeric Salmon with Cream
122 Delicious Umami Calamari
123 Air-Fried Tilapia
123 Paprika Cod with Endives
123 Peppered Tuna Skewers
123 Sea Scallops with tangy Cherry Sauce
123 Steamed Crab
123 Lemon Salmon with Dill
123 Nut-Crusted Halibut
124 Paprika Catfish with Tarragon
124 Tropical Sea Bass
124 Country Boil
124 Mediterranean Spicy Cod
124 Delicious Lobster Risotto
124 Creamy Crab
125 Mussels in White Wine
125 Mahi-Mahi with a Lemon-Caper Sauce
125 Steamed Shrimp with Asparagus
125 Delicious Louisiana Grouper
125 Steaming Clams
125 Crab Legs
126 Delicious Seafood Gumbo
126 Curried Coconut Shrimp
126 Cod with Olives and Fennel
126 Fish Stew
126 Garlicky Shrimp Scampi
126 Tilapia with Tomatoes
127 Fish Chowder
127 Lobster with Butter Sauce
127 Shrimp with tangy Risotto
127 Healthy Jambalaya
127 Regular Pad Thai

Crab Cakes With Aioli

Prep Time: 10 minutes. | Cook Time: 20 minutes. | Serves: 4

2 (8-ounce) cans crabmeat, drained and picked over to remove any bits of shell
2 eggs
¼ cup almond flour
Lemon Aioli
¼ cup mayo
2 teaspoons fresh lemon juice
1 teaspoon Dijon mustard
3 tablespoons mayo
1 tablespoon Dijon mustard
1 teaspoon Old Bay seasoning
1 tablespoon chopped fresh parsley
½ teaspoon salt

½ teaspoon garlic powder
½ teaspoon Old Bay seasoning

1. Place the Cook & Crisp Basket in your Ninja Foodi Pressure Cooker Steam Fryer. 2. Line the basket with parchment paper. 3. In a suitable bowl, mix the crabmeat, eggs, almond flour, mayo, Dijon mustard, Old Bay seasoning, parsley, and salt. Use a silicone spatula to fold until mixed, taking care not to break up the crabmeat too much. 4. Use an ice cream scoop to form the crab mixture patties. Place in a single layer on the lined Cook & Crisp Basket, then press lightly with the bottom of the scoop to flatten the patties into a circle about ½ inch thick. 5. Put on the Smart Lid on top of the Ninja Foodi Steam Fryer. 6. Move the Lid Slider to the "Air Fry/Stovetop". 7. Pausing halfway through the cooking time flip the patties, cook on "Air Fry" Mode at 350°F/175°C for about 10 minutes until lightly browned. 8. To make the lemon aioli: In a suitable bowl, mix the mayo, lemon juice, Dijon mustard, garlic powder, and Old Bay seasoning. Stir until mixed. 9. Serve the crab cakes topped with the aioli sauce.
Per Serving: Calories 319; Fat 21.2 g; Sodium 63 mg; Carbs 14g; Fiber 3.5g; Sugar 8.9g; Protein 19.6g

BBQ Shrimp With Butter Sauce

Prep Time: 10 minutes. | Cook Time: 20 minutes. | Serves: 4

6 tablespoons unsalted butter
⅓ cup Worcestershire sauce
3 cloves garlic, minced
Juice of 1 lemon
1 teaspoon paprika
1 teaspoon Creole seasoning
1½ pounds shrimp, peeled and deveined
2 tablespoons fresh parsley

1. Place the Cook & Crisp Basket in your Ninja Foodi Pressure Cooker Steam Fryer and place a reversible rack in it. 2. In any suitable microwave-safe bowl, mix the butter, Worcestershire, and garlic. Microwave on high for about 1 to 2 minutes until the butter is melted. Stir in the lemon juice, paprika, and Creole seasoning. Add the shrimp and toss until coated. 3. Transfer the prepare mixture to Cook & Crisp Basket. 4. Put on the Smart Lid on top of the Ninja Foodi Steam Fryer. 5. Move the Lid Slider to the "Air Fry/Stovetop". 6. Pausing halfway through the cooking time flip the shrimp, cook on "Air Fry" Mode at 370°F/185°C for about 12 to 15 minutes, until the shrimp are cooked through. Top with the parsley just before serving.
Per Serving: Calories 629; Fat 40.5 g; Sodium 584 mg; Carbs 16.9g; Fiber 4.1g; Sugar 9.3g; Protein 50.3g

Shrimp Kebabs

Prep Time: 10 minutes. | Cook Time: 20 minutes. | Serves: 4

1½ pounds large shrimp, peeled and deveined
1 large bell pepper, chopped
2 tablespoons olive oil
1 teaspoon smoked paprika
¾ teaspoon salt
3 cloves garlic, minced
8 ounces smoked chorizo, sliced into ½-inch rounds

1. Place the Cook & Crisp Basket in your Ninja Foodi Pressure Cooker Steam Fryer. 2. In a suitable bowl, mix the shrimp, bell pepper, olive oil, paprika, salt, and garlic. Toss gently until coated. 3. Thread the shrimp, peppers, and sausage onto the skewers, alternating ingredients as you go. 4. Put on the Smart Lid on top of the Ninja Foodi Steam Fryer. 5. Move the Lid Slider to the "Air Fry/Stovetop". 6. Working in batches if necessary and once cooked halfway through, flip the skewers, cook on "Air Fry" Mode at 400°F/200°C for about 12 to 15 minutes, until the peppers are tender and the shrimp are cooked through.
Per Serving: Calories 248; Fat 11.8 g; Sodium 421 mg; Carbs 2.2g; Fiber 0.4g; Sugar 1.5g; Protein 33.3g

Shrimp with Spicy Dipping Sauce

Prep Time: 10 minutes. | Cook Time: 20 minutes. | Serves: 4

1 (2½-ounce) bag pork rinds
¾ cup unsweetened shredded coconut flakes
¾ cup coconut flour
1 teaspoon onion powder
1 teaspoon garlic powder
2 eggs
1½ pounds large shrimp, peeled
and deveined
½ teaspoon salt
¼ teaspoon black pepper
Spicy Dipping Sauce
½ cup mayo
2 tablespoons sriracha
Zest and juice of ½ lime
1 clove garlic, minced

1. Place the Cook & Crisp Basket in your Ninja Foodi Pressure Cooker Steam Fryer. 2. In a food processor with metal blade, mix the pork rinds and coconut flakes. Pulse until the mixture resembles coarse crumbs. Transfer to any shallow bowl. 3. In another shallow bowl, mix the coconut flour, onion powder, and garlic powder; mix until mixed. 4. In another shallow bowl, beat the eggs until slightly frothy. 5. In a suitable bowl, season the prepared shrimp with the salt and black pepper. 6. Dredge the shrimp in the flour mixture, then dip in the eggs, and coat with the pork rind crumb mixture. 7. Arrange the coated shrimp on a baking sheet until ready to air fry. 8. Working in batches if necessary, arrange the shrimp in a single layer in your Ninja Foodi Cook & Crisp Basket. 9. Put on the Smart Lid on top of the Ninja Foodi Steam Fryer. 10. Move the Lid Slider to the "Air Fry/Stovetop". 11. Once cooked halfway through, flip the shrimp, cook on "Air Fry" Mode at 390°F/200°C for about 8 minutes until cooked through. To make the sauce: In a suitable bowl, mix the mayo, sriracha, lime zest and juice, and garlic. Whisk until mixed. Serve alongside the shrimp.
Per Serving: Calories 360; Fat 30.8 g; Sodium 584 mg; Carbs 1.3g; Fiber 0.5g; Sugar 0.2g; Protein 18.6g

Sesame Salmon

Prep Time: 10 minutes. | Cook Time: 20 minutes. | Serves: 4

¼ cup mixed black and brown sesame seeds
1 tablespoon reduced-sodium soy sauce
1 teaspoon sesame oil
1 teaspoon honey
4 (6-ounce) salmon filets, skin removed
2 tablespoons chopped fresh marjoram, for garnish (optional)

1. Place the Cook & Crisp Basket in your Ninja Foodi Pressure Cooker Steam Fryer. 2. Place the sesame seeds on a plate or in a small shallow bowl. In a separate small bowl, mix the soy sauce, sesame oil, and honey. 3. Brush all sides of the salmon with the soy sauce mixture until coated. Press the top of each filet into the sesame seeds to create a coating. 4. Arrange the fish in a single layer in the basket of your Ninja Foodi Pressure Cooker Steam Fryer, seed-side up. 5. Put on the Smart Lid on top of the Ninja Foodi Steam Fryer. 6. Move the Lid Slider to the "Air Fry/Stovetop". 7. Cook on "Air Fry" Mode at 360°F/180°C for about 10 minutes until the fish is firm and flakes easily with a fork. Top with the marjoram, if desired, before serving.
Per Serving: Calories 416; Fat 8.3 g; Sodium 208 mg; Carbs 22.9g; Fiber 0.5g; Sugar 19g; Protein 60.6g

Blackened Snapper

Prep Time: 13 minutes. | Cook Time: 8–10 minutes. | Serves: 4

1½ teaspoons black pepper
¼ teaspoon thyme
¼ teaspoon garlic powder
⅛ teaspoon cayenne pepper
1 teaspoon olive oil
4 4-ounce red snapper fillet portions, skin on
4 thin slices lemon
Cooking spray

1. Place the Cook & Crisp Basket in your Ninja Foodi Pressure Cooker Steam Fryer. 2. Mix the spices and oil together to make a paste. Rub into both sides of the fish. 3. Spray Cook & Crisp Basket with nonstick cooking spray and lay snapper steaks in basket, skin-side down. 4. Place a lemon slice on each piece of fish. 5. Put on the Smart Lid on top of the Ninja Foodi Steam Fryer. 6. Move the Lid Slider to the "Air Fry/Stovetop". 7. Cook on "Air Fry" Mode at 390°F/200°C for about 8 to 10 minutes. The fish will not flake when done, but it should be white through the center.
Per Serving: Calories 303; Fat 3.1 g; Sodium 343 mg; Carbs 24.9g; Fiber 1.5g; Sugar 0.9g; Protein 22.6g

Breaded Salmon

Prep Time: 10 minutes. | **Cook Time: 20 minutes.** | **Serves: 4**

2 cups breadcrumbs
4 salmon fillets

2 eggs, beaten
1 cup Swiss cheese, shredded

1. Place the Cook & Crisp Basket in your Pressure Cooker Steam Fryer. 2. Dip each salmon filet into eggs. Top with Swiss cheese. Dip into breadcrumbs, coating entire fish. Put into the Cook & Crisp Basket. Put on the Smart Lid on top of the Ninja Foodi Steam Fryer. Move the Lid Slider to the "Air Fry/Stovetop". Select the "Air Fry" mode for cooking. Adjust the cooking temperature to 390°F/200°C. Cook for around 20 minutes.
Per serving: Calories 347; Fat: 17.7g; Sodium 1655mg; Carbs: 6.8g; Fiber: 1.2g; Sugars 2.8g; Protein 33.3g

Fish Sticks with Tartar Sauce

Prep Time: 10 minutes. | **Cook Time: 20 minutes.** | **Serves: 4**

1½ pounds cod fillets, cut into 1-inch strips
1 teaspoon salt
½ teaspoon black pepper
2 eggs
¾ cup almond flour
¼ cup grated Parmesan cheese
Olive oil
Tartar Sauce

½ cup sour cream
½ cup mayo
3 tablespoons chopped dill pickle
2 tablespoons capers, drained and chopped
½ teaspoon dried dill
1 tablespoon dill pickle liquid (optional)

1. Place the Cook & Crisp Basket in your Ninja Foodi Pressure Cooker Steam Fryer. 2. Season the cod fillet strips with the salt and black pepper; then set this fish aside. 3. In any shallow bowl, lightly beat the eggs. In a second shallow bowl, mix the almond flour and Parmesan cheese. Stir until mixed. 4. Dip the fish into the egg mixture followed by the flour mixture. Press lightly to ensure an even coating. 5. Working in batches if necessary, arrange the fish in a single layer in the Ninja Foodi Cook & Crisp Basket and spray with olive oil. 6. Put on the Smart Lid on top of the Ninja Foodi Steam Fryer. 7. Move the Lid Slider to the "Air Fry/Stovetop". 8. Once cooked halfway through, flip the fish, cook on "Air Fry" Mode at 400°F/200°C for about 15 minutes. 9. In a suitable bowl, mix the sour cream, mayo, pickle, capers, and dill. 10. Serve the fish with this sauce.
Per Serving: Calories 413; Fat 30.8 g; Sodium 1279 mg; Carbs 2.4g; Fiber 0.5g; Sugar 1.3g; Protein 31.6g

Scallops in Butter Sauce

Prep Time: 10 minutes. | **Cook Time: 20 minutes.** | **Serves: 2**

8 large dry sea scallops (about ¾ pound)
Salt and black pepper
2 tablespoons olive oil
2 tablespoons unsalted butter, melted
2 tablespoons chopped flat-leaf

parsley
1 tablespoon fresh lemon juice
2 teaspoons capers, drained and chopped
1 teaspoon grated lemon zest
1 clove garlic, minced

1. Place the Cook & Crisp Basket in your Ninja Foodi Pressure Cooker Steam Fryer. 2. Use a paper towel to pat the scallops dry. Sprinkle lightly with salt and pepper. Brush with the olive oil. Arrange the scallops in a single layer in your Ninja Foodi Cook & Crisp Basket. 3. Put on the Smart Lid on top of the Ninja Foodi Steam Fryer. 4. Move the Lid Slider to the "Air Fry/Stovetop". 5. Once cooked halfway through, flip the scallops, cook on "Air Fry" Mode at 400°F/200°C for about 6 minutes until firm and opaque. 6. Meanwhile, in a suitable bowl, mix the oil, butter, parsley, lemon juice, capers, lemon zest, and garlic. Drizzle over the scallops just before serving.
Per Serving: Calories 404; Fat 20.3 g; Sodium 8 mg; Carbs 3.4g; Fiber 1g; Sugar 1.2g; Protein 53.4g

Stuffed Flounder

Prep Time: 10 minutes. | **Cook Time: 20 minutes.** | **Serves: 4**

¼ cup pine nuts
2 tablespoons olive oil

½ cup chopped tomatoes
1 (6-ounce) bag spinach, chopped

2 cloves garlic, chopped
Salt and black pepper
2 tablespoons unsalted butter

4 flounder filets (about 1½ pounds)
Dash of paprika
½ lemon, sliced into 4 wedges

1. Place the Cook & Crisp Basket in your Ninja Foodi Pressure Cooker Steam Fryer. 2. Place the pine nuts in Cook & Crisp Basket. 3. Put on the Smart Lid on top of the Ninja Foodi Steam Fryer. 4. Move the Lid Slider to the "Air Fry/Stovetop". 5. Cook on "Air Fry" Mode at 400°F/200°C for about 4 minutes until the nuts are lightly browned and fragrant. Remove the Cook & Crisp Basket. from your Ninja Foodi Pressure Cooker Steam Fryer, tip the nuts onto a plate to cool. Chop them into fine pieces. 6. In the Cook & Crisp Basket , mix the oil, tomatoes, spinach, and garlic. Use tongs to toss until mixed. 7. Put on the Smart Lid on top of the Ninja Foodi Steam Fryer. 8. Move the Lid Slider to the "Air Fry/Stovetop". 9. Cook on "Air Fry" Mode at 400°F/200°C for about 5 minutes until the tomatoes are softened and the spinach is wilted. 10. Transfer the vegetables to a suitable bowl and stir in the toasted pine nuts. 11. Place 1 tablespoon of the butter in the bottom of the Cook & Crisp Basket. Lower the heat on your Ninja Foodi Pressure Cooker Steam Fryer to 350°F/175°C. 12. Place the flounder on a clean work surface. Sprinkle both sides with salt and black pepper. Divide the vegetable mixture among the flounder filets and carefully roll up, securing with toothpicks. 13. Working in batches if necessary, arrange the filets seam-side down in the Cook & Crisp Basket along with 1 tablespoon of water. Top the filets with remaining 1 tablespoon butter and sprinkle with a dash of paprika. Cover loosely with foil. Cook on "Air Fry" Mode at 350°F/175°C for about 10 to 15 minutes until the fish is opaque and flakes easily with a fork. Remove the toothpicks before serving with the lemon wedges.
Per Serving: Calories 602; Fat 38 g; Sodium 3163 mg; Carbs 0.3g; Fiber 0.1g; Sugar 0g; Protein 61.4g

Cucumber Salmon Salad

Prep Time: 10 minutes. | **Cook Time: 20 minutes.** | **Serves: 2**

1-pound salmon filet
1½ tablespoons olive oil
1 tablespoon sherry vinegar
1 tablespoon capers, rinsed and drained

1 seedless cucumber, thinly sliced
¼ Vidalia onion, thinly sliced
2 tablespoons chopped fresh parsley
Salt and black pepper

1. Place the Cook & Crisp Basket in your Ninja Foodi Pressure Cooker Steam Fryer. 2. Lightly coat the salmon with ½ tablespoon of the olive oil. Place skin-side down in the Ninja Foodi Cook & Crisp Basket. 3. Put on the Smart Lid on top of the Ninja Foodi Steam Fryer. 4. Move the Lid Slider to the "Air Fry/Stovetop". 5. Cook on "Air Fry" Mode at 400°F/200°C for about 8 to 10 minutes until the fish is opaque and flakes easily with a fork. Transfer the salmon to a plate and let cool to room temperature. Remove the skin and carefully flake the fish into bite-size chunks. 6. In a suitable bowl, whisk the remaining 1 tablespoon olive oil, salt, black pepper and the vinegar until mixed. Add the flaked fish, capers, cucumber, onion, and parsley. Toss gently to coat. 7. Serve.
Per Serving: Calories 382; Fat 32.5 g; Sodium 1363 mg; Carbs 3.2g; Fiber 0.2g; Sugar 1.9g; Protein 19.1g

Crusted Flounder Fillets

Prep Time: 10 minutes. | **Cook Time: 5–8 minutes.** | **Serves: 4**

1 egg white
1 tablespoon water
1 cup panko breadcrumbs
2 tablespoons extra-light virgin

olive oil
4 4-ounce flounder fillets
Salt and pepper
Oil for misting or cooking spray

1. Place the Cook & Crisp Basket in your Ninja Foodi Pressure Cooker Steam Fryer. 2. Beat together egg white and water in shallow dish. 3. In another shallow dish, mix panko crumbs and oil until well mixed and crumbly (best done by hand). 4. Season flounder fillets with salt and pepper to taste. Dip each fillet into egg mixture and then roll in panko crumbs, pressing in crumbs so that fish is nicely coated. 5. Spray Cook & Crisp Basket with nonstick cooking spray and add fillets. 6. Put on the Smart Lid on top of the Ninja Foodi Steam Fryer. 7. Move the Lid Slider to the "Air Fry/Stovetop". 8. Cook on "Air Fry" Mode at 390°F/200°C for about 3 minutes. 9. Spray fish fillets but do not turn. Cook 2 to 5 minutes longer until golden brown and crispy. Using a spatula, carefully remove fish from basket and serve.
Per Serving: Calories 257; Fat 10.4g; Sodium 431mg; Total Carbs 20g; Fiber 0g; Sugar 1.6g; Protein 21g

Tuna Steaks with Tapenade

Prep Time: 10 minutes. | Cook Time: 20 minutes. | Serves: 4

4 (6-ounce) ahi tuna steaks	1 tablespoon olive oil
1 tablespoon olive oil	1 tablespoon chopped fresh parsley
Salt and black pepper	1 clove garlic
½ lemon, sliced into 4 wedges	2 teaspoons red wine vinegar
Olive Tapenade	1 teaspoon capers, drained
½ cup pitted kalamata olives	

1. Place the Cook & Crisp Basket in your Ninja Foodi Pressure Cooker Steam Fryer. 2. Drizzle the tuna steaks with the olive oil and sprinkle with salt and black pepper. Arrange the tuna steaks in a single layer in your Ninja Foodi Cook & Crisp Basket. 3. Put on the Smart Lid on top of the Ninja Foodi Steam Fryer. 4. Move the Lid Slider to the "Air Fry/Stovetop". 5. Pausing to turn the steaks halfway through the cooking time, cook on "Air Fry" Mode at 400°F/200°C for about 10 minutes until the fish is firm. 6. To make the tapenade: In a food processor fitted with a metal blade, mix the olives, olive oil, parsley, garlic, vinegar, and capers. Pulse until the mixture is chopped, pausing to scrape down the sides of the bowl if necessary. Spoon the tapenade over the top of the tuna steaks and serve with lemon wedges.
Per Serving: Calories 324; Fat 17.8 g; Sodium 363 mg; Carbs 8.9g; Fiber 0.5g; Sugar 1.9g; Protein 36.6g

Tuna Patties with Sriracha Sauce

Prep Time: 10 minutes. | Cook Time: 20 minutes. | Serves: 4

2 (6-ounce) cans tuna packed in oil	Pinch of salt and pepper
3 tablespoons almond flour	Spicy Sriracha Sauce
2 tablespoons mayo	¼ cup mayo
1 teaspoon dried dill	1 tablespoon sriracha sauce
½ teaspoon onion powder	1 teaspoon garlic powder

1. Place the Cook & Crisp Basket in your Ninja Foodi Pressure Cooker Steam Fryer. 2. Line the basket with parchment paper. 3. In a suitable bowl, mix the tuna, almond flour, mayo, dill, salt, pepper and onion powder. Use a fork to stir, mashing with the back of the fork as necessary, until mixed. 4. Use an ice cream scoop to form the tuna mixture patties. Place the patties in a single layer on the parchment paper in your Ninja Foodi Cook & Crisp Basket. Press lightly with the bottom of the scoop to flatten into a circle about ½ inch thick. 5. Put on the Smart Lid on top of the Ninja Foodi Steam Fryer. 6. Move the Lid Slider to the "Air Fry/Stovetop". 7. Once cooked halfway through, flip the patties, cook on "Air Fry" Mode at 380°F/195°C for about 10 minutes until lightly browned. 8. To make the sriracha sauce: In a suitable bowl, mix the mayo, sriracha, and garlic powder. Serve the tuna patties topped with the sriracha sauce.
Per Serving: Calories 398; Fat 37.8 g; Sodium 1463 mg; Carbs 2.5g; Fiber 0.2g; Sugar 0.5g; Protein 13.6g

Fish Fillets With Dill Sauce

Prep Time: 5 minutes. | Cook Time: 7 minutes. | Serves: 4

1-pound snapper, grouper, or salmon fillets	(homemade, here, or store-bought)
Salt	2 tablespoons dill, chopped, plus more for garnish
Black pepper	1 tablespoon freshly squeezed lemon juice
1 tablespoon avocado oil	½ teaspoon grated lemon zest
¼ cup sour cream	
¼ cup sugar-free mayo	

1. Place the Cook & Crisp Basket in your Ninja Foodi Pressure Cooker Steam Fryer. 2. Pat the fish dry with paper towels and season well with salt and pepper. Brush with the avocado oil. 3. Place the fillets in the Ninja Foodi Cook & Crisp Basket. Put on the Smart Lid on top of the Ninja Foodi Steam Fryer. 4. Move the Lid Slider to the "Air Fry/Stovetop". 5. Cook on "Air Fry" Mode at 400°F/200°C for about 1 minute. 6. Lower your Ninja Foodi Pressure Cooker Steam Fryer temperature to 325°F/160°C and continue cooking for about 5 minutes. Flip the half-cooked fish and cook for 7. 1 minute more or until an instant-read thermometer reads 145°F/60°C. (If using salmon, cook it to 125°F/50°C for medium-rare.) 8. While the fish is cooking, make the sauce by combining the sour cream, mayo, dill, lemon juice, and lemon zest in a suitable bowl. Add salt and pepper and stir until

mixed. Refrigerate until ready to serve. 9. Serve the fish with the sauce, garnished with the remaining dill.
Per Serving: Calories 267; Fat 15.2 g; Sodium 479 mg; Carbs 13.9g; Fiber 0.1g; Sugar 12.9g; Protein 20.6g

Shrimp Salad

Prep Time: 10 minutes | Cook Time: 4 to 6 minutes. | Serves: 4

12 ounces fresh large shrimp, peeled and deveined	¼ teaspoon black pepper, plus additional to season the marinade
1 tablespoon plus 1 teaspoon freshly squeezed lemon juice	⅓ cup sugar-free mayo (homemade, here, or store-bought)
4 tablespoons olive oil or avocado oil	2 tablespoons freshly grated Parmesan cheese
2 garlic cloves, minced	1 teaspoon Dijon mustard
¼ teaspoon salt, plus additional to season the marinade	1 tinned anchovy, mashed
	12 ounces romaine hearts, torn

1. Place the Cook & Crisp Basket in your Ninja Foodi Pressure Cooker Steam Fryer. 2. Place the shrimp in a suitable bowl. Add 1 tablespoon of lemon juice, 1 tablespoon of olive oil, and 1 minced garlic clove. Season with salt and pepper. Toss well and refrigerate for about 15 minutes. 3. While the shrimp marinates, make the dressing: In a blender, mix the mayo, Parmesan cheese, Dijon mustard, the remaining 1 teaspoon of lemon juice, the anchovy, the remaining minced garlic clove, ¼ teaspoon of salt, and ¼ teaspoon of pepper. Process until smooth. With the blender running, slowly stream in the remaining 3 tablespoons of oil. Transfer the mixture to a jar; seal and refrigerate until ready to serve. 4. Remove the shrimp from its marinade and place it in the Ninja Foodi Cook & Crisp Basket in a single layer. 5. Put on the Smart Lid on top of the Ninja Foodi Steam Fryer. 6. Move the Lid Slider to the "Air Fry/Stovetop". 7. Cook on "Air Fry" Mode at 400°F/200°C for about 2 minutes. Flip the half-cooked shrimp. Cook for about 2 to 4 minutes more, until the flesh turns opaque. 8. Place the romaine in a suitable bowl and toss with the desired amount of dressing. Top with the shrimp and serve immediately.
Per Serving: Calories: 329; Total Fat: 30g; Total Carbs: 4g; Fiber: 2g; Sugar: 0g; Protein: 16g

Crab Meat Cakes

Prep Time: 10 minutes| Cook Time: 14 minutes. | Serves: 4

Avocado oil spray	1 tablespoon sugar-free mayo (homemade, here, or store-bought)
⅓ cup red onion, diced	2 teaspoons Dijon mustard
¼ cup red bell pepper, diced	⅛ teaspoon cayenne pepper
8 ounces lump crabmeat, picked over for shells	Salt
3 tablespoons blanched almond flour	Black pepper
1 large egg, beaten	Elevated Tartar Sauce, for serving
	Lemon wedges, for serving

1. Place the Cook & Crisp Basket in your Ninja Foodi Pressure Cooker Steam Fryer and place a reversible rack in it. 2. Spray Cook & Crisp Basket with oil. Put the onion and red bell pepper in the it and give them a quick spray with oil. 3. Place the Cook & Crisp Basket in your Ninja Foodi Cook & Crisp Basket. 4. Put on the Smart Lid on top of the Ninja Foodi Steam Fryer. 5. Move the Lid Slider to the "Air Fry/Stovetop". 6. Cook the vegetables on "Air Fry" Mode at 400°F/200°C for about 7 minutes, until tender. 7. Transfer the vegetables to a suitable bowl. Add the crabmeat, almond flour, egg, mayo, mustard, and cayenne pepper and season with salt and pepper. Stir until the mixture is well mixed. 8. Form the mixture into four 1-inch-thick cakes. Cover with plastic wrap and refrigerate for about 1 hour. 9. Place the crab cakes in a single layer in the Ninja Foodi Cook & Crisp Basket and spray them with oil. 10. Put on the Smart Lid on top of the Ninja Foodi Steam Fryer. 11. Move the Lid Slider to the "Air Fry/Stovetop". 12. Cook on "Air Fry" Mode at 400°F/200°C for about 4 minutes. Flip the half-cooked crab cakes and spray with more oil. Cook for about 3 minutes more, until the internal temperature of the crab cakes reaches 155°F/70°C. 13. Serve with tartar sauce and a squeeze of fresh lemon juice.
Per Serving: Calories: 159; Fat 5.8 g; Sodium 198 mg; Carbs 9.5 g; Fiber 1.1g; Sugar 7.2g; Protein 16.6g

Scallops with Lemon Sauce

Prep Time: 5 minutes | Cook Time: 15 minutes. | Serves: 4

1-pound large sea scallops	1 tablespoon freshly squeezed
Salt and black pepper	lemon juice
Avocado oil spray	1 teaspoon minced garlic
¼ cup (4 tablespoons) unsalted	¼ teaspoon red pepper flakes
butter	

1. Place the Cook & Crisp Basket in your Ninja Foodi Pressure Cooker Steam Fryer and place a reversible rack in it. 2. If your scallops still have the adductor muscles attached, remove them. Dry the scallops with a paper towel. 3. Season scallops with salt and pepper, then place them on a plate and refrigerate for about 15 minutes. 4. Spray the Ninja Foodi Cook & Crisp Basket with oil, and arrange the scallops in a single layer. Spray the top of the scallops with oil. 5. Put on the Smart Lid on top of the Ninja Foodi Steam Fryer. 6. Move the Lid Slider to the "Air Fry/Stovetop". 7. Cook on "Air Fry" Mode at 350°F/175°C for about 6 minutes. Flip the half-cooked scallops. 8. Cook for about 6 minutes more, until an instant-read thermometer reads 145°F/60°C. 9. While the scallops cook, place the butter, lemon juice, garlic, and red pepper flakes in a small ramekin. 10. When the scallops have finished cooking, remove them from your Ninja Foodi Pressure Cooker Steam Fryer. Place the ramekin in your Ninja Foodi Pressure Cooker Steam Fryer. Cook until the butter melts, about 3 minutes. Stir. 11. Toss the scallops with the warm butter and serve.

Per Serving: Calories 341; Fat 24.6 g; Sodium 401 mg; Carbs 12g; Fiber 0.1g; Sugar 11.9g; Protein 18.6g

Swordfish Skewers

Prep Time: 10 minutes | Cook Time: 6 TO 8 minutes. |Serves: 4

1 pound filleted swordfish	2 teaspoons Dijon mustard
¼ cup avocado oil	Salt
2 tablespoons freshly squeezed	Black pepper
lemon juice	3 ounces cherry tomatoes
1 tablespoon minced fresh parsley	

1. Place the Cook & Crisp Basket in your Ninja Foodi Pressure Cooker Steam Fryer. 2. Cut the fish into 1½-inch chunks, picking out any remaining bones. 3. In a suitable bowl, mix well the oil, lemon juice, parsley, and Dijon mustard. Season to taste with salt and pepper. Add the fish and toss to coat the pieces. Cover and marinate the fish chunks in the refrigerator for about 30 minutes. 4. Remove the fish from the marinade. Thread the fish and cherry tomatoes on 4 skewers, alternating as you go. 5. Place the skewers in the Ninja Foodi Cook & Crisp Basket. 6. Put on the Smart Lid on top of the Ninja Foodi Steam Fryer. 7. Move the Lid Slider to the "Air Fry/Stovetop". 8. Cook on "Air Fry" Mode at 400°F/200°C for about 3 minutes. Flip the half-cooked skewers. Cook for about 3 to 5 minutes longer, until the fish is cooked through and an instant-read thermometer reads 140°F/60°C.

Per Serving: Calories 634; Fat 19.6 g; Sodium 1263 mg; Carbs 13.1g; Fiber 1.5g; Sugar 8.6g; Protein 96g

Coconut Crusted Shrimp

Prep Time: 15 minutes. | Cook Time: 17 minutes. |Serves: 4

¾ cup unsweetened shredded	Black pepper
coconut	2 large eggs
¾ cup coconut flour	1 pound fresh extra-large or jumbo
1 teaspoon garlic powder	shrimp, peeled and deveined
¼ teaspoon cayenne pepper	Avocado oil spray
Salt	

1. Place the Cook & Crisp Basket in your Ninja Foodi Pressure Cooker Steam Fryer. 2. In a suitable bowl, mix the shredded coconut, coconut flour, garlic powder, and cayenne pepper. Season to taste with salt and pepper. 3. In a suitable bowl, beat the eggs. 4. Pat the shrimp dry with paper towels. Dip each shrimp in the eggs and then the coconut mixture. Gently press the coating to the shrimp to help it adhere. 5. Spray the shrimp top with oil and place them in a single layer in your Ninja Foodi Cook & Crisp Basket, working in batches if necessary. 6. Put on the Smart Lid on top of the Ninja Foodi Steam Fryer. 7. Move the Lid Slider to the "Air Fry/Stovetop". 8. Cook the

shrimp at 400°F/200°C for about 9 minutes, then flip and spray them with more oil. Cook for about 8 minutes more, until the center of the shrimp is opaque and cooked through.

Per Serving: Calories 324; Fat 17.8 g; Sodium 363 mg; Carbs 8.9g; Fiber 0.5g; Sugar 1.9g; Protein 36.6g

Almond-Coated Fish

Prep Time: 15 minutes. | Cook Time: 10 minutes. | Serves: 4

4 4-ounce fish fillets	Salt and pepper
¾ cup breadcrumbs	¾ cup flour
¼ cup sliced almonds, crushed	1 egg, beaten with 1 tablespoon
2 tablespoons lemon juice	water
⅛ teaspoon cayenne	Oil for misting or cooking spray

1. Place the Cook & Crisp Basket in your Ninja Foodi Pressure Cooker Steam Fryer. 2. Split fish fillets lengthwise down the center to create 8 pieces. 3. Mix breadcrumbs and almonds together and set aside. 4. Mix the lemon juice and cayenne together. Brush on all sides of fish. 5. Season fish to taste with salt and pepper. 6. Place the flour on a sheet of wax paper. 7. Roll fillets in flour, dip in egg wash, and roll in the crumb mixture. 8. Mist both sides of fish with oil or cooking spray. 9. Spray Cook & Crisp Basket and lay fillets inside. 10. Put on the Smart Lid on top of the Ninja Foodi Steam Fryer. 11. Move the Lid Slider to the "Air Fry/Stovetop". 12. Cook on "Air Fry" Mode at 390°F/200°C for about 5 minutes, turn fish over,. Cook for an additional 5 minutes or until fish is done and flakes easily.

Per Serving: Calories 213; Fat 4.1 g; Sodium 303 mg; Carbs 37.9g; Fiber 1.5g; Sugar 1.9g; Protein 26.6g

Spicy Salmon

Prep Time: 5 minutes. | Cook Time: 10 to 12 minutes. |Serves: 4

½ cup sugar-free mayo	sauce, diced
(homemade, here, or store-bought)	1 teaspoon adobo sauce (from the
2 tablespoons brown sugar	canned chipotle)
substitute, such as Sukrin Gold	16 ounces salmon fillets
2 teaspoons Dijon mustard	Salt
1 canned chipotle chile in adobo	Black pepper

1. Place the Cook & Crisp Basket in your Ninja Foodi Pressure Cooker Steam Fryer. 2. In a small food processor, mix the mayo, brown sugar substitute, Dijon mustard, chipotle pepper, and adobo sauce. Process for about 1 minute until everything is mixed and the brown sugar substitute is no longer granular. 3. Season the salmon with salt and pepper. Spread half of the sauce over the fish, and reserve the remainder of the sauce for serving. 4. Place the salmon in your Ninja Foodi Cook & Crisp Basket. 5. Put on the Smart Lid on top of the Ninja Foodi Steam Fryer. 6. Move the Lid Slider to the "Air Fry/Stovetop". 7. Cook on "Air Fry" Mode at 400°F/200°C for about 5 minutes. Flip the half-cooked salmon. Cook for about 5 to 7 minutes more, until an instant-read thermometer reads 125°F/50°C (for medium-rare). 8. Serve warm with the remaining sauce.

Per Serving: Calories 398; Fat 27 g; Sodium 416mg; Carbs 34.9g; Fiber 6.5g; Sugar 6.9g; Protein 11.6g

Fish for Kids

Prep Time: 10 minutes. | Cook Time: 6–8 minutes. | Serves: 4

8 ounces fish fillets (pollock or	½ cup plain breadcrumbs
cod)	Oil for misting or cooking spray
Salt (optional)	

1. Place the Cook & Crisp Basket in your Ninja Foodi Pressure Cooker Steam Fryer. 2. Cut fish fillets into "fingers" about ½ x 3 inches. Sprinkle with salt to taste, if desired. 3. Roll fish in breadcrumbs. Spray all sides with oil or cooking spray. 4. Place in Cook & Crisp Basket in single layer. 5. Put on the Smart Lid on top of the Ninja Foodi Steam Fryer. 6. Move the Lid Slider to the "Air Fry/ Stovetop". 7. Cook on "Air Fry" Mode at 390°F/200°C for about 6 to 8 minutes, until golden brown and crispy.

Per Serving: Calories 297; Fat 1g; Sodium 291mg; Total Carbs 35g; Fiber 1g; Sugar 9g; Protein 29g

Garlicky Shrimp

Prep Time: 5 minutes. | Cook Time: 10 minutes. |Serves: 4

1 pound fresh large shrimp, peeled and deveined	Black pepper
1 tablespoon avocado oil	2 tablespoons unsalted butter, melted
2 teaspoons minced garlic	
½ teaspoon red pepper flakes	2 tablespoons chopped fresh parsley
Salt	

1. Place the Cook & Crisp Basket in your Ninja Foodi Pressure Cooker Steam Fryer. 2. Place the shrimp in a suitable bowl and toss with the avocado oil, 1 teaspoon of minced garlic, and red pepper flakes. Season with salt and pepper. 3. Arrange the shrimp in single layer in your Ninja Foodi Cook & Crisp Basket, working in batches if necessary. 4. Put on the Smart Lid on top of the Ninja Foodi Steam Fryer. 5. Move the Lid Slider to the "Air Fry/Stovetop". 6. Cook on "Air Fry" Mode at 350°F/175°C for about 6 minutes. Flip the half-cooked shrimp. Cook for about 2 to 4 minutes more, until the internal temperature of the shrimp reaches 120°F/50°C. (The time it takes to cook will depend on the size of the shrimp.) 7. While the shrimp are cooking, melt the butter in a small saucepan over medium heat and stir in the remaining 1 teaspoon of garlic. 8. Transfer the cooked shrimp to a suitable bowl, add the garlic butter, and toss well. Top with the parsley and serve warm.
Per Serving: Calories 399; Fat 13 g; Sodium 626 mg; Carbs 52.9g; Fiber 8.8g; Sugar 3.9g; Protein 19.6g

Mayo Fish Sticks

Prep Time: 10 minutes | Cook Time: 9 minutes. Serves: 4

1-pound cod fillets	¼ cup sugar-free mayo (homemade, here, or store-bought)
1½ cups blanched almond flour	
2 teaspoons Old Bay seasoning	1 large egg, beaten
½ teaspoon paprika	Avocado oil spray
Salt	Elevated Tartar Sauce, for serving
Black pepper	

1. Place the Cook & Crisp Basket in your Ninja Foodi Pressure Cooker Steam Fryer. 2. Cut the fish into ¾-inch-wide strips. In any shallow bowl, stir together the almond flour, Old Bay seasoning, paprika, and salt and pepper to taste. In another shallow bowl, mix well the mayo and egg. 3. Dip the cod strips in the egg mixture, then the almond flour, gently pressing with your fingers to help adhere the coating. 4. Place the coated fish on a parchment paper–lined baking sheet and freeze for about 30 minutes. 5. Spray the Ninja Foodi Cook & Crisp Basket with oil. Place the fish in the basket in a single layer, and spray each piece with oil. 6. Put on the Smart Lid on top of the Ninja Foodi Steam Fryer. 7. Move the Lid Slider to the "Air Fry/Stovetop". 8. Cook on "Air Fry" Mode at 400°F/200°C for about 5 minutes. Flip and spray with more oil. Cook on "Air Fry" Mode for about 4 minutes more, until the internal temperature reaches 140°F/60°C. Serve with the tartar sauce.
Per Serving: Calories 539; Fat 17.5 g; Sodium 1875 mg; Carbs 79.2g; Fiber 4.5g; Sugar 26.9g; Protein 15.6g

Fish Tacos

Prep Time: 25 minutes. | Cook Time: 7–10 minutes. | Serves: 4

Fish Tacos:

1-pound fish fillets	¼ teaspoon smoked paprika
¼ teaspoon cumin	1 teaspoon oil
¼ teaspoon coriander	Cooking spray
⅛ teaspoon red pepper	6–8 corn or flour tortillas (6-inch size)
1 tablespoon lime zest	

Jalapeño-Lime Sauce:

½ cup sour cream	½ teaspoon minced jalapeño (flesh only)
1 tablespoon lime juice	
¼ teaspoon grated lime zest	¼ teaspoon cumin

Napa Cabbage Garnish:

1 cup shredded Napa cabbage	pepper
¼ cup slivered red or green bell	¼ cup slivered onion

1. Place the Cook & Crisp Basket in your Ninja Foodi Pressure Cooker Steam Fryer. 2. Slice the fish fillets into strips approximately ½-inch thick. 3. Put the strips into a sealable plastic bag along with the cumin, coriander, red pepper, lime zest, smoked paprika, and oil. Massage seasonings into the fish until evenly distributed. 4. Spray Cook & Crisp Basket with nonstick cooking spray and place seasoned fish inside. 5. Put on the Smart Lid on top of the Ninja Foodi Steam Fryer. 6. Move the Lid Slider to the "Air Fry/Stovetop". 7. Cook on "Air Fry" Mode at 390°F/200°C for approximately 5 minutes. Shake basket to distribute fish. Cook an additional 2 to 5 minutes, until fish flakes easily. 8. While the fish is cooking, prepare the Jalapeño-Lime Sauce by mixing the sour cream, lime juice, lime zest, jalapeño, and cumin together to make a smooth sauce. Set aside. 9. Mix the cabbage, bell pepper, and onion together and set aside. 10. To warm refrigerated tortillas, wrap in damp paper towels and microwave for about 30 to 60 seconds. 11. To serve, spoon some of fish into a warm tortilla. Add one or two tablespoons Napa Cabbage Garnish and drizzle with Jalapeño-Lime Sauce.
Per Serving: Calories 348; Fat 30g; Sodium 660mg; Total Carbs 5g; Fiber 0g; Sugar 0g; Protein 14g

Italian Tuna

Prep Time: 15 minutes. | Cook Time: 21–24 minutes. | Serves: 8

Cooking spray	1 tuna loin (approximately 2 pounds, 3 to 4 inches thick, large enough to fill a 6 x 6-inch baking dish)
1 tablespoon Italian seasoning	
⅛ teaspoon black pepper	
1 tablespoon extra-light olive oil	
1 teaspoon lemon juice	

1. Place the Cook & Crisp Basket in your Ninja Foodi Pressure Cooker Steam Fryer. 2. Spray the Cook & Crisp Basket with cooking spray and place in Cook & Crisp Basket. 3. Mix together the Italian seasoning, pepper, oil, and lemon juice. 4. Using a dull table knife or butter knife, pierce top of tuna about every half inch. Insert knife into top of tuna roast and pierce almost all the way to the bottom. 5. Spoon oil mixture into each of the holes and use the knife to push seasonings into the tuna as deeply as possible. 6. Spread any remaining oil mixture on all outer surfaces of tuna. 7. Place tuna roast in Cook & Crisp Basket. 8. Put on the Smart Lid on top of the Ninja Foodi Steam Fryer. 9. Move the Lid Slider to the "Air Fry/Stovetop". 10. Cook on "Air Fry" Mode at 390°F/200°C for about 20 minutes. Check temperature with a meat thermometer. Cook for an additional 1 to 4 minutes until temperature reaches 145°F/60°C.
Per Serving: Calories 399; Fat 16g; Sodium 537mg; Total Carbs 28g; Fiber 3g; Sugar 10g; Protein 35g

Shrimp Po' Boys

Prep Time: 20 minutes. | Cook Time: 5 minutes | Serves: 4

½ cup cornstarch	Old Bay Seasoning
2 eggs	Oil for misting or cooking spray
2 tablespoons milk	2 large hoagie rolls
¾ cup shredded coconut	Honey mustard or light mayo
½ cup panko breadcrumbs	1½ cups shredded lettuce
1 pound (31–35 count) shrimp, peeled and deveined	1 large tomato, thinly sliced

1. Place the Cook & Crisp Basket in your Ninja Foodi Pressure Cooker Steam Fryer. 2. Place cornstarch in a shallow dish or plate. 3. In another shallow dish, beat together eggs and milk. 4. In a third dish mix the coconut and panko crumbs. 5. Sprinkle shrimp with Old Bay Seasoning to taste. 6. Dip shrimp in cornstarch to coat lightly, dip in egg mixture, shake off excess, and roll in coconut mixture to coat well. 7. Spray both sides of coated shrimp with oil or cooking spray. 8. Put on the Smart Lid on top of the Ninja Foodi Steam Fryer. 9. Move the Lid Slider to the "Air Fry/Stovetop". Cook half the shrimp in a single layer at 390°F/200°C on "Air Fry" Mode for about 5 minutes. 10. Repeat to cook remaining shrimp. 11. To Assemble 12. Split each hoagie lengthwise, leaving one long edge intact. 13. Put on the Smart Lid on top of the Ninja Foodi Steam Fryer. 14. Move the Lid Slider to the "Air Fry/Stovetop". 15. Place in Cook & Crisp Basket. Cook on "Air Fry" Mode at 390°F/200°C for about 1 to 2 minutes until heated through. 16. Remove buns, break apart, and place on 4 plates, cut side up. 17. Spread with honey mustard or mayo. 18. Top with shredded lettuce, tomato slices, and coconut shrimp.
Per Serving: Calories 249; Fat 5.7 g; Sodium 574 mg; Carbs 23.9g; Fiber 0.9g; Sugar 1.9g; Protein 3.6g

Crispy Salmon Croquettes

Prep Time: 10 minutes. | Cook Time: 7–8 minutes. | Serves: 4

1 tablespoon oil	⅓ cup crushed saltine crackers
½ cup breadcrumbs	(about 8 crackers)
1 14.75-ounce can salmon, drained	½ teaspoon Old Bay Seasoning
and all skin and fat removed	½ teaspoon onion powder
1 egg, beaten	½ teaspoon Worcestershire sauce

1. Place the Cook & Crisp Basket in your Ninja Foodi Pressure Cooker Steam Fryer. 2. In a shallow dish, mix oil and breadcrumbs until crumbly. 3. In a suitable bowl, mix the salmon, egg, cracker crumbs, Old Bay, onion powder, and Worcestershire. Mix well and shape into 8 small patties about ½-inch thick. 4. Gently dip each patty into breadcrumb mixture and turn to coat well on all sides. 5. Put on the Smart Lid on top of the Ninja Foodi Steam Fryer. 6. Move the Lid Slider to the "Air Fry/Stovetop". 7. Cook on "Air Fry" Mode at 390°F/200°C for about 7 to 8 minutes until outside is crispy and browned.
Per Serving: Calories 308; Fat 24g; Sodium 715mg; Total Carbs 0.8g; Fiber 0.1g; Sugar 0.1g; Protein 21.9g

Fish Cakes with Potatoes

Prep Time: 30 minutes. | Cook Time: 10–12 minutes. | Serves: 4

¾ cup mashed potatoes (about 1	1 large egg
large russet potato)	¼ cup potato starch
12 ounces cod or other white fish	½ cup panko breadcrumbs
Salt and black pepper, to taste	1 tablespoon fresh chopped chives
Oil for misting or cooking spray	2 tablespoons minced onion

1. Place the Cook & Crisp Basket in your Ninja Foodi Pressure Cooker Steam Fryer. 2. Peel potatoes, cut into cubes. Cook on stovetop till soft. 3. Salt and pepper raw fish to taste. Mist with oil or cooking spray. 4. Put on the Smart Lid on top of the Ninja Foodi Steam Fryer. 5. Move the Lid Slider to the "Air Fry/Stovetop". 6. Cook fish at 360°F/180°C on "Air Fry" Mode for about 6 to 8 minutes, until fish flakes easily. If fish is crowded, rearrange halfway through cooking to ensure all pieces cook evenly. 7. Transfer fish to a plate and break apart to cool. 8. Beat egg in a shallow dish. 9. Place potato starch in another shallow dish, and panko crumbs in a third dish. 10. When potatoes are done, drain in colander and rinse with cold water. 11. In a suitable bowl, mash the potatoes and stir in the chives and onion. Add salt and pepper to taste, then stir in the fish. 12. If needed, stir in a tablespoon of the beaten egg to help bind the mixture. 13. Shape into 8 small, fat patties. Dust lightly with potato starch, dip in egg, and roll in panko crumbs. Spray both sides with oil or cooking spray. 14. Put on the Smart Lid on top of the Ninja Foodi Steam Fryer. 15. Move the Lid Slider to the "Air Fry/Stovetop". 16. Cook on "Air Fry" Mode at 360°F/180°C for about 10 to 12 minutes, until golden brown and crispy.
Per Serving: Calories 351; Fat 20.3 g; Sodium 298 mg; Carbs 40.9g; Fiber 0.5g; Sugar 35.5g; Protein 33.6g

Fish Nuggets

Prep Time: 10 minutes. | Cook Time: 7–8 minutes. | Serves: 4

2 medium catfish Nuggets, cut in	2 eggs
chunks.	2 tablespoons skim milk
2 medium catfish fillets, cut in	½ cup cornstarch
chunks (approximately 1 x 2 inch)	1 cup panko breadcrumbs, crushed
Salt and pepper	Oil for misting or cooking spray

1. Place the Cook & Crisp Basket in your Ninja Foodi Pressure Cooker Steam Fryer. 2. Season catfish chunks with salt and pepper to your liking. 3. Beat together eggs and milk in a suitable bowl. 4. Place cornstarch in a second small bowl. 5. Place breadcrumbs in a third small bowl. 6. Dip catfish chunks in cornstarch, dip in egg wash, shake off excess, then roll in breadcrumbs. 7. Spray all sides of catfish chunks with oil or cooking spray. 8. Place chunks in Cook & Crisp Basket in a single layer, leaving space between for air circulation. 9. Put on the Smart Lid on top of the Ninja Foodi Steam Fryer. 10. Move the Lid Slider to the "Air Fry/Stovetop". 11. Cook on "Air Fry" Mode at 390°F/200°C for about 4 minutes, turn and cook an additional 3 to 4 minutes, until fish flakes easily and outside is crispy brown. 12.

Repeat to cook remaining catfish nuggets.
Per Serving: Calories 685; Fat 18.3 g; Sodium 865 mg; Carbs99.3g; Fiber 6.5g; Sugar 7.9g; Protein 27.6g

Crunchy Cod

Prep Time: 12 minutes. | Cook Time: 10 minutes. | Serves: 2

4 tablespoons butter, melted	2 (6-ounce) cod fillets
8 to 10 RITZ® crackers, crushed	Salt and black pepper
into crumbs	1 lemon

1. Place the Cook & Crisp Basket in your Ninja Foodi Pressure Cooker Steam Fryer. 2. Melt the butter in a small saucepan on the stovetop or in a microwavable dish in the microwave, and then transfer the butter to a shallow dish. Place the crushed RITZ® crackers into a second shallow dish. 3. Season the fish fillets with salt and black pepper. Dip them into the butter and then coat both sides with the RITZ® crackers. 4. Place the fish into the Ninja Foodi Cook & Crisp Basket. 5. Put on the Smart Lid on top of the Ninja Foodi Steam Fryer. 6. Move the Lid Slider to the "Air Fry/Stovetop". 7. Cook at 380°F/195°C on "Air Fry" Mode for about 8 to 10 minutes, flipping the fish over halfway through the cooking time. 8. Serve with a wedge of lemon to squeeze over the top.
Per Serving: Calories 351; Fat 11g; Sodium 150mg; Total Carbs 3.3g; Fiber 0.2g; Sugar 1g; Protein 33.2g

Crumbed Fish Sticks

Prep Time: 20 minutes. | Cook Time: 6–9 minutes. | Serves: 4

1-pound fish fillets	Crumb Coating:
½ teaspoon hot sauce	¾ cup panko breadcrumbs
1 tablespoon coarse brown mustard	¼ cup stone-cornmeal
1 teaspoon Worcestershire sauce	¼ teaspoon salt
Salt	Oil for misting or cooking spray

1. Place the Cook & Crisp Basket in your Ninja Foodi Pressure Cooker Steam Fryer. 2. Cut fish fillets crosswise into slices 1-inch wide. 3. Mix the hot sauce, mustard, and Worcestershire sauce together to make a paste and rub on all sides of the fish. Season to taste with salt. 4. Mix crumb coating ingredients together and spread on a sheet of wax paper. 5. Roll the fish fillets in the crumb mixture. 6. Spray all sides with olive oil or cooking spray and place in Cook & Crisp Basket in a single layer. 7. Put on the Smart Lid on top of the Ninja Foodi Steam Fryer. 8. Move the Lid Slider to the "Air Fry/Stovetop". 9. Cook on "Air Fry" Mode at 390°F/200°C for about 6 to 9 minutes, until fish flakes easily.
Per Serving: Calories 416; Fat 8.3 g; Sodium 208 mg; Carbs 22.9g; Fiber 0.5g; Sugar 19g; Protein 60.6g

Easy Crab Cakes

Prep Time: 20 minutes. | Cook Time: 10–12 minutes. | Serves: 4

8 ounces imitation crabmeat	1 tablespoon Worcestershire sauce,
4 ounces leftover cooked fish (such	plus 2 teaspoons
as cod, pollock, or haddock)	2 teaspoons dried parsley flakes
2 tablespoons minced green onion	½ teaspoon dried dill weed,
2 tablespoons minced celery	crushed
¾ cup crushed saltine cracker	½ teaspoon garlic powder
crumbs	½ teaspoon Old Bay Seasoning
2 tablespoons light mayo	½ cup panko breadcrumbs
1 teaspoon prepared yellow	Oil for misting or cooking spray
mustard	

1. Place the Cook & Crisp Basket in your Ninja Foodi Pressure Cooker Steam Fryer. 2. Use knives or a food processor to shred crabmeat and fish. 3. In a suitable bowl, mix all the recipe ingredients except panko and oil. Stir well. 4. Shape into 8 small, fat patties. 5. Carefully roll patties in panko crumbs to coat. Spray both sides with oil or cooking spray. 6. Place patties in Cook & Crisp Basket. 7. Put on the Smart Lid on top of the Ninja Foodi Steam Fryer. 8. Move the Lid Slider to the "Air Fry/Stovetop". 9. Cook on "Air Fry" Mode at 390°F/200°C for about 10 to 12 minutes until golden brown and crispy.
Per Serving: Calories 249; Fat 5.7 g; Sodium 574 mg; Carbs 23.9g; Fiber 0.9g; Sugar 1.9g; Protein 3.6g

Crisp Crawfish

Prep Time: 15 minutes. | Cook Time: 18–20 minutes. | Serves: 4

½ cup flour, plus 2 tablespoons
½ teaspoon garlic powder
1½ teaspoons Old Bay Seasoning
½ teaspoon onion powder
Coating:
1½ cups panko crumbs
1 teaspoon Old Bay Seasoning

½ cup beer, plus 2 tablespoons
12-ounce package frozen crawfish tail meat, thawed and drained
Oil for misting or cooking spray

½ teaspoon black pepper

1. Place the Cook & Crisp Basket in your Ninja Foodi Pressure Cooker Steam Fryer. 2. In a suitable bowl, mix together the flour, garlic powder, Old Bay Seasoning, and onion powder. Stir in beer to blend. 3. Add crawfish meat to batter and stir to coat. 4. Mix the coating ingredients in food processor and pulse to crush the crumbs. Transfer crumbs to shallow dish. 5. Pour the crawfish and batter into a colander to drain. Stir with a spoon to drain excess batter. 6. Working with a handful of crawfish at a time, roll in crumbs and place on a cookie sheet. It's okay if some of the smaller pieces of crawfish meat stick together. 7. Spray breaded crawfish with oil or cooking spray and place all at once into Cook & Crisp Basket. 8. Put on the Smart Lid on top of the Ninja Foodi Steam Fryer. 9. Move the Lid Slider to the "Air Fry/Stovetop". 10. Cook on "Air Fry" Mode at 390°F/200°C for about 5 minutes. Shake basket or stir and mist again with olive oil or spray. Cook 5 more minutes, shake basket again, and mist lightly again. Continue cooking 3 to 5 more minutes, until browned and crispy.
Per Serving: Calories 305; Fat 15g; Sodium 482mg; Total Carbs 17g; Fiber 3g; Sugar 2g; Protein 35g

Crusted Sea Scallops

Prep Time: 10 minutes. | Cook Time: 6–8 minutes | Serves: 4

1½ pounds sea scallops
Salt and pepper
2 eggs

½ cup flour
½ cup plain breadcrumbs
Oil for misting or cooking spray

1. Place the Cook & Crisp Basket in your Ninja Foodi Pressure Cooker Steam Fryer. 2. Rinse scallops and remove the tough side muscle. Sprinkle to taste with salt and pepper. 3. Beat eggs together in a shallow dish. Place flour in a second shallow dish and breadcrumbs in a third. 4. Dip scallops in flour, then eggs, and then roll in breadcrumbs. Mist with oil or cooking spray. 5. Place scallops in Cook & Crisp Basket in a single layer, leaving some space between. You should be able to cook about a dozen at a time. 6. Put on the Smart Lid on top of the Ninja Foodi Steam Fryer. 7. Move the Lid Slider to the "Air Fry/Stovetop". 8. Cook on "Air Fry" Mode at 390°F/200°C for about 6 to 8 minutes, watching carefully so as not to overcook. Scallops are done when they turn opaque all the way through. They will feel slightly firm when pressed with tines of a fork. 9. Repeat to cook remaining scallops.
Per Serving: Calories 275; Fat 1.4g; Sodium 582mg; Total Carbs 31.5g; Fiber 1.1g; Sugar 0.1g; Protein 29.8g

Marinated Shrimp

Prep Time: 1 hour 20 minutes. | Cook Time: 6–8 minutes | Serves: 4

Shrimp
1 pound (26–30 count) shrimp, peeled, deveined, and butterflied (last tail section of shell intact)
Marinade
1 5-ounce can evaporated milk
2 eggs, beaten
2 tablespoons white vinegar

1 tablespoon baking powder
Coating
1 cup crushed panko breadcrumbs
½ teaspoon paprika
½ teaspoon Old Bay Seasoning
¼ teaspoon garlic powder
Oil for misting or cooking spray

1. Place the Cook & Crisp Basket in your Ninja Foodi Pressure Cooker Steam Fryer. 2. Stir together all marinade ingredients until well mixed. Add shrimp and stir to coat. Refrigerate for about 1 hour. 3. Mix coating ingredients in shallow dish. 4. Remove shrimp from marinade, roll in crumb mixture, and spray with olive oil or cooking spray. 5. Put on the Smart Lid on top of the Ninja Foodi Steam Fryer. 6. Move the Lid Slider to the "Air Fry/Stovetop". 7. Cooking in two

batches, place shrimp in Cook & Crisp Basket in single layer, close but not overlapping. Cook on "Air Fry" Mode at 390°F/200°C for about 6 to 8 minutes, until light golden brown and crispy. 8. Repeat to cook remaining shrimp.
Per Serving: Calories 275; Fat 1.4g; Sodium 582mg; Total Carbs 31.5g; Fiber 1.1g; Sugar 0.1g; Protein 29.8g

Shrimp Grits

Prep Time: 15 minutes. | Cook Time: shrimp 5–7 minutes| Serves: 4

1-pound raw shelled shrimp, deveined (26–30 count or smaller)
Marinade
2 tablespoons lemon juice
2 tablespoons Worcestershire sauce
1 tablespoon olive oil
1 teaspoon Old Bay Seasoning
½ teaspoon hot sauce
Grits
¾ cup quick cooking grits (not instant)

3 cups water
½ teaspoon salt
1 tablespoon butter
½ cup chopped green bell pepper
½ cup chopped celery
½ cup chopped onion
½ teaspoon oregano
¼ teaspoon Old Bay Seasoning
2 ounces sharp Cheddar cheese, grated

1. Place the Cook & Crisp Basket in your Ninja Foodi Pressure Cooker Steam Fryer and place a reversible rack in it. 2. Stir together all marinade ingredients. Pour marinade over shrimp and set aside. 3. For grits, heat water and salt to boil in saucepan on stovetop. Stir in grits, lower heat to medium-low. Cook about 5 minutes until thick and done. 4. Place butter, bell pepper, celery, and onion in Cook & Crisp Basket . 5. Put on the Smart Lid on top of the Ninja Foodi Steam Fryer. 6. Move the Lid Slider to the "Air Fry/Stovetop". 7. Cook on "Air Fry" Mode at 390°F/200°C for about 2 minutes and stir. Cook 6 or 7 minutes longer, until crisp tender. 8. Add oregano and 1 teaspoon Old Bay to cooked vegetables. Stir in grits and cheese. Cook on "Air Fry" Mode at 390°F/200°C for about 1 minute. Cook 1 to 2 minutes longer to melt cheese. 9. Remove from Ninja Foodi Steam Fryer. Cover with plate to keep warm while shrimp cooks. 10. Drain marinade from shrimp. Place shrimp in Cook & Crisp Basket. Cook on "Air Fry" Mode at 360°F/180°C for about 3 minutes. Stir or shake basket. Cook 2 to 4 more minutes, until done. 11. To serve, spoon grits onto plates and top with shrimp.
Per Serving: Calories 275; Fat 1.4g; Sodium 582mg; Total Carbs 31.5g; Fiber 1.1g; Sugar 0.1g; Protein 29.8g

Pecan Crusted Striped Bass

Prep Time: 12 minutes. | Cook Time: 9 minutes. | Serves: 2

Flour, for dredging
2 egg whites, beaten
1 cup pecans, chopped
1 teaspoon chopped orange zest, plus more for garnish
½ teaspoon salt
2 (6-ounce) fillets striped bass

Salt and black pepper, to taste
Vegetable or olive oil
Orange Cream Sauce (Optional)
½ cup fresh orange juice
¼ cup heavy cream
1 sprig fresh thyme

1. Place the Cook & Crisp Basket in your Ninja Foodi Pressure Cooker Steam Fryer. 2. Spread the flour in one shallow dish. Place the beaten egg whites in a second shallow dish. Finally, mix the chopped pecans, orange zest and salt in a third shallow dish. 3. First season the fish fillets with salt and black pepper. Then coat each fillet in flour. Shake off any excess flour and dip the fish into the egg white. Let the excess egg drip off, and then immediately press the fish into the pecan-orange mixture. Set the crusted fish fillets aside. 4. Spray the crusted fish with oil and then transfer the fillets to your Ninja Foodi Cook & Crisp Basket. 5. Put on the Smart Lid on top of the Ninja Foodi Steam Fryer. 6. Move the Lid Slider to the "Air Fry/Stovetop". 7. Cook on "Air Fry" Mode for about 8 to 9 minutes at 400°F/200°C, flipping the fish over halfway through the cooking time. The nuts on top should be nice and toasty and the fish should feel firm to the touch. 8. If you'd like to make a sauce to go with the fish while it cooks, mix the freshly squeezed orange juice, heavy cream and sprig of thyme in a small saucepan. 9. Simmer on the stovetop for about 5 minutes and then set aside. 10. Remove the fish from your Ninja Foodi Pressure Cooker Steam Fryer. Then add a sprinkling of orange zest and a spoonful of the orange cream sauce over the top if desired.
Per Serving: Calories 268; Fat 10.4g; Sodium 411mg; Total Carbs 0.4g; Fiber 0.1g; Sugar 0.1g; Protein 40.6g

Shrimp cakes

Prep Time: 15 minutes. | Cook Time: 10–12 minutes | Serves: 4

½ pound shelled and deveined raw shrimp	½ teaspoon garlic powder
¼ cup chopped red bell pepper	½ teaspoon Old Bay Seasoning
¼ cup chopped green onion	½ teaspoon salt
¼ cup chopped celery	2 teaspoons Worcestershire sauce
2 cups cooked sushi rice	½ cup plain breadcrumbs
	Oil for misting or cooking spray

1. Place the Cook & Crisp Basket in your Ninja Foodi Pressure Cooker Steam Fryer. 2. Chop the shrimp finely. 3. Place shrimp in a suitable bowl and add all other ingredients except the breadcrumbs and oil. Stir until well mixed. 4. Shape shrimp mixture into 8 patties, no more than ½-inch thick. Roll patties in breadcrumbs and mist with oil or cooking spray. 5. Place 4 shrimp patties in Cook & Crisp Basket. 6. Put on the Smart Lid on top of the Ninja Foodi Steam Fryer. 7. Move the Lid Slider to the "Air Fry/Stovetop". 8. Cook on "Air Fry" Mode at 390°F/200°C for about 10 to 12 minutes, until shrimp cooks through and outside is crispy. 9. Repeat to cook remaining shrimp patties.
Per Serving: Calories 220; Fat 1.7g; Sodium 178mg; Total Carbs 1.7g; Fiber 0.2g; Sugar 0.2g; Protein 32.9g

Crab Stuffed Shrimp

Prep Time: 20 minutes. | Cook Time: 12 minutes | Serves: 4

16 tail-on shrimp, peeled and deveined	2 tablespoons chopped green bell pepper
¾ cup crushed panko breadcrumbs	½ cup crushed saltine crackers
Oil for misting or cooking spray	1 teaspoon Old Bay Seasoning
Stuffing	1 teaspoon garlic powder
2 6-ounce cans lump crabmeat	¼ teaspoon thyme
2 tablespoons chopped shallots	2 teaspoons dried parsley flakes
2 tablespoons chopped green onions	2 teaspoons fresh lemon juice
2 tablespoons chopped celery	2 teaspoons Worcestershire sauce
	1 egg, beaten

1. Chop 4 shrimp and keep them aside. Cut a deep slit in the remaining whole shrimp and keep them aside. 2. Place the Cook & Crisp Basket in your Ninja Foodi Pressure Cooker Steam Fryer. 3. Mix the chopped shrimp in a suitable bowl with all of the stuffing ingredients and stir to mix. 4. Divide the prepared shrimp stuffing into 12 parts. 5. Stuff each whole shrimp with one part of the prepared stuffing. 6. Gently roll each stuffed shrimp in the crumbs and mist them with oil or cooking spray. 7. Place 6 shrimp at a time in Cook & Crisp Basket. 8. Put on the Smart Lid on top of the Ninja Foodi Steam Fryer. 9. Move the Lid Slider to the "Air Fry/Stovetop". 10. Cook on "Air Fry" Mode at 360°F/180°C for about 10 minutes. 11. Spray them with oil or spray. Cook 2 minutes longer until stuffing cooks through inside and is crispy outside. 12. Repeat to cook remaining shrimp.
Per Serving: Calories 381; Fat 29g; Sodium 821mg; Total Carbs 34.6g; Fiber 0g; Sugar 0g; Protein 30g

Tilapia Teriyaki with Rice

Prep Time: 12 minutes. | Cook Time: 10–12 minutes. | Serves: 4

4 tablespoons teriyaki sauce	6 ounces frozen mixed peppers with onions, thawed and drained
1 tablespoon pineapple juice	2 cups cooked rice
1-pound tilapia fillets	
Cooking spray	

1. Mix the teriyaki sauce with pineapple juice in a suitable bowl. 2. Split tilapia fillets down the center lengthwise. 3. Place the Cook & Crisp Basket in your Ninja Foodi Pressure Cooker Steam Fryer. 4. Brush all sides of fish with the sauce, spray Cook & Crisp Basket with nonstick cooking spray, and place fish in the basket. 5. Stir the peppers and onions into the remaining sauce and spoon over the fish. Save any leftover sauce for drizzling over the fish when serving. 6. Put on the Smart Lid on top of the Ninja Foodi Steam Fryer. 7. Move the Lid Slider to the "Air Fry/Stovetop". 8. Cook on "Air Fry" Mode at 360°F/180°C for about 10 to 12 minutes, until fish flakes easily with a fork and is done in center. 9. Divide into 3 or 4 serving plates and serve each with approximately ½ cup cooked rice.
Per Serving: Calories 374; Fat 13g; Sodium 552mg; Total Carbs 25g; Fiber 1.2g; Sugar 1.2g; Protein 37.7g

Tuna Nuggets with Hoisin Sauce

Prep Time: 15 minutes. | Cook Time: 5–7 minutes. | Serves: 4

½ cup hoisin sauce	½ small onion, quartered and thinly sliced
2 tablespoons rice wine vinegar	8 ounces fresh tuna, cut into 1-inch cubes
2 teaspoons sesame oil	
1 teaspoon garlic powder	Cooking spray
2 teaspoons dried lemongrass	3 cups cooked jasmine rice
¼ teaspoon red pepper flakes	

1. Place the Cook & Crisp Basket in your Ninja Foodi Pressure Cooker Steam Fryer and place a reversible rack in it. 2. Mix the hoisin sauce, vinegar, sesame oil, and seasonings together. 3. Stir in the onions and tuna nuggets. 4. Spray the Cook & Crisp Basket with nonstick spray and pour in tuna mixture. 5. Put on the Smart Lid on top of the Ninja Foodi Steam Fryer. 6. Move the Lid Slider to the "Air Fry/Stovetop". 7. Cook on "Air Fry" Mode at 390°F/200°C for about 3 minutes. Stir gently. 8. Cook 2 minutes and stir again, checking for doneness. Tuna should be barely cooked through, just beginning to flake and still very moist. If necessary, continue cooking and stirring in 1-minute intervals until done. 9. Serve warm over hot jasmine rice.
Per Serving: Calories 351; Fat 16g; Sodium 777mg; Total Carbs 26g; Fiber 4g; Sugar 5g; Protein 28g

Red Snapper with Green Onions Salsa

Prep Time: 12 minutes. | Cook Time: 8 minutes. | Serves: 2

2 oranges, peeled, segmented and chopped	4 green onions, cut into 2-inch lengths
1 tablespoon minced shallot	Start by making the salsa. Cut the peel off the oranges, slicing around the oranges to expose the flesh. Segment the oranges by cutting in between the membranes of the orange. Chop the segments and mix in a suitable bowl with the shallot, Jalapeño or Serrano pepper, cilantro, lime juice and salt. Set the salsa aside.
1 to 3 teaspoons minced red Jalapeño or Serrano pepper	
1 tablespoon chopped fresh cilantro	
Lime juice, to taste	
2 (5- to 6-ounce) red snapper fillets	
½ teaspoon Chinese five-spice powder	
Salt and black pepper, to taste	
Vegetable or olive oil	

1. Place the Cook & Crisp Basket in your Ninja Foodi Pressure Cooker Steam Fryer. 2. Season the fish fillets with the five-spice powder, salt and black pepper. Spray both sides of the fish fillets with oil. Toss the green onions with a little oil. 3. Transfer the fish to the Ninja Foodi Cook & Crisp Basket and scatter the green onions around the fish. 4. Put on the Smart Lid on top of the Ninja Foodi Steam Fryer. 5. Move the Lid Slider to the "Air Fry/Stovetop". 6. Cook at 400°F/200°C on "Air Fry" Mode for about 8 minutes. 7. Remove the fish from your Ninja Foodi Pressure Cooker Steam Fryer, along with the fried green onions. Serve with white rice and a spoonful of the salsa on top.
Per Serving: Calories 353; Fat 5g; Sodium 818mg; Total Carbs 53.2g; Fiber 4.4g; Sugar 8g; Protein 17.3g

Grilled Salmon

Prep Time: 10 minutes. | Cook Time: 8 minutes. | Serves: 2

2 salmon fillets	⅓ cup of light soy sauce
2 tablespoons olive oil	⅓ cup of water
1 teaspoon liquid stevia	Salt and black pepper to taste

1. Place the Cook & Crisp Basket in your Pressure Cooker Steam Fryer. 2. Season salmon fillets with black pepper and salt. Mix the rest of the recipe ingredients in a suitable bowl. Allow the salmon fillets to marinate in mixture for around 2 hours. Drain salmon fillets. Put on the Smart Lid on top of the Ninja Foodi Steam Fryer. Move the Lid Slider to the "Air Fry/Stovetop". Select the "Air Fry" mode for cooking. Adjust the cooking temperature to 355°F/180°C. Air Fry for around 8 minutes.
Per serving: Calories 684; Fat: 30.1g; Sodium 1075mg; Carbs: 15.1g; Fiber: 1.5g; Sugars 10.1g; Protein 84.9g

Cod with Grapes

Prep Time: 10 minutes. | Cook Time: 15 minutes. | Serves: 2

2 fillets black cod (8-ounces)
3 cups kale, minced
2 teaspoons white balsamic vinegar
½ cup pecans
1 cup grapes, halved
1 small bulb fennel, cut into inch-thick slices
4 tablespoons extra-virgin olive oil
Salt and black pepper to taste

1. Place the Cook & Crisp Basket in your Pressure Cooker Steam Fryer. 2. Use black pepper and salt to season your fish fillets. Drizzle with 1 teaspoon of olive oil. Place the fish in the Cook & Crisp Basket with the skin side down . Put on the Smart Lid on top of the Ninja Foodi Steam Fryer. Move the Lid Slider to the "Air Fry/Stovetop". Select the "Air Fry" mode for cooking. Adjust the cooking temperature to 400°F/200°C. Cook for around 10 minutes. Take the fish out and cover loosely with aluminum foil. Mix fennel, pecans, and grapes. Pour 2 tablespoons of olive oil and season with black pepper and salt. Add to the Ninja Foodi Pressure Steam Fryer basket. Put on the Smart Lid on top of the Ninja Foodi Steam Fryer. 3. Move the Lid Slider to the "Air Fry/Stovetop". Select the "Air Fry" mode for cooking. 4. Cook for an additional 5 minutes. In a suitable bowl mix minced kale and cooked grapes, fennel and pecans. Cover ingredients with balsamic vinegar and remaining 1 tablespoon of olive oil. Toss gently. Serve fish with sauce and enjoy!
Per serving: Calories 194; Fat: 2.6g; Sodium 1257mg; Carbs: 35.4g; Fiber: 3.7g; Sugars 3.1g; Protein 9.4g

Salmon with Zucchini

Prep Time: 12 minutes. | Cook Time: 12 minutes. | Serves: 2

1 small zucchini, sliced into ¼-inch thick half moons
1 teaspoon olive oil
Salt and black pepper
2 (5-ounce) salmon fillets
1 beefsteak tomato, chopped (about 1 cup)
1 tablespoon capers, rinsed
10 black olives, pitted and sliced
2 tablespoons dry vermouth or white wine
2 tablespoons butter
¼ cup chopped fresh basil, chopped

1. Place the Cook & Crisp Basket in your Ninja Foodi Pressure Cooker Steam Fryer. 2. Toss the zucchini with the oil, salt and black pepper. Transfer the zucchini into the Ninja Foodi Put on the Smart Lid on top of the Ninja Foodi Steam Fryer. 3. Move the Lid Slider to the "Air Fry/Stovetop". 4. Cook on "Air Fry" Mode at 400°F/200°C for about 5 minutes, shaking the basket once or twice during the cooking process. 5. Cut 2 large rectangles out of a parchment sheet. Divide the zucchini between the two pieces of parchment paper, placing the vegetables in the center of each rectangle. 6. Set a fillet of salmon on each pile of zucchini. Season the fish with salt and black pepper. Toss the tomato, capers, olives and vermouth (or white wine) together in a suitable bowl. Divide the tomato mixture between the two fish packages, placing it on top of the fish fillets and pouring any juice out of the bowl onto the fish. Top each fillet with a tablespoon of melted butter. 7. Fold up each parchment square. Bring two edges together and fold them over a few times, leaving some space above the fish. Twist the open sides together and upwards so they can serve as handles for the packet, but don't let them extend beyond the top of your Ninja Foodi Cook & Crisp Basket. 8. Place the two packages into your Ninja Foodi Pressure Cooker Steam Fryer. 9. Put on the Smart Lid on top of the Ninja Foodi Steam Fryer. 10. Move the Lid Slider to the "Air Fry/Stovetop". 11. Cook on "Air Fry" Mode at 400°F/200°C on "Air Fry" Mode for about 12 minutes. 12. Once cooked, let the fish sit in the parchment for about 2 minutes. 13. Serve the fish in parchment paper, or if desired, remove the parchment paper before serving. Garnish with a little fresh basil.
Per Serving: Calories 346; Fat 16.1g; Sodium 882mg; Total Carbs 1.3g; Fiber 0.5g; Sugar 0.5g; Protein 48.2g

Fish Fingers

Prep Time: 10 minutes. | Cook Time: 10 minutes | Serves: 2

10-ounces codfish, sliced into strips
2 teaspoons mixed dried herbs
2 eggs
¼ teaspoon baking soda
1 teaspoon rice flour
2 teaspoons cornflower
2 tablespoons almond flour
½ lemon, juiced
1 teaspoon ginger garlic
½ teaspoon turmeric powder
½ teaspoon red chili flakes
2 teaspoons garlic powder
2 tablespoons olive oil
1 cup breadcrumbs
Tartar sauce or ketchup

1. Place the Cook & Crisp Basket in your Pressure Cooker Steam Fryer. 2. Place fish fingers in a suitable bowl. Add a teaspoon of mixed herbs, 1 teaspoon of garlic powder, red chili flakes, turmeric powder, ginger garlic, lemon juice, salt and black pepper. Stir well and set aside for around 10 minutes. In another bowl, mix almond flour, rice flour, corn flour and baking soda. Break eggs into this bowl. Stir well then add fish. Set aside for around 10 minutes. 3. Mix breadcrumbs and remaining 1 teaspoon of mixed herbs and 1 teaspoon of garlic powder. Cover fish with breadcrumb mixture. Lay aluminum foil in the Cook & Crisp Basket. Lay the fish fingers in the basket and cover with olive oil. Put on the Smart Lid on top of the Ninja Foodi Steam Fryer. 4. Move the Lid Slider to the "Air Fry/Stovetop". Select the "Air Fry" mode for cooking. 5. Adjust the cooking temperature to 360°F/180°C. Cook for around 10 minutes and serve with tartar sauce or ketchup.
Per serving: Calories 541; Fat: 12.4g; Sodium 250mg; Carbs: 85.4g; Fiber: 21.3g; Sugars 6.1g; Protein 26.5g

Asian Style Sea Bass

Prep Time: 10 minutes. | Cook Time: 20 minutes. | Serves: 2

1 medium sea bass or halibut (12-ounces)
2 garlic cloves, minced
1 tablespoon olive oil
3 slices of ginger, julienned
2 tablespoons cooking wine
1 tomato, cut into quarters
1 lime, cut
1 green onion, chopped
1 chili, diced

1. Place the Cook & Crisp Basket in your Pressure Cooker Steam Fryer. 2. Prepare ginger, garlic oil mixture: sauté ginger and garlic with oil until golden brown in a suitable saucepan over medium-heat on top of the stove. Prepare fish: clean, rinse, and pat dry. Cut in half to fit into basket. Place the fish inside of "cook & crisp basket" then drizzle it with cooking wine. Layer tomato and lime slices on top of fish. Cover with garlic ginger oil mixture. Top with green onion and slices of chili. Cover with aluminum foil. Put on the Smart Lid on top of the Ninja Foodi Steam Fryer. 3. Move the Lid Slider to the "Air Fry/Stovetop". Select the "Air Fry" mode for cooking. 4. Adjust the cooking temperature to 360°F/180°C. Cook for around 20 minutes.
Per serving: Calories 105; Fat: 2.4g; Sodium 812mg; Carbs: 12.2g; Fiber: 2.4g; Sugars 2.4g; Protein 9.5g

Shrimp Sliders

Prep Time: 12 minutes. | Cook Time: 10 minutes. | Serves: 4

16 raw jumbo shrimp, peeled, deveined and tails removed (about 1 pound)
1 rib celery, chopped
2 carrots, grated (about ½ cup)
2 teaspoons lemon juice
2 teaspoons Dijon mustard
¼ cup chopped fresh basil or parsley
½ cup breadcrumbs
½ teaspoon salt
Black pepper, to taste
Vegetable or olive oil, in a spray bottle
8 slider buns
Mayo
Butter lettuce
2 avocados, sliced and peeled

1. Place the Cook & Crisp Basket in your Ninja Foodi Pressure Cooker Steam Fryer. 2. Put the shrimp into a food processor and pulse it a few times to rough chop the shrimp. Remove three quarters of the shrimp and transfer it to a suitable bowl. Continue to process the remaining shrimp in the food process until it is a smooth purée. Transfer the purée to the bowl with the chopped shrimp. 3. Add the celery, carrots, lemon juice, mustard, basil, breadcrumbs, salt and pepper to the bowl and mix well. 4. Shape the shrimp mixture into 8 patties. Spray all sides of the patties with oil and transfer one layer of patties to your Ninja Foodi Cook & Crisp Basket. 5. Put on the Smart Lid on top of the Ninja Foodi Steam Fryer. 6. Move the Lid Slider to the "Air Fry/Stovetop". 7. Cook on "Air Fry" Mode at 380°F/195°C for about 10 minutes, flipping the patties over halfway through the cooking time. 8. Prepare the slider rolls by toasting them and spreading a little mayo on both halves. Place a piece of butter lettuce on the bottom bun, top with the shrimp slider and then finish with the avocado slices on top. Pop the top half of the bun on top and enjoy!
Per Serving: Calories 223; Fat 11.7g; Sodium 721mg; Total Carbs 13.6g; Fiber 0.7g; Sugar 8g; Protein 15.7g

Horseradish Salmon

Prep Time: 12 minutes. | Cook Time: 12 minutes. | Serves: 2

2 (5-ounce) salmon fillets	2 tablespoons prepared horseradish
Salt and black pepper	½ teaspoon chopped lemon zest
2 teaspoons Dijon mustard	1 tablespoon olive oil
½ cup panko breadcrumbs*	1 tablespoon chopped fresh parsley

1. Place the Cook & Crisp Basket in your Ninja Foodi Pressure Cooker Steam Fryer. 2. Season the salmon with salt and black pepper. Then spread the Dijon mustard on the salmon, coating the entire surface. 3. Mix the breadcrumbs, horseradish, lemon zest and olive oil in a suitable bowl. Spread the mixture over the top of the salmon and press down lightly with your hands, adhering it to the salmon using the mustard as "glue". 4. Transfer the salmon to the Ninja Foodi Cook & Crisp Basket. 5. Put on the Smart Lid on top of the Ninja Foodi Steam Fryer. 6. Move the Lid Slider to the "Air Fry/Stovetop". 7. Cook at 360°F/180°C on "Air Fry" Mode for about 12 to 14 minutes (depending on how thick your fillet is) until the fish feels firm to the touch. Sprinkle with the parsley.

Per Serving: Calories 400; Fat 32g; Sodium 721mg; Total Carbs 2.6g; Fiber 0g; Sugar 0g; Protein 27.4g

Shrimp Scampi

Prep Time: 12 minutes. | Cook Time: 5 minutes. | Serves: 2 to 4

16 to 20 raw large shrimp, peeled, deveined and tails removed	1 clove garlic, sliced
½ cup white wine	1 teaspoon olive oil
Black pepper	Salt, to taste
¼ cup + 1 tablespoon butter	Juice of ½ lemon, to taste
	¼ cup chopped fresh parsley

1. Place the Cook & Crisp Basket in your Ninja Foodi Pressure Cooker Steam Fryer. 2. Start by marinating the shrimp in the white wine and black pepper for at least 30 minutes, or as long as 2 hours in the refrigerator. 3. Melt ¼ cup of butter in a small saucepan on the stovetop. Add the garlic and let the butter simmer, but be sure to not let it burn. 4. Pour the shrimp and marinade into your Ninja Foodi Pressure Cooker Steam Fryer, letting the marinade drain through to the bottom drawer. Drizzle the olive oil on the shrimp and season well with salt. 5. Put on the Smart Lid on top of the Ninja Foodi Steam Fryer. 6. Move the Lid Slider to the "Air Fry/Stovetop". 7. Cook at 400°F/200°C on "Air Fry" Mode for about 3 minutes. Turn the shrimp over (don't shake the basket because the marinade will splash around) and pour the garlic butter over the shrimp. Cook for another 2 minutes. 8. Remove the shrimp from the Ninja Foodi Cook & Crisp Basket and transfer them to a suitable bowl. Squeeze lemon juice over all the shrimp and toss with the chopped parsley and remaining tablespoon of butter. Season to taste with salt and serve over rice or pasta, or on their own with some crusty bread.

Per Serving: Calories 316; Fat 12.2g; Sodium 587mg; Total Carbs 12.2g; Fiber 1g; Sugar 1.8g; Protein 25.8g

Grilled Salmon with Capers

Prep Time: 10 minutes. | Cook Time: 8 minutes. | Serves: 2

1 teaspoon capers, chopped	1 tablespoon olive oil
2 sprigs dill, chopped	4 slices lemon
1 lemon zest	11-ounce salmon fillet
Dressing:	
5 capers, chopped	Pinch of lemon zest
1 sprig dill, chopped	Salt and black pepper to taste
2 tablespoons plain yogurt	

1. Place the Cook & Crisp Basket in your Pressure Cooker Steam Fryer. 2. Mix dill, capers, lemon zest, olive oil and salt in a suitable bowl. Cover the salmon with this mixture. Put on the Smart Lid on top of the Ninja Foodi Steam Fryer. 3. Move the Lid Slider to the "Air Fry/Stovetop". Select the "Air Fry" mode for cooking. 4. Adjust the cooking temperature to 400°F/200°C. Cook salmon for around 8 minutes. Mix the dressing ingredients in another bowl. When salmon is cooked, place on serving plate and drizzle dressing over it. Place lemon slices at the side of the plate and serve.

Per serving: Calories 669; Fat: 53.8g; Sodium 905mg; Carbs: 41.7g; Fiber: 8.6g; Sugars 12.3g; Protein 14g

Shrimp and Fingerling Potatoes

Prep Time: 12 minutes. | Cook Time: 16 minutes. | Serves: 4

½ red onion, chopped into 1-inch chunks	sliced into 1-inch chunks
8 fingerling potatoes, sliced into 1-inch slices or halved lengthwise	16 raw large shrimp, peeled, deveined and tails removed
1 teaspoon olive oil	1 lime
Salt and black pepper	¼ cup chopped fresh cilantro
8 ounces raw chorizo sausage,	Chopped orange zest (optional)

1. Place the Cook & Crisp Basket in your Ninja Foodi Pressure Cooker Steam Fryer. 2. Mix the red onion and potato chunks in a suitable bowl and toss with the olive oil, salt and black pepper. 3. Transfer the vegetables to the Ninja Foodi Cook & Crisp Basket. 4. Put on the Smart Lid on top of the Ninja Foodi Steam Fryer. 5. Move the Lid Slider to the "Air Fry/Stovetop". 6. Cook on "Air Fry" Mode at 380°F/195°C for about 6 minutes, and shaking the basket a few times during the cooking process. 7. Add the chorizo chunks and continue to cook for another 5 minutes. 8. Add the shrimp, season with salt and continue to cook, shaking the basket every once in a while, for another 5 minutes. 9. Transfer the tossed shrimp, chorizo and potato to a suitable bowl and squeeze some lime juice over the top to taste. Toss in the fresh cilantro, orange zest and a drizzle of olive oil, and season again to taste. 10. Serve with a fresh green salad.

Per Serving: Calories 502; Fat 25g; Sodium 230mg; Total Carbs 1.5g; Fiber 0.2g; Sugar 0.4g; Protein 64.1g

Crispy Fish Sticks

Prep Time: 10 minutes. | Cook Time: 13 minutes. | Serves: 4

3 eggs	1 cup almond flour
2 cups breadcrumbs	3 tablespoons skim milk
1 lb. codfish	Salt and black pepper to taste

1. Place the Cook & Crisp Basket in your Pressure Cooker Steam Fryer. 2. Mix milk and egg in a suitable mixing bowl. In another bowl, add breadcrumbs, and in a third bowl mix flour. Slice the fish into strips and season with black pepper and salt. Dip each piece into flour, then into egg mixture and then into breadcrumbs. Put on the Smart Lid on top of the Ninja Foodi Steam Fryer. Move the Lid Slider to the "Air Fry/Stovetop". Select the "Air Fry" mode for cooking. Put on the Smart Lid on top of the Ninja Foodi Steam Fryer. 3. Move the Lid Slider to the "Air Fry/Stovetop". Select the "Air Fry" mode for cooking. 4. Adjust the cooking temperature to 340°F/170°C. Cook for around 13 minutes. Turn once during cooking.

Per serving: Calories 357; Fat: 16.1g; Sodium 80mg; Carbs: 26g; Fiber: 7.3g; Sugars 9.2g; Protein 29.4g

Vegetable with Salmon Fillets

Prep Time: 20 minutes. | Cook Time: 12 minutes. | Serves: 2

¼ cup soy sauce	2 minced garlic cloves
½ teaspoon salt	2 (5 ounces) salmon fillets
½ cup fresh juiced orange	2 teaspoons grated orange zest
1 tablespoon avocado oil	3 tablespoons rice vinegar
1 tablespoon chopped ginger	
For the Veggies	
½ teaspoon toasted sesame seeds	mushrooms
1 tablespoon sesame oil	2 halved heads baby bok choy
2 ounces stemmed dry shiitake	Salt, to taste

1. Place the Cook & Crisp Basket in your Pressure Cooker Steam Fryer. 2. Using a suitable mixing bowl, add in the avocado oil, soy sauce, salt, vinegar, orange juice, zest, ginger, garlic and mix until mixed. 3. Divide the marinade into 2 and reserve one then add the salmon fillets into a Ziploc bag and pour the remaining soy sauce mix in to marinate for an hour. 4. Transfer the marinated salmon into the "cook & crisp basket" then put on the Smart Lid on top of the Ninja Foodi Steam Fryer. 5. Move the Lid Slider to the "Air Fry/Stovetop". Select the "Air Fry" mode for cooking. air fry for around 6 minutes at 400°F/200°C. 6. In the meantime, coat the mushroom and bok choy with the oil, season with the salt then set aside. 7. Add the vegetables into the "cook & crisp basket" along with the salmon fillets and cook for an extra 6 minutes. 8. Serve, drizzled with the reserved marinade, a garnish of the sesame seeds and enjoy.

Per serving: Calories 404; Fat: 19.4g; Sodium 187mg; Carbs: 5g; Fiber: 1.1g; Sugars 0.8g; Protein 52g

Fish Capers Cakes

Prep Time: 10 minutes. | Cook Time: 8 minutes| Serves: 4

14-ounces of potatoes, boiled and mashed	¼ cup almond flour
10-ounces cooked salmon, flaked	1 handful parsley, fresh, chopped
1 teaspoon olive oil	1 handful of capers
	1 teaspoon lemon zest

1. Place the Cook & Crisp Basket in your Pressure Cooker Steam Fryer. 2. Brush salmon with olive oil. Place the potatoes, flaked salmon, lemon zest, parsley, and capers in a suitable bowl and mix well. Make 4 large cakes out of the mixture. Dust fish cakes with flour. Place them in the fridge for an hour. Add salmon cakes to the Cook & Crisp Basket . Put on the Smart Lid on top of the Ninja Foodi Steam Fryer. Move the Lid Slider to the "Air Fry/Stovetop". Select the "Air Fry" mode for cooking. 3. Adjust the cooking temperature to 350°F/175°C. Cook for around 8 minutes. Serve warm.
Per serving: Calories 303; Fat: 10.4g; Sodium 703mg; Carbs: 9.2g; Fiber: 0g; Sugars 8.7g; Protein 40.6g

Parmesan Tilapia

Prep Time: 10 minutes. | Cook Time: 5 minutes | Serves: 4

1 tablespoon olive oil	1 tablespoon parsley, chopped
4 tilapia fillets	2 teaspoons paprika
¾ cup grated Parmesan cheese	Pinch of garlic powder

1. Place the Cook & Crisp Basket in your Pressure Cooker Steam Fryer. 2. Brush oil over tilapia fillets. Mix the remaining recipe ingredients in a suitable bowl. Coat tilapia fillets with parmesan mixture. Line the Cook & Crisp Basket with parchment paper and arrange fillets. Place in Pressure Cooker Steam Fryer. Put on the Smart Lid on top of the Ninja Foodi Steam Fryer. 3. Move the Lid Slider to the "Air Fry/Stovetop". Select the "Air Fry" mode for cooking. 4. Adjust the cooking temperature to 350°F/175°C. Cook for around 5 minutes.
Per serving: Calories 323; Fat: 17.9g; Sodium 838mg; Carbs: 4.3g; Fiber: 1.5g; Sugars 1g; Protein 35.5g

Red Salmon Croquettes

Prep Time: 10 minutes. | Cook Time: 10 minutes. | Serves: 4

14-ounce tin of red salmon, drained	2 tablespoons spring onions, chopped
2 free-range eggs	Black pepper and salt to taste
5 tablespoons olive oil	Pinch of herbs
½ cup breadcrumbs	

1. Place the Cook & Crisp Basket in your Pressure Cooker Steam Fryer. 2. Add drained salmon into a suitable bowl and mash well. Break in the egg, add herbs, spring onions, salt, pepper and mix well. In another bowl, mix breadcrumbs and oil and mix well. Take a spoon of the salmon mixture and shape it into a croquette shape in your hand. Roll it in the breadcrumbs and place inside the Cook & Crisp Basket. Put on the Smart Lid on top of the Ninja Foodi Steam Fryer. 3. Move the Lid Slider to the "Air Fry/Stovetop". Select the "Air Fry" mode for cooking. 4. Set your Ninja Foodi Pressure Steam Fryer to 390°F/200°C for around 10 minutes.
Per serving: Calories 419; Fat: 15.8g; Sodium 3342mg; Carbs: 0.4g; Fiber: 0.2g; Sugars 0g; Protein 65.4g

Salmon with Veggies

Prep Time: 10 minutes. | Cook Time: 10 minutes. |Serves: 2

2 (6-ounce) salmon fillets, skin on	½ garlic clove, minced
Black pepper and salt to taste	Small handful cherry tomatoes, halved
1 teaspoon olive oil	
2 large zucchinis, trimmed and spiralized	Small handful of black olives, chopped
1 avocado, peeled and chopped	2 tablespoons pine nuts, toasted
Small handful of parsley, chopped	

1. Place the Cook & Crisp Basket in your Pressure Cooker Steam Fryer. 2. Brush salmon with olive oil and season with black pepper and salt. Place salmon in the Cook & Crisp Basket. Put on the Smart Lid on top of the Ninja Foodi Steam Fryer. Move the Lid Slider to the "Air Fry/Stovetop". Select the "Air Fry" mode for cooking. Adjust the cooking temperature to 350°F/175°C. Cook for around 10 minutes. Blend the avocado, garlic, and parsley in a food processor until smooth. Toss in a suitable bowl with zucchini, olives, and tomatoes. Divide vegetables between two plates, top each portion with salmon fillet, sprinkle with pine nuts, and serve.
Per serving: Calories 609; Fat: 19.5g; Sodium 132mg; Carbs: 49g; Fiber: 6g; Sugars 13.3g; Protein 57.5g

Cajun Lemon Salmon

Prep Time: 10 minutes. | Cook Time: 7 minutes. | Serves: 1

1 salmon fillet	1 teaspoon liquid stevia
1 teaspoon Cajun seasoning	½ lemon, juiced
2 lemon wedges, for serving	

1. Place the Cook & Crisp Basket in your Pressure Cooker Steam Fryer. 2. Mix lemon juice and liquid stevia and coat salmon with this mixture. Sprinkle Cajun seasoning all over salmon. Place salmon on parchment paper in the Cook & Crisp Basket. Put on the Smart Lid on top of the Ninja Foodi Steam Fryer. Move the Lid Slider to the "Air Fry/Stovetop". Select the "Air Fry" mode for cooking. Adjust the cooking temperature to 350°F/175°C. Cook for around 7-minutes. Serve with lemon wedges.
Per serving: Calories 570; Fat: 29.3g; Sodium 845mg; Carbs: 5.8g; Fiber: 1.6g; Sugars 2.7g; Protein 68.6g

Salmon Potato Patties

Prep Time: 10 minutes. | Cook Time: 10 minutes. | Serves: 2

3 large russet potatoes, boiled, mashed	2 tablespoons olive oil
	Parsley, fresh, chopped
1 salmon fillet	Handful of parboiled vegetables
1 egg	½ teaspoon dill
Breadcrumbs	Black pepper and salt to taste

1. Place the Cook & Crisp Basket in your Pressure Cooker Steam Fryer. 2. Peel, chop, and mash cooked potatoes. Put potatoes in the Cook & Crisp Basket. Put on the Smart Lid on top of the Ninja Foodi Steam Fryer. Move the Lid Slider to the "Air Fry/Stovetop". Select the "Air Fry" mode for cooking. Air Fry salmon for 5 minutes. Use a fork to flake salmon then set aside. Add vegetables, parsley, flaked salmon, dill, salt, and pepper to mashed potatoes. Add egg and mix. Shape the mixture into six patties. Cover with breadcrumbs. Cook at 355°F/180°C for around 10 minutes.
Per serving: Calories 403; Fat: 23.8g; Sodium 782mg; Carbs: 4.4g; Fiber: 1.9g; Sugars 0.7g; Protein 48.9g

Fried Shrimp

Prep Time: 7 minutes. | Cook Time: 10 minutes. | Serves: 4

½ teaspoon oregano	2 pounds peeled and deveined jumbo cooked shrimp
⅔ cup shaved parmesan cheese	
1 teaspoon basil	4 minced garlic cloves
1 teaspoon pepper	quartered lime
1 teaspoon powdered onion	Cooking spray oil
2 tablespoons sesame oil	

1. Place the Cook & Crisp Basket in your Pressure Cooker Steam Fryer. 2. Using a suitable mixing bowl, add in the oil, powdered onion, basil, oregano, pepper, parmesan cheese, garlic and mix everything together. 3. Add the cooked shrimp into the mixture and toss until well coated. 4. Grease the "cook & crisp basket" with cooking spray oil then add in the coated shrimp. Put on the Smart Lid on top of the Ninja Foodi Steam Fryer. 5. Move the Lid Slider to the "Air Fry/Stovetop". Select the "Air Fry" mode for cooking. 6. Air fry for around 10 minutes at 350°F/175°C. 7. Serve with a garnish of the lime juice and enjoy as desired.
Per serving: Calories 506; Fat: 23.9g; Sodium 197mg; Carbs: 3.6g; Fiber: 0.7g; Sugars 1.2g; Protein 66.1g

Buttery Shrimp Scampi

Prep Time: 5 minutes. | Cook Time: 8 minutes. | Serves: 4

1-pound raw shrimp
1 tablespoon juiced lime
1 tablespoon minced garlic
1 tablespoon chopped chives

1 tablespoon fresh chopped basil
2 tablespoons chicken stock
2 teaspoons red pepper flakes
4 tablespoons melted butter

1. Place the Cook & Crisp Basket in your Pressure Cooker Steam Fryer. 2. Add the pepper flakes, garlic and melted butter into the "cook & crisp basket". Put on the Smart Lid on top of the Ninja Foodi Steam Fryer. 3. Move the Lid Slider to the "Air Fry/Stovetop". Select the "Air Fry" mode for cooking. 4. Air fry at 390°F/200°C for a minute, until the butter, garlic and pepper are all incorporated. Add in the remaining recipe ingredients into the "cook & crisp basket" then mix together. 5. Air fry the shrimp for around 7 minutes at 390°F/200°C. 6. Serve, garnished with extra herbs if desired and enjoy.
Per serving: Calories 340; Fat: 27.7g; Sodium 109mg; Carbs: 12.6g; Fiber: 0.3g; Sugars 3g; Protein 15.7g

Miso Salmon Fillets

Prep Time: 10 minutes. | Cook Time: 10 minutes. | Serves: 2

½ cup boiling water
½ teaspoon cracked black pepper
1 teaspoon diced ginger
1 teaspoon sesame seeds
1 teaspoons minced garlic cloves
2 tablespoons soy sauce

2 tablespoons white miso
2 chopped green scallions
2 tablespoons brown sugar
2 (5 ounces) salmon fillets
Non-stick cooking spray

1. Place the Cook & Crisp Basket in your Pressure Cooker Steam Fryer. 2. Using a suitable mixing bowl, add in the pepper, ginger, garlic, miso, brown sugar, soy sauce and boiling water then mix together. 3. Using a flat work station, place the salmon fillets then cover with the sauce mixture, ensuring even amount of coating all over. 4. Grease the "cook & crisp basket" with cooking spray then add in the coated fillets. Put on the Smart Lid on top of the Ninja Foodi Steam Fryer. Move the Lid Slider to the "Air Fry/Stovetop". Select the "Air Fry" mode for cooking. Air Fry for around 12 minutes at 400°F/200°C. 5. Serve with a garnish of scallions, sesame seeds and enjoy as desired.
Per serving: Calories 305; Fat: 16.7g; Sodium 148mg; Carbs: 2.5g; Fiber: 1.1g; Sugars 0.1g; Protein 36.5g

Creamy Scallops

Prep Time: 5 minutes. | Cook Time: 10 minutes. | Serves: 2

½ teaspoon salt
½ teaspoon black pepper
¾ cup heavy whipping cream
1 teaspoon coconut oil
1 teaspoon minced garlic
1 tablespoon tomato paste

1 tablespoon chopped fresh basil
8 jumbo sea scallops
12 ounces' pack frozen spinach, drained and thawed
Nonstick cooking oil spray
Black pepper and salt, to taste

1. Place the Cook & Crisp Basket in your Pressure Cooker Steam Fryer. 2. Grease the "cook & crisp basket" then add in the drained and thawed spinach and keep to the side. 3. Generously season the scallops all over with oil, a sprinkle of black pepper and salt then place inside the pan on the spinach. 4. Using a suitable mixing bowl, add in the extra pepper, salt, basil, tomato paste, garlic, heavy cream and mix together. 5. Then pour the cream mixture over the scallops and place in the Ninja Foodi Pressure Steam Fryer. 6. Air fry the scallops for around 10 minutes at 350°F/175°C then serve and enjoy as desired.
Per serving: Calories 315; Fat: 15g; Sodium 91mg; Carbs: 0g; Fiber: 0g; Sugars 0g; Protein 42.3g

Garlicky Salmon Fillets

Prep Time: 5 minutes. | Cook Time: 12 minutes. | Serves: 4

½ lime juice
½ lime wedges
1 tablespoon coconut oil
1 teaspoon powdered garlic

1 pound diced salmon fillets
2 teaspoons seafood seasoning
2 teaspoons lime pepper seasoning
Salt, to taste

1. Place the Cook & Crisp Basket in your Pressure Cooker Steam Fryer. 2. Ensure the salmon fillets are completely dry then mix the

lime juice and coconut oil together. 3. Coat the dry salmon with the oil mixture then sprinkle with the salt and remaining seasonings. 4. Prepare the "cook & crisp basket" with parchment paper then place in the salmon fillets. Put on the Smart Lid on top of the Ninja Foodi Steam Fryer. Move the Lid Slider to the "Air Fry/Stovetop". Select the "Air Fry" mode for cooking. Air Fry at 360°F/180°C for around 12 minutes. 5. Allow the fillets to cool off for a bit then serve, garnished with the lime wedges and enjoy.
Per serving: Calories 786; Fat: 24.2g; Sodium 252mg; Carbs: 31.6g; Fiber: 3.9g; Sugars 22.8g; Protein 106.9g

Salmon Cakes

Prep Time: 35 minutes. | Cook Time: 15 minutes. | Serves: 5

¼ cup mashed avocado
¼ cup chopped cilantro, with extra
¼ cup tapioca starch, with 4 extra teaspoons
½ teaspoon salt
For the Greens
½ teaspoon salt
2 teaspoons olive oil

½ cup coconut flakes
1-pound salmon
1 ½ teaspoon yellow curry powder
2 large eggs
Avocado oil

6 cups arugula and spinach mix

1. Place the Cook & Crisp Basket in your Pressure Cooker Steam Fryer. 2. Skin the salmon then chop into pieces and transfer into a suitable mixing bowl. 3. Add in the cilantro, salt, curry powder, avocado and incorporate together. 4. Pour in the teaspoons of tapioca then mix until mixed then mold the patties into 10 even sizes. 5. Transfer the molded patties into a parchment paper prepared baking sheet then freeze for about 30 minutes. 6. In the meantime, mix the eggs in a suitable mixing bowl and pour the coconut flakes, ¼ cup of tapioca into different bowls. 7. Coat the "cook & crisp basket" with oil. 8. Run the chilled patties through the tapioca until coated, then dredge in the egg mix and finally coat with the coconut flakes. 9. Transfer the covered patties into the basket then Put on the Smart Lid on top of the Ninja Foodi Steam Fryer. 10. Move the Lid Slider to the "Air Fry/Stovetop". Select the "Air Fry" mode for cooking. Cook at 400°F/200°C for around 15 minutes until the crispy and tenderized. 11. Using a suitable pan, heat the olive oil up over medium heat then add in the spinach, arugula, salt and stir cook for a minute until wilted. 12. Serve the salmon cakes and greens together, enjoying with a garnish of cilantro.
Per serving: Calories 367; Fat: 22.9g; Sodium 101mg; Carbs: 8g; Fiber: 1.9g; Sugars 3g; Protein 31.8g

Delicious Fish Tacos

Prep time: 15 minutes| Cook time: 3 minutes| Serves: 8

Slaw
½ cup grated cabbage
1 large carrot, peeled and grated
1 small jicama, peeled and julienned
Juice of ½ lime
Fish
1-pound cod, cubed
Juice from ½ lime
2 tablespoons fresh orange juice
1 teaspoon garlic salt
1 teaspoon ground cumin
1 tablespoon olive oil

1 tablespoon olive oil
2 dashes hot sauce
¼ cup chopped fresh cilantro
½ teaspoon sea salt

1 cup water
To Serve
½ cup guacamole
½ cup diced tomatoes
8 (6") soft corn tortillas

1. For Slaw: Combine slaw ingredients in a medium bowl. Refrigerate covered for 30 minutes up to overnight. 2. For Fish: In a large bowl, combine fish, lime juice, orange juice, garlic salt, cumin, and olive oil and refrigerate for 15 minutes. 3. Add 1 cup water to Ninja Foodi XL Pressure Cooker Steam Fryer with SmartLid cooking pot. Insert Deluxe reversible rack. Place Cook & Crisp Basket on top of Deluxe reversible rack. Add cod in an even row onto Cook & Crisp Basket. Pour in additional marinade for the steaming aromatics. 4. Lock lid; move slider towards PRESSURE. Adjust pressure release valve in the SEAL position. Close pressure-release valve. The cooking temperature will default to HIGH, which is accurate. Set time to 3 minutes. Select START/STOP and start cooking. When cooking is complete, let pressure release quickly by turning it into VENT position. Transfer fish to a serving bowl. 5. To Serve: Assemble fish tacos by adding equal amounts of fish, slaw, guacamole, and tomatoes to each corn tortilla.
Per Serving: Calories 346; Fat 22g; Sodium 1300mg; Carbs 1g; Fiber 0g; Sugar 0g; Protein 32g

Parmesan Cod

Prep Time: 5 minutes. | Cook Time: 15 minutes. | Serves: 4

4 cod fillets, boneless
Salt and black pepper to the taste
1 cup parmesan
4 tablespoons balsamic vinegar
A drizzle of olive oil
3 spring onions, chopped

1. Place the Cook & Crisp Basket in your Pressure Cooker Steam Fryer. 2. Season fish with salt, pepper, grease with the oil, and coat it in parmesan. Put the fillets in the Cook & Crisp Basket. Put on the Smart Lid on top of the Ninja Foodi Steam Fryer. Move the Lid Slider to the "Air Fry/Stovetop". Select the "Air Fry" mode for cooking. Air Fry at 370°F/185°C for around 14 minutes. Meanwhile, in a suitable bowl, mix the spring onions with salt, pepper and the vinegar and whisk. Divide the cod between plates, drizzle the spring onions mix all over and serve with a side salad.
Per serving: Calories 636; Fat: 25g; Sodium 259mg; Carbs: 0.9g; Fiber: 0.5g; Sugars 0g; Protein 95.6g

Bacon Wrapped Scallops

Prep Time: 15 minutes. | Cook Time: 7 minutes. | Serves: 4

1 teaspoon coriander
½ teaspoon paprika
¼ teaspoon salt
16 ounces scallops
4 ounces bacon, sliced
1 teaspoon sesame oil

1. Place the Cook & Crisp Basket in your Pressure Cooker Steam Fryer. 2. Sprinkle the scallops with coriander, paprika, and salt. Then wrap the scallops in the bacon slices and secure with toothpicks. Sprinkle the scallops with sesame oil. Put the scallops in the "cook & crisp basket". Put on the Smart Lid on top of the Ninja Foodi Steam Fryer. Move the Lid Slider to the "Air Fry/Stovetop". Select the "Air Fry" mode for cooking. 3. Adjust the cooking temperature to 400°F/200°C. 4. Cook for them for around 7 minutes.
Per serving: Calories 278; Fat: 15.4g; Sodium 321mg; Carbs: 1.3g; Fiber: 0.5g; Sugars 0.1g; Protein 32.1g

Cod with Spring Onions

Prep Time: 5 minutes. | Cook Time: 15 minutes. | Serves: 2

2 cod fillets, boneless
Salt and black pepper to the taste
1 bunch spring onions, chopped
3 tablespoons ghee, melted

1. In the Cook & Crisp Basket, mix all the recipe ingredients, toss gently. 2. Place the Cook & Crisp Basket in your Pressure Cooker Steam Fryer. Put on the Smart Lid on top of the Ninja Foodi Steam Fryer. Move the Lid Slider to the "Air Fry/Stovetop". Select the "Air Fry" mode for cooking. Air Fry at 360°F/180°C for around 15 minutes. Divide the fish and sauce between plates and serve.
Per serving: Calories 443; Fat: 16.3g; Sodium 305mg; Carbs: 37.4g; Fiber: 7.8g; Sugars 11.4g; Protein 38.5g

Salmon with Chives Sauce

Prep Time: 5 minutes. | Cook Time: 20 minutes. | Serves: 4

4 salmon fillets, boneless
A pinch of salt and black pepper
½ cup heavy cream
1 tablespoon chives, chopped
1 teaspoon lemon juice
1 teaspoon dill, chopped
2 garlic cloves, minced
¼ cup ghee, melted

1. In a suitable bowl, mix all the recipe ingredients except the salmon and mix well. Arrange the salmon in the Cook & Crisp Basket, drizzle the sauce all over. 2. Place the Cook & Crisp Basket in your Pressure Cooker Steam Fryer. 3. Put on the Smart Lid on top of the Ninja Foodi Steam Fryer. Move the Lid Slider to the "Air Fry/Stovetop". Select the "Air Fry" mode for cooking. Air Fry at 360°F/180°C for around 20 minutes. Divide everything between plates and serve.
Per serving: Calories 423; Fat: 18.4g; Sodium 137mg; Carbs: 4.6g; Fiber: 1.9g; Sugars 0.8g; Protein 56.2g

Garlic Shrimp

Prep Time: 10 minutes. | Cook Time: 5 minutes. | Serves: 3

1-pound shrimps, peeled
½ teaspoon garlic powder
¼ teaspoon minced garlic
1 teaspoon cumin
¼ teaspoon lemon zest, grated
½ tablespoon avocado oil
½ teaspoon dried parsley

1. Place the Cook & Crisp Basket in your Pressure Cooker Steam Fryer. 2. In the mixing bowl mix up shrimps, garlic powder, minced garlic, cumin, lemon zest, and dried parsley. Then add avocado oil and mix up the shrimps well. Put the shrimps in the "cook & crisp basket". Put on the Smart Lid on top of the Ninja Foodi Steam Fryer. Move the Lid Slider to the "Air Fry/Stovetop". Select the "Air Fry" mode for cooking. Adjust the cooking temperature to 400°F/200°C. Cook for around 5 minutes.
Per serving: Calories 681; Fat: 30.7g; Sodium 1245mg; Carbs: 54.9g; Fiber: 9.9g; Sugars 5g; Protein 42.5g

Tilapia with Tomato Salsa

Prep Time: 5 minutes. | Cook Time: 15 minutes. | Serves: 4

4 tilapia fillets, boneless
1 tablespoon olive oil
A pinch of salt and black pepper
12 ounces tomatoes, chopped
2 tablespoons green onions,
chopped
2 tablespoons sweet red pepper, chopped
1 tablespoon balsamic vinegar

1. Place the Cook & Crisp Basket in your Pressure Cooker Steam Fryer. 2. Arrange the tilapia in the Cook & Crisp Basket and season with black pepper and salt. In a suitable bowl, mix all the other ingredients, toss and spread over the fish. Put on the Smart Lid on top of the Ninja Foodi Steam Fryer. Move the Lid Slider to the "Air Fry/Stovetop". Select the "Air Fry" mode for cooking. Air Fry at 350°F/175°C for around 15 minutes. Divide the mix between plates and serve.
Per serving: Calories 397; Fat: 19.1g; Sodium 431mg; Carbs: 16.8g; Fiber: 5.3g; Sugars 6.4g; Protein 39.4g

Crusted Salmon

Prep Time: 15 minutes. | Cook Time: 8 minutes. | Serves: 4

12 ounces salmon fillet
¼ cup pistachios, grinded
1 teaspoon cream cheese
½ teaspoon nutmeg
2 tablespoons coconut flour
½ teaspoon turmeric
¼ teaspoon sage
½ teaspoon salt
1 tablespoon heavy cream
Cooking spray

1. Place the Cook & Crisp Basket in your Pressure Cooker Steam Fryer. 2. Cut the salmon fillet into 4 parts. In the mixing bowl mix up cream cheese, turmeric, sage, salt, and heavy cream. Then in the separated bowl mix up coconut flour and pistachios. Dip the salmon fillets in the cream cheese mixture and then coat in the pistachio mixture. Place the coated salmon fillets in the basket and grease them with the cooking spray. Put on the Smart Lid on top of the Ninja Foodi Steam Fryer. 3. Move the Lid Slider to the "Air Fry/Stovetop". Select the "Air Fry" mode for cooking. Adjust the cooking temperature to 380°F/195°C. Cook the fish for around 8 minutes.
Per serving: Calories 348; Fat: 11.1g; Sodium 139mg; Carbs: 7.9g; Fiber: 3g; Sugars 1.6g; Protein 52.8g

Catfish With Avocado

Prep Time: 5 minutes. | Cook Time: 15 minutes. | Serves: 4

2 teaspoons oregano, dried
2 teaspoons cumin,
2 teaspoons sweet paprika
A pinch of salt and black pepper
4 catfish fillets
1 avocado, peeled and cubed
½ cup spring onions, chopped
2 tablespoons cilantro, chopped
2 teaspoons olive oil
2 tablespoons lemon juice

1. In a suitable bowl, mix all the recipe ingredients except the fish and toss. Arrange them in the Cook & Crisp Basket, top with the fish. Place the Cook & Crisp Basket in your Pressure Cooker Steam Fryer. Put on the Smart Lid on top of the Ninja Foodi Steam Fryer. Move the Lid Slider to the "Air Fry/Stovetop". Select the "Air Fry" mode for cooking. Air Fry at 360°F/180°C for around 15 minutes, flipping the fish halfway. Divide between plates and serve.
Per serving: Calories 396; Fat: 11.4g; Sodium 448mg; Carbs: 30.7g; Fiber: 3.7g; Sugars 0.8g; Protein 40.2g

Herbed Shrimp Skewers

Prep Time: 10 minutes. | Cook Time: 5 minutes. | Serves: 5

4-pounds shrimps, peeled
2 tablespoons fresh cilantro, chopped
2 tablespoons apple cider vinegar
1 teaspoon coriander
1 tablespoon avocado oil
Cooking spray

1. Place the Cook & Crisp Basket in your Pressure Cooker Steam Fryer. 2. In the shallow bowl mix up avocado oil, coriander, apple cider vinegar, and fresh cilantro. Then put the shrimps in the big bowl and sprinkle with avocado oil mixture. Mix them well and leave for around 10 minutes to marinate. After this, string the shrimps on the skewers. Arrange the shrimp skewers in the Cook & Crisp Basket. Put on the Smart Lid on top of the Ninja Foodi Steam Fryer. Move the Lid Slider to the "Air Fry/Stovetop". Select the "Air Fry" mode for cooking. Adjust the cooking temperature to 400°F/200°C. Cook for them for around 5 minutes.
Per serving: Calories 654; Fat: 46.8g; Sodium 845mg; Carbs: 9.9g; Fiber: 3.5g; Sugars 3.5g; Protein 56.9g

Air-Fried Cod

Prep Time: 5 minutes. | Cook Time: 14 minutes. | Serves: 4

⅓ cup stevia
2 tablespoons coconut aminos
4 cod fillets, boneless
A pinch of salt and black pepper

1. In the Cook & Crisp Basket, mix all the recipe ingredients and toss gently. Place the Cook & Crisp Basket in your Pressure Cooker Steam Fryer. 2. Put on the Smart Lid on top of the Ninja Foodi Steam Fryer. Move the Lid Slider to the "Air Fry/Stovetop". Select the "Air Fry" mode for cooking. Air Fry at 350°F/175°C for around 14 minutes, flipping the fish halfway. Divide everything between plates and serve.
Per serving: Calories 375; Fat: 19.8g; Sodium 2105mg; Carbs: 29g; Fiber: 0.7g; Sugars 24.8g; Protein 24.3g

Crab Muffins

Prep Time: 15 minutes. | Cook Time: 20 minutes. | Serves: 2

5 ounces crab meat, chopped
2 eggs, beaten
2 tablespoons almond flour
¼ teaspoon baking powder
½ teaspoon apple cider vinegar
½ teaspoon paprika
1 tablespoon butter, softened
Cooking spray

1. Place the Cook & Crisp Basket in your Pressure Cooker Steam Fryer. 2. Grind the chopped crab meat and put it in the bowl. Add eggs, almond flour, baking powder, apple cider vinegar, paprika, and butter. Stir the mixture until homogenous. Grease the muffin molds with cooking spray. Then pour the crab meat batter in the muffin molds and place them in the Cook & Crisp Basket. Put on the Smart Lid on top of the Ninja Foodi Steam Fryer. 3. Move the Lid Slider to the "Air Fry/Stovetop". Select the "Air Fry" mode for cooking. Adjust the cooking temperature to 365°F/185°C. Cook the crab muffins for around 20 minutes or until they are light brown. Cool the cooked muffins to the room temperature and remove from the muffin mold.
Per serving: Calories 388; Fat: 21.8g; Sodium 787mg; Carbs: 5.4g; Fiber: 1.5g; Sugars 1.4g; Protein 49.3g

Tilapia with Kale

Prep Time: 5 minutes. | Cook Time: 20 minutes. | Serves: 4

4 tilapia fillets, boneless
Salt and black pepper to the taste
2 garlic cloves, minced
1 teaspoon fennel seeds
½ teaspoon red pepper flakes, crushed
1 bunch kale, chopped
3 tablespoons olive oil

1. In the Cook & Crisp Basket, mix all the recipe ingredients. 2. Place the Cook & Crisp Basket in your Pressure Cooker Steam Fryer. 3. Put on the Smart Lid on top of the Ninja Foodi Steam Fryer. Move the Lid Slider to the "Air Fry/Stovetop". Select the "Air Fry" mode for cooking. Air Fry at 360°F/180°C for around 20 minutes. Divide everything between plates and serve.
Per serving: Calories 585; Fat: 39.5g; Sodium 1687mg; Carbs: 10.4g; Fiber: 2.7g; Sugars 3.1g; Protein 43.2g

Chili Crispy Haddock

Prep Time: 10 minutes. | Cook Time: 8 minutes. | Serves: 4

12 ounces haddock fillet
1 egg, beaten
1 teaspoon cream cheese
1 teaspoon chili flakes
½ teaspoon salt
1 tablespoon flax meal
Cooking spray

1. Place the Cook & Crisp Basket in your Pressure Cooker Steam Fryer. 2. Cut the haddock on 4 pieces and sprinkle with chili flakes and salt. After this, in the small bowl mix up egg and cream cheese. Dip the haddock pieces in the egg mixture and generously sprinkle with flax meal. Spray the Cook & Crisp Basket with cooking spray. Put the prepared haddock pieces in the Cook & Crisp Basket in one layer. Put on the Smart Lid on top of the Ninja Foodi Steam Fryer. Move the Lid Slider to the "Air Fry/Stovetop". Select the "Air Fry" mode for cooking. 3. Adjust the cooking temperature to 400°F/200°C. 4. Cook them for around 4 minutes from each side or until they are golden brown.
Per serving: Calories 596; Fat: 24.6g; Sodium 316mg; Carbs: 36.8g; Fiber: 15.6g; Sugars 9.5g; Protein 58.8g

Lime paprika Cod

Prep Time: 5 minutes. | Cook Time: 14 minutes. | Serves: 4

4 cod fillets, boneless
1 tablespoon olive oil
Salt and black pepper to the taste
2 teaspoons sweet paprika
Juice of 1 lime

1. Place the Cook & Crisp Basket in your Pressure Cooker Steam Fryer. 2. In a suitable bowl, mix all the recipe ingredients, transfer the fish to the Cook & Crisp Basket. Put on the Smart Lid on top of the Ninja Foodi Steam Fryer. Move the Lid Slider to the "Air Fry/Stovetop". Select the "Air Fry" mode for cooking. Cook for 350°F/175°C for around 7 minutes on each side. Divide the fish between plates and serve with a side salad.
Per serving: Calories 343; Fat: 20.1g; Sodium 903mg; Carbs: 0.2g; Fiber: 0.1g; Sugars 0.2g; Protein 37.1g

Mackerel with Peppers

Prep Time: 15 minutes. | Cook Time: 20 minutes. | Serves: 5

1-pound mackerel, trimmed
1 tablespoon paprika
1 green bell pepper
½ cup spring onions, chopped
1 tablespoon avocado oil
1 teaspoon apple cider vinegar
½ teaspoon salt

1. Place the Cook & Crisp Basket in your Pressure Cooker Steam Fryer. 2. Wash the mackerel if needed and sprinkle with paprika. Chop the green bell pepper. Then fill the mackerel with bell pepper and spring onion. After this, sprinkle the fish with avocado oil, apple cider vinegar, and salt. Place the mackerel in the Ninja Foodi Pressure Steam Fryer basket. Put on the Smart Lid on top of the Ninja Foodi Steam Fryer. Move the Lid Slider to the "Air Fry/Stovetop". Select the "Air Fry" mode for cooking. 3. Adjust the cooking temperature to 375°F/190°C. Cook for it for around 20 minutes.
Per serving: Calories 416; Fat: 23.6g; Sodium 934mg; Carbs: 6g; Fiber: 2g; Sugars 0.6g; Protein 37.9g

Ginger Lime Salmon

Prep Time: 5 minutes. | Cook Time: 12 minutes. | Serves: 4

2 tablespoons lime juice
1-pound salmon fillets, boneless, skinless and cubed
1 tablespoon ginger, grated
4 teaspoons olive oil
1 tablespoon coconut aminos
1 tablespoon sesame seeds, toasted
1 tablespoon chives, chopped

1. In the Cook & Crisp Basket, mix all the recipe ingredients and toss. Place the Cook & Crisp Basket in your Pressure Cooker Steam Fryer. Put on the Smart Lid on top of the Ninja Foodi Steam Fryer. Move the Lid Slider to the "Air Fry/Stovetop". Select the "Air Fry" mode for cooking. Air Fry at 360°F/180°C for around 12 minutes. Divide into bowls and serve.
Per serving: Calories 372; Fat: 16.3g; Sodium 742mg; Carbs: 6.8g; Fiber: 0.8g; Sugars 1.8g; Protein 42.3g

Crusted Sardine Cakes

Prep Time: 15 minutes. | Cook Time: 10 minutes. | Serves: 5

12 ounces sardines, trimmed, cleaned	2 tablespoons flax meal
¼ cup coconut flour	1 teaspoon black pepper
1 egg, beaten	1 teaspoon salt
	Cooking spray

1. Place the Cook & Crisp Basket in your Pressure Cooker Steam Fryer. 2. Chop the sardines and put them in the bowl. Add coconut flour, egg, flax meal, black pepper, and salt. Mix up the mixture with the help of the fork. Then make 5 cakes from the sardine mixture. Grease the Ninja Foodi Pressure Steam Fryer basket with cooking spray and place the cakes inside. Put on the Smart Lid on top of the Ninja Foodi Steam Fryer. 3. Move the Lid Slider to the "Air Fry/Stovetop". Select the "Air Fry" mode for cooking. Adjust the cooking temperature to 390°F/200°C. Cook them for around 5 minutes from each side.
Per serving: Calories 326; Fat: 12g; Sodium 779mg; Carbs: 8.3g; Fiber: 2.9g; Sugars 1.3g; Protein 46.9g

Gingered Cod

Prep Time: 10 minutes. | Cook Time: 8 minutes. | Serves: 2

10 ounces cod fillet	1 tablespoon sunflower oil
½ teaspoon cayenne pepper	½ teaspoon salt
¼ teaspoon coriander	½ teaspoon dried rosemary
½ teaspoon ginger	½ teaspoon paprika
½ teaspoon black pepper	

1. Place the Cook & Crisp Basket in your Pressure Cooker Steam Fryer. 2. In the shallow bowl mix up cayenne pepper, coriander, ginger, black pepper, salt, dried rosemary, and paprika. Then rub the cod fillet with the spice mixture. After this, sprinkle it with sunflower oil. Place the cod fillet in the basket. Put on the Smart Lid on top of the Ninja Foodi Steam Fryer. Move the Lid Slider to the "Air Fry/Stovetop". Select the "Air Fry" mode for cooking. Adjust the cooking temperature to 390°F/200°C. Cook it for around 4 minutes. Then carefully flip the fish on another side. Cook for around 4 minutes more.
Per serving: Calories 565; Fat: 14.5g; Sodium 938mg; Carbs: 47g; Fiber: 3.8g; Sugars 5g; Protein 58g

Paprika Tilapia with Capers

Prep Time: 5 minutes. | Cook Time: 20 minutes. | Serves: 4

4 tilapia fillets, boneless	1 teaspoon garlic powder
3 tablespoons ghee, melted	½ teaspoon smoked paprika
A pinch of salt and black pepper	½ teaspoon oregano, dried
2 tablespoons capers	2 tablespoons lemon juice

1. Place the Cook & Crisp Basket in your Pressure Cooker Steam Fryer. 2. In a suitable bowl, mix all the recipe ingredients except the fish and toss. Arrange the fish in the Cook & Crisp Basket, pour the capers mix all over. Put on the Smart Lid on top of the Ninja Foodi Steam Fryer. Move the Lid Slider to the "Air Fry/Stovetop". Select the "Air Fry" mode for cooking. Cook for 360°F/180°C for around 20 minutes, shaking halfway. Divide between plates and serve hot.
Per serving: Calories 402; Fat: 19.9g; Sodium 1387mg; Carbs: 24g; Fiber: 8g; Sugars 12.7g; Protein 32.1g

Sesame Crusted Salmon

Prep Time: 10 minutes. | Cook Time: 9 minutes. | Serves: 6

18 ounces salmon fillet	1 tablespoon sesame seeds
2 tablespoons swerve	2 tablespoons lemon juice
1 tablespoon apple cider vinegar	½ teaspoon minced garlic
6 teaspoons liquid aminos	1 tablespoon avocado oil
1 teaspoon minced ginger	

1. Place the Cook & Crisp Basket in your Pressure Cooker Steam Fryer. 2. Cut the salmon fillet into 8 portions and sprinkle with apple cider vinegar, minced ginger, lemon juice, minced garlic, and liquid aminos. Leave the fish for around 10 to 15 minutes to marinate. After this, sprinkle the fish with avocado oil and put in the Cook & Crisp Basket in one layer. Cook the fish fillets for around 7 minutes. Then sprinkle them with swerve and sesame seeds. Put on the Smart Lid on top of the Ninja Foodi Steam Fryer. Move the Lid Slider to the "Air Fry/Stovetop". Select the "Air Fry" mode for cooking. Cook for around 2 minutes more at 400°F/200°C.
Per serving: Calories 347; Fat: 18.8g; Sodium 137mg; Carbs: 13.4g; Fiber: 8.5g; Sugars 1g; Protein 36.3g

Parsley Coconut Shrimp

Prep Time: 5 minutes. | Cook Time: 12 minutes. | Serves: 4

1 tablespoon ghee, melted	A pinch of red pepper flakes
1-pound shrimp, peeled and deveined	A pinch of salt and black pepper
¼ cup coconut cream	1 tablespoon parsley, chopped
	1 tablespoon chives, chopped

1. Place the Cook & Crisp Basket in your Pressure Cooker Steam Fryer. 2. In the Cook & Crisp Basket, mix all the recipe ingredients except the parsley. Place the Cook & Crisp Basket in your Pressure Cooker Steam Fryer. Put on the Smart Lid on top of the Ninja Foodi Steam Fryer. Move the Lid Slider to the "Air Fry/Stovetop". Select the "Air Fry" mode for cooking. Air Fry at 360°F/180°C for around 12 minutes. Divide the mix into bowls, sprinkle the parsley on top and serve.
Per serving: Calories 618; Fat: 13.5g; Sodium 96mg; Carbs: 98.7g; Fiber: 5.3g; Sugars 0.5g; Protein 24.4g

Bacon Halibut Steaks

Prep Time: 15 minutes. | Cook Time: 10 minutes. | Serves: 4

24 ounces halibut steaks (6 ounces each fillet)	½ teaspoon black pepper
½ teaspoon salt	4 ounces bacon, sliced
	1 tablespoon sunflower oil

1. Place the Cook & Crisp Basket in your Pressure Cooker Steam Fryer. 2. Cut every halibut fillet on 2 parts and sprinkle with salt and black pepper. Then wrap the fish fillets in the sliced bacon. Sprinkle the halibut bites with sunflower oil and put in the "cook & crisp basket". Put on the Smart Lid on top of the Ninja Foodi Steam Fryer. Move the Lid Slider to the "Air Fry/Stovetop". Select the "Air Fry" mode for cooking. Adjust the cooking temperature to 400°F/200°C. Cook the meal for around 5 minutes. Then flip the fish bites on another side. Cook for them for around 5 minutes more.
Per serving: Calories 412; Fat: 23.6g; Sodium 1495mg; Carbs: 4.8g; Fiber: 1.3g; Sugars 1.7g; Protein 37.9g

Trout with Herb Sauce

Prep time: 5 minutes | Cook time: 5 minutes | Serves: 4

Trout	2 teaspoons Italian seasoning
4 (½-pound) fresh river trout	1 small shallot, peeled and minced
1 teaspoon sea salt	2 tablespoons mayonnaise
4 cups torn lettuce leaves, divided	½ teaspoon fresh lemon juice
1 teaspoon white wine vinegar	¼ teaspoon sugar
½ cup water	Pinch of salt
Herb Sauce	2 tablespoons sliced almonds, toasted
½ cup minced fresh flat-leaf parsley	

1. For Trout: Rinse the trout inside and out; pat dry. Sprinkle with salt inside and out. Put 3 cups lettuce leaves in the bottom of the Ninja Foodi XL Pressure Cooker Steam Fryer with SmartLid cooking pot. Arrange the trout over the top of the lettuce and top fish with the remaining lettuce. 2. Pour vinegar and water into pot. 3. Lock lid; move slider towards PRESSURE. Adjust pressure release valve in the SEAL position. Close pressure-release valve. The cooking temperature will default to HIGH, which is accurate. Set time to 3 minutes. Select START/STOP and start cooking. When cooking is complete, let pressure release quickly by turning it into VENT position. 4. Transfer fish to a serving plate. Peel and discard the skin from the fish. Remove and discard the heads if desired. 5. For Herb Sauce: In a small bowl, mix together the parsley, Italian seasoning, shallot, mayonnaise, lemon juice, sugar, and salt. Evenly divide among the fish, spreading it over them. 6. Sprinkle toasted almonds over the top of the sauce. Serve.
Per Serving: Calories 239; Fat 9g; Sodium 901mg; Carbs 11g; Fiber 1g; Sugar 1g; Protein 27g

Parmesan Salmon

Prep Time: 5 minutes. | Cook Time: 15 minutes. | Serves: 4

4 salmon fillets, skinless
1 teaspoon mustard
A pinch of salt and black pepper

½ cup coconut flakes
1 tablespoon parmesan, grated
Cooking spray

1. Place the Cook & Crisp Basket in your Pressure Cooker Steam Fryer. 2. In a suitable bowl, mix the parmesan with the other ingredients except the fish and cooking spray and stir well. Coat the fish in this mixture, grease it with cooking spray and arrange in the Cook & Crisp Basket. Put on the Smart Lid on top of the Ninja Foodi Steam Fryer. Move the Lid Slider to the "Air Fry/Stovetop". Select the "Air Fry" mode for cooking. Air Fry these fillets at 400°F/200°C for around 15 minutes, divide between plates and serve with a side salad.
Per serving: Calories 413; Fat: 24.5g; Sodium 962mg; Carbs: 6.9g; Fiber: 1.1g; Sugars 2.9g; Protein 39.1g

Crusted Cheesy Shrimps

Prep Time: 15 minutes. | Cook Time: 5 minutes. | Serves: 4

14 ounces shrimps, peeled
2 eggs, beaten
¼ cup heavy cream
1 teaspoon salt
1 teaspoon black pepper

4 ounces Monterey jack cheese, shredded
5 tablespoons coconut flour
1 tablespoon lemon juice, for garnish

1. Place the Cook & Crisp Basket in your Pressure Cooker Steam Fryer. 2. In the mixing bowl mix up heavy cream, salt, and black pepper. Add eggs and mix the mixture until homogenous. After this, mix up coconut flour and Monterey jack cheese. Dip the shrimps in the heavy cream mixture and coat in the coconut flour mixture. Then dip the shrimps in the egg mixture again and coat in the coconut flour. Arrange the shrimps in the Cook & Crisp Basket in one layer . Put on the Smart Lid on top of the Ninja Foodi Steam Fryer. Move the Lid Slider to the "Air Fry/Stovetop". Select the "Air Fry" mode for cooking. 3. Adjust the cooking temperature to 400°F/200°C. 4. Cook for them for around 5 minutes. Repeat the same step with remaining shrimps. Sprinkle the shrimps with lemon juice.
Per serving: Calories 612; Fat: 38.2g; Sodium 76mg; Carbs: 39.1g; Fiber: 5.8g; Sugars 1.6g; Protein 30.6g

Salmon with Lime Sauce

Prep Time: 5 minutes. | Cook Time: 20 minutes. | Serves: 4

4 salmon fillets, boneless
¼ cup coconut cream
1 teaspoon lime zest, grated
⅓ cup heavy cream

¼ cup lime juice
½ cup coconut, shredded
A pinch of salt and black pepper

1. In a suitable bowl, mix all the recipe ingredients except the salmon and whisk. Arrange the fish in the Cook & Crisp Basket, drizzle the coconut sauce all over. Place the Cook & Crisp Basket in your Pressure Cooker Steam Fryer. 2. Put on the Smart Lid on top of the Ninja Foodi Steam Fryer. Move the Lid Slider to the "Air Fry/Stovetop". Select the "Air Fry" mode for cooking. Air Fry at 360°F/180°C for around 20 minutes. Divide between plates and serve.
Per serving: Calories 408; Fat: 23.1g; Sodium 412mg; Carbs: 27.7g; Fiber: 7.2g; Sugars 19.2g; Protein 24.4g

Catfish Fillet Bites

Prep Time: 10 minutes. | Cook Time: 10 minutes. | Serves: 4

¼ cup coconut flakes
3 tablespoons coconut flour
1 teaspoon salt

3 eggs, beaten
10 ounces catfish fillet
Cooking spray

1. Place the Cook & Crisp Basket in your Pressure Cooker Steam Fryer. 2. Cut the catfish fillet on the small pieces (nuggets) and sprinkle with salt. After this, dip the catfish pieces in the egg and coat in the coconut flour. Then dip the fish pieces in the egg again and coat in the coconut flakes. Spray the Cook & Crisp Basket with cooking spray. Place the catfish nuggets in the Ninja Foodi Pressure Steam Fryer basket. Put on the Smart Lid on top of the Ninja Foodi Steam Fryer. Move the Lid Slider to the "Air Fry/Stovetop". Select the "Air Fry" mode for cooking. Adjust the cooking temperature to 385°F/195°C. Cook them for around 6 minutes. Then flip the nuggets on another side. Cook for them for around 4 minutes more.
Per serving: Calories 347; Fat: 15.7g; Sodium 999mg; Carbs: 11.8g; Fiber: 1.1g; Sugars 7g; Protein 39.6g

Mustard Parmesan Cod

Prep Time: 10 minutes. | Cook Time: 14 minutes. | Serves: 4

1 cup parmesan, grated
4 cod fillets, boneless

Salt and black pepper to the taste
1 tablespoon mustard

1. Place the Cook & Crisp Basket in your Pressure Cooker Steam Fryer. 2. In a suitable bowl, mix the parmesan with salt, pepper and the mustard and stir. Spread them over the cod, arrange the fish in the Cook & Crisp Basket. Put on the Smart Lid on top of the Ninja Foodi Steam Fryer. Move the Lid Slider to the "Air Fry/Stovetop". Select the "Air Fry" mode for cooking. Air Fry at 370°F/190°C for around 7 minutes on each side. Divide between plates and serve with a side salad.
Per serving: Calories 236; Fat: 10.4g; Sodium 713mg; Carbs: 9.8g; Fiber: 0.5g; Sugars 0.1g; Protein 25.7g

Turmeric Salmon with Cream

Prep Time: 10 minutes. | Cook Time: 7 minutes. | Serves: 2

8 ounces salmon fillet
2 tablespoons coconut flakes
1 tablespoon coconut cream
½ teaspoon salt

½ teaspoon turmeric
½ teaspoon onion powder
1 teaspoon nut oil

1. Place the Cook & Crisp Basket in your Pressure Cooker Steam Fryer. 2. Cut the salmon fillet into halves and sprinkle with salt, turmeric, and onion powder. After this, dip the fish fillets in the coconut cream and coat in the coconut flakes. Sprinkle the salmon fillets with nut oil. Arrange the salmon fillets in the Ninja Foodi Pressure Steam Fryer basket. Put on the Smart Lid on top of the Ninja Foodi Steam Fryer. Move the Lid Slider to the "Air Fry/Stovetop". Select the "Air Fry" mode for cooking. Adjust the cooking temperature to 380°F/195°C. Cook for around 7 minutes.
Per serving: Calories 427; Fat: 18.1g; Sodium 676mg; Carbs: 13.7g; Fiber: 7.5g; Sugars 1.7g; Protein 51.2g

Delicious Umami Calamari

Prep time: 15 minutes| Cook time: 20 minutes| Serves: 4

1 tablespoon olive oil
1 small onion, peeled and diced
2 cloves garlic, minced
¼ cup dry red wine
1 (14.5-ounce) can diced tomatoes, including juice
1 cup chicken broth
¼ cup chopped fresh parsley
6 tablespoons chopped fresh basil,

divided
1 teaspoon sea salt
½ teaspoon ground black pepper
2 teaspoons anchovy paste
1 bay leaf
1 pound calamari tubes, cut into ¼" rings
¼ cup grated Parmesan cheese

1. Move the slider towards "AIR FRY/STOVETOP" and set Ninja Foodi XL Pressure Cooker Steam Fryer with SmartLid to SEAR/SAUTÉ mode. Adjust the temperature to "Hi5" by using up arrow. Press START/STOP to begin cooking. Add olive oil and heat. Add onion and sauté for 3–5 minutes until onions are translucent. Add garlic and sauté for an additional minute. Add red wine, press Adjust button to change temperature to less, and simmer unlidded for 5 minutes. 2. Add remaining ingredients except 2 tablespoons basil and Parmesan cheese. 3. Lock lid; move slider towards PRESSURE. Adjust pressure release valve in the SEAL position. Close pressure-release valve. The cooking temperature will default to HIGH, which is accurate. Set time to 3 minutes. Select START/STOP and start cooking. 4. When cooking is complete, let pressure release naturally for 10 minutes, then quick-release any remaining pressure by turning it into VENT position. 5. Remove bay leaf. Use a slotted spoon to transfer pot ingredients to four bowls. Garnish each bowl with equal amounts Parmesan cheese and ½ tablespoon basil.
Per Serving: Calories 194; Fat 6g; Sodium 481mg; Carbs 6g; Fiber 1.5g; Sugar 3g; Protein 27g

Air-Fried Tilapia

Prep Time: 15 minutes. | Cook Time: 9 minutes. | Serves: 2

1 chili pepper, chopped
1 teaspoon chili flakes
1 tablespoon sesame oil
½ teaspoon salt
10 ounces tilapia fillet
¼ teaspoon onion powder

1. Place the Cook & Crisp Basket in your Pressure Cooker Steam Fryer. 2. In the shallow bowl mix up chili pepper, chili flakes, salt, and onion powder. Gently churn the mixture and add sesame oil. After this, slice the tilapia fillet and sprinkle with chili mixture. Massage the fish with the help of the fingertips gently and leave for around 10 minutes to marinate. Put the tilapia fillets in the Ninja Foodi Pressure Steam Fryer basket. Put on the Smart Lid on top of the Ninja Foodi Steam Fryer. Move the Lid Slider to the "Air Fry/Stovetop". Select the "Air Fry" mode for cooking. Adjust the cooking temperature to 390°F/200°C. Cook for around 5 minutes. Then flip the fish on another side. Cook for around 4 minutes more.
Per serving: Calories 232; Fat: 8.4g; Sodium 300mg; Carbs: 8.6g; Fiber: 0.9g; Sugars 0.1g; Protein 30.1g

Paprika Cod with Endives

Prep Time: 5 minutes. | Cook Time: 20 minutes. | Serves: 4

2 endives, shredded
2 tablespoons olive oil
Salt and black pepper to the taste
4 salmon fillets, boneless
½ teaspoon sweet paprika

1. In the Cook & Crisp Basket, mix the fish with the rest of the ingredients and toss. 2. Place the Cook & Crisp Basket in your Pressure Cooker Steam Fryer. Put on the Smart Lid on top of the Ninja Foodi Steam Fryer. Move the Lid Slider to the "Air Fry/ Stovetop". Select the "Air Fry" mode for cooking. Air Fry at 350°F/175°C for around 20 minutes, flipping the fish halfway. Divide between plates and serve right away.
Per serving: Calories 314; Fat: 8.7g; Sodium 337mg; Carbs: 21.2g; Fiber: 4.1g; Sugars 16g; Protein 37.9g

Peppered Tuna Skewers

Prep Time: 5 minutes. | Cook Time: 12 minutes. | Serves: 4

1-pound tuna steaks, boneless and cubed
1 chili pepper, minced
4 green onions, chopped
2 tablespoons lime juice
A drizzle of olive oil
Salt and black pepper to the taste

1. Place the Cook & Crisp Basket in your Pressure Cooker Steam Fryer. 2. In a suitable bowl mix all the recipe ingredients and toss them. Thread the tuna cubes on skewers, arrange them in the Cook & Crisp Basket. Put on the Smart Lid on top of the Ninja Foodi Steam Fryer. Move the Lid Slider to the "Air Fry/Stovetop". Select the "Air Fry" mode for cooking. Air Fry at 370°F/190°C for around 12 minutes. Divide between plates and serve with a side salad.
Per serving: Calories 344; Fat: 10g; Sodium 251mg; Carbs: 4.7g; Fiber: 0.5g; Sugars 2.2g; Protein 55.7g

Sea Scallops with tangy Cherry Sauce

Prep time: 5 minutes| Cook time: 1 minutes| Serves: 2

¼ cup cherry preserves
1 teaspoon lemon juice
1 teaspoon tamari
1 tablespoon unsalted butter
1-pound fresh sea scallops
½ teaspoon salt
1 cup water

1. In a small bowl, whisk together preserves, lemon juice, and tamari. Set aside. 2. Move the slider towards "AIR FRY/STOVETOP" and set Ninja Foodi XL Pressure Cooker Steam Fryer with SmartLid to SEAR/SAUTÉ mode. Adjust the temperature to "Hi5" by using up arrow. Press START/STOP to begin cooking. Add butter to pot and heat 30 seconds. Season scallops with salt, add to pot, and sear 30 seconds per side. Transfer to Cook & Crisp Basket. Top scallops with preserve mixture. 3. Add water to the Ninja Foodi XL Pressure Cooker Steam Fryer with SmartLid cooking pot. Insert Cook & Crisp Basket. 4. Lock lid; move slider towards PRESSURE. Adjust pressure release valve in the SEAL position. Close pressure-release valve. The cooking temperature will default to HIGH, which is accurate. Set time to 0 minutes. Select START/STOP and start cooking. When cooking is complete, let pressure release quickly by turning it into VENT position. 5. Transfer scallops to two plates. Serve warm.
Per Serving: Calories 311; Fat 17g; Sodium 1110mg; Carbs 3g; Fiber 0g; Sugar 0g; Protein 34g

Steamed Crab

Prep time: 5 minutes| Cook time: 3 minutes| Serves: 2

1 cup water
4 cloves garlic, quartered
1 small onion, peeled and diced large
1 tablespoon Old Bay Seasoning
2 sprigs fresh thyme
2 pounds crab legs

1. Add water, garlic, onion, Old Bay Seasoning, and thyme to the Ninja Foodi XL Pressure Cooker Steam Fryer; stir to combine. 2. Insert Deluxe reversible rack. Add crab legs. 3. Lock lid; move slider to AIR FRY/STOVETOP. Select STEAM, and set time to 3 minutes. Press START/STOP to begin cooking. When cooking is complete, let pressure release quickly by turning it into VENT position. Carefully unlock lid. 4. Transfer crab legs to a serving platter.
Per Serving: Calories 251; Fat 14g; Sodium 411mg; Carbs 6g; Fiber 5g; Sugar 1g; Protein 12g

Lemon Salmon with Dill

Prep time: 5 minutes| Cook time: 5 minutes| Serves: 2

2 (5-ounce) salmon fillets
½ teaspoon sea salt
4 lemon slices
2 teaspoons chopped fresh dill
1 cup water

1. Pat fillets dry with a paper towel and place on a Cook & Crisp Basket. Season salmon with salt. Place 2 lemon slices on each fillet. Sprinkle with chopped dill. 2. Place water in Ninja Foodi XL Pressure Cooker Steam Fryer with SmartLid cooking pot. Insert Deluxe reversible rack. Place Cook & Crisp Basket onto Deluxe reversible rack. 3. Lock lid; move slider towards PRESSURE. Adjust pressure release valve in the SEAL position. Close pressure-release valve. The cooking temperature will default to HIGH, which is accurate. Set time to 5 minutes. Select START/STOP and start cooking. When cooking is complete, let pressure release quickly by turning it into VENT position. 4. Remove fish to plates and serve immediately.
Per Serving: Calories 282; Fat 13g; Sodium 359mg; Carbs 6g; Fiber 2.5g; Sugar 1g; Protein 36g

Nut-Crusted Halibut

Prep time: 5 minutes| Cook time: 7 minutes| Serves: 2

1 tablespoon Dijon mustard
1 teaspoon fresh lemon juice
2 tablespoons panko bread crumbs
¼ cup chopped unsalted pistachios
½ teaspoon salt
2 (5-ounce) halibut fillets
1 cup water

1. Preheat the oven to broiler for 500°F/260°C. 2. In a small bowl, combine mustard, lemon juice, bread crumbs, pistachios, and salt to form a thick paste. 3. Pat the halibut fillets dry with a paper towel. Rub the paste on the top of each fillet and place in Cook & Crisp Basket. 4. Pour 1 cup water in the Ninja Foodi XL Pressure Cooker Steam Fryer with SmartLid cooking pot. Insert Deluxe reversible rack. Place Cook & Crisp Basket on Deluxe reversible rack. 5. Lock lid; move slider towards PRESSURE. Adjust pressure release valve in the SEAL position. Close pressure-release valve. The cooking temperature will default to HIGH, which is accurate. Set time to 5 minutes. Select START/STOP and start cooking. 6. When cooking is complete, let pressure release quickly by turning it into VENT position. Transfer fillets to a parchment-paper-lined baking sheet. 7. Broil for approximately 1–2 minutes until tops are browned. Remove from heat and serve hot.
Per Serving: Calories 283; Fat 14g; Sodium 1460mg; Carbs 0g; Fiber 0g; Sugar 0g; Protein 40g

Paprika Catfish with Tarragon

Prep time: 5 minutes| Cook time: 3 minutes| Serves: 2

1 (14.5-ounce) can diced tomatoes, including juice	tarragon
2 teaspoons dried minced onion	1 medium green bell pepper, seeded and diced
¼ teaspoon onion powder	1 stalk celery, finely diced
1 teaspoon dried minced garlic	1 teaspoon salt
¼ teaspoon garlic powder	¼ teaspoon ground black pepper
2 teaspoons smoked paprika	pound catfish fillets, rinsed and cut into bite-sized pieces
1 tablespoon chopped fresh	

1. Add all ingredients except fish to the Ninja Foodi XL Pressure Cooker Steam Fryer with SmartLid cooking pot and stir to mix. Once mixed, add the fish on top. 2. Lock lid; move slider towards PRESSURE. Adjust pressure release valve in the SEAL position. Close pressure-release valve. The cooking temperature will default to HIGH, which is accurate. Set time to 3 minutes. Select START/STOP and start cooking. When cooking is complete, let pressure release quickly by turning it into VENT position. 3. Transfer all ingredients to a serving bowl. Serve warm.
Per Serving: Calories 355; Fat 16g; Sodium 750mg; Carbs 25g; Fiber 1g; Sugar 13g; Protein 25g

Tropical Sea Bass

Prep time: 5 minutes| Cook time: 3 minutes| Serves: 3

1 (14.5-ounce) can coconut milk	1 teaspoon ground turmeric
Juice of 1 lime	1 teaspoon ground ginger
1 tablespoon red curry paste	½ teaspoon sea salt
1 teaspoon fish sauce	½ teaspoon white pepper
1 teaspoon coconut aminos	1-pound sea bass, cut into 1" cubes
1 teaspoon honey	¼ cup chopped fresh cilantro
2 teaspoons sriracha	3 lime wedges
2 cloves garlic, minced	

1. In a large bowl, whisk together coconut milk, lime juice, red curry paste, fish sauce, coconut aminos, honey, sriracha, garlic, turmeric, ginger, sea salt, and white pepper. 2. Place sea bass in the bottom of Ninja Foodi XL Pressure Cooker Steam Fryer with SmartLid cooking pot. Pour coconut milk mixture over the fish. 3. Lock lid; move slider towards PRESSURE. Adjust pressure release valve in the SEAL position. Close pressure-release valve. The cooking temperature will default to HIGH, which is accurate. Set time to 3 minutes. Select START/STOP and start cooking. When cooking is complete, let pressure release quickly by turning it into VENT position. 4. Transfer fish and broth into three bowls. Garnish each with equal amounts of chopped cilantro and a lime wedge. Serve.
Per Serving: Calories 262; Fat 11g; Sodium 482mg; Carbs 26g; Fiber 1.5g; Sugar 1g; Protein 13g

Country Boil

Prep time: 10 minutes| Cook time:5 minutes| Serves: 6

1 large sweet onion, peeled and chopped	sausage, cut in 1" sections
4 cloves garlic, quartered	1 pound frozen tail-on shrimp
6 small red potatoes, cut in sixths	1 tablespoon Old Bay Seasoning
3 ears corn, cut in thirds	2 cups chicken broth
1½ pounds fully cooked andouille	1 lemon, cut into 6 wedges
	½ cup chopped fresh parsley

1. Layer onions in an even layer in the Ninja Foodi XL Pressure Cooker Steam Fryer with SmartLid cooking pot. Scatter the garlic on top of onions. Add red potatoes in an even layer, then do the same for the corn and sausage. Add the shrimp and sprinkle with Old Bay Seasoning. Pour in broth. 2. Squeeze lemon wedges into the Ninja Foodi XL Pressure Cooker Steam Fryer with SmartLid cooking pot and place squeezed lemon wedges into the pot. 3. Lock lid; move slider towards PRESSURE. Adjust pressure release valve in the SEAL position. Close pressure-release valve. The cooking temperature will default to HIGH, which is accurate. Set time to 5 minutes. Select START/STOP and start cooking. 4. When cooking is complete, let pressure release quickly by turning it into VENT position. Transfer ingredients to a serving platter and garnish with parsley.
Per Serving: Calories 440; Fat 17g; Sodium 590mg; Carbs 44g; Fiber 6g; Sugar 3g; Protein 27g

Mediterranean Spicy Cod

Prep time: 5 minutes| Cook time: 6 minutes| Serves: 2

2 (5-ounce) cod fillets, divided	1 small Roma tomato, diced, divided
2 teaspoons olive oil, divided	3 tablespoons chopped fresh basil leaves, divided
1½ teaspoons sea salt, divided	
10 pitted kalamata olives, divided	

1. Place a piece of cod on a 10" × 10" square of aluminum foil. Drizzle with 1 teaspoon olive oil. Sprinkle with ½ teaspoon salt. Scatter 5 olives, ½ the tomatoes, and 1 tablespoon basil on top of fish. Bring up the sides of the foil and crimp at the top to create a foil pocket. 2. Repeat with remaining piece of fish. Place both fish packs in the Ninja Foodi XL Pressure Cooker Steam Fryer with SmartLid cooking pot. 3. Lock lid; move slider towards PRESSURE. Adjust pressure release valve in the SEAL position. Close pressure-release valve. The cooking temperature will default to HIGH, which is accurate. Set time to 6 minutes. Select START/STOP and start cooking. When cooking is complete, let pressure release quickly by turning it into VENT position. 4. Remove foil packets and transfer fish and toppings to two plates. Garnish each plate with ½ tablespoon basil and ¼ teaspoon salt.
Per Serving: Calories 340; Fat 18.5g; Sodium 396mg; Carbs 8g; Fiber 4g; Sugar 2g; Protein 35g

Delicious Lobster Risotto

Prep time: 5 minutes| Cook time: 20 minutes| Serves: 4

4 tablespoons butter	3 tablespoons grated Parmesan cheese
1 small onion, peeled and finely diced	½ teaspoon salt
2 cloves garlic, minced	¼ teaspoon ground black pepper
1½ cups Arborio rice	Meat from 3 small lobster tails, diced
1 cup chardonnay	¼ cup chopped fresh parsley
3 cups vegetable broth	
½ teaspoon lemon zest	

1. Move the slider towards "AIR FRY/STOVETOP" and set Ninja Foodi XL Pressure Cooker Steam Fryer with SmartLid to SEAR/SAUTÉ mode. Adjust the temperature to "Hi5" by using up arrow. Press START/STOP to begin cooking and add the butter. Heat until melted. Add onion and stir-fry for 3–5 minutes until translucent. Add garlic and rice and cook for an additional minute. Add white wine and slowly stir unlidded for 5 minutes until liquid is absorbed by the rice. 2. Add broth, lemon zest, Parmesan, salt, and pepper. 3. Lock lid; move slider to AIR FRY/STOVETOP. Select STEAM, and set time to 10 minutes. Press START/STOP to begin cooking. Carefully unlock lid. 4. Stir in lobster, garnish with fresh parsley, and serve warm.
Per Serving: Calories 461; Fat 21.5g; Sodium 652mg; Carbs 41g; Fiber 3.5g; Sugar 5g; Protein 26g

Creamy Crab

Prep time: 5 minutes| Cook time: 8 minutes| Serves: 4

4 tablespoons butter	¼ cup chicken broth
½ stalk celery, finely diced	½ cup heavy cream
1 small red onion, peeled and finely diced	½ teaspoon sea salt
1-pound uncooked lump crabmeat	½ teaspoon ground black pepper

1. Move the slider towards "AIR FRY/STOVETOP" and set Ninja Foodi XL Pressure Cooker Steam Fryer with SmartLid to SEAR/SAUTÉ mode. Adjust the temperature to "Hi5" by using up arrow. Press START/STOP to begin cooking. Add the butter and melt. Add the celery and red onion. Stir-fry for 3–5 minutes until celery begins to soften. Stir in the crabmeat and broth. 2. Lock lid; move slider towards PRESSURE. Adjust pressure release valve in the SEAL position. Close pressure-release valve. The cooking temperature will default to HIGH, which is accurate. Set time to 3 minutes. Select START/STOP and start cooking. When cooking is complete, let pressure release quickly by turning it into VENT position. 3. Carefully stir in the cream, add salt and pepper, and serve warm.
Per Serving: Calories 273; Fat 9.9g; Sodium 258mg; Carbs 3.4g; Fiber 1.6g; Sugar 0.3g; Protein 39.8g

Mussels in White Wine

Prep time: 10 minutes| Cook time: 8 minutes| Serves: 4

2 tablespoons ghee
1 medium onion, peeled and diced
3 cloves garlic, minced
½ cup dry white wine
1 (14.5-ounce) can diced tomatoes, including juice
1 teaspoon cayenne pepper
1 teaspoon sea salt
Juice of 1 lemon
2 pounds fresh mussels, cleaned and debearded
4 tablespoons chopped fresh parsley

1. Move the slider towards "AIR FRY/STOVETOP" and set Ninja Foodi XL Pressure Cooker Steam Fryer with SmartLid to SEAR/SAUTÉ mode. Adjust the temperature to "Hi5" by using up arrow. Press START/STOP to begin cooking. Add the ghee and melt. Add onion and sauté for 3–5 minutes until translucent. Add garlic and cook for an additional minute. Stir in white wine and let cook 2 minutes. Add tomatoes, cayenne pepper, salt, and lemon juice. 2. Insert Cook & Crisp Basket. Place mussels on top. 3. Lock lid; move slider towards PRESSURE. Adjust pressure release valve in the SEAL position. Close pressure-release valve. The cooking temperature will default to HIGH, which is accurate. Set time to 0 minutes. Select START/STOP and start cooking. When cooking is complete, let pressure release quickly by turning it into VENT position. 4. Remove mussels and discard any that haven't opened. Transfer mussels to four bowls and pour liquid from Pot equally among bowls. Garnish each bowl with 1 tablespoon parsley. Serve immediately.
Per Serving: Calories 251; Fat 10g; Sodium 233mg; Carbs 4g; Fiber 3g; Sugar 1g; Protein 8g

Mahi-Mahi with a Lemon-Caper Sauce

Prep time: 5 minutes| Cook time: 7 minutes| Serves: 2

2 (6-ounce, 1"-thick) mahi-mahi fillets
2 tablespoons fresh lemon juice
2 tablespoons capers
1 teaspoon sea salt
1 teaspoon lemon zest
2 tablespoons butter, cut into 2 pats
1 tablespoon chopped fresh parsley

1. Place a piece of foil on the Ninja Foodi XL Pressure Cooker Steam Fryer Cook & Crisp Basket. Set both fillets on the foil. Create a "boat" with the foil by bringing up the edges. Pour lemon juice on fish. Add capers. Season fish with salt and zest. Add a pat of butter to each fillet. Set Deluxe reversible rack in the Ninja Foodi XL Pressure Cooker Steam Fryer and place the Cook & Crisp Basket on the rack. 2. Lock lid; move slider towards PRESSURE. Adjust pressure release valve in the SEAL position. Close pressure-release valve. The cooking temperature will default to HIGH, which is accurate. Set time to 7 minutes. Select START/STOP and start cooking. When cooking is complete, let pressure release quickly by turning it into VENT position. 3. Transfer fish to two plates. Garnish each with ½ tablespoon chopped parsley.
Per Serving: Calories 436; Fat 26.5g; Sodium 616mg; Carbs 24g; Fiber 4g; Sugar 5g; Protein 28g

Steamed Shrimp with Asparagus

Prep time: 5 minutes| Cook time: 1 minutes| Serves: 2

1 cup water
1 bunch asparagus
1 teaspoon sea salt, divided
1-pound shrimp, peeled and
deveined
½ lemon
2 tablespoons butter, cut into 2 pats

1. Pour water into Ninja Foodi XL Pressure Cooker Steam Fryer with SmartLid cooking pot. Insert Deluxe reversible rack. Place Cook & Crisp Basket on rack. 2. Prepare asparagus by finding the natural snap point on the stalks and discarding the woody ends. 3. Spread the asparagus on the bottom of the Cook & Crisp Basket. Sprinkle with ½ teaspoon salt. Add the shrimp. Squeeze lemon into it, then sprinkle shrimp with remaining ½ teaspoon salt. Place pats of butter on shrimp. 4. Lock lid; move slider towards PRESSURE. Adjust pressure release valve in the SEAL position. Close pressure-release valve. The cooking temperature will default to HIGH, which is accurate. Set time to 1 minutes. Select START/STOP and start cooking. When cooking is complete, let pressure release quickly by turning it into VENT position. 5. Transfer shrimp and asparagus to a platter and serve.
Per Serving: Calories 45; Fat 3g; Sodium 100mg; Carbs 0.9g; Fiber

0g; Sugar 0g; Protein 3.5g

Delicious Louisiana Grouper

Prep time: 10 minutes| Cook time: 20 minutes| Serves: 4

2 tablespoons olive oil
1 small onion, peeled and diced
1 stalk celery, diced
1 small green bell pepper, seeded and diced
1 (15-ounce) can diced tomatoes
¼ cup water
1 tablespoon tomato paste
1 teaspoon honey
Pinch of dried basil
2 teaspoons Creole seasoning
4 grouper fillets, rinsed and cut into bite-sized pieces
½ teaspoon sea salt
¼ teaspoon ground black pepper

1. Move the slider towards "AIR FRY/STOVETOP" and set Ninja Foodi XL Pressure Cooker Steam Fryer with SmartLid to SEAR/SAUTÉ mode. Adjust the temperature to "Hi5" by using up arrow. Press START/STOP to begin cooking. Heat oil and add onion, celery, and bell pepper. Sauté for 3–5 minutes until onions are translucent and peppers are tender. 2. Stir in undrained tomatoes, water, tomato paste, honey, basil, and Creole seasoning. 3. Sprinkle fish with salt and pepper. Gently toss the fish pieces into the sauce in the Ninja Foodi XL Pressure Cooker Steam Fryer with SmartLid cooking pot. 4. Lock lid; move slider towards PRESSURE. Adjust pressure release valve in the SEAL position. Close pressure-release valve. The cooking temperature will default to HIGH, which is accurate. Set time to 5 minutes. Select START/STOP and start cooking. When cooking is complete, let pressure release quickly by turning it into VENT position. 5. Transfer fish to a serving platter. Move the slider towards "AIR FRY/STOVETOP" and set Ninja Foodi XL Pressure Cooker Steam Fryer with SmartLid to SEAR/SAUTÉ mode. Adjust the temperature to "Hi5" by using up arrow. Press START/STOP to begin cooking and simmer juices unlidded for 10 minutes. 6. Transfer tomatoes and preferred amount of sauce over fish. Serve immediately.
Per Serving: Calories 366; Fat 16.6g; Sodium 256mg; Carbs 7.5g; Fiber 0.2g; Sugar 0.3g; Protein 4.6g

Steaming Clams

Prep time: 5 minutes| Cook time: 10 minutes| Serves: 4

2 pounds fresh clams, rinsed and purged
1 tablespoon olive oil
1 small white onion, peeled and
diced
1 clove garlic, quartered
½ cup chardonnay
½ cup water

1. Place clams in the Cook & Crisp Basket. Set aside. 2. Move the slider towards "AIR FRY/STOVETOP" and set Ninja Foodi XL Pressure Cooker Steam Fryer with SmartLid to SEAR/SAUTÉ mode. Adjust the temperature to "Hi5" by using up arrow. Press START/STOP to begin cooking. Heat olive oil. Add onion and sauté 3–5 minutes until translucent. Add garlic and cook another minute. Pour in white wine and water. Insert Cook & Crisp Basket. 3. Lock lid; move slider towards PRESSURE. Adjust pressure release valve in the SEAL position. Close pressure-release valve. The cooking temperature will default to HIGH, which is accurate. Set time to 4 minutes. Select START/STOP and start cooking. When cooking is complete, let pressure release quickly by turning it into VENT position. 4. Transfer clams to four serving bowls and top with a generous scoop of cooking liquid.
Per Serving: Calories 338; Fat 5.6g; Sodium 239mg; Carbs 5.5g; Fiber 0.6g; Sugar 0.6g; Protein 62.2g

Crab Legs

Prep time: 3 minutes| Cook time: 3 minutes| Serves: 4

2 lbs. wild-caught Snow Crab legs
1 cup water
⅓ cup ghee or clarified butter
Lemon slices

1. Place the Cook & Crisp Basket in the Ninja Foodi XL Pressure Cooker Steam Fryer with SmartLid cooking pot with 1 cup water. Put the crab legs in the pot and seal the lid. 2. Lock lid; move slider to AIR FRY/STOVETOP. Select STEAM, and set time to 3 minutes. Press START/STOP to begin cooking. 3. When cooking is complete, let pressure release naturally. Melt the ghee or clarified butter in a microwave or on the stovetop. 4. Serve the legs with ghee and with lemon slices on the side.
Per Serving: Calories 221; Fat 11g; Sodium 256mg; Carbs 6g; Fiber 4g; Sugar 2g; Protein 9g

Delicious Seafood Gumbo

Prep time: 10 minutes| Cook time: 10 minutes| Serves: 8

24 ounces sea bass fillets
3 tablespoons olive oil
3 tablespoons Cajun seasoning
2 yellow onions
2 bell peppers
4 celery ribs

4 cups tomatoes, chopped
¼ cup tomato paste
3 bay leaves
2 cups bone broth
2 lbs. medium raw shrimp, deveined

1. Pat the fish dry and cut into 2 inch cubes. Chop the onions, peppers, and celery. Season the fish with salt, pepper, and half of the Cajun seasoning. 2. Move the slider towards "AIR FRY/STOVETOP" and set Ninja Foodi XL Pressure Cooker Steam Fryer with SmartLid to SEAR/SAUTÉ mode. Adjust the temperature to "Hi5" by using up arrow. 3. Press START/STOP to begin cooking and add the oil. Add the fish and cook for about 4 minutes, flipping a few times to make sure it's evenly cooked. 4. Remove the fish with a slotted spoon and set aside. Add the pepper, onions, celery, and remaining Cajun seasoning and Sauté for another few minutes. Return the fish to the pot and add the tomatoes, paste, broth, and bay leaves. 5. Lock lid; move slider towards PRESSURE. Adjust pressure release valve in the SEAL position. Close pressure-release valve. The cooking temperature will default to HIGH, which is accurate. Set time to 5 minutes. Select START/STOP and start cooking. 6. When cooking is complete, let pressure release naturally. Set Ninja Foodi XL Pressure Cooker Steam Fryer with SmartLid to SEAR/SAUTÉ mode again. 7. Add the shrimp and cook for 4 minutes. Season with more salt and pepper to taste before serving.
Per Serving: Calories 271; Fat 12g; Sodium 354mg; Carbs 6g; Fiber 4g; Sugar 2g; Protein 11g

Curried Coconut Shrimp

Prep time: 10 minutes| Cook time: 10 minutes| Serves: 4

1 lb. shrimp, shelled, deveined
1 tablespoon ginger
1 tablespoon garlic
½ teaspoon turmeric

1 teaspoon salt
½ teaspoon cayenne pepper
1 teaspoon garam masala
½ can unsweetened coconut milk

1. Mince the ginger and garlic. Mix all the ingredients in a casserole dish. Put the Cook & Crisp Basket in the Ninja Foodi XL Pressure Cooker Steam Fryer with SmartLid cooking pot. 2. Pour two cups of water in the pot and put the dish on the Cook & Crisp Basket. Cover the dish with foil and seal the pot. 3. Lock lid; move slider to AIR FRY/STOVETOP. Select STEAM, and set time to 4 minutes. 4. Serve with extra coconut milk if desired, poured over rice.
Per Serving: Calories 367; Fat 10.3g; Sodium 222mg; Carbs 3.5g; Fiber 1.6g; Sugar 2.3g; Protein 62.1g

Cod with Olives and Fennel

Prep time: 15 minutes| Cook time: 25 minutes| Serves: 2

2 tablespoons olive oil
½ white onion
1 head garlic
1-½ cups chicken broth
¼ cup olive brine
¼ cup canned tomato purée

Salt and pepper, to taste
½ cup green olives
1 head fennel
One 12-ounce Alaskan cod fillet
¼ bunch basil

1. Cut the garlic head in half and cut cod fillet into 3 inch squares. Pit the olives and crush them, then cut the fennel into quarters. 2. Move the slider towards "AIR FRY/STOVETOP" and Set Ninja Foodi XL Pressure Cooker Steam Fryer with SmartLid to SEAR/SAUTÉ mode. Adjust the temperature to "Hi5" by using up arrow. 3. Press START/STOP to begin cooking and add the oil. Place the garlic and onion cut side down in the oil and sauté for a few minutes. When the garlic and onion start to brown flip them over and add the broth, olive brine and tomato purée to pot and turn it off. Add the olives and fennel to the pot and season with salt and pepper. 4. Lock lid; move slider towards PRESSURE. Adjust pressure release valve in the SEAL position. Close pressure-release valve. The cooking temperature will default to HIGH, which is accurate. Cook on LOW pressure for 10 minutes. Select START/STOP and start cooking. 5. When cooking is complete, let pressure release naturally. Season the cod with salt and pepper and put it in the pot. Seal the pot and cook the cod on Low pressure for 4 minutes. 6. Remove the fish and transfer it to serving bowls. Tear the basil leaves into the pot. Top the fish with the vegetables then spoon the basil broth over the fish to serve.

Per Serving: Calories 215; Fat 10.4g; Sodium 214mg; Carbs 23.1g; Fiber 1.8g; Sugar 2.8g; Protein 7.6g

Fish Stew

Prep time: 5 minutes| Cook time: 15 minutes| Serves: 4

4 tablespoons olive oil
1 red onion
4 cloves garlic
½ cup dry white wine
8-ounce bottle clam juice
2-½ cups water
2 cups diced tomatoes

Salt, pepper, and red pepper to taste
2 lbs. boneless, skinless sea bass fillets
2 tablespoons fresh lemon juice
2 tablespoons chopped fresh dill

1. Cut the bass into 2 inch pieces. Mince the garlic and thinly slice the onion. Move the slider towards "AIR FRY/STOVETOP" and set Ninja Foodi XL Pressure Cooker Steam Fryer with SmartLid to SEAR/SAUTÉ mode. Adjust the temperature to "Hi5" by using up arrow. 2. Press START/STOP to begin cooking and add 2 tablespoons of oil. Add the onions and cook until they begin to soften. Add the garlic and continue to sauté for another minute. Add the wine and scrape up any brown bits from the bottom of the pot. Mix in the clam juice, tomatoes, salt, and peppers. 3. Lock lid; move slider towards PRESSURE. Adjust pressure release valve in the SEAL position. Close pressure-release valve. The cooking temperature will default to HIGH, which is accurate. Set time to 5 minutes. Select START/STOP and start cooking. 4. When cooking is complete, let pressure release naturally. Add the fish and continue to cook on SEAR/SAUTÉ mode for about 5 minutes or until the fish is cooked. Mix in the remaining oil, lemon juice, and dill before serving.
Per Serving: Calories 95; Fat 7g; Sodium 210mg; Carbs 8.4g; Fiber 3.6g; Sugar 4.7g; Protein 1.5g

Garlicky Shrimp Scampi

Prep time: 5 minutes| Cook time: 10 minutes| Serves: 6

2 tablespoons butter
1 lb. shrimp
4 cloves garlic
½ teaspoon red pepper flakes
½ teaspoon paprika

1 cup chicken broth
½ cup half and half
½ cup parmesan cheese
Pepper, to taste

1. Mince the garlic. Move the slider towards "AIR FRY/STOVETOP" and set Ninja Foodi XL Pressure Cooker Steam Fryer with SmartLid to SEAR/SAUTÉ mode. Adjust the temperature to "Hi5" by using up arrow. Press START/STOP to begin cooking and add the butter. Add the garlic and red pepper and sauté for 2 minutes. Add the paprika, shrimp, broth, and pepper. 2. Lock lid; move slider towards PRESSURE. Adjust pressure release valve in the SEAL position. Close pressure-release valve. The cooking temperature will default to HIGH, which is accurate. Set and time to 2 minutes. Select START/STOP and start cooking. 3. When cooking is complete, let pressure release naturally. Select the SEAR/SAUTÉ mode again then stir in the half and half and parmesan until the parmesan is completely melted. 4. Serve over linguini.
Per Serving: Calories 216; Fat 7.9g; Sodium 147mg; Carbs 6.3g; Fiber 0.6g; Sugar 0.6g; Protein 0.2g

Tilapia with Tomatoes

Prep time: 5 minutes| Cook time: 5 minutes| Serves: 4

4 tilapia fillets
Salt and pepper
3 roma tomatoes
2 cloves garlic
¼ cup basil

2 tablespoons olive oil
Salt and pepper, to taste
Balsamic vinegar
Mince the garlic and chop the basil.

1. Season the fish with salt and pepper and place in a Cook & Crisp Basket Deluxe Reversible Rack. Place the basket in the pot with ½ cup water. 2. Lock lid; move slider towards PRESSURE. Adjust pressure release valve in the SEAL position. Close pressure-release valve. The cooking temperature will default to HIGH, which is accurate. Set time to 4 minutes. Select START/STOP and start cooking. 3. When cooking is complete, let pressure release naturally. Dice the tomatoes, toss them in a bowl with garlic, basil, olive oil, salt, pepper, and vinegar. Transfer the fish to a serving plate. 4. Top with the tomato mixture and serve.
Per Serving: Calories 145; Fat 13.7g; Sodium 411mg; Carbs 6g; Fiber 1.7g; Sugar 3.5g; Protein 1.3g

Fish Chowder

Prep time: 10 minutes| Cook time: 5 minutes| Serves: 4

¾ cup chopped bacon	2 tablespoons butter
1 shallot	1 lb. frozen wild caught haddock
2 ribs celery	fillets
1 carrot	1 cup frozen corn
2 cloves garlic	White pepper, to taste
3 Yukon gold potatoes	2 cups heavy cream
4 cups vegetable broth	1 tablespoon potato starch

1. Chop the vegetables and bacon and mince the garlic. Peel and cube the potatoes into small cubes. Move the slider towards "AIR FRY/ STOVETOP" and set Ninja Foodi XL Pressure Cooker Steam Fryer with SmartLid to SEAR/SAUTÉ mode. Adjust the temperature to "Hi5" by using up arrow. 2. Press START/STOP to begin cooking and melt the butter. Add the bacon and cook until browned. Add the veggies and continue to cook until the vegetables begin to soften. Add the fish, corn, and broth to the pot and seal the pot. 3. Lock lid; move slider towards PRESSURE. Adjust pressure release valve in the SEAL position. Close pressure-release valve. The cooking temperature will default to HIGH, which is accurate. Set time to 5 minutes. Select START/STOP and start cooking. 4. When cooking is complete, let pressure release naturally. Mix the starch and cream in a small bowl then stir it into the pot. 5. Allow the mixture to thicken for a few minutes before serving.
Per Serving: Calories 133; Fat 7g; Sodium 236mg; Carbs 8.1g; Fiber 1.4g; Sugar 0.5g; Protein 10.5g

Lobster with Butter Sauce

Prep time: 5 minutes| Cook time: 5 minutes| Serves: 4

1 tablespoon old bay seasoning	½ teaspoon salt
4 lobster tails	½ teaspoon pepper
1 cup butter	2 teaspoons lemon juice
1 clove garlic	1 teaspoon dill weed

1. Mince the garlic. Put 1 cup of water in the pot and mix in the old bay seasoning. Put the lobster in the Cook & Crisp Basket and put the basket in the pot. 2. Lock lid; move slider towards PRESSURE. Adjust pressure release valve in the SEAL position. Close pressure-release valve. The cooking temperature will default to HIGH, which is accurate. Set time to 4 minutes. Select START/STOP and start cooking. 3. When cooking is complete, let pressure release naturally. While the lobster cooks, heat 1 tablespoon of butter in a saucepan over medium heat until the butter starts to brown. Add the remaining butter and garlic and cook for another minute. 4. Mix in the remaining ingredients and transfer the melted butter to a bowl for serving. Serve the lobster with butter sauce.
Per Serving: Calories 210; Fat 19.2g; Sodium 410mg; Carbs 6.2g; Fiber 3.5g; Sugar 1.5g; Protein 6.7g

Shrimp with tangy Risotto

Prep time: 10 minutes| Cook time: 30 minutes| Serves: 6

1 tablespoon olive oil	24 medium shrimp, deveined,
5 teaspoons butter	peeled and tailed
1 cup onion, chopped fine	2 lemons, one juiced, one cut into
½ cup red bell pepper	wedges
1 tablespoon lemon zest	½ cup parmesan cheese, grated
1 cup Arborio rice	⅛ teaspoon coarse black pepper
¼ cup white wine, like Sauvignon	1 tablespoon fresh parsley,
Blanc	chopped
3 cups chicken broth	Olive oil, for drizzling

1. Move the slider towards "AIR FRY/STOVETOP" and set Ninja Foodi XL Pressure Cooker Steam Fryer with SmartLid to SEAR/ SAUTÉ mode. Adjust the temperature to "Hi5" by using up arrow. Press START/STOP to begin cooking. 2. When the bottom of the cooking pot gets hot, add olive oil and butter. Add onion and red bell pepper when butter is melted and sauté for about 3 minutes or until softened. Stir in lemon zest. Fold in rice until completely coated. Sauté for about 5 minutes or until mostly translucent. Stir in wine and cook for 3 to 4 minutes or until evaporated. Stir in broth. 3. Lock lid; move slider to AIR FRY/STOVETOP. Select STEAM, and set

time to 20 minutes. Press START/STOP to begin cooking. Open the lid and stir the risotto. Fold in shrimp and lemon juice. Set STEAM for 5 minutes. Shrimp should be pink and opaque; if risotto is too 'al dente' cook for an additional 5 minutes. Fold in parmesan and black pepper. 4. Serve garnished with parsley, lemon wedges, and an olive oil drizzle on top.
Per Serving: Calories 169; Fat 11.1g; Sodium 347mg; Carbs 1.7g; Fiber 0.6g; Sugar 1.1g; Protein 13.6g

Healthy Jambalaya

Prep time: 10 minutes| Cook time: 50 minutes| Serves: 6

⅓ cup onion, diced	1 jalapeño chili, chopped
1 rib celery, very thinly sliced	1 (15 oz.) can black-eyed peas,
1 teaspoon olive oil	undrained
½ lb. andouille sausage, sliced	1-½ cups white or brown rice,
12 medium shrimp, deveined and	uncooked
peeled	1 teaspoon cayenne pepper
1 cup chicken stock	1 teaspoon paprika
2 cups tomatoes, diced	1 teaspoon garlic powder

1. Add olive oil to pressure cooker and move the slider towards "AIR FRY/STOVETOP" and set Ninja Foodi XL Pressure Cooker Steam Fryer with SmartLid to SEAR/SAUTÉ mode. Adjust the temperature to "Hi5" by using up arrow. Press START/STOP to begin cooking. Add onion and celery. 2. Close and lock lid. Continue sautéing for an additional 5 minutes. Open the lid and add remaining ingredients. Stir to combine. 3. Lock lid; move slider to AIR FRY/STOVETOP. Select STEAM, and set time to 25 minutes. Press START/STOP to begin cooking. Once finished, let sit for 5 minutes; do not remove the lid. Select STEAM for 10 additional minutes. Stir and check rice to make sure it is fully cooked. If not, add a little more water (about 2 tablespoons), stir, and set it to cook again for an additional 5 minutes. 4. Serve with your favorite salad or on its own with a light beer or glass of lemonade.
Per Serving: Calories 225; Fat 14.8g; Sodium 366mg; Carbs 7.2g; Fiber 1.4g; Sugar 3.2g; Protein 17.6g

Regular Pad Thai

Prep time: 8 minutes| Cook time: 25 minutes| Serves: 4

1 lb. chicken breast, cut into 2-inch	2 eggs
strips	1-½ cups chicken broth
8 large shrimp deveined, peeled	½ cup unsalted roasted peanuts,
and tailed	crushed, for garnish
8 oz. Thai Rice Noodles	1 lime cut into wedges, for garnish
¼ cup grapeseed oil	Pad Thai Sauce:
3 scallions, topped and thinly	3 tablespoons tamarind paste
sliced	⅓ cup light brown sugar
1 medium carrot, shaved into	2 tablespoons fish sauce
ribbons	1 tablespoon fresh lime juice
1 cup bean sprouts	1 tablespoon tomato paste
1-½ teaspoons fresh garlic,	1 teaspoon ground chili paste, like
chopped	Sambal Oelek

1. Soak noodles in hot water for 1-2 minutes and drain; noodles should bend slightly. Add pad thai sauce ingredients to a glass mixing bowl and whisk until well-blended. Move the slider towards "AIR FRY/STOVETOP" and set Ninja Foodi XL Pressure Cooker Steam Fryer with SmartLid to SEAR/SAUTÉ mode. Adjust the temperature to "Hi5" by using up arrow. 2. Press START/STOP to begin cooking. Add olive oil, garlic, carrots, bean sprouts, and scallions to cooking pot. Sauté for 1 minute. Add chicken and sauté for 1 minute. Push ingredients to one side of the cooking pot and crack eggs into the empty spot and scramble until almost firm. Fold into other ingredients. Add broth. Fold in Pad Thai sauce and stir until well-combined. Gently fold noodles into the sauce. 3. Lock lid; move slider to AIR FRY/STOVETOP. Select STEAM, and set time to 10 minutes. Press START/STOP to begin cooking. Open the lid and lay shrimp on top of the Pad Thai. Place on Keep Warm for 5 minutes. 4. Plate Pad Thai and serve garnished with peanuts and a lime wedge.
Per Serving: Calories 181; Fat 8.8g; Sodium 230mg; Carbs 17g; Fiber 3.5g; Sugar 4.1g; Protein 11.1g

Chapter 6 Snacks and Appetizer Recipes

129 Crispy Thai Prawns

129 Bacon Wrapped Onion

129 Crispy Brussels Sprout

129 Eggplant Crisps

129 Fried Leek with Mustard

129 Brussels Sprouts With Cheese

129 Broccoli with Coriander and Cheese

130 Crispy Chicken Wings

130 Spicy Hot Dogs

130 Kale Chips

130 Bacon Shrimp

130 Broccoli Pecorino Toscano bites

130 Spinach with Parsley Dip

130 Roasted Zucchini Cubes

131 Chicken Wings with Sage

131 Crackling Bites

131 Celery Chips With Harissa Sauce

131 Carrot Chips with Cheese

131 Onion Rings

131 Cocktail Wieners

131 Deviled Eggs

132 Chinese Glazed Baby Carrots

132 Crispy Zucchini Fries

132 Brie and Artichoke Dip

132 Teriyaki Chicken

132 Fish Sauce Wings

132 Crispy Wings with Thai Chili Sauce

132 Crispy Pork Meatballs

133 Crispy Cocktail Meatballs

133 Crispy Cheeseburger Bites

133 Crispy BBQ Smokies

133 Crispy Broccoli Fries with Spicy Dip

133 Picnic Chicken Chunks

133 Crispy Wings with Blue Cheese

133 Crispy Celery Fries with Aioli

134 Fried Shallots

134 Crispy Ranch Kale Chips

134 Avocado Fries Wrapped in Bacon

134 Crispy Calamari Appetizer

134 Crispy Zucchini Chips with Sauce

134 Grilled Meatball

134 Mediterranean Cocktail Meatballs

135 Grandma's Crispy Wings

135 Crispy Cauliflower

135 Bacon Fat Bombs

135 Mexican Zucchini Cakes Ole

135 Crispy Tomato Chips

135 Bell Pepper Chips with Parmesan

135 Paprika Cheese Chips

135 Thai Turkey Bites

136 Spinach Chips

136 Romano Crispy Zucchini Fries

136 Parmesan Chicken Meatballs

136 Greek Keftedes with Tzatziki Dip

136 Cheese Breadsticks

136 Avocado Fries with Salsa Fresca

137 Scallops Bacon Kabobs

137 Bacon Bell Pepper Skewers

137 Crispy Japanese Yakitori

137 Asian Short Ribs

137 Olive-Stuffed Jalapeños

137 Cheese Quesadillas

137 Deviled Eggs with Swiss Cheese

138 Hot Wings

138 Mustard Wings

138 Shrimp Sesame Toasts

138 Pizza Bombs with Marinara Sauce

138 Cauliflower Pizza Crusts

138 Dill Pickles with Ranch Dip

139 Party Chex Snack

139 Air-Fried Pumpkin Seeds

139 Trail Chex Snack

139 Grilled Pimento Croutons

139 Eggplant Fries

139 French Fries

139 Zucchini Fries

140 Pickle Chips

140 Barbecue Chips

140 Avocado Fries

140 Ranch Potato Chips

140 Brie with Tomatoes

140 Mozzarella Bites

141 Mushroom Bites

141 Mozzarella with Puttanesca Sauce

141 Chicken Bites

141 Pizza Cheese Bites

141 Parsley Olives Fritters

141 Crispy Zucchini Crackers

142 Tacon Mexican Muffins

142 Mushroom Basil Bites

142 Bacon Chaffle

142 Crispy Zucchini Chips

142 Cheddar Cheese Rounds

142 Cheese Sticks

142 Bacon Sprouts Wraps

142 Crusted Zucchini Chips

143 Coconut Granola

143 Beef Smokies

143 Shrimp Balls

143 Turmeric Chicken Bites

143 Cashew Dip

143 Bacon Bites

143 Pickled Bacon

143 Air-Fried Pork Rinds

144 Avocado Balls

144 Avocado Wraps

144 Flavored Chicken Meatballs

144 Crusted Hot Dogs

144 Salmon Bites

144 Eggplant Chips

144 Meatballs

144 Duck Wraps

145 Sushi

145 Classic Pork Meatballs

Crispy Thai Prawns

Prep Time: 10 minutes. | Cook Time: 10 minutes. | Serves: 4

16 prawns, cleaned and deveined
Salt and black pepper, to your liking
½ teaspoon cumin powder
1 teaspoon fresh lemon juice
1 medium-sized egg, whisked
⅓ cup of beer
1 teaspoon baking powder
1 tablespoon curry powder
½ teaspoon grated fresh ginger
½ cup coconut flour

1. Place the Cook & Crisp Basket in your Ninja Foodi Pressure Cooker Steam Fryer. 2. Toss the prawns with salt, pepper, cumin powder, and lemon juice. 3. In a mixing dish, place the whisked egg, beer, baking powder, curry powder, and the ginger; mix well. 4. In another mixing dish, place the coconut flour. 5. Now, dip the prawns in the beer mixture; roll your prawns over the coconut flour. 6. Cook at 360°F/180°C on "Air Fry" Mode for about 5 minutes; turn them over, press the power button again. 7. Put on the Smart Lid on top of the Ninja Foodi Steam Fryer. 8. Move the Lid Slider to the "Air Fry/Stovetop". 9. Cook on "Air Fry" Mode for additional 2 to 3 minutes. Bon appétit!
Per Serving: Calories 396; Fat 23.2g; Sodium 622mg; Total Carbs 0.7g; Fiber 0g; Sugar 0g; Protein 45.6g

Bacon Wrapped Onion

Prep Time: 10 minutes. | Cook Time: 30 minutes. | Serves: 2

1 onion, cut into ½-inch slices
1 teaspoon curry powder
1 teaspoon cayenne pepper
Salt and black pepper, to your liking
8 strips bacon
¼ cup spicy ketchup
Cooking spray

1. Place the Cook & Crisp Basket in your Ninja Foodi Pressure Cooker Steam Fryer. 2. Place the onion rings in the bowl with cold water; let them soak approximately 20 minutes; drain the onion rings and pat dry using a kitchen towel. 3. Sprinkle curry powder, cayenne pepper, salt, and black pepper over onion rings. 4. Wrap one layer of bacon around onion, trimming any excess. Secure the rings with toothpicks. 5. Spritz the Ninja Foodi Cook & Crisp Basket with cooking spray; arrange the breaded onion rings in your Ninja Foodi Cook & Crisp Basket. 6. Put on the Smart Lid on top of the Ninja Foodi Steam Fryer. 7. Move the Lid Slider to the "Air Fry/Stovetop". 8. Cook at 360°F/180°C on "Air Fry" Mode for about 15 minutes, turning them over halfway through the cooking time. Serve with spicy ketchup. Bon appétit!
Per Serving: Calories 437; Fat 28g; Sodium 1221mg; Total Carbs 22.3g; Fiber 0.9g; Sugar 8g; Protein 30.3g

Crispy Brussels Sprout

Prep Time: 10 minutes. | Cook Time: 20 minutes. | Serves: 4

1 pound Brussels sprouts, ends and yellow leaves removed and halved lengthwise
Salt and black pepper, to taste
1 tablespoon toasted sesame oil
1 teaspoon fennel seeds
Chopped fresh parsley, for garnish

1. Place the Cook & Crisp Basket in your Ninja Foodi Pressure Cooker Steam Fryer. 2. Place the Brussels sprouts, salt, pepper, sesame oil, and fennel seeds in a resalable plastic bag. Seal the bag and shake to coat. Place the mixture in the Cook & Crisp Basket. 3. Put on the Smart Lid on top of the Ninja Foodi Steam Fryer. 4. Move the Lid Slider to the "Air Fry/Stovetop". 5. Cook at 380°F/195°C on "Air Fry" Mode for about 15 minutes until tender. Make sure to flip the half-cooked over halfway through the cooking time. 6. Serve sprinkled with fresh parsley. Bon appétit!
Per Serving: Calories 352; Fat 9.1g; Sodium 1294mg; Total Carbs 3.9g; Fiber 1g; Sugar 1g; Protein 61g

Eggplant Crisps

Prep Time: 10 minutes. | Cook Time: 45 minutes. | Serves: 4

1 eggplant, peeled and thinly sliced
Salt
½ cup almond meal
¼ cup canola oil
½ cup water
1 teaspoon garlic powder

½ teaspoon dried dill weed
½ teaspoon black pepper, to taste

1. Place the Cook & Crisp Basket in your Ninja Foodi Pressure Cooker Steam Fryer. 2. Salt the eggplant slices and let them stay for about 30 minutes. Squeeze the eggplant slices and rinse them under cold running water. 3. Toss the eggplant slices with the other ingredients. 4. Put on the Smart Lid on top of the Ninja Foodi Steam Fryer. 5. Move the Lid Slider to the "Air Fry/Stovetop". 6. Cook on "Air Fry" Mode at 390°F/200°C for about 13 minutes, working in batches. 7. Serve with a sauce for dipping. Bon appétit!
Per Serving: Calories 374; Fat 25g; Sodium 275mg; Total Carbs 7.3g; Fiber 0g; Sugar 6g; Protein 12.3g

Fried Leek with Mustard

Prep Time: 10 minutes. | Cook Time: 15 minutes. | Serves: 4

1 large-sized leek, cut into ½-inch wide rings
Salt and pepper, to taste
1 teaspoon mustard
1 cup milk
1 egg
½ cup almond flour
½ teaspoon baking powder
½ cup pork rinds, crushed

1. Place the Cook & Crisp Basket in your Ninja Foodi Pressure Cooker Steam Fryer. 2. Toss your leeks with salt and pepper. 3. In a mixing bowl, whisk the mustard, milk and egg until frothy and pale. 4. Now, mix almond flour and baking powder in another mixing bowl. In the third bowl, place the pork rinds. 5. Coat the leek slices with the almond meal mixture. Dredge the floured leek slices into the milk and egg mixture, coating well. Finally, roll them over the pork rinds. 6. Put on the Smart Lid on top of the Ninja Foodi Steam Fryer. 7. Move the Lid Slider to the "Air Fry/Stovetop". Cook on "Air Fry" Mode for approximately 10 minutes at 370°F/185°C. Bon appétit!
Per Serving: Calories 391; Fat 24g; Sodium 142mg; Total Carbs 38.5g; Fiber 3.5g; Sugar 21g; Protein 6.6g

Brussels Sprouts With Cheese

Prep Time: 10 minutes. | Cook Time: 20 minutes. | Serves: 4

¾ pound Brussels sprouts, trimmed and cut off the ends
1 teaspoon kosher salt
1 tablespoon lemon zest
Non-stick cooking spray
1 cup feta cheese, cubed

1. Place the Cook & Crisp Basket in your Ninja Foodi Pressure Cooker Steam Fryer. 2. Firstly, peel the Brussels sprouts using a small paring knife. Toss the leaves with salt and lemon zest; spritz them with a cooking spray, coating all sides. 3. Put on the Smart Lid on top of the Ninja Foodi Steam Fryer. 4. Move the Lid Slider to the "Air Fry/Stovetop". 5. Cook on "Air Fry" Mode at 380°F/195°C or about 8 minutes; shake the cooking basket halfway through the cooking time. Cook on "Air Fry" Mode for about 7 more minutes. 6. Make sure to work in batches so everything can cook evenly. Taste and adjust the seasonings. Serve with feta cheese. Bon appétit!
Per Serving: Calories 258; Fat 12.4g; Sodium 79mg; Total Carbs 34.3g; Fiber 1g; Sugar 17g; Protein 3.2g

Broccoli with Coriander and Cheese

Prep Time: 10 minutes. | Cook Time: 20 minutes. | Serves: 6

2 eggs, well whisked
2 cups Colby cheese, shredded
½ cup almond meal
2 tablespoons sesame seeds
Seasoned salt, to taste
¼ teaspoon black pepper
1 head broccoli, grated
1 cup parmesan cheese, grated
Cooking oil

1. Place the Cook & Crisp Basket in your Ninja Foodi Pressure Cooker Steam Fryer. 2. Mix the eggs, Colby cheese, almond meal, sesame seeds, salt, black pepper, and broccoli to make the consistency of dough. 3. Chill for about 1 hour and shape into small balls; roll the patties over parmesan cheese. Spritz them with cooking oil on all sides. 4. Put on the Smart Lid on top of the Ninja Foodi Steam Fryer. 5. Move the Lid Slider to the "Air Fry/Stovetop". 6. Cook on "Air Fry" Mode at 360°F/180°C for about 10 minutes. Check for doneness and cook for about 8 to 10 more minutes. Serve with a sauce for dipping. Bon appétit!
Per Serving: Calories 149; Fat 1.2g; Sodium 3mg; Total Carbs 37.6g; Fiber 5.8g; Sugar 29g; Protein 1.1g

Crispy Chicken Wings

Prep Time: 10 minutes. | Cook Time: 20 minutes. | Serves: 6

For the Sauce:

1 tablespoon yellow mustard	Salt and black pepper, to your
1 tablespoon apple cider vinegar	liking
1 tablespoon olive oil	⅛ teaspoon allspice
¼ cup ketchup, no sugar added	¼ cup water
1 garlic clove, minced	

For the Wings:

2 pounds chicken wings	¼ cup habanero hot sauce
¼ teaspoon celery salt	Chopped fresh parsley, or garnish

1. Place the Cook & Crisp Basket in your Ninja Foodi Pressure Cooker Steam Fryer and place a reversible rack in it. 2. In a sauté pan that is preheated over a medium-high flame, place all the ingredients for the sauce and bring it to a boil. Then, reduce the temperature and simmer until it has thickened. 3. Place the chicken wings in the Cook & Crisp Basket. 4. Put on the Smart Lid on top of the Ninja Foodi Steam Fryer. 5. Move the Lid Slider to the "Air Fry/Stovetop". 6. Cook the chicken wings at 400°F/200°C on "Air fry" Mode for about 6 minutes; flip the half-cooked over. Cook for additional 6 minutes. Season them with celery salt. 7. Serve with the prepared sauce and habanero hot sauce, garnished with fresh parsley leaves. Bon appétit!
Per Serving: Calories 327; Fat 14.2g; Sodium 672mg; Total Carbs 47.2g; Fiber 1.7g; Sugar 24.8g; Protein 4.4g

Spicy Hot Dogs

Prep Time: 10 minutes. | Cook Time: 20 minutes. | Serves: 6

6 hot dogs	6 tablespoons ketchup, no sugar
1 tablespoon mustard	added

1. Place the Cook & Crisp Basket in your Ninja Foodi Pressure Cooker Steam Fryer. 2. Place the hot dogs in the lightly greased Cook & Crisp Basket. 3. Put on the Smart Lid on top of the Ninja Foodi Steam Fryer. 4. Move the Lid Slider to the "Air Fry/Stovetop". 5. Cook on "Air Fry" Mode at 380°F/195°C for about 15 minutes, turning them over halfway through the cooking time to promote even cooking. 6. Serve on cocktail sticks with the mustard and ketchup. Enjoy!
Per Serving: Calories 386; Fat 10.3 g; Sodium 238 mg; Carbs 72.9g; Fiber 4.5g; Sugar 59g; Protein 2.6g

Kale Chips

Prep Time: 10 minutes. | Cook Time: 5 minutes. | Serves: 4

2 ½ tablespoons olive oil	pieces
1 ½ teaspoons garlic powder	2 tablespoons lemon juice
1 bunch of kale, torn into small	1 ½ teaspoons seasoned salt

1. Place the Cook & Crisp Basket in your Ninja Foodi Pressure Cooker Steam Fryer. 2. Toss your kale with the other ingredients. 3. Put on the Smart Lid on top of the Ninja Foodi Steam Fryer. 4. Move the Lid Slider to the "Air Fry/Stovetop". 5. Cook on "Air Fry" Mode at 195°F/90°C for about 4 to 5 minutes, tossing kale halfway through. 6. Serve with your favorite dipping sauce.
Per Serving: Calories 93; Fat 4.1 g; Sodium 303 mg; Carbs 37.9g; Fiber 1.5g; Sugar 1.9g; Protein 6.6g

Bacon Shrimp

Prep Time: 10 minutes. | Cook Time: 45 minutes. | Serves: 10

1 ¼ pounds shrimp, peeled and	1 tablespoon salt
deveined	1 teaspoon chili powder
1 teaspoon paprika	1 tablespoon shallot powder
½ teaspoon black pepper	¼ teaspoon cumin powder
½ teaspoon red pepper flakes,	1 ¼ pounds thin bacon slices
crushed	

1. Place the Cook & Crisp Basket in your Ninja Foodi Pressure Cooker Steam Fryer. 2. Toss the shrimps with all the seasoning until they are coated well. 3. Next, wrap a slice of bacon around the shrimps, securing with a toothpick; repeat with the remaining ingredients; chill for about 30 minutes. 4. Put on the Smart Lid on top of the Ninja Foodi Steam Fryer. 5. Move the Lid Slider to the "Air

Fry/Stovetop". 6. Cook them at 360°F/180°C on "Air Fry" Mode for about 7 to 8 minutes, working in batches. Serve with cocktail sticks if desired. Enjoy!
Per Serving: Calories 192; Fat 9.3g; Sodium 133mg; Total Carbs 27.1g; Fiber 1.4g; Sugar 19g; Protein 3.2g

Broccoli Pecorino Toscano bites

Prep Time: 10 minutes. | Cook Time: 20 minutes. | Serves: 6

1 large-sized head of broccoli,	1 teaspoon groundnut oil
broken into small florets	1 cup bacon bits
½ teaspoon salt	1 cup Pecorino Toscano, freshly
¼ teaspoon black pepper	grated
1 tablespoon Shoyu sauce	Paprika, to taste

1. Place the Cook & Crisp Basket in your Ninja Foodi Pressure Cooker Steam Fryer. 2. Add the broccoli florets to boiling water; boil approximately 4 minutes; drain well. 3. Season with salt and pepper; drizzle with Shoyu sauce and groundnut oil. Mash with a suitable potato masher. 4. Add the bacon and cheese to the mixture; shape the mixture into bite-sized balls. 5. Put on the Smart Lid on top of the Ninja Foodi Steam Fryer. 6. Move the Lid Slider to the "Air Fry/Stovetop". 7. Cook at 390°F/200°C on "Air Fry" Mode for about 10 minutes; shake your Ninja Foodi Cook & Crisp Basket and continue to cook for about 5 minutes more. 8. Toss the fried bombs with paprika. Bon appétit!
Per Serving: Calories 204; Fat 9g; Sodium 91mg; Total Carbs 27g; Fiber 2.4g; Sugar 15g; Protein 1.3g

Spinach with Parsley Dip

Prep Time: 10 minutes. | Cook Time: 20 minutes. | Serves: 4

Spinach Melts:

2 cups spinach, torn into pieces	1 teaspoon baking powder
1 ½ cups cauliflower	½ teaspoon salt
1 tablespoon sesame oil	½ teaspoon black pepper
½ cup scallions, chopped	¼ teaspoon dried dill
2 garlic cloves, minced	½ teaspoon dried basil
½ cup almond flour	1 cup cheddar cheese, shredded
¼ cup coconut flour	

Parsley Yogurt Dip:

½ cup Greek-Style yoghurt	chopped
2 tablespoons mayo	1 tablespoon fresh lemon juice
2 tablespoons fresh parsley,	½ teaspoon garlic, smashed

1. Place the Cook & Crisp Basket in your Ninja Foodi Pressure Cooker Steam Fryer. 2. Place spinach in a mixing dish; pour in hot water. Drain and rinse well. 3. Add cauliflower to the steamer basket; steam until the cauliflower is tender about 5 minutes. 4. Mash the cauliflower; add the remaining ingredients for Spinach Melts and mix to mix well. Shape the mixture into patties and transfer them to the lightly greased cooking basket. 5. Put on the Smart Lid on top of the Ninja Foodi Steam Fryer. 6. Move the Lid Slider to the "Air Fry/Stovetop". 7. Cook on "Air Fry" Mode at 330°F/165°C for about 14 minutes until heated. 8. Meanwhile, make your dipping sauce by whisking the remaining ingredients. Place in your refrigerator until ready to serve. 9. Serve the Spinach Melts with the chilled sauce on the side. Enjoy!
Per Serving: Calories 477; Fat 13.3 g; Sodium 128 mg; Carbs 89.5g; Fiber 6.5g; Sugar 59.2g; Protein 5.4g

Roasted Zucchini Cubes

Prep Time: 10 minutes. | Cook Time: 20 minutes. | Serves: 6

1 ½ pounds zucchini, peeled and	A pinch of pepper
cut into ½-inch chunks	2 tablespoons sage, chopped
2 tablespoons melted coconut oil	Zest of 1 small-sized lemon
A pinch of coarse salt	⅛ teaspoon allspice

1. Place the Cook & Crisp Basket in your Ninja Foodi Pressure Cooker Steam Fryer. 2. Toss the squash chunks with the other items. 3. Put on the Smart Lid on top of the Ninja Foodi Steam Fryer. 4. Move the Lid Slider to the "Air Fry/Stovetop". 5. Roast in your Ninja Foodi Pressure Cooker Steam Fryer cooking basket at 350°F/175°C on "Air Fry" Mode at 350°F/175°C for about 10 minutes. 6. Pause the machine, and turn the temperature to 400°F/200°C; stir and roast for additional 8 minutes. Bon appétit!
Per Serving: Calories 157; Fat 1.3g; Sodium 27mg; Total Carbs 1.3g; Fiber 1g; Sugar 2.2g; Protein 8.2g

Chicken Wings with Sage

Prep Time: 10 minutes. | Cook Time: 1 hour 10 minutes. | Serves: 4

⅓ cup almond flour
⅓ cup buttermilk
1 ½ pound chicken wings
1 tablespoon tamari sauce
⅓ teaspoon fresh sage
1 teaspoon mustard seeds
½ teaspoon garlic paste
½ teaspoon mixed peppercorns
½ teaspoon seasoned salt
2 teaspoons fresh basil

1. Place the Cook & Crisp Basket in your Ninja Foodi Pressure Cooker Steam Fryer. 2. Place the seasonings along with the garlic paste, chicken wings, buttermilk, and tamari sauce in a large-sized mixing dish. Let it soak about 55 minutes; drain the wings. 3. Dredge the wings in the almond flour and transfer them to your Ninja Foodi Pressure Cooker Steam Fryer cooking basket. 4. Put on the Smart Lid on top of the Ninja Foodi Steam Fryer. 5. Move the Lid Slider to the "Air Fry/Stovetop". 6. Cook for about 16 minutes at 355°F/180°C. Serve on a nice serving platter with a dressing on the side. Bon appétit!
Per Serving: Calories 284; Fat 16g; Sodium 252mg; Total Carbs 31.6g; Fiber 0.9g; Sugar 6.6g; Protein 3.7g

Crackling Bites

Prep Time: 10 minutes. | Cook Time: 50 minutes. | Serves: 10

1-pound pork rind raw, scored by the butcher
1 tablespoon salt
2 tablespoons smoked paprika

1. Place the Cook & Crisp Basket in your Ninja Foodi Pressure Cooker Steam Fryer. 2. Sprinkle and rub salt on the skin side of the pork rind. Allow it to rest for about 30 minutes. 3. Put on the Smart Lid on top of the Ninja Foodi Steam Fryer. 4. Move the Lid Slider to the "Air Fry/Stovetop". 5. Roast at 380°F/195°C on "Air Fry" Mode for about 8 minutes; turn them over. Cook for a further 8 minutes until blistered. 6. Sprinkle the smoked paprika all over the pork crackling and serve. Bon appétit!
Per Serving: Calories 116; Fat 4.3 g; Sodium 28 mg; Carbs 32.9g; Fiber 2.5g; Sugar 29g; Protein 1.6g

Celery Chips With Harissa Sauce

Prep Time: 10 minutes. | Cook Time: 30 minutes. | Serves: 3

½-pound celery root
2 tablespoons olive oil
Harissa Mayo:
¼ cup mayo
2 tablespoons sour cream
½ tablespoon harissa paste
Salt and black pepper, to taste
Cooking spray

¼ teaspoon cumin
Salt, to taste

1. Place the Cook & Crisp Basket in your Ninja Foodi Pressure Cooker Steam Fryer. 2. Cut the celery root into desired size and shape. 3. Now, spritz the Ninja Foodi Cook & Crisp Basket with cooking spray. 4. Toss the celery chips with the olive oil, salt, and black pepper. 5. Put on the Smart Lid on top of the Ninja Foodi Steam Fryer. 6. Move the Lid Slider to the "Air Fry/Stovetop". 7. Cook on "Air Fry" Mode at 400°F/200°C for about 25 to 30 minutes, turning them over every 10 minutes to promote even cooking. 8. Meanwhile, mix all the recipe ingredients for the harissa mayo. Place in your refrigerator until ready to serve. Bon appétit!
Per Serving: Calories 426; Fat 36.3 g; Sodium 248 mg; Carbs 22.1g; Fiber 2g; Sugar 10.9g; Protein 6.6g

Carrot Chips with Cheese

Prep Time: 10 minutes. | Cook Time: 20 minutes. | Serves: 3

3 carrots, sliced into sticks
1 tablespoon coconut oil
⅓ cup Romano cheese, preferably
freshly grated
2 teaspoons granulated garlic
Salt and black pepper, to taste

1. Place the Cook & Crisp Basket in your Ninja Foodi Pressure Cooker Steam Fryer. 2. Toss all the recipe ingredients in a mixing bowl until the carrots are coated on all sides. 3. Put on the Smart Lid

on top of the Ninja Foodi Steam Fryer. 4. Move the Lid Slider to the "Air Fry/Stovetop". 5. Cook on "Air Fry" Mode at 380°F/195°C for about 15 minutes, and shaking the basket halfway through the cooking time. 6. Serve with your favorite dipping sauce. Bon appétit!
Per Serving: Calories 148; Fat 0.3 g; Sodium 3 mg; Carbs 38.9g; Fiber 0.5g; Sugar 33.9g; Protein 0.6g

Onion Rings

Prep Time: 10 minutes. | Cook Time: 25 minutes. | Serves: 4

2 eggs, beaten
2 tablespoons olive oil
2 onions, sliced
1 green chili, deseeded and chopped
2 ounces almond flour
1-ounce coconut flour
Salt and black pepper, to taste
1 teaspoon cumin seeds
½ teaspoon turmeric

1. Place the Cook & Crisp Basket in your Ninja Foodi Pressure Cooker Steam Fryer. 2. Place all ingredients, except for the onions, in a mixing dish; mix to mix well, adding a little water to the mixture. 3. Once you've got a thick batter, add the onions; stir to coat well. 4. Put on the Smart Lid on top of the Ninja Foodi Steam Fryer. 5. Move the Lid Slider to the "Air Fry/Stovetop". 6. Cook at 370°F/185°C on "Air Fry" Mode for about 20 minutes, and flipping them halfway through the cooking time. 7. Work in batches and transfer to a serving platter. Enjoy!
Per Serving: Calories 551; Fat 29.3 g; Sodium 74 mg; Carbs 73.9g; Fiber 3.5g; Sugar 55.9g; Protein 5g

Cocktail Wieners

Prep Time: 10 minutes. | Cook Time: 20 minutes. | Serves: 4

1-pound pork cocktail sausages
For the Sauce:
¼ cup mayo
¼ cup cream cheese
1 whole grain mustard
1 teaspoon balsamic vinegar
1 garlic clove, minced
1 teaspoon chili powder

1. Place the Cook & Crisp Basket in your Ninja Foodi Pressure Cooker Steam Fryer. 2. Take your sausages, give them a few pricks using a fork and place them on the Cook & Crisp Basket . 3. Put on the Smart Lid on top of the Ninja Foodi Steam Fryer. 4. Move the Lid Slider to the "Air Fry/Stovetop". 5. Cook on "Air Fry" Mode at 350°F/175°C for 15 minutes; after 8 minutes, pause your Ninja Foodi Pressure Cooker Steam Fryer, turn the sausages over. Cook for further 7 minutes. 6. Check for doneness and take the sausages out of the machine. 7. In the meantime, mix all the ingredients for the sauce. Serve with warm sausages and enjoy!
Per Serving: Calories 116; Fat 2.3 g; Sodium 15 mg; Carbs 18.9g; Fiber 4.5g; Sugar 2.2g; Protein 6g

Deviled Eggs

Prep Time: 10 minutes. | Cook Time: 25 minutes. | Serves: 3)

6 eggs
6 slices bacon
2 tablespoons mayo
1 teaspoon hot sauce
½ teaspoon Worcestershire sauce
2 tablespoons green onions, chopped
1 tablespoon pickle relish
Salt and black pepper, to taste
1 teaspoon smoked paprika

1. Place the Cook & Crisp Basket in your Ninja Foodi Pressure Cooker Steam Fryer. 2. Place the wire rack in your Ninja Foodi Cook & Crisp Basket; lower the eggs onto the wire rack. 3. Put on the Smart Lid on top of the Ninja Foodi Steam Fryer. 4. Move the Lid Slider to the "Air Fry/Stovetop". 5. Cook on "Air Fry" Mode at 270°F/130°C for about 15 minutes. 6. Transfer them to an ice-cold water bath to stop the cooking. Peel the eggs under cold running water; slice them into halves. 7. Place the bacon in the Cook & Crisp Basket. Cook the bacon at 400°F/200°C on "Air Fry" Mode for about 3 minutes; flip the half-cooked bacon over. Cook an additional 3 minutes; chop the bacon and reserve. 8. Mash the egg yolks with the mayo, hot sauce, Worcestershire sauce, green onions, pickle relish, salt, and black pepper; add the reserved bacon and add the yolk mixture into the egg whites with a spoon. 9. Garnish with smoked paprika. Bon appétit!
Per Serving: Calories 416; Fat 8.3 g; Sodium 208 mg; Carbs 22.9g; Fiber 0.5g; Sugar 19g; Protein 60.6g

Chinese Glazed Baby Carrots

Prep Time: 10 minutes. | Cook Time: 20 minutes. | Serves: 6

1-pound baby carrots
2 tablespoons sesame oil
½ teaspoon Szechuan pepper
1 teaspoon Wuxiang powder (Five-spice powder)

3-4 drops liquid Stevia
1 large garlic clove, crushed
1 (1-inch) piece fresh ginger root, peeled and grated
2 tablespoons tamari sauce

1. Place the Cook & Crisp Basket in your Ninja Foodi Pressure Cooker Steam Fryer. 2. Toss all the recipe ingredients together and place them in your Ninja Foodi Cook & Crisp Basket. 3. Put on the Smart Lid on top of the Ninja Foodi Steam Fryer. 4. Move the Lid Slider to the "Air Fry/Stovetop". 5. Cook on "Air Fry" Mode at 380°F/195°C for about 15 minutes, and shaking the basket halfway through the cooking time. Enjoy!
Per Serving: Calories 399; Fat 13 g; Sodium 626 mg; Carbs 52.9g; Fiber 8.8g; Sugar 3.9g; Protein 19.6g

Crispy Zucchini Fries

Prep Time: 10 minutes. | Cook Time: 26 minutes. | Serves: 4

2 zucchinis, slice into sticks
2 teaspoons shallot powder
¼ teaspoon dried dill weed
2 teaspoons garlic powder
½ cup Parmesan cheese, preferably freshly grated

⅓ teaspoon cayenne pepper
3 egg whites
⅓ cup almond meal
Cooking spray
Salt and black pepper, to your liking

1. Place the Cook & Crisp Basket in your Ninja Foodi Pressure Cooker Steam Fryer. 2. Pat the zucchini sticks dry using a kitchen towel. 3. Grab a mixing bowl and beat the egg whites until pale; then, add all the seasonings in the order listed above and beat again 4. Take another mixing bowl and mix together almond meal and the Parmesan cheese. 5. Then, coat the zucchini sticks with the seasoned egg mixture; then, roll them over the parmesan cheese mixture. 6. Lay the breaded zucchini sticks in a single layer on the tray that is coated lightly with cooking spray. 7. Put on the Smart Lid on top of the Ninja Foodi Steam Fryer. 8. Move the Lid Slider to the "Air Fry/Stovetop". 9. Cook on "Air Fry" Mode at 375°F/190°C for about 20 minutes until the sticks are golden brown. Serve with your favorite sauce for dipping.
Per Serving: Calories 175; Fat 13.1g; Sodium 154mg; Total Carbs 14g; Fiber 0.8g; Sugar 8.9g; Protein 0.7g

Brie and Artichoke Dip

Prep Time: 10 minutes. | Cook Time: 22 minutes. | Serves: 10

2 cups arugula leaves, torn into pieces
⅓ can artichoke hearts, drained and chopped
½ cup Mozarella cheese, shredded
⅓ cup sour cream
3 cloves garlic, minced

⅓ teaspoon dried basil
1 teaspoon salt
7 ounces Brie cheese
½ cup mayo
⅓ teaspoon black pepper
A pinch of allspice

1. Place the Cook & Crisp Basket in your Ninja Foodi Pressure Cooker Steam Fryer. 2. Mix together the Brie cheese, mayo, sour cream, garlic, basil, salt, black pepper, and the allspice. 3. Throw in the artichoke hearts and arugula; gently stir to mix. Transfer the prepared mixture to the Cook & Crisp Basket. Now, scatter the Mozarella cheese evenly over the top. 4. Put on the Smart Lid on top of the Ninja Foodi Steam Fryer. 5. Move the Lid Slider to the "Air Fry/Stovetop". 6. Cook on "Air Fry" Mode at 325°F/160°C for about 17 minutes. Serve with veggie sticks. Bon appétit!
Per Serving: Calories 391; Fat 24g; Sodium 142mg; Total Carbs 38.5g; Fiber 3.5g; Sugar 21g; Protein 6.6g

Teriyaki Chicken

Prep Time: 10 minutes. | Cook Time: 40 minutes. | Serves: 6

1 ½ pounds chicken drumettes
Salt and cracked black pepper, to taste
Teriyaki Sauce:
1 tablespoon sesame oil

2 tablespoons fresh chives, chopped

¼ cup soy sauce

½ cup water
½ teaspoon Five-spice powder
2 tablespoons rice wine vinegar

½ teaspoon fresh ginger, grated
2 cloves garlic, crushed

1. Place the Cook & Crisp Basket in your Ninja Foodi Pressure Cooker Steam Fryer and place a reversible rack in it. 2. Rub the chicken drumettes with salt and cracked black pepper. 3. Place the drumettes in the Cook & Crisp Basket . 4. Put on the Smart Lid on top of the Ninja Foodi Steam Fryer. 5. Move the Lid Slider to the "Air Fry/Stovetop". 6. Cook on "Air Fry" Mode at 380°F/195°C for approximately 15 minutes. Turn them over. Cook an additional 7 minutes. 7. While the chicken drumettes are roasting, mix the sesame oil, soy sauce, water, Five-spice powder, vinegar, ginger, and garlic in a pan over medium heat. 8. Cook for about 5 minutes, stirring occasionally. 9. Now, reduce its heat and let it simmer until the glaze thickens. 10. After that, brush the glaze all over the chicken drumettes. Cook on "Air Fry" Mode for a further 6 minutes until the surface is crispy. Serve topped with the remaining glaze and garnished with fresh chives. Bon appétit!
Per Serving: Calories 416; Fat 8.3 g; Sodium 208 mg; Carbs 22.9g; Fiber 0.5g; Sugar 19g; Protein 6.6g

Fish Sauce Wings

Prep Time: 10 minutes. | Cook Time: 1 hour 15 minutes. | Serves: 4

2 teaspoons coriander seeds
1 ½ tablespoons soy sauce
⅓ cup vermouth
¾-pound chicken wings

1 ½ tablespoons each fish sauce
2 tablespoons melted butter
1 teaspoon seasoned salt
Black pepper, to taste

1. Place the Cook & Crisp Basket in your Ninja Foodi Pressure Cooker Steam Fryer. 2. Rub the chicken wings with the black pepper and seasoned salt; now, add the other ingredients. 3. Next, soak the chicken wings in this mixture for about 55 minutes in the refrigerator. 4. Put on the Smart Lid on top of the Ninja Foodi Steam Fryer. 5. Move the Lid Slider to the "Air Fry/Stovetop". 6. Cook the chicken wings at 365°F/185°C on "Air Fry" Mode for about 16 minutes until warmed through. Bon appétit!
Per Serving: Calories 327; Fat 14.2g; Sodium 672mg; Total Carbs 47.2g; Fiber 1.7g; Sugar 24.8g; Protein 4.4g

Crispy Wings with Thai Chili Sauce

Prep Time: 10 minutes. | Cook Time: 25 minutes. | Serves: 6

2 ½ tablespoons dry sherry
2 teaspoons ginger powder
1 ½ pound chicken wings
Lime wedges, to serve

2 teaspoons garlic powder
⅓ cup Thai chili sauce
1 teaspoon smoked paprika
Salt and black pepper, to taste

1. Place the Cook & Crisp Basket in your Ninja Foodi Pressure Cooker Steam Fryer. 2. Toss the chicken wings with the ginger powder, garlic powder, paprika, salt, black pepper, and dry sherry. 3. Put on the Smart Lid on top of the Ninja Foodi Steam Fryer. 4. Move the Lid Slider to the "Air Fry/Stovetop". 5. Cook the chicken wings for about 16 minutes at 365°F/185°C until they are heated. 6. Serve with the Thai chili sauce and the lime wedges. Bon appétit!
Per Serving: Calories 157; Fat 1.3g; Sodium 27mg; Total Carbs 1.3g; Fiber 1g; Sugar 2.2g; Protein 8.2g

Crispy Pork Meatballs

Prep Time: 10 minutes. | Cook Time: 25 minutes. | Serves: 8

1 teaspoon cayenne pepper
2 teaspoons mustard
2 tablespoons Brie cheese, grated
5 garlic cloves, minced

2 small-sized yellow onions, peeled and chopped
1½ pounds pork
Salt and black pepper, to taste

1. Place the Cook & Crisp Basket in your Ninja Foodi Pressure Cooker Steam Fryer. 2. Mix all of the above ingredients until everything is well incorporated. 3. Now, form the mixture into balls (the size of golf a ball). 4. Put on the Smart Lid on top of the Ninja Foodi Steam Fryer. 5. Move the Lid Slider to the "Air Fry/Stovetop". 6. Cook on "Air Fry" Mode for about 17 minutes at 375°F/190°C. Serve with your favorite sauce.
Per Serving: Calories 258; Fat 12.4g; Sodium 79mg; Total Carbs 34.3g; Fiber 1g; Sugar 17g; Protein 3.2g

Crispy Cocktail Meatballs

Prep Time: 10 minutes. | Cook Time: 20 minutes. | Serves: 8

½ teaspoon fine salt
1 cup Romano cheese, grated
3 cloves garlic, minced
1½ pound pork
½ cup scallions, chopped

2 eggs, well whisked
⅓ teaspoon cumin powder
⅔ teaspoon black pepper
2 teaspoons basil

1. Place the Cook & Crisp Basket in your Ninja Foodi Pressure Cooker Steam Fryer. 2. Simply mix all the ingredients in a large-sized mixing bowl. 3. Shape into bite-sized balls; cook the meatballs in your Ninja Foodi Pressure Cooker Steam Fryer. 4. Put on the Smart Lid on top of the Ninja Foodi Steam Fryer. 5. Move the Lid Slider to the "Air Fry/Stovetop". 6. Cook on "Air Fry" Mode for about 18 minutes at 345°F/175°C. Serve with some tangy sauce such as marinara sauce if desired. Bon appétit!
Per Serving: Calories 192; Fat 9.3g; Sodium 133mg; Total Carbs 27.1g; Fiber 1.4g; Sugar 19g; Protein 3.2g

Crispy Cheeseburger Bites

Prep Time: 10 minutes. | Cook Time: 20 minutes. | Serves: 4

1 tablespoon Dijon mustard
2 tablespoons minced scallions
1-pound beef
1 ½ teaspoons minced green garlic
½ teaspoon cumin

Salt and black pepper, to savor
12 cherry tomatoes
12 cubes cheddar cheese
Mini burgers, as desired

1. Place the Cook & Crisp Basket in your Ninja Foodi Pressure Cooker Steam Fryer. 2. In a large-sized mixing dish, place the mustard, beef, cumin, scallions, garlic, salt, and pepper; then mix with your hands or a spatula so that everything is evenly coated. 3. Form into 12 meatballs. 4. Put on the Smart Lid on top of the Ninja Foodi Steam Fryer. 5. Move the Lid Slider to the "Air Fry/Stovetop". 6. Cook on "Air Fry" Mode for about 15 minutes at 375°F/190°C, until they are cooked in the middle. 7. Thread cherry tomatoes, mini burgers and cheese on cocktail sticks. Bon appétit!
Per Serving: Calories 204; Fat 9g; Sodium 91mg; Total Carbs 27g; Fiber 2.4g; Sugar 15g; Protein 1.3g

Crispy BBQ Smokies

Prep Time: 10 minutes. | Cook Time: 20 minutes. | Serves: 6

1-pound beef cocktail wieners
10 ounces barbecue sauce, no

sugar added

1. Place the Cook & Crisp Basket in your Ninja Foodi Pressure Cooker Steam Fryer. 2. Prick holes into your sausages using a fork and transfer them to the Cook & Crisp Basket. 3. Put on the Smart Lid on top of the Ninja Foodi Steam Fryer. 4. Move the Lid Slider to the "Air Fry/Stovetop". 5. Cook on "Air Fry" Mode at 380°F/195°C for about 13 minutes. Spoon the barbecue sauce into the Cook & Crisp Basket . Cook an additional 2 minutes. 6. Serve with toothpicks. Bon appétit!
Per Serving: Calories 284; Fat 16g; Sodium 252mg; Total Carbs 31.6g; Fiber 0.9g; Sugar 6.6g; Protein 3.7g

Crispy Broccoli Fries with Spicy Dip

Prep Time: 10 minutes. | Cook Time: 15 minutes. | Serves: 4

¾-pound broccoli florets
½ teaspoon onion powder
1 teaspoon granulated garlic
½ teaspoon cayenne pepper
Spicy Dip:
¼ cup mayo
¼ cup Greek yogurt

Salt and black pepper, to taste
2 tablespoons sesame oil
4 tablespoons parmesan cheese, preferably freshly grated

¼ teaspoon Dijon mustard
1 teaspoon hot sauce

1. Place the Cook & Crisp Basket in your Ninja Foodi Pressure Cooker Steam Fryer. 2. Add the broccoli to the salted boiling water to blanch it until all dente, about 3 to 4 minutes. Drain well and transfer to the lightly greased Cook & Crisp Basket. 3. Add the onion powder, garlic, cayenne pepper, salt, black pepper, sesame oil, and parmesan cheese. 4. Put on the Smart Lid on top of the Ninja Foodi Steam Fryer. 5. Move the Lid Slider to the "Air Fry/Stovetop". 6. Cook on "Air Fry" Mode at 400°F/200°C for about 6 minutes, tossing halfway through the cooking time. 7. Meanwhile, mix all of the spicy dip ingredients. Serve broccoli fries with chilled dipping sauce. Bon appétit!
Per Serving: Calories 416; Fat 8.3 g; Sodium 208 mg; Carbs 22.9g; Fiber 0.5g; Sugar 19g; Protein 60.6g

Picnic Chicken Chunks

Prep Time: 10 minutes. | Cook Time: 20 minutes. | Serves: 6

1-pound chicken breasts, slice into tenders
½ teaspoon cayenne pepper
Salt and black pepper, to taste
¼ cup almond meal

1 egg, whisked
½ cup parmesan cheese, freshly grated
¼ cup mayo
¼ cup barbecue sauce

1. Place the Cook & Crisp Basket in your Ninja Foodi Pressure Cooker Steam Fryer. 2. Season the chicken with the cayenne pepper, salt, and black pepper. 3. Dip the boneless chicken tenders into the almond meal, then coat them with the egg. 4. Press the egg-dipped chicken tenders into the parmesan cheese and coat evenly. 5. Spread the evenly coated chicken tenders in the greased Ninja Foodi Cook & Crisp Basket. 6. Put on the Smart Lid on top of the Ninja Foodi Steam Fryer. 7. Move the Lid Slider to the "Air Fry/Stovetop". 8. Cook on "Air Fry" Mode at 360°F/180°C or about 9 to 12 minutes, turning them over to cook evenly. 9. In a suitable mixing bowl, mix the mayo with the barbecue sauce. 10. Serve the chicken chunks with the sauce for dipping. Bon appétit!
Per Serving: Calories 239; Fat 48.3 g; Sodium 598 mg; Carbs 98g; Fiber 2.5g; Sugar 4.9g; Protein 7.6g

Crispy Wings with Blue Cheese

Prep Time: 10 minutes. | Cook Time: 20 minutes. | Serves: 6

1 ½ pounds chicken wings
2 teaspoons sesame oil
Kosher salt and black pepper, to taste

2 tablespoons tamari sauce
1 tablespoon rice vinegar
2 garlic cloves, minced
1 cup blue cheese, crumbled

1. Place the Cook & Crisp Basket in your Ninja Foodi Pressure Cooker Steam Fryer. 2. Toss the chicken wings with the sesame oil, salt, and pepper. Add chicken wings to a lightly greased Cook & Crisp Basket. 3. Put on the Smart Lid on top of the Ninja Foodi Steam Fryer. 4. Move the Lid Slider to the "Air Fry/Stovetop". 5. Roast the chicken wings on "Air Fry" Mode at 390°F/200°C for about 7 minutes. Turn them over once or twice to ensure even cooking. 6. In a mixing dish, mix the tamari sauce, vinegar, garlic, and blue cheese. 7. Pour the sauce all over the chicken wings; Cook on "Air Fry" Mode an additional 5 minutes. Bon appétit!
Per Serving: Calories 426; Fat 36.3 g; Sodium 248 mg; Carbs 22.1g; Fiber 2g; Sugar 10.9g; Protein 6.6g

Crispy Celery Fries with Aioli

Prep Time: 10 minutes. | Cook Time: 20 minutes. | Serves: 4

1-pound celery, peel long strips
2 tablespoons sesame oil
Salt and black pepper, to taste
1 teaspoon red pepper flakes, crushed
½ teaspoon curry powder

½ teaspoon mustard seeds
Spicy Citrus Aioli:
¼ cup mayo
1 tablespoon fresh lime juice
1 clove garlic, smashed
Salt and black pepper, to taste

1. Place the Cook & Crisp Basket in your Ninja Foodi Pressure Cooker Steam Fryer. 2. Toss the celery chips with the sesame oil, salt, black pepper, red pepper, curry powder, and mustard seeds. 3. Put on the Smart Lid on top of the Ninja Foodi Steam Fryer. 4. Move the Lid Slider to the "Air Fry/Stovetop". 5. Cook on "Air Fry" Mode at 380°F/195°C for about 15 minutes, shaking the Ninja Foodi Cook & Crisp Basket periodically. 6. Meanwhile, make the sauce by whisking the mayo, lime juice, garlic, salt, and pepper. Place in the refrigerator until ready to use. Bon appétit!
Per Serving: Calories 477; Fat 13.3 g; Sodium 128 mg; Carbs 89.5g; Fiber 6.5g; Sugar 59.2g; Protein 5.4g

Fried Shallots

Prep Time: 10 minutes. | Cook Time: 25 minutes. | Serves: 4

½ cup almond flour
2 large-sized eggs
½ teaspoon baking powder
⅔ teaspoon red pepper flakes, crushed

1 cup shallots, sliced into rings
½ cup beer
½ teaspoon fine salt
1 cup pork rinds

1. Place the Cook & Crisp Basket in your Ninja Foodi Pressure Cooker Steam Fryer. 2. Use a medium-sized bowl to mix almond flour with eggs, baking powder, salt, beer and crushed red pepper flakes. 3. Dip shallots rings into the prepared batter; make sure to coat them on all sides. Now, coat them with the pork rinds. 4. Put on the Smart Lid on top of the Ninja Foodi Steam Fryer. 5. Move the Lid Slider to the "Air Fry/Stovetop". 6. Cook the shallots on "Air Fry" Mode at 345°F/175°C for about 11 minutes. 7. Eat warm.
Per Serving: Calories 398; Fat 37.8 g; Sodium 1463 mg; Carbs 2.5g; Fiber 0.2g; Sugar 0.5g; Protein 3.6g

Crispy Ranch Kale Chips

Prep Time: 10 minutes. | Cook Time: 7 minutes. | Serves: 4

1 ½ teaspoons Ranch seasoning mix
2 tablespoons sesame oil
Salt and pepper, to taste

3 heads of kale, torn into small pieces
2 tablespoons Worchester sauce

1. Place the Cook & Crisp Basket in your Ninja Foodi Pressure Cooker Steam Fryer. 2. Toss all the recipe ingredients together in a mixing bowl. 3. Put on the Smart Lid on top of the Ninja Foodi Steam Fryer. 4. Move the Lid Slider to the "Air Fry/Stovetop". 5. Then, cook on "Air Fry" Mode at 195°F/90°C for about 4 minutes. Enjoy!
Per Serving: Calories 80; Fat 7g; Sodium 168mg; Carbs 4g; Fiber 1g; Sugar 1.5g; Protein 1g

Avocado Fries Wrapped in Bacon

Prep Time: 10 minutes. | Cook Time: 10 minutes. | Serves: 5

2 teaspoons chili powder
2 avocados, pitted and cut into 10 pieces
1 teaspoon salt

½ teaspoon garlic powder
1 teaspoon black pepper
5 rashers back bacon, cut into halves

1. Place the Cook & Crisp Basket in your Ninja Foodi Pressure Cooker Steam Fryer. 2. Lay the bacon rashers on a clean surface; then, place one piece of avocado slice on each bacon slice. Add the salt, black pepper, chili powder, and garlic powder. 3. Then, wrap the bacon slice around the avocado and repeat with the remaining rolls; secure them with a cocktail sticks or toothpicks. 4. Put on the Smart Lid on top of the Ninja Foodi Steam Fryer. 5. Move the Lid Slider to the "Air Fry/Stovetop". 6. Cook on "Air Fry" Mode at 370°F/185°C for about 5 minutes and serve with your favorite sauce for dipping.
Per Serving: Calories 382; Fat 32.5 g; Sodium 1363 mg; Carbs 3.2g; Fiber 0.2g; Sugar 1.9g; Protein 9.1g

Crispy Calamari Appetizer

Prep Time: 10 minutes. | Cook Time: 20 minutes. | Serves: 6

1 ½ pounds calamari tubes, cleaned, cut into rings
Salt and black pepper, to taste
2 tablespoons lemon juice

½ cup almond meal
2 eggs, whisked
¼ cup buttermilk
Cooking oil

1. Place the Cook & Crisp Basket in your Ninja Foodi Pressure Cooker Steam Fryer. 2. Rinse the calamari and pat it dry. Season with salt and black pepper. Drizzle lemon juice all over the calamari. 3. Now, mix the almond meal, eggs, and buttermilk. Dredge the calamari in the batter. 4. Arrange them in your Ninja Foodi Pressure Cooker Steam Fryer cooking basket. Spritz with cooking oil. 5. Put on the Smart Lid on top of the Ninja Foodi Steam Fryer. 6. Move the Lid Slider to the "Air Fry/Stovetop". 7. Cook on "Air Fry" Mode at 390°F/200°C for about 9 to 12 minutes, shaking the basket occasionally. Work in batches. 8. Serve with toothpicks. Bon appétit!
Per Serving: Calories 276; Fat 2.1 g; Sodium 18 mg; Carbs 65.9g;

Fiber 4.5g; Sugar 59g; Protein 2.6g

Crispy Zucchini Chips with Sauce

Prep Time: 10 minutes. | Cook Time: 25 minutes. | Serves: 4

⅓ cup almond meal
½ cup Parmesan cheese, grated
Salt and black pepper, to taste
¼ teaspoon oregano
Sauce:
½ cup Greek-style yogurt
1 tablespoon fresh cilantro, chopped

1 medium-sized zucchini, cut into slices
2 tablespoons grapeseed oil

1 garlic clove, minced
Black pepper, to your liking

1. Place the Cook & Crisp Basket in your Ninja Foodi Pressure Cooker Steam Fryer. 2. In any shallow bowl, mix the almond meal, Parmesan, salt, black pepper, and oregano. 3. Dip the zucchini slices in the prepared batter, pressing to adhere. 4. Brush with the grapeseed oil. 5. Put on the Smart Lid on top of the Ninja Foodi Steam Fryer. 6. Move the Lid Slider to the "Air Fry/Stovetop". 7. Cook on "Air Fry" Mode at 400°F/200°C for about 12 minutes. Shake the Ninja Foodi Cook & Crisp Basket periodically to ensure even cooking. Work in batches. 8. While the chips are baking, whisk the sauce ingredients; place in your refrigerator until ready to serve. Enjoy!
Per Serving: Calories 267; Fat 15.2 g; Sodium 479 mg; Carbs 13.9g; Fiber 0.1g; Sugar 12.9g; Protein 2.6g

Grilled Meatball

Prep Time: 10 minutes. | Cook Time: 20 minutes. | Serves: 6

½-pound pork
½-pound beef
1 teaspoon dried onion flakes
1 teaspoon fresh garlic, minced
1 teaspoon dried parsley flakes

Salt and black pepper, to taste
1 red pepper, 1-inch pieces
1 cup pearl onions
½ cup barbecue sauce, no sugar added

1. Place the Cook & Crisp Basket in your Ninja Foodi Pressure Cooker Steam Fryer. 2. Mix the meat with the onion flakes, garlic, parsley flakes, salt, and black pepper. Shape the mixture into 1-inch balls. 3. Thread the meatballs, pearl onions, and peppers alternately onto skewers. Place the skewers on the Cook & Crisp Basket. 4. Microwave the barbecue sauce for about 10 seconds. 5. Put on the Smart Lid on top of the Ninja Foodi Steam Fryer. 6. Move the Lid Slider to the "Air Fry/Stovetop". 7. Cook on "Air Fry" Mode at 380°F/195°Cor about 5 minutes. Turn the skewers over halfway through the cooking time. Brush with the sauce. Cook for a further 5 minutes. Work in batches. 8. Serve with the remaining barbecue sauce and enjoy!
Per Serving: Calories 368; Fat 32.8 g; Sodium 507 mg; Carbs 0.6g; Fiber 0.1g; Sugar 1.1g; Protein 8.5g

Mediterranean Cocktail Meatballs

Prep Time: 10 minutes. | Cook Time: 15 minutes. | Serves: 4

For the Meatballs:
1 ½ tablespoons melted butter
2 teaspoons red pepper flakes, crushed
½ tablespoon fresh cilantro, chopped
2 eggs
For Mediterranean Dipping sauce:
⅓ cup black olives, chopped
2 tablespoons fresh Italian parsley
½ teaspoon lemon zest
⅓ cup Greek-style yogurt

2 tablespoons fresh mint leaves, chopped
1 teaspoon kosher salt
4 garlic cloves, minced
1-pound pork
2 tablespoons capers

½ teaspoon dill, fresh or dried and chopped
2 tablespoons fresh rosemary

1. Place the Cook & Crisp Basket in your Ninja Foodi Pressure Cooker Steam Fryer. 2. In a large-sized mixing dish, place all the recipe ingredients for the meatballs; mix to mix well. Shape the prepared mixture into golf ball sized meatballs. 3. Put on the Smart Lid on top of the Ninja Foodi Steam Fryer. 4. Move the Lid Slider to the "Air Fry/Stovetop". 5. Cook the meatballs on "Air Fry" Mode at 395°F/200°C for about 9 minutes, working in batches. 6. In the meantime, make the dipping sauce by whisking all the sauce ingredients. Serve warm meatballs with the prepared Mediterranean dipping sauce.
Per Serving: Calories 404; Fat 20.3 g; Sodium 8 mg; Carbs 3.4g; Fiber 1g; Sugar 1.2g; Protein 3.4g

Grandma's Crispy Wings

Prep Time: 10 minutes. | Cook Time: 40 minutes | Serves: 4

2 cloves garlic, smashed
3 tablespoons melted butter
Black pepper and fine salt, to taste
8 chicken wings
A few dashes of hot sauce

1. Place the Cook & Crisp Basket in your Ninja Foodi Pressure Cooker Steam Fryer. 2. First of all, steam chicken wings for about 8 minutes; pat them dry and place in the refrigerator for about 55 minutes. 3. Put on the Smart Lid on top of the Ninja Foodi Steam Fryer. 4. Move the Lid Slider to the "Air Fry/Stovetop". 5. Now, cook on "Air Fry" Mode at 335°F/170°C for about 28 minutes, turning halfway through. While the chicken wings are cooking, combine the other ingredients to make the sauce. 6. To finish, toss chicken wings with the sauce and serve immediately.
Per Serving: Calories 319; Fat 14.7 g; Sodium 92 mg; Carbs 30.3g; Fiber 4g; Sugar 12.3g; Protein 24g

Crispy Cauliflower

Prep Time: 10 minutes. | Cook Time: 20 minutes. | Serves: 2

3 cups cauliflower florets
2 tablespoons sesame oil
1 teaspoon onion powder
1 teaspoon garlic powder
1 teaspoon thyme
1 teaspoon sage
1 teaspoon rosemary
Salt and cracked black pepper, to taste
1 teaspoon paprika

1. Place the Cook & Crisp Basket in your Ninja Foodi Pressure Cooker Steam Fryer. 2. Toss the cauliflower with the remaining ingredients; toss to coat well. 3. Put on the Smart Lid on top of the Ninja Foodi Steam Fryer. 4. Move the Lid Slider to the "Air Fry/Stovetop". 5. Cook on "Air Fry" Mode at 400°F/200°C for about 12 minutes, shaking the cooking basket halfway through the cooking time. They will crisp up as they cool. Bon appétit!
Per Serving: Calories 148; Fat 0.3 g; Sodium 3 mg; Carbs 38.9g; Fiber 0.5g; Sugar 33.9g; Protein 0.6g

Bacon Fat Bombs

Prep Time: 10 minutes. | Cook Time: 15 minutes. | Serves: 6

2 onions, sliced
1 cup bacon, chopped
½ cup Colby cheese, shredded
8 ounces soft cheese
2 ½ tablespoons canola oil
2 eggs

1. Place the Cook & Crisp Basket in your Ninja Foodi Pressure Cooker Steam Fryer. 2. Mix all the recipe ingredients in a mixing dish. Roll the mixture into bite-sized balls. 3. Put on the Smart Lid on top of the Ninja Foodi Steam Fryer. 4. Move the Lid Slider to the "Air Fry/Stovetop". 5. Cook them on "Air Fry" Mode at 390°F/200°C for about 5 minutes. Work in batches. 6. Serve with toothpicks and enjoy!
Per Serving: Calories 273; Fat 24 g; Sodium 1181 mg; Carbs 12.8g; Fiber 1g; Sugar 1.4g; Protein 20g

Mexican Zucchini Cakes Ole

Prep Time: 10 minutes. | Cook Time: 22 minutes. | Serves: 4

⅓ cup Swiss cheese, grated
⅓ teaspoon fine salt
⅓ teaspoon baking powder
⅓ cup scallions, chopped
½ tablespoon fresh basil, chopped
1 zucchini, trimmed and grated
½ teaspoon freshly cracked black pepper
1 teaspoon Mexican oregano
1 cup bacon, chopped
¼ cup almond meal
¼ cup coconut flour
2 small eggs, lightly beaten
1 cup Cotija cheese, grated
Cooking oil

1. Place the Cook & Crisp Basket in your Ninja Foodi Pressure Cooker Steam Fryer. 2. Mix all ingredients, except for Cotija cheese and cooking oil, until everything is well mixed. 3. Then, gently flatten each ball. Spritz the cakes with a nonstick cooking oil. 4. Put on the Smart Lid on top of the Ninja Foodi Steam Fryer. 5. Move the Lid Slider to the "Air Fry/Stovetop". 6. Cook on "Air Fry" Mode for about 13 minutes at 305°F/150°C; work with batches. Serve warm with tomato ketchup and mayo.

Per Serving: Calories 373; Fat 8.5 g; Sodium 4928 mg; Carbs 0.8g; Fiber 0.3g; Sugar 7.6g; Protein 74.5g

Crispy Tomato Chips

Prep Time: 10 minutes. | Cook Time: 15 minutes. | Serves: 4

4 Roma tomatoes, sliced
2 tablespoons olive oil
Salt and white pepper, to taste
1 teaspoon Italian seasoning mix
½ cup Parmesan cheese, grated

1. Place the Cook & Crisp Basket in your Ninja Foodi Pressure Cooker Steam Fryer. 2. Generously grease the Ninja Foodi Cook & Crisp Basket with nonstick cooking oil. 3. Toss the sliced tomatoes with the remaining ingredients. Transfer them to the cooking basket without overlapping. 4. Put on the Smart Lid on top of the Ninja Foodi Steam Fryer. 5. Move the Lid Slider to the "Air Fry/Stovetop". 6. Cook on "Air Fry" Mode at 350°F/175°C for about 5 minutes. Shake the cooking basket. Cook an additional 5 minutes. Work in batches. 7. Serve with Mediterranean aioli for dipping, if desired. Bon appétit!
Per Serving: Calories 596; Fat 10.8 g; Sodium 7429 mg; Carbs 14.9g; Fiber 1.9g; Sugar 21.9g; Protein 112.2g

Bell Pepper Chips with Parmesan

Prep Time: 10 minutes. | Cook Time: 20 minutes. | Serves: 4

1 egg, beaten
½ cup parmesan, grated
1 teaspoon salt
½ teaspoon red pepper flakes,
crushed
¾-pound bell peppers, deveined and cut to ¼-inch strips
2 tablespoons grapeseed oil

1. Place the Cook & Crisp Basket in your Ninja Foodi Pressure Cooker Steam Fryer. 2. In a mixing bowl, mix together the egg, parmesan, salt, and red pepper flakes; mix to mix well. 3. Dip bell peppers into the batter and transfer them to the cooking basket. Brush with the grapeseed oil. 4. Put on the Smart Lid on top of the Ninja Foodi Steam Fryer. 5. Move the Lid Slider to the "Air Fry/Stovetop". 6. Cook on "Air Fry" Mode at 390°F/200°C for about 4 minutes. Shake the basket. Cook for a further 3 minutes. Work in batches. 7. Taste, adjust the seasonings and serve. Bon appétit!
Per Serving: Calories 363; Fat 17.1 g; Sodium 1065 mg; Carbs 19.8g; Fiber 3.4g; Sugar 12.9g; Protein 33.7g

Paprika Cheese Chips

Prep Time: 2 minutes. | Cook Time: 5 minutes. | Serves: 4

8 ounces cheddar cheese, shredded   1 teaspoon sweet paprika

1. Divide the cheese in small heaps in the Cook & Crisp Basket, sprinkle the paprika on top. Place the Cook & Crisp Basket in your Pressure Cooker Steam Fryer. Put on the Smart Lid on top of the Ninja Foodi Steam Fryer. Move the Lid Slider to the "Air Fry/Stovetop". Select the "Air Fry" mode for cooking. Air Fry at 400°F/200°C for around 5 minutes. Cool the chips down and serve them.
Per serving: Calories 128; Fat: 1.7g; Sodium 771mg; Carbs: 22.1g; Fiber: 4.5g; Sugars 3.9g; Protein 7.1g

Thai Turkey Bites

Prep Time: 10 minutes. | Cook Time: 20 minutes. | Serves: 6

1 ½ pounds turkey wings, cut into pieces
1 teaspoon ginger-garlic paste
1 ½ tablespoons rice wine
1 ½ tablespoons coconut oil, melted
½ palmful minced lemongrass
1 teaspoon cayenne pepper
Salt flakes and black pepper, to savor
⅓ cup Thai chili sauce

1. Place the Cook & Crisp Basket in your Ninja Foodi Pressure Cooker Steam Fryer. 2. Toss turkey wings with all of the above ingredients. 3. Put on the Smart Lid on top of the Ninja Foodi Steam Fryer. 4. Move the Lid Slider to the "Air Fry/Stovetop". 5. Cook them on "Air Fry" Mode at 355°F/180°C for about 18 minutes until they are cooked. 6. Serve with Thai chili sauce and lemon wedges. Bon appétit!
Per Serving: Calories 157; Fat 10.1 g; Sodium 423 mg; Carbs 1.6g; Fiber 0.5g; Sugar 0.4g; Protein 14.9g

Spinach Chips

Prep Time: 10 minutes. | Cook Time: 20 minutes. | Serves: 3

3 cups fresh spinach leaves
1 tablespoon olive oil
1 teaspoon salt
½ teaspoon cayenne pepper
1 teaspoon garlic powder

Chili Yogurt Dip:
¼ cup yogurt
2 tablespoons mayo
½ teaspoon chili powder

1. Place the Cook & Crisp Basket in your Ninja Foodi Pressure Cooker Steam Fryer. 2. Toss the spinach leaves with the olive oil and seasonings. 3. Put on the Smart Lid on top of the Ninja Foodi Steam Fryer. 4. Move the Lid Slider to the "Air Fry/Stovetop". 5. Cook on "Air Fry" Mode at 350°F/175°C for about 10 minutes, shaking the cooking basket occasionally. 6. Cook until the edges brown, working in batches. 7. In the meantime, make the sauce by whisking all the recipe ingredients in a mixing dish. Serve immediately.
Per Serving: Calories 297; Fat 18.4 g; Sodium 1151 mg; Carbs 11.6g; Fiber 0.6g; Sugar 10.9g; Protein 20.5g

Romano Crispy Zucchini Fries

Prep Time: 10 minutes. | Cook Time: 20 minutes. | Serves: 2

1 zucchini, slice into strips
2 tablespoons mayo
¼ cup almond meal
½ cup Romano cheese, shredded

Salt and black pepper, to your liking
1 tablespoon garlic powder
½ teaspoon red pepper flakes

1. Place the Cook & Crisp Basket in your Ninja Foodi Pressure Cooker Steam Fryer. 2. Coat the zucchini with mayo. 3. Mix the almond meal, Romano cheese, and spices in a shallow dish. 4. Then, coat the zucchini sticks with the cheese mixture. 5. Put on the Smart Lid on top of the Ninja Foodi Steam Fryer. 6. Move the Lid Slider to the "Air Fry/Stovetop". 7. Cook those zucchini sticks on "Air Fry" Mode at 400°F/200°C for about 12 minutes, shaking the basket halfway through the cooking time. 8. Work in batches until the sticks are crispy and golden brown. Bon appétit!
Per Serving: Calories 384; Fat 20.5g; Sodium 449 mg; Carbs 5.1g; Fiber 2.1g; Sugar 0.7g; Protein 45g

Parmesan Chicken Meatballs

Prep Time: 10 minutes. | Cook Time: 15 minutes. | Serves: 4

½ cup almond flour
2 eggs
1 ½ tablespoons melted butter
⅓ teaspoon mustard seeds
1-pound chicken
2 garlic cloves, minced
1 teaspoon dried basil

½ teaspoon Hungarian paprika
⅓ cup Parmesan cheese, preferably freshly grated
½ lime, zested
1 teaspoon fine salt
⅓ teaspoon black pepper

1. Place the Cook & Crisp Basket in your Ninja Foodi Pressure Cooker Steam Fryer. 2. In a nonstick skillet that is preheated over a moderate flame, place the chicken and garlic; cook until the chicken is no longer pink and the garlic is just browned, about 3 minutes. 3. Throw in the remaining ingredients; shape the mixture into balls (e.g. the size of a golf ball). 4. Transfer them to the greased cooking basket. 5. Put on the Smart Lid on top of the Ninja Foodi Steam Fryer. 6. Move the Lid Slider to the "Air Fry/Stovetop". 7. Cook on "Air Fry" Mode at 385°F/195°C for about 8 minutes, or till they're thoroughly heated.
Per Serving: Calories 362; Fat 22.6 g; Sodium 242 mg; Carbs 2.9g; Fiber 1.4g; Sugar 0.5g; Protein 37.4g

Greek Keftedes with Tzatziki Dip

Prep Time: 10 minutes. | Cook Time: 20 minutes. | Serves: 6

Greek Keftedes:
½ pound mushrooms, chopped
½-pound pork sausage, chopped
1 teaspoon shallot powder
1 teaspoon granulated garlic
1 teaspoon dried rosemary
Tzatziki Dip:

1 teaspoon dried basil
1 teaspoon dried oregano
2 eggs
2 tablespoons golden flaxseed meal

½ Lebanese cucumbers, grated, juice squeezed out
1 cup full-fat Greek yogurt
1 tablespoon fresh lemon juice

1 garlic clove, minced
1 tablespoon olive oil
½ teaspoon salt

1. Place the Cook & Crisp Basket in your Ninja Foodi Pressure Cooker Steam Fryer. 2. In a mixing bowl, mix all the recipe ingredients for the Greek keftedes. 3. Shape the meat mixture into bite-sized balls. 4. Put on the Smart Lid on top of the Ninja Foodi Steam Fryer. 5. Move the Lid Slider to the "Air Fry/Stovetop". 6. Cook on "Air Fry" Mode at 380°F/195°C or about 10 minutes, shaking the cooking basket once or twice to ensure even cooking. 7. Meanwhile, make the tzatziki dip by mixing all ingredients. Serve the keftedes with cocktail sticks and tzatziki dip on the side. Enjoy!
Per Serving: Calories 328; Fat 28.7 g; Sodium 95 mg; Carbs 7.4g; Fiber 2.8g; Sugar 0.7g; Protein 13g

Cheese Breadsticks

Prep Time: 10 minutes. | Cook Time: 30 minutes. | Serves: 6

½ cup almond meal
Salt and black pepper, to taste
¼ teaspoon smoked paprika
½ teaspoon celery seeds

6 ounces mature Cheddar, cold, freshly grated
2 tablespoons cream cheese
2 tablespoons cold butter

1. Place the Cook & Crisp Basket in your Ninja Foodi Pressure Cooker Steam Fryer. 2. Line the Ninja Foodi Cook & Crisp Basket with parchment paper. 3. In a mixing bowl, mix the almond meal, salt, black pepper, paprika, and celery seeds. 4. Then, mix the cheese and butter in the bowl of a stand mixer. Slowly stir in the almond meal mixture and mix to mix well. 5. Then, pack the batter into a cookie press fitted with a star disk. Pipe the long ribbons of dough across the parchment paper. Then cut into six-inch lengths. 6. Put on the Smart Lid on top of the Ninja Foodi Steam Fryer. 7. Move the Lid Slider to the "Air Fry/Stovetop". 8. Cook on "Air Fry" Mode at 330°F/165°C for about 15 minutes. 9. Repeat with the remaining dough. Let the cheese straws cool on a rack. You can store them between sheets of parchment in an airtight container. Bon appétit!
Per Serving: Calories 370; Fat 10.5 g; Sodium 503 mg; Carbs 21.4g; Fiber 3.1g; Sugar 1.9g; Protein 46.6g

Avocado Fries with Salsa Fresca

Prep Time: 10 minutes. | Cook Time: 6 minutes. | Serves: 6

½ cup flour
2 teaspoons salt
2 eggs, beaten
1 cup panko breadcrumbs
⅛ teaspoon cayenne pepper
Quick Salsa Fresca
1 cup cherry tomatoes
1 tablespoon-sized chunk of shallot or red onion
2 teaspoons fresh lime juice

¼ teaspoon smoked paprika (optional)
2 large avocados, just ripe
Vegetable oil, in a spray bottle

1 teaspoon chopped fresh cilantro or parsley
Salt and black pepper

1. Place the Cook & Crisp Basket in your Pressure Cooker Steam Fryer. 2. Set up your dredging station with three shallow dishes. Place the flour and salt in the first shallow dish. Place the eggs into the second dish. Mix the breadcrumbs, cayenne pepper and paprika (if using) in the third dish. 3. Cut the avocado in half around the pit and separate the two sides. Slice the avocados into long strips while still in their skin. Run a spoon around the slices, separating them from the avocado skin. Try to keep the slices whole, but don't worry if they break – you can still coat. 4. Coat the avocado slices by dredging them first in the flour, then the egg and then the breadcrumbs, pressing the crumbs on gently with your hands. Set the coated avocado fries on the Cook & Crisp Basket and grease them on all sides with vegetable oil. 5. Put on the Smart Lid on top of the Ninja Foodi Steam Fryer. 6. Move the Lid Slider to the "Air Fry/Stovetop". Select the "Air Fry" mode for cooking. 7. Air-fry the avocado fries, one layer at a time, at 400°F/200°C for 6 minutes, turning them over halfway through the cooking time and spraying again if necessary. When the fries are nicely browned on all sides, season with salt and remove. 8. While the avocado fries are cooking, make the salsa fresca by combining everything in a food processor. Pulse several times until the salsa is a chunky purée. Serve the fries warm with the salsa on the side for dipping.
Per serving: Calories 282; Fat: 15.4g; Sodium 646mg; Carbs: 16.4g; Fiber: 7g; Sugars 6.5g; Protein 22.5g

Scallops Bacon Kabobs

Prep Time: 10 minutes. | Cook Time: 40 minutes. | Serves: 6

1-pound sea scallops
½ cup coconut milk
1 tablespoon vermouth
Salt and black pepper, to taste

½-pound bacon, diced
1 shallot, diced
1 teaspoon garlic powder
1 teaspoon paprika

1. Place the Cook & Crisp Basket in your Ninja Foodi Pressure Cooker Steam Fryer. 2. In a ceramic bowl, place the sea scallops, coconut milk, vermouth, salt, and black pepper; let it marinate for about 30 minutes. 3. Assemble the skewers alternating the scallops, bacon, and shallots. Sprinkle garlic powder and paprika all over the skewers. 4. Put on the Smart Lid on top of the Ninja Foodi Steam Fryer. 5. Move the Lid Slider to the "Air Fry/Stovetop". 6. Cook on "Air Fry" Mode at 400°F/200°C for about 6 minutes. Serve warm and enjoy!
Per Serving: Calories 206; Fat 6.4 g; Sodium 911 mg; Carbs 28.9g; Fiber 3.6g; Sugar 20.4g; Protein 11g

Bacon Bell Pepper Skewers

Prep Time: 10 minutes. | Cook Time: 20 minutes. | Serves: 4

16 cocktail sausages, halved
4 ounces bacon, diced
1 red bell pepper, cut into 1 ½-inch pieces
1 green bell pepper, cut into 1

½-inch pieces
Salt and cracked black pepper, to taste
½ cup tomato chili sauce

1. Place the Cook & Crisp Basket in your Ninja Foodi Pressure Cooker Steam Fryer. 2. Thread the cocktail sausages, bacon, and peppers alternately onto skewers. Sprinkle with salt and black pepper. 3. Put on the Smart Lid on top of the Ninja Foodi Steam Fryer. 4. Move the Lid Slider to the "Air Fry/Stovetop". 5. Cook on "Air Fry" Mode at 380°F/195°Cor about 15 minutes, turning the skewers over once or twice to ensure even cooking. 6. Serve with the tomato chili sauce on the side. Enjoy!
Per Serving: Calories 467; Fat 19.8 g; Sodium 958 mg; Carbs 2.6g; Fiber 0.1g; Sugar 2.2g; Protein 65.7g

Crispy Japanese Yakitori

Prep Time: 10 minutes. | Cook Time: 15 minutes | Serves: 4

1-pound chicken tenders, cut bite-sized pieces
1 clove garlic, minced
1 teaspoon coriander seeds
Salt and pepper, to taste

2 tablespoons Shoyu sauce
2 tablespoons sake
1 tablespoon fresh lemon juice
2 tablespoons sesame oil

1. Place the Cook & Crisp Basket in your Ninja Foodi Pressure Cooker Steam Fryer. 2. Place the chicken tenders, garlic, coriander, salt, black pepper, Shoyu sauce, sake, and lemon juice in a ceramic dish; cover and let it marinate for about 2 hours. 3. Then, discard the marinade and tread the chicken tenders onto bamboo skewers. 4. Place the skewered chicken in the lightly greased Cook & Crisp Basket. Drizzle sesame oil all over the skewered chicken. 5. Put on the Smart Lid on top of the Ninja Foodi Steam Fryer. 6. Move the Lid Slider to the "Air Fry/Stovetop". 7. Cook on "Air Fry" Mode at 360°F/180°Cor about 6 minutes. Turn the skewered chicken over; brush with the reserved marinade. Cook for a further 6 minutes. Enjoy!
Per Serving: Calories 322; Fat 14 g; Sodium 679 mg; Carbs 1.1g; Fiber 0.2g; Sugar 0.7g; Protein 45.5g

Asian Short Ribs

Prep Time: 10 minutes. | Cook Time: 35 minutes. | Serves: 4

1 pound meaty short ribs
½ rice vinegar
2 tablespoons soy sauce
1 tablespoons Sriracha sauce
2 garlic cloves, minced
1 tablespoon doenjang (soybean

paste)
1 teaspoon kochukaru (chili pepper flakes)
Salt and black pepper, to taste
1 tablespoon sesame oil
¼ cup green onions, chopped

1. Place the Cook & Crisp Basket in your Ninja Foodi Pressure

Cooker Steam Fryer. 2. Place the short ribs, vinegar, soy sauce, Sriracha, garlic, and spices in Ziploc bag; let it marinate overnight. 3. Rub the sides and bottom of the Ninja Foodi Cook & Crisp Basket with sesame oil. Discard the marinade and transfer the ribs to the prepared cooking basket. 4. Put on the Smart Lid on top of the Ninja Foodi Steam Fryer. 5. Move the Lid Slider to the "Air Fry/Stovetop". 6. Cook the marinated on "Air Fry" Mode at 365°F/185°Cor about 17 minutes. Turn the ribs over, brush with the reserved marinade. Cook an additional 15 minutes. 7. Garnish with green onions. Bon appétit!
Per Serving: Calories 360; Fat 30.8 g; Sodium 584 mg; Carbs 1.3g; Fiber 0.5g; Sugar 0.2g; Protein 18.6g

Olive-Stuffed Jalapeños

Prep Time: 10 minutes. | Cook Time: 8 minutes. | Serves: 5

¼ cup plain cream cheese
¼ cup finely grated Cheddar cheese

2 tablespoons chopped black olives
5 medium jalapeño peppers, cut lengthwise, seeded

1. Place the Cook & Crisp Basket in your Pressure Cooker Steam Fryer. 2. In a suitable bowl, cream cheese, Cheddar cheese, and black olives. 3. Press cream cheese mixture into each jalapeño half. 4. Lay stuffed peppers in ungreased "cook & crisp basket". 5. Put on the Smart Lid on top of the Ninja Foodi Steam Fryer. 6. Move the Lid Slider to the "Air Fry/Stovetop". Select the "Air Fry" mode for cooking. 7. Adjust the cooking temperature to 350°F/175°C for 8 minutes. 8. Once done, transfer stuffed peppers to a suitable serving plate and serve warm.
Per serving: Calories 319; Fat: 15.6g; Sodium 99mg; Carbs: 4.8g; Fiber: 0.7g; Sugars 2.9g; Protein 38.5g

Cheese Quesadillas

Prep Time: 10 minutes. | Cook Time: 24 minutes. | Serves: 4

8 tablespoons Mexican blend shredded cheese

8 (6") soft corn tortillas
2 teaspoons olive oil

1. Place the Cook & Crisp Basket in your Pressure Cooker Steam Fryer. 2. Evenly sprinkle cheese over four tortillas. Top each with a remaining tortilla and brush the tops with oil. 3. Place one quesadilla in ungreased "cook & crisp basket". 4. Put on the Smart Lid on top of the Ninja Foodi Steam Fryer. 5. Move the Lid Slider to the "Air Fry/Stovetop". Select the "Air Fry" mode for cooking. 6. Adjust the cooking temperature to 350°F/175°C for 6 minutes. 7. Remove and repeat with remaining quesadillas. 8. Transfer quesadillas to a suitable serving tray and serve warm.
Per serving: Calories 349; Fat: 15.1g; Sodium 157mg; Carbs: 25.6g; Fiber: 2.6g; Sugars 22.5g; Protein: 29.7g

Deviled Eggs with Swiss Cheese

Prep Time: 5 minutes. | Cook Time: 15 minutes. | Serves: 4

4 large eggs
1 cup ice cubes
1 cup water
2 tablespoons mayonnaise
1 tablespoon Thousand Island dressing
⅛ teaspoon salt

⅛ teaspoon black pepper
2 tablespoons finely chopped corned beef
1 teaspoon caraway seeds
2 tablespoons finely chopped Swiss cheese

1. Place the Cook & Crisp Basket in your Pressure Cooker Steam Fryer. 2. Place eggs in silicone cupcake liners to avoid eggs from moving around or cracking during cooking process. Add silicone cups to "cook & crisp basket". 3. Put on the Smart Lid on top of the Ninja Foodi Steam Fryer. 4. Move the Lid Slider to the "Air Fry/Stovetop". Select the "Air Fry" mode for cooking. Cook at 250°F/120°C for 15 minutes. 5. Add ice and water to a suitable bowl. Transfer cooked eggs to water bath immediately to stop cooking process. After 5 minutes, carefully peel eggs. 6. Cut eggs in half lengthwise. Spoon yolks into a suitable bowl. Arrange white halves on a suitable plate. 7. Using a fork, blend egg yolks with mayonnaise, dressing, salt, pepper, corned beef, and caraway seeds. Fold in cheese. Spoon mixture into egg white halves. Serve.
Per serving: Calories 182; Fat: 14.1g; Sodium 18mg; Carbs: 8.9g; Fiber: 4.1g; Sugars 4g; Protein 7.2g

Hot Wings

Prep Time: 15 minutes. | Cook Time: 44 minutes. | Serves: 6

2 pounds chicken wings, split at the joint
1 tablespoon water
1 tablespoon butter, room temperature
½ cup buffalo wing sauce
Cooking oil

1. Place the Cook & Crisp Basket in your Pressure Cooker Steam Fryer. 2. Place water in bottom of the Cook & Crisp Basket to ensure minimum smoke from fat: drippings. 3. Place half of chicken wings in "cook & crisp basket" greased with cooking oil. Put on the Smart Lid on top of the Ninja Foodi Steam Fryer. Move the Lid Slider to the "Air Fry/Stovetop". Select the "Air Fry" mode for cooking. 4. Adjust the cooking temperature to 250°F/120°C. 5. Cook 6 minutes. Flip wings, then cook an additional 6 minutes. 6. While wings are cooking, mix butter and wing sauce in a suitable bowl. 7. Increase temperature on air fryer to 400°F/200°C. Flip wings and cook for 5 minutes. 8. Once done, transfer to bowl with sauce and toss. Set aside. 9. Repeat process with remaining wings. Serve warm.
Per serving: Calories 271; Fat: 19.2g; Sodium 124mg; Carbs: 7.2g; Fiber: 2.9g; Sugars 0.5g; Protein 18.6g

Mustard Wings

Prep Time: 15 minutes. | Cook Time: 44 minutes. | Serves: 6

2 pounds chicken wings, split at the joint
1 tablespoon butter, melted
1 tablespoon water
1 tablespoon Dijon mustard
2 tablespoons yellow mustard
¼ cup honey
1 teaspoon apple cider vinegar
⅛ teaspoon salt
Cooking oil

1. Place the Cook & Crisp Basket in your Pressure Cooker Steam Fryer. 2. Place water in bottom of the Cook & Crisp Basket to ensure minimum smoke from fat: drippings. 3. Place half of wings in "cook & crisp basket" greased with cooking oil. Put on the Smart Lid on top of the Ninja Foodi Steam Fryer. Move the Lid Slider to the "Air Fry/Stovetop". Select the "Air Fry" mode for cooking. Adjust the cooking temperature to 250°F/120°C. 4. Cook for 6 minutes. Flip wings, then cook an additional 6 minutes. 5. While wings are cooking, mix butter, Dijon mustard, yellow mustard, honey, cider vinegar, and salt in a suitable bowl. 6. Raise temperature to 400°F/200°C. Flip wings and cook for 5 minutes. Flip wings once more. Cook for an additional 5 minutes. 7. Transfer cooked wings to bowl with sauce and toss. Repeat process with remaining wings. Serve warm.
Per serving: Calories 309; Fat: 5.1g; Sodium 245mg; Carbs: 43g; Fiber: 9.6g; Sugars 14.2g; Protein 25.8g

Shrimp Sesame Toasts

Prep Time: 10 minutes. | Cook Time: 8 minutes. | Serves: 6

½ pound raw shrimp, peeled and de-veined
1 egg (or 2 egg whites)
2 scallions, more for garnish
2 teaspoons grated fresh ginger
1 teaspoon soy sauce
½ teaspoon toasted sesame oil
2 tablespoons chopped fresh cilantro or parsley
1 to 2 teaspoons sriracha sauce
6 slices thinly-sliced white sandwich bread (Pepperidge Farm®)
½ cup sesame seeds
Thai chili sauce

1. Place the Cook & Crisp Basket in your Pressure Cooker Steam Fryer. 2. Mix the shrimp, egg, scallions, fresh ginger, soy sauce, sesame oil, cilantro (or parsley) and sriracha sauce in a food processor and process into a chunky paste, scraping down the sides of the food processor bowl as necessary. 3. Cut the crusts off the sandwich bread and generously spread the shrimp paste onto each slice of bread. Place the sesame seeds on a plate and invert each shrimp toast into the sesame seeds to coat, pressing down gently. Cut each slice of bread into 4 triangles. 4. Transfer one layer of shrimp toast triangles to the Cook & Crisp Basket. 5. Put on the Smart Lid on top of the Ninja Foodi Steam Fryer. 6. Move the Lid Slider to the "Air Fry/Stovetop". Select the "Air Fry" mode for cooking. 7. Cook on the "Air Fry" mode at 400°F/200°C for 6 to 8 minutes, or until the sesame seeds are toasted on top. 8. Serve warm with a little Thai chili sauce and some sliced scallions as garnish.
Per serving: Calories 223; Fat: 10.6g; Sodium 646mg; Carbs: 4.1g; Fiber: 2.4g; Sugars 1.6g; Protein 29.5g

Pizza Bombs with Marinara Sauce

Prep Time: 10 minutes. | Cook Time: 12 minutes. | Serves: 9 pizza bites

⅓ cup gluten-free all-purpose flour
¼ teaspoon salt
¼ teaspoon baking powder
½ cup small-diced pepperoni
2 ounces cream cheese, room temperature
¼ cup shredded mozzarella cheese
½ teaspoon Italian seasoning
2 tablespoons whole milk
1 teaspoon olive oil
½ cup marinara sauce, warmed

1. Place the Cook & Crisp Basket in your Pressure Cooker Steam Fryer. 2. In a suitable bowl, mix flour, salt, and baking powder. 3. In a suitable bowl, mix remaining ingredients, except marinara sauce. Add dry recipe ingredients to bowl and mix until well mixed. 4. Form mixture into nine (1") balls and place on the Cook & Crisp Basket. Put on the Smart Lid on top of the Ninja Foodi Steam Fryer. 5. Move the Lid Slider to the "Air Fry/Stovetop". Select the "Air Fry" mode for cooking. Adjust the cooking temperature to 325°F/160°C. 6. Cook for 12 minutes. 7. Transfer balls to a suitable plate. Serve warm with marinara sauce.
Per serving: Calories 217; Fat: 5.1g; Sodium 624mg; Carbs: 6.8g; Fiber: 0.8g; Sugars 1.8g; Protein 31.1g

Cauliflower Pizza Crusts

Prep Time: 10 minutes. | Cook Time: 30 minutes. | Serves: 2

1 cup cauliflower rice
1 large egg
½ cup grated mozzarella cheese
1 tablespoon grated Parmesan cheese
1 clove garlic, peeled and minced
1 teaspoon Italian seasoning
⅛ teaspoon salt
Cooking oil

1. Place the deluxe reversible rack in your Pressure Cooker Steam Fryer. 2. In a suitable bowl, mix all the recipe ingredients. 3. Divide mixture in half and spread into two pizza suitable pans greased with preferred cooking oil. 4. Place one pan in the deluxe reversible rack. Put on the Smart Lid on top of the Ninja Foodi Steam Fryer. Move the Lid Slider to the "Air Fry/Stovetop". Select the "Air Fry" mode for cooking. 5. Adjust the cooking temperature to 400°F/200°C. 6. Cook for 12 minutes. Once done, remove pan and repeat with second pan. 7. Top crusts with your favorite toppings. Cook for an additional 3 minutes.
Per serving: Calories 309; Fat: 17.4g; Sodium 348mg; Carbs: 4.8g; Fiber: 1.9g; Sugars 0.6g; Protein 33.4g

Dill Pickles with Ranch Dip

Prep Time: 10 minutes. | Cook Time: 8 minutes. | Serves: 4

4 to 6 dill pickles, sliced in half or quartered lengthwise
½ cup all-purpose flour
2 eggs, beaten
1 cup plain breadcrumbs
Light Ranch Dip
¼ cup reduced-fat: mayonnaise
¼ cup buttermilk
¼ cup non-fat: Greek yogurt
1 tablespoon chopped fresh chives
1 teaspoon salt
⅛ teaspoon cayenne pepper
2 tablespoons fresh dill leaves, dried well
Vegetable oil, in a spray bottle

1 tablespoon chopped fresh parsley
1 tablespoon lemon juice
salt and black pepper

1. Place the Cook & Crisp Basket in your Pressure Cooker Steam Fryer. 2. Set up your dredging station using three shallow dishes. Place the flour in the first shallow dish. Place the eggs into the second dish. Mix the breadcrumbs, salt, cayenne and fresh dill in a food processor and process until everything is mixed and the crumbs are very fine. Place the crumb mixture in the third dish. 3. Coat the pickles pieces by dredging them first in the flour, then the egg, and then the breadcrumbs, pressing the crumbs on gently with your hands. Set the coated pickles on the Cook & Crisp Basket and grease them on all sides with vegetable oil. 4. Put on the Smart Lid on top of the Ninja Foodi Steam Fryer. 5. Move the Lid Slider to the "Air Fry/Stovetop". Select the "Air Fry" mode for cooking. 6. Cook one layer of pickles at a time at 400°F/200°C for 8 minutes, turning them over halfway through the cooking process and spraying again. 7. While the pickles are cooking, make the light ranch dip by mixing everything in a suitable bowl. 8. Serve the pickles warm with the dip on the side.
Per serving: Calories 353; Fat: 18.5g; Sodium 682mg; Carbs: 2.3g; Fiber: 0.8g; Sugars 1g; Protein 45.8g

Party Chex Snack

Prep Time: 5 minutes. | Cook Time: 5 minutes. | Serves: 4

2 cups Rice Chex
2 cups Corn Chex
¼ cup mixed nuts

¼ teaspoon salt
3 tablespoons butter, melted

1. Place the Cook & Crisp Basket in your Pressure Cooker Steam Fryer. 2. In a suitable bowl, mix all the recipe ingredients. 3. Place Chex mixture into ungreased "cook & crisp basket". 4. Put on the Smart Lid on top of the Ninja Foodi Steam Fryer. 5. Move the Lid Slider to the "Air Fry/Stovetop". Select the "Air Fry" mode for cooking. Adjust the cooking temperature to 350°F/175°C. Cook for 3 minutes. 6. Shake basket, then cook an additional 2 minutes. 7. Transfer mixture to a serving bowl. Let cool 5 minutes, then serve warm.
Per serving: Calories 307; Fat: 15.5g; Sodium 720mg; Carbs: 6.6g; Fiber: 1g; Sugars 2.8g; Protein 36.6g

Air-Fried Pumpkin Seeds

Prep Time: 10 minutes. | Cook Time: 13 minutes. | Serves: 4

2 cups fresh pumpkin seeds, rinsed
and dried
2 teaspoons olive oil

½ teaspoon, ¼ teaspoon salt,
divided

1. Place the Cook & Crisp Basket in your Pressure Cooker Steam Fryer. 2. In a suitable bowl, toss seeds with oil and ½ teaspoon salt. 3. Place seeds in ungreased "cook & crisp basket". 4. Put on the Smart Lid on top of the Ninja Foodi Steam Fryer. 5. Move the Lid Slider to the "Air Fry/Stovetop". Select the "Air Fry" mode for cooking. 6. Adjust the cooking temperature to 325°F/160°C. 7. Cook for 7 minutes. Using a spatula, turn seeds, then cook an additional 6 minutes. 8. Transfer seeds to a suitable bowl and let cool 5 minutes before serving.
Per serving: Calories 481; Fat: 14.6g; Sodium 285mg; Carbs: 57.5g; Fiber: 7.3g; Sugars 1g; Protein 31.1g

Trail Chex Snack

Prep Time: 5 minutes. | Cook Time: 5 minutes. | Serves: 4

3 cups Rice Chex
¼ cup salted pumpkin seeds
¼ cup crushed pecans
¼ teaspoon cinnamon
1 tablespoon light brown sugar
¼ teaspoon salt

3 tablespoons butter, melted
2 tablespoons raisins
2 tablespoons unsweetened
coconut flakes
¼ cup mini chocolate chips

1. Place the Cook & Crisp Basket in your Pressure Cooker Steam Fryer. 2. In a suitable bowl, mix Rice Chex, pumpkin seeds, pecans, cinnamon, brown sugar, salt, and butter. 3. Place Rice Chex mixture into ungreased "cook & crisp basket". 4. Put on the Smart Lid on top of the Ninja Foodi Steam Fryer. 5. Move the Lid Slider to the "Air Fry/Stovetop". Select the "Air Fry" mode for cooking. 6. Adjust the cooking temperature to 350°F/175°C. Cook for 3 minutes. 7. Shake basket, then cook an additional 2 minutes. 8. Transfer Rice Chex mixture to a suitable bowl. Let cool 15 minutes. 9. Once mixture cools, toss in raisins, coconut, and chocolate chips. Serve.
Per serving: Calories 322; Fat: 15.9g; Sodium 104mg; Carbs: 5.1g; Fiber: 0.9g; Sugars 2.9g; Protein 38.4g

Grilled Pimento Croutons

Prep Time: 10 minutes. | Cook Time: 24 minutes. | Serves: 4

8 ounces shredded sharp Cheddar
cheese
1 (4-ounce) jar chopped pimientos,
including juice
½ cup mayonnaise

¼ teaspoon salt
¼ teaspoon black pepper
8 slices gluten-free sandwich bread
4 tablespoons butter, melted

1. Place the Cook & Crisp Basket in your Pressure Cooker Steam Fryer. 2. Mix cheese, pimientos including juice, mayonnaise, salt, and pepper in a suitable bowl. Refrigerate covered 30 minutes. 3. Spread pimento cheese mixture evenly over four slices gluten-free bread.

Top each slice with a plain slice and press down just enough to not smoosh cheese out of edges of sandwich. 4. Brush top and bottom of each sandwich with melted butter. Place one sandwich at a time in ungreased "cook & crisp basket". Put on the Smart Lid on top of the Ninja Foodi Steam Fryer. Move the Lid Slider to the "Air Fry/Stovetop". Select the "Air Fry" mode for cooking. 5. Adjust the cooking temperature to 350°F/175°C. 6. Cook for 3 minutes. Flip sandwich. Cook for an additional 3 minutes. Repeat with remaining sandwiches. 7. Slice each sandwich into sixteen sections and serve warm.
Per serving: Calories 384; Fat: 23.6g; Sodium 80mg; Carbs: 20.7g; Fiber: 8.3g; Sugars 3.5g; Protein 24.6g

Eggplant Fries

Prep Time: 10 minutes. | Cook Time: 12 minutes. | Serves: 2

2 large eggs
2 tablespoons whole milk
½ cup gluten-free bread crumbs
½ cup grated Parmesan cheese

1 teaspoon salt
1 medium eggplant, cut into ½"
rounds, then sliced
½ cup marinara sauce, warmed

1. Place the Cook & Crisp Basket in your Pressure Cooker Steam Fryer. 2. Mix eggs and milk in a suitable bowl. In a separate shallow dish, mix bread crumbs, Parmesan cheese, and salt. 3. Dip eggplant in egg mixture. Dredge in bread crumb mixture. 4. Place eggplant fries in ungreased "cook & crisp basket". Put on the Smart Lid on top of the Ninja Foodi Steam Fryer. Move the Lid Slider to the "Air Fry/Stovetop". Select the "Air Fry" mode for cooking. 5. Adjust the cooking temperature to 400°F/200°C. 6. Cook for 5 minutes. Flip fries, then cook an additional 5 minutes. Flip once more. Cook for an additional 2 minutes. 7. Transfer fries to a suitable plate and serve with warmed marinara sauce on the side for dipping.
Per serving: Calories 314; Fat: 8.7g; Sodium 337mg; Carbs: 21.2g; Fiber: 4.1g; Sugars 16g; Protein 37.9g

French Fries

Prep Time: 10 minutes. | Cook Time: 15 minutes. | Serves: 4

2 russet potatoes, scrubbed and cut
into ¼" fries

3 teaspoons salt

1. Place the Cook & Crisp Basket in your Pressure Cooker Steam Fryer. 2. Place fries in a suitable saucepan. Add water to pan to cover fries. Add 1 teaspoon salt. Bring to a boil over high heat. Boil 3 minutes until fork tender. Drain. Toss fries with 1 teaspoon salt. Place salted fries in ungreased "cook & crisp basket". Put on the Smart Lid on top of the Ninja Foodi Steam Fryer. Move the Lid Slider to the "Air Fry/Stovetop". Select the "Air Fry" mode for cooking. 4. Adjust the cooking temperature to 400°F/200°C. 5. Cook for 5 minutes. Shake basket, then cook an additional 5 minutes. Shake basket once more and season with remaining teaspoon salt. Cook an additional 5 minutes. 6. Transfer fries to a suitable plate and serve warm.
Per serving: Calories 422; Fat: 7.3g; Sodium 1093mg; Carbs: 26.9g; Fiber: 5.9g; Sugars 2.4g; Protein 58.5g

Zucchini Fries

Prep Time: 10 minutes. | Cook Time: 20 minutes. | Serves: 2

1 large zucchini, cut into ¼" fries
1 teaspoon salt
½ cup buttermilk

¾ cup gluten-free bread crumbs
2 teaspoons dried thyme

1. Place the Cook & Crisp Basket in your Pressure Cooker Steam Fryer. 2. Scatter zucchini fries evenly over a paper towel. Sprinkle with salt. Let sit 10 minutes, then pat with paper towels. 3. Pour buttermilk into a shallow dish. Place bread crumbs in a second shallow dish. Dip zucchini in buttermilk, then dredge in bread crumbs. 4. Place half of zucchini fries in ungreased "cook & crisp basket". Put on the Smart Lid on top of the Ninja Foodi Steam Fryer. Move the Lid Slider to the "Air Fry/Stovetop". Select the "Air Fry" mode for cooking. 5. Adjust the cooking temperature to 375°F/190°C. 6. Cook for 5 minutes. Flip fries, then cook an additional 5 minutes. 7. Transfer fries to a suitable serving dish. Repeat cooking steps with remaining fries. Season with thyme and serve warm.
Per serving: Calories 393; Fat: 11.7g; Sodium 591mg; Carbs: 16.4g; Fiber: 4.3g; Sugars 6.6g; Protein 56.4g

Pickle Chips

Prep Time: 10 minutes. | Cook Time: 16 minutes. | Serves: 4

2 large eggs
¼ cup whole milk
1 teaspoon Worcestershire sauce
½ cup gluten-free bread crumbs
½ cup Bob's Red Mill Gluten Free

Cornbread Mix
1 teaspoon garlic powder
1 teaspoon salt
1 (16-ounce) jar dill pickle chips, drained and patted dry

1. Place the Cook & Crisp Basket in your Pressure Cooker Steam Fryer. 2. Mix eggs, milk, and Worcestershire sauce in a suitable bowl. 3. Mix bread crumbs, cornbread mix, garlic powder, and salt in a shallow dish. 4. Dip pickle slices in egg mixture. Dredge in Cornmeal mixture, shaking off any excess. 5. Add half of pickle slices to ungreased "cook & crisp basket". Put on the Smart Lid on top of the Ninja Foodi Steam Fryer. Move the Lid Slider to the "Air Fry/Stovetop". Select the "Air Fry" mode for cooking. 6. Adjust the cooking temperature to 400°F/200°C. 7. Cook for 4 minutes. Shake basket and flip pickles. Cook an additional 4 minutes. 8. Transfer cooked chips to a suitable plate. Repeat with remaining pickles. Serve.
Per serving: Calories 428; Fat: 29g; Sodium 546mg; Carbs: 10.8g; Fiber: 3.1g; Sugars 0.2g; Protein 30.6g

Barbecue Chips

Prep Time: 10 minutes. | Cook Time: 17 minutes. | Serves: 2

½ teaspoon smoked paprika
¼ teaspoon chili powder
¼ teaspoon garlic powder
⅛ teaspoon onion powder
⅛ teaspoon cayenne pepper

⅛ teaspoon light brown sugar
1 teaspoon salt
1 medium russet potato, scrubbed and sliced into ⅛"-thick circles
2 teaspoons olive oil

1. Place the Cook & Crisp Basket in your Pressure Cooker Steam Fryer.2. In a suitable bowl, mix smoked paprika, chili powder, garlic powder, onion powder, cayenne pepper, brown sugar, and ½ teaspoon salt. Set aside. 3. In a separate large bowl, toss chips with olive oil and ½ teaspoon salt. 4. Place chips in ungreased "cook & crisp basket". Put on the Smart Lid on top of the Ninja Foodi Steam Fryer. Move the Lid Slider to the "Air Fry/Stovetop". Select the "Air Fry" mode for cooking. 5. Adjust the cooking temperature to 400°F/200°C. 6. Cook for 6 minutes. Shake basket, then cook an additional 5 minutes. Shake basket once more. Cook for an additional 6 minutes. 7. Transfer chips to bowl with seasoning mix and toss. Let rest 15 minutes before serving.
Per serving: Calories 342; Fat: 13.7g; Sodium 678mg; Carbs: 32.3g; Fiber: 4.5g; Sugars 22.1g; Protein 26.7g

Avocado Fries

Prep Time: 10 minutes. | Cook Time: 10 minutes. | Serves: 2

1 large egg
2 tablespoons whole milk
1 cup crushed chili corn chips

1 medium avocado, halved, peeled, pitted, and sliced into 12 "fries"
Cooking oil

1. Place the Cook & Crisp Basket in your Pressure Cooker Steam Fryer. 2. Mix egg and milk in a suitable bowl. Add chili corn chip crumbs to a separate shallow dish. 3. Dip avocado slices into egg mixture. Dredge in chip crumbs to coat. 4. Place half of avocado slices in "cook & crisp basket" greased with cooking oil. 5. Put on the Smart Lid on top of the Ninja Foodi Steam Fryer. 6. Move the Lid Slider to the "Air Fry/Stovetop". Select the "Air Fry" mode for cooking. 7. Adjust the cooking temperature to 375°F/190°C. 8. Cook for 5 minutes. Transfer to serving plate and repeat with remaining avocado slices. 9. Serve fries warm.
Per serving: Calories 275; Fat: 2.2g; Sodium 486mg; Carbs: 27.3g; Fiber: 0.4g; Sugars 17.5g; Protein 36.3g

Ranch Potato Chips

Prep Time: 10 minutes. | Cook Time: 16 minutes. | Serves: 2

1 teaspoon dry ranch seasoning mix
½ teaspoon salt

¼ teaspoon black pepper
2 cups sliced scrubbed fingerling potatoes

2 teaspoons olive oil

1. Place the Cook & Crisp Basket in your Pressure Cooker Steam Fryer. 2. Mix ranch seasoning mix, salt, and pepper in a suitable bowl. Set aside ½ teaspoon for garnish. 3. Toss sliced potatoes with oil in a suitable bowl. Sprinkle with seasoning mix, except reserved ½ teaspoon, to coat. 4. Place chips in ungreased "cook & crisp basket". Put on the Smart Lid on top of the Ninja Foodi Steam Fryer. Move the Lid Slider to the "Air Fry/Stovetop". Select the "Air Fry" mode for cooking. 5. Adjust the cooking temperature to 400°F/200°C. 6. Cook for 3 minutes. Shake basket. Cook an additional 3 minutes. 7. basket. Cook for 5 minutes. Shake basket once more. Cook an additional 5 minutes. 8. nsfer chips to a suitable bowl. Garnish with remaining seasoning, then let rest 15 minutes before serving.
Per serving: Calories 385; Fat: 13.2g; Sodium 929mg; Carbs: 31.6g; Fiber: 4.2g; Sugars 2.6g; Protein 36.4g

Brie with Tomatoes

Prep Time: 10 minutes. | Cook Time: 15 minutes. | Serves: 8

1 baguette
2 pints red and yellow cherry tomatoes
1 tablespoon olive oil
Salt and black pepper
1 teaspoon balsamic vinegar

1 tablespoon chopped fresh parsley
1 (8-ounce) wheel of Brie cheese
Olive oil
½ teaspoon Italian seasoning
1 tablespoon chopped fresh basil

1. Place the Cook & Crisp Basket in your Pressure Cooker Steam Fryer. 2. Start by making the crostini. Slice the baguette diagonally into ½-inch slices and brush the slices with olive oil on both sides. Transfer them into the Cook & Crisp Basket. Put on the Smart Lid on top of the Ninja Foodi Steam Fryer. Move the Lid Slider to the "Air Fry/Stovetop". Select the "Air Fry" mode for cooking. Air fry the baguette slices at 350°F/175°C in batches for around 6 minutes or until browned on all sides. Set the bread aside on your serving platter. 3. Toss the cherry tomatoes in a suitable bowl with the olive oil, black pepper and salt. Put on the Smart Lid on top of the Ninja Foodi Steam Fryer. Move the Lid Slider to the "Air Fry/Stovetop". Select the "Air Fry" mode for cooking. Air fry the cherry tomatoes at 350°F/175°C for around 3 to 5 minutes, shaking the basket a few times during the cooking process. The tomatoes should be soft and some of them will burst open. Toss the warm tomatoes with the balsamic vinegar and fresh parsley and set aside. 4. Cut a circle of parchment paper the same size as your wheel of Brie cheese. Brush both sides of the Brie wheel with olive oil and sprinkle with Italian seasoning, if using. Place the circle of parchment paper on one side of the Brie and transfer the Brie to the Ninja Foodi Pressure Steam Fryer basket, parchment side down. Put on the Smart Lid on top of the Ninja Foodi Steam Fryer. Move the Lid Slider to the "Air Fry/Stovetop". Select the "Air Fry" mode for cooking. Air Fry the brie at 350°F/175°C for 10 minutes. 5. Watch carefully and remove the Brie before the rind cracks and the cheese starts to leak out. Transfer the wheel to your serving platter and top with the roasted tomatoes. Sprinkle with basil and serve with the toasted bread slices.
Per serving: Calories 476; Fat: 37.7g; Sodium 742mg; Carbs: 15.3g; Fiber: 6g; Sugars 5g; Protein 24.8g

Mozzarella Bites

Prep Time: 5 minutes. | Cook Time: 5 minutes. | Serves: 8

2 cups mozzarella, shredded
¾ cup almond flour

2 teaspoons psyllium husk powder
¼ teaspoon sweet paprika

1. Place the Cook & Crisp Basket in your Pressure Cooker Steam Fryer. 2. Put the mozzarella in a suitable bowl, melt it in the microwave for around 2 minutes, add all the other ingredients quickly and stir really until you obtain a dough. Divide the prepared dough into 2 balls, roll them on 2 baking sheets and cut into triangles. Arrange the tortillas in the Cook & Crisp Basket. Put on the Smart Lid on top of the Ninja Foodi Steam Fryer. Move the Lid Slider to the "Air Fry/Stovetop". Select the "Air Fry" mode for cooking. Air Fry at 370°F/190°C for around 5 minutes. Transfer to bowls and serve as a snack.
Per serving: Calories 283; Fat: 3.6g; Sodium 381mg; Carbs: 55.4g; Fiber: 8.1g; Sugars 3.1g; Protein 8.7g

Mushroom Bites

Prep Time: 10 minutes. | Cook Time: 7 minutes. | Serves: 6

6 cremini mushroom caps
3 ounces Parmesan, grated
1 tablespoon olive oil

½ tomato, chopped
½ teaspoon dried basil
1 teaspoon ricotta cheese

1. Place the Cook & Crisp Basket in your Pressure Cooker Steam Fryer. 2. Sprinkle the mushroom caps with olive oil and put in the Ninja Foodi Pressure Steam Fryer basket in one layer. Put on the Smart Lid on top of the Ninja Foodi Steam Fryer. 3. Move the Lid Slider to the "Air Fry/Stovetop". Select the "Air Fry" mode for cooking. 4. Cook them at 400°F/200°C for around 3 minutes. After this, mix up tomato and ricotta cheese. Fill the mushroom caps with tomato mixture. Then top them with parmesan and sprinkle with dried basil. 5. Put on the Smart Lid on top of the Ninja Foodi Steam Fryer. 6. Move the Lid Slider to the "Air Fry/Stovetop". Select the "Air Fry" mode for cooking. 7. Cook the mushroom pizzas for around 4 minutes at 400°F/200°C.
Per serving: Calories 254; Fat: 2.6g; Sodium 482mg; Carbs: 49.1g; Fiber: 4.8g; Sugars 0.2g; Protein 7.8g

Mozzarella with Puttanesca Sauce

Prep Time: 10 minutes. | Cook Time: 8 minutes. | Serves: 8

Puttanesca Sauce
2 teaspoons olive oil
1 anchovy, chopped
2 cloves garlic, minced
1 (14-ounce) can petite diced tomatoes
½ cup chicken stock or water
⅓ cup Kalamata olives, chopped
2 tablespoons capers
½ teaspoon dried oregano
¼ teaspoon crushed red pepper flakes
Salt and black pepper

1 tablespoon fresh parsley, chopped
8 slices of sliced white bread (Pepperidge Farm®)
8 ounces mozzarella cheese, sliced
½ cup all-purpose flour
3 eggs, beaten
1½ cups seasoned panko breadcrumbs
½ teaspoon garlic powder
½ teaspoon salt
Black pepper
Olive oil, in a spray bottle

1. Place the Cook & Crisp Basket in your Pressure Cooker Steam Fryer. 2. Start by making the puttanesca sauce. Heat the olive oil in a suitable saucepan on the stovetop. Stir in anchovies and garlic and sauté for around 3 minutes. Stir in the tomatoes, chicken stock, olives, capers, oregano and crushed red pepper flakes and simmer the sauce for around 20 minutes. Season with salt and black pepper and stir in the parsley. 3. Cut the bread crust. Keep four slices of the bread on a cutting board. Divide the cheese between the four slices of bread. Top the cheese with the remaining four slices of bread to make little sandwiches and cut each sandwich into 4 triangles. 4. Set up your dredging station using three shallow dishes. Place the flour in the first shallow dish, the eggs in the second dish and in the third dish, mix the garlic powder, panko breadcrumbs, salt and black pepper. 5. Dredge each little triangle in the flour first and then dip them into the egg. 6. Let the excess egg drip off and then press the triangles into the breadcrumb mixture, pressing the crumbs on with your hands so they adhere. Place the coated triangles in the freezer for around 2 hours, until the cheese is frozen. 7. Grease all sides of the mozzarella triangles with oil and transfer a single layer of triangles to the Ninja Foodi Pressure Steam Fryer basket. Put on the Smart Lid on top of the Ninja Foodi Steam Fryer. Move the Lid Slider to the "Air Fry/Stovetop". Select the "Air Fry" mode for cooking. Air fry in batches at 390°F/200°C for 5 minutes. 8. Serve with the warm puttanesca sauce.
Per serving: Calories 371; Fat: 4.9g; Sodium 1207mg; Carbs: 57.5g; Fiber: 25g; Sugars 7g; Protein 25.6g

Chicken Bites

Prep Time: 5 minutes. | Cook Time: 20 minutes. | Serves: 4

2 teaspoons garlic powder
2 eggs
Salt and black pepper to the taste
¾ cup coconut flakes

Cooking spray
1-pound chicken breasts, skinless, boneless and cubed

1. Place the Cook & Crisp Basket in your Pressure Cooker Steam

Fryer. 2. Put the coconut in a suitable bowl and mix the eggs with garlic powder, black pepper and salt in a second one. Dredge the chicken cubes in eggs and then in coconut and arrange them all in the Cook & Crisp Basket. Grease with cooking spray. 3. Put on the Smart Lid on top of the Ninja Foodi Steam Fryer. 4. Move the Lid Slider to the "Air Fry/Stovetop". Select the "Air Fry" mode for cooking. 5. Air Fry at 370°F/185°C for around 20 minutes. Arrange the chicken bites on a platter and serve as an appetizer.
Per serving: Calories 339; Fat: 14g; Sodium 556mg; Carbs: 44.6g; Fiber: 6.4g; Sugars 3.8g; Protein 10.5g

Pizza Cheese Bites

Prep Time: 15 minutes. | Cook Time: 3 minutes. | Serves: 10

10 Mozzarella cheese slices   10 pepperoni slices

1. Place the Cook & Crisp Basket in your Pressure Cooker Steam Fryer. 2. Line the Cook & Crisp Basket with baking paper and put Mozzarella in it in one layer. Put on the Smart Lid on top of the Ninja Foodi Steam Fryer. Move the Lid Slider to the "Air Fry/Stovetop". Select the "Air Fry" mode for cooking. Cook for the cheese at 400°F/200°C for around 3 minutes or until it is melted. After this, remove the cheese from the Ninja Foodi Pressure Steam Fryer and cool it to room temperature. Then remove the melted cheese from the baking paper and put the pepperoni slices on it. Fold the cheese in the shape of turnovers.
Per serving: Calories 373; Fat: 3.1g; Sodium 687mg; Carbs: 69.2g; Fiber: 9.6g; Sugars 3.4g; Protein 17.8g

Parsley Olives Fritters

Prep Time: 5 minutes. | Cook Time: 12 minutes. | Serves: 6

Cooking spray
½ cup parsley, chopped
1 egg
½ cup almond flour
Salt and black pepper to the taste

3 spring onions, chopped
½ cup kalamata olives, pitted and minced
3 zucchinis, grated

1. Place the Cook & Crisp Basket in your Pressure Cooker Steam Fryer. 2. In a suitable bowl, mix all the recipe ingredients except the cooking spray, stir well and shape medium fritters out of this mixture. Place the fritters in the Cook & Crisp Basket grease them with cooking spray. Put on the Smart Lid on top of the Ninja Foodi Steam Fryer. Move the Lid Slider to the "Air Fry/Stovetop". Select the "Air Fry" mode for cooking. Air Fry at 380°F/195°C for around 6 minutes on each side. Serve them as an appetizer.
Per serving: Calories 194; Fat: 2.6g; Sodium 1257mg; Carbs: 35.4g; Fiber: 3.7g; Sugars 3.1g; Protein 9.4g

Crispy Zucchini Crackers

Prep Time: 15 minutes. | Cook Time: 20 minutes. | Serves: 16

1 cup zucchini, grated
2 teaspoons flax meal
1 teaspoon salt
3 tablespoons almond flour
¼ teaspoon baking powder

¼ teaspoon chili flakes
1 tablespoon xanthan gum
1 tablespoon butter, softened
1 egg, beaten
Cooking spray

1. Place the Cook & Crisp Basket in your Pressure Cooker Steam Fryer. 2. Squeeze the zucchini to get rid of vegetable juice and transfer in the big bowl. Add flax meal, salt, almond flour, baking powder, chili flakes, xanthan gum, and stir well. After this, add butter and egg. Knead the non-sticky dough. Place it on the baking paper and cover with the second sheet of baking paper. Roll up the prepared dough into the flat square. After this, remove the baking paper from the prepared dough surface. Cut it on medium size crackers. Line the Ninja Foodi Pressure Steam Fryer basket with baking paper and put the crackers inside in one layer. Grease them with cooking spray. 3. Put on the Smart Lid on top of the Ninja Foodi Steam Fryer. 4. Move the Lid Slider to the "Air Fry/Stovetop". Select the "Air Fry" mode for cooking. 5. Cook them at 355°F/180°C for 20 minutes.
Per serving: Calories 244; Fat: 9.1g; Sodium 1399mg; Carbs: 34.3g; Fiber: 8.7g; Sugars 15.7g; Protein 8.3g

Tacon Mexican Muffins

Prep Time: 10 minutes. | Cook Time: 15 minutes. | Serves: 4

1 cup beef	shredded
1 teaspoon taco seasonings	1 teaspoon tomato sauce
2 ounces Mexican blend cheese,	Cooking spray

1. Place the Cook & Crisp Basket in your Pressure Cooker Steam Fryer. 2. Meanwhile, in the mixing bowl mix up beef and taco seasonings. Grease the muffin molds with cooking spray. Then transfer the beef mixture in the muffin molds and top them with cheese and tomato sauce. Transfer the muffin molds in the Cook & Crisp Basket . Put on the Smart Lid on top of the Ninja Foodi Steam Fryer. Move the Lid Slider to the "Air Fry/Stovetop". Select the "Air Fry" mode for cooking. Adjust the cooking temperature to 375°F/190°C. 3. Cook for them for around 15 minutes.
Per serving: Calories 105; Fat: 2.4g; Sodium 812mg; Carbs: 12.2g; Fiber: 2.4g; Sugars 2.4g; Protein 9.5g

Mushroom Basil Bites

Prep Time: 5 minutes. | Cook Time: 12 minutes. | Serves: 6

Salt and black pepper to the taste	½ pound mushrooms, minced
1 and ¼ cups coconut flour	1 egg, whisked
2 garlic clove, minced	Cooking spray
2 tablespoons basil, minced	

1. Place the Cook & Crisp Basket in your Pressure Cooker Steam Fryer. 2. In a suitable bowl, mix all the recipe ingredients except the cooking spray, stir well and shape medium balls out of this mix. Arrange the balls in the Cook & Crisp Basket, grease them with cooking spray. Put on the Smart Lid on top of the Ninja Foodi Steam Fryer. Move the Lid Slider to the "Air Fry/Stovetop". Select the "Air Fry" mode for cooking. Air Fry at 350°F/175°C for around 6 minutes on each side. Serve as an appetizer.
Per serving: Calories 151; Fat: 10.4g; Sodium 703mg; Carbs: 9.2g; Fiber: 0g; Sugars 8.7g; Protein 6g

Bacon Chaffle

Prep Time: 10 minutes. | Cook Time: 25 minutes. | Serves: 4

4 eggs, beaten	¼ teaspoon salt
2 ounces bacon, chopped, cooked	½ teaspoon black pepper
1 cucumber, pickled, grated	Cooking spray
2 ounces Cheddar cheese, shredded	

1. Place the Cook & Crisp Basket in your Pressure Cooker Steam Fryer. 2. In the mixing bowl mix up eggs, bacon, pickled cucumber, cheese, salt, and black pepper. Mix the mixture gently. 3. Then grease the Cook & Crisp Basket with cooking spray. Pour ¼ part of the liquid inside. 4. Put chaffle in the "cook & crisp basket" . Put on the Smart Lid on top of the Ninja Foodi Steam Fryer. Move the Lid Slider to the "Air Fry/Stovetop". Select the "Air Fry" mode for cooking. 5. Adjust the cooking temperature to 400°F/200°C. 6. Cook for it for around 6 minutes. 7. Then transfer the cooked chaffle in the plate. 8. Repeat the same steps with the remaining chaffle batter. In the end, you should get 4 chaffles.
Per serving: Calories 209; Fat: 15.8g; Sodium 3342mg; Carbs: 0.4g; Fiber: 0.2g; Sugars 0g; Protein 5.4g

Crispy Zucchini Chips

Prep Time: 5 minutes. | Cook Time: 15 minutes. | Serves: 6

3 zucchinis, sliced	2 eggs, whisked
Salt and black pepper to the taste	1 cup almond flour

1. Place the Cook & Crisp Basket in your Pressure Cooker Steam Fryer. 2. In a suitable bowl, mix the eggs with black pepper and salt. Put the flour in a second bowl. Dredge the zucchinis in flour and then in eggs. Arrange the chips in the Cook & Crisp Basket. Put on the Smart Lid on top of the Ninja Foodi Steam Fryer. 3. Move the Lid Slider to the "Air Fry/Stovetop". Select the "Air Fry" mode for cooking. 4. Air Fry at 350°F/175°C for around 15 minutes and serve as a snack.

Per serving: Calories 270; Fat: 8.4g; Sodium 1761mg; Carbs: 35.7g; Fiber: 13.3g; Sugars 4.1g; Protein 4.8g

Cheddar Cheese Rounds

Prep Time: 10 minutes. | Cook Time: 6 minutes. | Serves: 4

1 cup Cheddar cheese, shredded

1. Place the Cook & Crisp Basket in your Pressure Cooker Steam Fryer. 2. Then line the Ninja Foodi Pressure Steam Fryer basket with baking paper. Sprinkle the cheese on the baking paper in the shape of small rounds. 3. Put on the Smart Lid on top of the Ninja Foodi Steam Fryer. 4. Move the Lid Slider to the "Air Fry/Stovetop". Select the "Air Fry" mode for cooking. 5. Adjust the cooking temperature to 400°F/200°C. 6. Cook them for around 6 minutes or until the cheese is melted and starts to be crispy.
Per serving: Calories 291; Fat: 10.8g; Sodium 2153mg; Carbs: 12.1g; Fiber: 1.6g; Sugars 5.6g; Protein 7g

Cheese Sticks

Prep Time: 10 minutes. | Cook Time: 4 minutes. | Serves: 4

1 egg, beaten	6 ounces Provolone cheese
4 tablespoons coconut flakes	Cooking spray
1 teaspoon paprika	

1. Place the Cook & Crisp Basket in your Pressure Cooker Steam Fryer. 2. Cut the cheese into sticks. Then dip every cheese stick in the beaten egg. After this, mix up coconut flakes and paprika. Coat the cheese sticks in the coconut mixture. Put the cheese sticks in the Cook & Crisp Basket and grease them with cooking spray. 3. Put on the Smart Lid on top of the Ninja Foodi Steam Fryer. 4. Move the Lid Slider to the "Air Fry/Stovetop". Select the "Air Fry" mode for cooking. 5. Adjust the cooking temperature to 400°F/200°C. 6. Cook the meal for around 2 minutes from each side. Cool them well before serving.
Per serving: Calories 285; Fat: 7.5g; Sodium 367mg; Carbs: 50.6g; Fiber: 9.6g; Sugars 18.2g; Protein 4.4g

Bacon Sprouts Wraps

Prep Time: 5 minutes. | Cook Time: 20 minutes. | Serves: 12

12 bacon strips	A drizzle of olive oil
12 Brussels sprouts	

1. Place the Cook & Crisp Basket in your Pressure Cooker Steam Fryer. 2. Wrap each Brussels sprouts in a bacon strip, brush them with some oil, put them in the Cook & Crisp Basket. Put on the Smart Lid on top of the Ninja Foodi Steam Fryer. Move the Lid Slider to the "Air Fry/Stovetop". Select the "Air Fry" mode for cooking. Air Fry at 350°F/175°C for around 20 minutes. Serve as an appetizer.
Per serving: Calories 330; Fat: 29.1g; Sodium 348mg; Carbs: 12.6g; Fiber: 1.6g; Sugars 0g; Protein 7.7g

Crusted Zucchini Chips

Prep Time: 10 minutes. | Cook Time: 13 minutes. | Serves: 8

2 zucchinis, sliced	2 eggs, beaten
4 tablespoons almond flour	½ teaspoon white pepper
2 ounces Parmesan	Cooking spray

1. Place the Cook & Crisp Basket in your Pressure Cooker Steam Fryer. 2. In a suitable bowl, mix up almond flour, Parmesan, and white pepper. Then dip the zucchini slices in the egg and coat in the almond flour mixture. Place the prepared zucchini slices in the Cook & Crisp Basket in one layer . Put on the Smart Lid on top of the Ninja Foodi Steam Fryer. Move the Lid Slider to the "Air Fry/Stovetop". Select the "Air Fry" mode for cooking. Cook them at 355°F/180°C for around 10 minutes. Then flip the vegetables on another side. Cook for them for around 3 minutes more or until crispy.
Per serving: Calories 195; Fat: 12.7g; Sodium 1131mg; Carbs: 27.7g; Fiber: 3.5g; Sugars 5.9g; Protein 2.1g

Coconut Granola

Prep Time: 10 minutes. | Cook Time: 12 minutes. | Serves: 4

1 teaspoon monk fruit	2 tablespoons coconut flakes
1 teaspoon almond butter	2 tablespoons pumpkin seeds,
1 teaspoon coconut oil	crushed
2 tablespoons almonds, chopped	1 teaspoon hemp seeds
1 teaspoon pumpkin puree	1 teaspoon flax seeds
½ teaspoon pumpkin pie spices	Cooking spray

1. Place the Cook & Crisp Basket in your Pressure Cooker Steam Fryer. 2. In the big bowl mix up almond butter and coconut oil. Microwave the mixture until it is melted. After this, in the separated bowl mix up monk fruit, pumpkin spices, coconut flakes, pumpkin seeds, hemp seeds, and flax seeds. Add the melted coconut oil and pumpkin puree. Then stir the mixture until it is homogenous. Then put the pumpkin mixture on the baking paper and make the shape of the square. After this, cut the square on the serving bars and transfer in the Cook & Crisp Basket Put on the Smart Lid on top of the Ninja Foodi Steam Fryer. 3. Move the Lid Slider to the "Air Fry/Stovetop". Select the "Air Fry" mode for cooking. Adjust the cooking temperature to 350°F/175°C. Cook the pumpkin granola for around 12 minutes.
Per serving: Calories 194; Fat: 10.9g; Sodium 292mg; Carbs: 21.7g; Fiber: 6.4g; Sugars 9g; Protein 6.4g

Beef Smokies

Prep Time: 15 minutes. | Cook Time: 10 minutes. | Serves: 10

12 ounces pork and beef smokies	1 teaspoon erythritol
3 ounces bacon, sliced	1 teaspoon olive oil
1 teaspoon keto tomato sauce	½ teaspoon cayenne pepper

1. Place the Cook & Crisp Basket in your Pressure Cooker Steam Fryer. 2. Sprinkle the smokies with cayenne pepper and tomato sauce. Then sprinkle them with erythritol and olive oil. After this, wrap every smokie in the bacon and secure it with the toothpick. Place the bacon smokies in the Cook & Crisp Basket. Put on the Smart Lid on top of the Ninja Foodi Steam Fryer. Move the Lid Slider to the "Air Fry/Stovetop". Select the "Air Fry" mode for cooking. 3. Adjust the cooking temperature to 400°F/200°C. 4. Cook for them for around 10 minutes. Shake them gently during cooking to avoid burning.
Per serving: Calories 171; Fat: 10g; Sodium 2629mg; Carbs: 18.6g; Fiber: 2.6g; Sugars 13.8g; Protein 4.3g

Shrimp Balls

Prep Time: 5 minutes. | Cook Time: 15 minutes. | Serves: 4

1-pound shrimp, peeled, deveined	½ cup coconut flour
and minced	1 tablespoon avocado oil
1 egg, whisked	1 tablespoon cilantro, chopped
3 tablespoons coconut, shredded	

1. Place the Cook & Crisp Basket in your Pressure Cooker Steam Fryer. 2. In a suitable bowl, mix all the recipe ingredients, stir well and shape medium balls out of this mix. Place the balls in your the Cook & Crisp Basket. 3. Put on the Smart Lid on top of the Ninja Foodi Steam Fryer. 4. Move the Lid Slider to the "Air Fry/Stovetop". Select the "Air Fry" mode for cooking. 5. Air Fry at 350°F/175°C for around 15 minutes and serve as an appetizer.
Per serving: Calories 120; Fat: 2.3g; Sodium 2mg; Carbs: 24.1g; Fiber: 2.3g; Sugars 10g; Protein 3.6g

Turmeric Chicken Bites

Prep Time: 10 minutes. | Cook Time: 12 minutes. | Serves: 6

8 ounces chicken fillet	½ teaspoon paprika
½ teaspoon black pepper	3 egg whites, whisked
½ teaspoon turmeric	4 tablespoons almond flour
¼ teaspoon coriander	Cooking spray

1. Place the Cook & Crisp Basket in your Pressure Cooker Steam Fryer. 2. In the shallow bowl mix up black pepper, turmeric, coriander, and paprika. Then chop the chicken fillet on the small cubes and sprinkle them with spice mixture. Stir well and add egg white. Mix up the chicken and egg whites well. After this, coat every chicken cube in the almond flour. Put the chicken cubes in the Ninja Foodi Pressure Steam Fryer basket in one layer and gently spray with cooking spray. Put on the Smart Lid on top of the Ninja Foodi Steam Fryer. Move the Lid Slider to the "Air Fry/Stovetop". Select the "Air Fry" mode for cooking. Adjust the cooking temperature to 375°F/190°C. Cook the chicken popcorn for around 7 minutes. Then shake the chicken popcorn well .Cook for it for around 5 minutes more.
Per serving: Calories 139; Fat: 11.9g; Sodium 60mg; Carbs: 5.4g; Fiber: 3.1g; Sugars 1g; Protein 5g

Cashew Dip

Prep Time: 5 minutes. | Cook Time: 8 minutes. | Serves: 6

½ cup cashews, soaked in water	1 teaspoon lime juice
for around 4 hours and drained	A pinch of salt and black pepper
3 tablespoons cilantro, chopped	2 tablespoons coconut milk
2 garlic cloves, minced	

1. Place the Cook & Crisp Basket in your Pressure Cooker Steam Fryer. 2. In a blender, mix all the recipe ingredients, pulse well and transfer to the Cook & Crisp Basket. Put on the Smart Lid on top of the Ninja Foodi Steam Fryer. Move the Lid Slider to the "Air Fry/Stovetop". Select the "Air Fry" mode for cooking. Air Fry at 350°F/175°C for around 8 minutes. Serve as a party dip.
Per serving: Calories 187; Fat: 18.3g; Sodium 596mg; Carbs: 4.9g; Fiber: 1.1g; Sugars 0g; Protein 3.1g

Bacon Bites

Prep Time: 5 minutes. | Cook Time: 10 minutes. | Serves: 4

4 bacon slices, halved	A pinch of pink salt
1 cup dark chocolate, melted	

1. Place the Cook & Crisp Basket in your Pressure Cooker Steam Fryer. 2. Dip each bacon slice in some chocolate, sprinkle pink salt over them, put them in the Cook & Crisp Basket. Put on the Smart Lid on top of the Ninja Foodi Steam Fryer. Move the Lid Slider to the "Air Fry/Stovetop". Select the "Air Fry" mode for cooking. Air Fry at 350°F/175°C for around 10 minutes. Serve as a snack.
Per serving: Calories 68; Fat: 7g; Sodium 475mg; Carbs: 1.8g; Fiber: 0.3g; Sugars 0g; Protein 0.5g

Pickled Bacon

Prep Time: 5 minutes. | Cook Time: 20 minutes. | Serves: 4

4 dill pickle spears, sliced in half	8 bacon slices, halved
and quartered	1 cup avocado mayonnaise

1. Place the Cook & Crisp Basket in your Pressure Cooker Steam Fryer. 2. Wrap each pickle spear in a bacon slice, put them in the Cook & Crisp Basket. Put on the Smart Lid on top of the Ninja Foodi Steam Fryer. Move the Lid Slider to the "Air Fry/Stovetop". Select the "Air Fry" mode for cooking. Air Fry at 400°F/200°C for around 20 minutes. Divide into bowls and serve as a snack with the mayonnaise.
Per serving: Calories 98; Fat: 7.2g; Sodium 475mg; Carbs: 8.7g; Fiber: 3.9g; Sugars 1.6g; Protein 2.2g

Air-Fried Pork Rinds

Prep Time: 10 minutes. | Cook Time: 10 minutes. | Serves: 3

6 ounces pork skin	1 teaspoon olive oil
1 tablespoon keto tomato sauce	

1. Place the Cook & Crisp Basket in your Pressure Cooker Steam Fryer. 2. Chop the pork skin into the rinds and sprinkle with the sauce and olive oil. Mix up well. Place the pork skin rinds in the Ninja Foodi Pressure Steam Fryer basket in one layer. Put on the Smart Lid on top of the Ninja Foodi Steam Fryer. Move the Lid Slider to the "Air Fry/Stovetop". Select the "Air Fry" mode for cooking. Adjust the cooking temperature to 400°F/200°C. 3. Cook for around 10 minutes. Flip the rinds on another side after 5 minutes of cooking.
Per serving: Calories 342; Fat: 0g; Sodium 1mg; Carbs: 10.6g; Fiber: 2g; Sugars 7.8g; Protein 0.2g

Avocado Balls

Prep Time: 5 minutes. | Cook Time: 5 minutes. | Serves: 4

1 avocado, peeled, pitted and mashed
¼ cup ghee, melted
2 garlic cloves, minced
2 spring onions, minced
1 chili pepper, chopped
1 tablespoon lime juice
2 tablespoons cilantro
A pinch of salt and black pepper
4 bacon slices, cooked and crumbled
Cooking spray

1. Place the Cook & Crisp Basket in your Pressure Cooker Steam Fryer. 2. In a suitable bowl, mix all the recipe ingredients except the cooking spray, stir well and shape medium balls out of this mix. Place them in the Cook & Crisp Basket, grease with cooking spray. Put on the Smart Lid on top of the Ninja Foodi Steam Fryer. Move the Lid Slider to the "Air Fry/Stovetop". Select the "Air Fry" mode for cooking. Air Fry at 370°F/185°C for around 5 minutes. Serve as a snack.
Per serving: Calories 52; Fat: 3.5g; Sodium 702mg; Carbs: 3g; Fiber: 1.4g; Sugars 0.1g; Protein 1.4g

Avocado Wraps

Prep Time: 5 minutes. | Cook Time: 15 minutes. | Serves: 4

2 avocados, peeled, and cut into 12 wedges
12 bacon strips
1 tablespoon ghee, melted

1. Place the Cook & Crisp Basket in your Pressure Cooker Steam Fryer. 2. Wrap each avocado wedge in a bacon strip, brush them with the ghee, put them in the Cook & Crisp Basket. Put on the Smart Lid on top of the Ninja Foodi Steam Fryer. Move the Lid Slider to the "Air Fry/Stovetop". Select the "Air Fry" mode for cooking. Air Fry at 360°F/180°C for around 15 minutes. Serve as an appetizer.
Per serving: Calories 137; Fat: 7.1g; Sodium 167mg; Carbs: 16.2g; Fiber: 3.8g; Sugars 4.7g; Protein 3.1g

Flavored Chicken Meatballs

Prep Time: 5 minutes. | Cook Time: 20 minutes. | Serves: 12

2-pound chicken breast, skinless, boneless and
A pinch of salt and black pepper
2 garlic cloves, minced
2 spring onions, chopped
2 tablespoons ghee, melted
6 tablespoons keto hot sauce
¾ cup almond meal
Cooking spray

1. Place the Cook & Crisp Basket in your Pressure Cooker Steam Fryer. 2. In a suitable bowl, mix all the recipe ingredients except the cooking spray, stir well and shape medium meatballs out of this mix. Arrange the meatballs in the Cook & Crisp Basket, grease them with cooking spray. Put on the Smart Lid on top of the Ninja Foodi Steam Fryer. Move the Lid Slider to the "Air Fry/Stovetop". Select the "Air Fry" mode for cooking. Air Fry at 360°F/180°C for around 20 minutes. Serve as an appetizer.
Per serving: Calories 136; Fat: 14.3g; Sodium 9mg; Carbs: 3.5g; Fiber: 0g; Sugars 0g; Protein 0.3g

Crusted Hot Dogs

Prep Time: 15 minutes. | Cook Time: 5 minutes. | Serves: 4

4 hot dogs
1 egg, beaten
⅓ cup coconut flour
½ teaspoon turmeric

1. Place the Cook & Crisp Basket in your Pressure Cooker Steam Fryer. 2. In the bowl mix up egg, coconut flour, and turmeric. Then dip the hot dogs in the mixture. Transfer the hot dogs in the freezer and freeze them for around 5 minutes. Place the frozen hot dogs in the Ninja Foodi Pressure Steam Fryer basket. Put on the Smart Lid on top of the Ninja Foodi Steam Fryer. Move the Lid Slider to the "Air Fry/Stovetop". Select the "Air Fry" mode for cooking. Adjust the cooking temperature to 400°F/200°C. Cook for them for around 6 minutes or until they are light brown.
Per serving: Calories 236; Fat: 8.1g; Sodium 14mg; Carbs: 42.1g; Fiber: 6.3g; Sugars 0.8g; Protein 2.3g

Salmon Bites

Prep Time: 5 minutes. | Cook Time: 10 minutes. | Serves: 12

2 avocados, peeled, pitted and mashed
4 ounces smoked salmon, skinless, boneless and chopped
2 tablespoons coconut cream
1 teaspoon avocado oil
1 teaspoon dill, chopped
A pinch of salt and black pepper

1. Place the Cook & Crisp Basket in your Pressure Cooker Steam Fryer. 2. In a suitable bowl, mix all the recipe ingredients, stir well and shape medium balls out of this mix. Place them in the Cook & Crisp Basket. Put on the Smart Lid on top of the Ninja Foodi Steam Fryer. Move the Lid Slider to the "Air Fry/Stovetop". Select the "Air Fry" mode for cooking. Air Fry at 350°F/175°C for around 10 minutes. Serve as an appetizer.
Per serving: Calories 122; Fat: 10.1g; Sodium 143mg; Carbs: 4.9g; Fiber: 1.2g; Sugars 1.1g; Protein 3.6g

Eggplant Chips

Prep Time: 10 minutes. | Cook Time: 25 minutes. | Serves: 4

1 eggplant, sliced
1 teaspoon garlic powder
1 tablespoon olive oil

1. Place the Cook & Crisp Basket in your Pressure Cooker Steam Fryer. 2. Mix up olive oil and garlic powder. Then brush every eggplant slice with a garlic powder mixture. Place the eggplant slices in the Ninja Foodi Pressure Steam Fryer basket in one layer. Put on the Smart Lid on top of the Ninja Foodi Steam Fryer. Move the Lid Slider to the "Air Fry/Stovetop". Select the "Air Fry" mode for cooking. Cook them at 400°F/200°C for around 15 minutes. Then flip the eggplant slices on another side. 3. Cook for around 10 minutes.
Per serving: Calories 36; Fat: 1g; Sodium 1159mg; Carbs: 2.1g; Fiber: 0.6g; Sugars 1.3g; Protein 3.9g

Meatballs

Prep Time: 5 minutes. | Cook Time: 20 minutes. | Serves: 6

1-pound beef meat,
1 teaspoon onion powder
1 teaspoon garlic powder
A pinch of salt and black pepper
2 tablespoons chives, chopped
Cooking spray

1. Place the Cook & Crisp Basket in your Pressure Cooker Steam Fryer. 2. In a suitable bowl, mix all the recipe ingredients except the cooking spray, stir well and shape medium meatballs out of this mix. Pace them in the Cook & Crisp Basket, grease with cooking spray. Put on the Smart Lid on top of the Ninja Foodi Steam Fryer. Move the Lid Slider to the "Air Fry/Stovetop". Select the "Air Fry" mode for cooking. Air Fry at 360°F/180°C for around 20 minutes. Serve as an appetizer.
Per serving: Calories 176; Fat: 9.6g; Sodium 122mg; Carbs: 15.7g; Fiber: 4.5g; Sugars 3.8g; Protein 7.8g

Duck Wraps

Prep Time: 15 minutes. | Cook Time: 6 minutes. | Serves: 6

1-pound duck fillet, boiled
1 tablespoon mascarpone
1 teaspoon chili flakes
1 teaspoon onion powder
6 wonton wraps
1 egg yolk, whisked
Cooking spray

1. Place the Cook & Crisp Basket in your Pressure Cooker Steam Fryer. 2. Shred the boiled duck fillet and mix it up with mascarpone, chili flakes, and onion powder. After this, fill the wonton wraps with the duck mixture and roll them in the shape of pies. Brush the duck pies with the egg yolk. Put the duck pies in the Cook & Crisp Basket and grease them with the cooking spray. Put on the Smart Lid on top of the Ninja Foodi Steam Fryer. 3. Move the Lid Slider to the "Air Fry/Stovetop". Select the "Air Fry" mode for cooking. 4. Adjust the cooking temperature to 385°F/195°C. Cook the snack for around 3 minutes from each side.
Per serving: Calories 72; Fat: 5g; Sodium 70mg; Carbs: 0.4g; Fiber: 0g; Sugars 0.4g; Protein 6.3g

Sushi

Prep Time: 10 minutes. | Cook Time: 10 minutes. | Serves: 10

10 bacon slices
2 tablespoons cream cheese

1 cucumber

1. Place the Cook & Crisp Basket in your Pressure Cooker Steam Fryer. 2. Place the bacon slices in the Cook & Crisp Basket in one layer . Put on the Smart Lid on top of the Ninja Foodi Steam Fryer. Move the Lid Slider to the "Air Fry/Stovetop". Select the "Air Fry" mode for cooking. Cook for around 10 minutes at 400°F/200°C. Meanwhile, cut the cucumber into small wedges. When the bacon is cooked, cool it to the room temperature and spread with cream cheese. Then place the cucumber wedges over the cream cheese and roll the bacon into the sushi.
Per serving: Calories 110; Fat: 4.3g; Sodium 81mg; Carbs: 16.4g; Fiber: 5.4g; Sugars 6.1g; Protein 3.8g

Classic Pork Meatballs

Prep Time: 5 minutes. | Cook Time: 20 minutes. | Serves: 12

1-pound pork meat,
3 spring onions, minced
3 tablespoons cilantro, chopped
1 tablespoon ginger, grated
2 garlic cloves, minced

1 chili pepper, minced
A pinch of salt and black pepper
1 and ½ tablespoons coconut aminos
Cooking spray

1. Place the Cook & Crisp Basket in your Pressure Cooker Steam Fryer. 2. In a suitable bowl, mix all the recipe ingredients except the cooking spray, stir really well and shape medium meatballs out of this mix. Arrange them in the Cook & Crisp Basket, grease with cooking spray. Put on the Smart Lid on top of the Ninja Foodi Steam Fryer. Move the Lid Slider to the "Air Fry/Stovetop". Select the "Air Fry" mode for cooking. Air Fry at 380°F/195°C for around 20 minutes. Serve as an appetizer.
Per serving: Calories 110; Fat: 3.4g; Sodium 1446mg; Carbs: 13.9g; Fiber: 5.4g; Sugars 3.8g; Protein 8.2g

Chapter 7 Dessert Recipes

147 Nutty Cake
147 Spiced Pumpkin Pudding
147 Lemon Cheesecake
147 Sweet Raspberry Curd
147 Chocolate Pudding Cake
147 Delicious Banana Bread
148 Poached Spiced Pears with Pomegranate
148 Matcha Cake
148 Flan
148 Creamy Raspberry Jam
148 Sweet Pecans
148 Red Cherry Compote
148 Baked Avocado
149 Tangy Fruit Salad Jam
149 Delicious Cranberry Pudding
149 syrupy Crème Brulee
149 Regular Chocolate Pudding
149 Caramel Pear Pudding
149 Fudge Brownies
150 Sweet Tapioca
150 nutty Chocolate Candy
150 Vegan Coconut Yogurt
150 yellow Marmalade
150 Delicious Blueberries Yogurt
150 Air Fried Walnut Bars
150 Blondies
151 sweet Quiche
151 Easy Chocolate Cream
151 Ricotta Vanilla Cookies
151 Cream Cheese Cinnamon Pie
151 Greece Style Yogurt Cake
151 Easy Pecan Cobbler
151 Homemade Pecan Nutella
151 Cocoa Ricotta Pudding
152 Zesty Lemon Biscotti
152 Chia Egg Pie
152 Ricotta Cheese Muffins
152 Orange Nutmeg Galettes
152 Rhubarb Cream Pie
152 Lemon Cream Pie
152 Sponge Cake
152 Baked Sweet Cantaloupe
153 Mini Cheesecakes
153 Orange Custard

153 Carambola Chips
153 Sweet Blueberries Muffins
153 Cinnamon Plum
153 Peanuts Cupcakes
153 Blackberry Butter Cake
154 Rum Lava Cake
154 Easy Chocolate Cake
154 Roasted Apple Crisp
154 Macaroons
154 Rice Cake
154 Strawberry Rolls
155 Vanilla Custard
155 Fried Pancake Oreos
155 Sweet Gingerbread
155 Grilled Pineapple
155 Easy Peach Cobbler
155 Swiss Roll
156 Sweet Potato Donut
156 Fried Pies
156 Zesty Raspberry Muffins
156 Vanilla Pecan Pie
156 Honey Chocolate Cookies
156 Easy Butter Cake
157 Chocolate Mug Cake
157 Pound Cake
157 Almond Pears
157 Baked Butter Apple
157 Coconut Pie
157 Butter Peach Crumble
157 Banana Cake
158 Lemon Cake
158 Dough Dippers with Chocolate Sauce
158 Pumpkin Pudding
158 Air-Fried Peach Slices
158 Marshmallow Fluff Turnover
158 Easy Vanilla Soufflé
159 Blackberry Granola Crisp
159 Dark Brownies
159 Quick Peanut Butter Cookies
159 Walnut Bread
159 Sugary Churros
159 Avocado Cocoa Pudding
159 Chia Coconut Pudding
160 Toasted Flakes

160 Poppy Seed Cake
160 Strawberry Shortcake
160 Ginger Bacon Bites
160 Chocolate Cake
161 Pear Crumble
161 Pineapple Galette
161 Apple Butter
161 Crispy Pork Rinds
161 Chocolate-Covered Bacon
161 Apple Almond Turnovers
162 Espresso Brownies
162 Prune Muffins
162 Chocolate Muffins
162 Cranberry Cake
162 White Chocolate Cookies
162 Sweet Lemon Bars
163 Macadamia Cookies
163 Almond Cookies
163 Soft Raisin Muffins
163 Coconut Cake
163 Crispy Profiteroles
163 Pineapple with Macadamia Batter
164 Cranberry Brownies
164 Prune Cookies
164 Pudding with Sultanas
164 Clafoutis
164 Orange Cake
164 Apricots in Whiskey Sauce
164 Cracker S'mores
165 Cinnamon Pear Clafoutis
165 Frosted Blackberry Shortcake
165 Peach Walnut Parfaits
165 Cinnamon Flour Twists
165 Chocolate Egg Rolls
165 Confetti Cake
166 Blueberry Oats Crisp
166 Cinnamon Stuffed Apples
166 Raspberry Pineapple Sundaes
166 Gooey Brownies
166 Chocolate Cookie Cups
166 Vegan Apple Pies
167 Spice Monkey Bread
167 Cinnamon Beignets
167 Flaxseed Carrot Cake
167 Chia Pudding Tarts

Nutty Cake

Prep time: 10 minutes| Cook time: 40 minutes| Serves: 8

½ cup almond flour
½ cup unbleached flour
½ cup unsweetened shredded coconut
⅓ cup sugar

1 teaspoon baking powder
1 teaspoon apple pie spice
2 eggs
¼ cup butter
½ cup heavy whipping cream

1. Blend the dry ingredients in a medium bowl. Mix the wet ingredients in the bowl one at a time. Pour the mix into a greased cake pan and cover with foil. Pour 2 cups of water into the pot. Put the cake pan on the Deluxe Reversible Rack and lower it into the pan in Ninja Foodi XL Pressure Cooker Steam Fryer. 2. Lock lid; move slider towards PRESSURE. Adjust pressure release valve in the SEAL position. Close pressure-release valve. The cooking temperature will default to HIGH, which is accurate. Set time to 40 minutes. Select START/STOP and start cooking. 3. When cooking is complete, let pressure release naturally for 10 minutes. Remove from the pot and allow to cool an additional 15 minutes before serving.
Per Serving: Calories 118; Fat 7.2g; Sodium 232mg; Carbs 14g; Fiber 1g; Sugar 11g; Protein 2g

Spiced Pumpkin Pudding

Prep time: 2 minutes| Cook time: 6 minutes| Serves: 4

1 tablespoon vanilla
1 teaspoon pumpkin pie spice
2 eggs
¼ cup sugar

3 tablespoons cornstarch
15 ounce can pumpkin puree
12 ounce can evaporated milk

1. Beat the eggs in a medium bowl. Mix in half the milk, the pumpkin puree, and the vanilla into the eggs and set aside. Mix the sugar, spice, and starch together in the cooking pot. 2. Move the slider towards "AIR FRY/STOVETOP" and set Ninja Foodi XL Pressure Cooker Steam Fryer with SmartLid to SEAR/SAUTÉ mode. Adjust the temperature to "Hi5" by using up arrow. Press START/STOP to begin cooking. Slowly stir in the remaining milk to the pot. Continue stirring on Sauté for about 3 minutes. 3. Press the START/STOP and mix in the pumpkin spice mix. Turn the pot back to SEAR/SAUTÉ and stir continuously for another 3 minutes. 4. Remove from heat and allow to cool before eating. Add a dollop of whipped cream or vanilla ice cream for a treat.
Per Serving: Calories 350; Fat 22.5g; Sodium 166mg; Carbs 38g; Fiber 1g; Sugar 25g; Protein 1g

Lemon Cheesecake

Prep time: 10 minutes| Cook time: 35 minutes| Serves: 8

¾ cup almond flour
⅔ cup sugar
⅛ teaspoon salt
2 tablespoons butter
1 lb. cream cheese
¼ cup lemon juice

1 teaspoon lemon zest
1 teaspoon lemon extract
2 eggs
2 tablespoons heavy whipping cream

1. Line Cook & Crisp Basket with parchment paper and set aside. Melt the butter in a bowl and mix in the salt, almond flour, and 2 tablespoons sugar to make crust mixture. Press the crust into the Cook & Crisp Basket and set aside. 2. Beat the cream cheese in a medium bowl until smooth, then mix in the lemon juice, zest, and extract. Beat in the eggs one at a time. Beat in the cream then pour the mixture onto the prepared crust. 3. Wrap the Cook & Crisp Basket in foil and place it on the Deluxe Reversible Rack. Pour 1 cup of water into the pot and lower the Deluxe Reversible Rack into the pot. 4. Lock lid; move slider towards PRESSURE. Adjust pressure release valve in the SEAL position. Close pressure-release valve. 5. The cooking temperature will default to HIGH, which is accurate. Set time to 35 minutes. Select START/STOP and start cooking. 6. When cooking is complete, let pressure release naturally. Transfer the cake to the refrigerator for a few hours before serving.
Per Serving: Calories 429; Fat 32g; Sodium 325mg; Carbs 5g; Fiber 1g; Sugar 3g; Protein 5g

Sweet Raspberry Curd

Prep time: 5 minutes| Cook time: 25 minutes| Serves: 8

18 oz. raspberries
1½ cups sugar
3 tablespoon lemon juice

3 egg yolks
3 tablespoon butter

1. In the Ninja Foodi XL Pressure Cooker Steam Fryer, combine the raspberries, sugar and lemon juice. Lock lid; move slider towards PRESSURE. Adjust pressure release valve in the SEAL position. Close pressure-release valve. The cooking temperature will default to HIGH, which is accurate. Set time to 2 minutes. Select START/STOP and start cooking. When cooking is complete, let pressure release naturally for 5 minutes, then quickly release by turning it into VENT position. 2. Open the lid. Use the mesh strainer to puree the raspberries and remove the seeds. In a bowl, whisk egg yolks and combine with the raspberries puree. Return the mixture to the pot. Move the slider towards "AIR FRY/STOVETOP" and set Ninja Foodi XL Pressure Cooker Steam Fryer with SmartLid to SEAR/SAUTÉ mode. Adjust the temperature to "Hi5" by using up arrow. Press START/STOP to begin cooking. 3. Bring the mixture to a boil, stirring constantly. Press the START/STOP key to stop the SAUTÉ function. Add the butter and stir to combine. Serve chilled.
Per Serving: Calories 354; Fat 7.9g; Sodium 704mg; Carbs 6g; Fiber 3.6g; Sugar 6g; Protein 18g

Chocolate Pudding Cake

Prep time: 15 minutes| Cook time: 15 minutes| Serves: 2

¾ cup butter
2 ounces unsweetened chocolate
½ cup heavy cream
2 tablespoons instant coffee crystals
1 teaspoon vanilla extract

4 tablespoons unsweetened cocoa powder
⅓ cup almond flour
⅛ teaspoon salt
5 eggs
⅔ cup sugar

1. Move the slider towards "AIR FRY/STOVETOP" and set Ninja Foodi XL Pressure Cooker Steam Fryer with SmartLid to SEAR/SAUTÉ mode. Adjust the temperature to "Hi5" by using up arrow. Press START/STOP to begin cooking. 2. Add the butter and chocolate. Stir continuously until melted then remove from heat. In one small bowl mix together the heavy cream, coffee crystals, and vanilla. 3. In a separate small bowl mix the cocoa, flour, and salt. In a third small bowl beat the eggs then mix in the sugar. Mix the eggs into the pot. Add the cocoa, stirring continuously. Add in the cream mix stirring continuously until an even batter forms. 4. Lock lid; move slider to STEAMCRISP. Select STEAM & BAKE, set temperature to 400°F/200°C, and set time to 9 minutes. Press START/STOP to begin cooking.
Per Serving: Calories 173; Fat 13.6g; Sodium 281mg; Carbs 3g; Fiber 1g; Sugar 1g; Protein 10g

Delicious Banana Bread

Prep time: 15 minutes| Cook time: 1 hour 10 minutes | Serves: 6

1-½ cups unbleached flour
½ cup sugar or sugar substitute
2 teaspoons baking powder
½ teaspoon baking soda
½ teaspoon vanilla extract
½ teaspoon sea salt

1 cup ripe bananas, mashed
⅓ cup softened butter
¼ cup milk
1 egg
¼ cup walnuts, chopped

1. Combine the flour, sugar, baking powder, baking soda and salt in a large mixing bowl; whisk until the ingredients are well mixed. Fold in the bananas, butter, milk, egg and vanilla extract. 2. Use an electric mixer to mix until the batter has a uniform thick consistency. Fold in chopped walnuts. Grease the bottom of the cooking pot with non-stick cooking spray. Pour batter into cooking pot. 3. Lock lid; move slider to AIR FRY/STOVETOP. Select STEAM, and set time to 30 minutes. Press START/STOP to begin cooking. Cook for 30 minutes more. 4. Transfer to plate and let cool for one hour before serving.
Per Serving: Calories 105; Fat 5g; Sodium 233mg; Carbs 7g; Fiber 2g; Sugar 4g; Protein 8g

Poached Spiced Pears with Pomegranate

Prep time: 10 minutes| Cook time: 55 minutes| Serves: 4

2 firm Anjou or Bosc pears, peeled, halved, and cored
2 cups pomegranate juice
2 cups apple cider
2 cinnamon sticks
1 large orange peel, about 1 inch
thick
2 whole cloves
1 pinch of freshly shaved nutmeg
1-piece fresh ginger peeled, cut into thin slivers
Vanilla ice cream, optional

1. Add all ingredients to the cooking pot of the Ninja Foodi XL Pressure Cooker Steam Fryer. 2. Lock lid; move slider to AIR FRY/STOVETOP. Select STEAM, and set time to 30 minutes. Press START/STOP to begin cooking. Cook for 20 minutes more. 3. Open the lid and flip the pears over; let rest for 1 hour. Turn pears over again and let sit for another hour. 4. Serve warm with vanilla ice cream, or refrigerate overnight for a more intense flavor and color.
Per Serving: Calories 200; Fat 15.6g; Sodium 165mg; Carbs 5g; Fiber 1g; Sugar 2g; Protein 10g

Matcha Cake

Prep time: 8 minutes| Cook time: 30 minutes | Serves: 4

2 large eggs
1 cup unbleached flour
½ cup sugar
½ cup butter
1 tablespoon green tea matcha powder
½ teaspoon baking powder

1. Combine all of the ingredients in a large mixing bowl. Grease the cooking pot of the Ninja Foodi XL Pressure Cooker Steam Fryer with non-stick cooking spray. 2. Add the cake mix to the cooking pot. Lock lid; move slider to STEAMCRISP. Select STEAM & BAKE, set temperature to 400°F/200°C, and set time to 30 minutes. Press START/STOP to begin cooking. 3. Open the lid. Transfer to a plate to cool for 20 minutes and serve!
Per Serving: Calories 138; Fat 10.6g; Sodium 102mg; Carbs 1g; Fiber 0g; Sugar 1g; Protein 9g

Flan

Prep time: 15 minutes| Cook time: 1 HOUR 10 minutes|
Serves: 4

6 egg yolks
1 (12 oz.) can evaporated milk
1 (12 oz.) can condensed milk
1 teaspoon pure vanilla extract
¼ cup granulated sugar, for caramel sauce
One flan mold

1. Gently combine the egg yolk, condensed milk, evaporated milk and vanilla in a large mixing bowl and set aside. Add granulated sugar to a saucepan and heat on a stove at medium-low, while stirring; turn off the heat when sugar is melted and caramel colored, and assemble flan. Pour the custard into the flan mold. 2. Add caramel sauce evenly over custard. Place flan in the Cook & Crisp Basket. 3. Lock lid; move slider to AIR FRY/STOVETOP. Select STEAM, and set time to 30 minutes. Press START/STOP to begin cooking. Cook for 30 minutes more. 4. Let it cool completely, transfer to a plate, and serve!
Per Serving: Calories 311; Fat 6g; Sodium 112mg; Carbs 15g; Fiber 6g; Sugar 12g; Protein 2g

Creamy Raspberry Jam

Prep time: 5 minutes| Cook time: 25 minutes| Serves: 8

4 cups raspberries (fresh or frozen)
1 cup sugar or ⅔ cup light honey
3 tablespoon lemon juice
1½ tablespoon cornstarch
1½ tablespoon water

1. In the Ninja Foodi XL Pressure Cooker Steam Fryer, combine the raspberries, sugar and lemon. Stir well. 2. Lock lid; move slider towards PRESSURE. Adjust pressure release valve in the SEAL position. Close pressure-release valve. The cooking temperature will default to HIGH, which is accurate. Set time to 3 minutes. Select START/STOP and start cooking. 3. When cooking is complete, let pressure release naturally for 10 minutes, then quickly release by turning it into VENT position. 4. Uncover the pot. In a cup, whisk together the cornstarch and water until combined. Pour this mixture in the pot and stir. 5. Let the jam cool and use up within a week, or freeze for later.
Per Serving: Calories 354; Fat 7.9g; Sodium 704mg; Carbs 6g; Fiber 3.6g; Sugar 6g; Protein 18g

Sweet Pecans

Prep time: 15 minutes| Cook time: 15 minutes| Serves: 2

3 cups pecan halves
⅓ teaspoon nutmeg
⅓ tablespoon cinnamon
⅓ tablespoon vanilla extract
½ cup maple syrup
⅓ teaspoon salt
½ cup water
¼ cup white sugar
¼ cup brown sugar

1. Move the slider towards "AIR FRY/STOVETOP" and set Ninja Foodi XL Pressure Cooker Steam Fryer with SmartLid to SEAR/SAUTÉ mode. Adjust the temperature to "Hi5" by using up arrow. Press START/STOP to begin cooking. In the Ninja Foodi XL Pressure Cooker Steam Fryer cooking pot, combine the pecans, nutmeg, cinnamon, vanilla, maple syrup and salt. Stirring constantly, cook for 7-10 minutes, until the pecans are tender. Press the START/STOP to stop the SAUTÉ function. Pour in the water. 2. Lock lid; move slider towards PRESSURE. Adjust pressure release valve in the SEAL position. Close pressure-release valve. The cooking temperature will default to HIGH, which is accurate. Set time to 20 minutes. Select START/STOP and start cooking. 3. When cooking is complete, let pressure release quickly by turning it into VENT position. Pour the pecans mixture onto the Cook & Crisp Basket. 4. Lock lid; move slider to STEAMCRISP. Select STEAM & BAKE, set temperature to 375°F/190°C, and set time to 10 minutes. Press START/STOP to begin cooking. Bake for 5 minutes then flip and cook for another 5 minutes. 5. Transfer the pecans to the bowl and let them cool for 10 minutes. Add sugar and mix well. Serve.
Per Serving: Calories 354; Fat 7.9g; Sodium 704mg; Carbs 6g; Fiber 3.6g; Sugar 6g; Protein 18g

Red Cherry Compote

Prep time: 15 minutes| Cook time: 15 minutes| Serves: 2

3 cups cherries, fresh or frozen
1 cup apples, peeled and diced
1 tablespoon coconut oil
¾ cup water
1½ tablespoon maple syrup
A pinch of salt
2 tablespoon cornstarch

1. In the Ninja Foodi XL Pressure Cooker Steam Fryer, combine the cherries, apples, coconut oil, water, maple syrup, and salt. 2. Lock lid; move slider towards PRESSURE. Adjust pressure release valve in the SEAL position. Close pressure-release valve. The cooking temperature will default to HIGH, which is accurate. Set time to 4 minutes. Select START/STOP and start cooking. 3. When cooking is complete, let pressure quickly release by turning it into VENT position. Carefully unlock the lid. Stir well. 4. Move the slider towards "AIR FRY/STOVETOP" and set Ninja Foodi XL Pressure Cooker Steam Fryer with SmartLid to SEAR/SAUTÉ mode. Adjust the temperature to "Hi5" by using up arrow. Press START/STOP to begin cooking. 5. Add the cornstarch, and stirring occasionally, bring the mixture to a boil. Press the START/STOP to stop the SAUTÉ function. Let the compote cool for 10 minutes. Serve.
Per Serving: Calories 354; Fat 7.9g; Sodium 704mg; Carbs 6g; Fiber 3.6g; Sugar 6g; Protein 18g

Baked Avocado

Prep Time: 5 minutes. | Cook Time: 20 minutes. | Serves: 2

1 avocado, pitted, halved
2 teaspoons sugar
1 teaspoon vanilla extract
2 teaspoons butter

1. Place the Cook & Crisp Basket in your Ninja Foodi Pressure Cooker Steam Fryer. 2. Sprinkle the avocado with sugar, vanilla extract, and butter. 3. Put the avocado in your Ninja Foodi Pressure Cooker Steam Fryer. 4. Put on the Smart Lid on top of the Ninja Foodi Steam Fryer. 5. Move the Lid Slider to the "Air Fry/Stovetop". 6. Cook on "Air Fry" Mode at 350°F/175°C for about 20 minutes.
Per Serving: Calories 212; Fat 11.8g; Sodium 321mg; Total Carbs 24.6g; Fiber 4.4g; Sugar 8g; Protein 7.3g

Tangy Fruit Salad Jam

Prep time: 15 minutes| Cook time: 15 minutes| Serves: 2

1 cup blueberries	1 teaspoon lemon zest
1 medium orange, peeled	½ teaspoon cinnamon
1 medium apple, diced	1½ cups water
1 cup sugar	

1. In the Ninja Foodi XL Pressure Cooker Steam Fryer, combine the blueberries, orange, apple, sugar, lemon zest, cinnamon and water. 2. Lock lid; move slider towards PRESSURE. Adjust pressure release valve in the SEAL position. Close pressure-release valve. The cooking temperature will default to HIGH, which is accurate. Set time to 4 minutes. Select START/STOP and start cooking. 3. When cooking is complete, let pressure release naturally for 10 minutes, then quickly release any remaining pressure by turning it into VENT position. Carefully unlock the lid. 4. Move the slider towards "AIR FRY/STOVETOP" and set Ninja Foodi XL Pressure Cooker Steam Fryer with SmartLid to SEAR/SAUTÉ mode. Adjust the temperature to "Hi5" by using up arrow. Press START/STOP to begin cooking. 5. Simmer the sauce until thickened. Let it cool and serve.
Per Serving: Calories 354; Fat 7.9g; Sodium 704mg; Carbs 6g; Fiber 3.6g; Sugar 6g; Protein 18g

Delicious Cranberry Pudding

Prep time: 15 minutes| Cook time: 15 minutes| Serves: 2

1 cup water	1 teaspoon vanilla extract
3 large eggs, beaten	⅓ cup dried cranberries
½ cup sugar, granulated	3 cups bread cubes
2 cups milk	⅓ cup pecans, chopped

1. Prepare the Ninja Foodi XL Pressure Cooker Steam Fryer by adding the water to the pot and placing the Deluxe Reversible Rack in it. 2. In a bowl, whisk together the eggs, sugar and milk until combined. Add the vanilla, stir. Grease the Cook & Crisp Basket and add the cranberries and bread cubes. Pour the egg mixture in the Cook & Crisp Basket. Cover tightly with tin aluminum foil. Place the dish on the Deluxe Reversible Rack. Close and lock the lid. 3. Lock lid; move slider to AIR FRY/STOVETOP. Select STEAM, and set time to 25 minutes. Press START/STOP to begin cooking. Open the lid, uncover the Cook & Crisp Basket and sprinkle with pecans. 4. Serve or cover and chill up to 24 hours.
Per Serving: Calories 354; Fat 7.9g; Sodium 704mg; Carbs 6g; Fiber 3.6g; Sugar 6g; Protein 18g

syrupy Crème Brulee

Prep time: 15 minutes| Cook time: 15 minutes| Serves: 2

1 cup water	1 and ⅓ cups heavy whipping
3 large egg yolks	cream, warm
¼ teaspoon ground cinnamon	½ teaspoon maple extract
½ cup brown sugar	1½ teaspoon sugar

1. Pour the water into the Ninja Foodi XL Pressure Cooker Steam Fryer and set a Deluxe Reversible Rack in the pot. In a medium bowl, whisk together egg yolks, cinnamon and sugar until combined. 2. Add the warm cream and stir well. Add the maple extract, stir. Divide the mixture between the ramekins and sprinkle sugar for the topping. Place the ramekins on the Deluxe Reversible Rack. 3. Lock lid; move slider to AIR FRY/STOVETOP. Select STEAM, and set time to 30 minutes. Press START/STOP to begin cooking. 4. Let the ramekins cool, and then refrigerate them for 10-15 minutes. Serve.
Per Serving: Calories 354; Fat 7.9g; Sodium 704mg; Carbs 6g; Fiber 3.6g; Sugar 6g; Protein 18g

Regular Chocolate Pudding

Prep time: 15 minutes| Cook time: 15 minutes| Serves: 2

1½ cups water	2 teaspoon vanilla extract
1½ cups whipping cream	Dash of salt
½ cup milk	¼ teaspoon cinnamon
6 oz. bittersweet chocolate slivers	¼ cup brown sugar
5 egg yolks	

1. Prepare the Ninja Foodi XL Pressure Cooker Steam Fryer by adding the water to the pot and placing the Deluxe Reversible Rack in it. 2. In a saucepan, combine the cream and milk and bring to a simmer. Remove from heat. Add the chocolate. Stir until the chocolate is melted. In a bowl, whisk together the egg yolks, vanilla extract, salt, cinnamon and sugar until combined. Stirring constantly, add hot chocolate to yolk mixture. Pour the mixture in the Cook & Crisp Basket. Cover the pan tightly with aluminum foil. 3. Lock lid; move slider towards PRESSURE. Adjust pressure release valve in the SEAL position. Close pressure-release valve. The cooking temperature will default to HIGH, which is accurate. Cook on LOW pressure for 20 minutes. Select START/STOP and start cooking. 4. When cooking is complete, let pressure naturally release for 5 minutes, then quickly release any remaining pressure by turning it into VENT position. Remove the Cook & Crisp Basket from the pot. 5. Let it cool to room temperature, cover and chill at least 4 hours or up to 2 days. Serve.
Per Serving: Calories 354; Fat 7.9g; Sodium 704mg; Carbs 6g; Fiber 3.6g; Sugar 6g; Protein 18g

Caramel Pear Pudding

Prep time: 15 minutes| Cook time: 15 minutes| Serves: 2

1 cup water	½ cup pecans, chopped
1 cup flour	⅛ teaspoon ground cloves
4 medium pears, peeled and cubed	½ teaspoon ground cinnamon
1½ cups baking powder	¾ cup brown sugar
½ cup milk	¼ cup butter, soft
½ cup sugar	¾ cup boiling water
¼ teaspoon salt	

1. Prepare the Ninja Foodi XL Pressure Cooker Steam Fryer by adding the water to the pot and placing the Deluxe Reversible Rack in it. 2. In the Cook & Crisp Basket, combine the flour, pears, baking powder, milk, sugar, salt, pecans, cloves, and cinnamon. In a bowl, whisk together the butter, sugar and boiling water until combined. Pour this mixture into the Cook & Crisp Basket, don't stir. Place the Cook & Crisp Basket on the Deluxe Reversible Rack. 3. Lock lid; move slider towards PRESSURE. Adjust pressure release valve in the SEAL position. Close pressure-release valve. The cooking temperature will default to HIGH, which is accurate. Set time to 35 minutes. Select START/STOP and start cooking. 4. When cooking is complete, let pressure quickly release by turning it into VENT position. 5. Let the pudding cool, and then refrigerate before serving.
Per Serving: Calories 354; Fat 7.9g; Sodium 704mg; Carbs 6g; Fiber 3.6g; Sugar 6g; Protein 18g

Fudge Brownies

Prep Time: 10 minutes. | Cook Time: 35 minutes. | Serves: 8

1 cup granulated swerve	1 teaspoon vanilla
2 tablespoons unsweetened cocoa powder, sifted	2 tablespoons Baileys
½ cup almond flour	2 ounces unsweetened chocolate chips
½ cup coconut flour	½ cup sour cream
¼ teaspoon salt	⅓ cup powdered sugar
¼ teaspoon baking powder	3 ounces Ricotta cheese, room temperature
½ cup butter, melted then cooled	
2 eggs room temperature	

1. Place the Cook & Crisp Basket in your Ninja Foodi Pressure Cooker Steam Fryer. 2. In a mixing bowl, mix granulated swerve, cocoa powder, flour, salt, and baking powder. 3. Mix in butter, eggs, and vanilla. Add the batter to a lightly-greased Cook & Crisp Basket. 4. Put on the Smart Lid on top of the Ninja Foodi Steam Fryer. 5. Move the Lid Slider to the "Air Fry/Stovetop". 6. Cook on "Air Fry" Mode for about 25 minutes at 355°F/180°C. Allow them to cool slightly on a wire rack. 7. Microwave the chocolate chips until everything's melted; allow the mixture to cool at room temperature. 8. After that, add Ricotta cheese, Baileys, sour cream, and powdered sugar; mix until everything is blended. 9. Spread this mixture onto the top of your brownie. Serve well chilled.
Per Serving: Calories 113; Fat 3g; Sodium 152mg; Total Carbs 20g; Fiber 3g; Sugar 1.1g; Protein 3.5g

Sweet Tapioca

Prep time: 15 minutes| Cook time: 15 minutes| Serves: 2

1 cup pearl tapioca, rinsed	4 egg yolks
5 cups coconut milk	1 cup sugar
2 teaspoon ginger, grated	½ teaspoon salt
16-inch lemongrass, diced	1 cup cashew nuts, toasted

1. In the Ninja Foodi XL Pressure Cooker Steam Fryer, combine the tapioca and coconut milk. Add the ginger and lemongrass, stir. 2. Lock lid; move slider to AIR FRY/STOVETOP. Select STEAM, and set time to 6 minutes. Press START/STOP to begin cooking. Uncover the pot. In a bowl, whisk together the egg yolks, sugar and salt until combined. 3. Move the slider towards "AIR FRY/STOVETOP" and set Ninja Foodi XL Pressure Cooker Steam Fryer with SmartLid to SEAR/SAUTÉ mode. Adjust the temperature to "Hi5" by using up arrow. Press START/STOP to begin cooking and add the egg mixture. 4. Simmer until the mixture has thickened. Sprinkle with toasted cashew nuts and serve.
Per Serving: Calories 354; Fat 7.9g; Sodium 704mg; Carbs 6g; Fiber 3.6g; Sugar 6g; Protein 18g

nutty Chocolate Candy

Prep time: 15 minutes| Cook time: 15 minutes| Serves: 2

14 oz. condensed coconut milk	2 cups water
12 oz. dark chocolate chips	1 cup almonds, chopped

1. In the Cook & Crisp Basket, combine the chocolate chips and coconut milk. Cover the Cook & Crisp Basket tightly with aluminum foil. Place the Deluxe reversible rack in the bottom of cooking pot. Place the Cook & Crisp Basket on the rack. 2. Lock lid; move slider towards PRESSURE. Adjust pressure release valve in the SEAL position. Close pressure-release valve. The cooking temperature will default to HIGH, which is accurate. Set time to 3 minutes. Select START/STOP and start cooking. 3. When cooking is complete, let pressure release quickly by turning it into VENT position. Carefully unlock the lid. Add the almonds and mix well. Line a sheet pan with a parchment paper. 4. With a tablespoon, drop the candy onto the paper. Slip the pan into the freezer for about 10-20 minutes. Serve.
Per Serving: Calories 354; Fat 7.9g; Sodium 704mg; Carbs 6g; Fiber 3.6g; Sugar 6g; Protein 18g

Vegan Coconut Yogurt

Prep time: 15 minutes| Cook time: 15 minutes| Serves: 2

3 cans (14 oz. each) coconut milk	1 tablespoon maple syrup
4 capsules probiotics	2 tablespoon gelatin

1. Remove the top cream from the coconut milk and add to the Ninja Foodi XL Pressure Cooker Steam Fryer. 2. Lock lid; move slider to AIR FRY/STOVETOP and select the YOGURT. The default temperature setting will display. Use the up and down arrows to the left of the display to select "FEr". Press START/STOP to begin cooking. Bring the milk to a boil. Then press START/STOP to stop cooking. 3. When the temperature drops to 100°F/40°C, open the probiotics capsules and add to the milk. Stir until combined. Close and lock the lid. Select the YOGURT again and set the cooking time for 8 hours. 4. Open the lid. Add the maple syrup and gelatin and gently stir well. Pour equally into the jars. Let it cool completely and refrigerate for 1-2 hours before serving.
Per Serving: Calories 354; Fat 7.9g; Sodium 704mg; Carbs 6g; Fiber 3.6g; Sugar 6g; Protein 18g

yellow Marmalade

Prep time: 15 minutes| Cook time: 15 minutes| Serves: 6

1 lb. lemons, quartered, deseeded, and sliced with a mandolin	½ cup water
	2 lbs. sugar

1. Add the lemons and water to the Ninja Foodi XL Pressure Cooker Steam Fryer. 2. Lock lid; move slider towards PRESSURE. Adjust pressure release valve in the SEAL position. Close pressure-release valve. The cooking temperature will default to HIGH, which is accurate. Set time to 2 minutes. Select START/STOP and start cooking. 3. When cooking is complete, let pressure release naturally for 10 minutes. Uncover the pot. Add the sugar and stir for 2 minutes until the sugar melts. 4. Move the slider towards "AIR FRY/STOVETOP" and set Ninja Foodi XL Pressure Cooker Steam Fryer with SmartLid to SEAR/SAUTÉ mode. Adjust the temperature to "Hi5" by using up arrow. Press START/STOP to begin cooking. 5. Bring to a boil, cook for 5 minutes. Transfer the mixture into clean or sterilized jars. Serve chilled or store in the refrigerator.
Per Serving: Calories 354; Fat 7.9g; Sodium 704mg; Carbs 6g; Fiber 3.6g; Sugar 6g; Protein 18g

Delicious Blueberries Yogurt

Prep time: 15 minutes| Cook time: 15 minutes| Serves: 4

¼ cup sugar	2 cups drained low-fat yogurt
2 cups blueberries	1 tablespoon pistachios, shelled
½ teaspoon balsamic vinegar	and diced
1 tablespoon lime juice	

1. In the Ninja Foodi XL Pressure Cooker Steam Fryer, combine the sugar, blueberries, vinegar and lime juice. 2. Lock lid; move slider towards PRESSURE. Adjust pressure release valve in the SEAL position. Close pressure-release valve. The cooking temperature will default to HIGH, which is accurate. Set time to 10minutes. Select START/STOP and start cooking. 3. When cooking is complete, let pressure release naturally for 10 minutes by turning it into VENT position. Uncover the pot. Prepare the yogurt jars. Pour ¼ cup of yogurt into each jars. Then add 2 tablespoon of blueberry sauce into jars. Make another layer of yogurt and top with blueberry sauce again. 4. Sprinkle with pistachios at the end. Refrigerate until ready to serve.
Per Serving: Calories 354; Fat 7.9g; Sodium 704mg; Carbs 6g; Fiber 3.6g; Sugar 6g; Protein 18g

Air Fried Walnut Bars

Prep Time: 15 minutes. | Cook Time: 16 minutes. | Serves: 4

1 egg, beaten	¼ cup coconut flour
2 tablespoons sugar	1 ounce walnuts, chopped
7 tablespoons coconut oil, softened	½ teaspoon baking powder
1 teaspoon vanilla extract	

1. Place the Cook & Crisp Basket in your Ninja Foodi Pressure Cooker Steam Fryer and place a reversible rack in it. 2. Mix egg with sugar, coconut oil, vanilla extract, coconut flour, and baking powder. 3. Stir the mixture gently, add walnuts, and mix the mixture until homogenous. 4. Pour the mixture in the Ninja Foodi Cook & Crisp Basket and flatten gently. 5. Put on the Smart Lid on top of the Ninja Foodi Steam Fryer. 6. Move the Lid Slider to the "Air Fry/Stovetop". 7. Cook the walnut on "Air Fry" Mode at 375°F/190°C for about 16 minutes. 8. Cool the dessert well and cut into bars.
Per Serving: Calories 413; Fat 30.8 g; Sodium 1279 mg; Carbs 2.4g; Fiber 0.5g; Sugar 1.3g; Protein 31.6g

Blondies

Prep Time: 10 minutes. | Cook Time: 15 minutes. | Serves: 2

1 egg, beaten	½ teaspoon vanilla extract
1 tablespoon almond butter	1 teaspoon Splenda
½ teaspoon baking powder	2 tablespoons almond flour
1 teaspoon lime juice	

1. Place the Cook & Crisp Basket in your Ninja Foodi Pressure Cooker Steam Fryer and place a reversible rack in it. 2. Put all the recipe ingredients in the mixer bowl and mix until smooth. 3. Pour the mixture in your Ninja Foodi Cook & Crisp Basket, flatten gently. 4. Put on the Smart Lid on top of the Ninja Foodi Steam Fryer. 5. Move the Lid Slider to the "Air Fry/Stovetop". 6. Cook on "Air Fry" Mode at 375°F/190°C for about 15 minutes. 7. Then cut the cooked dessert into servings.
Per Serving: Calories 101; Fat 2g; Sodium 480mg; Total Carbs 4g; Fiber 2g; Sugar 0g; Protein 18g

sweet Quiche

Prep time: 5 minutes| Cook time: 35 minutes| Serves: 2

3 large eggs
¼ cup milk
Salt and ground black pepper to taste

1 tablespoon chives, chopped
½ cup cheddar cheese, shredded
Cooking spray
1 cup water

1. In a medium bowl, whisk together eggs, milk, salt, pepper, and chives until combined. Grease the Cook & Crisp Basket with cooking spray. Add the cheese to the Cook & Crisp Basket. 2. Pour the egg mixture into the pan and spread evenly. Pour the water into the Ninja Foodi XL Pressure Cooker Steam Fryer and set a Deluxe Reversible Rack in the pot. Place the Cook & Crisp Basket on the rack. 3. Lock lid; move slider towards PRESSURE. Adjust pressure release valve in the SEAL position. Close pressure-release valve. The cooking temperature will default to HIGH, which is accurate. Set time to 30 minutes. Select START/STOP and start cooking. 4. When cooking is complete, let pressure quickly release by turning it into VENT position. Carefully unlock the lid. Serve.
Per Serving: Calories 30; Fat 13g; Sodium 12mg; Carbs 49g; Fiber 4g; Sugar 6g; Protein 3g

Easy Chocolate Cream

Prep Time: 10 minutes. | Cook Time: 15 minutes. | Serves: 3

1-ounce dark chocolate, chopped
1 cup coconut cream

1 teaspoon vanilla extract
1 tablespoon sugar

1. Place the Cook & Crisp Basket in your Ninja Foodi Pressure Cooker Steam Fryer and place a reversible rack in it. 2. Pour the coconut cream into the Cook & Crisp Basket and place it in your Ninja Foodi Pressure Cooker Steam Fryer. 3. Add chocolate, vanilla extract, and sugar. 4. Put on the Smart Lid on top of the Ninja Foodi Steam Fryer. 5. Move the Lid Slider to the "Air Fry/Stovetop". 6. Cook the chocolate cream on "Air Fry" Mode at 360°F/180°C for about 15 minutes. Stir the liquid from time to time during cooking.
Per Serving: Calories 180; Fat 3.2g; Sodium 133mg; Total Carbs 32g; Fiber 1.1g; Sugar 1.8g; Protein 9g

Ricotta Vanilla Cookies

Prep Time: 15 minutes. | Cook Time: 12 minutes. | Serves: 6

1 teaspoon vanilla extract
1 cup ricotta cheese
1 cup coconut flour

1 egg, beaten
2 tablespoons swerve

1. Place the Cook & Crisp Basket in your Ninja Foodi Pressure Cooker Steam Fryer. 2. Mix coconut flour with vanilla extract, ricotta cheese, egg, and swerve. 3. Knead the dough and make cookies. 4. Put the cookies in your Ninja Foodi Pressure Cooker Steam Fryer. 5. Put on the Smart Lid on top of the Ninja Foodi Steam Fryer. 6. Move the Lid Slider to the "Air Fry/Stovetop". 7. Cook on "Air Fry" Mode at 365°F/185°C for about 12 minutes.
Per Serving: Calories 185; Fat 11g; Sodium 355mg; Total Carbs 21g; Fiber 5.8g; Sugar 3g; Protein 4.7g

Cream Cheese Cinnamon Pie

Prep Time: 15 minutes. | Cook Time: 30 minutes. | Serves: 6

2 eggs, beaten
6 tablespoons almond flour
½ teaspoon vanilla extract
6 tablespoons cream cheese
½ teaspoon baking powder

1 teaspoon apple cider vinegar
½ teaspoon cinnamon
3 tablespoons sugar
1 tablespoon coconut oil, melted

1. Place the Cook & Crisp Basket in your Ninja Foodi Pressure Cooker Steam Fryer and place a reversible rack in it. 2. Brush the Cook & Crisp Basket with coconut oil. 3. Then mix eggs with almond flour, vanilla extract, cream cheese, baking powder, apple cider vinegar, cinnamon, and sugar. 4. Blend this cinnamon egg mixture until smooth and pour it in the Cook & Crisp Basket. 5. Put on the Smart Lid on top of the Ninja Foodi Steam Fryer. 6. Move the Lid Slider to the "Air Fry/Stovetop". 7. Cook the pie in your Ninja Foodi Pressure Cooker Steam Fryer at 350°F/175°C on "Air Fry" Mode for about 30 minutes. 8. Then cool the cooked pie well.
Per Serving: Calories 122; Fat 1.8g; Sodium 794mg; Total Carbs 17g; Fiber 8.9g; Sugar 1.6g; Protein 14.9g

Greece Style Yogurt Cake

Prep Time: 10 minutes. | Cook Time: 30 minutes. | Serves: 12

6 eggs, beaten
1 teaspoon vanilla extract
1 teaspoon baking powder

2 cups almond flour
4 tablespoons sugar
1 cup Plain yogurt

1. Place the Cook & Crisp Basket in your Ninja Foodi Pressure Cooker Steam Fryer and place a reversible rack in it. 2. Mix all the recipe ingredients in a suitable mixing bowl. 3. Then pour the mixture into Cook & Crisp Basket and place it in your Ninja Foodi Pressure Cooker Steam Fryer and flatten it gently. 4. Put on the Smart Lid on top of the Ninja Foodi Steam Fryer. 5. Move the Lid Slider to the "Air Fry/Stovetop". 6. Cook the cake at 350°F/175°C on "Air Fry" Mode for about 30 minutes.
Per Serving: Calories 163; Fat 11.5g; Sodium 918mg; Total Carbs 8.3g; Fiber 4.2g; Sugar 0.2g; Protein 7.4g

Easy Pecan Cobbler

Prep Time: 15 minutes. | Cook Time: 30 minutes. | Serves: 4

¼ cup coconut cream
1 egg, beaten
½ cup coconut flour

1 teaspoon vanilla extract
2 tablespoons coconut oil, softened
3 pecans, chopped

1. Place the Cook & Crisp Basket in your Ninja Foodi Pressure Cooker Steam Fryer and place a reversible rack in it. 2. Mix coconut oil with pecans, add the mixture into the Cook & Crisp Basket and place it in your Ninja Foodi Pressure Cooker Steam Fryer. Flatten the mixture gently. 3. In a suitable mixing bowl, mix coconut cream with egg, coconut flour, and vanilla extract. 4. Put the mixture over the pecans, flatten it gently. 5. Put on the Smart Lid on top of the Ninja Foodi Steam Fryer. 6. Move the Lid Slider to the "Air Fry/Stovetop". 7. Cook on "Air Fry" Mode at 350°F/175°C for about 30 minutes. 8. Cool the cooked meal and transfer in the plates.
Per Serving: Calories 134; Fat 5.9g; Sodium 343mg; Total Carbs 9.5g; Fiber 0.5g; Sugar 1.1g; Protein 10.4g

Homemade Pecan Nutella

Prep Time: 20 minutes. | Cook Time: 5 minutes. | Serves: 4

4 pecans, chopped
5 teaspoons butter, softened
½ teaspoon vanilla extract

1 tablespoon Splenda
1 teaspoon of cocoa powder

1. Put all the recipe ingredients in your Ninja Foodi Pressure Cooker Steam Fryer's cooking pot and stir gently. 2. Put on the Smart Lid on top of the Ninja Foodi Steam Fryer. 3. Move the Lid Slider to the "Air Fry/Stovetop". 4. Cook the mixture at 400°F/200°C on "Bake" Mode for about 5 minutes. 5. Then transfer the mixture in the serving bowl and refrigerate for about 15-20 minutes before serving.
Per Serving: Calories 229; Fat 1.9 |Sodium 567mg; Total Carbs 1.9g; Fiber 0.4g; Sugar 0.6g; Protein 11.8g

Cocoa Ricotta Pudding

Prep Time: 10 minutes. | Cook Time: 20 minutes. | Serves: 8

2 cups ricotta cheese
2 tablespoons coconut flour
3 tablespoons Splenda
3 eggs, beaten

1 tablespoon vanilla extract
½ cup coconut cream
1 tablespoon cocoa powder

1. Whisk the coconut cream with cocoa powder. 2. Then add eggs, Splenda, ricotta cheese, vanilla extract and coconut flour. 3. Mix the mixture until smooth and pour in your Ninja Foodi Pressure Cooker Steam Fryer's pot. 4. Put on the Smart Lid on top of the Ninja Foodi Steam Fryer. 5. Move the Lid Slider to the "Air Fry/Stovetop". 6. Cook the pudding at 350°F/175°C on "Bake" Mode for about 20 minutes. Stir the pudding every 5 minutes during cooking.
Per Serving: Calories 186; Fat 3g; Sodium 223mg; Total Carbs 31g; Fiber 8.7g; Sugar 5.5g; Protein 9.7g

Zesty Lemon Biscotti

Prep Time: 15 minutes. | Cook Time: 40 minutes. | Serves: 6

2 ounces almonds, chopped
2 tablespoons coconut oil
2 eggs, beaten
1 teaspoon vanilla extract
1 cup coconut flour
1 teaspoon lemon zest, grated

½ teaspoon baking powder
1 teaspoon lemon juice
¼ cup coconut cream
1 teaspoon sesame oil
3 tablespoons sugar

1. Place the Cook & Crisp Basket in your Ninja Foodi Pressure Cooker Steam Fryer. 2. Mix all the recipe ingredients in a suitable mixing bowl. 3. Then knead the dough and put in your Ninja Foodi Cook & Crisp Basket. 4. Put on the Smart Lid on top of the Ninja Foodi Steam Fryer. 5. Move the Lid Slider to the "Air Fry/Stovetop". 6. Cook the dough on "Air Fry" Mode for about 38 minutes at 375°F/190°C. 7. Then slice the dough into biscotti. Cook on "Air Fry" Mode at 400°F/200°C for about 2 minutes more.
Per Serving: Calories 103; Fat 8.4g; Sodium 117mg; Total Carbs 3.5g; Fiber 0.9g; Sugar 1.5g; Protein 5.1g

Chia Egg Pie

Prep Time: 10 minutes. | Cook Time: 30 minutes. | Serves: 8

1 cup almond flour
2 tablespoons chia seeds
4 eggs, beaten

4 tablespoons sugar
1 teaspoon vanilla extract
2 tablespoons coconut oil, melted

1. Place the Cook & Crisp Basket in your Ninja Foodi Pressure Cooker Steam Fryer and place a reversible rack in it. 2. Brush the Ninja Foodi Cook & Crisp Basket with coconut oil. 3. Then mix almond flour with chia seeds, eggs, vanilla extract, and sugar. 4. Pour the mixture into Cook & Crisp Basket and place it in your Ninja Foodi Cook & Crisp Basket, flatten it in the shape of the pie. 5. Put on the Smart Lid on top of the Ninja Foodi Steam Fryer. 6. Move the Lid Slider to the "Air Fry/Stovetop". 7. Cook on "Air Fry" Mode at 365°F/185°C for about 30 minutes.
Per Serving: Calories 197; Fat 8.6g; Sodium 510mg; Total Carbs 22.2g; Fiber 1.4g; Sugar 13g; Protein 7.6g

Ricotta Cheese Muffins

Prep Time: 15 minutes. | Cook Time: 11 minutes. | Serves: 4

4 teaspoons ricotta cheese
1 egg, beaten
½ teaspoon baking powder
1 teaspoon vanilla extract

8 teaspoons coconut flour
3 tablespoons coconut cream
2 teaspoons sugar
Cooking spray

1. Place the Cook & Crisp Basket in your Ninja Foodi Pressure Cooker Steam Fryer. 2. Spray the muffin molds with cooking spray. 3. Then mix all the recipe ingredients in a suitable mixing bowl. 4. When you get a smooth batter, pour it in the muffin molds and place in your Ninja Foodi Cook & Crisp Basket. 5. Put on the Smart Lid on top of the Ninja Foodi Steam Fryer. 6. Move the Lid Slider to the "Air Fry/Stovetop". 7. Cook the muffins on "Air Fry" Mode at 365°F/185°C for about 11 minutes.
Per Serving: Calories 284; Fat 7.9g; Sodium 704mg; Total Carbs 38.1g; Fiber 1.9g; Sugar 1.9g; Protein 14.8g

Orange Nutmeg Galettes

Prep Time: 10 minutes. | Cook Time: 15 minutes. | Serves: 6

1 cup almond meal
½ cup coconut flour
3 eggs
⅓ cup milk
2 tablespoons monk fruit

2 teaspoons grated lemon peel
⅓ teaspoon nutmeg, preferably
1 ½ teaspoons baking powder
3 tablespoons orange juice
A pinch of turmeric

1. Place the Cook & Crisp Basket in your Ninja Foodi Pressure Cooker Steam Fryer and place a reversible rack in it. 2. Grab two mixing bowls. Mix dry ingredients in the first bowl. 3. In the second bowl, mix all wet ingredients. Add wet mixture to the dry mixture and mix until smooth and uniform. 4. Pour the mixture in the Cook & Crisp Basket. 5. Put on the Smart Lid on top of the Ninja Foodi Steam Fryer. 6. Move the Lid Slider to the "Air Fry/Stovetop". 7. Cook on

"Air Fry" Mode for about 4 to 5 minutes at 345°F/175°C. Work in batches. Dust with confectioners' swerve if desired. Bon appétit!
Per Serving: Calories 248; Fat 30g; Sodium 660mg; Total Carbs 5g; Fiber 0g; Sugar 0g; Protein 4g

Rhubarb Cream Pie

Prep Time: 15 minutes. | Cook Time: 20 minutes. | Serves: 6

4-ounce rhubarb, chopped
¼ cup coconut cream
1 teaspoon vanilla extract
¼ cup sugar

1 cup coconut flour
1 egg, beaten
4 tablespoons coconut oil, softened

1. Place the Cook & Crisp Basket in your Ninja Foodi Pressure Cooker Steam Fryer and place a reversible rack in it. 2. Mix coconut cream with vanilla extract, sugar, coconut flour, egg, and coconut oil. 3. When the mixture is smooth, add rhubarb and stir gently. 4. Pour the mixture into the Cook & Crisp Basket and place it in your Ninja Foodi Pressure Cooker Steam Fryer. 5. Put on the Smart Lid on top of the Ninja Foodi Steam Fryer. 6. Move the Lid Slider to the "Air Fry/Stovetop". 7. Cook the pie on "Air Fry" Mode at 375°F/190°C for about 20 minutes. 8. Cool the cooked pie and cut into servings.
Per Serving: Calories 206; Fat 3.4g; Sodium 174mg; Total Carbs 35g; Fiber 9.4g; Sugar 5.9g; Protein 10.6g

Lemon Cream Pie

Prep Time: 10 minutes. | Cook Time: 35 minutes. | Serves: 6

1 cup coconut flour
½ lemon, sliced
¼ cup heavy cream
2 eggs, beaten

2 tablespoons sugar
1 teaspoon baking powder
Cooking spray

1. Place the Cook & Crisp Basket in your Ninja Foodi Pressure Cooker Steam Fryer and place a reversible rack in it. 2. Spray the Ninja Foodi Cook & Crisp Basket with cooking spray. 3. Then line the bottom Cook & Crisp Basket with lemon. 4. In a suitable mixing bowl, mix coconut flour with heavy cream, eggs, sugar, and baking powder. 5. Pour the batter over the lemons. 6. Put on the Smart Lid on top of the Ninja Foodi Steam Fryer. 7. Move the Lid Slider to the "Air Fry/Stovetop". 8. Cook the pie on "Air Fry" Mode at 365°F/185°C for about 35 minutes.
Per Serving: Calories 270; Fat 14.6g; Sodium 394mg; Total Carbs 31.3g; Fiber 7.5g; Sugar 9.7g; Protein 6.4g

Sponge Cake

Prep Time: 10 minutes. | Cook Time: 30 minutes. | Serves: 6

2 cups coconut flour
5 eggs, beaten
½ cup sugar

1 teaspoon baking powder
1 teaspoon vanilla extract
Cooking spray

1. Place the Cook & Crisp Basket in your Ninja Foodi Pressure Cooker Steam Fryer and place a reversible rack in it. 2. Whisk the coconut flour with eggs, sugar, baking powder, and vanilla extract. 3. Spray Cook & Crisp Basket with cooking spray and pour the coconut flour mixture inside. 4. Put on the Smart Lid on top of the Ninja Foodi Steam Fryer. 5. Move the Lid Slider to the "Air Fry/Stovetop". 6. Cook on "Air Fry" Mode at 355°F/180°C for about 30 minutes.
Per Serving: Calories 131; Fat 0.1g; Sodium 271mg; Total Carbs 32.8g; Fiber 6.4g; Sugar 7g; Protein 6.3g

Baked Sweet Cantaloupe

Prep Time: 10 minutes. | Cook Time: 10 minutes. | Serves: 2

1 cup cantaloupe, chopped
1 teaspoon vanilla extract

1 tablespoon sugar
1 teaspoon olive oil

1. Place the Cook & Crisp Basket in your Ninja Foodi Pressure Cooker Steam Fryer. 2. Put the cantaloupe in the Ninja Foodi Cook & Crisp Basket and sprinkle with vanilla extract, sugar, and olive oil. 3. Put on the Smart Lid on top of the Ninja Foodi Steam Fryer. 4. Move the Lid Slider to the "Air Fry/Stovetop". 5. Cook the dessert on "Air Fry" Mode for at 375°F/190°C for about 10 minutes.
Per Serving: Calories 208; Fat 5g; Sodium 1205mg; Total Carbs 34.1g; Fiber 7.8g; Sugar 2.5g; Protein 5.9g

Mini Cheesecakes

Time: 10 minutes. | Cook Time: 30 minutes. | Serves: 8

For the Crust:

⅓ teaspoon grated nutmeg	8 tablespoons melted butter
1 ½ tablespoons sugar	1 teaspoon cinnamon
1 ½ cups almond meal	A pinch of kosher salt

For the Cheesecake:

2 eggs	4 ounces soft cheese
½ cups unsweetened chocolate chips	½ cup swerve
1 ½ tablespoons sour cream	½ teaspoon vanilla essence

1. Place the Cook & Crisp Basket in your Ninja Foodi Pressure Cooker Steam Fryer and place a reversible rack in it. 2. Firstly, line eight cups of mini muffin pan with paper liners. 3. To make the crust, mix the almond meal together with sugar, cinnamon, nutmeg, and kosher salt. 4. Now, add melted butter and stir well to moisten the crumb mixture. 5. Divide the crust mixture among the muffin cups and press gently to make even layers. 6. In another bowl, whip together the soft cheese, sour cream and swerve until uniform and smooth. Fold in the eggs and the vanilla essence. 7. Then, divide chocolate chips among the prepared muffin cups. Then, add the cheese mixture to each muffin cup. 8. Put on the Smart Lid on top of the Ninja Foodi Steam Fryer. 9. Move the Lid Slider to the "Air Fry/Stovetop". 10. Cook on "Air Fry" Mode for about 18 minutes at 345°F/175°C. To finish, transfer the mini cheesecakes to a cooling rack; store in the fridge.
Per Serving: Calories 297; Fat 1g; Sodium 291mg; Total Carbs 35g; Fiber 1g; Sugar 9g; Protein 2g

Orange Custard

Prep Time: 10 minutes. | Cook Time: 35 minutes. | Serves: 6

6 eggs	½ teaspoon orange rind, grated
7 ounces cream cheese	1 ½ cardamom pods, bruised
2 ½ cans condensed milk, sweetened	2 teaspoons vanilla paste
½ cup swerve	¼ cup fresh orange juice

1. Place the Cook & Crisp Basket in your Ninja Foodi Pressure Cooker Steam Fryer and place a reversible rack in it. 2. In a suitable saucepan, melt swerve over a moderate flame; it takes about 10 to 12 minutes. Immediately but carefully pour the melted sugar into six ramekins, tilting to coat their bottoms; allow them to cool slightly. 3. In a mixing dish, beat the cheese until smooth; now, fold in the eggs, one at a time, and continue to beat until pale and creamy. 4. Add the orange rind, cardamom, vanilla, orange juice, and the condensed milk; mix again. Pour the mixture over the caramelized sugar. 5. Put on the Smart Lid on top of the Ninja Foodi Steam Fryer. 6. Move the Lid Slider to the "Air Fry/Stovetop". 7. Cook on "Air Fry" Mode at 325°F/160°C for about 28 minutes until it has thickened. 8. Refrigerate overnight; garnish with berries or other fruits and serve.
Per Serving: Calories 399; Fat 16g; Sodium 537mg; Total Carbs 28g; Fiber 3g; Sugar 10g; Protein 5g

Carambola Chips

Prep Time: 10 minutes. | Cook Time: 50 minutes. | Serves: 6

10-ounce carambola, sliced	1 tablespoon sugar
1 teaspoon coconut oil, melted	

1. Place the Cook & Crisp Basket in your Ninja Foodi Pressure Cooker Steam Fryer. 2. Mix carambola with coconut oil and sugar. 3. Then put it in your Ninja Foodi Pressure Cooker Steam Fryer. 4. Put on the Smart Lid on top of the Ninja Foodi Steam Fryer. 5. Move the Lid Slider to the "Air Fry/Stovetop". 6. Cook on "Air Fry" Mode at 340°F/170°C for about 50 minutes. Shake the carambola slices every 5 minutes.
Per Serving: Calories 166; Fat 3.2g; Sodium 437mg; Total Carbs 28.8g; Fiber 1.8g; Sugar 2.7g; Protein 5.8g

Sweet Blueberries Muffins

Prep Time: 10 minutes. | Cook Time: 20 minutes. | Serves: 6

2 teaspoons blueberries	1 teaspoon baking powder

4 tablespoons coconut flour	3 tablespoons sugar
4 tablespoons coconut oil, softened	

1. Place the Cook & Crisp Basket in your Ninja Foodi Pressure Cooker Steam Fryer. 2. Put all the recipe ingredients in a suitable mixing bowl and mix until smooth. 3. Then pour the mixture in the muffin molds. 4. Place the muffin molds in the Ninja Foodi Cook & Crisp Basket. 5. Put on the Smart Lid on top of the Ninja Foodi Steam Fryer. 6. Move the Lid Slider to the "Air Fry/Stovetop". 7. Cook on "Air Fry" Mode at 350°F/175°C for about 20 minutes.
Per Serving: Calories 193; Fat 1g; Sodium 395mg; Total Carbs 38.7g; Fiber 1.6g; Sugar 0.9g; Protein 6.6g

Cinnamon Plum

Prep Time: 5 minutes. | Cook Time: 10 minutes. | Serves: 4

4 plums, pitted, halved	1 teaspoon coconut oil, melted
1 teaspoon cinnamon	

1. Place the Cook & Crisp Basket in your Ninja Foodi Pressure Cooker Steam Fryer. 2. Put the plum in the Ninja Foodi Cook & Crisp Basket in one layer. 3. Then sprinkle them with cinnamon and coconut oil. 4. Put on the Smart Lid on top of the Ninja Foodi Steam Fryer. 5. Move the Lid Slider to the "Air Fry/Stovetop". 6. Cook the plums on "Air Fry" Mode at 360°F/180°C for about 10 minutes.
Per Serving: Calories 288; Fat 6.9g; Sodium 761mg; Total Carbs 46g; Fiber 4g; Sugar 12g; Protein 9.6g

Peanuts Cupcakes

Prep Time: 10 minutes. | Cook Time: 15 minutes. | Serves: 8

4 egg whites	½ stick butter, softened
2 whole egg	⅓ teaspoon almond extract
½ teaspoon pure vanilla extract	1 cup almond flour
½ cup swerve	½ cup coconut flour
½ cup confectioners' swerve	2 tablespoons unsalted peanuts,
⅓ teaspoon cream of tartar	

1. Place the Cook & Crisp Basket in your Ninja Foodi Pressure Cooker Steam Fryer. 2. First of all, beat the softened butter and swerve until it is fluffy. 3. After that, fold in the egg and mix again; carefully throw in the flour along with peanuts; stir in the almond extract and vanilla extract. 4. Divide the batter among the muffin cups that are lined with muffin papers. 5. Put on the Smart Lid on top of the Ninja Foodi Steam Fryer. 6. Move the Lid Slider to the "Air Fry/Stovetop". 7. Cook on "Air Fry" Mode at 325°F/160°C for about 10 minutes. 8. Meanwhile, prepare the topping; simply whip the egg whites and cream of tartar until it has an airy texture. 9. Now, gradually add the confectioners' swerve; continue mixing until stiff glossy peaks form. To finish, decorate the cupcakes and serve them on a nice serving platter.
Per Serving: Calories 257; Fat 10.4g; Sodium 431mg; Total Carbs 20g; Fiber 0g; Sugar 1.6g; Protein 2g

Blackberry Butter Cake

Prep Time: 10 minutes. | Cook Time: 30 minutes. | Serves: 8

⅓ cup fresh blackberries	1 teaspoon baking soda
½ cup butter, room temperature	4 whole eggs
⅓ teaspoon baking powder	1 cup almond flour
2 ounces swerve	1 teaspoon orange zest
½ cup cocoa powder, melted	

1. Place the Cook & Crisp Basket in your Ninja Foodi Pressure Cooker Steam Fryer. 2. In a suitable bowl, beat the butter, swerve and orange zest with an electric mixer. Carefully fold in the eggs, one at a time; beat well with your electric mixer after each addition. 3. Next, throw in the almond flour, baking soda, baking powder, cocoa powder, and orange juice. 4. Pour the prepared batter into the Cook & Crisp Basket. Top with fresh blackberries. 5. Put on the Smart Lid on top of the Ninja Foodi Steam Fryer. 6. Move the Lid Slider to the "Air Fry/Stovetop". 7. Cook on "Air Fry" Mode for about 22 minutes at 335°F/170°C. 8. Check the cake for doneness; allow it to cool on a wire rack. Bon appétit!
Per Serving: Calories 155; Fat 4.2g; Sodium 963mg; Total Carbs 21.5g; Fiber 0.8g; Sugar 5.7g; Protein 8.1g

Rum Lava Cake

Prep Time: 10 minutes. | Cook Time: 20 minutes. | Serves: 4

2 ½ ounces butter	½ cup almond flour
3 ounces chocolate, unsweetened	1 teaspoon rum extract
2 eggs, beaten	1 teaspoon vanilla extract
½ cup confectioners' swerve	

1. Place the Cook & Crisp Basket in your Ninja Foodi Pressure Cooker Steam Fryer and place a reversible rack in it. 2. Spritz the Cook & Crisp Basket with cooking spray. 3. Melt the butter with chocolate in a microwave-safe bowl. Mix the eggs and confectioners' swerve until frothy. 4. Pour the butter/chocolate mixture into the egg mixture. Stir in the almond flour, rum extract, and vanilla extract. Mix until everything is well incorporated. 5. Scrape the batter into the Cook & Crisp Basket . 6. Put on the Smart Lid on top of the Ninja Foodi Steam Fryer. 7. Move the Lid Slider to the "Air Fry/Stovetop". 8. Cook on "Air Fry" Mode at 370°F/185°C for about 9 to 11 minutes. 9. Let stand at room temperature for about 2 to 3 minutes. Invert on a plate while warm and serve. Bon appétit!
Per Serving: Calories 275; Fat 1.4g; Sodium 582mg; Total Carbs 31.5g; Fiber 1.1g; Sugar 0.1g; Protein 9.8g

Easy Chocolate Cake

Prep Time: 10 minutes. | Cook Time: 20–23 minutes | Serves: 8

½ cup sugar	¼ teaspoon salt
¼ cup flour, 3 tablespoons	1 egg
3 tablespoons cocoa	2 tablespoons oil
½ teaspoon baking powder	½ cup milk
½ teaspoon baking soda	½ teaspoon vanilla extract

1. Place the Cook & Crisp Basket in your Ninja Foodi Pressure Cooker Steam Fryer. 2. Lightly grease and dust with flour in the Cook & Crisp Basket. 3. In a suitable bowl, stir together the sugar, flour, cocoa, baking powder, baking soda, and salt. 4. Add all other ingredients and beat with a wire whisk until smooth. 5. Pour batter into the Cook & Crisp Basket. 6. Put on the Smart Lid on top of the Ninja Foodi Steam Fryer. 7. Move the Lid Slider to the "Air Fry/ Stovetop". 8. Cook on "Air Fry" Mode at 330°F/165°C for about 20 to 23 minutes, until toothpick inserted in center comes out clean or with crumbs clinging to it.
Per Serving: Calories 220; Fat 13g; Sodium 542mg; Total Carbs 0.9g; Fiber 0.3g; Sugar 0.2g; Protein 5.6g

Roasted Apple Crisp

Prep Time: 10 minutes. | Cook Time: 16–18 minutes | Serves: 4–6

Filling

3 Granny Smith apples, thinly sliced (about 4 cups)	1½ teaspoons lemon juice
¼ teaspoon cinnamon	2 tablespoons honey
⅛ teaspoon salt	1 tablespoon brown sugar
Cooking spray	

Crumb Topping

2 tablespoons oats	2 tablespoons chopped walnuts
2 tablespoons oat bran	2 tablespoons brown sugar
2 tablespoons cooked quinoa	2 teaspoons coconut oil

1. Place the Cook & Crisp Basket in your Ninja Foodi Pressure Cooker Steam Fryer and place a reversible rack in it. 2. Mix all filling ingredients and stir well so that apples are evenly coated. 3. Spray the Cook & Crisp Basket with nonstick cooking spray and spoon in the apple mixture. 4. Put on the Smart Lid on top of the Ninja Foodi Steam Fryer. 5. Move the Lid Slider to the "Air Fry/Stovetop". 6. Cook on "Air Fry" Mode at 360°F/180°C for about 5 minutes. Stir well, scooping up from the bottom to mix apples and sauce. 7. At this point, the apples should be crisp-tender. Continue cooking in 3-minute intervals until apples are as soft as you like. 8. While apples are cooking, mix all topping ingredients in a suitable bowl. Stir until coconut oil mixes in well and distributes evenly. 9. When apples are cooked to your liking, sprinkle crumb mixture on top. 10. Cook on "Air Fry" Mode at 360°F/180°C for about 8 to 10 minutes until crumb topping is golden brown and crispy.
Per Serving: Calories 220; Fat 1.7g; Sodium 178mg; Total Carbs 1.7g; Fiber 0.2g; Sugar 0.2g; Protein 2.9g

Macaroons

Prep Time: 5 minutes. | Cook Time: 8–10 minutes. | Yields: 12 macaroons

1⅓ cups shredded, sweetened coconut	2 tablespoons sugar
4½ teaspoons flour	1 egg white
	½ teaspoon almond extract

1. Place the Cook & Crisp Basket in your Ninja Foodi Pressure Cooker Steam Fryer and place a reversible rack in it. 2. Mix all the recipe ingredients together. 3. Shape coconut mixture into 12 balls. 4. Place all 12 macaroons in Cook & Crisp Basket. 5. Put on the Smart Lid on top of the Ninja Foodi Steam Fryer. 6. Move the Lid Slider to the "Air Fry/Stovetop". 7. Cook on "Air Fry" Mode at 330°F/165°C for about 8 to 10 minutes, until golden.
Per Serving: Calories 346; Fat 16.1g; Sodium 882mg; Total Carbs 1.3g; Fiber 0.5g; Sugar 0.5g; Protein 4.2g

Rice Cake

Prep Time: 8 minutes. | Cook Time: 30–35 minutes | Serves: 8

1 cup all-natural coconut water	4 tablespoons honey
1 cup unsweetened coconut milk	Cooking spray
1 teaspoon almond extract	¾ cup raw jasmine rice
¼ teaspoon salt	2 cups sliced or cubed fruit

1. Place the Cook & Crisp Basket in your Ninja Foodi Pressure Cooker Steam Fryer and place a reversible rack in it. 2. In a suitable bowl, mix well the coconut milk, almond extract, coconut water, salt, and honey. 3. Grease the Cook & Crisp Basket with cooking spray then add the rice. 4. Pour liquid mixture over rice. 5. Put on the Smart Lid on top of the Ninja Foodi Steam Fryer. 6. Move the Lid Slider to the "Air Fry/Stovetop". 7. Cook on "Air Fry" Mode at 360°F/180°C for about 15 minutes. 8. Stir again. Cook on "Air Fry" Mode for about 20 minutes longer until rice are soft. 9. Allow the rice cake to cool slightly. 10. Garnish with fruit and serve.
Per Serving: Calories 223; Fat 11.7g; Sodium 721mg; Total Carbs 13.6g; Fiber 0.7g; Sugar 8g; Protein 5.7g

Strawberry Rolls

Prep Time: 20 minutes. | Cook Time: 5–6 minutes. | Serves: 4

3 ounces low-fat cream cheese	8 sheets phyllo dough
2 tablespoons plain yogurt	Butter-flavored cooking spray
2 teaspoons sugar	¼–½ cup dark chocolate chips
¼ teaspoon pure vanilla extract	(optional)
8 ounces fresh strawberries	

1. Place the Cook & Crisp Basket in your Ninja Foodi Pressure Cooker Steam Fryer. 2. In a suitable bowl, mix well the cream cheese, yogurt, sugar, and vanilla. Beat with hand mixer at high speed until smooth, about 1 minute. 3. Wash strawberries and destem. Chop enough of them to measure ½ cup. Stir into cheese mixture. 4. Phyllo dough dries out quickly, so cover your stack of phyllo sheets with waxed paper and then place a damp dish towel on top of that. Remove only one sheet at a time as you work. 5. To create one pastry roll, lay out a single sheet of phyllo. Spray lightly with butter-flavored spray, top with a second sheet of phyllo, and spray the second sheet lightly. 6. Place a quarter of the filling (about 3 tablespoons) about ½ inch from the edge of one short side. Fold one end of the phyllo over the filling and keep rolling a turn or two. Fold in both the left and right sides so that the edges meet in the middle of your roll. Then roll up completely. Spray outside of pastry roll with butter spray. 7. When you have 4 rolls, place them in your Ninja Foodi Cook & Crisp Basket, seam side down, leaving some space in between each. 8. Put on the Smart Lid on top of the Ninja Foodi Steam Fryer. 9. Move the Lid Slider to the "Air Fry/Stovetop". 10. Cook on "Air Fry" Mode at 330°F/165°C for about 5 to 6 minutes, until they turn a delicate golden brown. 11. Repeat to make the remaining rolls. 12. Allow pastries to cool to room temperature. 13. When ready to serve, slice the remaining strawberries. If desired, melt the chocolate chips in microwave or double boiler. Place 1 pastry on each dessert plate, and top with sliced strawberries. Drizzle melted chocolate over strawberries and onto plate.
Per Serving: Calories 282; Fat 15g; Sodium 526mg; Total Carbs 20g; Fiber 0.6g; Sugar 3.3g; Protein 16g

Vanilla Custard

Prep Time: 8 minutes. | Cook Time: 45–60 minutes | Serves: 4-6

2 cups whole milk	¼ teaspoon vanilla
2 eggs	Cooking spray
¼ cup sugar	⅛ teaspoon nutmeg
⅛ teaspoon salt	

1. Place the Cook & Crisp Basket in your Ninja Foodi Pressure Cooker Steam Fryer and place a reversible rack in it. 2. In a blender, process milk, egg, sugar, salt, and vanilla until smooth. 3. Spray the Cook & Crisp Basket with nonstick spray and pour the custard into it. 4. Put on the Smart Lid on top of the Ninja Foodi Steam Fryer. 5. Move the Lid Slider to the "Air Fry/Stovetop". 6. Cook on "Air Fry" Mode at 300°F/150°C for about 45 to 60 minutes. Custard is done when the center sets. 7. Sprinkle top with the nutmeg. 8. Allow custard to cool slightly. 9. Serve it warm, or chilled.
Per Serving: Calories 256; Fat 16.4g; Sodium 1321mg; Total Carbs 19.2g; Fiber 2.2g; Sugar 4.2g; Protein 5.2g

Fried Pancake Oreos

Prep Time: 7 minutes. | Cook Time: 6 minutes | Yield: 12 cookies

Oil for misting or nonstick spray	½ cup water, plus 2 tablespoons
1 cup complete pancake and waffle mix	12 Oreos or other chocolate sandwich cookies
1 teaspoon vanilla extract	1 tablespoon confectioners' sugar

1. Place the Cook & Crisp Basket in your Ninja Foodi Pressure Cooker Steam Fryer and place a reversible rack in it. 2. Spray the Cook & Crisp Basket with oil or nonstick spray. 3. In a suitable bowl, mix together the pancake mix, vanilla, and water. 4. Dip 4 cookies in batter and place in the Cook & Crisp Basket. 5. Put on the Smart Lid on top of the Ninja Foodi Steam Fryer. 6. Move the Lid Slider to the "Air Fry/Stovetop". 7. Cook on "Air Fry" Mode at 390°F/200°C for about 6 minutes, until browned. 8. Repeat those steps for the remaining cookies. 9. Sift sugar over warm cookies.
Per Serving: Calories 105; Fat 25g; Sodium 532mg; Total Carbs 2.3g; Fiber 0.4g; Sugar 2g; Protein 8.3g

Sweet Gingerbread

Prep Time: 5 minutes. | Cook Time: 20 minutes | Serves: 6–8

Cooking spray	1 teaspoon baking powder
1 cup flour	⅛ teaspoon salt
2 tablespoons sugar	¼ cup molasses
¾ teaspoon ginger	½ cup buttermilk
½ teaspoon baking soda	2 tablespoons oil
1 egg	1 teaspoon pure vanilla extract
¼ teaspoon cinnamon	

1. Place the Cook & Crisp Basket in your Ninja Foodi Pressure Cooker Steam Fryer. 2. Spray the Cook & Crisp Basket lightly with cooking spray. 3. In a suitable bowl, mix together all the dry ingredients. 4. In a separate bowl, beat the egg. Add molasses, buttermilk, oil, and vanilla and stir until well mixed. 5. Pour liquid mixture into dry ingredients and stir until well blended. 6. Pour batter into the Cook & Crisp Basket. 7. Put on the Smart Lid on top of the Ninja Foodi Steam Fryer. 8. Move the Lid Slider to the "Air Fry/Stovetop". 9. Cook on "Air Fry" Mode at 330°F/165°C for about 20 minutes until toothpick inserted in center of loaf comes out clean.
Per Serving: Calories 190; Fat 18g; Sodium 150mg; Total Carbs 0.6g; Fiber 0.4g; Sugar 0.4g; Protein 7.2g

Grilled Pineapple

Prep Time: 5 minutes. | Cook Time: 12 minutes | Serves: 4

Oil for misting or cooking spray	¼ teaspoon brandy
4 ½-inch-thick slices fresh pineapple, core removed	2 tablespoons slivered almonds, toasted
1 tablespoon honey	Vanilla frozen yogurt or coconut

sorbet

1. Place the Cook & Crisp Basket in your Ninja Foodi Pressure Cooker Steam Fryer. 2. Spray both sides of pineapple slices with oil or cooking spray. Place on grill plate or directly into Cook & Crisp Basket. 3. Put on the Smart Lid on top of the Ninja Foodi Steam Fryer. 4. Move the Lid Slider to the "Air Fry/Stovetop". 5. Cook on "Air Fry" Mode at 390°F/200°C for about 6 minutes. Turn slices over. Cook on "Air Fry" Mode for an additional 6 minutes. 6. Mix together the honey and brandy. 7. Remove cooked pineapple slices, sprinkle with toasted almonds, and drizzle with honey mixture. 8. Serve with a scoop of frozen yogurt or sorbet on the side.
Per Serving: Calories 267; Fat 12g; Sodium 165mg; Total Carbs 39g; Fiber 1.4g; Sugar 22g; Protein 3.3g

Easy Peach Cobbler

Prep Time: 15 minutes. | Cook Time: 12–14 minutes. | Serves: 4

16 ounces frozen peaches, thawed, with juice (do not drain)	½ cup flour
6 tablespoons sugar	¼ teaspoon salt
1 tablespoon cornstarch	3 tablespoons butter
1 tablespoon water	1½ tablespoons cold water
Crust	¼ teaspoon sugar

1. Place the Cook & Crisp Basket in your Ninja Foodi Pressure Cooker Steam Fryer. 2. Place peaches, including juice, and sugar in Cook & Crisp Basket. Stir to mix well. 3. In a small cup, dissolve cornstarch in the water. Stir into peaches. 4. In a suitable bowl, mix the flour and salt. Cut in butter using knives or a pastry blender. Stir in the cold water to make a stiff dough. 5. On a floured board or wax paper, pat dough into a square or circle slightly smaller than your Ninja Foodi Pressure Cooker Steam Fryer baking pan. Cut diagonally into 4 pieces. 6. Place dough pieces on top of peaches, leaving a tiny bit of space between the edges. Sprinkle very lightly with sugar, no more than about ¼ teaspoon. 7. Put on the Smart Lid on top of the Ninja Foodi Steam Fryer. 8. Move the Lid Slider to the "Air Fry/Stovetop". 9. Cook on "Air Fry" Mode at 360°F/180°C for about 12 to 14 minutes, until fruit bubbles and crust browns.
Per Serving: Calories 183; Fat 15g; Sodium 402mg; Total Carbs 2.5g; Fiber 0.4g; Sugar 1.1g; Protein 10g

Swiss Roll

Prep Time: 10 minutes. | Cook Time: 1 hour 20 minutes. | Serves: 6

½ cup milk	¼ teaspoon salt
¼ cup swerve	1 cup almond flour
1 tablespoon yeast	1 cup coconut flour
½ stick butter	2 tablespoons fresh orange juice
1 egg	
Filling:	
2 tablespoons butter	¼ teaspoon cinnamon
4 tablespoons swerve	1 teaspoon vanilla paste
1 teaspoon star anise	½ cup confectioners' swerve

1. Place the Cook & Crisp Basket in your Ninja Foodi Pressure Cooker Steam Fryer and place a reversible rack in it. 2. Heat a cup of milk in any microwave safe bowl and transfer the warm milk to the bowl of a stand electric mixer. Add the ¼ cup of swerve and yeast, and mix to mix well. Cover and let it sit until the yeast is foamy. 3. Then, beat the butter on low speed. Fold in the egg and mix again. Add salt and flour. Add the orange juice and mix on medium speed until a soft dough forms. 4. Knead the dough on a floured surface. Cover it loosely and let it sit in a warm place about 1 hour until doubled in size. Then, spritz the bottom and sides of Cook & Crisp Basket with cooking oil (butter flavored). 5. Roll your dough out into a rectangle. 6. Spread 2 tablespoons of butter all over the dough. In a mixing dish, mix 4 tablespoons of swerve, star anise, cinnamon, and vanilla; sprinkle evenly over the dough. 7. Then, roll up your dough to form a log. Cut into 6 equal rolls and place them in the parchment-lined Cook & Crisp Basket. 8. Put on the Smart Lid on top of the Ninja Foodi Steam Fryer. 9. Move the Lid Slider to the "Air Fry/Stovetop". 10. Cook on "Air Fry" Mode at 350°F/175°Cor about 12 minutes, turning them halfway through the cooking time. Dust with confectioners' swerve and enjoy!
Per Serving: Calories 260; Fat 16g; Sodium 585mg; Total Carbs 3.1g; Fiber 1.3g; Sugar 0.2g; Protein 5.5g

Sweet Potato Donut

Prep Time: 10 minutes. | Cook Time: 4–5 minutes. | Serves: 18

1 cup flour	sweet potatoes
⅓ cup sugar	1 egg, beaten
¼ teaspoon baking soda	2 tablespoons butter, melted
1 teaspoon baking powder	1 teaspoon pure vanilla extract
⅛ teaspoon salt	Oil for misting or cooking spray
½ cup cooked mashed purple	

1. Place the Cook & Crisp Basket in your Ninja Foodi Pressure Cooker Steam Fryer. 2. In a suitable bowl, stir together the flour, sugar, baking soda, baking powder, and salt. 3. In a separate bowl, mix the potatoes, egg, butter, and vanilla and mix well. 4. Add potato mixture to dry ingredients and stir into a soft dough. 5. Shape dough into 1½-inch balls. Mist lightly with oil or cooking spray. 6. Place 9 donut holes in Cook & Crisp Basket, leaving a little space in between. 7. Put on the Smart Lid on top of the Ninja Foodi Steam Fryer. 8. Move the Lid Slider to the "Air Fry/Stovetop". 9. Cook on "Air Fry" Mode at 390°F/200°C for about 4 to 5 minutes, until done in center and lightly browned outside. 10. Repeat to cook remaining donut holes.
Per Serving: Calories 209; Fat 7.5g; Sodium 321mg; Total Carbs 34.1g; Fiber 4g; Sugar 3.8g; Protein 4.3g

Fried Pies

Prep Time: 10 minutes. | Cook Time: 5 minutes. | Yield: 12 pies

12 small flour tortillas (4-inch diameter)	2 tablespoons shredded, unsweetened coconut
½ cup fig preserves	Oil for misting or cooking spray
¼ cup sliced almonds	

1. Wrap refrigerated tortillas in damp paper towels and heat in microwave 30 seconds to warm. Making with one tortilla at a time, place 2 teaspoons fig preserves, 1 teaspoon sliced almonds, and ½ teaspoon coconut in the center of each. 2. Moisten outer edges of tortilla all around. 3. Fold one side of tortilla over filling to make a half-moon shape and press down lightly on center. With the tines of a fork, press down firmly on edges of tortilla to seal in filling. 4. Mist both sides with oil or cooking spray. 5. Place hand pies in Cook & Crisp Basket close but not overlapping. It's fine to lean some against the sides and corners of the basket. 6. Put on the Smart Lid on top of the Ninja Foodi Steam Fryer. 7. Move the Lid Slider to the "Air Fry/Stovetop". 8. Cook on "Air Fry" Mode at 390°F/200°C for about 5 minutes until lightly browned. Serve hot. 9. Refrigerate any leftover pies in a closed container. To serve later, toss them back in the Ninja Foodi Cook & Crisp Basket. Cook for about 2 or 3 minutes to reheat.
Per Serving: Calories 180; Fat 3.2g; Sodium 133mg; Total Carbs 32g; Fiber 1.1g; Sugar 1.8g; Protein 9g

Zesty Raspberry Muffins

Prep Time: 10 minutes. | Cook Time: 35 minutes. | Serves: 10

1 egg	2 teaspoon baking powder
1 cup frozen raspberries, coated with some flour	Yogurt, as needed
	1 teaspoon lemon zest
1 ½ cups flour	2 tablespoon lemon juice
½ cup sugar	Pinch of sea salt
⅓ cup vegetable oil	

1. Place the Cook & Crisp Basket in your Pressure Cooker Steam Fryer. 2. Place all of the dry recipe ingredients in a bowl and mix well. 3. Beat the egg and pour it into a cup. Mix it with the oil and lemon juice. Add in the yogurt, to taste. 4. Mix the dry and wet recipe ingredients. 5. Add in the lemon zest and raspberries. 6. Coat the insides of 10 muffin tins with a little butter. 7. Spoon an equal amount of the mixture into each muffin tin. 8. Transfer to the Cook & Crisp Basket. Put on the Smart Lid on top of the Ninja Foodi Steam Fryer. Move the Lid Slider to the "Air Fry/Stovetop". Select the "Air Fry" mode for cooking. Adjust the cooking temperature to 350°F/175°C. 9. Cook for around 10 minutes, in batches if necessary.
Per serving: Calories 257; Fat: 16.5g; Sodium 1031mg; Carbs: 23.6g; Fiber: 3.4g; Sugars 6.1g; Protein 4.7g

Vanilla Pecan Pie

Prep Time: 10 minutes. | Cook Time: 1 hour 10 minutes. | Serves: 4

1x 8-inch pie dough	2 tablespoon butter
½ teaspoon cinnamon	1 tablespoon butter, melted
¾ teaspoon vanilla extract	2 tablespoon sugar
2 eggs	½ cup chopped pecans
¾ cup maple syrup	Oil
⅛ teaspoon nutmeg	

1. Place the Cook & Crisp Basket in your Pressure Cooker Steam Fryer. 2. In a suitable bowl, coat the pecans in the melted butter. 3. Transfer the pecans to the Cook & Crisp Basket. Put on the Smart Lid on top of the Ninja Foodi Steam Fryer. Move the Lid Slider to the "Air Fry/Stovetop". Select the "Air Fry" mode for cooking. Cook at 370°F/185°C for 10 minutes. Then grease the Cook & Crisp Basket with oil. Put the pie dough in it and add the pecans on top. 4. In a suitable bowl, mix the rest of the ingredients. Pour this over the pecans. 5. Put on the Smart Lid on top of the Ninja Foodi Steam Fryer. Move the Lid Slider to the "Air Fry/Stovetop". Select the "Air Fry" mode for cooking. Adjust the cooking temperature to 370°F/190°C. 6. Air Fry for around 25 minutes.
Per serving: Calories 194; Fat: 13g; Sodium 208mg; Carbs: 30.6g; Fiber: 5.6g; Sugars 20.7g; Protein 9.1g

Honey Chocolate Cookies

Prep Time: 10 minutes. | Cook Time: 30 minutes. | Serves: 8

3 ounces sugar	6 ounces flour
4 ounces butter	1 ½ tablespoon milk
1 tablespoon honey	2 ounces chocolate chips

1. Place the Cook & Crisp Basket in your Pressure Cooker Steam Fryer. 2. Mix the sugar and butter using an electric mixer, until a fluffy texture is achieved. 3. Stir in the remaining ingredients, minus the chocolate chips. 4. Gradually fold in the chocolate chips. 5. Spoon equal portions of the mixture onto a lined baking sheet and flatten out each one with a spoon. Ensure the cookies are not touching. 6. Place in the Cook & Crisp Basket . Put on the Smart Lid on top of the Ninja Foodi Steam Fryer. Move the Lid Slider to the "Air Fry/Stovetop". Select the "Air Fry" mode for cooking. Adjust the cooking temperature to 350°F/175°C. 7. Cook for around 18 minutes.
Per serving: Calories 148; Fat: 0.7g; Sodium 3mg; Carbs: 57.4g; Fiber: 5.1g; Sugars 40.4g; Protein 2g

Easy Butter Cake

Prep Time: 10 minutes. | Cook Time: 25 minutes. | Serves: 2

1 egg	6 tablespoon sugar
1 ½ cup flour	Pinch of sea salt
7 tablespoon butter, at room temperature	Cooking spray
	Dusting of sugar to serve
6 tablespoon milk	

1. Place the Cook & Crisp Basket in your Pressure Cooker Steam Fryer. 2. Spritz the inside of a suitable ring cake tin with cooking spray. 3. In a suitable bowl, mix the butter and sugar using a whisk. 4. Stir in the egg and continue to mix everything until the mixture is smooth and fluffy. 5. Pour the flour through a sieve into the bowl. 6. Pour in the milk, before adding a pinch of salt, and mix once again to incorporate everything well. 7. Pour the prepared batter into the tin and use the back of a spoon to made sure the surface is even. 8. Place in the Cook & Crisp Basket. Put on the Smart Lid on top of the Ninja Foodi Steam Fryer. Move the Lid Slider to the "Air Fry/Stovetop". Select the "Air Fry" mode for cooking. Adjust the cooking temperature to 360°F/180°C. 9. Cook for around 15 minutes. 10. Before removing it from Pressure Cooker Steam Fryer, ensure the cake is cooked through by inserting a toothpick into the center and checking that it comes out clean. 11. Allow the cake to cool and serve with dusting of sugar.
Per serving: Calories 281; Fat: 6.7g; Sodium 187mg; Carbs: 52.7g; Fiber: 6.6g; Sugars 29g; Protein 5.1g

Chocolate Mug Cake

Prep Time: 10 minutes. | Cook Time: 15 minutes. | Serves: 1

1 tablespoon cocoa powder
3 tablespoon coconut oil
¼ cup flour

3 tablespoons whole milk
5 tablespoon sugar

1. Place the Cook & Crisp Basket in your Pressure Cooker Steam Fryer. 2. In a suitable bowl, stir all of the recipe ingredients to mix them completely. 3. Take a short, stout mug and pour the mixture into it. 4. Put the mug in your Ninja Foodi Pressure Steam Fryer. Put on the Smart Lid on top of the Ninja Foodi Steam Fryer. Move the Lid Slider to the "Air Fry/Stovetop". Select the "Air Fry" mode for cooking. Cook for around 10 minutes at 390°F/200°C.
Per serving: Calories 361; Fat: 31.3g; Sodium 385mg; Carbs: 13.8g; Fiber: 7.3g; Sugars 2.5g; Protein 9.7g

Pound Cake

Prep Time: 10 minutes. | Cook Time: 35 minutes. | Serves: 8

1 stick butter
1 cup swerve
4 eggs
1 ½ cups coconut flour
½ teaspoon baking powder
½ teaspoon baking soda

¼ teaspoon salt
A pinch of freshly grated nutmeg
A pinch of star anise
½ cup buttermilk
1 teaspoon vanilla essence
Cooking spray

1. Place the Cook & Crisp Basket in your Ninja Foodi Pressure Cooker Steam Fryer and place a reversible rack in it. 2. Spritz the Cook & Crisp Basket with cooking spray. 3. Beat the butter and swerve with a hand mixer until creamy. Then, fold in the eggs, one at a time, and mix well until fluffy. 4. Stir in the flour along with the remaining ingredients. Mix to mix well. Scrape the batter into the Cook & Crisp Basket. 5. Put on the Smart Lid on top of the Ninja Foodi Steam Fryer. 6. Move the Lid Slider to the "Air Fry/Stovetop". 7. Cook on "Air Fry" Mode at 320°F/160°C for about 15 minutes; rotate the basket. Cook for another 15 minutes, until the top of the cake springs back when gently pressed with your fingers. Bon appétit!
Per Serving: Calories 196; Fat 7.1g; Sodium 492mg; Total Carbs 21.6g; Fiber 2.9g; Sugar 0.8g; Protein 13.4g

Almond Pears

Prep Time: 10 minutes. | Cook Time: 15–20 minutes | Serves: 4

Yogurt Topping
1 container vanilla Greek yogurt (5–6 ounces)
¼ teaspoon almond flavoring

2 whole pears
¼ cup crushed Biscoff cookies
1 tablespoon sliced almonds
1 tablespoon butter

1. Place the Cook & Crisp Basket in your Ninja Foodi Pressure Cooker Steam Fryer. 2. Stir almond flavoring into yogurt and set aside while preparing pears. 3. Halve each pear and spoon out the core. 4. Place pear halves in Cook & Crisp Basket. 5. Stir together the cookie crumbs and almonds. Add ¼ of this almond mixture into the hollow cavity of each pear half. 6. Cut butter into 4 pieces and place one piece on top of crumb mixture in each pear. 7. Put on the Smart Lid on top of the Ninja Foodi Steam Fryer. 8. Move the Lid Slider to the "Air Fry/Stovetop". 9. Cook on "Air Fry" Mode at 360°F/180°C for about 15 to 20 minutes until pears have cooked through but are still slightly firm. 10. Serve pears warm with a dollop of yogurt topping.
Per Serving: Calories 275; Fat 1.4g; Sodium 582mg; Total Carbs 31.5g; Fiber 1.1g; Sugar 0.1g; Protein 2.8g

Baked Butter Apple

Prep Time: 10 minutes. | Cook Time: 20 minutes | Yield: 6 apple halves

3 small Honey Crisp or other baking apples
3 tablespoons maple syrup

3 tablespoons chopped pecans
1 tablespoon firm butter, cut into 6 pieces

1. Place the Cook & Crisp Basket in your Ninja Foodi Pressure Cooker Steam Fryer. 2. Wash apples well and dry them. 3. Cut the apples in half. Remove their cores and a little of the flesh from the center to make a cavity for the pecans. 4. Set the cut apple halves in Cook & Crisp Basket, with their cut side up. 5. Add ½ teaspoons pecans into each apple cavity. 6. Spoon ½ tablespoon maple syrup over the added pecan filling in each apple. 7. Top each apple half with pecans with ½ teaspoon butter. 8. Put on the Smart Lid on top of the Ninja Foodi Steam Fryer. 9. Move the Lid Slider to the "Air Fry/Stovetop". 10. Cook on "Air Fry" Mode at 360°F/180°C for about 20 minutes, until apples are tender.
Per Serving: Calories 220; Fat 1.7g; Sodium 178mg; Total Carbs 1.7g; Fiber 0.2g; Sugar 0.2g; Protein 2.9g

Coconut Pie

Prep Time: 10 minutes. | Cook Time: 20–23 minutes | Serves: 4

1 cup milk
¼ cup plus 2 tablespoons sugar
¼ cup biscuit baking mix
1 teaspoon vanilla
2 eggs

2 tablespoons melted butter
Cooking spray
½ cup shredded, sweetened coconut

1. Place the Cook & Crisp Basket in your Ninja Foodi Pressure Cooker Steam Fryer and place a reversible rack in it. 2. Place all the recipe ingredients except coconut in a suitable bowl. 3. Using a hand mixer to beat on high speed for about 3 minutes. 4. Let sit for about 5 minutes. 5. Spray the Cook & Crisp Basket with cooking spray. 6. Pour filling into Cook & Crisp Basket and sprinkle coconut over top. 7. Put on the Smart Lid on top of the Ninja Foodi Steam Fryer. 8. Move the Lid Slider to the "Air Fry/Stovetop". 9. Cook pie on "Air Fry" Mode at 330°F/165°C for about 20 to 23 minutes until center sets.
Per Serving: Calories 353; Fat 5g; Sodium 818mg; Total Carbs 53.2g; Fiber 4.4g; Sugar 8g; Protein 1.3g

Butter Peach Crumble

Prep Time: 10 minutes. | Cook Time: 35 minutes. | Serves: 6

1 ½ lb. peaches, peeled and chopped
2 tablespoon lemon juice
1 cup flour

1 tablespoon water
½ cup sugar
5 tablespoons cold butter
Pinch of sea salt

1. Place the Cook & Crisp Basket in your Pressure Cooker Steam Fryer. 2. Mash the peaches a little with a fork to achieve a lumpy consistency. 3. Add in two tablespoons of sugar and the lemon juice. 4. In a bowl, mix the flour, salt, and sugar. Throw in a tablespoon of water before adding in the cold butter, mixing until crumbly. 5. Grease the Cook & Crisp Basket and arrange the berries at the bottom. Top with the crumbs. 6. Put on the Smart Lid on top of the Ninja Foodi Steam Fryer. Move the Lid Slider to the "Air Fry/Stovetop". Select the "Air Fry" mode for cooking. Air Fry for around 20 minutes at 390°F/200°C.
Per serving: Calories 363; Fat: 10.7g; Sodium 253mg; Carbs: 63.7g; Fiber: 3.8g; Sugars 22.9g; Protein 4.9g

Banana Cake

Prep Time: 10 minutes. | Cook Time: 55 minutes. | Serves: 6

16 ounces bananas, mashed
8 ounces flour
6 ounces sugar
3.5 ounces walnuts, chopped

2.5 ounces butter
2 eggs
¼ teaspoon baking soda
Oil

1. Place the Cook & Crisp Basket in your Pressure Cooker Steam Fryer. 2. Coat the Cook & Crisp Basket with a little oil. 3. In a suitable bowl mix the sugar, butter, egg, flour and soda using a whisk. Throw in the bananas and walnuts. 4. Transfer the mixture to the Cook & Crisp Basket. Put on the Smart Lid on top of the Ninja Foodi Steam Fryer. Move the Lid Slider to the "Air Fry/Stovetop". Select the "Air Fry" mode for cooking. Adjust the cooking temperature to 355°F/180°C. 5. Cook for around 10 minutes. 6. Reduce its heat to 330°F/165°C. Cook for another 15 minutes. Serve hot.
Per serving: Calories 363; Fat: 10.7g; Sodium 253mg; Carbs: 63.7g; Fiber: 3.8g; Sugars 22.9g; Protein 4.9g

Lemon Cake

Prep Time: 10 minutes. | Cook Time: 60 minutes. | Serves: 6

17.5 ounces ricotta cheese
5.4 ounces sugar
3 eggs
3 tablespoon flour

1 lemon, juiced and zested
2 teaspoon vanilla extract
[optional]

1. Place the Cook & Crisp Basket in your Pressure Cooker Steam Fryer. 2. Mix all of the recipe ingredients until a creamy consistency is achieved. 3. Place the mixture in a cake tin. 4. Transfer the tin to the Cook & Crisp Basket. Put on the Smart Lid on top of the Ninja Foodi Steam Fryer. Move the Lid Slider to the "Air Fry/Stovetop". Select the "Air Fry" mode for cooking. Adjust the cooking temperature to 320°F/160°C. 5. Cook for the cakes for around 25 minutes. 6. Remove the cake from the fryer, allow to cool, and serve.
Per serving: Calories 420; Fat: 17.1g; Sodium 282mg; Carbs: 65.7g; Fiber: 4.5g; Sugars 35.1g; Protein 7g

Dough Dippers with Chocolate Sauce

Prep Time: 10 minutes. | Cook Time: 45 minutes. | Serves: 5

¾ cup sugar
1 lb. friendly bread dough
1 cup heavy cream
12 ounces high quality semi-sweet

chocolate chips
½ cup butter, melted
2 tablespoon extract

1. Place the Cook & Crisp Basket in your Pressure Cooker Steam Fryer. 2. Coat the inside of the basket with a little melted butter. 3. Halve and roll up the prepared dough to create two 15-inch logs. Slice each log into 20 disks. 4. Halve each disk and twist it 3 or 4 times. 5. Lay out a cookie sheet and lay the twisted dough pieces on top. Brush the pieces with some more melted butter and sprinkle on the sugar. 6. Place the sheet in the Cook & Crisp Basket. Put on the Smart Lid on top of the Ninja Foodi Steam Fryer. Move the Lid Slider to the "Air Fry/Stovetop". Select the "Air Fry" mode for cooking. 7. Adjust the cooking temperature to 350°F/175°C. 8. Air Fry for around 5 minutes. Flip the prepared dough twists over, and brush the other side with more butter. Cook for an additional 3 minutes. It may be necessary to complete this step in batches. 9. In the meantime, make the chocolate sauce. Firstly, put the heavy cream into a suitable saucepan over the medium heat and allow it to simmer. 10. Put the chocolate chips into a large bowl and add the simmering cream on top. Mix the chocolate chips everything until a smooth consistency is achieved. Stir in 2 tablespoons of extract. 11. Transfer the fried cookies in a shallow dish, pour over the rest of the melted butter and sprinkle on the sugar. 12. Drizzle on the chocolate sauce before serving.
Per serving: Calories 469; Fat: 36.5g; Sodium 46mg; Carbs: 31.4g; Fiber: 4.5g; Sugars 17.9g; Protein 9.1g

Pumpkin Pudding

Prep Time: 10 minutes. | Cook Time: 25 minutes. | Serves: 4

3 cups pumpkin puree
3 tablespoon honey
1 tablespoon ginger
1 tablespoon cinnamon
1 teaspoon clove

1 teaspoon nutmeg
1 cup full-fat: cream
2 eggs
1 cup sugar

1. Place the Cook & Crisp Basket in your Pressure Cooker Steam Fryer. 2. In a suitable bowl, stir all of the recipe ingredients to mix. 3. Grease inside of the Cook & Crisp Basket. 4. Pour the mixture into the Cook & Crisp Basket. 5. Put on the Smart Lid on top of the Ninja Foodi Steam Fryer. 6. Move the Lid Slider to the "Air Fry/Stovetop". Select the "Air Fry" mode for cooking. 7. Adjust the cooking temperature to 390°F/200°C. 8. Cook for around 15 minutes. Serve with whipped cream if desired.
Per serving: Calories 360; Fat: 7.8g; Sodium 280mg; Carbs: 74.4g; Fiber: 8g; Sugars 47.4g; Protein 2.7g

Air-Fried Peach Slices

Prep Time: 10 minutes. | Cook Time: 40 minutes. | Serves: 4

4 cups peaches, sliced   2 – 3 tablespoon sugar

2 tablespoon flour
⅓ cup oats
2 tablespoons unsalted butter

¼ teaspoon vanilla extract
1 teaspoon cinnamon

1. Place the Cook & Crisp Basket in your Pressure Cooker Steam Fryer. 2. In a large bowl, mix the peach slices, sugar, vanilla extract, and cinnamon. Pour the prepared mixture into the Cook & Crisp Basket. 3. Put on the Smart Lid on top of the Ninja Foodi Steam Fryer. 4. Move the Lid Slider to the "Air Fry/Stovetop". Select the "Air Fry" mode for cooking. 5. Cook for around 20 minutes on 290°F/145°C. 6. In the meantime, mix the oats, flour, and unsalted butter in a separate bowl. 7. Once the peach slices cooked, pour the butter mixture on top of them. 8. Cook for around 10 minutes at 310°F/155°C. 9 .Remove from the Pressure Cooker Steam Fryer and allow to crisp up for around 5 –10 minutes. Serve with ice cream if desired.
Per serving: Calories 130; Fat: 3.9g; Sodium 3mg; Carbs: 21.6g; Fiber: 1.6g; Sugars 9.8g; Protein 3.6g

Marshmallow Fluff Turnover

Prep Time: 10 minutes. | Cook Time: 35 minutes. | Serves: 4

4 sheets filo pastry, defrosted
4 tablespoons chunky peanut butter
4 teaspoon marshmallow fluff

2 ounces butter, melted
Pinch of sea salt

1. Place the Cook & Crisp Basket in your Pressure Cooker Steam Fryer. 2. Roll out the pastry sheets. Coat one with a light brushing of butter. 3. Lay a second pastry sheet on top of the first one. Brush once again with butter. Repeat until all 4 sheets have been used. 4. Slice the filo layers into four strips, measuring 3 inches x 12 inches. 5. Spread one tablespoon of peanut butter and one teaspoon of marshmallow fluff on the underside of each pastry strip. 6. Take the tip of each sheet and fold it backwards over the filling, forming a triangle. Repeat this action in a zigzag manner until the filling is completely enclosed. 7. Seal the ends of each turnover with a light brushing of butter. 8. Put the turnovers in the Cook & Crisp Basket. Put on the Smart Lid on top of the Ninja Foodi Steam Fryer. Move the Lid Slider to the "Air Fry/Stovetop". Select the "Air Fry" mode for cooking. Adjust the cooking temperature to 360°F/180°C. 9. Cook for around 3 to 5 minutes, until they turn golden brown and puffy. 10. Sprinkle a little sea salt over each turnover before serving.
Per serving: Calories 281; Fat: 6.7g; Sodium 187mg; Carbs: 52.7g; Fiber: 6.6g; Sugars 29g; Protein 5.1g

Easy Vanilla Soufflé

Prep Time: 10 minutes. | Cook Time: 50 minutes. | Serves: 6

¼ cup flour
¼ cup butter, softened
1 cup whole milk
¼ cup sugar
2 teaspoon vanilla extract

1 vanilla bean
5 egg whites
4 egg yolks
1 ounces sugar
1 teaspoon cream of tartar

1. Mix the flour and butter to create a smooth paste. 2. In a saucepan, heat up the milk. Add the ¼ cup sugar and allow it to dissolve. 3. Put the vanilla bean in the mixture and bring it to a boil. 4. Pour in the flour-butter mixture. Beat the contents of the saucepan with wire whisk, removing all the lumps. 5. Reduce its heat and allow the mixture to simmer and thicken for a number of minutes. 6. Take the saucepan off the heat. Remove the vanilla bean and let the mixture cool for around 10 minutes in an ice bath. 7. In the meantime, grease six 3-ounces ramekins or soufflé dishes with butter and add a sprinkling of sugar to each one. 8. In a separate bowl quickly, rigorously stir the egg yolks and vanilla extract together. Mix with the milk mixture. 9. In another bowl, beat the egg whites, 1 ounces sugar and cream of tartar to form medium stiff peaks. 10. Fold the egg whites into the soufflé base. Transfer everything to the ramekins, smoothing the surfaces with a knife or the back of a spoon. 11. Put the ramekins in the cook and crisp basket. Place the Cook & Crisp Basket in your Pressure Cooker Steam Fryer. 12. Put on the Smart Lid on top of the Ninja Foodi Steam Fryer. Move the Lid Slider to the "Air Fry/Stovetop". Select the "Air Fry" mode for cooking. Adjust the cooking temperature to 330°F/165°C. 13. Cook for around 14 to 16 minutes. You may need to complete this step in multiple batches. 14. Serve the soufflés topped with powdered sugar and with a side of chocolate sauce.
Per serving: Calories 182; Fat: 0.7g; Sodium 7mg; Carbs: 46.3g; Fiber: 6.2g; Sugars 40.7g; Protein 1.9g

Blackberry Granola Crisp

Prep Time: 10 minutes. | Cook Time: 18 minutes. | Serves: 1

2 tablespoon lemon juice
⅓ cup powdered erythritol
¼ teaspoon xanthan gum

2 cup blackberries
1 cup crunchy granola

1. Place the Cook & Crisp Basket in your Pressure Cooker Steam Fryer. 2. In a suitable bowl, mix the lemon juice, erythritol, xanthan gum, and blackberries. Transfer to the Cook & Crisp Basket and seal with aluminum foil. Put on the Smart Lid on top of the Ninja Foodi Steam Fryer. Move the Lid Slider to the "Air Fry/Stovetop". Select the "Air Fry" mode for cooking. 3. Cook for 12 minutes at 350°F/175°C. 4. Take care when removing the dish from the Pressure Cooker Steam Fryer. Give the blackberries another stir and top with the granola. 5. Return the dish to the Pressure Cooker Steam Fryer. Put on the Smart Lid on top of the Ninja Foodi Steam Fryer. Move the Lid Slider to the "Air Fry/Stovetop". Select the "Air Fry" mode for cooking. Cook for minutes at 320°F/160°C. Serve once the granola has turned brown and enjoy.
Per serving: Calories 420; Fat: 17.1g; Sodium 282mg; Carbs: 65.7g; Fiber: 4.5g; Sugars 35.1g; Protein 7g

Dark Brownies

Prep Time: 10 minutes. | Cook Time: 11–13 minutes | Serves: 4

1 egg
½ cup granulated sugar
¼ teaspoon salt
½ teaspoon vanilla
¼ cup butter, melted
¼ cup flour, plus 2 tablespoons

¼ cup cocoa
Cooking spray
Optional
vanilla ice cream
caramel sauce
whipped cream

1. Place the Cook & Crisp Basket in your Ninja Foodi Pressure Cooker Steam Fryer and place a reversible rack in it. 2. Beat well sugar, salt, egg, and vanilla until the mixture turns light in color. 3. Stir in melted butter and mix well. 4. Add in flour and cocoa. 5. Spray the Cook & Crisp Basket with cooking spray. 6. Spread the prepared cocoa batter in the Cook & Crisp Basket. 7. Put on the Smart Lid on top of the Ninja Foodi Steam Fryer. 8. Move the Lid Slider to the "Air Fry/Stovetop". 9. Cook on "Air Fry" Mode this batter at 330°F/165°C for about 13 minutes. Cool the baked cake at room temperature and cut into 4 large squares or 16 small brownie bites.
Per Serving: Calories 268; Fat 10.4g; Sodium 411mg; Total Carbs 0.4g; Fiber 0.1g; Sugar 0.1g; Protein 4.6g

Quick Peanut Butter Cookies

Prep Time: 10 minutes. | Cook Time: 15 minutes. | Serves: 1

¼ teaspoon salt
4 tablespoon erythritol

½ cup peanut butter
1 egg

1. Place the Cook & Crisp Basket in your Pressure Cooker Steam Fryer. 2. Mix the salt, erythritol, and peanut butter in a suitable bowl, incorporating everything well. Break the egg over the mixture and mix to create a dough. 3. Flatten the prepared dough using a rolling pin and cut into shapes with a knife or cookie cutter. Make a crisscross on the top of each cookie with a fork. 4. Put the cookies inside the Cook & Crisp Basket. Put on the Smart Lid on top of the Ninja Foodi Steam Fryer. 5. Move the Lid Slider to the "Air Fry/Stovetop". Select the "Air Fry" mode for cooking. Adjust the cooking temperature to 360°F/180°C. 6. Leave to cook for 10 minutes. Take care when taking them out and allow to cool before enjoying.
Per serving: Calories 360; Fat: 7.8g; Sodium 280mg; Carbs: 74.4g; Fiber: 8g; Sugars 47.4g; Protein 2.7g

Walnut Bread

Prep Time: 10 minutes. | Cook Time: 40 minutes. | Serves: 1 loaf

7 ounces flour
¼ teaspoon baking powder
2.5 ounces butter

5.5 ounces sugar
2 medium eggs
14 ounces bananas, peeled

2.8 ounces chopped walnuts

1. Place the Cook & Crisp Basket in your Pressure Cooker Steam Fryer. 2. Grease the Cook & Crisp Basket with butter. 3. Mix the flour and the baking powder in a suitable bowl. 4. In a separate bowl, beat the sugar and butter until fluffy and pale. Gradually add in the flour and egg. Stir. 5. Throw in the walnuts and mix again. 6. Mash the bananas using a fork and transfer to the bowl. Mix once more, until everything is incorporated. 7. Pour the mixture into the Cook & Crisp Basket. Put on the Smart Lid on top of the Ninja Foodi Steam Fryer. Move the Lid Slider to the "Air Fry/Stovetop". Select the "Air Fry" mode for cooking. 8. Adjust the cooking temperature to 350°F/175°C. 9. Cook for around 10 minutes.
Per serving: Calories 488; Fat: 34.3g; Sodium 130mg; Carbs: 42.4g; Fiber: 1.7g; Sugars 21.5g; Protein 4.8g

Sugary Churros

Prep Time: 10 minutes. | Cook Time: 15 minutes. | Serves: 1

½ cup water
¼ cup butter
½ cup flour

3 eggs
2 ½ teaspoon sugar

1. Place the Cook & Crisp Basket in your Pressure Cooker Steam Fryer. 2. In a suitable saucepan, bring the water and butter to a boil. Once it is bubbling, add the flour and mix to create a doughy consistency. 3. Remove from the heat, allow to cool, and crack the eggs into the saucepan. Blend with a hand mixer until the prepared dough turns fluffy. 4. Transfer the prepared dough into a piping bag. 5. Pipe the prepared dough into the Cook & Crisp Basket in several three-inch-long segments. 6. Put on the Smart Lid on top of the Ninja Foodi Steam Fryer. 7. Move the Lid Slider to the "Air Fry/Stovetop". Select the "Air Fry" mode for cooking. 8. Adjust the cooking temperature to 380°F/195°C. 9. Cook for 10 minutes before removing from the fryer and coating in the sugar. 10. Serve with the low-carb chocolate sauce of your choice.
Per serving: Calories 256; Fat: 3.5g; Sodium 7mg; Carbs: 54.2g; Fiber: 10.7g; Sugars 32.2g; Protein 4.9g

Avocado Cocoa Pudding

Prep Time: 10 minutes. | Cook Time: 5 minutes. | Serves: 1

1 avocado
3 teaspoon liquid sugar
1 tablespoon cocoa powder

4 teaspoons unsweetened milk
¼ teaspoon vanilla extract

1. Place the Cook & Crisp Basket in your Pressure Cooker Steam Fryer. 2. Halve the avocado, twist to open, and scoop out the pit. 3. Spoon the flesh into a suitable bowl and mash it with a fork. Throw in the sugar, cocoa powder, milk, and vanilla extract, and mix everything with a hand mixer. 4. Transfer this mixture to the Cook & Crisp Basket. Put on the Smart Lid on top of the Ninja Foodi Steam Fryer. Move the Lid Slider to the "Air Fry/Stovetop". Select the "Air Fry" mode for cooking. Adjust the cooking temperature to 360°F/180°C. 5. Cook for 3 minutes.
Per serving: Calories 488; Fat: 34.3g; Sodium 130mg; Carbs: 42.4g; Fiber: 1.7g; Sugars 21.5g; Protein 4.8g

Chia Coconut Pudding

Prep Time: 10 minutes. | Cook Time: 10 minutes. | Serves: 1

1 cup chia seeds
1 cup unsweetened coconut milk
1 teaspoon liquid sugar

1 tablespoon coconut oil
1 teaspoon butter

1. Place the Cook & Crisp Basket in your Pressure Cooker Steam Fryer. 2. In a suitable bowl, gently mix the chia seeds with the milk and sugar, before mixing the coconut oil and butter. Spoon seven equal-sized portions into seven ramekins and set these inside the Cook & Crisp Basket. 3. Put on the Smart Lid on top of the Ninja Foodi Steam Fryer. 4. Move the Lid Slider to the "Air Fry/Stovetop". Select the "Air Fry" mode for cooking. Adjust the cooking temperature to 360°F/180°C. 5. Cook for 4 minutes. Take care when removing the ramekins from the fryer and allow to cool for 4 minutes before serving.
Per serving: Calories 130; Fat: 3.9g; Sodium 3mg; Carbs: 21.6g; Fiber: 1.6g; Sugars 9.8g; Protein 3.6g

Toasted Flakes

Prep Time: 10 minutes. | Cook Time: 5 minutes. | Serves: 1

1 cup unsweetened coconut flakes	¼ cup granular erythritol
2 teaspoon coconut oil, melted	Salt

1. Place the Cook & Crisp Basket in your Pressure Cooker Steam Fryer. 2. In a suitable bowl, mix the coconut flakes, oil, granular erythritol, and a pinch of salt, ensuring that the flakes are coated completely. 3. Place the coconut flakes in the Cook & Crisp Basket. Put on the Smart Lid on top of the Ninja Foodi Steam Fryer. Move the Lid Slider to the "Air Fry/Stovetop". Select the "Air Fry" mode for cooking. Air Fry at 300°F/150°C for 3 minutes, giving the basket a good shake a few times throughout the cooking time. Fry until golden and serve.

Per serving: Calories 363; Fat: 10.7g; Sodium 253mg; Carbs: 63.7g; Fiber: 3.8g; Sugars 22.9g; Protein 4.9g

Poppy Seed Cake

Prep Time: 10 minutes. | Cook Time: 15 minutes. | Serves: 8

For the Cake:

1½ cups all-purpose flour	butter, melted
2 teaspoons baking powder	2 large eggs
1 teaspoon salt	½ cup whole milk
½ cup granulated sugar	1 tablespoon poppy seeds
6 tablespoons (¾ stick) unsalted	Finely grated zest of 1 lemon

For the Syrup:

3 tablespoons fresh lemon juice	¼ cup granulated sugar

For the Glaze:

1 cup powdered sugar	lemon juice
1 tablespoon 1 teaspoon fresh	

To make the cake: 1. In a suitable bowl, mix the flour, baking powder, and salt until evenly mixed. In a suitable bowl, mix the granulated sugar, melted butter, and eggs until smooth, then mix in the milk, poppy seeds, and lemon zest. Pour the liquid ingredients over the dry recipe ingredients and mix until just mixed. Pour the prepared batter into a greased the Cook & Crisp Basket and smooth the top. 2. Place the Cook & Crisp Basket in your Pressure Cooker Steam Fryer. 3. Put on the Smart Lid on top of the Ninja Foodi Steam Fryer. Move the Lid Slider to the "Air Fry/Stovetop". Select the "Air Fry" mode for cooking. Air Fry at 310°F/155°C until a toothpick inserted into the center of the cake comes out clean, about 30 to 35 minutes. 4. Meanwhile, make the syrup: In a microwave-safe bowl, heat the lemon juice and granulated sugar in the microwave, stirring until the sugar dissolves. 5. Remove the pan from the Ninja Foodi Pressure Steam Fryer and transfer to a wire rack set over a rimmed baking sheet. Let cool for around 5 minutes in the pan, then turn the cake out onto the rack and invert it so it's right-side up. As soon as you unmold it, use a toothpick to stab the top of the warm cake all over, making as many holes as you can. Slowly pour the warm lemon syrup over the top of the cake so that it absorbs as you pour it on. Let the cake cool completely on the rack to allow the syrup to hydrate the cake fully. 6. To make the glaze: In a glass bowl, mix the powdered sugar and lemon juice and stir into a thick glaze. Microwave the glaze until loose and pourable, about 30 seconds, then stir until completely smooth. Pour the hot glaze over the top of the cake, still on the rack, letting it drip over the edges. Let the cake stand for at least 10 minutes to allow the glaze to set. Transfer the cake to a plate before serving.

Per serving: Calories 161; Fat: 12.4g; Sodium 375mg; Carbs: 9.8g; Fiber: 1.5g; Sugars 2.6g; Protein 3.8g

Strawberry Shortcake

Prep Time: 10 minutes. | Cook Time: 15 minutes. | Serves: 4 to 6

1⅓ cups all-purpose flour	Turbinado sugar, such as Sugar In
3 tablespoons granulated sugar	The Raw, for sprinkling
1½ teaspoons baking powder	2 tablespoons powdered sugar,
1 teaspoon salt	more for dusting
8 tablespoons butter, cubed and	½ teaspoon vanilla extract
chilled	1 cup quartered fresh strawberries
1⅓ cups heavy cream, chilled	

1. In a suitable bowl, mix the flour, granulated sugar, baking powder, and salt. Add the butter and use your fingers to break apart the butter pieces while working them into the flour mixture, until pea-size pieces form. Pour ⅔ cup of the cream over the flour mixture and, using a rubber spatula, mix the ingredients until just mixed. 2. Transfer the prepared dough to a work surface and form into a 7-inch-wide disk. Brush the top with water, then sprinkle with some turbinado sugar. Using a suitable metal spatula, transfer the prepared dough to the Cook & Crisp Basket. Place the Cook & Crisp Basket in your Pressure Cooker Steam Fryer. 3. Put on the Smart Lid on top of the Ninja Foodi Steam Fryer. Move the Lid Slider to the "Air Fry/Stovetop". Select the "Air Fry" mode for cooking. Air Fry at 350°F/175°C until golden brown and fluffy, about 20 minutes. Let cool in the "cook & crisp basket" for around 5 minutes, then turn out onto a wire rack, right-side up, to cool completely. 4. Meanwhile, in a suitable bowl, beat the remaining ⅔ cup cream, the powdered sugar, and vanilla until stiff peaks form. Split the scone like a hamburger bun and spread the strawberries over the bottom. Top with the whipped cream and cover with the top of the scone. Dust with powdered sugar and cut into wedges to serve.

Per serving: Calories 339; Fat: 14g; Sodium 556mg; Carbs: 44.6g; Fiber: 6.4g; Sugars 3.8g; Protein 10.5g

Ginger Bacon Bites

Prep Time: 10 minutes. | Cook Time: 15 minutes. | Serves: 2

¼ teaspoon ginger	2 tablespoon Swerve
⅕ teaspoon baking soda	3 slices bacon, cooked and
⅔ cup peanut butter	chopped

1. Place the Cook & Crisp Basket in your Pressure Cooker Steam Fryer. 2. In a suitable bowl, mix the ginger, baking soda, peanut butter, and Swerve together, making sure to mix everything well. 3. Stir in the chopped bacon. 4. With clean hands, shape the mixture into a cylinder and cut in six. Press down each slice into a cookie with your palm. 5. Put the cookies inside the Cook & Crisp Basket . Put on the Smart Lid on top of the Ninja Foodi Steam Fryer. Move the Lid Slider to the "Air Fry/Stovetop". Select the "Air Fry" mode for cooking. Adjust the cooking temperature to 350°F/175°C. 6. Cook for 7 minutes. Take care when taking them out of the fryer and allow to cool before serving.

Per serving: Calories 182; Fat: 0.7g; Sodium 7mg; Carbs: 46.3g; Fiber: 6.2g; Sugars 40.7g; Protein 1.9g

Chocolate Cake

Prep Time: 10 minutes. | Cook Time: 20 minutes. | Serves: 4

⅛ teaspoon fine sea salt	1 egg 1 egg white, whisked
1 tablespoon candied ginger	¼ cup unsalted butter, room
½ teaspoon cinnamon	temperature
2 tablespoons cocoa powder	2 tablespoons Truvia for baking
3-ounces almond flour	

For Filling:

6-ounces raspberries, fresh	1 teaspoon lime juice, fresh
1 tablespoon Truvia	

1. Place the Cook & Crisp Basket in your Pressure Cooker Steam Fryer. 2. Then, spritz the inside of two cakes pans with buttered-flavored cooking spray. In a suitable mixing bowl, beat Truvia and butter until creamy. Then, stir in the whisked eggs. Stir in the cocoa powder, flour, cinnamon, ginger and salt. Press the prepared batter dividing it evenly into cake pans; use a wide spatula to level the surface of batter. Put the cake pan on the Cook & Crisp Basket. Put on the Smart Lid on top of the Ninja Foodi Steam Fryer. Move the Lid Slider to the "Air Fry/Stovetop". Select the "Air Fry" mode for cooking. Adjust the cooking temperature to 315°F/155°C. Air Fry for around 20 minutes. 3. While your cake is baking, stir the ingredients for filling in a suitable saucepan. Cook over high heat, stirring often and mashing; bring to a boil and decrease the temperature. Cook for about 7 minutes or until mixture thickens. Allow filling to cool at room temperature. 4. Spread half of raspberry filling over first cake, then top with other cake and spread the remaining raspberry filling on top.

Per serving: Calories 592; Fat: 40g; Sodium 104mg; Carbs: 65.1g; Fiber: 13.2g; Sugars 41.2g; Protein 18.6g

Pear Crumble

Prep Time: 10 minutes. | Cook Time: 15 minutes. | Serves: 4

2 ripe d'Anjou pears (1 pound), peeled, cored, and chopped
¼ cup packed light brown sugar
2 tablespoons cornstarch
1 teaspoon salt
¼ cup granulated sugar
3 tablespoons unsalted butter, at room temperature
⅓ cup all-purpose flour
2½ tablespoons Dutch-process cocoa powder
¼ cup chopped blanched hazelnuts
Vanilla ice cream or whipped cream (optional)

1. In the Cook & Crisp Basket, mix the pears, brown sugar, cornstarch, and ½ teaspoon salt and toss until the pears are evenly coated in the sugar. 2. In a suitable bowl, mix the remaining ½ teaspoon salt with the granulated sugar, butter, flour, and cocoa powder and pinch and press the butter into the other ingredients with your fingers until a sandy, shaggy crumble dough forms. Stir in the hazelnuts. Sprinkle the crumble topping evenly over the pears. 3. Place the Cook & Crisp Basket in your Pressure Cooker Steam Fryer. Put on the Smart Lid on top of the Ninja Foodi Steam Fryer. Move the Lid Slider to the "Air Fry/Stovetop". Select the "Air Fry" mode for cooking. Air Fry at 320°F/160°C until the crumble is crisp and the pears are bubbling in the center, about 30 minutes. 4. Carefully remove the basket from the Ninja Foodi Pressure Steam Fryer and serve the hot crumble in bowls, topped with ice cream or whipped cream, if you like.
Per serving: Calories 254; Fat: 2.6g; Sodium 482mg; Carbs: 49.1g; Fiber: 4.8g; Sugars 0.2g; Protein 7.8g

Pineapple Galette

Prep Time: 10 minutes. | Cook Time: 15 minutes. | Serves: 2

¼ medium-size pineapple, peeled, crosswise into ¼-inch-thick slices
2 tablespoons dark rum
1 teaspoon vanilla extract
½ teaspoon salt
Grated zest of ½ lime
1 sheet puff pastry, cut into an 8-inch round
3 tablespoons granulated sugar
2 tablespoons unsalted butter, cubed and chilled
Coconut ice cream, for serving

1. In a suitable bowl, mix the pineapple slices, rum, vanilla, salt, and lime zest and let stand for at least 10 minutes to allow the pineapple to soak in the rum. 2. Press the puff pastry round into the bottom and up the Cook & Crisp Basket and use the tines of a fork to dock the bottom and sides. 3. Place the pineapple slices on the bottom of the pastry in more or less a single layer, then sprinkle with the sugar and dot with the butter. Drizzle with the leftover juices from the bowl. 4. Place the Cook & Crisp Basket in your Pressure Cooker Steam Fryer. 5. Put on the Smart Lid on top of the Ninja Foodi Steam Fryer. Move the Lid Slider to the "Air Fry/Stovetop". Select the "Air Fry" mode for cooking. Air Fry at 310°F/155°C until the pastry is puffed and golden brown and the pineapple is caramelized on top, about 40 minutes. 6. Transfer the basket to a wire rack to cool for around 15 minutes. Serve warm with coconut ice cream.
Per serving: Calories 128; Fat: 1.7g; Sodium 771mg; Carbs: 22.1g; Fiber: 4.5g; Sugars 3.9g; Protein 7.1g

Apple Butter

Prep Time: 10 minutes. | Cook Time: 15 minutes. | Serves: 1 ¼ cups

MAKES 1¼ CUPS
Cooking spray
2 cups store-bought unsweetened applesauce
⅔ cup packed light brown sugar
3 tablespoons fresh lemon juice
½ teaspoon salt
¼ teaspoon cinnamon
⅛ teaspoon allspice

1. Spray the Cook & Crisp Basket with cooking spray. Mix all the recipe ingredients in a suitable bowl until smooth, then pour into the Cook & Crisp Basket. 2. Place the Cook & Crisp Basket in your Pressure Cooker Steam Fryer. 3. Put on the Smart Lid on top of the Ninja Foodi Steam Fryer. Move the Lid Slider to the "Air Fry/Stovetop". Select the "Air Fry" mode for cooking. Air Fry at 340°F/170°C until the apple mixture is caramelized, reduced to a thick puree, and fragrant, about 1 hour. 4. Remove the Cook & Crisp Basket in your Pressure Cooker Steam Fryer., stir to mix the caramelized bits at the edge with the rest, then let cool completely to thicken. Scrape the apple butter into a jar and store in the refrigerator for up to 2 weeks.

Crispy Pork Rinds

Prep Time: 10 minutes. | Cook Time: 10 minutes. | Serves: 2

2 ounces pork rinds
2 teaspoons unsalted butter, melted
¼ cup powdered erythritol
½ teaspoon cinnamon

1. Place the Cook & Crisp Basket in your Pressure Cooker Steam Fryer. 2. Coat the rinds with the melted butter. 3. In a separate bowl, mix the erythritol and cinnamon and pour over the pork rinds, ensuring the rinds are covered completely and evenly. 4. Transfer the pork rinds into the Cook & Crisp Basket. Put on the Smart Lid on top of the Ninja Foodi Steam Fryer. Move the Lid Slider to the "Air Fry/Stovetop". Select the "Air Fry" mode for cooking. Air Fry at 400°F/200°C for 5 minutes.
Per serving: Calories 469; Fat: 36.5g; Sodium 46mg; Carbs: 31.4g; Fiber: 4.5g; Sugars 17.9g; Protein 9.1g

Chocolate-Covered Bacon

Prep Time: 10 minutes. | Cook Time: 25 minutes. | Serves: 4

8 slices sugar-free bacon
1 tablespoon granular erythritol
⅓ cup low-carb sugar-free
chocolate chips
1 teaspoon coconut oil
½ teaspoon maple extract

1. Place the Cook & Crisp Basket in your Pressure Cooker Steam Fryer. 2. Place the bacon in the Cook & Crisp Basket and add the erythritol on top. 3. Put on the Smart Lid on top of the Ninja Foodi Steam Fryer. 4. Move the Lid Slider to the "Air Fry/Stovetop". Select the "Air Fry" mode for cooking. 5. Cook for 6 minutes at 350°F/175°C and turn the bacon over. Leave to cook another 6 minutes or until the bacon is sufficiently crispy. 6. Take the bacon out of the fryer and leave it to cool. 7. Microwave the chocolate chips and coconut oil for half a minute. Remove from the microwave and mix before stirring in the maple extract. 8. Set the bacon flat on a piece of parchment paper and pour the mixture over. Allow to harden in the refrigerator for 5 minutes before serving.
Per serving: Calories 361; Fat: 31.3g; Sodium 385mg; Carbs: 13.8g; Fiber: 7.3g; Sugars 2.5g; Protein 9.7g

Apple Almond Turnovers

Prep Time: 10 minutes. | Cook Time: 15 minutes. | Serves: 8

3 apples, cored, peeled and diced
⅓ cup almonds, chopped
½ tablespoon cinnamon
½ teaspoon vanilla extract
½ teaspoon star anise,
2 tablespoons Truvia for baking
1 tablespoon cornstarch
½ pack phyllo pastry sheets
½ stick butter, melted
1 teaspoon orange peel, grated

1. In a suitable pan, cook the apples, cornstarch, Truvia, vanilla and orange peel. Cook for around 5 minutes or until apple filling thickens. Remove from heat and set aside. 2. Brush a piece of phyllo dough with melted butter; use a pastry brush. Cover with another sheet and brush again. Continue with two more sheets of phyllo dough. Then, cut the phyllo dough in half lengthwise. 3. Add 1 tablespoon of the apple filling at the end of the prepared dough; scatter chopped almonds over the top. Fold to create a triangle. It is important that the apple filling is completely enclosed. 4. Continue with remaining phyllo dough. Brush with extra butter. Place into the Cook & Crisp Basket in a single layer. Place the Cook & Crisp Basket in your Pressure Cooker Steam Fryer. 5. Put on the Smart Lid on top of the Ninja Foodi Steam Fryer. Move the Lid Slider to the "Air Fry/Stovetop". Select the "Air Fry" mode for cooking. Air Fry at 345°F/175°C for around 15 minutes; cook in batches. 6. Meanwhile, mix Truvia, star anise and cinnamon. When your turnovers are done, brush them with some extra butter. Dust them with the seasoned sweetener and serve.
Per serving: Calories 541; Fat: 12.4g; Sodium 250mg; Carbs: 85.4g; Fiber: 21.3g; Sugars 6.1g; Protein 6.5g

Espresso Brownies

Prep Time: 10 minutes. | Cook Time: 36 minutes. | Serves: 8

8-ounces dark chocolate, chopped into chunks
1 teaspoon pure coffee extract
2 tablespoons liquid Stevia
1 tablespoon cocoa powder
2 tablespoons instant espresso powder
½ cup almond butter
¾ cup almond flour
½ teaspoon lime peel zest
¼ cup almond meal
2 eggs and 1 egg yolk
½ teaspoon baking soda
½ teaspoon baking powder
½ teaspoon cinnamon

1. Melt the chocolate and almond butter in your microwave. Allow the mixture to cool at room temperature. Then, mix the eggs, stevia, cinnamon, espresso powder, coffee extract and lime zest. 2. Next, add the egg mixture to the chocolate butter mixture. Stir in almond flour and almond meal along with baking soda, baking powder, and cocoa powder. 3. Finally, press the prepared batter into a buttered Cook & Crisp Basket. Place the Cook & Crisp Basket in your Pressure Cooker Steam Fryer Put on the Smart Lid on top of the Ninja Foodi Steam Fryer. Move the Lid Slider to the "Air Fry/Stovetop". Select the "Air Fry" mode for cooking. Air fry for around 35 to minutes at 345°F/175°C.
Per serving: Calories 244; Fat: 9.1g; Sodium 1399mg; Carbs: 34.3g; Fiber: 8.7g; Sugars 15.7g; Protein 8.3g

Prune Muffins

Prep Time: 10 minutes. | Cook Time: 13 minutes. | Serves: 6

⅓ cup walnut meal
⅓ cup walnuts, chopped
¼ teaspoon salt
½ teaspoon pure hazelnut extract
⅓ teaspoon cloves
½ teaspoon pure vanilla extract
⅓ teaspoon cinnamon
1 teaspoon baking powder
½ teaspoon baking soda
2 teaspoons fresh apple juice
1 cup yogurt
2 eggs
¾ stick butter, room temperature
2 tablespoons Truvia for baking
¾ cup almond flour
⅓ cup prunes, chopped

1. In a suitable bowl, mix walnut meal, almond flour, baking soda, baking powder, cloves, cinnamon, and Truvia. Take another bowl, mix eggs, yogurt, butter and apple juice; mix to mix well. Next, add your wet mixture to the dry mixture. Fold in the prunes and walnuts. 2. Press the prepared batter mixture into a greased muffin tin. Transfer them to the Cook & Crisp Basket. Place the Cook & Crisp Basket in your Pressure Cooker Steam Fryer. Put on the Smart Lid on top of the Ninja Foodi Steam Fryer. Move the Lid Slider to the "Air Fry/Stovetop". Select the "Air Fry" mode for cooking. Air Fry at 355°F/180°C for around 13 to minutes.
Per serving: Calories 669; Fat: 53.8g; Sodium 905mg; Carbs: 41.7g; Fiber: 8.6g; Sugars 12.3g; Protein 14g

Chocolate Muffins

Prep Time: 10 minutes. | Cook Time: 15 minutes. | Serves: 6

3 teaspoons cocoa powder
¾ dried apricots, chopped
1 ¼ cups almond flour
1 teaspoon pure rum extract
1 ½ tablespoons Truvia for baking
2 eggs
1 stick butter, room temperature
¼ cup maple syrup, sugar-free
1 cup rice milk
½ teaspoon baking soda
1 teaspoon baking powder
¼ teaspoon nutmeg, grated
½ teaspoon cinnamon
⅛ teaspoon salt

1. In a suitable bowl, mix Truvia, almond flour, baking soda, baking powder, salt, nutmeg, cinnamon and cocoa powder. In another bowl, add butter and cream it, also add egg, rum extract, rice milk, sugar-free maple syrup; mix to mix. Next, add your wet mixture to the dry mixture and fold in the apricots. 2. Press the prepared batter into a greased muffin tin. Transfer them to the Cook & Crisp Basket. Place the Cook & Crisp Basket in your Pressure Cooker Steam Fryer. 3. Put on the Smart Lid on top of the Ninja Foodi Steam Fryer. Move the Lid Slider to the "Air Fry/Stovetop". Select the "Air Fry" mode for cooking. Air Fry at 345°F/175°C for around 15 minutes.
Per serving: Calories 344; Fat: 3g; Sodium 603mg; Carbs: 73.8g; Fiber: 11.5g; Sugars 8.6g; Protein 9.4g

Cranberry Cake

Prep Time: 10 minutes. | Cook Time: 20 minutes. | Serves: 8

1 cup almond flour
⅓ teaspoon baking soda
⅓ teaspoon baking powder
1 tablespoon Truvia for baking
½ teaspoon cloves
½ cup cranberries, fresh or thawed
2 eggs, 1 egg yolk, beaten
½ teaspoon vanilla paste
1 stick butter
½ teaspoon cardamom
⅓ teaspoon cinnamon
1 tablespoon browned butter

1. In a suitable bowl, mix the flour with baking soda, baking powder, Truvia, cloves, cinnamon, and cardamom. In another bowl, add stick of butter, vanilla paste, mix in the eggs and mix until light and fluffy. Add the flour or sweetener mixture to butter or egg mixture and fold in cranberries and browned butter. Add the mixture into the greased Cook & Crisp Basket. Place the Cook & Crisp Basket in your Pressure Cooker Steam Fryer. 2. Put on the Smart Lid on top of the Ninja Foodi Steam Fryer. Move the Lid Slider to the "Air Fry/Stovetop". Select the "Air Fry" mode for cooking. Adjust the cooking temperature to 355°F/180°C. Air Fry for around 20 minutes.
Per serving: Calories 192; Fat: 6.6g; Sodium 15mg; Carbs: 34.5g; Fiber: 4g; Sugars 27.3g; Protein 2.9g

White Chocolate Cookies

Prep Time: 10 minutes. | Cook Time: 11 minutes. | Serves: 10

2 eggs, beaten
8-ounces white chocolate, chopped
¼ teaspoon fine sea salt
⅓ teaspoon nutmeg, grated
⅓ teaspoon allspice,
⅓ teaspoon anise star,
2 tablespoons Truvia
½ cup quick-cooking oats
2 ¼ cup almond flour
¾ cup butter

1. Put all the recipe ingredients, except 1 egg, into a suitable mixing bowl. Knead with hands until a soft dough is formed. Place the prepared dough into fridge for around 20 minutes. Roll the chilled dough into small balls; flatten the balls in the Cook & Crisp Basket. 2. Make an egg wash by using the remaining egg. Then, glaze the cookies with the egg wash; Place the Cook & Crisp Basket in your Pressure Cooker Steam Fryer. 3. Put on the Smart Lid on top of the Ninja Foodi Steam Fryer. 4. Move the Lid Slider to the "Air Fry/Stovetop". Select the "Air Fry" mode for cooking. 5. Adjust the cooking temperature to 350°F/175°C. 6. Cook for around 11 minutes.
Per serving: Calories 385; Fat: 28.3g; Sodium 80mg; Carbs: 27.4g; Fiber: 0.7g; Sugars 16.7g; Protein 4.6g

Sweet Lemon Bars

Prep Time: 10 minutes. | Cook Time: 22 minutes. | Serves: 6

4 tablespoon coconut oil, melted
¼ teaspoon 1 pinch of salt
1 teaspoon pure vanilla extract
½ cup 3 tablespoon granulated sugar
½ cup 2 tablespoon all-purpose flour
¼ cup freshly squeezed lemon juice
Zest of 1 lemon
½ cup canned coconut cream
4 tablespoon cornstarch
Powdered sugar

1. In a suitable bowl, mix the coconut oil, ¼ teaspoon of salt, vanilla extract, and 3 tablespoons of sugar. Mix in the flour until a soft dough forms. Transfer the mixture to the Cook & Crisp Basket and gently press the prepared dough to cover the bottom. 2. Place the Cook & Crisp Basket in your Pressure Cooker Steam Fryer. 3. Put on the Smart Lid on top of the Ninja Foodi Steam Fryer. Move the Lid Slider to the "Air Fry/Stovetop". Select the "Air Fry" mode for cooking. Air Fry at 350°F/175°C until golden, about 10 minutes. Remove the crust from the "cook & crisp basket" and set aside to cool slightly. 4. In a suitable saucepan on the stovetop over medium heat, mix the lemon juice and zest, coconut cream, the pinch of salt, and the remaining ½ cup of sugar. Mix in the cornstarch and . cook for until thickened, about 5 minutes. Pour the lemon mixture over the crust. 5. Place them in the "cook & crisp basket" . Put on the Smart Lid on top of the Ninja Foodi Steam Fryer. Move the Lid Slider to the "Air Fry/Stovetop". Select the "Air Fry" mode for cooking. Adjust the cooking temperature to 350°F/175°C. 6. Cook for until the mixture is bubbly and almost completely set, about 10 to 12 minutes. 7. Remove them from the "cook & crisp basket" and set aside to cool completely. Transfer to a dish and put in the refrigerator for at least 4 hours. Dust with the powdered sugar and slice into 6 bars before serving.
Per serving: Calories 194; Fat: 2.6g; Sodium 1257mg; Carbs: 35.4g; Fiber: 3.7g; Sugars 3.1g; Protein 9.4g

Macadamia Cookies

Prep Time: 10 minutes. | Cook Time: 25 minutes. | Serves: 10

¾ cup coconut oil, room temperature
1½ cups coconut flour
1¼ cups macadamia nuts, unsalted and chopped
½ teaspoon pure vanilla extract
⅓ teaspoon baking soda
½ teaspoon baking powder

⅓ teaspoon cloves,
¼ teaspoon nutmeg, freshly grated
2 tablespoons Truvia for baking
2 cups almond flour
3 eggs and egg yolk, whisked
½ teaspoon pure coconut extract
⅛ teaspoon fine sea salt

1. In a suitable bowl, mix both types of flour, baking soda and baking powder. In suitable bowl, beat the eggs with coconut oil. Mix the egg mixture with the flour mixture. Add other ingredients and shape into cookies. Transfer them to the Cook & Crisp Basket. Place the Cook & Crisp Basket in your Pressure Cooker Steam Fryer. 2. Put on the Smart Lid on top of the Ninja Foodi Steam Fryer. Move the Lid Slider to the "Air Fry/Stovetop". Select the "Air Fry" mode for cooking. Air Fry at 370°F/185°C for around 25 minutes.
Per serving: Calories 433; Fat: 26.6g; Sodium 694mg; Carbs: 36.8g; Fiber: 2.8g; Sugars 28.4g; Protein 17.3g

Almond Cookies

Prep Time: 10 minutes. | Cook Time: 13 minutes. | Serves: 8

½ cup slivered almonds
1 stick butter, room temperature
2 tablespoons Truvia
⅓ cup almond flour

⅓ cup coconut flour
⅓ teaspoons cloves
1 tablespoon candied ginger
¾ teaspoon pure vanilla extract

1. In a mixing dish, beat Truvia, butter, vanilla extract, cloves, and ginger until light and fluffy. Then, throw in the both kinds of flour and slivered almonds. Continue to mix until soft dough is formed. Cover and place into fridge for around 35 to minutes. 2. Roll the prepared dough into small cookies and place them on the Cook & Crisp Basket; gently press each cookie using the back of a spoon. Place the Cook & Crisp Basket in your Pressure Cooker Steam Fryer. 3. Put on the Smart Lid on top of the Ninja Foodi Steam Fryer. Move the Lid Slider to the "Air Fry/Stovetop". Select the "Air Fry" mode for cooking. Adjust the cooking temperature to 315°F/155°C. 4. Air Fry cookies for around 13 minutes.
Per serving: Calories 221; Fat: 3.9g; Sodium 154mg; Carbs: 50g; Fiber: 3.4g; Sugars 26.1g; Protein 1.8g

Soft Raisin Muffins

Prep Time: 10 minutes. | Cook Time: 15 minutes. | Serves: 6

¼ teaspoon salt
½ teaspoon lemon zest, grated
⅓ teaspoon anise star
⅓ teaspoon allspice,
2 eggs
2 cups almond flour

1 ¼ teaspoons baking powder
1 cup sour cream
½ cup coconut oil
2 tablespoons Truvia for baking
¾ cup raisins

1. Place the Cook & Crisp Basket in your Pressure Cooker Steam Fryer. 2. In a suitable bowl, mix flour, baking powder, Truvia, salt, anise star, allspice and lemon zest. In another bowl, mix coconut oil, sour cream, eggs, and mix to mix. Now, add the wet mixture to the dry mixture and fold in the raisins. 3. Press the prepared batter mixture into a greased muffin tin. Transfer them to the Cook & Crisp Basket. Put on the Smart Lid on top of the Ninja Foodi Steam Fryer. Move the Lid Slider to the "Air Fry/Stovetop". Select the "Air Fry" mode for cooking. Air Fry at 345°F/175°C for around 15 minutes.
Per serving: Calories 490; Fat: 37g; Sodium 183mg; Carbs: 29.7g; Fiber: 7.8g; Sugars 11.6g; Protein 19.3g

Coconut Cake

Prep Time: 10 minutes. | Cook Time: 17 minutes. | Serves: 6

¾ cup shredded coconut
¼ teaspoon salt
⅓ teaspoon nutmeg, grated
½ teaspoon baking powder

1 ¼ cups almond flour
2 eggs
2 tablespoons Truvia
1 stick butter

2 tablespoons orange jam   ⅓ coconut milk

1. Spritz the Cook & Crisp Basket with cooking spray. Then, beat the butter with Truvia until fluffy. 2. Fold in the eggs; continue mixing until smooth. Add nutmeg, salt, and flour; then, slowly pour in the coconut milk. Finally, add the shredded coconut and orange jam; mix to create cake batter. 3. Then, press the prepared batter into the Cook & Crisp Basket. Place the Cook & Crisp Basket in your Pressure Cooker Steam Fryer. Put on the Smart Lid on top of the Ninja Foodi Steam Fryer. Move the Lid Slider to the "Air Fry/Stovetop". Select the "Air Fry" mode for cooking. Adjust the cooking temperature to 355°F/180°C. Air Fry cake for around 17 minutes, then transfer the cake to a cooling rack. Serve chilled.
Per serving: Calories 194; Fat: 2.6g; Sodium 1257mg; Carbs: 35.4g; Fiber: 3.7g; Sugars 3.1g; Protein 9.4g

Crispy Profiteroles

Prep Time: 10 minutes. | Cook Time: 10 minutes. | Serves: 2

2 tablespoon vegan butter
¼ cup unsweetened soy milk
1 teaspoon pure vanilla extract
1 tablespoon maple syrup
3 tablespoon liquid egg substitute
For the Cream
14oz (400g) canned coconut milk, refrigerated overnight
For the Drizzle
¼ cup vegan chocolate chips

1 cup all-purpose flour
1 teaspoon baking powder
¼ teaspoon salt
Nonstick cooking spray

1½ tablespoon powdered sugar

½ teaspoon coconut oil

1. Place the Cook & Crisp Basket in your Pressure Cooker Steam Fryer. 2. Grease the "cook & crisp basket" with nonstick cooking spray. 3. In a suitable saucepan on the stovetop over medium-low heat, melt the butter. Add the soy milk, vanilla extract, maple syrup, and egg. Mix to mix. Add the flour, baking powder, and salt. Mix well with a wooden spoon until a sticky dough forms. Turn off the heat and allow to cool for around 2 minutes. Add the warm dough to a piping bag with a wide tip. 4. Pipe the prepared dough directly into the Cook & Crisp Basket, forming 10 mounds the size of golf balls. Dampen your finger with water and gently press down the top of each mound to prevent burning. Put on the Smart Lid on top of the Ninja Foodi Steam Fryer. 5. Move the Lid Slider to the "Air Fry/Stovetop". Select the "Air Fry" mode for cooking. 6. Adjust the cooking temperature to 375°F/190°C. 7. Cook until puffed and golden, about 10 minutes. 8. Transfer the profiteroles to a platter and allow to cool. 9. Add the coconut cream, and powdered sugar to bowl and mix until fluffy, about 2 to 3 minutes. Set aside. 10. Place the chocolate chips and coconut oil in a microwave-safe dish. Microwave for around 60 to 90 seconds. Stir until mixed and glossy. 11. Use a serrated knife to slice each profiterole in half and fill with a heaping spoonful of cream. (You'll have about half the cream left over. Refrigerate for up to 3 days for another use.) Drizzle the profiteroles with the chocolate sauce and serve immediately.
Per serving: Calories 130; Fat: 3.9g; Sodium 3mg; Carbs: 21.6g; Fiber: 1.6g; Sugars 9.8g; Protein 3.6g

Pineapple with Macadamia Batter

Prep Time: 10 minutes. | Cook Time: 7 minutes. | Serves: 8

2 cups pineapple peeled and sliced
½ cup macadamia nuts,
¾ cup almond flour
¼ cup cornstarch flour
½ teaspoon nutmeg, grated
½ teaspoon vanilla extract
1 teaspoon orange extract

¼ teaspoon salt
½ teaspoon baking powder
½ teaspoon baking soda
2 tablespoons Truvia
1 ⅓ cups milk
2 tablespoons coconut oil

1. Place the Cook & Crisp Basket in your Pressure Cooker Steam Fryer. 2. To make batter mix all the recipe ingredients, except for pineapple, in a suitable mixing bowl. Dip the slices of pineapple into batter. Transfer them to the Cook & Crisp Basket. Put on the Smart Lid on top of the Ninja Foodi Steam Fryer. Move the Lid Slider to the "Air Fry/Stovetop". Select the "Air Fry" mode for cooking. Adjust the cooking temperature to 380°F/195°C. Air fry for around 7 minutes or until golden.
Per serving: Calories 257; Fat: 16.5g; Sodium 1031mg; Carbs: 23.6g; Fiber: 3.4g; Sugars 6.1g; Protein 4.7g

Cranberry Brownies

Prep Time: 10 minutes. | Cook Time: 35 minutes. | Serves: 8

1 teaspoon pure rum extract
¼ teaspoon cardamom
2 tablespoons Truvia for baking
2 eggs and an egg yolk, whisked
½ cup coconut oil
3 tablespoons coconut flakes
¾ cup almond flour
8-ounces white chocolate
3 tablespoons whiskey
⅓ cup cranberries

1. Place the Cook & Crisp Basket in your Pressure Cooker Steam Fryer. 2. Microwave white chocolate and coconut oil until melted. Allow mixture to cool at room temperature. Next, mix eggs, Truvia, rum extract, and cardamom, mix well. Add the rum mixture to the chocolate mixture, stirring in flour and coconut flakes. Mix the cranberries with whiskey let soak for around 15 minutes. Fold them into the prepared batter. Press the butter into buttered Cook & Crisp Basket. 3. Put on the Smart Lid on top of the Ninja Foodi Steam Fryer. 4. Move the Lid Slider to the "Air Fry/Stovetop". Select the "Air Fry" mode for cooking. 5. Air-fry for around 35 minutes at 340°F/170°C. Allow them to cool on a wire rack before serving.
Per serving: Calories 194; Fat: 13g; Sodium 208mg; Carbs: 30.6g; Fiber: 5.6g; Sugars 20.7g; Protein 9.1g

Prune Cookies

Prep Time: 10 minutes. | Cook Time: 20 minutes. | Serves: 10

½ teaspoon baking soda
½ teaspoon baking powder
½ teaspoon orange zest
1 teaspoon vanilla paste
⅓ teaspoon cinnamon
1 stick butter, softened
1 ½ cups almond flour
2 tablespoons Truvia for baking
⅓ cup prunes, chopped
⅓ coconut, shredded

1. Mix the butter with Truvia until mixture becomes fluffy; sift in the flour and add baking powder, as well as baking soda. Add the remaining recipe ingredients and mix well. Knead the prepared dough and transfer it to the fridge for around 20 minutes. 2. To finish, shape the chilled dough into bite-size balls; arrange the balls on the Cook & Crisp Basket and gently flatten them with the back of a spoon. Place the Cook & Crisp Basket in your Pressure Cooker Steam Fryer. 3. Put on the Smart Lid on top of the Ninja Foodi Steam Fryer. Move the Lid Slider to the "Air Fry/Stovetop". Select the "Air Fry" mode for cooking. Air fry for around 20 minutes at 315°F/155°C.
Per serving: Calories 375; Fat: 28.4g; Sodium 128mg; Carbs: 22.4g; Fiber: 6.3g; Sugars 9.7g; Protein 14.9g

Pudding with Sultanas

Prep Time: 10 minutes. | Cook Time: 25 minutes. | Serves: 8

1 teaspoon vanilla extract
1 ½ tablespoons coffee liqueur
1 loaf stale Italian bread, torn into pieces
⅓ cup white chocolate chunks
3 eggs, whisked
¼ cup Sultanas
1 ⅓ cup skim milk
2 tablespoons Truvia for baking

1. Place the Cook & Crisp Basket in your Pressure Cooker Steam Fryer. 2. Prepare two mixing bowls. Dump bread pieces into first bowl. In the second bowl, mix the remaining ingredients, except the white chocolate and Sultanas; mix until smooth. 3. Pour the egg or milk mixture over the bread pieces. Allow to soak for around 20 minutes; using a suitable spatula gently press down. Now, scatter chocolate chunks and Sultanas over the top. Divide the bread pudding between two mini loaf pans. Transfer them to the Cook & Crisp Basket. Put on the Smart Lid on top of the Ninja Foodi Steam Fryer. Move the Lid Slider to the "Air Fry/Stovetop". Select the "Air Fry" mode for cooking. Air Fry for around 25 minutes at 320°F/160°C.
Per serving: Calories 320; Fat: 28.8g; Sodium 1mg; Carbs: 18.2g; Fiber: 4.2g; Sugars 11.6g; Protein 1.8g

Clafoutis

Prep Time: 10 minutes. | Cook Time: 25 minutes. | Serves: 6

¼ teaspoon nutmeg, grated
½ teaspoon crystalized ginger
⅓ teaspoon cinnamon
½ teaspoon baking soda
½ teaspoon baking powder
2 tablespoons Truvia for baking

½ cup coconut cream
¾ cup coconut milk
3 eggs, whisked
4 medium-sized pears, cored and
sliced
1 ½ cups plums, pitted
¾ cup almond flour

1. Place the deluxe reversible racking your Pressure Cooker Steam Fryer. 2. grease 2 mini pie pans using a non-stick cooking spray. Lay the plums and pears on the bottom of pie pans. In a suitable saucepan that is preheated over medium heat, warm the cream along with the coconut milk until heated. Remove the pan from heat; mix in the flour along with baking soda and baking powder. 3. In a suitable bowl, mix the eggs, Truvia, spices until the mixture is creamy. Add the creamy milk mixture. Carefully spread this mixture over your fruit in pans. Put the pans on the rack. Put on the Smart Lid on top of the Ninja Foodi Steam Fryer. Move the Lid Slider to the "Air Fry/Stovetop". Select the "Air Fry" mode for cooking. Air Fry at 320°F/160°C for around 25 minutes.
Per serving: Calories 281; Fat: 6.7g; Sodium 187mg; Carbs: 52.7g; Fiber: 6.6g; Sugars 29g; Protein 5.1g

Orange Cake

Prep Time: 10 minutes. | Cook Time: 20 minutes. | Serves: 6

⅓ cup almonds, chopped
3 tablespoons orange marmalade
1 stick butter
½ teaspoon allspice,
½ teaspoon anise seed,
½ teaspoon baking powder
1 teaspoon baking soda
6-ounces almond flour
2 tablespoons Truvia for baking
2 eggs 1 egg yok, beaten
Olive oil cooking spray for pans

1. Place the deluxe reversible rack in your Pressure Cooker Steam Fryer. 2. Grease cake pan with olive oil cooking spray. Mix the butter and Truvia until nice and smooth. Fold in the eggs, almonds, marmalade; beat again until well mixed. Add flour, baking soda, baking powder, allspice, star anise and cinnamon. Put the cake pan on the rack. Put on the Smart Lid on top of the Ninja Foodi Steam Fryer. Move the Lid Slider to the "Air Fry/Stovetop". Select the "Air Fry" mode for cooking. Air Fry at 310°F/155°C for around 20 minutes.
Per serving: Calories 361; Fat: 31.3g; Sodium 385mg; Carbs: 13.8g; Fiber: 7.3g; Sugars 2.5g; Protein 9.7g

Apricots in Whiskey Sauce

Prep Time: 10 minutes. | Cook Time: 35 minutes. | Serves: 4

1 lb. apricot, pitted and halved
¼ cup whiskey
1 teaspoon pure vanilla extract
½ stick butter, room temperature
½ cup maple syrup sugar-free

1. In a suitable saucepan over medium heat, heat the maple syrup, vanilla, butter; simmer until the butter is melted. Add the whiskey and stir to mix. Arrange the apricots on the bottom of greased Cook & Crisp Basket. 2. Pour the sauce over the apricots; scatter whole cloves over the top. Then, place the Cook & Crisp Basket in your Pressure Cooker Steam Fryer. 3. Put on the Smart Lid on top of the Ninja Foodi Steam Fryer. 4. Move the Lid Slider to the "Air Fry/Stovetop". Select the "Air Fry" mode for cooking. 5. Air-fry at 380°F/195°C for around 35 minutes.
Per serving: Calories 469; Fat: 36.5g; Sodium 46mg; Carbs: 31.4g; Fiber: 4.5g; Sugars 17.9g; Protein 9.1g

Cracker S'mores

Prep Time: 10 minutes. | Cook Time: 3 minutes. | Serves: 4

4 squares vegan dark chocolate
4 large vegan marshmallows
4 full graham crackers, halved

1. Place the Cook & Crisp Basket in your Pressure Cooker Steam Fryer. 2. Place 1 chocolate square and 1 marshmallow on 1 cracker half. Repeat this step with 3 more cracker halves. 3. Place the s'mores in the "cook & crisp basket". Put on the Smart Lid on top of the Ninja Foodi Steam Fryer. Move the Lid Slider to the "Air Fry/Stovetop". Select the "Air Fry" mode for cooking. Adjust the cooking temperature to 350°F/175°C. 4. Cook for until the marshmallow is puffed and golden, about 2 to 3 minutes. 5. Transfer the s'mores to a platter. Top each with a remaining cracker half and serve immediately.
Per serving: Calories 363; Fat: 10.7g; Sodium 253mg; Carbs: 63.7g; Fiber: 3.8g; Sugars 22.9g; Protein 4.9g

Cinnamon Pear Clafoutis

Prep Time: 10 minutes. | Cook Time: 25 minutes. | Serves: 4

2 cups medium pears, finely chopped
juice of ½ lemon
½ cup granulated sugar
¼ cup whole wheat pastry flour
1 teaspoon baking powder
⅛ teaspoon salt
½ teaspoon cinnamon
½ cup unsweetened soy milk
1 tablespoon canola oil

1. In the Cook & Crisp Basket, mix the pears, lemon juice, and 2 tablespoons of sugar. 2. In a suitable bowl, mix the pastry flour, baking powder, salt, and cinnamon. Add the soy milk, canola oil, and the remaining 6 tablespoons of sugar. Mix until a smooth batter forms. Pour the prepared batter over the pears. 3. Place the Cook & Crisp Basket in your Pressure Cooker Steam Fryer. 4. Put on the Smart Lid on top of the Ninja Foodi Steam Fryer. Move the Lid Slider to the "Air Fry/Stovetop". Select the "Air Fry" mode for cooking. Adjust the cooking temperature to 340°F/170°C. 5. Air Fry until the cake is puffed and golden, about 20 to 25 minutes. 6. Remove the cake from the "cook & crisp basket" and allow the cake to cool before serving.
Per serving: Calories 420; Fat: 17.1g; Sodium 282mg; Carbs: 65.7g; Fiber: 4.5g; Sugars 35.1g; Protein 7g

Frosted Blackberry Shortcake

Prep Time: 10 minutes. | Cook Time: 12 minutes. | Serves: 4

1 cup all-purpose flour
2 tablespoon granulated sugar
1½ teaspoon baking powder
⅛ teaspoon salt
For the Cream
14oz (400g) canned coconut milk, refrigerated overnight
2 tablespoon coconut oil
¼ cup unsweetened soy milk
2 cups fresh blackberries

1½ tablespoon powdered sugar
2 teaspoons orange zest

1. To make the cream, mix coconut milk with the powdered sugar and orange zest and mix until fluffy, 2. In a suitable bowl, mix the flour, granulated sugar, baking powder, and salt. Add the coconut oil and use a pastry cutter to work the oil into the flour until distributed throughout the dry recipe ingredients. 3. Add the soy milk and use clean hands to gently mix. Be careful not to overmix. Gently press the prepared dough into the Cook & Crisp Basket. 4. Place the Cook & Crisp Basket in your Pressure Cooker Steam Fryer. 5. . Put on the Smart Lid on top of the Ninja Foodi Steam Fryer. Move the Lid Slider to the "Air Fry/Stovetop". Select the "Air Fry" mode for cooking. Adjust the cooking temperature to 320°F/160°C. 6. Air Fry until the edges are golden, about 12 minutes. 7. Remove from the "cook & crisp basket" and allow the shortcake to cool for around 10 minutes. 8. Place the baked shortcake onto a serving platter and cut into 4 slices. Top each slice with 2 tablespoons of cream and an equal amount of the blackberries before serving.
Per serving: Calories 256; Fat: 3.5g; Sodium 7mg; Carbs: 54.2g; Fiber: 10.7g; Sugars 32.2g; Protein 4.9g

Peach Walnut Parfaits

Prep Time: 10 minutes. | Cook Time: 12 minutes. | Serves: 2

3 tablespoon light brown sugar
⅓ cup chopped walnuts
¼ teaspoon sea salt
4 peaches, halved and pits removed
6oz (170g) dairy-free plain yogurt

1. Place the Cook & Crisp Basket in your Pressure Cooker Steam Fryer. 2. In a suitable bowl, mix the brown sugar, walnuts, and salt. Mix well. 3. Place the peaches in the Cook & Crisp Basket. Evenly sprinkle the walnut mixture over the peaches. 4. Put on the Smart Lid on top of the Ninja Foodi Steam Fryer. 5. Move the Lid Slider to the "Air Fry/Stovetop". Select the "Air Fry" mode for cooking. 6. Adjust the cooking temperature to 350°F/175°C. 7. Cook until the peaches are tender and the sugar has begun to caramelize, about 10 to 12 minutes. 8. Transfer the peaches to a platter to cool slightly. Top with the yogurt before serving.
Per serving: Calories 488; Fat: 34.3g; Sodium 130mg; Carbs: 42.4g; Fiber: 1.7g; Sugars 21.5g; Protein 4.8g

Cinnamon Flour Twists

Prep Time: 10 minutes. | Cook Time: 12 minutes. | Serves: 20

2 cups all-purpose flour, more
½ teaspoon salt
½ cup canola oil
5 to 8 tablespoon cold water
¼ cup granulated sugar
1½ teaspoon cinnamon

1. Place the Cook & Crisp Basket in your Pressure Cooker Steam Fryer. 2. In a suitable bowl, mix the flour and salt. 3. In a separate medium bowl, mix the oil and 5 to 6 tablespoons of the water. Make a well in the center of the flour mixture and pour in the oil mixture. Mix with a fork until just mixed. Add 1 to 2 more tablespoons of water as needed. 4. In a suitable bowl, mix the sugar and cinnamon. 5. On a floured surface, roll out the prepared dough into a 10-inch (25cm) round. Cut the prepared dough into 10 strips and then cut each strip in half. Sprinkle the sugar and cinnamon mixture on both sides and gently twist each strip. 6. Working in batches, place 10 twists in the "cook & crisp basket". Put on the Smart Lid on top of the Ninja Foodi Steam Fryer. Move the Lid Slider to the "Air Fry/Stovetop". Select the "Air Fry" mode for cooking. Adjust the cooking temperature to 330°F/165°C. 7. Cook for until golden brown, about 5 to 6 minutes. 8. Transfer the cinnamon twists to a platter and allow to cool before serving.
Per serving: Calories 182; Fat: 0.7g; Sodium 7mg; Carbs: 46.3g; Fiber: 6.2g; Sugars 40.7g; Protein 1.9g

Chocolate Egg Rolls

Prep Time: 10 minutes. | Cook Time: 6 minutes. | Serves: 4

4 egg roll wrappers
4 tablespoon vegan chocolate and hazelnut spread or nut butter
2 small bananas, halved
Powdered sugar
Oil

1. Place the Cook & Crisp Basket in your Pressure Cooker Steam Fryer. 2. Place 1 wrapper on a flat surface, with the pointed end facing up. Spread the butter in the middle and top with half a banana. Fold in the sides over the filling and then roll up from bottom to top. Repeat this step with the remaining wrappers and filling. Grease the egg rolls with oil. 3. Place the egg rolls in the "cook & crisp basket". Put on the Smart Lid on top of the Ninja Foodi Steam Fryer. Move the Lid Slider to the "Air Fry/Stovetop". Select the "Air Fry" mode for cooking. Adjust the cooking temperature to 370°F/185°C. 4. Cook for 5 to 6 minutes until golden brown. 5. Transfer the egg rolls to a platter and allow to cool for at least 10 minutes. Dust with the powdered sugar before serving.
Per serving: Calories 149; Fat: 15.4g; Sodium 313mg; Carbs: 1.1g; Fiber: 0.1g; Sugars 0.1g; Protein 2.2g

Confetti Cake

Prep Time: 10 minutes. | Cook Time: 30 minutes. | Serves: 4

1½ cups vegan vanilla cake mix
¾ cup unsweetened applesauce
2 tablespoon canola oil
For The Frosting
3 tablespoon vegan butter (Earth Balance recommended)
1 cup powdered sugar
½ teaspoon pure vanilla extract
¼ cup water
2 tablespoon colored sprinkles
Nonstick cooking spray

pinch of salt
1 to 2 tablespoon unsweetened soy milk

1. Spray the Cook & Crisp Basket with nonstick cooking spray. 2. In a suitable bowl, mix the cake mix, applesauce, canola oil, and water. Fold in the sprinkles. Place the mixture in the Cook & Crisp Basket. 3. Place the Cook & Crisp Basket in your Pressure Cooker Steam Fryer. 4. Put on the Smart Lid on top of the Ninja Foodi Steam Fryer. Move the Lid Slider to the "Air Fry/Stovetop". Select the "Air Fry" mode for cooking. Adjust the cooking temperature to 310°F/155°C. Air Fry until the top is golden and a toothpick comes out clean from the center, about 30 minutes. 5. In a suitable bowl, make the frosting by beating the butter, powdered sugar, vanilla extract, and salt until well mixed. Continue to mix while adding 1 to 2 tablespoons of soy milk to reach the desired consistency. 6. Remove the "cook & crisp basket" and allow the cake to cool completely. Spread the buttercream over the cake before serving.
Per serving: Calories 93; Fat: 1.6g; Sodium 465mg; Carbs: 15.2g; Fiber: 5g; Sugars 3.8g; Protein 4.5g

Blueberry Oats Crisp

Prep Time: 10 minutes. | Cook Time: 17 minutes. | Serves: 4

2 cups fresh blueberries
Juice of ½ orange
1 tablespoon maple syrup
2 teaspoon cornstarch
1 tablespoon vegan butter (Earth Balance recommended)
½ cup rolled oats
¼ cup almond flour
½ teaspoon cinnamon
2 tablespoon coconut sugar or granulated sugar
Pinch of salt

1. In the Cook & Crisp Basket, mix the blueberries, orange juice, maple syrup, and cornstarch. Mix well. 2. In a suitable bowl, mix the butter, oats, almond flour, cinnamon, sugar, and salt. Use clean hands to mix until a soft, crumbly dough forms. Evenly sprinkle the prepared dough over the blueberries. 3. Place the Cook & Crisp Basket in your Pressure Cooker Steam Fryer. 4. Put on the Smart Lid on top of the Ninja Foodi Steam Fryer. Move the Lid Slider to the "Air Fry/Stovetop". Select the "Air Fry" mode for cooking. Adjust the cooking temperature to 370°F/185°C. 5. Air Fry until the topping is crispy and the berries are thick and bubbly, about 15 to 17 minutes. 6. Remove the crisp from the "cook & crisp basket" and allow the crisp to cool for at least 10 minutes before serving.
Per serving: Calories 360; Fat: 7.8g; Sodium 280mg; Carbs: 74.4g; Fiber: 8g; Sugars 47.4g; Protein 2.7g

Cinnamon Stuffed Apples

Prep Time: 10 minutes. | Cook Time: 20 minutes. | Serves: 4

2 small red or green apples, halved horizontally
4 teaspoon vegan butter (Earth Balance recommended)
¼ teaspoon cardamom
2 teaspoon cinnamon
¼ cup chopped walnuts
¼ cup raisins
Pinch of salt

1. Remove the seeds and core from both halves of each apple and place all 4 halves cut side up in the Cook & Crisp Basket. Pour about 1 inch (2.5cm) of water into the bottom of the basket. 2. In a suitable bowl, mix the butter, cardamom, cinnamon, walnuts, raisins, and salt. Mix well. Equally divide the filling among the apple halves. 3. Place the Cook & Crisp Basket in your Pressure Cooker Steam Fryer. 4. Put on the Smart Lid on top of the Ninja Foodi Steam Fryer. Move the Lid Slider to the "Air Fry/Stovetop". Select the "Air Fry" mode for cooking. Adjust the cooking temperature to 350°F/175°C. 5. Air Fry until the apples are tender, about 20 minutes. 6. Remove the apples from the "cook & crisp basket" and allow the apples to cool for around 10 minutes before serving.
Per serving: Calories 241; Fat: 9.8g; Sodium 605mg; Carbs: 29.8g; Fiber: 8.5g; Sugars 1.1g; Protein 9.8g

Raspberry Pineapple Sundaes

Prep Time: 10 minutes. | Cook Time: 5 minutes. | Serves: 4

2 cups diced pineapple
½ teaspoon cinnamon
½ teaspoon granulated sugar
1 cup raspberries
¾ cup dairy-free ice cream
½ cup Agave and Pistachio Granola
Nonstick cooking spray

1. Place the Cook & Crisp Basket in your Pressure Cooker Steam Fryer. 2. Grease the "cook & crisp basket" with nonstick cooking spray. 3. In a suitable bowl, mix the pineapple, cinnamon, and sugar. Toss well to coat. 4. Place the pineapple in the "cook & crisp basket". Put on the Smart Lid on top of the Ninja Foodi Steam Fryer. Move the Lid Slider to the "Air Fry/Stovetop". Select the "Air Fry" mode for cooking. Adjust the cooking temperature to 400°F/200°C. Cook for until sizzling and the sugar begins to caramelize, about 5 minutes. 5. Remove the pineapple from the "cook & crisp basket" and allow to cool slightly. Serve the pineapple over the ice cream. Top each sundae with an equal amount of Agave and Pistachio Granola and raspberries.
Per serving: Calories 49; Fat: 3.8g; Sodium 638mg; Carbs: 3; Fiber: 1.6g; Sugars 0.4g; Protein 2.1g

Gooey Brownies

Prep Time: 10 minutes. | Cook Time: 15 minutes. | Serves: 4 to

6

1 cup granulated sugar
⅓ cup Dutch-process cocoa powder
½ teaspoon salt
8 tablespoons (1 stick) unsalted butter, melted
1 teaspoon vanilla extract
2 large eggs, beaten
¼ cup all-purpose flour
½ cup chopped bittersweet chocolate
Vanilla ice cream and flaky sea salt, for serving

1. Place the Cook & Crisp Basket in your Pressure Cooker Steam Fryer. 2. In a suitable bowl, mix the sugar, cocoa powder, and salt. Then add the melted butter, vanilla, and eggs and mix until smooth. Stir in the flour and chocolate and pour the prepared batter into the Cook & Crisp Basket. 3. Place the Cook & Crisp Basket in your Pressure Cooker Steam Fryer. 4. Put on the Smart Lid on top of the Ninja Foodi Steam Fryer. Move the Lid Slider to the "Air Fry/Stovetop". Select the "Air Fry" mode for cooking. Air Fry at 310°F/155°C until the brownie "pudding" is set at the edges but still jiggly in the middle (it may form a "skin" in the middle, but it doesn't affect the taste), about 30 minutes. 5. Let the brownie cool in the Ninja Foodi Pressure Steam Fryer for around 5 minutes, enough time to grab some bowls and allow the ice cream to soften to the perfect scooping consistency. Divide the gooey brownies among serving bowls and top with a scoop of ice cream and, if you like, a decent pinch of flaky sea salt.
Per serving: Calories 373; Fat: 3.1g; Sodium 687mg; Carbs: 69.2g; Fiber: 9.6g; Sugars 3.4g; Protein 7.8g

Chocolate Cookie Cups

Prep Time: 10 minutes. | Cook Time: 10 minutes. | Serves: 4

1 tablespoon flaxseed
3 tablespoon water
1 cup all-purpose flour
½ teaspoon baking powder
¼ teaspoon salt
3 tablespoon maple syrup
2 tablespoon coconut oil, melted
¼ cup vegan chocolate chips
Nonstick cooking spray

1. Place the Cook & Crisp Basket in your Pressure Cooker Steam Fryer. 2. Spray 4 ramekins with nonstick cooking spray. Set aside. 3. In a suitable bowl, mix the flaxseed and water. 4. In a suitable bowl, mix the flour, baking powder, and salt. Add the flaxseed mixture, maple syrup, and coconut oil. Mix until just mixed. Fold in the chocolate chips. Add an equal amount of batter into each ramekin. 5. Place the prepared ramekins in the Cook & Crisp Basket. Put on the Smart Lid on top of the Ninja Foodi Steam Fryer. Move the Lid Slider to the "Air Fry/Stovetop". Select the "Air Fry" mode for cooking. Adjust the cooking temperature to 340°F/170°C. Air Fry until puffed and golden, about 8 to 10 minutes. 6. Remove the ramekins from the "cook & crisp basket" and allow the cookie cups to cool before serving.
Per serving: Calories 195; Fat: 7.3g; Sodium 592mg; Carbs: 31.8g; Fiber: 4.7g; Sugars 0.6g; Protein 1.8g

Vegan Apple Pies

Prep Time: 10 minutes. | Cook Time: 10 minutes. | Serves: 4

1 medium apple (Gala or Granny Smith recommended), peeled and finely diced
Juice of ½ orange
2 tablespoon granulated sugar
½ teaspoon cinnamon
2 teaspoon cornstarch
10oz (285g) vegan pie dough
All-purpose flour

1. Place the Cook & Crisp Basket in your Pressure Cooker Steam Fryer. 2. In a suitable bowl, mix the apple, orange juice, sugar, cinnamon, and cornstarch. Mix well. 3. Roll out the prepared dough on a floured surface. Cut the prepared dough into 4 rounds. Place 2 tablespoons of the apple mixture in the center of each. Fold the prepared dough in half and seal the edges with a fork. Make a suitable slit in the top for steam to escape. 4. Place the pies in the "cook & crisp basket". Put on the Smart Lid on top of the Ninja Foodi Steam Fryer. Move the Lid Slider to the "Air Fry/Stovetop". Select the "Air Fry" mode for cooking. Adjust the cooking temperature to 350°F/175°C. 5. Cook for until golden brown, about 10 minutes. 6. Transfer the pies to a wire rack to cool before serving.
Per serving: Calories 339; Fat: 14g; Sodium 556mg; Carbs: 44.6g; Fiber: 6.4g; Sugars 3.8g; Protein 10.5g

Spice Monkey Bread

Prep Time: 10 minutes. | Cook Time: 15 minutes. | Serves: 6 to 8

1 can (16.3 ounces) store-bought refrigerated biscuit dough
¼ cup packed light brown sugar
1 teaspoon cinnamon
½ teaspoon freshly grated nutmeg
½ teaspoon ginger
½ teaspoon salt
¼ teaspoon allspice
⅛ teaspoon cloves
4 tablespoons (½ stick) unsalted butter, melted
½ cup powdered sugar
2 teaspoons bourbon
2 tablespoons chopped candied cherries
2 tablespoons chopped pecans

1. Open the can and separate the biscuits, then cut each into quarters. Toss the biscuit quarters in a suitable bowl with the brown sugar, cinnamon, nutmeg, ginger, salt, allspice, and cloves until evenly coated. Transfer the prepared dough pieces and any sugar left in the bowl to the Cook & Crisp Basket and drizzle evenly with the melted butter. 2. Place the Cook & Crisp Basket in your Pressure Cooker Steam Fryer. 3. Put on the Smart Lid on top of the Ninja Foodi Steam Fryer. Move the Lid Slider to the "Air Fry/Stovetop". Select the "Air Fry" mode for cooking. Air Fry at 310°F/155°C until the monkey bread is golden brown and cooked through in the middle, about 25 minutes. Transfer the pan to a wire rack and let cool completely. Unmold from the pan. 4. In a suitable bowl, mix the powdered sugar and the bourbon into a smooth glaze. Drizzle the glaze over the cooled monkey bread and, while the glaze is still wet, sprinkle with the cherries and pecans to serve.
Per serving: Calories 231; Fat: 2.1g; Sodium 816mg; Carbs: 38.1g; Fiber: 14.4g; Sugars 4.5g; Protein 16.6g

Cinnamon Beignets

Prep Time: 10 minutes. | Cook Time: 15 minutes. | Serves: 16

3 tablespoons unsalted butter, cut into small cubes
½ teaspoon salt
1 teaspoon vanilla extract
1 cup 2 tablespoons all-purpose
flour, more for dusting
2 large eggs
1 cup granulated sugar
2 teaspoons cinnamon
Vegetable oil, for brushing

1. In a suitable saucepan, mix the butter, salt, vanilla, and 1 cup water and bring to a boil over high heat. Add the flour and cook, with constant stirring with a wooden spoon, until a smooth dough forms, about 30 seconds. Transfer the prepared dough to a suitable bowl, let cool for around 1 minute, then add 1 egg, stirring vigorously until the prepared dough is smooth again. Repeat with the remaining egg. 2. Transfer the prepared dough to a floured work surface and sprinkle the top with more flour. Pat the prepared dough into a 9-inch square about ¼ inch thick. Flip the prepared dough sheet over from time to time and add more flour if it's sticking to the surface (don't worry about adding too much flour since you will brush it off later). Cut the prepared dough square into 16 smaller squares and transfer them to a foil-lined baking sheet. Using a dry pastry brush, dust off as much of the excess flour as you can on both sides. Chill the beignets on the sheet in the freezer until frozen solid, at least 1 hour. 3. Meanwhile, mix the sugar and cinnamon in a suitable brown paper bag. 4. Using a pastry brush, brush 4 squares all over with enough oil to coat well. Place them in one layer in the Cook & Crisp Basket. Place the Cook & Crisp Basket in your Pressure Cooker Steam Fryer. 5. Put on the Smart Lid on top of the Ninja Foodi Steam Fryer. Move the Lid Slider to the "Air Fry/Stovetop". Select the "Air Fry" mode for cooking. Air Fry at 400°F/200°C until golden brown and puffed, about 13 minutes. As soon as the beignets are done, use tongs to immediately transfer them to the paper bag and shake them in the cinnamon-sugar to coat. Repeat with the remaining dough squares and cinnamon-sugar in three more batches. Serve the beignets hot.
Per serving: Calories 283; Fat: 3.6g; Sodium 381mg; Carbs: 55.4g; Fiber: 8.1g; Sugars 3.1g; Protein 8.7g

Flaxseed Carrot Cake

Prep Time: 10 minutes. | Cook Time: 30 minutes. | Serves: 6

1 tablespoon flaxseed
3 tablespoon water
½ cup cake flour
¼ teaspoon baking soda
Pinch of salt
½ teaspoon cinnamon
½ cup granulated sugar
¼ cup canola oil
½ teaspoon pure vanilla extract
¼ cup unsweetened applesauce
¾ cup grated carrots
For The Glaze
⅓ cup powdered sugar
½ teaspoon pure vanilla extract
2 tablespoon raisins
2 tablespoon chopped walnuts
Nonstick cooking spray

2 teaspoons dairy-free milk (soy recommended)

1. Spray the Cook & Crisp Basket with nonstick cooking spray. Set aside. 2. In a suitable bowl, mix the flaxseed and water. Set aside for at least 5 minutes. 3. In a suitable bowl, mix the cake flour, baking soda, salt, and cinnamon. Add the sugar, canola oil, vanilla extract, applesauce, and flaxseed mixture. Mix well. Fold in the carrots, raisins, and walnuts. Place the prepared batter in the Cook & Crisp Basket. 4. Place the Cook & Crisp Basket in your Pressure Cooker Steam Fryer. 5. Put on the Smart Lid on top of the Ninja Foodi Steam Fryer. Move the Lid Slider to the "Air Fry/Stovetop". Select the "Air Fry" mode for cooking. Adjust the cooking temperature to 310°F/155°C. Air Fry until a toothpick comes out clean from the center, about 25 to 30 minutes. 6. Transfer the cake to a serving platter and allow to cool completely. 7. In a suitable bowl, make the glaze by whisking the ingredients. Drizzle the prepared glaze over the cake and allow to set. 8. Cut the cake into 6 slices before serving.
Per serving: Calories 344; Fat: 3g; Sodium 603mg; Carbs: 73.8g; Fiber: 11.5g; Sugars 8.6g; Protein 9.4g

Chia Pudding Tarts

Prep Time: 10 minutes. | Cook Time: 10 minutes. | Serves: 6

1 cup chocolate soy milk
¼ cup chia seeds
1 tablespoon orange zest
Pinch of sea salt
2 cups all-purpose flour
½ teaspoon salt
½ cup canola oil
8 tablespoons cold water

1. In a 16-ounce (475-milliliter) glass jar, mix the soy milk, chia seeds, orange zest, and sea salt. Allow the prepared mixture to sit for around 10 minutes before whisking again. Cover and refrigerate for at least 6 hours. In a suitable bowl, mix the flour and salt. 2. In a separate medium bowl, mix the oil and 5 to 6 tablespoons of the water. Make a small well in the center of the flour mixture and pour in the oil mixture. Mix with a fork until just mixed. Add 2 more tablespoons of water as needed. Shape the prepared dough into a ball. 3. Roll out the prepared dough between 2 sheets of wax or parchment paper. Use a 4.5-inch (5cm) ring mold to cut out 6 rounds. Transfer the prepared dough to ramekins and press in gently to form the cups. 4. Place the prepared ramekins in the Cook & Crisp Basket. Place the Cook & Crisp Basket in your Pressure Cooker Steam Fryer. 5. Put on the Smart Lid on top of the Ninja Foodi Steam Fryer. Move the Lid Slider to the "Air Fry/Stovetop". Select the "Air Fry" mode for cooking. Adjust the cooking temperature to 350°F/175°C. 6. Air Fry until the crust is golden, about 10 minutes. 7. Remove the ramekins from the "cook & crisp basket" and allow the cups to cool completely. Transfer the cups to a platter. Fill the cups with the chia pudding and serve immediately.
Per serving: Calories 336; Fat: 9.9g; Sodium 1672mg; Carbs: 42.6g; Fiber: 1.7g; Sugars 2.1g; Protein 12.3g

Chapter 8 Soup, Stew, and Chili Recipes

169 Regular Chicken Broth

169 Regular Vegetable Broth

169 Chicken and Vegetable Broth

169 Traditional Beef Chili

169 Tortellini Soup with pesto

169 Tomato Soup with basil

170 Pot Pie Soup

170 Potato Soup with cheese

170 Delicious Minestrone

170 Bean Ham Soup

170 Corn Chowder with Potatoes

171 Clam Corn Chowder

171 Clam Chowder

171 Healthy White Chicken Chili

171 Kale Sausage Soup

171 Healthy Three Bean Chili

172 Chicken Soup

172 Spicy Curried Cauliflower Soup

172 Beefy Minestrone Soup

172 Delicious Moroccan Carrot Soup

172 Italian Tuscan Soup

173 Mexican-Style Chicken Noodle Soup

173 Chicken with Dumplings

173 Spicy Beef with Broccoli Zoodle Soup

173 Cheesy Creamy Spinach Soup

174 Dropped Egg Soup

174 Ham with Split Pea Soup

174 Tomatoes Stuffed Pepper Soup

174 Delicious Zuppa Toscana

174 Five-Ingredient Bean Soup

175 Spicy Buffalo Chicken Chowder

175 Beef Spicy Pho

175 Delicious Colombian Chicken Soup

175 Garlicky Green Chickpea Soup

176 Creamy Tomato Soup with Basil

176 Thai Tropical red Soup

176 Cheesy Broccoli Soup

176 Creamy Lasagna Soup

177 Two-Bean Chili stew

177 "Noodle" Soup

177 Thai Chicken Curry Soup with Veggies "Ramen"

177 Bean Tuscan Soup

Regular Chicken Broth

Prep time: 5 minutes| Cook time: 30 minutes| Serves: 12

Leftover bones and skin from 1 (4-pound) chicken
1 medium onion, peeled and roughly chopped
2 medium carrots, roughly chopped
2 medium stalks celery, roughly chopped
1 bay leaf
2 teaspoons salt
12 cups water

1. Place chicken bones and skin in Ninja Foodi XL Pressure Cooker Steam Fryer with SmartLid cooking pot. 2. Place onion, carrots, and celery on top of chicken bones. 3. Add in bay leaf, salt, and water. Mix. 4. Lock lid; move slider towards PRESSURE. Adjust pressure release valve in the SEAL position. Close pressure-release valve. The cooking temperature will default to HIGH, which is accurate. Set the time for 30 minutes. Select START/STOP and start cooking. When cooking is complete, let pressure release naturally and unlock lid. 5. Strain Chicken Broth through a mesh strainer into a large bowl. 6. Ladle Chicken Broth into jars for refrigerator storage or freezer bags for freezer storage. Store in refrigerator up to one week or in freezer for up to three months.
Per Serving: Calories 27; Fat 0g; Sodium 477mg; Carbs 2g; Fiber 1g; Sugar 1g; Protein 4g

Regular Vegetable Broth

Prep time: 5 minutes| Cook time: 30 minutes| Serves: 12

2 medium stalks celery, roughly chopped
2 large carrots, roughly chopped
1 medium yellow onion, peeled and roughly chopped
4 cloves garlic, roughly chopped
1 tablespoon tomato paste
2 teaspoons salt
⅛ teaspoon black pepper
12 cups water

1. Place celery, carrots, onion, garlic, tomato paste, salt, and pepper in Ninja Foodi XL Pressure Cooker Steam Fryer with SmartLid cooking pot. 2. Pour water into pot. Mix until tomato paste is evenly distributed. 3. Lock lid; move slider towards PRESSURE. Adjust pressure release valve in the SEAL position. Close pressure-release valve. The cooking temperature will default to HIGH, which is accurate. Set the time for 30 minutes. Select START/STOP and start cooking. When cooking is complete, let pressure release naturally. 4. Strain Vegetable Broth through a mesh strainer into a large bowl. 5. Ladle Vegetable Broth into jars for refrigerator storage or freezer bags for freezer storage. Store in the refrigerator up to one week or in the freezer up to three months.
Per Serving: Calories 12; Fat 0g; Sodium 451mg; Carbs 3g; Fiber 1g; Sugar 3g; Protein 0g

Chicken and Vegetable Broth

Prep time: 10 minutes| Cook time: 20 minutes| Serves: 6

4 thick-cut bacon slices cut into cubes
4 cups chicken broth
3 pounds Yukon gold potatoes, peeled
1 teaspoon salt
½ teaspoon black pepper
4 ounces cream cheese, melted
1 pint half-and-half
1 cup shredded sharp Cheddar cheese
2 medium green onions, sliced

1. Move the slider towards "AIR FRY/STOVETOP" and set Ninja Foodi XL Pressure Cooker Steam Fryer with SmartLid to SEAR/SAUTÉ mode. Adjust the temperature to "Hi5" by using up arrow. Press START/STOP to begin cooking and cook bacon pieces until crisp. Press START/STOP button. 2. Drain bacon fat and place cooked bacon in-between two paper towels. Set aside. 3. Pour in broth and deglaze pot. 4. Place whole potatoes, salt, and pepper into cooking pot. Lock lid; move slider towards PRESSURE. Adjust pressure release valve in the SEAL position. Close pressure-release valve. The cooking temperature will default to HIGH, which is accurate. Set the time for 10 minutes. Select START/STOP and start cooking. When cooking is complete, let pressure release quickly by turning it into VENT position and unlock the lid. 5. Using an immersion blender or potato masher, blend up potatoes and broth until only a few chunks are left. 6. Turn Ninja Foodi XL Pressure Cooker Steam Fryer back on and select Sauté setting. Whisk in cream cheese and half-and-half. Let cook an additional 10 minutes, stirring occasionally. 7. Mix in half of the cooked bacon. 8. Serve topped with cheese, green onions, and remaining bacon.
Per Serving: Calories 578; Fat 36g; Sodium 823mg; Carbs 49g; Fiber

5g; Sugar 6g; Protein 17g

Traditional Beef Chili

Prep time: 10 minutes| Cook time: 55 minutes| Serves: 6

1 tablespoon olive oil
1 medium yellow onion, peeled and diced
2 medium jalapeños, seeded and diced
2 pounds ground beef
1 teaspoon salt
1 teaspoon black pepper
3 cloves garlic, minced
2 (15-ounce) cans tomato sauce
2 (15.5-ounce) cans kidney beans, drained and rinsed
3 teaspoons chili powder
½ teaspoon cayenne pepper
¼ teaspoon red pepper flakes

1. Move the slider towards "AIR FRY/STOVETOP" and set Ninja Foodi XL Pressure Cooker Steam Fryer with SmartLid to SEAR/SAUTÉ mode. Adjust the temperature to "Hi5" by using up arrow. Press START/STOP to begin cooking. Add oil. 2. Pour in onion, jalapeños, and ground beef. Sprinkle with salt and pepper. Stir and cook until onions are soft and meat is no longer pink, about 8 minutes. 3. Add in garlic and cook an additional 30 seconds. Turn Ninja Foodi XL Pressure Cooker Steam Fryer with SmartLid cooking pot off. Drain fat from the pot. 4. Mix in tomato sauce, kidney beans, chili powder, cayenne pepper, and red pepper flakes. Make sure to scrape the bottom of the pot for any stuck-on food. 5. Lock lid; move slider towards PRESSURE. Adjust pressure release valve in the SEAL position. Close pressure-release valve. The cooking temperature will default to HIGH, which is accurate. Set the time for 45 minutes. Select START/STOP and start cooking. 6. When cooking is complete, let pressure release naturally and unlock lid. Serve.
Per Serving: Calories 502; Fat 26g; Sodium 1382mg; Carbs 29g; Fiber 8g; Sugar 6g; Protein 38g

Tortellini Soup with pesto

Prep time: 5 minutes| Cook time: 1 minutes| Serves: 6

6 cups chicken broth
3 cups frozen tortellini
8 medium green onions, sliced
⅓ cup frozen chopped spinach
1½ teaspoons salt
¾ teaspoon black pepper
½ teaspoon dried oregano
½ cup basil pesto

1. Combine broth, tortellini, green onions, spinach, salt, pepper, and oregano in Ninja Foodi XL Pressure Cooker Steam Fryer with SmartLid cooking pot. 2. Lock lid; move slider towards PRESSURE. Adjust pressure release valve in the SEAL position. Close pressure-release valve. The cooking temperature will default to HIGH, which is accurate. Set the time for 1 minutes. Select START/STOP and start cooking. 3. When cooking is complete, let pressure release quickly by turning it into VENT position. 4. Unlock lid and remove it. 5. Ladle soup into bowls and top with pesto.
Per Serving: Calories 294; Fat 13g; Sodium 1105mg; Carbs 32g; Fiber 4g; Sugar 2g; Protein 14g

Tomato Soup with basil

Prep time: 5 minutes| Cook time: 9 minutes| Serves: 4

2 tablespoons olive oil
1 medium yellow onion, peeled and chopped
2 cloves garlic, minced
4 (14.5-ounce) cans diced tomatoes
2 cups vegetable broth
¼ cup fresh basil, chopped
2 tablespoons granulated sugar
1 teaspoon salt
1 cup heavy whipping cream

1. Move the slider towards "AIR FRY/STOVETOP" and set Ninja Foodi XL Pressure Cooker Steam Fryer with SmartLid to SEAR/SAUTÉ mode. Adjust the temperature to "Hi5" by using up arrow. Press START/STOP to begin cooking. Put oil and onion into cooking pot. Cook onion 2 minutes until soft. 2. Add in garlic and cook 30 seconds. Turn off. 3. Add tomatoes, vegetable broth, basil, sugar, and salt to pot and stir to combine. 4. Lock lid; move slider towards PRESSURE. Adjust pressure release valve in the SEAL position. Close pressure-release valve. The cooking temperature will default to HIGH, which is accurate. Set QUICK RELEASE and time to 7 minutes. Select START/STOP and start cooking. 5. When cooking is complete, let pressure release quickly by turning it into VENT position. 6. Blend soup with an immersion blender. 7. Once blended, whisk in heavy whipping cream and serve.
Per Serving: Calories 341; Fat 29g; Sodium 822mg; Carbs 20g; Fiber 3g; Sugar 15g; Protein 4g

Pot Pie Soup

Prep time: 10 minutes| Cook time: 5 minutes| Serves: 4

2 tablespoons olive oil	2 teaspoons salt
1 medium yellow onion, peeled and chopped	½ teaspoon black pepper
	½ teaspoon dried parsley
2 cloves garlic, minced	¼ teaspoon dried sage
4 cups chicken broth	1 bay leaf
1 cup diced cooked chicken	1 cup heavy whipping cream
1 (12-ounce) bag frozen mixed vegetables	⅓ cup all-purpose flour

1. Move the slider towards "AIR FRY/STOVETOP" and set Ninja Foodi XL Pressure Cooker Steam Fryer with SmartLid to SEAR/SAUTÉ mode. Adjust the temperature to "Hi5" by using up arrow. Press START/STOP to begin cooking. Put oil and onion into pot. Cook onion 2 minutes until soft. 2. Add in garlic and cook 30 seconds. Turn pot off. 3. Add broth, chicken, mixed vegetables, salt, pepper, parsley, sage, and bay leaf. 4. Lock lid; move slider towards PRESSURE. Adjust pressure release valve in the SEAL position. Close pressure-release valve. The cooking temperature will default to HIGH, which is accurate. Set the time for 2 minutes. Select START/STOP and start cooking. When cooking is complete, let pressure release quickly by turning it into VENT position and unlock lid. 5. In a small bowl, whisk together cream and flour. Whisk cream mixture into soup. 6. Remove bay leaf and serve.
Per Serving: Calories 472; Fat 31g; Sodium 1321mg; Carbs 29g; Fiber 4g; Sugar 8g; Protein 21g

Potato Soup with cheese

Prep time: 10 minutes| Cook time: 20 minutes| Serves: 8

3 pounds red potatoes, quartered	½ teaspoon onion powder
4 cups vegetable broth	½ teaspoon dried oregano
4 cups water	¼ teaspoon black pepper
2 teaspoons salt	2 (15-ounce) cans Cheddar cheese sauce
½ teaspoon garlic powder	

1. Combine potatoes, broth, water, salt, garlic powder, onion powder, oregano, and pepper in Ninja Foodi XL Pressure Cooker Steam Fryer with SmartLid cooking pot. 2. Lock lid; move slider towards PRESSURE. Adjust pressure release valve in the SEAL position. Close pressure-release valve. The cooking temperature will default to HIGH, which is accurate. Set the time for 10 minutes. Select START/STOP and start cooking. When cooking is complete, let pressure release quickly by turning it into VENT position and unlock lid. 3. Blend soup using an immersion blender until smooth. 4. Mix in Cheddar cheese sauce. Move the slider towards "AIR FRY/STOVETOP" and Set Ninja Foodi XL Pressure Cooker Steam Fryer with SmartLid to SEAR/SAUTÉ mode. Adjust the temperature to "Hi5" by using up arrow. Press START/STOP to begin cooking. 5. Let cook, stirring occasionally, 10 minutes. Serve.
Per Serving: Calories 342; Fat 15g; Sodium 968mg; Carbs 36g; Fiber 4g; Sugar 11g; Protein 14g

Delicious Minestrone

Prep time: 10 minutes| Cook time: 13 minutes| Serves: 6

2 tablespoons olive oil	2 teaspoons salt
1 medium yellow onion, peeled and chopped	1 teaspoon dried oregano
	½ teaspoon black pepper
2 cloves garlic, minced	4 cups chopped kale
4 cups vegetable broth	1 (15.5-ounce) can cannelloni beans, drained and rinsed
2 cups water	
3 medium russet potatoes, peeled and cubed	1 (15.5-ounce) can red kidney beans, drained and rinsed
2 medium carrots, diced	
1 cup chopped green beans	½ cup medium shell-shaped pasta

1. Move the slider towards "AIR FRY/STOVETOP" and set Ninja Foodi XL Pressure Cooker Steam Fryer with SmartLid to SEAR/SAUTÉ mode. Adjust the temperature to "Hi5" by using up arrow. Press START/STOP to begin cooking. Put oil and onion into pot. Cook onion 2 minutes until soft. 2. Add in garlic and cook 30 seconds. Turn Pot off. 3. Add broth, water, potatoes, carrots, green beans, salt, oregano, and pepper to pot and mix. 4. Lock lid; move slider towards PRESSURE. Adjust pressure release valve in the SEAL position. Close pressure-release valve. The cooking temperature will default to HIGH, which is accurate. Set QUICK RELEASE and time to 2 minutes. Select START/STOP and start cooking. When cooking is complete, let pressure release quickly by turning it into VENT position. 5. Move the slider towards "AIR FRY/STOVETOP" and set Ninja Foodi XL Pressure Cooker Steam Fryer with SmartLid to SEAR/SAUTÉ mode. Adjust the temperature to "Hi5" by using up arrow. Press START/STOP to begin cooking. Mix in kale, cannelloni beans, kidney beans, and pasta. Let cook 8 minutes. 6. Turn off and serve.
Per Serving: Calories 278; Fat 6g; Sodium 1044mg; Carbs 47g; Fiber 9g; Sugar 9g; Protein 11g

Bean Ham Soup

Prep time: 10 minutes| Cook time: 7 minutes| Serves: 6

1 pound great northern beans	with bone reserved
2 tablespoons olive oil	6 cups chicken broth
1 small yellow onion, peeled and chopped	2 medium carrots, diced
	1 teaspoon dried parsley
6 cloves garlic, minced	½ teaspoon black pepper
1 (16-ounce) ham steak, cubed	1 bay leaf

1. Soak beans overnight. 2. Move the slider towards "AIR FRY/STOVETOP" and set Ninja Foodi XL Pressure Cooker Steam Fryer with SmartLid to SEAR/SAUTÉ mode. Adjust the temperature to "Hi5" by using up arrow. Press START/STOP to begin cooking. Put oil and onion into cooking pot. Cook onion 2 minutes until soft. 3. Add in garlic and cook 30 seconds. Turn off. 4. Add beans, ham and ham bone, broth, carrots, parsley, pepper, and bay leaf to cooking pot. 5. Lock lid; move slider towards PRESSURE. Adjust pressure release valve in the SEAL position. Close pressure-release valve. The cooking temperature will default to HIGH, which is accurate. Set the time for 4 minutes. Select START/STOP and start cooking. 6. When cooking is complete, let pressure release quickly by turning it into VENT position. 7. Unlock lid and remove it. 8. Remove bay leaf and ham bone. Serve.
Per Serving: Calories 435; Fat 9g; Sodium 1068mg; Carbs 53g; Fiber 14g; Sugar 5g; Protein 37g

Corn Chowder with Potatoes

Prep time: 15 minutes| Cook time: 20 minutes| Serves: 8

1-pound bacon, cut into ½" strips	quartered
2 medium stalks celery, diced	1 (15-ounce) can corn
1 medium yellow onion, peeled and chopped	1 (14.75-ounce) can creamed corn
	2 teaspoons salt
1 medium carrot, diced	¼ teaspoon black pepper
2 cloves garlic, minced	¼ teaspoon cayenne pepper
4 cups vegetable broth	1 cup whole milk
1½ pounds baby yellow potatoes,	4 medium green onions, sliced

1. Move the slider towards "AIR FRY/STOVETOP" and set Ninja Foodi XL Pressure Cooker Steam Fryer with SmartLid to SEAR/SAUTÉ mode. Adjust the temperature to "Hi5" by using up arrow. Press START/STOP to begin cooking. Add sliced bacon into cooking pot. Cook, stirring occasionally, for 7 minutes. 2. Remove bacon and place in between two paper towels. Set aside. 3. Remove bacon grease, reserving 2 tablespoons bacon grease inside cooking pot. Add celery, onion, and carrots. Cook, stirring occasionally, 7 minutes. 4. Add in garlic and cook an additional 30 seconds. 5. Pour in broth and deglaze the pot. Turn pot off. 6. Mix in corn, creamed corn, salt, black pepper, and cayenne. 7. Lock lid; move slider towards PRESSURE. Adjust pressure release valve in the SEAL position. Close pressure-release valve. The cooking temperature will default to HIGH, which is accurate. Set time to 3 minutes. Select START/STOP and start cooking. When cooking is complete, let pressure release quickly by turning it into VENT position. 8. Unlock lid and remove it. 9. Slowly whisk in milk. Serve topped with cooked bacon and green onions.
Per Serving: Calories 392; Fat 24g; Sodium 1170mg; Carbs 33g; Fiber 4g; Sugar 9g; Protein 12g

Clam Corn Chowder

Prep time: 10 minutes| Cook time: 15 minutes| Serves: 6

2 tablespoons (28g) grass-fed butter
1 large yellow onion, finely diced
4 fresh cloves garlic, finely chopped
2 tablespoons (15g) gluten-free all-purpose flour
2 large celery ribs, sliced about ¼" (6mm) thick
1 large carrot, peeled and diced
1 large russet potato, peeled and diced
10 oz. (280g) fresh or frozen corn kernels
¼ cup (15g) chopped fresh flat-leaf parsley
1 cup (237ml) clam juice
1 cup (237ml) fish, chicken or vegetable stock
1 teaspoon sea salt
1 teaspoon dried thyme
1 teaspoon dried dill
1 teaspoon dried basil
½ teaspoon freshly ground black pepper
½ teaspoon dried oregano
Zest of 1 lemon
13 oz. (370g) canned clams, drained
1 cup (237ml) milk
¾ cup (175ml) heavy cream

1. Move the slider towards "AIR FRY/STOVETOP" and set Ninja Foodi XL Pressure Cooker Steam Fryer with SmartLid to SEAR/SAUTÉ mode. Adjust the temperature to "Hi5" by using up arrow. Press START/STOP to begin cooking. Place the butter in. Once the butter has melted, add the onion and sauté for 4 minutes, stirring occasionally. 2. Add the garlic and sauté for 1 minute, stirring occasionally. Add the flour and stir for 1 more minute. Add the celery, carrot, potato, corn, parsley, clam juice, stock, salt, thyme, dill, basil, pepper, oregano, lemon zest and clams, then give the mixture a quick stir. 3. Lock lid; move slider towards PRESSURE. Adjust pressure release valve in the SEAL position. Close pressure-release valve. The cooking temperature will default to HIGH, which is accurate. Set time to 9 minutes. Select START/STOP and start cooking. 4. When cooking is complete, let pressure release quickly by turning it into VENT position. 5. Move the slider towards "AIR FRY/STOVETOP" and set Ninja Foodi XL Pressure Cooker Steam Fryer with SmartLid to SEAR/SAUTÉ mode. Adjust the temperature to "Hi5" by using up arrow. Press START/STOP to begin cooking, add the milk and cream, then stir until they are fully mixed in. 6. Allow to come to a simmer and cook for about 5 minutes, or until the chowder slightly thickens. Taste for seasoning and adjust the salt to taste. Allow to rest for 10 minutes. 7. Serve immediately.
Per Serving: Calories 232; Fat 11.2g; Sodium 554mg; Carbs 10.6g; Fiber 3g; Sugar 1g; Protein 13.2g

Clam Chowder

Prep time: 10 minutes| Cook time: 13 minutes| Serves: 4

2 tablespoons olive oil
1 medium yellow onion, peeled and chopped
3 cloves garlic, minced
1 cup chicken broth
3 small russet potatoes, peeled and
cubed
1 (8-ounce) bottle clam juice
2 teaspoons salt
½ teaspoon black pepper
2 cups half-and-half
2 (6.5-ounce) cans minced clams

1. Move the slider towards "AIR FRY/STOVETOP" and set Ninja Foodi XL Pressure Cooker Steam Fryer with SmartLid to SEAR/SAUTÉ mode. Adjust the temperature to "Hi5" by using up arrow. Press START/STOP to begin cooking. Cook onion 2 minutes until soft. 2. Add in garlic and cook 30 seconds. Turn pot off. 3. Add broth, potatoes, clam juice, salt, and pepper to cooking pot. 4. Lock lid; move slider towards PRESSURE. Adjust pressure release valve in the SEAL position. Close pressure-release valve. The cooking temperature will default to HIGH, which is accurate. Set the time for 10 minutes. Select START/STOP and start cooking. 5. When cooking is complete, let pressure release quickly by turning it into VENT position. 6. unlock lid and remove it. 7. Whisk in half-and-half to the chowder. Mix in clams. 8. Serve.
Per Serving: Calories 420; Fat 30g; Sodium 1737mg; Carbs 31g; Fiber 2g; Sugar 6g; Protein 9g

Healthy White Chicken Chili

Prep time: 10 minutes| Cook time: 30 minutes| Serves: 6

4 cups chicken broth
3 (14.5-ounce) cans cannellini beans
1 pound boneless, skinless chicken
breasts
1 (16-ounce) can creamed corn
2 (4-ounce) cans mild diced green chilies
1 medium yellow onion, peeled and chopped
2 cloves garlic, minced
1 tablespoon chili powder
1 teaspoon salt
1 teaspoon dried oregano
½ teaspoon black pepper
½ teaspoon crushed red pepper
1 cup full-fat sour cream

1. Combine broth, beans, chicken, corn, green chilies, onion, garlic, chili powder, salt, oregano, black pepper, and crushed red pepper inside Ninja Foodi XL Pressure Cooker Steam Fryer with SmartLid cooking pot. 2. Lock lid; move slider towards PRESSURE. Adjust pressure release valve in the SEAL position. Close pressure-release valve. The cooking temperature will default to HIGH, which is accurate. 3. Set the time for 30 minutes. Select START/STOP and start cooking. 4. When cooking is complete, let pressure release naturally for 10 minutes, then quick-release any remaining pressure by turning it into VENT position. 5. Remove chicken from pot and shred using two forks. Place chicken back into cooking pot. Mix in sour cream. 6. Serve hot.
Per Serving: Calories 403; Fat 10g; Sodium 1119mg; Carbs 49g; Fiber 10g; Sugar 13g; Protein 33g

Kale Sausage Soup

Prep time: 10 minutes| Cook time: 18 minutes| Serves: 8

1 tablespoon olive oil
1 pound hot Italian sausage, casings removed
4 cups chicken broth
4 cups water
6 medium russet potatoes, peeled and cubed
4 cups kale, stems removed
1 small yellow onion, peeled and chopped
3 cloves garlic, minced
½ teaspoon salt
⅛ teaspoon black pepper
1 cup heavy whipping cream
1 tablespoon flour

1. Move the slider towards "AIR FRY/STOVETOP" and set Ninja Foodi XL Pressure Cooker Steam Fryer with SmartLid to SEAR/SAUTÉ mode. Adjust the temperature to "Hi5" by using up arrow. Press START/STOP to begin cooking. Put oil and sausage into cooking pot. Cook sausage 8 minutes until brown, breaking it up into pieces while cooking. Turn Ninja Foodi XL Pressure Cooker Steam Fryer off. 2. Add broth, water, potatoes, kale, onion, garlic, salt, and pepper and stir to combine. 3. Lock lid; move slider towards PRESSURE. Adjust pressure release valve in the SEAL position. Close pressure-release valve. The cooking temperature will default to HIGH, which is accurate. Set the time for 10 minutes. Select START/STOP and start cooking. When cooking is complete, let pressure release quickly by turning it into VENT position. 4. Whisk in heavy cream and flour. Serve.
Per Serving: Calories 350; Fat 21g; Sodium 426mg; Carbs 31g; Fiber 3g; Sugar 3g; Protein 11g

Healthy Three Bean Chili

Prep time: 5 minutes| Cook time: 16 minutes| Serves: 4

2 tablespoons olive oil
1 medium yellow onion, peeled and chopped
1 medium green bell pepper, seeded and chopped
4 cloves garlic, minced
1 cup water
2 (15.5-ounce) cans red kidney beans, drained and rinsed
2 (15.5-ounce) cans black beans, drained and rinsed
2 (15.5-ounce) cans cannelloni beans, drained and rinsed
1 (15-ounce) can tomato sauce
1 (6-ounce) can tomato paste
1 tablespoon chili powder
1 teaspoon dried oregano
½ teaspoon cayenne pepper

1. Move the slider towards "AIR FRY/STOVETOP" and set Ninja Foodi XL Pressure Cooker Steam Fryer with SmartLid to SEAR/SAUTÉ mode. Adjust the temperature to "Hi5" by using up arrow. Press START/STOP to begin cooking. Add oil to pot. Add in onion and bell pepper and cook 5 minutes until soft. 2. Add in garlic and cook an additional 30 seconds until fragrant. 3. Pour in water and deglazed bottom of pot. Turn pot off. 4. Add in kidney beans, black beans, cannelloni beans, tomato sauce, tomato paste, chili powder, oregano, and cayenne pepper. Mix well. 5. Lock lid; move slider towards PRESSURE. Adjust pressure release valve in the SEAL position. Close pressure-release valve. The cooking temperature will default to HIGH, which is accurate. Set the time for 10 minutes. Select START/STOP and start cooking. 6. When cooking is complete, let pressure release quickly by turning it into VENT position and unlock lid. 7. Serve.
Per Serving: Calories 625; Fat 11g; Sodium 1355mg; Carbs 102g; Fiber 28g; Sugar 11g; Protein 36g

Chicken Soup

Prep time: 5 minutes| Cook time: 25 minutes| Serves: 6

6 cups chicken broth
1 (6-ounce) can tomato paste
1 pound boneless, skinless chicken breasts
1 (15.25-ounce) can corn, drained
1 (14.5-ounce) can black beans, rinsed and drained

2 (7-ounce) cans mild diced green chilies
1 teaspoon salt
¼ teaspoon black pepper
2 cups tortilla chips
¼ cup cilantro, roughly chopped

1. Pour broth into Ninja Foodi XL Pressure Cooker Steam Fryer with SmartLid cooking pot. Whisk tomato paste into broth. 2. Add in chicken breasts, corn, beans, green chilies, salt, and pepper. Stir to combine. 3. Lock lid; move slider towards PRESSURE. Adjust pressure release valve in the SEAL position. Close pressure-release valve. 4. The cooking temperature will default to HIGH, which is accurate. Set time to 15 minutes. Select START/STOP and start cooking. 5. When cooking is complete, let pressure release naturally for 10 minutes, then quick-release any remaining pressure by turning it into VENT position. Unlock lid and remove it. 6. Remove chicken. Shred chicken using two forks and then place it back into Ninja Foodi XL Pressure Cooker Steam Fryer with SmartLid cooking pot. 7. Serve soup topped with tortilla chips and cilantro.
Per Serving: Calories 289; Fat 6g; Sodium 920mg; Carbs 32g; Fiber 6g; Sugar 10g; Protein 30g

Spicy Curried Cauliflower Soup

Prep time: 10 minutes| Cook time: 25 minutes| Serves: 4

2 teaspoons (10ml) olive oil
1 medium onion, chopped
3 cloves garlic, minced
1 tablespoon (15g) red curry paste
3 cups (710ml) chicken stock

1 large head cauliflower, broken into florets, core discarded
1 (13.5-oz [400m]) can coconut milk
1 teaspoon coarse salt

1. Move the slider towards "AIR FRY/STOVETOP" and set Ninja Foodi XL Pressure Cooker Steam Fryer with SmartLid to SEAR/SAUTÉ mode. Adjust the temperature to "Hi5" by using up arrow. Press START/STOP to begin cooking. 2. Add the olive oil, then the onion. Cook, stirring occasionally, until the onion is soft, about 5 minutes. Add the garlic and red curry paste. Cook for about another minute, stirring frequently. 3. Press START/STOP to turn off. Add the chicken stock, taking care to scrape up any browned bits from the bottom of the pot. Add the cauliflower florets. 4. Lock lid; move slider towards PRESSURE. Adjust pressure release valve in the SEAL position. Close pressure-release valve. The cooking temperature will default to HIGH, which is accurate. Set time to 20 minutes. Select START/STOP and start cooking. 5. When cooking is complete, let pressure release naturally for 10 minutes, then quick-release any remaining pressure by turning it into VENT position. 6. Carefully remove the lid. Stir in the coconut milk and salt. Using an immersion blender, puree the soup until smooth. 7. Serve immediately.
Per Serving: Calories 242; Fat 12.2g; Sodium 222mg; Carbs 10.5g; Fiber 1.6g; Sugar 2g; Protein 11.6g

Beefy Minestrone Soup

Prep time: 15 minutes| Cook time: 15 minutes| Serves: 6

2 tablespoons (30ml) avocado oil or extra-virgin olive oil
1 yellow onion, diced
2 cloves garlic, minced
1 lb. (455g) ground beef
1 medium zucchini, diced
3 carrots, sliced and diced
3 celery ribs, diced
1 (14.5-oz [411g]) can diced tomatoes
3 tablespoons (48g) tomato paste

1 (15-oz [425g]) can cannellini beans, drained and rinsed
1 tablespoon (6g) Italian seasoning
5 cups (1.2L) chicken stock
2 tablespoons (30ml) red wine vinegar
1 teaspoon salt, plus more to taste
¼ cup (10g) chopped fresh basil
⅓ cup (30g) shredded Parmesan cheese, for garnish

1. Move the slider towards "AIR FRY/STOVETOP" and set Ninja Foodi XL Pressure Cooker Steam Fryer with SmartLid to SEAR/SAUTÉ mode. Adjust the temperature to "Hi5" by using up arrow. Press START/STOP to begin cooking. 2. Once hot, add the oil to the pot, then the onion and garlic. Cook for 2 to 3 minutes, then add the ground beef. Continue to cook for another 5 to 6 minutes, or until the ground beef is mostly cooked. Seleet START/STOP. 3. Add the zucchini, carrots, celery, diced tomatoes, tomato paste, beans, Italian seasoning, stock, vinegar and salt. Lock lid; move slider towards PRESSURE. Adjust pressure release valve in the SEAL position. Close pressure-release valve. The cooking temperature will default to HIGH, which is accurate. Set time to 6 minutes. Select START/STOP and start cooking. 4. When cooking is complete, let pressure release quickly by turning it into VENT position. Serve hot and garnish with fresh basil and Parmesan cheese.
Per Serving: Calories 252; Fat 11.3g; Sodium 321mg; Carbs 10.2g; Fiber 3g; Sugar 1g; Protein 12.2g

Delicious Moroccan Carrot Soup

Prep time: 10 minutes| Cook time: 15 minutes| Serves: 6

1 yellow onion, diced
2 cloves garlic, minced
½ teaspoon ground cinnamon
½ teaspoon ground cumin
¼ to ½ teaspoon cayenne pepper
Salt
Freshly ground black pepper
1 teaspoon grated fresh ginger
Juice of ½ lemon

1 lb. (455g) carrots, peeled and roughly chopped
2 cups (475ml) vegetable stock
1 cup (237ml) water
1 teaspoon honey
¾ cup (175ml) canned coconut milk
Chopped green onion, for topping
Pomegranate seeds, for topping

1. In the Ninja Foodi XL Pressure Cooker Steam Fryer with SmartLid cooking pot, combine the onion, garlic, cinnamon, cumin, cayenne, salt and black pepper to taste, ginger, lemon juice, carrots, stock and water. Stir to combine. 2. Lock lid; move slider towards PRESSURE. Adjust pressure release valve in the SEAL position. Close pressure-release valve. The cooking temperature will default to HIGH, which is accurate. Set time to 12 minutes. Select START/STOP and start cooking. 3. When cooking is complete, let pressure release quickly by turning it into VENT position. Remove the lid. Stir in the honey and coconut milk. Puree the soup until smooth and creamy, using an immersion blender. Adjust the salt, black pepper and cayenne to taste. 4. Serve with green onion and pomegranate seeds on top, if desired.
Per Serving: Calories 223; Fat 10.2g; Sodium 211mg; Carbs 9.4g; Fiber 2g; Sugar 2g; Protein 14.3g

Italian Tuscan Soup

Prep time: 5 minutes| Cook time: 15 minutes| Serves: 4

2 tablespoons (30ml) olive or avocado oil
1 medium yellow onion, chopped
3 cloves garlic, minced
1 lb. (455g) Italian sausage
5 cups (1.2L) chicken stock
3 large russet potatoes, peel on, cut into 1" (2.5cm) chunks
2 teaspoons (3g) dried basil
1 teaspoon dried fennel

1 teaspoon sea salt, plus more to taste
2 cups (134g) chopped large-leaf curly kale
½ cup (120ml) full-fat coconut milk or heavy cream
1 to 2 teaspoon (1 to 2 g) crushed red pepper flakes
Freshly ground black pepper

1. Move the slider towards "AIR FRY/STOVETOP" and set Ninja Foodi XL Pressure Cooker Steam Fryer with SmartLid to SEAR/SAUTÉ mode. Adjust the temperature to "Hi5" by using up arrow. Press START/STOP to begin cooking. Once hot, coat the bottom of the pot with the oil. Add the onion and sauté for 2 to 3 minutes, then toss in the garlic and sausage. Brown the sausage until cooked, about 5 minutes. Select START/STOP. Pour the chicken stock over the sausage, then add the potatoes, basil, fennel and salt. 2. Lock lid; move slider towards PRESSURE. Adjust pressure release valve in the SEAL position. Close pressure-release valve. The cooking temperature will default to HIGH, which is accurate. Set time to 7 minutes. Select START/STOP and start cooking. 3. When cooking is complete, let pressure release quickly by turning it into VENT position. 4. Remove the lid and move the slider towards "AIR FRY/STOVETOP" and set Ninja Foodi XL Pressure Cooker Steam Fryer with SmartLid to SEAR/SAUTÉ mode. Adjust the temperature to "Hi5" by using up arrow. Press START/STOP to begin cooking. Add the kale. 5. Stir for a few minutes until the kale begins to wilt. Add the coconut milk. Season with red pepper flakes, and additional salt and pepper to taste.
Per Serving: Calories 246; Fat 12.3g; Sodium 114mg; Carbs 9.2g; Fiber 4g; Sugar 2g; Protein 10.3g

Mexican-Style Chicken Noodle Soup

Prep time: 5 minutes| Cook time: 15 minutes| Serves: 8

2 tablespoons (28g) grass-fed butter, ghee or avocado oil
1 large yellow onion, thickly sliced
5 cloves garlic, finely minced
½ cup (90g) crushed tomatoes or diced fresh tomatoes
½ small green cabbage, thickly sliced
1 large celery rib, thickly sliced
2½ lb. (1.1kg) organic skinless, boneless chicken breast or thighs
6 cups (1.4L) chicken stock
1½ cups (355ml) filtered water
1 tablespoon (8g) chili powder
1½ teaspoon (9g) sea salt
1½ teaspoon (4g) ground cumin
½ teaspoon ground coriander
½ teaspoon dried oregano
½ teaspoon dried thyme
⅓ cup (80ml) fresh lime juice
2 cups (210g) gluten-free dried pasta; e.g., fusilli, macaroni, penne, egg noodles or broken-up tagliatelle
Fresh cilantro, for garnish
Lime wedges, for garnish

1. Move the slider towards "AIR FRY/STOVETOP" and set Ninja Foodi XL Pressure Cooker Steam Fryer with SmartLid to SEAR/SAUTÉ mode. Adjust the temperature to "Hi5" by using up arrow. Press START/STOP to begin cooking. 2. Place your healthy fat of choice in it. Once the fat has melted, add the onion and sauté for 7 minutes, stirring occasionally, then add the garlic and continue to sauté for 1 minute, stirring occasionally. Add the tomatoes, cabbage, celery, chicken, stock, water, chili powder, salt, cumin, coriander, oregano, thyme and lime juice, then give the mixture a stir. Press START/STOP. 3. Lock lid; move slider towards PRESSURE. Adjust pressure release valve in the SEAL position. Close pressure-release valve. The cooking temperature will default to HIGH, which is accurate. Set time to 12 minutes. Select START/STOP and start cooking. 4. When cooking is complete, let pressure release quickly by turning it into VENT position. Transfer the chicken to a large plate and shred the meat, using the tines of two forks. Set aside. Move the slider towards "AIR FRY/STOVETOP" and set Ninja Foodi XL Pressure Cooker Steam Fryer with SmartLid to SEAR/SAUTÉ mode. Adjust the temperature to "Hi5" by using up arrow. 5. As soon as the soup comes to a boil, add the pasta. Cook your pasta al dente according to the package directions—usually this is anywhere from 4 to 8 minutes. Return the shredded chicken to the pot and give it a stir. 6. Serve immediately, garnished with chopped fresh cilantro and lime wedges.

Per Serving: Calories 265; Fat 11.3g; Sodium 188mg; Carbs 9.2g; Fiber 1g; Sugar 1g; Protein 12.4g

Chicken with Dumplings

Prep time: 10 minutes| Cook time: 16 minutes| Serves: 6

1 cup all-purpose flour
2 teaspoons baking powder
1¼ teaspoons salt, divided
1½ cups whole milk, divided
6 tablespoons olive oil, divided
4 medium carrots, diced
2 pounds boneless, skinless chicken thighs, cut into 1" pieces
2 medium stalks celery, diced
1 medium yellow onion, peeled and diced
1½ cups sliced mushrooms
2 cloves garlic, minced
4 cups chicken broth
2 (10.5-ounce) cans cream of mushroom soup
½ teaspoon red pepper flakes
½ teaspoon black pepper

1. In a medium bowl, whisk together flour, baking powder, and 1 teaspoon salt. 2. Make a well in center of dry mixture and pour in ½ cup milk and 2 tablespoons olive oil. 3. Mix together with a fork until combined. This is your dumpling dough. Set aside. 4. Move the slider towards "AIR FRY/STOVETOP" and set Ninja Foodi XL Pressure Cooker Steam Fryer with SmartLid to SEAR/SAUTÉ mode. Adjust the temperature to "Hi5" by using up arrow. Press START/STOP to begin cooking. Pour in remaining 4 tablespoons olive oil. 5. Add in carrots, chicken, celery, onion, and mushrooms. Cover and cook 5 minutes until soft. Stir occasionally while it is cooking. 6. Remove lid and stir in minced garlic. Cook an additional 30 seconds. 7. Pour in chicken broth and deglaze pot. 8. Turn pot off and whisk in cream of mushroom soup, remaining 1 cup milk, red pepper flakes, black pepper, and remaining ¼ teaspoon salt. 9. Rip dumpling dough into 1" pieces and toss on top of soup so they evenly over top of the soup. A few might sink down. 10. Lock lid; move slider towards PRESSURE. Adjust pressure release valve in the SEAL position. Close pressure-release valve. The cooking temperature will default to HIGH, which is accurate. Set time to 10 minutes. Select START/STOP and start cooking. 11. When cooking is complete, let pressure release naturally. Serve.

Per Serving: Calories 529; Fat 24g; Sodium 1165mg; Carbs 34g; Fiber 3g; Sugar 9g; Protein 45g

Spicy Beef with Broccoli Zoodle Soup

Prep time: 10 minutes| Cook time: 15 minutes| Serves: 5

2 tablespoons (30ml) avocado oil
3 tablespoons (18g) minced fresh ginger
2 cloves garlic, minced
1½ lb. (680g) top sirloin steak tips, about 1" (2.5cm) pieces
3 level cups (270g) fresh broccoli florets
8 oz. (225g) sliced cremini mushrooms
6 cups (1.4L) beef stock
¼ cup (60ml) rice vinegar
¼ cup (60ml) coconut aminos or soy sauce
¼ cup (60ml) buffalo hot sauce or sriracha
1 large zucchini, spiralized into noodles
⅓ cup (33g) chopped fresh green onion

1. Move the slider towards "AIR FRY/STOVETOP" and set Ninja Foodi XL Pressure Cooker Steam Fryer with SmartLid to SEAR/SAUTÉ mode. Adjust the temperature to "Hi5" by using up arrow. Press START/STOP to begin cooking. 2. Once hot, add the oil, ginger, garlic and steak tips. Cook for a few minutes, until the beef is lightly browned on each side and the garlic and ginger are fragrant. Select START/STOP. Add the broccoli, mushrooms, beef stock, vinegar, coconut aminos and hot sauce and stir. At this point, you can remove and set aside the broccoli and add with the noodles after the soup has cooked, if you want the broccoli to be crisper. 3. Lock lid; move slider towards PRESSURE. Adjust pressure release valve in the SEAL position. Close pressure-release valve. The cooking temperature will default to HIGH, which is accurate. Set time to 8 minutes. Select START/STOP and start cooking. 4. When cooking is complete, let pressure release quickly by turning it into VENT position. Open the lid and add more hot sauce if you desire a spicier broth. 5. Add the spiralized zucchini, top with fresh green onion and serve hot.

Per Serving: Calories 262; Fat 11.3g; Sodium 369mg; Carbs 10.4g; Fiber 2g; Sugar 1g; Protein 7.2g

Cheesy Creamy Spinach Soup

Prep time: 10 minutes| Cook time: 15 minutes| Serves: 6

2 tablespoons (28g) grass-fed butter, ghee or avocado oil
1 yellow onion, peeled and diced
5 fresh cloves garlic, finely minced
2 large celery ribs, thickly sliced
1 lb. (455g) frozen organic spinach, thawed and moisture squeezed out
2 organic russet potatoes, peeled and cubed
1 teaspoon sea salt
1 teaspoon dried thyme
1 teaspoon dried dill
¼ teaspoon ground allspice
4 cups (946ml) chicken or vegetable stock
8 oz. (225g) sour cream, plus more for garnish
1 cup (115g) shredded cheddar cheese
Extra-virgin olive oil, for garnish

1. Move the slider towards "AIR FRY/STOVETOP" and set Ninja Foodi XL Pressure Cooker Steam Fryer with SmartLid to SEAR/SAUTÉ mode. Adjust the temperature to "Hi5" by using up arrow. Press START/STOP to begin cooking. Place your healthy fat of choice in the pot. 2. Once the fat has melted, add the onion and sauté for 7 minutes, stirring occasionally, then add the garlic and continue to sauté for 1 minute, stirring occasionally. Add the celery, spinach, potatoes, salt, thyme, dill, allspice and stock, then give the mixture a stir. Press START/STOP. 3. Lock lid; move slider towards PRESSURE. Adjust pressure release valve in the SEAL position. Close pressure-release valve. The cooking temperature will default to HIGH, which is accurate. Set NATURAL RELEASE and time to 9 minutes. Select START/STOP and start cooking. 4. When cooking is complete, let pressure release quickly by turning it into VENT position. In batches, ladle the soup into a blender, taking care to fill the blender only about halfway. Blend on a low setting just until pureed and combined. 5. Return the pureed soup to the pot and Move the slider towards "AIR FRY/STOVETOP" and set Ninja Foodi XL Pressure Cooker Steam Fryer with SmartLid to SEAR/SAUTÉ mode. Adjust the temperature to "Hi5" by using up arrow. Press START/STOP to begin cooking, bring to a boil and give it a few stirs. 6. Add the sour cream and cheese and stir until fully combined. Press START/STOP. 7. Serve immediately. Garnish with a dollop of sour cream or a drizzle of quality extra-virgin olive oil.

Per Serving: Calories 261; Fat 9.2g; Sodium 784mg; Carbs 7.3g; Fiber 1g; Sugar 2g; Protein 6.2g

Dropped Egg Soup

Prep time: 5 minutes| Cook time: 15 minutes| Serves: 6

4 cups (946ml) water
1 carrot, cut in half widthwise
2 celery ribs, cut in half widthwise
1 yellow onion, cut in half
1 clove garlic, peeled and smashed
1 teaspoon soy sauce
½ teaspoon salt, plus a pinch
½ teaspoon black peppercorns
1-star anise
1 (1" [2.5cm]) piece fresh ginger
4 large eggs
4 teaspoons (11g) cornstarch
Freshly ground black pepper
4 green onions, sliced

1. In the Ninja Foodi XL Pressure Cooker Steam Fryer with SmartLid cooking pot, combine the water, carrot, celery, onion, garlic, soy sauce, ½ teaspoon of salt, and the peppercorns, star anise and ginger. 2. Lock lid; move slider towards PRESSURE. Adjust pressure release valve in the SEAL position. Close pressure-release valve. The cooking temperature will default to HIGH, which is accurate. Set time to 10 minutes. Select START/STOP and start cooking. 3. When cooking is complete, let pressure release quickly by turning it into VENT position. Remove the lid. Insert a mesh strainer into a large bowl or stockpot. Pour the stock through the strainer into the bowl. Discard the vegetables and spices. Return the stock to the pot. 4. Move the slider towards "AIR FRY/STOVETOP" and set Ninja Foodi XL Pressure Cooker Steam Fryer with SmartLid to SEAR/SAUTÉ mode. Adjust the temperature to "Hi5" by using up arrow. Press START/STOP to begin cooking. 5. After 3 to 4 minutes, the stock should start to bubble up a bit. In small bowl, whisk together the eggs, cornstarch and a pinch each of salt and pepper. Slowly pour the eggs into the stock while whisking the whole time. The eggs should start to form fine ribbons as they cook. 6. Press START/STOP and adjust the salt and pepper to taste. Top with the green onions.
Per Serving: Calories 354; Fat 7.9g; Sodium 704mg; Carbs 6g; Fiber 3.6g; Sugar 6g; Protein 18g

Ham with Split Pea Soup

Prep time: 10 minutes| Cook time: 20 minutes| Serves: 6

2 teaspoons (10ml) olive oil
1 medium onion, chopped
2 celery ribs, chopped
3 carrots, chopped
6 cups (1.4L) chicken stock
1 ham bone
1 lb. (455g) dried split peas
1 bay leaf
Coarse salt
Freshly ground black pepper

1. Move the slider towards "AIR FRY/STOVETOP" and set Ninja Foodi XL Pressure Cooker Steam Fryer with SmartLid to SEAR/SAUTÉ mode. Adjust the temperature to "Hi5" by using up arrow. Press START/STOP to begin cooking. Add the olive oil, then the onion, celery and carrots. Cook, stirring occasionally, until the onion is soft, about 5 minutes. Press START/STOP. 2. Add the chicken stock, taking care to scrape up any browned bits from the bottom of the pot. Add the ham bone, split peas and bay leaf. 3. Lock lid; move slider towards PRESSURE. Adjust pressure release valve in the SEAL position. Close pressure-release valve. The cooking temperature will default to HIGH, which is accurate. Set time to 20 minutes. Select START/STOP and start cooking. 4. When cooking is complete, let pressure release naturally for 10 minutes, then quick-release any remaining pressure by turning it into VENT position. 5. Carefully remove the lid. Remove the ham bone, and any meat that fell from the ham bone, from the pot. Remove and discard the bay leaf. 6. Using an immersion blender, puree the soup until smooth. Remove the meat from the ham bone and add it and any other meat that was removed back to the pot. 7. Season well with salt and pepper, then serve.
Per Serving: Calories 253; Fat 11.2g; Sodium 333mg; Carbs 8.4g; Fiber 2g; Sugar 1g; Protein 6.5g

Tomatoes Stuffed Pepper Soup

Prep time: 15 minutes| Cook time: 15 minutes| Serves: 5

2 tablespoons (30ml) avocado oil or extra-virgin olive oil
1 yellow onion, diced
3 cloves garlic, minced
1 lb. (455g) ground beef
2 green bell peppers, seeded and diced
1 red bell pepper, seeded and diced
2 (14.5-oz [411g]) cans fire-roasted diced tomatoes
1 (15-oz [425g]) can tomato sauce
2 cups (475ml) beef stock
2 tablespoons (30ml) red wine vinegar
2 teaspoons (4g) Italian seasoning
2 teaspoons (12g) sea salt
2 cups (340g) cooked rice or (220g) cauliflower rice
¼ cup (20g) shredded Parmesan cheese, for garnish
Fresh basil, for garnish

1. Move the slider towards "AIR FRY/STOVETOP" and set Ninja Foodi XL Pressure Cooker Steam Fryer with SmartLid to SEAR/SAUTÉ mode. Adjust the temperature to "Hi5" by using up arrow. Press START/STOP to begin cooking. 2. Coat the bottom of the pot with oil, then add the onion and garlic. Sauté for 3 to 4 minutes, then add the ground beef. Continue to cook until the beef is no longer pink, about 3 to 4 minutes. Select START/STOP. Top the beef mixture with the bell peppers, diced tomatoes, tomato sauce, beef stock, red wine vinegar, Italian seasoning and salt. 3. Lock lid; move slider towards PRESSURE. Adjust pressure release valve in the SEAL position. Close pressure-release valve. The cooking temperature will default to HIGH, which is accurate. Set time to 6 minutes. Select START/STOP and start cooking. 4. When cooking is complete, let pressure release quickly by turning it into VENT position. Stir in the rice or cauliflower rice. 5. Serve hot and garnish with Parmesan cheese and fresh basil.
Per Serving: Calories 263; Fat 11.2g; Sodium 218mg; Carbs 8.6g; Fiber 1.6g; Sugar 2.3g; Protein 8.2g

Delicious Zuppa Toscana

Prep time: 10 minutes| Cook time: 20 minutes| Serves: 6

1 lb. (455g) hot Italian sausage, casings removed
1 small onion, chopped
4 to 5 cloves garlic, minced
3 cups (450g) diced red potatoes
4 to 5 cups (946ml to 1.2 L) low-
sodium chicken stock
3 cups (201g) chopped kale
1 cup (237ml) heavy cream
Coarse salt
Freshly ground black pepper

1. Move the slider towards "AIR FRY/STOVETOP" and set Ninja Foodi XL Pressure Cooker Steam Fryer with SmartLid to SEAR/SAUTÉ mode. Adjust the temperature to "Hi5" by using up arrow. Press START/STOP to begin cooking. 2. Add the sausage. Cook until the sausage is browned, about 5 minutes. Add the onion and cook until the onion is soft, about 5 minutes, stirring frequently. Add the garlic and cook for 1 more minute, stirring frequently. Add the potatoes and chicken stock, taking care to scrape any browned bits from the bottom. 3. Lock lid; move slider towards PRESSURE. Adjust pressure release valve in the SEAL position. Close pressure-release valve. The cooking temperature will default to HIGH, which is accurate. Set time to 12 minutes. Select START/STOP and start cooking. 4. When cooking is complete, let pressure release quickly by turning it into VENT position. Carefully remove the lid. Add the kale and cream, stirring until the kale is wilted. 5. Season generously with salt and pepper.
Per Serving: Calories 253; Fat 12.2g; Sodium 245mg; Carbs 11.4g; Fiber 3g; Sugar 1g; Protein 7.6g

Five-Ingredient Bean Soup

Prep time: 5 minutes| Cook time: 5 minutes| Serves: 2

2 cups (475ml) chicken or vegetable stock
¾ cup (195g) jarred salsa
1 (30-oz [850g]) can black beans, drained and rinsed
1 jalapeño, seeded and diced
½ yellow onion, diced
Salt
Freshly ground black pepper
Fresh cilantro, lime, sour cream and avocado, for garnish

1. In the Ninja Foodi XL Pressure Cooker Steam Fryer with SmartLid cooking pot, combine all the ingredients except for the garnishes, including salt and pepper to taste. 2. Lock lid; move slider towards PRESSURE. Adjust pressure release valve in the SEAL position. Close pressure-release valve. The cooking temperature will default to HIGH, which is accurate. Set time to 5 minutes. Select START/STOP and start cooking. 3. When cooking is complete, let pressure release quickly by turning it into VENT position. Remove the lid and use an immersion blender to puree about half of the soup. 4. You still want to see a few beans in the soup. Adjust the salt and pepper to taste and top with cilantro, lime, sour cream and avocado.
Per Serving: Calories 252; Fat 10.3g; Sodium 277mg; Carbs 7.6g; Fiber 3g; Sugar 4g; Protein 8.7g

Spicy Buffalo Chicken Chowder

Prep time: 10 minutes| Cook time: 15 minutes| Serves: 4

2 tablespoons (30ml) olive or avocado oil
1 white or yellow onion, chopped
1⅓ lb. (600g) chicken breast
1 cup (120g) diced celery
1 cup (130g) diced carrot
1½ cups (225g) diced Yukon gold potato
5 cups (1.2L) chicken stock
¾ cup (175ml) buffalo hot sauce
⅔ cup (160ml) full-fat canned coconut milk or half-and-half
¼ cup (10g) fresh cilantro, for garnish

1. Move the slider towards "AIR FRY/STOVETOP" and set Ninja Foodi XL Pressure Cooker Steam Fryer with SmartLid to SEAR/SAUTÉ mode. Adjust the temperature to "Hi5" by using up arrow. Press START/STOP to begin cooking. 2. Coat the bottom of the pot with the oil once hot, add the onion and sauté for 2 to 3 minutes. Select START/STOP. Place the chicken in the Ninja Foodi XL Pressure Cooker Steam Fryer with SmartLid cooking pot first. Then add the celery, carrot, potato, chicken stock and buffalo sauce on top of the chicken. 3. Lock lid; move slider towards PRESSURE. Adjust pressure release valve in the SEAL position. Close pressure-release valve. The cooking temperature will default to HIGH, which is accurate. Set time to 12 minutes. Select START/STOP and start cooking. 4. When cooking is complete, let pressure release quickly by turning it into VENT position. Once the steam is completely released, remove the lid. Add the coconut milk. 5. Top with the fresh cilantro and serve.
Per Serving: Calories 243; Fat 8.4g; Sodium 404mg; Carbs 6.3g; Fiber 2g; Sugar 1.5g; Protein 6.2g

Beef Spicy Pho

Prep time: 5 minutes| Cook time: 15 minutes| Serves: 4

1 lb. (455g) boneless beef eye round
1 tablespoon (18g) salt, plus more to season the beef
Freshly ground black pepper
1 tablespoon (15ml) canola oil
2 small yellow onions, cut in half, skin on
2 cloves garlic, smashed
1 cinnamon stick
2 whole cloves
1 bay leaf
4 peppercorns
2-star anise
1 oz. (28g) dried shiitake mushrooms
5 cups (1.2L) water
3 cups (710ml) beef stock
9.5 oz. (270g) ramen or udon noodles
Toppings: shredded red cabbage, thinly sliced red onion, hot sauce, fresh cilantro, lime wedges, sliced jalapeño and sesame seeds

1. Season all sides of the beef with salt and pepper. Place the oil in the cooking pot. Move the slider towards "AIR FRY/STOVETOP" and set Ninja Foodi XL Pressure Cooker Steam Fryer with SmartLid to SEAR/SAUTÉ mode. Adjust the temperature to "Hi5" by using up arrow. Press START/STOP to begin cooking. 2. Once the oil is shimmering, add the beef. Sear each side of the beef for about 5 minutes. Add the onions, garlic, cinnamon stick, cloves, bay leaf, peppercorns, star anise and dried mushrooms to the pot as well. 3. Continue to sear the beef for 5 more minutes while stirring the vegetables and herbs around. Press START/STOP and then remove the beef, transferring it to a nearby plate. Tent with foil and let rest. Pour the water and stock into the pot and add the salt. Stir to combine. 4. Lock lid; move slider towards PRESSURE. Adjust pressure release valve in the SEAL position. Close pressure-release valve. The cooking temperature will default to HIGH, which is accurate. Set time to 20 minutes. Select START/STOP and start cooking. 5. When cooking is complete, let pressure release quickly by turning it into VENT position. Remove the lid. Use a fine-mesh strainer with a handle to remove the onions, garlic, mushrooms and spices from the broth. Discard the onions, garlic and spices, reserving the mushrooms. Add the mushrooms back to the pot. 6. Move the slider towards "AIR FRY/STOVETOP" and set Ninja Foodi XL Pressure Cooker Steam Fryer with SmartLid to SEAR/SAUTÉ mode. Adjust the temperature to "Hi5" by using up arrow. Press START/STOP to begin cooking and wait a minute or two until the stock starts to bubble. Add the noodles and cook for 5 minutes, or until tender. Ladle the broth into bowls. 7. Use tongs to transfer the noodles to the bowls. Top with red cabbage, sliced red onion, hot sauce, fresh cilantro, lime wedges, sliced jalapeño and sesame seeds.
Per Serving: Calories 275; Fat 11.3g; Sodium 511mg; Carbs 8.6g; Fiber 2g; Sugar 1g; Protein 9.5g

Delicious Colombian Chicken Soup

Prep time: 5 minutes| Cook time: 25 minutes| Serves: 6

2 teaspoons (10ml) olive oil
1 medium onion, chopped
1 celery rib, chopped
3 cloves garlic, minced
½ teaspoon dried oregano
4 cups (946ml) chicken stock
2 lb. (905g) boneless, skinless chicken breast, cut into bite-size pieces
1 lb. (455g) baby red potatoes, cut into bite-size pieces
1½ cups (195g) frozen corn kernels
1 tablespoon (15ml) fresh lime juice
¼ cup (10g) chopped fresh cilantro
Coarse salt
Freshly ground black pepper
1 avocado, peeled, pitted and chopped

1. Move the slider towards "AIR FRY/STOVETOP" and set Ninja Foodi XL Pressure Cooker Steam Fryer with SmartLid to SEAR/SAUTÉ mode. Adjust the temperature to "Hi5" by using up arrow. Press START/STOP to begin cooking. 2. Add the onion and celery to the pot. Cook, stirring frequently, until the onion is soft, about 5 minutes. Add the garlic, oregano and cook for 1 more minute. Press START/STOP to turn off the pot. 3. Add the chicken stock, taking care to scrape up any browned bits from the bottom of the pot. Add the chicken, potatoes and corn. 4. Lock lid; move slider towards PRESSURE. Make sure the pressure release valve is in the SEAL position. The cooking temperature will default to HIGH, which is accurate. And set time to 20 minutes. Press START/STOP to cooking. 5. When cooking is complete, let pressure release quickly by turning it into VENT position. Carefully remove the lid. Stir in the lime juice and cilantro. Season well with salt and pepper. 6. Serve in bowls, topped with avocado.
Per Serving: Calories 253; Fat 11.3g; Sodium 411mg; Carbs 8.6g; Fiber 1g; Sugar 2g; Protein 7.2g

Garlicky Green Chickpea Soup

Prep time: 5 minutes| Cook time: 10 minutes| Serves: 8

2 tablespoons (28g) grass-fed butter, ghee or avocado oil
1 yellow onion, peeled and diced
8 oz. (225g) cleaned white button or cremini mushrooms, thinly sliced
7 cloves garlic, finely minced
2 large celery ribs, thinly sliced
1 organic russet potato, peeled and diced
1 tablespoon (7g) ground cumin
1 teaspoon ground coriander
1 teaspoon sea salt
½ teaspoon dried thyme
½ teaspoon ground allspice
6 cups (1.4L) chicken or vegetable stock
2 large bunches fresh spinach (about 1½ lb. [680g] total), leaves only, cleaned well
2 cups (480g) canned or cooked chickpeas
Sour cream, for garnish
Quality extra-virgin olive oil, for garnish

1. Move the slider towards "AIR FRY/STOVETOP" and set Ninja Foodi XL Pressure Cooker Steam Fryer with SmartLid to SEAR/SAUTÉ mode. Adjust the temperature to "Hi5" by using up arrow. Press START/STOP to begin cooking. Place your healthy fat of choice in the pot. 2. Once the fat has melted, add the onion and mushrooms and sauté for 7 minutes, stirring occasionally, then add the garlic and continue to sauté for 1 minute, stirring occasionally. Add the celery, potato, cumin, coriander, salt, thyme, allspice and stock, then give the mixture a stir. Press START/STOP. 3. Lock lid; move slider towards PRESSURE. Adjust pressure release valve in the SEAL position. Close pressure-release valve. The cooking temperature will default to HIGH, which is accurate. Set time to 7 minutes. Select START/STOP and start cooking. 4. When cooking is complete, let pressure release quickly by turning it into VENT position. Carefully open the lid. 5. Move the slider towards "AIR FRY/STOVETOP" and set Ninja Foodi XL Pressure Cooker Steam Fryer with SmartLid to SEAR/SAUTÉ mode. Adjust the temperature to "Hi5" by using up arrow. Press START/STOP to begin cooking and add the spinach and chickpeas. Allow the soup to come to a simmer, stirring until the spinach has fully wilted. Press START/STOP. 6. Taste for seasoning and adjust the salt to taste. Serve immediately. Garnish with a dollop of sour cream or a drizzle of quality extra-virgin olive oil.
Per Serving: Calories 246; Fat 8.4g; Sodium 298mg; Carbs 7.2g; Fiber 1g; Sugar 2g; Protein 6.3g

Creamy Tomato Soup with Basil

Prep time: 5 minutes| Cook time: 10 minutes| Serves: 4

2 tablespoons (30ml) avocado oil or extra-virgin olive oil
1 yellow onion, diced
4 cloves garlic, minced
2 large carrots, peeled and diced
2 tablespoons (16g) arrowroot starch
3 cups (710ml) vegetable or chicken stock
1 (28-oz [800g]) can San Marzano whole tomatoes, with juice
2 teaspoons (4g) Italian seasoning
1 teaspoon sea salt, plus more to taste
1 cup (237ml) half-and-half or heavy cream
½ cup (20g) fresh basil leaves, chopped, divided
⅓ cup (33g) freshly grated Parmesan cheese

1. Move the slider towards "AIR FRY/STOVETOP" and set Ninja Foodi XL Pressure Cooker Steam Fryer with SmartLid to SEAR/SAUTÉ mode. Adjust the temperature to "Hi5" by using up arrow. Press START/STOP to begin cooking. 2. Once the pot is hot, coat the bottom of the pot with the oil. Add the onion, garlic and carrots. Cook until the vegetables are softened, about 5 minutes. Select START/STOP. Sprinkle the mixture with the arrowroot starch. Add the stock, tomatoes, Italian seasoning and salt. Give the mixture a stir. 3. Lock lid; move slider towards PRESSURE. Adjust pressure release valve in the SEAL position. Close pressure-release valve. The cooking temperature will default to HIGH, which is accurate. Set time to 6 minutes. Select START/STOP and start cooking. 4. When cooking is complete, let pressure release quickly by turning it into VENT. Stir in the half-and-half and ¼ cup (10g) of the basil. Blend the soup, using an immersion blender or high-powered blender, until smooth. 5. Serve hot, adding more salt to taste, garnishing with the remaining basil and topping with the Parmesan cheese.
Per Serving: Calories 243; Fat 8.7g; Sodium 647mg; Carbs 6.4g; Fiber 3g; Sugar 1g; Protein 6.5g

Thai Tropical red Soup

Prep time: 5 minutes| Cook time: 19 minutes| Serves: 6

1 tablespoon extra-virgin olive oil
½ yellow onion, chopped
1 pound carrots
1 pound sweet potatoes
2 cloves garlic, minced
2 teaspoons curry powder
1 tablespoon minced fresh ginger (about 1-inch knob)
3½ cups water
2 teaspoons fine sea salt
½ cup full-fat coconut milk
6 tablespoons dried cranberries
6 tablespoons hulled pumpkin seeds
6 tablespoons chopped fresh cilantro

1. Move the slider towards "AIR FRY/STOVETOP" and Set Ninja Foodi XL Pressure Cooker Steam Fryer with SmartLid to SEAR/SAUTÉ mode. Adjust the temperature to "Hi5" by using up arrow. Press START/STOP to begin cooking and add the olive oil to the pot. 2. Once the oil is hot but not smoking, add the onion and sauté until tender, about 8 minutes, stirring occasionally so it doesn't stick. Meanwhile, peel and chop the carrots and sweet potatoes into 1-inch chunks. 3. Once the onion is tender, add the garlic, curry powder, and ginger and stir with a wooden spoon or spatula just until fragrant, about 1 minute. Add the carrots, sweet potatoes, water, and salt and use the spoon to scrape the bottom of the cooking pot to make sure nothing has stuck. 4. Lock lid; move slider towards PRESSURE. Adjust pressure release valve in the SEAL position. Close pressure-release valve. The cooking temperature will default to HIGH, which is accurate. Set time to 10 minutes. Select START/STOP and start cooking. 5. When cooking is complete, let pressure release naturally. Remove the lid and use an immersion blender to blend the soup directly in the pot until very smooth. Stir in the coconut milk and adjust the seasonings to taste. 6. Serve warm with 1 tablespoon each dried cranberries, pumpkin seeds, and cilantro sprinkled over each serving. Store leftovers in an airtight container in the fridge for 5 days.
Per Serving: Calories 256; Fat 9.4g; Sodium 347mg; Carbs 8.6g; Fiber 5g; Sugar 2g; Protein 7.4g

Cheesy Broccoli Soup

Prep time: 7 minutes| Cook time: 3 minutes| Serves: 4

1 yellow onion, chopped
2 carrots, peeled and chopped
1 small head (8 ounces) cauliflower, cut into florets (about 3 cups)
1-pound broccoli, cut into florets (about 6 cups)
1 tablespoon spicy brown mustard
3 cups water
Fine sea salt
½ cup shredded sharp Cheddar cheese
¼ cup finely grated Parmesan cheese
½ cup almond milk, or any milk of your choice
Freshly ground black pepper

1. Combine the water, 2 teaspoons salt, onion, carrots, cauliflower, broccoli and mustard in the Ninja Foodi XL Pressure Cooker Steam Fryer with SmartLid cooking pot. 2. Lock lid; move slider towards PRESSURE. Adjust pressure release valve in the SEAL position. Close pressure-release valve. The cooking temperature will default to HIGH, which is accurate. Set time to 3 minutes. Select START/STOP and start cooking. 3. When cooking is complete, let pressure release quickly by turning it into VENT position. 4. Blend the soup with an immersion blender, leaving as much texture as you like. Then add the cheddar, parmesan and almond milk and blend until combined. 5. Sprinkle with salt and pepper to taste and serve warm. Store leftovers in an airtight container in the refrigerator for up to 5 days.
Per Serving: Calories 257; Fat 11.3g; Sodium 256mg; Carbs 10.6g; Fiber 6g; Sugar 2g; Protein 8.3g

Creamy Lasagna Soup

Prep time: 10 minutes| Cook time: 15 minutes| Serves: 8

3 tablespoons (43g) grass-fed butter, ghee or avocado oil
1 lb. (455g) grass-fed ground beef
1 medium yellow onion, peeled and diced
8 oz. (225g) cleaned white button or cremini mushrooms, thinly sliced
5 cloves garlic, finely minced
1 cup (180g) crushed tomatoes or diced fresh tomatoes
1 teaspoon sea salt
1 teaspoon dried thyme
½ teaspoon dried oregano
½ teaspoon finely chopped fresh rosemary leaves
6 cups (1.4L) chicken or vegetable stock
2 cups (210g) gluten-free dried pasta; e.g. broken-up lasagna or tagliatelle
2 large bunches fresh spinach, leaves only, cleaned well
¼ cup (6g) fresh basil leaves
½ cup (120ml) heavy cream
¼ cup (60g) mascarpone or cream cheese
¼ cup (30g) shredded mozzarella cheese, for garnish
¼ cup (20g) shredded Parmesan or Asiago cheese, for garnish
Quality extra-virgin olive oil, for garnish

1. Move the slider towards "AIR FRY/STOVETOP" and set Ninja Foodi XL Pressure Cooker Steam Fryer with SmartLid to SEAR/SAUTÉ mode. Adjust the temperature to "Hi5" by using up arrow. Press START/STOP to begin cooking. 2. And place your healthy fat of choice in the pot. Once the fat has melted, add the ground beef and sauté for 7 minutes, stirring often, allowing the meat to brown, then place the cooked beef to a plate, set aside. Add the onion and mushrooms to the pot and sauté for 5 minutes, stirring occasionally, then add the garlic and continue to sauté for 1 minute, stirring occasionally. Add the cooked meat, tomatoes, salt, thyme, oregano, rosemary and stock, then give the mixture a stir. Press START/STOP. 3. Lock lid; move slider towards PRESSURE. Adjust pressure release valve in the SEAL position. Close pressure-release valve. The cooking temperature will default to HIGH, which is accurate. Set time to 5 minutes. Select START/STOP and start cooking. 4. When cooking is complete, let pressure release quickly by turning it into VENT position. Carefully open the lid. 5. Move the slider towards "AIR FRY/STOVETOP" and set Ninja Foodi XL Pressure Cooker Steam Fryer with SmartLid to SEAR/SAUTÉ mode. Adjust the temperature to "Hi5" by using up arrow. Press START/STOP to begin cooking. As soon as the soup comes to a boil, add the pasta. Cook your pasta al dente usually this is anywhere from 4 to 8 minutes. Then, add the spinach and basil, stirring until the spinach has fully wilted. Press START/STOP. 6. Add the cream and mascarpone cheese, stirring until incorporated. Taste for seasoning and adjust the salt to taste. 7. Serve immediately. Garnish with the shredded cheeses and a drizzle of quality extra-virgin olive oil.
Per Serving: Calories 252; Fat 11.2g; Sodium 310mg; Carbs 10.3g; Fiber 3g; Sugar 1.5g; Protein 7.3g

Two-Bean Chili stew

Prep time: 10 minutes| Cook time: 25 minutes| Serves: 6

1 cup dried black beans, soaked for 8 hours
1 cup dried red kidney beans, soaked for 8 hours
1 yellow onion, chopped
3 carrots, peeled and chopped
3 celery stalks, chopped
4 cloves garlic, minced
1 tablespoon chili powder
2 teaspoons ground cumin
¼ teaspoon cayenne pepper
2 cups water
One 28-ounce can diced tomatoes
1 sweet potato, peeled and cut into 1-inch chunks
Freshly ground black pepper
2 teaspoons fine sea salt
Chopped green onions, tender white and green parts only, for garnish
Chopped fresh cilantro, for garnish

1. Drain the soaked beans and rinse well. Combine the beans, onion, carrots, celery, garlic, chili powder, cumin, cayenne, water, tomatoes with their juices, sweet potato, and several grinds of black pepper in the Ninja Foodi XL Pressure Cooker Steam Fryer with SmartLid cooking pot. Stir well to make sure the beans are submerged in the liquid. 2. Lock lid; move slider towards PRESSURE. Adjust pressure release valve in the SEAL position. Close pressure-release valve. The cooking temperature will default to HIGH, which is accurate. Set time to 10 minutes. Select START/STOP and start cooking. 3. When cooking is complete, let pressure release naturally for about 10 minutes, then quickly release any remaining pressure by turning it into VENT position. Remove the lid and add the salt. 4. Stir well, using the back of the spoon to mash some of the sweet potatoes against the side of the pot to thicken the chili. Adjust the seasonings to taste, and serve immediately with green onions and cilantro on top. 5. Store leftovers in an airtight container and put in the fridge for 1 week.
Per Serving: Calories 262; Fat 9.4g; Sodium 312mg; Carbs 8.6g; Fiber 1g; Sugar 1g; Protein 9.2g

"Noodle" Soup

Prep time: 10 minutes| Cook time: 16 minutes| Serves: 4

1 tablespoon extra-virgin olive oil
1 yellow onion, chopped
3 cloves garlic, minced
1 teaspoon dried thyme, or 2 teaspoons fresh thyme
½ teaspoon dried oregano
1 pound boneless, skinless chicken thighs
3 carrots, peeled and chopped
3 celery stalks, chopped
Fine sea salt and freshly ground black pepper
4 cups (1 quart) low-sodium vegetable broth
1-pound zucchini (about 2 medium)
Chopped fresh flat-leaf parsley, for garnish

1. Move the slider towards "AIR FRY/STOVETOP" and set Ninja Foodi XL Pressure Cooker Steam Fryer with SmartLid to SEAR/SAUTÉ mode. Adjust the temperature to "Hi5" by using up arrow. Press START/STOP to begin cooking and add the olive oil to the cooking pot. 2. Once the oil is hot but not smoking, add the onion and sauté until softened, about 3 minutes. Add the garlic, thyme, and oregano and cook until fragrant, about 1 minute more, then press START/STOP to stop the cooking cycle. Add the chicken, carrots, celery, 2 teaspoons salt, several grinds of pepper, and the broth to the pot. 3. Lock lid; move slider towards PRESSURE. Adjust pressure release valve in the SEAL position. Close pressure-release valve. The cooking temperature will default to HIGH, which is accurate. Set time to 12 minutes. Select START/STOP and start cooking. Meanwhile, use a spiralizer or vegetable peeler to cut noodle like strips from the zucchini; set the noodles aside. 4. When cooking is complete, let pressure release quickly by turning it into VENT position. Use tongs to place the cooked chicken to a cutting board, then use two forks to shred the chicken. 5. Add the shredded chicken and zucchini noodles to the pot, and stir well. The noodles will soften quickly from the heat. 6. Sprinkle with additional salt and pepper, to taste, and serve immediately with parsley on top.
Per Serving: Calories 263; Fat 9.2g; Sodium 211mg; Carbs 8.6g; Fiber 2g; Sugar 1g; Protein 8.7g

Thai Chicken Curry Soup with Veggies "Ramen"

Prep time: 5 minutes| Cook time: 15 minutes| Serves: 6

2 tablespoons (30ml) avocado oil or coconut oil
½ large white onion, diced
1 tablespoon (6g) chopped fresh ginger
3 cloves garlic, minced
3 cups (710ml) chicken stock
1 (14.5-oz [411g]) can fire-roasted diced tomatoes
2 tablespoons (30g) Thai red curry paste
1 teaspoon sea salt, plus more to
taste
1 yellow bell pepper, seeded and diced
3 carrots, peeled and diced
1½ lb. (680g) chicken breast
1 (13.5-oz [400ml]) can full-fat coconut milk
Juice of 1 lime
2 large zucchinis, spiralized into noodles
¼ cup (10g) chopped fresh cilantro

1. Move the slider towards "AIR FRY/STOVETOP" and set Ninja Foodi XL Pressure Cooker Steam Fryer with SmartLid to SEAR/SAUTÉ mode. Adjust the temperature to "Hi5" by using up arrow. Press START/STOP to begin cooking. Coat the bottom of the pot with the oil, and once hot, add the onion. Cook for 2 to 3 minutes, then toss in the ginger and garlic. Once the vegetables are gently browned, about another 3 minutes, select START/STOP. 2. Add the chicken stock, fire-roasted tomatoes, Thai curry paste, salt, bell pepper, carrots and chicken. 3. Lock lid; move slider towards PRESSURE. Adjust pressure release valve in the SEAL position. Close pressure-release valve. The cooking temperature will default to HIGH, which is accurate. Set time to 8 minutes. Select START/STOP and start cooking. 4. When cooking is complete, let pressure release quickly by turning it into VENT position. 5. Remove the chicken breast and then shred with a fork and knife, then place the chicken back in the pot. Stir in the coconut milk, lime juice and spiralized zucchini. Let stand for about 10 minutes before serving. 6. Pour into individual bowls and add additional salt to taste. Garnish with fresh cilantro.
Per Serving: Calories 246; Fat 9.3g; Sodium 489mg; Carbs 8.1g; Fiber 2g; Sugar 3g; Protein 7.4g

Bean Tuscan Soup

Prep time: 10 minutes| Cook time: 25 minutes| Serves: 6

2 teaspoons (10ml) olive oil
1 medium onion, chopped
2 celery ribs, chopped
2 carrots, chopped
3 cloves garlic, minced
½ teaspoon Italian seasoning
4 cups (946ml) chicken stock
2 (14.5-oz [411g]) cans fire-roasted
diced tomatoes
2 (15-oz [425g]) cans white beans
1 bay leaf
12 oz. (340g) fresh spinach leaves
Coarse salt
Freshly ground black pepper
½ cup (50g) grated Parmesan cheese

1. Move the slider towards "AIR FRY/STOVETOP" and set Ninja Foodi XL Pressure Cooker Steam Fryer with SmartLid to SEAR/SAUTÉ mode. Adjust the temperature to "Hi5" by using up arrow. Press START/STOP to begin cooking. Add the olive oil, then the onion, celery and carrots to the pot. Cook, stirring frequently, until the onion is soft, about 5 minutes. 2. Add the garlic, Italian seasoning. Then cook for 1 minute more. Press START/STOP to turn off the pot. Add the chicken stock to the pot, taking care to scrape up any browned bits from the bottom of the pot. Add the fire-roasted tomatoes, beans and bay leaf. 3. Lock lid; move slider towards PRESSURE. Adjust pressure release valve in the SEAL position. Close pressure-release valve. The cooking temperature will default to HIGH, which is accurate. Set time to 20 minutes. Select START/STOP and start cooking. 4. When cooking is complete, let pressure release quickly by turning it into VENT position. Remove the bay leaf. Add the spinach leaves and then stir until wilted. 5. Season well with salt and pepper. Top each bowl with some grated Parmesan.
Per Serving: Calories 246; Fat 10.4g; Sodium 368mg; Carbs 8.6g; Fiber 4g; Sugar 4g; Protein 8.4g

Conclusion

In this fast-paced world, everything moves quickly, and your lifestyle needs to match that. For this reason, many cooking appliances are made to make it easier and take less time to make a tasty, healthy, and nutritious meal. Ninja Foodi XL Pressure Cooker Steam Fryer is one of the best appliances for today's fast-paced world because it lets you cook quickly, gives you a healthy meal that meets your dietary needs, and doesn't break the bank. With this appliance, you can quickly cook, bake, slow cook, and steam food.

The Ninja Foodi XL Pressure Cooker Steam Fryer cookbook is the perfect guidance that shows you how to use your device like a pro and gives you quick, easy, and healthy recipes. You can spend your time in the kitchen and do other things simultaneously. You and your family can enjoy a fantastic meal when you're done.

This fantastic cookbook has recipes for food from all over the world. Even if you don't cook often or professionally, it's easy to make food. This fantastic cookbook shows you how to prepare and cook your meal like a pro. So, guys, let's start our Ninja Foodi XL Pressure Cooker Steam Fryer journey and enjoy our fast-forward life with delicious food.

Appendix 1 Measurement Conversion Chart

VOLUME EQUIVALENTS (LIQUID)

US STANDARD	US STANDARD (OUNCES)	METRIC (APPROXIMATE)
2 tablespoons	1 fl.oz	30 mL
¼ cup	2 fl.oz	60 mL
½ cup	4 fl.oz	120 mL
1 cup	8 fl.oz	240 mL
1½ cup	12 fl.oz	355 mL
2 cups or 1 pint	16 fl.oz	475 mL
4 cups or 1 quart	32 fl.oz	1 L
1 gallon	128 fl.oz	4 L

TEMPERATURES EQUIVALENTS

FAHRENHEIT(F)	CELSIUS(C) (APPROXIMATE)
225 °F	107 °C
250 °F	120 °C
275 °F	135 °C
300 °F	150 °C
325 °F	160 °C
350 °F	180 °C
375 °F	190 °C
400 °F	205 °C
425 °F	220 °C
450 °F	235 °C
475 °F	245 °C
500 °F	260 °C

VOLUME EQUIVALENTS (DRY)

US STANDARD	METRIC (APPROXIMATE)
⅛ teaspoon	0.5 mL
¼ teaspoon	1 mL
½ teaspoon	2 mL
¾ teaspoon	4 mL
1 teaspoon	5 mL
1 tablespoon	15 mL
¼ cup	59 mL
½ cup	118 mL
¾ cup	177 mL
1 cup	235 mL
2 cups	475 mL
3 cups	700 mL
4 cups	1 L

WEIGHT EQUIVALENTS

US STANDARD	METRIC (APPROXIMATE)
1 ounce	28 g
2 ounces	57 g
5 ounces	142 g
10 ounces	284 g
15 ounces	425 g
16 ounces (1 pound)	455 g
1.5 pounds	680 g
2 pounds	907 g

Appendix 2 Air Fryer Cooking Chart

Vegetables	Temp (°F)	Time (min)
Asparagus	375	4 to 6
Baked Potatoes	400	35 to 45
Broccoli	400	8 to 10
Brussels Sprouts	350	15 to 18
Butternut Squash (cubed)	375	20 to 25
Carrots	375	15 to 25
Cauliflower	400	10 to 12
Corn on the Cob	390	6
Eggplant	400	15
Green Beans	375	16 to 20
Kale	250	12
Mushrooms	400	5
Peppers	375	8 to 10
Sweet Potatoes (whole)	380	30 to 35
Tomatoes (halved, sliced)	350	10
Zucchini (½-inch sticks)	400	12

Frozen Foods	Temp (°F)	Time (min)
Breaded Shrimp	400	9
Chicken Burger	360	11
Chicken Nudgets	400	10
Corn Dogs	400	7
Curly Fries (1 to 2 lbs.)	400	11 to 14
Fish Sticks (10 oz.)	400	10
French Fries	380	15 to 20
Hash Brown	360	15 to 18
Meatballs	380	6 to 8
Mozzarella Sticks	400	8
Onion Rings (8 oz.)	400	8
Pizza	390	5 to 10
Pot Pie	360	25
Pot Sticks (10 oz.)	400	8
Sausage Rolls	400	15
Spring Rolls	400	15 to 20

Meat and Seafood	Temp (°F)	Time (min)
Bacon	400	5 to 10
Beef Eye Round Roast (4 lbs.)	390	45 to 55
Bone to in Pork Chops	400	4 to 5 per side
Brats	400	8 to 10
Burgers	350	8 to 10
Chicken Breast	375	22 to 23
Chicken Tender	400	14 to 16
Chicken Thigh	400	25
Chicken Wings (2 lbs.)	400	10 to 12
Cod	370	8 to 10
Fillet Mignon (8 oz.)	400	14 to 18
Fish Fillet (0.5 lb., 1-inch)	400	10
Flank Steak(1.5 lbs.)	400	10 to 14
Lobster Tails (4 oz.)	380	5 to 7
Meatballs	400	7 to 10
Meat Loaf	325	35 to 45
Pork Chops	375	12 to 15
Salmon	400	5 to 7
Salmon Fillet (6 oz.)	380	12
Sausage Patties	400	8 to 10
Shrimp	375	8
Steak	400	7 to 14
Tilapia	400	8 to 12
Turkey Breast (3 lbs.)	360	40 to 50
Whole Chicken (6.5 lbs.)	360	75

Desserts	Temp (°F)	Time (min)
Apple Pie	320	30
Brownies	350	17
Churros	360	13
Cookies	350	5
Cupcakes	330	11
Doughnuts	360	5
Roasted Bananas	375	8
Peaches	350	5

Appendix 3 Recipes Index

"Noodle" Soup   177

A

Air Fried Bacon Slices   103
Air Fried Bell Peppers   38
Air Fried Grapefruit   18
Air Fried Olives   33
Air Fried Rack Of Lamb   93
Air Fried Turkey Breast   62
Air Fried Walnut Bars   150
Air-Fried Bacon Slices   102
Air-Fried Brown Mushrooms   43
Air-Fried Brussels Sprouts   46
Air-Fried Cheese Lings   44
Air-Fried Chicken Breasts   68
Air-Fried Chicken Legs   68
Air-Fried Cod   120
Air-Fried Green Beans   42
Air-Fried Meatballs   56
Air-Fried Peach Slices   158
Air-Fried Pork Rinds   143
Air-Fried Portobello Steak   40
Air-Fried Pumpkin Seeds   139
Air-Fried Tilapia   123
Air-Fried Turkey   55
Air-Fried Turkey Mash   57
Air-Fried Turkey Wings   70
Air-Fried Vegetables   45
Almond Cookies   163
Almond Egg Bread   23
Almond Pears   157
Almond-Coated Fish   110
Apple Almond Turnovers   161
Apple Butter   161
Apple Cider Pulled Pork   87
Apricots in Whiskey Sauce   164
Argula Cream Spread   13
Artichoke Pizza   16
Artichoke Stuffed Eggplant   47
Asian Short Ribs   137
Asian Style Sea Bass   115
Asian-Spiced Duck   66
Austrian Beef with Root Vegetables   86
Avocado Balls   144
Avocado Cocoa Pudding   159
Avocado Fries   140
Avocado Fries with Salsa Fresca   136
Avocado Fries Wrapped in Bacon   134
Avocado Wedges   39
Avocado Wraps   144

B

Bacon and Sausage Omelet   30
Bacon Bell Pepper Skewers   137
Bacon Bites   143
Bacon Brussels Sprouts   52
Bacon Brussels Sprouts with Orange Zest   37
Bacon Brussels Sprouts   37
Bacon Burger   25
Bacon Chaffle   142
Bacon Chicken   73
Bacon Cups   104
Bacon Egg Cups   23
Bacon Fat Bombs   135
Bacon Halibut Steaks   121
Bacon Hot Dogs   94

Bacon Knots   18
Bacon Shrimp   130
Bacon Sprouts Wraps   142
Bacon with Brussels Sprouts   37
Bacon with Cauliflower   100
Bacon Wrapped Chicken   55
Bacon Wrapped Onion   129
Bacon Wrapped Scallops   119
Bacon-Wrapped Asparagus   51
Bacon-Wrapped Onion   40
Baked Avocado   148
Baked Beef   89
Baked Butter Apple   157
Baked Cheesy Hash Brown Bake   29
Baked Egg   29
Baked Eggs   18
Baked Potatoes with Yogurt   51
Baked Sweet Cantaloupe   152
Balsamic Drumettes   72
Banana Cake   157
Barbecue Chips   140
Barbeque Sauce Chicken   63
Basic Chicken Nuggets   62
Basil Beef Steak   91
Basil Chicken Breast   57
BBQ Baby Ribs   104
BBQ Cheeseburgers   96
BBQ Ribs   98
BBQ Shrimp With Butter Sauce   107
Bean Ham Soup   170
Bean Tuscan Soup   177
Beef and Bean Stew with Tomatoes and Dill   82
beef and Chickpea Stew with Cilantro   82
Beef Artichoke Sauté   92
Beef Bites   88
Beef Brisket with BBQ Sauce   94
Beef Cabbage Rolls   89
Beef Carne Asada   102
Beef Chili   25
Beef Dinner Rolls   99
Beef Greens Bowl   88
Beef Marinara Wraps   93
Beef Meat Loaf   104
Beef Meatloaf Cups   96
Beef Provolone Casserole   92
Beef Reuben Fritters   103
Beef Roll   90
Beef Shoulder   98
Beef Smokies   143
Beef Spicy Pho   175
Beef Steak   89
Beef Steak Nuggets   103
Beef With Carrots   97
Beef, Red Pepper and Paprika Stew   81
Beefy Minestrone Soup   172
Beefy Poppers   97
Bell Pepper Chips with Parmesan   135
Bell Pepper Cups   27
Bell Peppers Salad   14
Blackberry Butter Cake   153
Blackberry Granola Crisp   159
Blackened Snapper   107
Blondies   150
Blueberry Morning Muffins   19
Blueberry Muffins   15

Blueberry Oats Crisp   166
Braised Beef with Pancettaand Red Wine   85
Bread-crumbed Onion Rings   52
Breaded Chicken   75
Breaded Salmon   108
Breakfast Chicken Sandwich   22
Breakfast Egg Pizza   14
Breakfast Eggs with Cream   22
Breakfast Scotch Eggs   19
Brie and Artichoke Dip   132
Brie with Tomatoes   140
Broccoli Cheese Gnocchi   40
Broccoli- Chicken   54
Broccoli Cranberry Salad   47
Broccoli Feta Balls   36
Broccoli- Frittata   10
Broccoli Gratin   52
Broccoli Pecorino Toscano bites   130
Broccoli Quiche   18
Broccoli Tofu Scramble   25
Broccoli with Coriander and Cheese   129
Broccoli with Mushrooms   34
Broccoli with Parmesan   48
Brussel Sprouts Egg Bake   12
Brussel Sprouts With Feta   39
Brussels Sprouts With Cheese   129
Buffalo Cauliflower   49
Buffalo Cauliflower Florets   37
Buffalo Chicken   58
Buffalo Ranch Cauliflower   40
Burrito Bowls with Chicken And Beans   77
Butter Peach Crumble   157
Buttered Marjoram Chicken   72
Buttery Shrimp Scampi   118

C

Cabbage Egg Fritters   39
Cajun Chicken   74
Cajun Lemon Salmon   117
Cajun Sausage   15
Cajun Spiced Okra   38
Cajun- Turkey Fingers   71
Cajusn Eggplants   38
Carambola Chips   153
Caramel Pear Pudding   149
Carrot Chips with Cheese   131
Carrot Leek Croquettes   42
Cashew Dip   143
Catfish Fillet Bites   122
Catfish With Avocado   119
Cauliflower Cheese Tots   41
Cauliflower Coconut Balls   38
Cauliflower Frittata With Almond Mike   12
Cauliflower Mash   35
Cauliflower Nuggets   52
Cauliflower Pizza Crusts   138
Cayenne Parsnip Burgers   46
Celery Chicken   57
Celery Chips With Harissa Sauce   131
Cheddar Breakfast   12
Cheddar Cheese Rounds   142
Cheddar Coconut Biscuits   11
Cheese & Avocado Melt   15
Cheese Breadsticks   136
Cheese Broccoli Pizza   47
Cheese Egg Scramble   11
Cheese Flatbread   40

Cheese Potato Gratin   43
Cheese Quesadillas   137
Cheese Ribeye Steak   97
Cheese Rolls   14
Cheese Sticks   142
Cheese Stuffed Chicken   70
Cheese Stuffed Peppers   47
Cheese Zucchini Skewers   39
Cheesy Asparagus   36
Cheesy Bacon Muffins   20
Cheesy Bacon Quiche   26
Cheesy Broccoli Casserole   10
Cheesy Broccoli Soup   176
Cheesy Creamy Spinach Soup   173
Cheesy Meaty Sausage Frittata   29
Cheesy Parsley Zucchini   39
Chia Coconut Pudding   159
Chia Egg Pie   152
Chia Pudding Tarts   167
Chicken and Cheese Taquitos   65
Chicken and Vegetable Broth   169
Chicken BBQ Burgers   66
Chicken Beans Bowl   57
Chicken Bites   141
Chicken Cabbage Pan   58
Chicken Egg Roll   76
Chicken Egg Rolls   61
Chicken Filling   60
Chicken Fritters   67
Chicken Ham Cordon Bleu   62
Chicken Ham Rochambeau   67
Chicken Hash   22
Chicken Hot Dogs   63
Chicken Muffins   11
Chicken Mushroom Kabobs   72
Chicken Nuggets   72
Chicken Omelet   70
Chicken Parmesan   68
Chicken Parmesan with Spaghetti   62
Chicken Parsley Nuggets   74
Chicken Pepper Fajitas   69
Chicken Pies   62
Chicken Roll   55
Chicken Roll-Ups   61
Chicken Sausages   56
Chicken Soup   172
Chicken Strips   56
Chicken Taquitos   68
Chicken Tenders   59
Chicken Turnip Curry   72
Chicken Wing Stir-Fry   67
Chicken Wings with Piri Piri Sauce   71
Chicken Wings with Sage   131
Chicken with Apricot-Ginger Sauce   63
Chicken with Broccoli Stir-Fry   78
Chicken with Chimichangas Sauce   61
Chicken with Dumplings   173
Chicken with Marinara Sauce   79
Chicken with Pineapple   69
Chili Crispy Haddock   120
Chili Egg Bake   11
Chinese Glazed Baby Carrots   132
Chives Mixed Beef   92
Chocolate Cake   160
Chocolate Cookie Cups   166
Chocolate Egg Rolls   165
Chocolate Muffins   162
Chocolate Mug Cake   157
Chocolate Pudding Cake   147
Chocolate Rolls   18
Chocolate-Covered Bacon   161
Cinnamon Applesauce Chops   87

Cinnamon Beignets   167
Cinnamon Flour Twists   165
Cinnamon Garlic   37
Cinnamon Pear Clafoutis   165
Cinnamon Plum   153
Cinnamon Stuffed Apples   166
Citrus-Glazed Pork Chops   101
Clafoutis   164
Clam Chowder   171
Clam Corn Chowder   171
Classic Pork Meatballs   145
Classical Hard-Boiled Eggs   28
Cocktail Wieners   131
Cocoa Ricotta Pudding   151
Coconut Cake   163
Coconut Cauliflower Curry   35
Coconut Cream Beef   88
Coconut Crusted Fish Sticks   12
Coconut Crusted Mozarella Sticks   14
Coconut Crusted Shrimp   110
Coconut Granola   143
Coconut Pie   157
Coconut Porridge   24
Cod with Grapes   115
Cod with Olives and Fennel   126
Cod with Spring Onions   119
Cola Pulled Pork   81
Colorful Steamed Vegetables   32
Colorful Vegetable Buddha Bowl   32
Confetti Cake   165
Corn Broccoli   42
Corn Chowder with Potatoes   170
Corn Cob   36
Corn Fritters   43
Corn on The Cob   46
Cornbread   44
Cornish Hens With Honey-Glaze   64
Coulotte Roast   97
Country Boil   124
Country Style Ribs   100
Crab Cakes With Aioli   107
Crab Legs   125
Crab Meat Cakes   109
Crab Muffins   120
Crab Stuffed Shrimp   114
Cracker S'mores   164
Crackled Pork Loin   100
Crackling Bites   131
Cranberry Brownies   164
Cranberry Cake   162
Cranberry Nutty Grits   29
Cream Cheese Cinnamon Pie   151
Creamy Cauliflower Frittata   10
Creamy Crab   124
Creamy Egg Cups   10
Creamy Garlicky Artichoke, Zucchini   35
Creamy Lasagna Soup   176
Creamy Macadamia Spinach   38
Creamy Mashed Sweet Potatoes   33
Creamy Raspberry Jam   148
Creamy Scallops   118
Creamy Seed Porridge   22
Creamy Spaghetti Squash   49
Creamy Tomato Soup with Basil   176
Crisp Brussels Sprout Chips   41
Crisp Crawfish   113
Crispy BBQ Smokies   133
Crispy Broccoli Fries with Spicy Dip   133
Crispy Brussels Sprout   129
Crispy Brussels Sprouts   34
Crispy Calamari Appetizer   134
Crispy Cauliflower   135

Crispy Celery Fries with Aioli   133
Crispy Cheeseburger Bites   133
Crispy Chicken Wings   130
Crispy Cocktail Meatballs   133
Crispy Fish Sticks   116
Crispy Fried Chicken   67
Crispy Honey Chicken Wings   66
Crispy Japanese Yakitori   137
Crispy Parmesan Artichokes   48
Crispy Pork Bites   105
Crispy Pork Meatballs   132
Crispy Pork Rinds   161
Crispy Profiteroles   163
Crispy Ranch Kale Chips   134
Crispy Salmon Croquettes   112
Crispy Sweet Potatoes   46
Crispy Thai Prawns   129
Crispy Tomato Chips   135
Crispy Turkey Burgers   62
Crispy Wings with Blue Cheese   133
Crispy Wings with Thai Chili Sauce   132
Crispy Zucchini Chips   142
Crispy Zucchini Chips with Sauce   134
Crispy Zucchini Crackers   141
Crispy Zucchini Fries   132
Crispy Zucchini Patties   39
Crumbed Fish Sticks   112
Crumbed Wax Beans   42
Crunchy Cod   112
Crunchy Kale   35
Crusted Cheesy Shrimps   122
Crusted Chicken Chunks   60
Crusted Chicken Drumsticks   73
Crusted Chicken Fingers   68
Crusted Chicken Schnitzel   70
Crusted Chicken Tenders   74
Crusted Chicken   57
Crusted Eggplant   46
Crusted Flounder Fillets   108
Crusted Hot Dogs   144
Crusted Lamb Chops   104
crusted Okra   37
Crusted Pork Cutlets   93
Crusted Portobello Mushrooms   46
Crusted Salmon   119
Crusted Sardine Cakes   121
Crusted Sea Scallops   113
Crusted Zucchini Chips   142
Cucumber Salmon Salad   108
Curried Beef   91
Curried Chicken Wings   54
Curried Coconut Shrimp   126
Curried Sweet Potato Fries   45

D

Dark Brownies   159
Delicious Banana Bread   147
Delicious Beef Picadillo   83
Delicious Blueberries Yogurt   150
Delicious Chili Con Carne   82
Delicious Colombian Chicken Soup   175
Delicious Cranberry Pudding   149
Delicious Fish Tacos   118
Delicious Lobster Risotto   124
Delicious Louisiana Grouper   125
Delicious Minestrone   170
Delicious Moroccan Carrot Soup   172
Delicious Mushroom Frittata   30
Delicious Prosciutto Wrapped Asparagus   36
Delicious Pumpkin Stew   35
Delicious Ropa Vieja   86
Delicious Seafood Gumbo   126
Delicious Sesame Chicken   75

Delicious Sweet Potatoes   32
Delicious Teriyaki Chicken   78
Delicious Umami Calamari   122
Delicious Zuppa Toscana   174
Delightful Eggs   28
Deviled Eggs with Swiss Cheese   137
Deviled Eggs   131
Dijon Glazed Pork Loin   101
Dill Bacon Bites   13
Dill Chicken   56
Dill Egg Omelet   14
Dill Pickles with Ranch Dip   138
Dough Dippers with Chocolate Sauce   158
Dropped Egg Soup   174
Duck Wraps   144

E

Easy Burgers   92
Easy Butter Cake   156
Easy Cauliflower Patties   35
Easy Chicken Paillard   60
Easy Chicken Pate   55
Easy Chocolate Cake   154
Easy Chocolate Cream   151
Easy Crab Cakes   112
Easy Nacho Chicken Fries   63
Easy Peach Cobbler   155
Easy Pecan Cobbler   151
Easy Pork Chops   101
Easy Vanilla Soufflé   158
Egg Breakfast   10
Egg Quesadillas   20
Egg Scramble   24
Egg with Green Beans   38
Eggplant Beef Sauté   90
Eggplant Chips   144
Eggplant Crisps   129
Eggplant Fries   139
Eggplant Pepper Spread   12
Eggs and Sausage Muffins   26
Eggs Dish   27
Eggs Ham   15
Eggs with Kalamata Olives   11
English Bacon Breakfast   25
Espresso Brownies   162

F

Fajita Rollups   66
Farro with Berries and Walnuts   26
Fat Air Fried Eggplant   40
FatPotato Bites   44
Feta Stuffed Portobellos   50
Fiesta Chicken   63
Fish Cakes with Potatoes   112
Fish Capers Cakes   117
Fish Chowder   127
Fish Fillets With Dill Sauce   109
Fish Fingers   115
Fish for Kids   110
Fish Nuggets   112
Fish Sauce Wings   132
Fish Stew   126
Fish Sticks with Tartar Sauce   108
Fish Tacos   111
Five-Ingredient Bean Soup   174
Flan   148
Flank Steak   98
Flavored Chicken Meatballs   144
Flaxseed Carrot Cake   167
Flaxseed Muffins   21
French Fries   139
French Meat and Vegetable Stew with
Tarragon   82

French Toasts   11
Fried Buffalo Chicken Wings   60
Fried Cabbage   49
Fried Celery   37
Fried Cheese Chicken   56
Fried Chicken   70
Fried Chicken Strips   64
Fried Drumsticks   61
Fried Eggplant   52
Fried Lamb Chops   93
Fried Lamb Steak   93
Fried Leek with Mustard   129
Fried Pancake Oreos   155
Fried PB&J Sandwich   21
Fried Pies   156
Fried Pork Loin Chops   94
Fried Rib Eye Steaks   90
Fried Shallots   134
Fried Shrimp   117
Frosted Blackberry Shortcake   165
Fudge Brownies   149

G

Garlic Beef Bread   89
Garlic Beef Meatballs   88
Garlic London Broil   96
Garlic Shrimp   119
Garlic Toast   28
Garlicky Beef Steak   90
Garlicky Green Chickpea Soup   175
Garlicky Roasted Cauliflower   47
Garlicky Salmon Fillets   118
Garlicky Shrimp Scampi   126
Garlicky Shrimp   111
German Roulade   95
Ginger Bacon Bites   160
Ginger Lime Salmon   120
Gingered Cod   121
Gingered Turkey   57
Glazed Ham   100
Gooey Brownies   166
Grandma's Crispy Wings   135
Greece Style Yogurt Cake   151
Greek Beef Stew with Tomatoes   83
Greek Keftedes with Tzatziki Dip   136
Greek Olives   39
Green Beans Salad   46
Grilled Cheese   45
Grilled Meatball   134
Grilled Pimento Croutons   139
Grilled Pineapple   155
Grilled Salmon   114
Grilled Salmon with Capers   116

H

Ham Casserole   28
Ham Cornmeal Muffins   19
Ham Eggs   21
Ham with Split Pea Soup   174
Hamburgers   103
Hasselback Potatoes   50
Hawaiian Roll Sliders   69
Healthy Blueberry Oat Mini Muffins   25
Healthy Egg Muffins   28
Healthy Jambalaya   127
Healthy Three Bean Chili   171
Healthy White Chicken Chili   171
Herbed Chicken Drumsticks   54
Herbed Chicken Wings   76
Herbed Filet Mignon   96
Herbed Green Beans   42
Herbed Lamb Chops   97
Herbed Olives   38

Herbed Pork Casserole   95
Herbed Radishes   41
Herbed Shrimp Skewers   120
Herbes de Provence Chops   85
Hoisin Glazed Drumsticks   72
Hoisin Pork Steak   95
Holiday Chicken Wings   73
Homemade Pecan Nutella   151
Homemade turkey Pot Pie   60
Honey Bratwurst with Brussels
Sprouts   101
Honey Carrots   49
Honey Chocolate Cookies   156
Honey Cornbread   51
Honey Turkey Breast   71
Horseradish Gorgonzola Mushrooms   47
Horseradish Salmon   116
Hot Wings   138
Hush Puffs   17

I

Indian Chicken Marsala   77
Indian Lamb Steaks   101
Indonesian Nutty Beef   84
Italian Beef   90
Italian Chicken Fillets   74
Italian Chicken Parmesan   57
Italian Frittata   25
Italian Pork Cut   99
Italian Pork Loin   104
Italian Tuna   111
Italian Turkey Sausage   71
Italian Tuscan Soup   172

J

Jacket Potatoes   32
Jalapeño Chicken   61
Jelly stuffed Muffins   20
Jerk-Spiced Chicken Wings   68

K

Kale Chips   130
Kale Cream Eggs   14
Kale Fritters   23
Kale Sausage Soup   171
KFC Chicken   67
Kielbasa Egg Scramble   12
Korean Braised Ribs   84
Korean Wings   65

L

Lamb Avocado Bowl   94
Lamb Cauliflower Fritters   90
Lamb Chops with Mint Sauce   89
Lamb Chops With Olive Spread   88
Lamb Meatballs   94
Lamb Skewers   93
Lemon Cake   158
Lemon Cheesecake   147
Lemon Chicken   54
Lemon Chicken with Herbed Potatoes   75
Lemon Cream Pie   152
Lemon Garlic Chicken   73
Lemon Salmon with Dill   123
Lemon-Dijon Chicken   58
Lemony Broccoli Salad   48
Lemony Brussels Sprout Salad   49
Lemony Lamb Chops   93
Lemony Peppers   40
Lemony Steamed Artichokes   36
Lime paprika Cod   120
Limey Duck Breast   70
Liver Pate   24
Lo Mein   75

Lobster with Butter Sauce   127

M

Macadamia Cookies   163
Macaroons   154
Mackerel with Peppers   120
Madeira Glazed Ham   105
Mahi-Mahi with a Lemon-Caper Sauce   125
Marinated Beef Loin   93
Marinated Shrimp   113
Marshmallow Fluff Turnover   158
Matcha Cake   148
Mayo Chicken Salad   66
Mayo Egg Salad   29
Mayo Fish Sticks   111
Meatball Lettuce Wraps   96
Meatballs   144
Meatballs in Spicy Tomato Sauce   83
Meatloaf   99
Meatloaf Slices   24
Mediterranean Chicken Fillets   69
Mediterranean Cocktail Meatballs   134
Mediterranean Spicy Cod   124
Mexican Brisket Salad   84
Mexican Burgers   66
Mexican Carnitas   96
Mexican Casserole   26
Mexican Corn   50
Mexican Meatloaf   96
Mexican Zucchini Cakes Ole   135
Mexican-Style Chicken Noodle Soup   173
Minced Beef Sandwich   24
Minced Beef Sauté   91
Mini Cheesecakes   153
Miso Salmon Fillets   118
Mongolian Beef   89
Morning Herbed Eggs   11
Morning Sausages   23
Mozarella Chicken   58
Mozarella Egg Bake   12
Mozzarella Bites   140
Mozzarella with Puttanesca Sauce   141
Muffin Burgers   101
Mushroom Basil Bites   142
Mushroom Beef Patties   98
Mushroom Bites   141
Mushroom Boat Eggs   20
Mushroom Burgers   103
Mushroom Cheese Loaf   51
Mushroom Puff Pastry   41
Mushroom Stuffed Turkey   59
Mussels in White Wine   125
Mustard Chicken Bites   55
Mustard Chicken Thighs   69
Mustard Glazed Beef Loin   91
Mustard Parmesan Cod   122
Mustard Tender Filet Mignon   98
Mustard Wings   138

N

Nashville Chicken   59
Nut-Crusted Halibut   123
Nutty Cake   147
nutty Chocolate Candy   150

O

Oat Muffins   19
Olive-Stuffed Jalapeños   137
Omelet Cups   27
Omelet with Herbs   13
Onion Beef Delights   90
Onion Rings   131
Orange Cake   164
Orange Creamy Rolls   19

Orange Custard   153
Orange Nutmeg Galettes   152
Orange Pumpkin Puree   36
Oregano Beef   89
Oregano Cauliflower Florets   33

P

Pancake Hash   22
Paprika Cabbage Steaks   48
Paprika Catfish with Tarragon   124
Paprika Cheese Chips   135
Paprika Chicken Breast   57
Paprika Chicken Cutlets   69
Paprika Cod with Endives   123
Paprika Tilapia with Capers   121
Parmesan Bread   16
Parmesan Cauliflower   45
Parmesan Cheeseburger Meatballs   94
Parmesan Chicken Meatballs   136
Parmesan Cod   119
Parmesan Green Bean Casserole   48
Parmesan Kale   48
Parmesan Meatballs   88
Parmesan Omelet   23
Parmesan Potatoes   49
Parmesan Salmon   122
Parmesan Tilapia   117
Parmesan Zucchini Bites   41
Parmesan Zucchini Gratin   48
Parsley Coconut Shrimp   121
Parsley Olives Fritters   141
Parsnips Meal   46
Party Chex Snack   139
Peach Vanilla Fritters   17
Peach Walnut Parfaits   165
Peachy Chicken With Cherries   64
Peanuts Cupcakes   153
Pear Crumble   161
Pecan Crusted Striped Bass   113
Pepper Bread   17
Pepper Chicken Halves   58
Pepper Eggs   13
Peppered Tuna Skewers   123
Pepperoni Cheese Pizza   16
Peppery Beef   99
Pesto Turkey Meatballs with Pasta   78
Pickle Chips   140
Pickled Bacon   143
Picnic Chicken Chunks   133
Pineapple Galette   161
Pineapple with Macadamia Batter   163
Pita Bread   16
Pita Chips   39
Pizza Bombs with Marinara Sauce   138
Pizza Cheese Bites   141
Pizza Crust   41
Poached Spiced Pears with
Pomegranate   148
Poblano Turkey Bake   64
Pomegranate Brussels Sprouts   32
Poppy Seed Cake   160
Pork Bun Thit Nuong   98
Pork Burgers   99
Pork Casserole   13
Pork Chops with Peppers   100
Pork Cutlets   99
Pork Kebab With Dill Sauce   91
Pork Kebabs With Pepper   95
Pork Quiche Cups   20
Pork Ragu   87
Pork Roast with Applesauce   100
Pork Sausage With Cauliflower   94
Pork Skewers   98

Pork Steak With Herbs   95
Pork Tenderloin with Herbs   95
Pork Tenderloin with Pepper Glaze   85
Pork With Herbs and Onions   89
Pork with Vegetables   92
Pork Wrapped Scotch Eggs   10
Porridge   27
Portobello Eggs   11
Pot Pie Soup   170
Potato Patties   42
Potato Soup with cheese   170
Potatoes & Cheese   44
Potatoes and Brussels Sprouts   34
Potatoes Fries   50
Pound Cake   157
Prune Cookies   164
Prune Muffins   162
Pudding with Sultanas   164
Pumpkin Pudding   158

Q

Quick Peanut Butter Cookies   159
Ranch Potato Chips   140
Raspberry Pineapple Sundaes   166

R

Red Cherry Compote   148
Red Salmon Croquettes   117
Red Snapper with Green Onions Salsa   114
Refresh Steamed Broccoli   32
Refreshing Chicken Tacos   75
Refreshing Quinoa and Pomegranate
Salad   32
Refreshing Vegetable Dish   34
Regular Chicken Broth   169
Regular Chocolate Pudding   149
Regular Pad Thai   127
Regular Vegetable Broth   169
Rhubarb Cream Pie   152
Rib Ragu with Pappardelle   85
Rice Cake   154
Rice Paper Breakfast   22
Ricotta Cheese Muffins   152
Ricotta Cheese Potatoes   43
Ricotta Chicken Wraps   71
Ricotta Vanilla Cookies   151
Roasted Apple Crisp   154
Roasted Artichoke   38
Roasted Bell Peppers   45
Roasted Broccoli   45
Roasted Chicken   77
Roasted Corn   48
Roasted Country-Style Vegetables   43
Roasted Garlic Asparagus   49
Roasted Mushroom   35
Roasted Sweet Potatoes   51
Roasted Turkey   69
Roasted Zucchini Cubes   130
Romano Crispy Zucchini Fries   136
Rosemary Meatballs   91
Rosemary Potatoes   50
Rosemary Spiced Chicken   74
Rum Lava Cake   154
Rump Roast   97

S

Sage Rubbed Turkey Breast   54
Salisbury Steak with Mushroom Gravy   102
Salmon Bites   144
Salmon Cakes   118
Salmon Jerky   42
Salmon Potato Patties   117
Salmon with Chives Sauce   119
Salmon with Lime Sauce   122

Salmon with Veggies   117
Salmon with Zucchini   115
Salsa Pulled Pork   84
Saucy BBQ Beef   91
Saucy Chicken Wings   54
Saucy Turkey Leg   56
Sausage Patties   100
Sausage with Fennel   99
Sausage with Peppers   87
 Savory-Sweet Braised Beef   87
Scallions Chicken   54
Scallops Bacon Kabobs   137
Scallops in Butter Sauce   108
Scallops with Lemon Sauce   110
Scrambled Spinach Eggs   44
Sea Scallops with tangy Cherry Sauce   123
Seasoned Artichoke   38
Sesame Carrots   47
Sesame Crusted Salmon   121
Sesame Flax Meal Porridge   22
Sesame Green Beans   51
Sesame Salmon   107
Sesame-Ginger Tenderloin   83
Shredded Greek-Style Chicken   78
Shrimp and Fingerling Potatoes   116
Shrimp Balls   143
Shrimp cakes   114
Shrimp Grits   113
Shrimp Kebabs   107
Shrimp Po' Boys   111
Shrimp Salad   109
Shrimp Scampi   116
Shrimp Sesame Toasts   138
Shrimp Sliders   115
Shrimp with Spicy Dipping Sauce   107
Shrimp with tangy Risotto   127
Simple Teriyaki Chicken   65
Smoked BBQ Sausages   40
 Smoky Barbecue Chicken   79
Smoky Barbecue Pork Chop Sandwiches   86
Smoky Chicken Quarters   60
Smoky Ribs   86
Soft Eggs   28
Soft Raisin Muffins   163
Soft-Boiled Eggs   13
Southern Chicken Livers   64
Soy Dipped Beef Tenderloin   97
Spanish Paella   33
Spice Monkey Bread   167
Spiced Chicken Thighs   66
Spiced Pumpkin Pudding   147
Spiced Turkey Breast   58
Spicy Acorn Squash   51
Spicy Bacon Pieces   102
Spicy Beef Stew with Caraway   81
Spicy Beef Stew with Olives   81
Spicy Beef with Broccoli Zoodle Soup   173
Spicy Buffalo Chicken Chowder   175
Spicy Buffalo Chicken Wings   65
Spicy Buffalo Wings   78
Spicy Chicken Alfredo   77
Spicy Curried Cauliflower Soup   172
Spicy Hot Dogs   130
Spicy Jicama Fries   41
Spicy Lamb Steak   94
Spicy Pork Gratin   92
Spicy Potato Wedges   33
Spicy Potatoes   45
Spicy Salmon   110
Spicy Teriyaki Chicken   77
Spicy Turkey Wings   73
Spinach Cheddar Quiche   23

Spinach Cheese Quesadilla   14
Spinach Chips   136
Spinach Egg Frittata   10
Spinach Muffins   14
Spinach Parsley Omelet   24
Spinach- Rollups   21
Spinach with Parsley Dip   130
Spinach-Feta Cups   27
Sponge Cake   152
Sriracha Glazed Ribs   98
Steak Bulgogi   100
Steak Salad   99
Steamed Crab   123
Steamed Shrimp with Asparagus   125
Steaming Clams   125
Stewed Lamb   88
Strawberry Morning Toast   16
Strawberry Rolls   154
Strawberry Shortcake   160
Stuffed Chicken Kiev   59
Stuffed Flounder   108
Stuffed Mushrooms   43
Stuffed Roulade   72
Stuffed Turkey Breast with Gravy   76
Stuffed Venison Tenderloin   101
Sugary Churros   159
Sushi   145
Swedish Beef Meatloaf   102
Sweet Blueberries Muffins   153
Sweet Chicken Wings   54
Sweet Cinnamon Muffins   15
Sweet Gingerbread   155
Sweet Lemon Bars   162
Sweet Pecans   148
Sweet Potato Donut   156
Sweet Potato Fries   50
Sweet Potato Toast   17
Sweet Potatoes with nuts   33
sweet Quiche   151
Sweet Raspberry Curd   147
Sweet Tangy Ham   88
Sweet Tapioca   150
Swiss Chard Egg Frittata   13
Swiss Roll   155
Swordfish Skewers   110
syrupy Crème Brulee   149
Szechuan Beans   45

T

Taco Broccoli   37
Taco Seasoned Meatballs   104
Tacon Mexican Muffins   142
Tangy Fruit Salad Jam   149
Tasty Chicken Meatballs   56
Tasty Steamed Asparagus   36
Tasty Tomato Spinach Quiche   29
Tender Beef Salad   91
Teriyaki Chicken   132
Thai Chicken Curry Soup with Veggies "Ramen"   177
Thai Chicken Rice   79
Thai Tropical red Soup   176
Thai Turkey Bites   135
Thanksgiving Turkey   68
Thymed Beef   92
Tilapia Teriyaki with Rice   114
Tilapia with Kale   120
Tilapia with Tomato Salsa   119
Tilapia with Tomatoes   126
Toast Sticks   19
Toasted Flakes   160
Tomato and Spinach Healthy Breakfast   27
Tomato Breakfast Wrap   15

Tomato Drumsticks   55
Tomato Egg Omelet   13
Tomato Soup with basil   169
Tomatoes Stuffed Pepper Soup   174
Tortellini Soup with pesto   169
Tostones With Green Sauce   52
Traditional Beef Chili   169
Traditional Broccoli Salad   34
Traditional French Eggs   28
Traditional Ratatouille   34
Trail Chex Snack   139
Tropical Oats   26
Tropical Sea Bass   124
Trout with Herb Sauce   121
Tuna Nuggets with Hoisin Sauce   114
Tuna Patties with Sriracha Sauce   109
Tuna Steaks with Tapenade   109
Turkey Cheese Cups   56
Turkey Cheese Pockets   58
Turkey Cream Spread   55
Turkey Cutlets   64
Turkey Meatballs   59
Turkey Meatloaf   73
Turkey Pepper Meatballs   71
Turkey Potatoes   43
Turkey Sandwiches   70
Turkey Sausage Roll-Ups   17
Turkey Scramble   10
Turkey Sliders   73
 Turkey with Gravy   76
Turkey With Mustard Glaze   65
Turkey With Sweet Sauce   55
Turkey Wraps   65
Turmeric Chicken Bites   143
Turmeric Salmon with Cream   122
Tuscan Chicken   74
Two-Bean Chili stew   177

V

Vanilla Custard   155
Vanilla Pecan Pie   156
Vegan Apple Pies   166
Vegan Coconut Yogurt   150
Vegetable Cheese Omelet   44
Vegetable with Salmon Fillets   116
Veggies on Toast   26
Vinegar Glazed Beef Shank   92

W

Walnut Apple Muffins   18
Walnut Bread   159
Walnut Granola   12
Walnut Vanilla Pancake   21
Western Cheese Omelet   21
White Chocolate Cookies   162
Worcester Pork Meatballs   95
Wrapped Bacon with Eggs   15

Y

yellow Marmalade   150

Z

Za'Atar Chops   90
Zesty Lemon Biscotti   152
Zesty Raspberry Muffins   156
Zucchini Fries   139
Zucchini Hash   24
Zucchini Spread   13
Zucchini with Sweet Potatoes   44

Made in the USA
Las Vegas, NV
02 January 2023

64764854R00111